Canada's Aviation Pioneers

Alice Gibson-Sutherland

Canada's Aviation Pioneers
50 Years of McKee Trophy Winners

Alice Gibson Sutherland

Foreword by Fred W. Hotson

McGRAW-HILL RYERSON LIMITED

Toronto   Montreal   New York   St.Louis
San Francisco   Auckland   Beirut   Bogotá   Düsseldorf
Johannesburg   Lisbon   London   Lucerne   Madrid   Mexico
New Delhi   Panama   Paris   San Juan   São Paulo   Singapore
Sidney   Tokyo

CANADA'S AVIATION PIONEERS

ISBN 0-07-082704-4

1 2 3 4 5 6 7 8 9 10 BP 7 6 5 4 3 2 1 0 9 8

Printed and bound in Canada

Canadian Cataloguing in Publication Data

Sutherland, Alice Gibson, date
    Canada's aviation pioneers

Includes index.
ISBN 0-07-082704-4

1. Air pilots - Canada - Biography.
2. Aeronautics - Canada - History. 3. Trans-
Canada Trophy (Aeronautics). I. Title.

TL539.S85   629.13'092'2   C78-001538-X

ERRATA

. . . .

"CANADA'S AVIATION PIONEERS"

by

ALICE GIBSON-SUTHERLAND

Published by McGraw-Hill Ryerson Limited, Toronto, in December, 1978.

. . . .

Page 17 — Column 1, para. 3, line 8, change "Vickers Aircraft Company" to read "Canadian Vickers Limited".
Column 1, para. 4, line 1, change "Vickers Aircraft" to read "Canadian Vickers Limited".
Column 2, para. 1, lines 15 and 16, change "Vickers Aircraft Company to read "Canadian Vickers Limited".

Page 21 — Column 2, para. 4, lines 14 and 15, change "March, 1927" to read "December 10, 1926".
Column 3, para. 3, line 2, delete the word "Bay".

Page 22 — Column 1, para. 2, line 4, change "G-CADL" to read "G-CAGE".

Page 34 — Column 1, para. 1, lines 8, 9 and 10, delete the following sentence: "The Fairchild, the other aircraft, however, had found its last resting place on the shore".

Page 42 — Caption under photo, amend as follows:
Line 3, change "E. A. Broadway" to read "Major Riddell of the R.C.C.S., Aklavik", and change "S. R. McMillan" to read "R.C.M.P. Sgt. Frank Hersey".
Line 3, delete "D.A."
Line 4, change "Mash" to "Nash".

Page 63 — Caption under photo, line 1, change "seaplane" to read "skiplane".

Page 156 — Caption under photo, line 2, delete the word "Trimotor".
Column 1, para. 2, line 4, delete the word "Trimotor".

Page 171 — Caption under photo, line 6, insert the following line after December: "1934, G-CAHJ was sold to United Air Transport, Edmonton; in June, 1938". The last sentence under the caption should now read as follows: "Then in December, 1934, G-CAHJ was sold to United Air Transport, Edmonton; in June, 1938, to Fleet Aircraft of Canada; and finally to Peace River Airways, Peace River, Alta., in July, 1938".

Page 205 — Caption under photo, line 1, change "A/V/M. W. A. Curtis" to read "A/M. W. A. Curtis".

Page 290 — Column 2, para. 2, lines 17 and 18, change "Vickers Aircraft Company" to read "Canadian Vickers Limited".

Page 293 — Caption over photo, line 1, change "V.C." to read "V.D.".

September, 1980.

AUTHOR   SUTHERLAND, ALICE GIBSON   TITLE   CANADA'S AVIATION PIONEERS

REVIEWED IN   Canadian Geographic   DATE   April/May 1979

Canada's Aviation Pioneers: 50 Years of McKee Trophy Winners, by Alice Gibson Sutherland (McGraw-Hill Ryerson Ltd., Toronto, 1978, 304 pp., $24.95).

This book is based on the biographies of the men who have won the McKee Trophy, Canada's top aviation award presented annually since 1927 in recognition of the most outstanding contribution in the field of operational flying. It is seldom given for a single brilliant exploit, but rather for excellence of performance and dedication to aviation over a period of years. The recipient need not necessarily be a pilot, though he generally is, and the honour has also been bestowed on navigators, engineers and other non-pilot airmen. In some years, the award has gone to men who made their greatest mark in aviation as captains of industry, managers and directors after their active flying careers were over. All of the recipients have played a decisive part in making Canadian aviation what it is today.

In writing about the McKee Trophy winners, the author does not overlook the achievements of their associates, helpers and advisers. The story that emerges is a history of Canadian aviation from the flight of the fragile Silver Dart at Baddeck, Nova Scotia, in February 1909, to the age of the big air transports.

have been added, however, to depict some of the more famous flights such as that of Punch Dickins across the unexplored Barren Lands in 1928.

Although the author gives credit to those who were helpful during her extensive research, some readers will be disappointed to find that a full listing of source materials is not included.

Alice Gibson Sutherland is exceptionally well qualified to write about the McKee Trophy and the men who have had the distinction of winning it. As secretary to the director of civil aviation in the Department of Transport, she was personally acquainted with many of the leading lights in aviation, civil, commercial and military. She has previously published articles on some of them, and for her current book she had access to many personal papers, as well as to government records.

Canada's Aviation Pioneers contains a wealth of information and is an invaluable reference work on the history of Canadian aviation. It is also an attractive item for the bookshelf or coffee table.

F.J. Hatch

Dr. Hatch is an historian with the National Defence Department's directorate of history and author of "Ship-to-Shore airmail services in the '20s" (CG, Aug/Sept 1978).

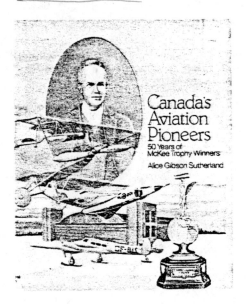

The reader will also find much in the way of human interest as the biographies, particularly those of the Arctic flyers and bush pilots, are enlivened by numerous anecdotes.

The photographs well illustrate the events described in the text, while maps trace the development of the principal air routes. A few smaller map inserts might

History of aviation pioneers outstanding

Canada's Aviation Pioneers: Fifty Years of McKee Trophy Winners, by Alice Gibson Sutherland; McGraw-Hill Ryerson; 304 pages; five maps; index; $24.95

By Elizabeth Wright

This excellent book results from a happy quirk of fate. When Murton Seymour, honorary counsel for the Royal Flying Clubs Association, visited the office of the controller of civil aviation in the 1940s, he regularly passed the desk of the controller's secretary, Alice Gibson. A casual remark sparked her idea of writing biographies of early McKee Trophy winners for *Canadian Aviation.* Later she expanded them into a book, which was published on the eve of the award's 50th anniversary. It is a meticulously researched labor of love, done in spare hours over a 20-year period.

The Trans-Canada (McKee) Trophy, which can be seen at the Museum of Science and Technology, came into existence to commemorate the first trans-Canada seaplane flight, made in 1926 by Captain James Dalzell McKee, a wealthy American pilot and aviation enthusiast. (He flew a Douglas seaplane from Montreal to Vancouver.) The first pilot and navigator on the arduous and frequently hazardous flight was Squadron Leader A. Earl Godfrey, M.C., A.F.M. (later A/V/M Godfrey) who was awarded the trophy in 1977.

To show his appreciation of courtesies extended to him by the RCAF and civil-aviation organizations, Captain McKee pre-

Alice Gibson Sutherland
Life's labor of love

sented the trophy, requesting that it be awarded annually to the person most meritoriously advancing aviation in Canada during the year, with emphasis on year-long continuous service rather than a single brilliant exploit.

The citations reflect Canada's history and development during a half century. During the 1920s and 1930s they recognized pioneer work on the frontiers, for example, "outstanding work in carrying out airway surveys preliminary to the inauguration of an airmail service in Canada. . . exploratory flights in northern Canada . . . service in the inauguration of Trans-Canada Airlines."

Many of the incidental adventures were heroic. "Wop" May and his co-pilot, on Jan. 1, 1929, flew 600 miles from Edmonton to Fort Vermilion with diptheria anti-toxin. The temperature was minus-40 degrees F., the only available plane an Avro 2 seater with no skis and an open cockpit. On arrival at Vermilion, frostbitten, bleeding from cuts inflicted by the biting winds, both men were so chilled that they had to be lifted from the cockpit. A fast dog team rushed the antitoxin to Little Red River; the Indians in the settlement all recovered.

Hitler war

During the war against Hitler, Canada's aviation resources expanded to the limit. One pioneer was cited for "wholehearted support . . . everything worthwhile in aviation." After the war, aviators were still "opening up Canada's vast hinterland. . . developing new methods of aerial navigation in the Arctic . . . mapping the Arctic . . . developing landing gear for light aircraft operating from unprepared surfaces in the Arctic." They were competing internationally with new navigation computer systems, record-breaking high-altitude flying, research in high-altitude

physiology, test-flying new types of planes at shows all over the world, etc.

Overall, McKee Trophy winners were men sinewy of mind and body, backed by teams equally absorbed in work they felt to be challenging and worthwhile.

The author, now a Merrickville resident, has done a remarkable job in condensing an immense amount of fascinating material. The record is presented in sufficiently detached fashion, but she is by no means a bloodless recorder. Part of her brief lament for the Avro Arrow (the C.F.105 cancelled in mid-production in February, 1959) shows her empathy. "Not one of the Arrows was kept as a work of art for a Canadian museum. Not one of the Arrows was kept to show its magnificent design. Not one of these six Arrows was to remain intact. Blueprints, brochures, reports and photographs were all reduced to ashes. Why, one asks? What a pity!"

An outstanding source book, and one for aviation buffs, this is also a book for all Canadians, as full of atmosphere and excitement as those of Robert Service, W. O. Mitchell or Arthur Hailey; but the events narrated by Gibson Sutherland are historical-factual, and the reader's imagination has to react and interpret accordingly. The 231 excellent photographs add immediacy to a work that should be read slowly and savored.

What topic and genre will this writer select next from her wealth of experience and background — the Canadian Aviation Hall of Fame, the bush pilots, a book for young adults, fiction? Her first book off-sets the tedious and destructive vogue of the anti-hero. We could use more.

Contents

*No awards were given for the years 1962, 1964, 1965, 1968 to 1972.

Foreword

It was May 1950 that the magazine, *Canadian Aviation*, began a series of small biographies covering early McKee Trophy winners. The author was Alice Gibson and few people realized that her interest in the subject stemmed from a very close association with the aviation hierarchy in Ottawa. As secretary to the Controller of Civil Aviation, she had daily contact with the people who were in the forefront of the industry. It was a casual remark by one of these people who visited Dan McLean's office in the 1940s which sparked the idea of recording the McKee Trophy story. The instigator was the 1939 winner, M.A. "Murt" Seymour, who kept up the theme whenever he passed Miss Gibson's desk en route to his appointment with the Controller. The resulting articles in *Canadian Aviation* set the scene for further research and writing on her favourite topic — the "Trans-Canada Trophy" — as it was known then. Now, as Alice Gibson Sutherland, she puts together the results of her dedicated research and provides a unique look at the people who built the aviation industry in Canada.

It is fortunate that the full significance of the trophy and its colourful background has at last been put into print along with the biographies of those who won it during fifty years. The planning of the award and the generous gift of the trophy by Captain James Dalzell McKee are both explained, including the tragic death of the donor only four months after the endowment was established. Outlined also is the near calamity during the Paul Hellyer years when it seemed politically expedient to retire the award with all its prestige and high motives. The trophy itself suffered physical damage during one of its many moves, but, as in the case of the early retirement, interested groups rallied to keep the long-standing tradition alive.

The story Mrs. Sutherland tells is one of people, and, although the sphere of their efforts was wide and varied over fifty years, the common denominator was one of achievement. The fact that these men were leaders in their field has placed their names in the forefront of aviation in Canada. Some have written of their work and all have received wide acclaim, but nowhere have their accumulated biographies appeared under one cover. The book's value as a research source will be greatly appreciated in the future and the author is to be congratulated on her dedication to the subject.

McKee's desire in 1926 was to recognize those who contributed to the advancement of aviation in Canada and it becomes quite clear that his objectives have been admirably fulfilled. This broad biographical coverage tells a story of human endeavour that touches every branch of aviation and still remains uniquely Canadian. Destiny placed these men in a position of decision during a vital period in Canada's history. An accounting of their efforts in the light of passing years indicates that these responsibilities have been well and truly discharged. This narrative of achievement within the industry tends to emphasize the stories of all who contributed to the development of aviation in Canada. The men selected for honour through the conditions of the award are the first to acclaim the accomplishments of their colleagues who joined them in the task.

James Dalzell McKee would be justifiably pleased that the story of his trophy over fifty years has now been recorded.

Fred W. Hotson, President
Canadian Aviation
Historical Society, 1978

Preface

The story of the illustrious winners of
the Trans-Canada Trophy, also
known as the McKee Trophy, has
been completed on the eve of the
fiftieth anniversary of its award.

This book was visualized twenty or
more long years ago, and much of
the research and writing was done
over a period of time whenever
precious moments could be found.
During those years when the early
winners of the Trans-Canada Trophy
were alive and well, and more
recently, these trophy winners gave
me invaluable assistance by providing
me with information on their
activities, including reports,
documents, letters, notes, historic
news clippings, photographs,
suggestions, personal interviews
and/or advice or guidance, so that
each story could be told and recorded
for posterity.

It is fitting that this aspect of
Canada's historic past be included in
the annals of Canada's aviation
history, especially on the golden
anniversary of the award of the
trophy.

Alice Gibson Sutherland
Ottawa, Ontario, Canada
October, 1977

Acknowledgements

I am indebted to many people and sources for the assistance which was so kindly given to me in the preparation of this work.

First of all, I wish to thank the winners of the Trans-Canada Trophy who provided me with invaluable assistance.

Also, I wish to acknowledge and thank the following sources for permission to quote passages from their publications: *Canadian Aviation; Aircraft; Hawker Siddeley Review; Imperial Oil Review; Engineering and Contract Record;* and the *Canadian Armed Forces Sentinel.* In addition, I acknowledge and thank Canada's Aviation Hall of Fame for permission to use simple excerpts from their publication; and the Canadian Aviation Historical Society for permission to quote a passage from a talk given by Group Captain Z.L. Leigh to their convention in June, 1976. I acknowledge and thank Walter Gilbert for permission to quote from the book *Arctic Pilot,* by Walter Gilbert as told to Kathleen Shackleton, published by Thomas Nelson & Sons, Ltd., 1939. I acknowledge and thank the following organizations, associations, magazines, newspapers, companies, government departments, libraries, etc., which were valuable sources of information: *Canadian Aircraft Operator; Canadian Flight; Canadian Air Line Pilot; The de Havilland Aircraft of Canada News Letters; The Lethbridge Herald; Canadian Airways Bulletin; Western Wings; Wings Over the Bush; Encyclopedia Canadiana; Roundel; The Okanagan Helicopter Group; Okanagan Helicopters Ltd.; Western Business and Industry; The Bee Hive;* the Royal Canadian Flying Clubs Association; *Arctic Circular; The Edmonton Journal;* Trans-Canada Air Lines; the Canadian Aeronautics and Space Institute; the Ontario Provincial Air Service; the Ontario Department of Lands and Forests; *The Pittsburgh Post;* the Carnegie Library, Pittsburgh, Pa.; *The Halifax Mail;* JGW Systems, Ottawa; Hunting Associates Ltd.; PSC Applied Research Ltd., Toronto; *The Ottawa Journal; The Ottawa Citizen; Saturday Night; Canadian Mining Journal; The Nelson Daily News;* Cominco, Trail, B.C.; *Canadian Militia Reports;* Red Lake District Chamber of Commerce; the Toronto Public Library; *The Northern Miner; The Fort Nelson News; The Vancouver Sun; Canadian Saturday Night; Imperial Oil Review; Canadian Armed Forces Sentinel; Armed Forces News;* the Department of Transport; the Department of National Defence; J.A. Wilson's Reports; *Civil Aviation Reports; Air Board Reports; Annual Reports of the Department of National Defence; Annual Reports of the Department of Transport;* J.A. Wilson's papers and articles; news releases from The de Havilland Aircraft of Canada; Directorate of History, Department of National Defence; the Air Transport Association of Canada; the Ministry of Natural Resources, Toronto; The Royal Canadian Navy; Western Electric Company, New York; press releases from the Department of National Defence; Hansard; House of Commons Debates; *Public Information Report from the Military Sea Transportation Service;* The Foundation Company of Canada; the Department of National Defence — General Information — Community Relations; *Between Ourselves; CAE Newsletter;* Canadian Pacific Air Lines; Aviation and Space Division, National Museum of Science and Technology, Ottawa; Okanagan Air Services, Kelowna, B.C.; *Air Age; The Condulet; The Polar Record;* the Department of Mines and Resources; the Public Archives of Canada; the Canadian Aviation Historical Society; the Library of Congress, Washington; the Public Archives of Nova Scotia; the Alexander Graham Bell National Historic Park; the National Library, Ottawa; the Department of Transport Library; *The National Geographic Magazine;* Walter Gilbert Realty; *Canadian Aviation Directory; Who's Who in Canada; Who's Who in World Aviation; Who's Who in Aviation; American Aviation Directory; Aviation Directory of Canada;* the National Research Council; *SAE Journal;* the Calgary Flying Club; *The Toronto Star;* The Military Sea Transportation Service (MSTS) (U.S.); the Department of the Navy (U.S.); the Defence Research Board; Maritime Central Airways; Federal Electric Company, Paramus, N.J.; *Financial Post; Hawker Siddeley Review;* the Ottawa Public Library; the Air Industries and Transport Association; and others whose names may have slipped my memory at this time.

I acknowledge and thank the following persons who very kindly assisted me through providing information, photographs, suggestions and/or advice or guidance: R.W. Bradford (Curator, Aviation and Space, National Museum of Science and Technology); J.C. Floyd; Miss Anita Jacobsen; Donald K. Archibald; W.G. Jewitt; David Willock; J. Clark Ruse; D.F. Parrott; Mrs. Mary Roberts; Fred W. Hotson; A.L. Sawle; Commander Frederick B. Watt; Mrs. W.R. (Violet) May; H.C. Ingram; Maurice Giles; A.R. Fenwick; Kathleen M. Clarke; Keith Edgar; Major Robert Dodds, O.B.E., M.C.; G.A. "Tommy" Thompson; A.G. Lester; Frank Reilly; W.A. MacIntosh; A.F. "Sandy" MacDonald; Ross Wilmot; J.L. McKelvie; W.F. Haehnel; D.J. Dalzell; John Best; Bruce West; Ethel M. Kirkpatrick; Don. S. Robertson; C.K. Le Capelain; Gordon Bulger; Mac West; W.G. Anderson; A.C. Morrison; Les Edwards; Gordon B. Rayner; George S. Lace; Mrs. Ada (A.B.) Carlson; Miss Dorothy Drew; Squadron Leader O.G. Nelson; Wing Commander J.H. Hitchins (former Air Historian with the Department of National Defence); Major A.W. Parrott, U.S.A.F., Edmonton; R.A. Keith; J.K. Reynolds; Commander J.P. Croal (Defence Research Board); Wing Commander J.A. Wiseman; J.S. Terrill (M.S.T.S.); N.S. Novikoff; Mrs. Geraldine Trudel; Emma Keates; Norman Avery; Miss Irene Williams; D.L. Buchanan, D.F.C.; Bill Bryant; Robert B. Gayner; Douglas Dewar; Peter Robertson; John Reid; Kenneth John Christie; John Gordon, J.P. De Wet; Richard Finnie; Miss Bernice Dow; Miss Gertrude Jones; Miss B.V. Scott; R.J. Crossley; Earl Hickson; A.J. "Fred" Shortt; Miss Dorothy E. Ryder; Mrs. A.D. McLean; G. Lusignan; Peter Cobbett; G.C. Finlayson; Robert F. Shaw; Air Marshall W.A. Curtis, C.B., C.B.E., etc; Mayor Allan A. Lamport; Group Captain Charles B. Limbrick (Ret.) (former Director of Radar Warfare, R.C.A.F.); Arnold Edinborough; J.E.R. Ross; Herbert Hollick-Kenyon; G.L. McGee; Hal Carey; M.C. Eames; Miss J. Kennedy; J.L. Harrison; Mrs. Romeo Vachon; Mrs. J.H. Tudhope; those who wish to remain anonymous; and those whose names may have slipped my memory at this time.

Then, too, I would like to thank my husband, the Reverend William S. Sutherland, for assisting me in various ways in the preparation of this work through his patience and understanding; his excellent suggestions; and his helpful criticism in reading some of the material.

A.G.S.

Canada's
Aviation
Pioneers

Landmarks in Canadian Aviation

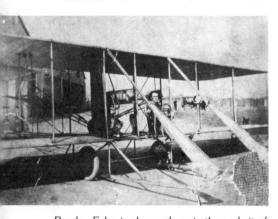

Royden Foley is shown above in the cockpit of a Wright plane, Model B, at Mineola, Long Island, N.Y., in 1916. It was just after Royden Foley had graduated from the Pratt Institute of Technology in New York that he joined Orville and Wilbur Wright in their flying experiments at Mineola Field, Long Island, in August, where he learned to fly at the Wright Brothers' flying school during the summer and fall of 1916. He trained on Wright's Model B plane. He received F.A.I. License No. 615. He flew his first aeroplane, a Martin-Curtiss, in November, 1916, from New York to Philadelphia. Later he flew a Sloan biplane for Aeromarine Corpn., New York, and then a Nieuport monoplane for a Mrs. Pearce of New York. Late in 1916 he joined the Royal Flying Corps, flying with No. 81 Squadron, using D.H. 6 aircraft. It was early in 1929 that Royden Foley sold the sole rights to manufacture Avro Avian aircraft in Canada to the Ottawa Car and Manufacturing Company Limited, Ottawa. He had purchased the rights earlier from A.V. Roe Company, England. He did well for himself. In World War II, Royden Foley served as a W/Cdr., at Ottawa, Windsor and Vancouver. Royden Foley was born in Saint John, N.B., and was a brother of Sam Foley, who was employed by the Department of Transport.

Photo courtesy of Gordon B. Rayner.

G-CAAB, A Curtiss JN-4, the second plane to be registered in Canada, belonged to McClelland and Lobb of Saskatoon. Its home base was "McClelland Field" at Saskatoon. Likewise, Captain H. S. McClelland held Commercial Air Pilot's License No. 2 — the second one to be issued in Canada. G-CAAB was used for barnstorming during 1919 and 1920, until the time of its accident in May, 1920. From left to right: H. S. McClelland, not known, H.N. Hyslop and H. D. Barley, all of Saskatoon.

The Aerial Service Company's hangar at Regina in 1920, with G-CAAA, a Curtiss JN-4 in front of the hangar. At the right is R. J. Groome of Moose Jaw and Regina who first owned G-CAAA, shown above. Also it was R. J. Groome who received Canadian Commercial Air Pilot's License No. 1 dated April 20, 1920 — the first ever issued in Canada. G-CAAA was later bought by registration markings, G-CAAA, ever issued in Canada. It was registered on April 20, 1920. Shown at the left is Robert McCombie of Regina, who received Canadian Air Engineer's License No. 1, dated April 20, 1920 — the first ever issued in Canada. G-CAAA was later bought by O. H. Clearwater of Saskatoon. R. J. Groome, a Flying Instructor at Regina, and student pilot A. J. Sims were killed in an aircraft crash on September 20, 1935, at 8:40 a.m. at Regina in Avro Avian CF-CDX on an instruction flight when the elevator control system of the aircraft failed in flight. The student pilot was at the controls and Groome was helpless to do anything. So ended the life of one of Canada's great pioneer pilots.

N-CACM, an H.S.2L flying boat, belonging to Pacific Airways, Seattle, Washington and Vancouver, B.C. It was made by Boeing Airplane Co., and carried three passengers. This was the year 1921. Five Canadian-registered aircraft in the early days bore the designation "N", rather than the designation "G". Those aircraft bearing the designation "N" were from the U.S., Seattle, New York and Dayton, but had special permission to operate in Canada. The five "N" Canadian registrations were: N-CACM, as above; N-CADR, a C.L.45 seaplane belonging to E. Hubbard of Seattle; N-CADS, a B1 flying boat, also belonging to E. Hubbard of Seattle; N-CADT, a Junkers 6, belonging to J.L. Larsen, New York; and N-CAED, a Dayton Wright F.P.2 with Twin Liberty engines, belonging to Dayton Wright Co., Dayton, Ohio, but based at Sault Ste. Marie, Ontario.

J. Scott-Williams of Vancouver with his Curtiss JN-4 aircraft, G-CAAG, on a landing field at Vernon, B.C., in 1921. He had bought the aircraft from Pacific Aviation Company of Minoru Park, Vancouver. J. Scott-Williams held Commercial Pilot's Certificate No. 138, dated July 11, 1921.

CF-CAK, a D.H. 60 Moth, was the first aircraft registered in the "CF" Series. It was owned by the Hamilton Aero Club. The aircraft was built in 1928 and its Certificate of Airworthiness was issued on January 28, 1929. The aircraft is shown with its wings folded for storage, while the one in the background has its wings open for flight. The plane changed hands several times and the whereabouts of the first aircraft registered in the "CF" Series is unknown today.

Photo courtesy of Gordon B. Rayner, formerly Chief Airworthiness Inspector with the Civil Aviation Branch of the Department of Transport.

Aircraft CF-AAA was the first aircraft operated by the Canadian Flying Clubs Association. By June 1, 1932, this aircraft (Moth) had made four trans-Canada flights. CF-AAA was a D.H. 60M Moth, with a Gypsy 1 Engine, registered in the name of the Aviation League of Canada, Ottawa, operated by the Canadian Flying Clubs Association. It was sold to the Cape Breton Flying Club of Sydney, N.S., on July 17, 1934, for $750. Then it was sold to Mr. C.R. Rogers, Director of the Cape Breton Flying Club, Sydney for $1,200 on July 22, 1934, as the club was in debt. It was next sold to Russell Smith, businessman, Sydney, N.S., for $950 on April 17, 1935. CF-AAA was sold to Colin McMillan of Fort William on July 13, 1938, for $950; then to Howard Disano, a service station operator, and Ralph Carroll of Sault Ste. Marie on April 22, 1940, for $200. By January, 1950, the aircraft was not to be used again. Its certificates were lost, and the aircraft was scrapped. That was the end of CF-AAA.

Photo courtesy of Murton Seymour.

"EU", the first Vickers "Viking" flying boat to be built in Canada, about to be launched at the Vickers Basin, Montreal, on July 25, 1923. It was the first post war Canadian-built aircraft.

Norseman CF-AYO, Mark I. The Norseman, a high wing single-engine monoplane, was designed in Canada at Cartierville, P.Q. This rugged aircraft was to become well-known throughout Canada and was outstanding amongst Canadian produced aircraft. When Bob Noorduyn organized the Noorduyn Aircraft Co. at Cartierville in 1934, he began work on the design of the famous Norseman. In 1935 Noorduyn Aviation Ltd. was formed to produce the Norseman. The first Norseman, Mk. I, built in 1935, was registered as CF-AYO. It was powered with a 420 h.p. Wright Whirlwind R-975-E3 engine, and had a Hamilton Standard controllable pitch propeller and Handley Page flaps. The Norseman was not a landplane equipped with floats as an afterthought, but seaplane and skiplane requirements were studied as part of the original design. Leigh Capreol made the test flights on the Norseman prototype in November, 1935, except the first one which was made by John McDonough. A.G. "Tim" Sims took delivery of CF-AYO for Dominion Skyways of Montreal in January, 1936. CF-AYO was used by Warner Brothers during the summer of 1941 while making the film "Captains of the Clouds" in Canada. It was hired from Dominion Skyways. CF-AYO continued to fly through the years for other companies such as Canadian Pacific Air Lines, Cap Airways Ltd., Gold Belt Air Service and Mont-Laurier Aviation Co. Ltd., who sold it to Orillia Air Services, Orillia. CF-AYO made its last flight on August 28, 1953, when it had an accident at Round Island Lake in the Georgian Bay area. Roy Downing, the pilot, was killed. Only one Mk. I Norseman, CF-AYO, was built; while three Mk. IIs were built each powered with the same Wright Whirlwind engine. These were CF-AZA, CF-AZE and CF-AZS.

Norseman CF-BAM, Mark III. Norseman CF-BAM, shown above on floats, was the Mk. III prototype. It was powered with a 550 h.p. Pratt and Whitney Wasp SC1 engine. Some four or five of these Mk. III Norseman were built. Leigh Brintnell of Mackenzie Air Service, Edmonton, picked up CF-BAM at St. Hubert on December 7, 1936, and flew it to Edmonton. CF-BAM saw service with the company until it was transferred to the R.C.A.F. in February, 1940. CF-BAW marked the beginning of the Norseman Mk. IV aircraft, which was powered with a 600 h.p. Pratt and Whitney Wasp H engine. Close to 100 Mk. IVs were built. The Mk. IVs were also used as navigation training 'planes under the B.C.A.T.P. By 1943, the Mk. VI Norseman was on the way. Some 767 Mk. VIs were built, 746 of which went to the U.S.A.A.F. The Mk. VI was basically the same as the Mk. IV, except for the addition of specialized military equipment for use during the war years, and a few other minor changes. The Mk. V followed Mk. VI, as Bob Noorduyn, the designer, had set aside the Mk. V (for Victory) for his post-war Norseman. The first Mk. V, CF-OBG, was purchased by the Ontario Provincial Air Service in June, 1945. It was, of course, the civil version without the military equipment, with a 500 lb. increase in payload. It was powered with the same engine as Mk. VI, the Pratt and Whitney R-1340-AN1 Wasp engine. Some 55 of these were built. From 1935 to 1945, Bob Noorduyn was Vice-President and General Manager of Noorduyn Aircraft Company, Cartierville, P.Q. During this time the company built over 900 Norseman, mostly for the R.C.A.F. and the U.S.A.A.F. In April, 1946, the rights and licence to build and sell the Norseman were sold to the Canadian Car and Foundry Co. of Montreal, and Bob Noorduyn then severed his connection with the further development of the Norseman. The Canadian Car then developed the Mk. VII, which made its first flight in the summer of 1951. When the Korean War came along, the St. Laurent plant where the Mk. VII was being developed was closed down, and the company's operations were transferred to Fort William, Ontario. No further development work was done on the Mk. VII at Fort William, and it was stored in the hangar belonging to Superior Airways. (The hangar was destroyed by fire in 1958, and the Mk. VII Norseman as well.) Since the company's production licence from the D.O.T. expired in 1953, Canadian Car decided to dispose of the licence to build the Norseman. So Bob Noorduyn's interest in the Norseman was rekindled, and Noorduyn Norseman Aircraft Ltd. was formed as an independent company in Montreal to give continued service to Norseman users. Bob Noorduyn was President and consultant. CF-LFR was the last Norseman to be built and it was test flown on December 17, 1959, by veteran test pilot and bush pilot Phil Lariviere of Montreal. CF-LFR was the 918th Norseman to be built. Bob Noorduyn, the designer of the famous Norseman, died in Burlington, Vermont, on February 22, 1959 — the year that the last Norseman was produced.

Replica.
Photo courtesy of the R.C.A.F.

History of the Trans-Canada Trophy

The "Trans-Canada Trophy," also known as the "McKee Trophy," came into existence in 1927 to commemorate the first trans-Canada seaplane flight made in September, 1926, by Captain James Dalzell McKee, a wealthy American pilot and owner of the Douglas seaplane used on this historic flight. Squadron Leader (now Air Vice-Marshal) A. Earl Godfrey was first pilot and navigator of the seaplane.

In the course of this historic seaplane flight Captain Dalzell McKee and Squadron Leader Earl Godfrey had to make an unexpected landing at Lake Traverse, Ontario, due to the weather, where they remained overnight. During their conversation that evening the topic of a trophy first came up as they were talking over many things.

When they arrived at Lac du Bonnet, Manitoba, they were met by Flight Lieutenant George Mercer, Commanding Officer of the Lac du Bonnet Air Force Station. The subject of a trophy to commemorate the flight came up again in the course of their talks in the evening. Dalzell McKee, Earl Godfrey and George Mercer discussed the pros and cons in a three-way, round-table parley.

When their flight across Canada to San Francisco, California, was completed, Captain McKee and Squadron Leader Godfrey returned to Ottawa to visit J. A. Wilson, the Secretary of the Royal Canadian Air Force. Captain

McKee's plans for a Trans-Canada Trophy to commemorate this flight were explained to him. In due course arrangements were completed, and the "Trans-Canada Trophy" came into existence.

To show his appreciation of the courtesies extended to him and for the assistance given to him during his flight across Canada by the Royal Canadian Air Force, the Ontario Provincial Air Service and other civil aviation organizations in Canada, Captain McKee presented this trophy with the request that it be awarded annually to the person rendering the most meritorious service during the year in the advancement of aviation in Canada.

The trophy is about three feet high and takes the form of a winged figure flying over the world, holding aloft a seaplane. The globe, winged figure and miniature Douglas seaplane, all of which are in sterling silver, rest on a marble base, on the front of which is a silver shield bearing the inscription "Trans-Canada Trophy." On the reverse face there is another shield bearing the following inscription:
Presented by J. Dalzell McKee, Esq., to commemorate the first Trans-Canada Seaplane Flight, September, 1926, to be awarded annually for meritorious service in the advancement of aviation in Canada.

Smaller shields on which were to be engraved the names of the winners were also provided.

A generous endowment to provide a replica for each winner was also given by Captain McKee at the time. The replica was a sterling silver vase suitably engraved with a representation of the trophy, the date and the winner's name. The replica was for the permanent retention of the recipient, and was presented at the same time as the trophy, or forwarded to the recipient. However, with the award of the trophy for 1967, a suitable wall plaque was presented instead of the silver vase. This change in policy was due to the rising price of silver.

The Minister of National Defence was the trustee for the trophy under the Deed of Gift. In accordance with the Deed of Gift from J. Dalzell McKee to the Minister of National Defence, the conditions governing the award of the Trans-Canada Trophy were laid down by a committee; and having been laid down should not be changed, except for good reason. The following conditions were, therefore, recommended by the Committee of Award for 1927, as being suitable for this and future awards. These considerations governing the award of the trophy, which were laid down in 1927, were as follows:

(1) The recipient should be one who is domiciled in Canada and who is identified with Canadian flying, either military or civil.

(2) Qualification as a pilot is a prior claim to consideration, but lack of such qualification does not exclude from consideration the claims of others connected with aviation who perform meritorious service.

(3) Continuous performance throughout the year should receive greater consideration than a single brilliant exploit.

(4) Operations tending to advance the cause of aviation should receive consideration over exploits of a difficult or dangerous character serving no useful end.

(5) The extension of the operation of aircraft into new fields should receive special consideration.

Officers commanding the R.C.A.F. units, both military and civil government operations, were invited to make recommendations from the personnel under their command for meritorious service during the year under consideration. All civil and commercial operating companies and provincial government services operating aircraft were also invited to submit recommendations on any of their personnel. In addition, any person claiming to have performed meritorious service could forward his own qualifications for the consideration of the committee. Also, the Committee of Award itself could enquire into any claimants for recognition who were not otherwise nominated.

The recommendations of the committee were to be forwarded to the Minister of National Defence on or before the first of April each year. The award was to be made by the minister as soon as possible after recommendations were received. The trophy was to be given into the custody of the recipient, and was to be returned to the Minister of National Defence not later than the 15th of January of the following year.

Prior to accepting the trophy, the recipient was required to provide a suitable bond to guarantee the safekeeping of the trophy and its return to the custody of the minister. Should this not be agreeable to the recipient, he could leave the trophy in the custody of the minister.

The Department of National Defence defrayed the cost of transportation of the trophy anywhere in Canada to and from the address of the recipient each year.

The conditions of this award were drawn up by Mr. J. A. Wilson, Squadron Leader Earl Godfrey and Squadron Leader A. T. Cowley. These conditions embodied any specific wishes that Dalzell McKee had in mind.

In accordance with the expressed wish of Dalzell McKee, the Committee of Award was to consist of not less than three persons. The Controller of Civil Aviation and, at that time, the Staff Officer in Charge of Civil Government Air Operations, Royal Canadian Air Force, were to be two of the members of this committee.

Although Dalzell McKee had completed the arrangements regarding the donation of the trophy before his untimely and unfortunate death on June 9, 1927, while attempting to land his Vedette flying boat on Lac la Pêche, Quebec, his secretary, Miss McCandless, kept in touch with the R.C.A.F. to assist in completing any remaining details.

His intentions as to the award of the trophy were carried out in the spirit in which he gave it. And awards were made from year to year.

Then the Trans-Canada Trophy was loaned permanently to the National Museum of Science and Technology (then the National Aviation Museum) in July, 1963, and placed in their custody, while proceedings were under way in an endeavour to retire the trophy.

And so the Minister of National Defence, then the Honourable Paul Hellyer, announced in April, 1965, that the Trans-Canada Trophy had been retired after having been awarded on thirty-five occasions. There would be no award for 1964. The trophy had already been placed in the museum. The Committee of Award had recommended retirement of the trophy because the members felt that individual contributions to aviation had become team efforts rather than individual efforts, it was reported, and individual efforts were not likely to be outstanding.

This caused concern amongst a number of winners of the Trans-Canada Trophy who felt that there was still room for individual effort. Accordingly, Philip Garratt called a meeting at The de Havilland Aircraft Company to discuss the matter. Those present were Philip Garratt, "Punch" Dickins, Murt Seymour, George Phillips and Group Captain Lewis Leigh. Also present was Air Vice-Marshal John L. Plant. They concluded that there was still room for individual winners, but that the trophy should be awarded only when a clearly warranted winner was available and not necessarily on an annual basis, as before. They commissioned Punch Dickins and Air Vice-Marshal Plant to go to Ottawa to talk to

Trans-Canada Trophy.
Photo courtesy of the R.C.A.F.

the Minister of National Defence, to put forward their views. This was done and the minister agreed with them. So the trophy was again to become active, to be awarded along the lines which they had suggested.[1]

In addition, John Gordon, author and writer, Ottawa, had previously spoken with the Honourable Paul Hellyer, Minister of National Defence, concerning the importance of reinstating the annual award of the Trans-Canada Trophy.

Therefore, plans to reinstate the annual award of the Trans-Canada Trophy, and withdraw it from retirement, were announced by Mr. Paul Hellyer, Minister of National Defence, while speaking at a testimonial dinner held in Ottawa on March 30, 1966, in honour of Philip Garratt, who had been selected by the minister as honorary winner of the trophy for 1966. The dinner honouring Mr. Garratt was sponsored by the Air Industries Association of Canada. The trophy had last been awarded to Frank MacDougall for 1963. This presentation generated renewed interest in the award of the trophy and resulted in its being permanently reinstated.

As a result, upon directions from the Minister of National Defence, new conditions for the award of the Trans-Canada Trophy were drafted by a joint civil and military Committee of Award, which were approved by the minister in the spring of 1968 just in time for the 1967 award. The new conditions for presentation of the award placed special emphasis on excellence in the field of flying operations. The award would be made only in those years where the contribution of the nominees was deemed worthy of such recognition. The trophy would remain on display in the National Museum of Science and Technology, and be removed for formal presentations.

As a result, the terms governing the award of the Trans-Canada Trophy were amended in 1968, as follows:

(1) The recipient shall be one who is domiciled in Canada who is identified with Canadian flying, either military or civil.

(2) Qualification as aircrew is a prior claim to consideration, but lack of such qualification does not exclude others from consideration providing they qualify in all other respects as included in these Conditions of Award.

(3) Operations which advance the cause of aviation shall receive consideration over exploits of a dangerous nature serving no useful end.

(4) Continuous performance throughout the year is worthy of consideration, however the trophy is awarded primarily for recognition of an outstanding contribution or spectacular achievement in the field of Air Operations.

(5) Pioneering of new areas of Aircraft Operations is to receive special consideration.

Then, through an arrangement, the Department of National Defence transferred the administration of the Trans-Canada Trophy to the Canadian Aeronautics and Space Institute early in 1972.

The Minister of National Defence approved the administrative transfer of the award to the Canadian Aeronautics and Space Institute on condition that the trophy remains in the custody of the National Museum of Science and Technology, and that a representative from the Department of National Defence continues to be in a position to uphold the interests of that department in administering the trophy.

As nominations for the Trans-Canada

Trophy would be considered by the senior Committee of Award of the Canadian Aeronautics and Space Institute, the Committee of Award for this trophy within the Department of National Defence would no longer be required. Therefore, the committee was dissolved at the direction of the Minister of National Defence.

The Canadian Aeronautics and Space Institute solicits nominations for the award of the Trans-Canada Trophy in the same way and at the same time as it solicits nominations for other awards. This involves inviting nominations in the *Canadian Aeronautics and Space Journal*, and the distribution of this invitation to a fairly wide mailing list of senior people concerned with aviation in Canada. The list includes all fellows of the institute, members of the institute's council, chairmen of the institute's branches, members of the institute, heads of government agencies, companies, universities, aviation publications, and others, about two hundred or so.

The Committee of Award, aside from its representative from the Department of National Defence, consists of fellows of the institute, as representative as possible of various fields of aerospace activity. The representative from the Department of National Defence must be satisfied that the committee makes a proper selection, to meet with the approval of the minister, who is responsible for the Trans-Canada Trophy. He does not represent military aviation, as such, as distinct from civil aviation.

The terms governing the award of the

---

[1]From a talk given by Group Captain Z. L. Leigh to the Canadian Aviation Historical Society Convention in June, 1976.

Trans-Canada Trophy, as laid down in 1972, are as follows:

Summary of terms

For outstanding achievement in the field of Air Operations, particularly in pioneering, as aircrew, new areas and applications of aviation. The achievement shall be of recent years and the recipient shall have been a resident of Canada at the time of achievement.

Terms

(1) The trophy shall be awarded annually (except when no qualified recipient is nominated) for outstanding achievement in the field of Air Operations; this achievement may be a single brilliant exploit within the previous year or a sustained high level of performance in recent years. To maintain the prestige of the trophy, it shall not be awarded for less than outstanding achievement.

(2) Pioneering of new areas of Air Operations shall receive special consideration.

(3) Achievements which advance the use of aviation shall receive consideration over achievements serving no useful end.

(4) The recipient shall be one who was domiciled in Canada and who was identified with Canadian flying, either military or civil, at the time of the achievement for which the trophy is awarded.

(5) Qualification as aircrew shall be a prior claim to consideration, but lack of such qualification shall not exclude others from consideration, provided they qualify in all other respects under these Conditions of Award.

COPY OF THE ORIGINAL AGREEMENT

THIS AGREEMENT made this . . . . 11th . . . . day of . . . . .February . . . . A.D. 1927.

BETWEEN:

> **JAMES DALZELL McKEE,** of the City of Pittsburg, in the State of Pennsylvania, one of the United States of America, hereinafter called "the Donor",

Of the First Part

-AND-

> **THE HONOURABLE, THE MINISTER OF NATIONAL DEFENCE,** of the Dominion of Canada, hereinafter called "the Minister",

Of the Second Part

WHEREAS the donor, a citizen of the United States of America, is desirous of expressing in a tangible manner his appreciation of the continuous courtesy shown him by Canadians; and

WHEREAS the donor has expressed his desire to show such tangible appreciation by presenting a trophy, together with an endowment fund, for the purpose of providing annually a replica of said trophy, or medallion in lieu; and

WHEREAS the donor is desirous that such trophy and endowment fund shall be held in trust in the manner and under the terms and conditions as hereinafter provided.

NOW, THEREFORE, THIS AGREEMENT WITNESSETH:

1.   That the donor doth hereby give, grant and donate unto the said Minister a certain trophy to be known and described as "The Trans-Canada Trophy", to be held in trust by the said Minister under the terms and conditions hereunder set forth.

2.   The said trophy shall constitute a Memorial of the first Trans-Continental Seaplane Flight made successfully in September, 1926, by the donor and Squadron Leader Godfrey, MC, AFC, R.C.A.F., in which the assistance of the Royal Canadian Air Force played no small part, as well as a perpetual trophy *for the encouragement of aviation* to be awarded in theory each year according to fixed principles, to such Canadian whether civilian, or a member of His Majesty's naval, land or air forces, who, in the opinion of an executive committee, hereunder mentioned, is best entitled to such award.

3.   The said executive committee shall consist of at least three persons who shall be appointed by the Minister, and without limiting the generality of the foregoing, the persons holding the offices of Controller of Civil Aviation and Staff Officer in charge of Civil Operations shall, if possible, be members of the said Committee, and, further, that the said Committee shall, as far as possible, be comprised of persons prominently identified with flying in the Dominion.

4.   The donor further gives, grants and donates unto the said Minister to be held in trust by him the sum of One Thousand ($1,000.00) Dollars, which shall be invested or re-invested from time to time in such securities as are authorized for the investment of trust funds, the interest accruing therefrom to be applied annually in perpetuity to the purchase of a replica or medallion of the said trophy, which

said replica or medallion shall be awarded annually by the executive committee in the manner aforesaid.

5.   The said executive committee shall determine the principles, conditions and rules which shall govern the annual award of the trophy, together with the replica or medallion thereof, having regard to the intentions of the donor as herein recited, and such principles, conditions and rules when once determined and settled by the said Committee, with the approval of the Minister, shall remain unchanged, so far as may be practicable, and shall govern such award in perpetuity, and, moreover, such principles, conditions and rules shall be given such publicity as shall, in the opinion of the said executive committee, encourage public interest in aviation and confidence in the justice and fairness governing the awarding of the said trophy.

6.   The Minister for himself and his successors in office hereby accepts the trusteeship of the said trophy and endowment fund, and hereby agrees to administer the same in accordance with the terms and conditions herein provided, and in such manner as will give effect to the intention of the donor.

IN WITNESS WHEREOF the parties hereto have hereunto set their hands and seals the day and year first above written.

SIGNED, SEALED & DELIVERED
    In the presence of:
    (sgd.) R. J. Orde (Colonel)   (sgd.) James Dalzell McKee
    (sgd.) T. W. MacDowell   (sgd.) J. L. Ralston

Captain James Dalzell McKee, Pittsburgh, Pa.
Photo courtesy of A/V/M. A.E. Godfrey, M.C., A.F.C., V.C.

Captain James Dalzell McKee, the Donor of the Trans-Canada (McKee) Trophy

Captain James Dalzell McKee was born in Pittsburgh, Pennsylvania, in 1893. He was a civil pilot and a keen aviation enthusiast who liked to explore new country. He was thirty-three years of age when he came to Canada and made his first flight to Sudbury, Ontario, in the spring of 1926. During his flight to Sudbury, his desire to explore new territory was whetted so, in August, 1926, Captain McKee returned to Canada to make a flight to northern Ontario, James Bay and Hudson Bay.

Captain McKee planned on using his Douglas Corps Observation aeroplane. For this flight, his aeroplane was to be converted into a seaplane by equipping it with a set of pontoons. Upon receiving permission from the Canadian Government to make the flight, this conversion job was carried out by the personnel of the Naval Air Station at Washington, D.C. Arrangements were made for Captain Wick, Officer Commanding the Naval Air Station, Washington, to accompany McKee on this flight through northern Ontario to Hudson Bay.

Upon the completion of this work on the aircraft, they left Washington to start their summer flight to Sudbury, Ontario, and points north. Their trip to Sudbury was enjoyable. However, when they went to take off from Sudbury to continue their flight, they discovered that the Douglas seaplane would not take off from fresh water with a full load. This came as a big disappointment to them as they had high hopes of reaching Hudson Bay, and seeing as much of the north country as possible. Faced with this unexpected problem, they had no choice but to cancel their flight to northern Ontario and Hudson Bay. The seaplane's load was lightened considerably, and it was flown to Montreal where it was left with Canadian Vickers Limited for certain modifications and repairs. A new metal propeller was ordered, and the Liberty engine was shipped to Washington, D.C., for overhaul.

Captain McKee got in touch with the Douglas Aircraft Company in Santa Monica, who told him that, by shortening the rear pontoon struts, there would be considerable improvement in take-off performance. Further, to obtain the best possible results, they advised returning the aircraft to their factory so that they might do this experimental work. Captain McKee thought he would like to make the flight to the Douglas Aircraft Company's plant at Santa Monica, California, by way of Vancouver, British Columbia, which would take him all the way across Canada and down the west coast of the United States.

With this in mind, McKee got in touch with the Controller of Civil Aviation for Canada to enquire whether or not it was possible to fly a seaplane across Canada. He was told that, although it had never been done, it was considered feasible and that a fairly good water route could be followed across Canada. Should he decide to carry out his plans, the Department of National Defence would supply him with a set of maps showing a seaplane route and give him every possible assistance.

On receiving permission to make the flight, Captain McKee had also expressed his desire to have an officer from the Royal Canadian Air Force accompany him as pilot.

As information about a seaplane route across Canada would be of great value to the R.C.A.F. and, further, as Earl Godfrey had already received orders to visit R.C.A.F. units at Vancouver, High River, Winnipeg and sub-units, this was thought to be a very favourable opportunity. So, Godfrey was asked to accompany McKee as first pilot and navigator.

The purpose of the flight was, therefore, two-fold. In the first place, McKee's objective was to transport the aircraft to the Douglas Aircraft Company's plant at Santa Monica, California; and, in the second place, the objective of the R.C.A.F. was to obtain a report on the possibility of a seaplane route across Canada.

The Royal Canadian Air Force had few seaplane bases in 1926, and there were very few landing fields along the way for aircraft. Also, the pilot could not avail himself of radio or meteorological facilities to assist him in his flying in those days. On this flight, gas and oil had to be shipped in advance to all of their stopping places along the route. Further, they had to have Imperial Oil bring gasoline down to their bases in drums. The crew then had to transfer it from drums into small cans and pour it into the gas tanks.

On this first transcontinental seaplane flight, the Douglas seaplane had a Liberty war-time engine in it, and it was on wooden floats. The Liberty engine was water-cooled and had to be drained every evening and refilled in the morning to prevent the engine from freezing during the night when the temperature dropped to freezing. In the morning, the oil had to be heated in order to warm up the engine so it could be started. Drums had to be rolled to the banks of the rivers in places, and ladders improvised for getting up and down the banks.

The Controller of Civil Aviation arranged with the Imperial Oil Company to ship aviation gasoline and oil to Prince Albert, Wabamun Lake and Fort Fraser. Fort Fraser was to be used as a refuelling base had it been necessary to fly to Prince Rupert, if bad weather had been encountered along the North Thompson and Fraser River route. McKee and Godfrey also obtained permission from Roy Maxwell, Director of the Ontario Provincial Air Service, to refuel at any of their bases en route or use their facilities. This courtesy was extended at Sudbury, Orient Bay and Sioux Lookout and, thanks to the R.C.A.F., at Ottawa, Lac du Bonnet, near Winnipeg, and Vancouver.

With the combined facilities of the R.C.A.F. and the Ontario Provincial Air Service, it was necessary to refuel at only two places between Montreal and Vancouver which were not air harbours.

Captain McKee and Squadron Leader Godfrey planned the transcontinental flight together, and made all the arrangements. They flew across Canada under trying conditions and, yes, in fact, in some instances very hazardous ones. They worked together, and lived together all the way from Montreal to San Francisco. On this flight they talked over their past and their future plans for their next year's flight to Herschel Island.

Godfrey arrived at Canadian Vickers Limited in Montreal by train at eleven o'clock on the morning of September 11, 1926. Captain McKee and Squadron Leader Godfrey planned on leaving Montreal around one o'clock the same day to start their flight. They hoped to go as far as Sudbury that day. However, as Dalzell McKee was delayed by the customs officials, he did not reach Canadian Vickers until after two o'clock. By the time the aircraft was completely loaded and ready to take off, it was about three o'clock. As it was rather late to try to make Sudbury that day, they decided to fly as far as Ottawa. Furthermore, as the engine had just been overhauled, they thought it advisable to make a short flight to Ottawa and then have the engine checked over before going any farther. Also, Canadian Vickers had just shortened the rear pontoon struts four and one-half inches to give better aircraft performance on take-off from fresh water with a full load. The aircraft had not been flown since these changes had been made; but when flown it took off easily with a full load.

It was on a Saturday afternoon, on September 11, 1926, when Captain James Dalzell McKee and Squadron Leader Earl Godfrey left Montreal on the first leg of their historic trans-Canada seaplane flight. The seaplane left the water at 3:05 hours, E.S.T., in the presence of two R.C.A.F. officers, one of whom was Flight Lieutenant A. L. Johnson, and a few officials of Canadian Vickers. Godfrey was first pilot and navigator of McKee's Douglas Corps Observation seaplane. They climbed to an altitude of 2,000 feet. As Canadian Vickers was located on the east side of the city, it gave them an excellent opportunity to see Montreal. In a few minutes they had left the city behind them and were heading west for Vancouver.

After leaving the St. Lawrence River, they followed the Ottawa River to Ottawa. They landed at Shirley's Bay about 4:30 in the afternoon, where No. 3 Operations Squadron of the R.C.A.F. was stationed. The seaplane was taxied to the slipway and handed over to the station personnel who checked the engine, cleaned the distributor heads and moored it to a buoy for the night. From Montreal to Ottawa, the route was found to be ideal for seaplanes, as it was possible to land at any place on the Ottawa River.

Next morning, Sunday, the 12th, McKee and Godfrey reached the station at 6:00 A.M. to resume their journey from Ottawa to Lake Traverse, Ontario. The mechanics had everything in readiness. They were taken to the seaplane in a row boat, and they took off at 7:40 A.M., with a strong east wind blowing and an overcast sky. Leaving Ottawa behind, they followed a westerly course along the Ottawa River for thirty miles. They encountered rain clouds at Mink Lake, so they attempted to climb above them, but soon became engulfed and were forced to glide down until they were level with the tree tops. They sighted the Canadian National Railway line and attempted to follow it, but as the clouds were about down to the tracks they were forced to alight on Lake Traverse, which is about 100 miles from Ottawa.

Choosing a sandy beach, they taxied to it and tied up. It was raining very hard

Douglas seaplane in which J. Dalzell McKee made his historic flight across Canada in 1926, accompanied by S/Ldr. A.E. Godfrey, M.C., A.F.C., V.C., of the R.C.A.F. This photo was taken by Punch Dickins, just north of the Saskatchewan River.
Via A/V/M. A.E. Godfrey.

and there was not a sign of habitation so they started to walk toward the railway. After an hour's walk through the wet woods they came to a log cabin where a provincial fire ranger lived. His name was John Culhane. He was pleased to see them, but needless to say they were more than pleased to see him. John Culhane looked after them well, loaning them dry shoes and clothing, giving them their meals and his own bed, while he slept on the floor. That was real hospitality, given when it was needed most. They telephoned a message through to their headquarters to give news of their whereabouts, and say that they were O.K.

Late in the afternoon a wind came up, so McKee and Godfrey went to look at the aircraft to make certain that it was secure — as they were short of rope in tying it up.

During the night the sky cleared. Rising at three in the early morning, they had breakfast and went out to the seaplane. They pumped water out of the wooden pontoons, and were hoping to get an early start. They had spent a day there waiting for the weather to clear up so that they could get off the lake.

On Monday, the 13th, McKee and Godfrey took off a few minutes before eleven o'clock under an overcast sky, with good visibility up to about 1,000 feet, to continue their flight to Sudbury.

Over Lake Nipissing the clouds began to lift and, by the time they reached Sudbury, the sky was fairly clear. This route was ideal for seaplanes too, as there were many rivers and lakes where a seaplane could land safely. They alighted on Ramsay Lake, south of the City of Sudbury, where an Ontario Provincial Air Service's base was located. They were taken care of by the O.P.A.S., whose personnel refuelled the seaplane, inspected the engine and pumped out the wooden floats.

Leaving Sudbury the next day, the 14th, shortly after 7:30 in the morning, they flew to Orient Bay, where G. A. "Tommy" Thompson was based. Here they stopped for lunch. The route from Sudbury to Delmage Lake was northwesterly and followed the Canadian Pacific Railway, thence turning in a northerly direction crossing the Algoma Central and Hudson Bay Railway at Oba Lake. From Mountain Lake to Orient Bay it followed the Canadian National Railway. Refuelling, they left for Sioux Lookout. Visibility was not good en route and the clouds were below 500 feet over the lake, with rain-squalls. However, with the use of their compass, they had no difficulty in picking out the main line of the Canadian National Railway at Collins Lake, and they followed it all the way in to Sioux Lookout. Upon alighting, they tied up at the Ontario Provincial Air

Service's dock and refuelled at once, assisted by Mr. Ross, the station superintendent, and his men. They were guests of Mr. Ross for dinner that evening, and he also provided them with sleeping accommodation.

The morning of Wednesday, the 15th, was very calm at Sioux Lookout. As there was no wind and the water was smooth, they were unable to take off until a breeze came up. After three attempts, they finally managed to take off shortly after 11:00 A.M. There were clouds most of the way to Swan Lake, Malachi Lake and Lac du Bonnet. An attempt was made to follow the Winnipeg River from Minaki, but as the clouds were below 200 feet and as there were numerous lakes or waterways adjoining the river it was not possible to do this. They then decided to fly south, pick up the railway, return to Minaki, and then fly a compass course across country to Lac du Bonnet. Upon leaving Minaki, a compass course was flown for some 45 miles. Then they flew close to the river banks, and landed near an Indian settlement at Swan Lake to check their bearings. When the engine failed to start again, the seaplane drifted to the shore. Then the batteries were changed so the self-starter would work. From Swan Lake, they returned to the railway and followed it as far as Malachi Lake where they alighted to send a wire to Lac du Bonnet to let them know the cause of their delay. Leaving there, they again followed the railway to Lac du Bonnet where they arrived around 5:30 in the afternoon. At Lac du Bonnet they were met by Flight Lieutenant George Mercer (later a Group Captain in the R.C.A.F.) who was Commanding Officer at the Air Force Station there. Due to inclement weather and engine trouble they had to spend a day at Lac du Bonnet.

The morning of Friday, the 17th, dawned clear, with a strong north wind blowing, which indicated good weather. So preparations for departure were hurried. They left Lac du Bonnet that day, and flew to Prince Albert via Grand Rapids and the Saskatchewan River under favourable conditions. They alighted at the old dock, east of the bridge on the south side of the Saskatchewan River, at Prince Albert. It was indeed an ideal place to beach a seaplane. However, they had to do their own refuelling. When they arrived at the hotel, they met Flying Officers Dickins and Walker, who loaned them the services of their mechanic, Sergeant Little, to help them check the engine the following morning and prepare the aircraft for flight. The following day they left Prince Albert and flew to Lake Wabamun, just west of Edmonton. (Flying Officers Dickins and Walker, in a D.H. 4B photographic aircraft, while flying near the Douglas seaplane in the vicinity of Prince Albert, snapped several pictures of the seaplane.) The sky was overcast, with many clouds; however, visibility below them was good. The surrounding country was covered with a mantle of snow as they drew closer to Edmonton, and it was quite cold. Upon alighting at Edmonton, they engaged a watchman to take care of the aircraft for the night.

The next day, Sunday, the 19th, appeared to be a beautiful morning and their spirits were high. This was the day of their flight through the mountains — and it was the first clear day that they had in two weeks of flying. They were also going to have a chance to see the mountains. However, clouds formed in the mountains around noon at that time of year, so they worked hurriedly to get off to an early start, but again they had difficulty in taking off due to the calm water of Lake Wabamun, which is about 2,400 feet above sea level. But by ten o'clock they were off for Vancouver. The flight went west from Lake Wabamun, then through the mountains via Yellowhead Pass, and down the North Thompson River to the Fraser River,

following it to Vancouver.

While they were passing through the mountains, a few clouds formed around the peaks. Mount Robson, 12,972 feet, the highest of the Canadian Rockies, towered above them. The scenery was magnificent, and on either side snow-clad mountain peaks were visible as far as the eye could see. The massiveness of the mountains, coupled with the magnificent natural colour scheme, seen from the air, created a picture never to be forgotten. Through the mountains, as well as over the other portions of the flight, the railroad was a great help to them in their navigation. Down the North Thompson River the valleys were wide, making a wonderful passage for the aircraft. Nearing Kamloops, which was in a dry belt at the time, the foliage and vegetation had a very arid appearance. Continuing down the Thompson and Fraser Rivers, they crossed the Cascade Range of mountains. When they reached Hope, they could see the waters of the Pacific in the distance, and were overcome with a sense of exhilaration.

It was on Sunday, September 19, at exactly 5:20 P.M. Pacific Time, that McKee and Godfrey alighted on English Bay, off Jericho Beach, the R.C.A.F. Station.

The Vancouver leg of their journey — on both sides of the Yellowhead Pass and in the Fraser River canyon — was, perhaps, the most dangerous part of their trip, as there were very few lakes to provide a landing place in case any trouble developed with the seaplane. Other than this section, the rest of the route could be safely flown by seaplane.

Strong headwinds and stormy weather with low clouds were encountered for the first four days of the flight, but from Prince Albert to Vancouver the weather was excellent.

So the first seaplane flight across Canada had been made!

After McKee and Godfrey completed their arrangements to enter the United

States, the Douglas seaplane left Vancouver on Wednesday, September 22, for Seattle, Washington, on a windy day. The route from Vancouver to Seattle followed the steamship lines of the inland water route. They alighted on Lake Washington, near Sand Point. The seaplane was refuelled by the Naval personnel of the Army and Naval Reserve Station there. Then Mr. Tidmarsh of the Boeing Airplane Company met them and took them to the plant where they met Bill Boeing and Phil Johnson, the Superintendent. Mr. Boeing and Mr. Johnson took them by car to Camp Lewis to see a Boeing single-seater pursuit aircraft with a 600 h.p. inverted Packard engine undergoing its flight tests. The aircraft made one short flight.

They left Seattle on the 23rd for Eureka (Yreka), California, with four inches of water in their wooden floats. A float landing wire broke during the take-off. They had a tail wind — their first since leaving Montreal. They reached Eureka at 4:10 P.M. Arrangements were made with the Standard Oil Company to refuel the aircraft the next morning. They also got in touch with a man who owned an old Curtiss JN-4. The next morning he rigged up some cables to replace the landing wire, broken during their take-off at Seattle. Water was emptied from the wooden pontoons, too, and other minor work was taken care of.

Captain McKee phoned Major Clagett, Air Officer of the 9th Corps area at Crissy Field, San Francisco, California. Major Clagett said he would fly to Eureka the next day and bring a mechanic with him to help to prepare the aircraft for the flight.

Major Clagett arrived at Eureka at 1:00 P.M. on September 24, having flown there in a Loening amphibian, piloted by Lieutenant Benton, whom Earl Godfrey had met a few years earlier. After the seaplane and its engine were checked and found to be in order, the two aircraft left Eureka together at 3:35 P.M. They flew along the coastal areas most of the way. The shoreline was quite rocky. The day was pleasant with a slight breeze coming from the south. A pall of smoke, caused by the forest fires, covered the land. Closer to San Francisco, they saw a bank of fog coming in from over the ocean, but it was easy for them to pick out the world-famous Golden Gate Bridge. They alighted on San Francisco Bay opposite Crissy Field at 6:05 P.M. on September 24, 1926, and their aircraft was made fast between two piers. Before they left the seaplane, the fog that they

had seen in the distance earlier had rolled in from the ocean enveloping the city in a heavy fog.

The aircraft was refuelled for a flight to San Diego. However, the fog was still heavy with no indication of it lifting for several days. Actually it hung like a blanket over the city for a week. So Captain McKee decided to end his flight at San Francisco. He made arrangements with Douglas Aircraft to have a pilot pick up the seaplane at San Francisco and fly it to Santa Monica, as a landplane if necessary, as the fog did not penetrate

very far inland. Then Captain McKee's historic seaplane was flown to Santa Monica the following week, where modifications were made.

During their fourteen days' elapsed time, they covered a distance of 3,955 miles in 43 hours and 49 minutes.

On September 26, 1926, Captain McKee left by train for Pittsburgh, Pa. and Squadron Leader Godfrey left by train for Vancouver, to return to their respective homes after a memorable and historic flight.

Flying Time and Distances from Montreal to Vancouver and San Francisco

DATE	FROM	TO	DEPART	ARRIVE	FLYING TIME HRS.	MINS.	DISTANCE
1926							
Sept. 11	Montreal, Quebec	Ottawa, Ontario	15:05	16:45	1	40	125
Sept. 12.	Ottawa, Ontario	Lake Traverse, Ont.	07:40	09:10	1	30	100
Sept. 13	Lake Traverse, Ontario	Sudbury, Ontario	10:57	12:32	1	35	175
Sept. 14	Sudbury, Ontario	Orient Bay, Ontario	07:44	12:24	4	40	415
Sept. 14	Orient Bay, Ontario	Sioux Lookout, Ont.	15:37	17:29	1	52	195
Sept. 15	Sioux Lookout, Ontario	Swan Lake, Manitoba	11:18	13:30	2	12	120
Sept. 15	Swan Lake, Manitoba	Malachi Lake, Man.	15:35	15:48		13	20
Sept. 15	Malachi Lake, Man.	Lac du Bonnet, Man.	16:30	17:35	1	05	150
Sept. 16	Lac du Bonnet, Manitoba	-	-	-	-	-	-
Sept. 17	Lac du Bonnet, Manitoba	Prince Albert, Sask.	09:06	16:30	7	24	545
Sept. 18	Prince Albert, Sask.	Lake Wabamun, Alta.	13:30	18:45	5	15	425
Sept. 19	Lake Wabamun, Alta.	Vancouver, B.C.	10:05	17:20	7	15	730
	Average m.p.h. was approximately 90.				34	41	3,000
Sept. 22	Vancouver, B.C.	Seattle, Wash.	08:53	10:15	1	22	125
Sept. 23	Seattle, Wash.	Eureka (Yreka), Cal.	10:54	16:10	5	16	550
Sept. 24	Eureka (Yreka), Cal.	San Francisco, Cal.	15:35	18:05	2	30	280
	Average m.p.h. was approximately 105.				9	08	955
				Grand Total	43	49	3,955

In the spring of 1927, Captain McKee again returned to Ottawa and was making preparations for another flight across Canada and through the northwest, which would be an equally significant one. He and his friends planned to follow the course of the Mackenzie River to Aklavik and Herschel Island. From there they would fly through the Yukon to Alaska and down the Pacific Coast to Vancouver, before returning to Montreal by a completely different route.

This was to be a flight of not just one, but three aircraft; the Douglas seaplane that McKee and Godfrey had flown on their trip to San Francisco, and two Vedette flying boats for Captain McKee's friends, Lieutenant Earl S. Hoag of the United States Army Air Corps, Washington, and Squadron Leader Tom Cowley, from the Office of the Controller of Civil Aviation. Again, Earl Godfrey was to fly the Douglas seaplane for Captain McKee.

Also, in the spring of 1927, it was decided to change the type of floats on the Douglas seaplane before making the trip. New Short floats had been introduced and were considered to be a better type of float. So Squadron Leader Godfrey flew the Douglas seaplane from Ottawa to Vickers Aircraft Company in Montreal to have it equipped with this new type of Short floats for their 1927 flight. Also, a Pratt and Whitney engine was installed in the Douglas seaplane — the first engine of this type ever to be installed in any seaplane in Canada. So, with the installation of this engine and the new type of Short floats, it actually was an "experimental" seaplane.

When Vickers Aircraft had completed this work, Godfrey test flew the seaplane and then test flew the two Vedette flying boats. After flying these Vedettes, Earl Godfrey spoke to Dal McKee at Lac la Pèche on the telephone from Montreal. Dal McKee wanted to have one of the Vedettes delivered to him at the camp where he was staying at Lac la Pèche, near Grand'Mère, Quebec. Lieutenant Earl S. Hoag, who was also well-known among Pittsburgh aviation circles, was in Montreal at the time. So, accompanied by Hoag, Godfrey flew one of the Vedettes to Dal McKee's camp at Lac la Pèche so McKee could get in as much practice flying on it as possible before leaving on their trip to the Canadian northwest. In fact, he had promised Godfrey that he would do this before the trip began. Godfrey then flew both Dal McKee and Hoag back to Vickers Aircraft Company in Montreal in the same Vedette. Then later, Dal McKee and Earl Hoag were to take the Vedette back to Lac la Pèche again for practice flying.

Most of the flying that Dal McKee had done had been in landplanes, so he was not familiar with flying seaplanes. He had attempted to make a landing on the water on a couple of occasions with the Douglas seaplane, but they did not turn out so well. From then on, Earl Godfrey did all the piloting — including landings and take-offs. Nevertheless, Dal McKee was receiving a lot of experience as second pilot during these landings and take-offs and in the air.

Earl Hoag was a good pilot, but he had never flown a seaplane or a flying boat. He was, moreover, a little dubious about flying one in the beginning. Before leaving Montreal, they had a discussion as to who would fly the Vedette to Lac la Pèche. Dal McKee offered to let Earl Hoag pilot the flying boat, but Earl Hoag said, "No, you fly it." So, on June 9, 1927, Dal McKee flew it, and Earl Hoag was the co-pilot. Dal McKee had the controls in taking off from the water. This was the first time that Dal McKee had flown a Vedette flying boat, other than as co-pilot with Earl Godfrey for the short distance of their trip from Lac la Pèche back to Montreal.

After they left, Earl Godfrey took delivery of the second Vedette which he had already test flown, and returned to Ottawa with it. He left Montreal about an hour after Dal McKee and Earl Hoag had left for Lac la Pèche. They both had roughly the same distance to fly. En route to Ottawa, Earl Godfrey flew through a terrific thunderstorm. Upon landing at Shirley's Bay, he was met by his wife and they drove to their home in Ottawa. They had no sooner arrived in the house when the telephone rang. It was Squadron Leader Basil D. Hobbs calling. He told Earl Godfrey that Dal McKee had just been killed in a crash landing he had made at Lac la Pèche in his Vedette flying boat.

Strange as it may seem, the accident could not necessarily be attributed to his inexperience on his Vedette flying boat, but perhaps to the evening shadows on the unusually tranquil lake which caused him to misjudge his distance from the water and strike it with such impact that the flying boat broke in two at the cockpit, while attempting to alight on Lac la Pèche, P.Q., in the Laurentian Mountains, on the evening of June 9, 1927. Earl Hoag was rescued as he clung to the wreckage. He was badly injured and was taken to the Laurentian Club at Lac la Pèche where he was treated for injuries and shock before being taken to a hospital in Montreal. Dal McKee's body was not found until the next evening when the Vedette flying boat was removed from the water. Earl Hoag was an invalid for a year or so before returning to the United State Army Air Corps.

After a very distinguished career, General Earl S. Hoag retired in 1949 after holding a number of very high commissions with the United States Department of Defense. He had learned to fly in 1917 at the Curtiss Flying School at Miami, Florida, and received his final flight training at Rockwell Field, California.

Earl Godfrey went to Pittsburgh as the Canadian representative at Dal McKee's funeral. At the time of his death, he was in his thirty-fifth year, and was in the investment business in Pittsburgh. He was the son of Stewart and Virginia McKee of Pittsburgh. He was a graduate of Princeton University and a member of several organizations, such as the Duquesne Club, Pittsburgh Golf Club, Aero Club of Pittsburgh and Pittsburgh Bankers' Club. During the First World War, he was a member of the Army Air Corps.

Dalzell McKee, a handsome man, was over six feet tall, well proportioned and exceptionally strong and muscular. He was a completely self-reliant person. He would be the first to take hold of a job and work harder at it than anyone else. He was very wealthy but used his money wisely. He was generous to everyone and

appreciated any kindnesses done for him, no matter how small.

Those who came in contact with him discovered his qualities quickly. He had a charming personality, and was an interesting conversationalist. His hobbies were yachting and flying and he was right at home talking about either one. One of his main ambitions was to master the art of flying seaplanes and flying boats, but he wanted to get this experience as he flew from place to place. Dal McKee learned to fly in the United States Army Air Corps and became an instructor. He volunteered to go overseas during the 1914-1918 war, but didn't make it. He was an only child and a bachelor who lived with his mother, who had been a widow since he was a small boy. He

loved the outdoors and the north country with its great open spaces, and often said he would like to have landed at some of the places they had flown over, especially at some of the fast-running rivers and deep gorges.

Aviation in Canada lost a really good friend in the death of Captain Dalzell McKee.

Nevertheless, Captain McKee's and Squadron Leader Godfrey's flight the year before had gone down in history to be remembered year after year in honour of Captain McKee, in the presentation of a trophy by him, known as the Trans-Canada Trophy, more widely known as the McKee Trophy in aviation circles today.

1927

Doc Oaks, 1927.
Photo courtesy of Doc Oaks.

Harold A. "Doc" Oaks

Citation: in recognition of his work in organizing air services to outlying districts

Captain Harold A. "Doc" Oaks, D.F.C., B.A.Sc., P.Eng., M.E.I.C., while Chief Pilot and Manager of Western Canada Airways, Winnipeg, received the first award of the Trans-Canada Trophy for meritorious service in the advancement of aviation in Canada during 1927 "in recognition of his work in organizing air services to outlying districts." The announcement of the award was made on April 16, 1928, by Colonel, the Honourable J.L. Ralston, Minister of National Defence.

In extending his congratulations, the minister conveyed his appreciation of the excellent work done by Captain Oaks in connection with the organization and operation of flying services in northern Ontario, Manitoba and Saskatchewan. He said he appreciated the difficulties and dangers faced, not only by Captain Oaks, but also by many other pilots and air engineers engaged in the pioneering work of developing aviation on a sound and self-sustaining basis in Canada. Through their notable and valiant efforts, progress was being made and the

---

He received his Commercial Air Pilot's Certificate, No. 199, on July 16, 1924, and his Air Engineer's Certificate, No. A-1220, on April 19, 1937.

Those who served on the first Committee of Award for the year 1927 were as follows:
Mr. J.A. Wilson, Controller of Civil Aviation, Department of National Defence, Ottawa.
Squadron Leader A.E. Godfrey, M.C., A.F.C., Royal Canadian Air Force, Department of National Defence, Ottawa.
Squadron Leader A.T.N. Cowley, Royal Canadian Air Force, Department of National Defence, Ottawa.

confidence of the public in the sphere of air services was increasing daily. The flying returns for 1927, which showed a great increase in air traffic, were evidence of this.

The minister felt that, in making this award to Captain Oaks, a high standard of achievement had been set which would be an incentive to all those engaged in flying in Canada. The individual records of many well-known pilots were perused before making this award and the minister was proud of the high quality of conscientious work that was being maintained in the face of many difficulties. Through Captain Oaks' energy and initiative, many isolated communities and mining fields became more easily accessible and travel in both summer and winter in northern Canada was revolutionized during the previous two years. His work in organizing winter flying was specially commendable.

During 1927, while Captain Oaks was Manager of Western Canada Airways, great strides were made in the organization of efficient flying services in northern Ontario, Manitoba and Saskatchewan. It was largely attributable to the organizing ability and skill of Captain Oaks that the transportation of men and supplies to the outlying mining camps was placed on an established footing. Flying was making possible the early development of mineral areas hitherto inaccessible for many months of the year. It was under his direction that methods of engine heating, and maintenance of both the engine and the aircraft in the field, in the coldest weather and under the most difficult conditions of winter and spring, were successfully developed.

Captain Oaks was a pioneer leader in the organization of air transport as applied to mining exploration and

G-CAFB, the Curtiss "Lark" belonging to Patricia Airways & Exploration Limited, on a lake in northwestern Ontario in 1926.
Photo courtesy of Doc Oaks.

transport in the north. A mining engineer by profession, as well as a pilot and an air engineer, he had the advantage of seeing this development from both sides.

During 1927, the year that he was awarded the trophy, Captain Oaks logged 336-1/2 hours, flying a distance of some 26,578 miles.

The Trans-Canada Trophy was officially presented to Captain Oaks in the spring of 1928 by Colonel J.L. Ralston, Minister of National Defence, at a ceremony in his office in the Parliament Buildings. Captain Oaks was the first person to be awarded the Trans-Canada Trophy. Mr. J.A. Wilson, Controller of Civil Aviation, was also in attendance. No pictures were taken of the presentation ceremony.

In expressing his thanks for this award, Captain Oaks said that it was very flattering to think that his efforts to establish air transportation in northern Ontario and Manitoba should receive this recognition from the Department of National Defence, but that the success of his operations was due to the hearty co-operation and hard work of the pilots and mechanics associated with him, as well as the courage and foresight of the financial backers of the enterprise.

Harold A. "Doc" Oaks was born at Hespeler, Ontario, on November 12, 1896. He was educated at the public schools at Hespeler and Preston, and at the secondary school of Galt Collegiate. In 1914 he enrolled at the University of Toronto to take an Arts Course (Economics), and completed his first year. In the summer of 1915, "Doc" Oaks, as he was nicknamed, enlisted in the Royal Canadian Corps of Signals, and went overseas that same year as a despatch rider. He was sent to France in March, 1916, and posted to the 1st Canadian Divisional Signals. Shortly after the battle of Vimy Ridge in May, 1917, he was transferred to the Royal Flying Corps.

Doc Oaks learned to fly Maurice

Farman Short Horns, B.E.'s and Bristol Fighters at Netheravon. He returned to France with the 48th Squadron of the Royal Flying Corps in March, 1918. He served with the Royal Air Force when it was formed on April 1, 1918, and was wounded in action. Doc Oaks was commissioned as a Captain on July 1, 1918. He was awarded the Distinguished Flying Cross in November of that same year.

Doc Oaks returned to Canada in May, 1919, and decided to take a Mining Engineering Course, hoping that later on he would be able to continue flying by combining his favourite occupations — mining and flying. He immediately enrolled at Queen's University and took a summer course from May until September. Then that fall he enrolled in Toronto University to enter his second year in mining. In 1922 Oaks graduated with his B.A.Sc. in mining.

By special permission of the head of the mining department, Professor H.E.T. Haultain, Oaks was allowed to do his fourth year thesis at Toronto University on a non-mining subject. This was done in the Department of Mechanical Engineering under Professor J. H. Parkin on an "investigation of the advantages of thick wing sections in commercial air-craft." At the time there was a small wind tunnel at Toronto University.

While working towards his mining engineering degree, Doc Oaks spent his summers in the field, as close to the mining work as possible. In 1920, he worked with the Teck Hughes Gold Mines at Kirkland Lake, Ontario, then just a prospect. In 1921, he went to the Northwest Territories as an assistant geologist with the Mackenzie River Oil Company on a party to Fort Norman, where oil had been discovered earlier. In 1922 he was hard at work with a Geological Survey of Canada party in the Michipicoten area, Ontario, under the late Dr. Ellis Thompson.

The Ontario Provincial Air Service was

organized in the spring of 1924 as a division of the Forestry Branch of the Province of Ontario by Roy Maxwell, and Doc Oaks joined the service that July, at Sudbury. Many of the resolute and experienced pilots engaged in northern work served their apprenticeship, as it were, in remote flying in the ranks of the Ontario Provincial Air Service. Doc Oaks then took a refresher course in flying which was given by G.A. "Tommy" Thompson, who was Superintendent of Operations for the Ontario Provincial Air Service at Sudbury. During the summers of 1924 and 1925 he flew for the Ontario Provincial Air Service around Sudbury, Temagami, Nipigon, Sioux Lookout and Port Arthur, on forest patrol work.

When the Red Lake gold rush started after discovery of gold by the Howey brothers in 1925, prospectors, and would-be prospectors, and mining engineers flocked to the Red Lake area in northwestern Ontario, District of Kenora, to stake claims. Doc Oaks and Tommy Thompson were two of those who felt a tug to go to the area in search of gold. They travelled from Hudson over the snow-laden ground by dog team and sled in the stark cold of January, 1926, on their own grubstake to try their luck. They staked claims but later turned them over to Patricia Airways and Exploration Limited for a minority interest.

Patricia Airways and Exploration Limited, formed in February, 1926, had its first base at Sioux Lookout, Ontario. An old Yukoner, Frank Davidson of Toronto, was the promoter and President. Doc Oaks stayed on with Patricia Airways and Exploration Limited as Pilot and Manager; while Tommy Thompson returned to the Ontario Provincial Air Service.

Patricia Airways and Exploration Limited purchased a Curtiss "Lark" aircraft, G-CAFB, in March, 1926, for their operations. It was a small open cockpit biplane powered by the first

Western Canada Airways' office and base at Pine Ridge (Goldpines) during the winter of 1926-27. Note the dog team to ferry the freight the one mile to town. G-CAGD, a Fokker Universal, The City of Toronto is in the foreground.

Wright Whirlwind engine ever used in Canada. The Lark carried two passengers, besides the pilot, and all were garbed in helmets and goggles, due to the open cockpit. It was said that the Lark was a "humdinger" of a ship and often made as many as ten flights a day. Previous to the purchase of the Lark, Jack V. Elliott shipped in by train three JN-4 Curtiss Jennies, war-time trainers, and ran a service to Red Lake until the Lark arrived. A. H. Farrington was Jack V. Elliott's pilot. As the Jennies were war-surplus aircraft, their usefulness was restricted. Doc Oaks was the pilot of the Lark, and Sammy Tomlinson was the mechanic. The company also employed one clerk. Throughout 1926, with the Lark on floats in summer and on skis in winter, the aircraft carried 260 passengers, 140,000 pounds of freight and 3,000 pounds of mail.

Patricia Airways and Exploration Limited operated a passenger, freight and air mail service from Sioux Lookout to Red Lake and Woman Lake in north-western Ontario, when the Red Lake gold rush was under way in 1926. The company made its inaugural air mail flight on June 27, 1926, with Doc Oaks piloting the Lark. A charge of twenty-five cents was made for each letter carried. Special air mail stickers were used. The company operated this service without assistance or subsidy from the government, and showed the possibility of a year-round operation of air mail services. In October, 1926, Dale Atkinson joined Patricia Airways and Exploration Limited and took over Doc Oaks' job of piloting the Lark. Doc Oaks then left the company to look for better financial backing to get away from a shoestring operation.

By chance, one day in Toronto in the fall of 1926, Doc Oaks met J. A. Wilson who, until his retirement in 1945, had held two important aviation positions with the government; one as Controller of Civil Aviation and the other as Director of Air Services. (He was awarded the Trans-Canada Trophy for 1944.) Mr. Wilson had suggested that Mr. James A. Richardson, a wealthy industrialist and grain broker, would be a good person to back a new flying company.

Mr. Richardson was President of James A. Richardson and Sons, Ltd., of Kingston, Toronto, Winnipeg, Calgary and Montreal. Born in Kingston in 1885, he moved to Winnipeg in the early 1920s, where he conducted his business. Mr. Richardson's business interests were many, as he possessed great organizing ability. In the years to come, Mr. Richardson was to provide much of his financial resources to assist in pioneering commercial aviation in Canada — and his enthusiasm for these ventures was boundless. So this was the man that Doc Oaks went to Winnipeg to see in the late fall, with his mind bursting with ideas about northern flying.

Oaks believed that an air service with good equipment and efficient manage-ment could further the development of mineral areas in Canada and would result in much benefit to the country as a whole. James Richardson became keenly interested and enthusiastic about the ideas that Doc Oaks had in mind, and agreed to financially back such a company.

So, in November, 1926, as a result of the outcome of their talks, Western Canada Airways Limited was organized to help meet the developing demand for aircraft in northern Ontario and Manitoba, for the purpose of carrying passengers, mail and freight, for photographic survey work and aerial mapping of timber limits. The company's main job, however, was to fly freight and passengers into the mining fields of the Red Lake area during the gold rush era. Although Western Canada Airways was formed in November, 1926, it was not incorporated as a company until March, 1927.

Doc Oaks was Western Canada Airways' first Manager. The company's first office was set up at Hudson, Ontario, as was also its base of operations.

In December, 1926, Oaks piloted the first aircraft purchased by Western Canada Airways from New York (Teterboro, New Jersey) to Hudson, Ontario, in 22 hours and 10 minutes, in the face of snowstorms and adverse weather conditions along the entire route, arriving at their base at Hudson, on Christmas Day, December 25. The aircraft was Fokker Universal monoplane G-CAFU, with an open cockpit, and a Wright Whirlwind J5 200 h.p. engine. Al Cheesman, mechanic, accompanied Doc Oaks on this stormy flight. H. A. Oaks, pilot; Al Cheesman, mechanic; and J. A. MacDougall, clerk, made up the operating personnel of Western Canada Airways.

On December 27, 1926, "FU" made her maiden flight from Hudson Bay to Narrow Lake with 700 pounds of general supplies and 50 pounds of dynamite for Bathurst Mines Limited. The flight covered 217 miles. By the end of the year, 31 hours had been flown, and 16 passengers and 850 pounds of freight had been carried.

During the year 1926, the Department of Railways and Canals sought assistance from an engineer from London, England, concerning the best location for a railway terminus and harbour works along Hudson Bay. Prior to his visit to Canada to inspect the natural conditions at Port Nelson and Churchill, the places in question, the engineer asked for information on the two locations, complete with maps and charts. These were furnished. However, in December, 1926, it was found that no data was available on the nature of the subsoil at Churchill, and that borings would be necessary.

Churchill was then icebound and separated from the railway by 280 miles of grim frozen waste, where there was no road and no habitation. Access by sea was impossible for six more months. The

First nose hangar at Hudson, January, 1927. Doc Oaks is standing by. The nose of CAFU is inside the structure.

Department of Railways and Canals then sent for Captain Oaks and offered him a contract for transporting machinery, supplies and the personnel of the party by air. Oaks accepted, and then made arrangements to purchase the aircraft required for the job as soon as possible.

So, in February, 1927, Oaks went to New York and purchased two aircraft for Western Canada Airways, both Fokker Universals (G-CAGD and G-CADL). Making two trips, Doc Oaks ferried them to Camp Borden, Ontario, where they were changed from wheels to skis, before being flown to Hudson, Ontario, in preparation for their winter expedition to Churchill. He was accompanied by air engineer Al Cheesman on the first flight, and by air engineer Bob Hodgins on the second flight. These monoplanes were powered with Wright Whirlwind engines.

On March 20, 1927, the two aircraft left from Hudson for Norway House and then to Cache Lake, complete with essential winter equipment, spares, and so on, from where the aerial freighting expedition would start. Western Canada Airways' contract with the Federal Department of Railways and Canals to undertake the aerial transportation of eight tons of material and equipment and a crew of fourteen government engineers from Cache Lake, at the end of steel on the Hudson Bay Railway, to Churchill, about 280 miles away, before the spring break-up commenced, was not signed until March, 1927.

The experience which Oaks had gained at Hudson during the past season operating under winter conditions was of great value when he organized this pioneer operation. G-CAFU, *The City of Winnipeg*, and G-CAGD, *The City of Toronto*, were the two aircraft used on this pioneering venture. In all, twenty-seven round trips were made, and the operation was completed in some thirty days. Notwithstanding the distance from any prepared base, and in spite of the severe winter conditions and hardships

endured by the pilots, engineers and others, this operation was a success and the men and equipment were landed safely at Fort Churchill. This assignment was the first major job the company had in the subarctic north.

The expedition was in charge of J. Rod Ross; and Bernt Balchen and F. J. Stevenson were the two pilots on these flights. Al Cheesman was the chief mechanic. It was Colonel Bernt Balchen who headed the search for Captain Roald Amundsen, the famous Norwegian explorer, and Lincoln Ellsworth, the famous and wealthy American explorer, when they were lost for a while in the Arctic white wastes while en route from Spitzbergen in May, 1925. Also, Colonel Bernt Balchen was to gain fame later in Antarctic flying as Admiral Richard E. Byrd's pilot, and in the air services of his country, Norway. F. J. Stevenson's name was to be remembered in Canadian aviation history with Stevenson Airport, Winnipeg, being named after him — until early in 1959 when the airport became officially known as Winnipeg International Airport. Stevenson was a Winnipeg lad.

The successful completion of this expedition pointed the way to further development in aviation, and greater flights to come, in spite of the hardships suffered by the pilots due to the cold, damp winter weather and the ever-constant storms around Churchill. This particular enterprise made engineers and prospectors realize the possibilities of using aircraft to open up mining areas in the north.

The decision which was made later on in 1927 to choose Fort Churchill as the ocean terminus for the Hudson Bay Railway was made possible by the success of these flights, as the engineering party was able to complete the necessary tests at Churchill.

These flights also established the usefulness of aircraft in distant areas, and the next move of the mining men was the

organizing of Northern Aerial Minerals Exploration Limited, Toronto, by Jack E. Hammell and Doc Oaks in 1928; and Dominion Explorers Limited by Thayer Lindsley and Colonel C. D. H. MacAlpine that same year. These companies planned to use aircraft for transportation purposes in their search for minerals in the north.

Apart from the Ontario Provincial Air Service and the Canadian Air Board's flying operations, there was practically no flying in Canada up to that time, except for the itinerant barnstorming outfits — and no winter flying.

Patricia Airways' Lark and Western Canada Airways' Fokkers broke the winter barrier to flying in the 1926-27 winter season.

A flight in the winter from New York to Winnipeg or Sioux Lookout is a routine affair now; but when Doc Oaks and Al Cheesman brought G-CAFU across to Ontario from New York via the northern route (i.e., Buffalo, Sudbury and Little Long Lac) in the cold of December, 1926, without mishap or unusual delay, it was an eye opener to hangar-bound aviators.

When the two aircraft left on the expedition to Churchill, the Patricia district operation by Western Canada Airways was left with only one aircraft. And Doc Oaks flew it, to keep their operation going.

From the middle of March to April 18, 1927, he spent twenty-five days flying in the Red Lake mining area, carrying 90 passengers and 13 tons of freight, and covered 9,737 miles during 119 hours and 40 minutes. Twenty-five days' flying in about one month in those days was really a lot for even the summer season.

By March, 1927, they had had much time to become acquainted with the various snow and slush conditions. Also, they were using their own skis which were built by the Elliott Brothers of Sioux Lookout. They were designed to minimize a lot of the snow difficulties,

A close-up of the Elliott Brothers' skis used on Fokker Universal Monoplane, G-CAFU.

and were in use on all Western Canada Airways' aircraft.

As the type of skis used at the beginning of operations by Western Canada Airways was unsatisfactory, a new type was designed and built in 1927 under Doc Oaks' direction, which was suitable for their subsequent operations. Oaks went to the Elliott Brothers, Carmen and Warner, of Sioux Lookout with the suggestion that they turn their skills gained from their business of building boats and making toboggans and sleighs to the making of aircraft skis. They hesitated as they did not think they should tackle a job like this. However, upon persuasion from Oaks their reluctance faded away and they went to work to devise a set.

That was in December, 1926, and that was how Oaks got the type of skis he wanted and how the Elliott Brothers got started in the work that brought them orders for skis from many firms in Canada, including the Department of National Defence, and from other countries as well.

The Elliott Brothers manufactured skis for the aircraft used by Admiral Richard Byrd on his three Antarctic Expeditions — skis for his Ford Trimotor for his 1929 Expedition; skis for his Curtiss Wright Condor in which he made the first flight over the South Pole in 1934; and skis for the two Curtiss Wright Condor biplanes and the Beechcraft used on his 1939-40 expedition. Elliott skis were also used on the Northrop aircraft *Polar Star*, flown by H. Hollick-Kenyon, on Lincoln Ellsworth's Antarctic Expedition in November, 1935.

The skis were made of varnished white ash, in three steps, the bottoms being covered with a specially prepared copper alloy. Each ski was held together with more than 1,400 rivets. All the work was done by hand by the Elliott Brothers themselves, without any assistance.

Nose hangars were designed and constructed by Doc Oaks and Al Cheesman so that the aircraft's engines

might be serviced in the field "in comfort." This distinctive type of nose hangar was peculiar to Canada around that time. It was a small tent or frame structure about twelve or fifteen feet square, of which three sides and the roof were boarded up and the front closed with a canvas curtain. The nose of the aircraft was drawn into the shelter and the front curtains were made fast around the bow of the fuselage. A stove could be placed in the structure and work undertaken on the engine with a fair degree of comfort and efficiency. These nose hangars, usually constructed on skids so that they might be moved from place to place, became a feature of all temporary flying bases in the north.

Next, Western Canada Airways purchased two Fairchild monoplanes and two de Havilland Moths for pilot training. The demand for air transportation in northern Ontario, Manitoba and Saskatchewan had been at all times more than could be handled and additional equipment was still being obtained. Also, Western Canada Airways opened an air mail service to the mining area of Red Lake from Rolling Portage in 1927. This air mail service was not subsidized by the government. The first regularly established passenger and express service was also operated by Western Canada Airways during the summer of 1927 covering various areas in northern Ontario and Manitoba, such as Hudson, Pine Ridge, Red Lake, Lac du Bonnet, Minaki, Long Lake and others.

Between the spring break-up period of 1927 and the opening of the navigation season, all aircraft were converted from ski landing gear to floats for the summer's work, and on May 10 the first trip of the summer season was made.

On June 1, 1927, an air base was established at Lac du Bonnet, Manitoba, for the convenience of prospectors and companies operating in the central Manitoba area. This provided a great

boon to those working in these districts.

The development of mining in northern Manitoba and Saskatchewan provided steady work throughout 1927. One contract alone for the development of the Sherritt-Gordon Mines, Limited, in the Cold Lake district of Manitoba, 100 miles or so from The Pas, involved transportation by air of 35 tons of supplies, diamond drills and other equipment, as well as forty men from Cormorant Lake to Cold Lake. By taking in this equipment by air, the mining group was able to prove its mineral deposits and proceed with the building of a railway to its claims months ahead of schedule. While the distance of some 75 miles was not great, the job was impressive and convinced others of the value of aircraft in roadless regions. Members of the Imperial Mining Congress were carried from Hudson, Ontario, and Minaki, Ontario, into the central Manitoba area and to Great Falls, Montana.

The company's aircraft were invaluable in time of emergency in the mining camps and, with their speedy means of transportation, saved a number of lives by making possible immediate medical attention whenever serious accidents occurred or illness developed.

Dale Atkinson joined the staff of Western Canada Airways in the fall of 1927 at Hudson, Ontario; while Francis Roy Brown joined the company in February, 1928, and was assigned to The Pas district, with his headquarters at Cranberry Portage. Roy Brown later joined Canadian Airways; became President of Wings Limited when it was formed in 1934; helped organize Central Northern Airways in 1947, and was its President at the time it was amalgamated with Arctic Wings to become Transair Limited, late in 1955. Later, he became a member of the Manitoba Legislature. Other pilots with Western Canada Airways during that period were W. Leigh Brintnell, who succeeded Doc Oaks as General Manager of Western

Returning to Hudson, Ontario, in the spring of 1927, upon the completion of the Churchill Expedition. Western Canada Airways' aircraft, G-CAFU, City of Winnipeg, *one of the two aircraft used on the expedition, is shown in the background. From left to right: Red Ross, in charge of the expedition, Bernt Balchen, Al Cheesman and Fred Stevenson.*

Canada Airways at Winnipeg in March, 1928; W. J. Buchanan; J. H. Holley and Al Cheesman, who was also employed as Maintenance Manager.

In the spring of 1928, Dale Atkinson was appointed District Manager of the base at Hudson, Ontario, and in the fall of that year, when the base was moved to Sioux Lookout, he became District Manager of the base there. By the time 1929 had dawned, a chain of operating bases had been completed across Canada adjacent to the Precambrian Shield and their fleet had grown to some thirty-seven aircraft.

The following excerpt from the February 16, 1928, issue of *The Northern Miner* by Norman C. Pearce, relating to flying done by Western Canada Airways, indicated the trend of the times:

. . . Here is what they do. In the winter they take a couple of prospectors away north to their centre of operations. They carry in their season's supplies and equipment, including a canoe that breaks down into three pieces, and can be put together quickly on the ground and an outboard motor for it, with a supply of gas. The prospectors camp until the snow goes, and then have the valuable break-up time for their work, which gives them a six weeks' jump on competitors.

The 'planes take in winter staking parties, too, that is people who know exactly where they want to stake. At a designated time the 'plane comes back and picks them up. This winter they have made trips as far as Reindeer Lake, the south end of which is 250 miles north of The Pas.

I feel rather sorry for the engineer or geologist who has no hankering for aeroplane trips. Today that mode of travel is practically necessary for the man whose time is valuable, or who wants to keep in touch with the new finds and make financial contact with their finders. Fortunately, Western Canada Airways is doing a splendid job in that field. They are blessed with strong money backing and a careful, skilful personnel. Last year they flew 200,000 passenger miles without an accident and carried a tremendous tonnage of freight without losing a pound.

Western Canada Airways also received a contract from the Post Office Department in 1928 to operate a weekly air mail service from Kississing to The Pas — a distance of 100 miles — to serve the newly developed Cold Lake mining district. On June 1, 1929, Western Canada Airways entered into a temporary agreement with the Post Office Department to carry air mail from Cranberry Portage to Kississing, superintending the service between The Pas and Kississing. Western Canada Airways also held another contract from the Post Office Department for the operation of an air mail service from Sioux Lookout-Gold Pines-Red Lake-Narrow Lake and Jackson Manion — some 320 miles (round trip), during 1928. This weekly service was operated throughout the Red Lake mining district in northern Ontario. Prior to this service by Western Canada Airways, the mail was taken in by canoes and dog teams.

On October 1, 1928, a new five-cent special air mail stamp was issued by the Post Office for letters weighing an ounce; and for each additional ounce extra air mail stamps were required

Some 277,184 pounds of mail was carried under contract from the Post Office Department during 1928, as well as a total of 316,631 pounds of mail.

Doc Oaks discussed aerial exploration with Jack E. Hammell in January, 1928, and invited him, as well as James Richardson, to come in and financially participate in backing a small $500,000 company that he was planning. Jack Hammell was so enthralled with the possibilities of such a company that he talked Oaks into letting him take it over on a bigger basis. The total money raised was $1,250,000, of which James Richardson put up $600,000. The name of the new company was Northern Aerial Minerals Exploration Limited, and it was incorporated on February 10, 1928. Oaks took over the direction of the company's flying, while Hammell took over the company's prospecting.

Al Cheesman joined the company in March as Superintendent of Flying. During these early years, Al Cheesman was a real asset to northern flying with his combined air engineer-pilot ability. He concentrated on working out methods to improve the heating of aircraft engines, as well as the maintenance of the aircraft and engine away from the base in winter weather. His ability to improvise in emergencies was unique. Also, Al Cheesman was chief pilot for Sir Hubert Wilkins on the 1929-30 Wilkins-Hearst Expedition to the Antarctic. Two Lockheed aircraft were used by the expedition. Al Cheesman, who had been living at Fort William, Ontario, died in April, 1958, after a short illness.

Much of the cold-weather equipment which Cheesman improvised was later redesigned by MacDonald Brothers Aircraft, Winnipeg, and used for many years in the north. There were improvements but no basic changes, until Tommy Siers developed the oil dilution system for cold weather starting.

Northern Aerial Minerals Exploration Company was classified as a commercial operating company, but its flying activities were distinct from most commercial operators in that there was no direct revenue from the operation of its aircraft. The company's fleet of aircraft was used solely for more effective prospecting. The company had an operating base at Sioux Lookout, Ontario. Out of this company, Pickle Crow Gold Mines came into existence, with the original find in 1928 remaining dormant until 1935.

In the spring of 1928 when Northern Aerial Minerals Exploration Company was started with much fanfare, and the first award of the Trans-Canada Trophy to Doc Oaks was announced, Professor Haultain, who in 1922 had given Oaks

permission to do a "flying" thesis on a mining course, wrote to congratulate him on receiving the award, and, in particular, he said, for following through on an idea. Oaks had linked up mining and flying. He had come back from four years of war with the intention of doing something that would enable him to continue to fly. Canada had a great unmapped and unexplored north country. The time that Oaks spent with the mining companies, on geological survey work, in prospecting, with the Ontario Provincial Air Service, with Patricia Airways and Exploration Limited and Western Canada Airways were all preliminaries towards a goal — a country-wide aerial exploration company.

Northern Aerial Minerals Exploration Company began flying operations in the middle of May, 1928. Before that, however, the organization of an efficient staff, and the purchase of suitable aircraft, transporting the new aircraft from manufacturing centres to the scene of their operations (an average distance of 1,500 miles), and establishing fuel caches at strategical centres to permit the uninterrupted operation of their aircraft in any part of northern Canada, all had to be undertaken. As some of the fuel caches were in very remote localities, it required many months to transport the fuel to its destination. One shipment, which left the railhead in May, 1928, was not expected to reach its destination until June, 1929! The organization of the mining activities required similar attention. Parties of geologists, field engineers and prospectors were completely equipped with all necessities, including 16-foot sectional canoes, and placed in chosen localities from Ungava Bay to the Yukon.

Two mining companies, Northern Aerial Minerals Exploration Company and Dominion Explorers Company, went into the field in the spring of 1928 with a view to examining the area along the northwestern side of Hudson Bay. Each

company sent a vessel with supplies, the former the *Patrick and Michael* from Saint John, and the latter the *Morso* from Halifax. At the same time canoe parties were worked into the area from the west, and aeroplanes from the south. The Northern Aerial Minerals Exploration Company established a base at the foot of Baker Lake where its vessel had been wrecked. Dominion Explorers organized their main base on the shore of Hudson Bay, which was called Tavanne.

Doc Oaks' log book for 1928 showed an unparalleled record of travel at all seasons of the year throughout northern Canada.

While with the Northern Aerial Minerals Exploration Company, Oaks made a flight in August, 1928, in a Fokker monoplane from New York to the headwaters of the South Nahanni River, an area in the southeast Yukon. From Winnipeg he went to The Pas, Fort McMurray, Fort Resolution and Fort Simpson. He was following up a story of a rich placer strike, called the Lost McLeod Mine, and a murder mystery which had been a lure to miners for years. Oaks had first heard the story when he was on his way to the Fort Norman oil fields in 1921 and tried to get a syndicate together to follow it up. With the aircraft and engines then available, this was not possible. Lieutenant-Colonel J. Scott Williams approached the area from the Pacific in 1926, and Oaks from the east by the Mackenzie Valley route in 1928. Oaks described the area as a "hunter's paradise." The valleys were well wooded, the streams full of fish, while moose, caribou, black and grizzly bears were plentiful, and mountain goats and big-horn sheep abounded in the mountains. Too, there were hot springs, similar to those reported by Scott Williams in the Valley of the Liard, above Hell's Gate.

While on the Nahanni, Doc Oaks thought it best to call in another machine, so he summoned one from

Winnipeg by the wireless service maintained in the north by the Royal Canadian Corps of Signals. Captain W. J. "John" McDonough received the message at lunch time in Winnipeg and left about three o'clock on an August afternoon. Refuelling at Ile à là Crosse and Fitzgerald on the Slave River, he had supper with Captain Oaks at Simpson the next evening.

John McDonough, alone in his Fairchild, had to attend to his own refuelling and mooring. When he travelled a distance of 1,400 miles cross country in a little over twenty-four hours, and over unsettled country at that, the flight made a very fascinating record for an ordinary commercial aircraft of that time.

Having met, the two 'planes took their party of nine prospectors, including Charlie McLeod and their guide, as well as the camp equipment, up the Liard River and the Nahanni River to where the Flat River joins the Nahanni River. Here the prospectors were left for the summer. However, by September 15, Doc Oaks was forced by the coming freeze-up to return to civilization, without the prospectors. Severe cold and snowstorms were a hazard on the outward journey, but he reached Edmonton on September 23, with no mishaps. The party of prospectors came out later to Fort Simpson, and were in an exhausted condition after their long trudge through the snow in the cold. They reached Fort Simpson just in time to take the last steamer of the season to Fort Smith — without ever having found Dead Man's Valley or the Lost McLeod Mine.

Oaks made another flight this same year from The Pas to Churchill via Nelson and the coast, to bring out a crew and to assist in the search for the tug *Yates*, missing from Churchill.

On December 27, 1928, Doc Oaks and T. M. "Pat" Reid, while both with Northern Aerial Minerals Exploration Company, left Remi Lake on the Canadian National Railways to make a flight up the eastern side of Hudson Bay as far as Richmond Gulf. Each was piloting an aircraft. They were to meet a prospecting party that had been left there the previous summer by schooner, on the understanding that they were to be picked up by 'plane in January, 1929. Oaks and Reid were accompanied by two honeymooners, an Anglican missionary and his wife, who wanted to return to the mission station at Rupert House. By dog team this trip would have taken six or eight weeks for the outward journey alone. There were only five settlements between the railway and Richmond Gulf, and the route lay over several hundred miles of the rocky eastern shore of James Bay and Hudson Bay, fully exposed to the sweep of the Arctic gales over the open areas. An hour after leaving, they arrived at Moose Factory where they left the mail, and continued their trip to Rupert House.

Without warning, while they were crossing Hannah Bay, a blinding snowstorm swept down on them preventing the two pilots from seeing each other. Visibility was zero. They both had flown over Rupert House, but were unable to see it due to the blizzard. About an hour before dusk, and at about the same time, each landed — Oaks on the coast seven miles north and Reid on the ice three miles offshore. Upon landing, Reid froze his skis to the surface of the ice to prevent the aircraft from being blown away, and he and Ken Murray, his mechanic, endeavoured to make themselves as "comfortable as possible" in the cabin of the 'plane until the storm subsided.

Oaks, with the honeymooning couple, and Kel Mews, his mechanic, taxied to shore to look for a sheltered spot from the storm where they could spend the night. He then noticed that one of his aircraft's skis was broken. They ate emergency rations for supper, heated over a blowtorch. Then they settled down for the night as best they could.

The weather was no better in the morning. The 'plane was disabled and frozen in — the blizzard was still raging and it was around -40° F. — so Oaks set out on foot to try to find Rupert House. After walking for miles along the coast, he came across a familiar landmark and realized that he was north of the post and not south, so he returned to the aircraft. He then found that an Indian trapper had passed by and had taken word of their predicament to Rupert House. About midnight, on New Year's Eve, a dog team arrived for the newlyweds and took them to the mission.

The following day the weather cleared and repairs were made to the aircraft's broken ski by a blacksmith from the mission station. Oaks and Reid and their mechanics then took off to continue their trail-blazing flight to Richmond Gulf, where they were to pick up their party of prospectors. They reached there on January 11, 1929, and between them brought back thirteen men to Remi Lake on the same day, thus completing safely another northern adventure. According to the records, this flight was the first one that was made to Richmond Gulf during the winter months.

During the first years of Northern Aerial Minerals Exploration's operations, thirty-three fuel caches were established, and the company was then able to place prospectors in any part of Canada within a short time. A permanent base was established at Sioux Lookout for their eastern operations. Hangars and workshops were erected for their aircraft maintenance headquarters. A total of 746 flights were made in 1,178 hours over a distance of 97,568 miles. They employed eight pilots and operated two Fairchild FC2's, two Fairchild FC2-W2's and one Fokker Super Universal aircraft, as well as one Loening amphibian and one D.H. 60X Moth seaplane.

Northern Aerial Minerals Exploration Company's operations — mining exploration and flying — were carried out in four main districts: Patricia District, Ontario, with headquarters at Hudson; northern Manitoba, with headquarters at The Pas; Alberta and Northwest Territories with headquarters at Edmonton; and on the east coast, Hudson Bay and Ungava, with headquarters at Richmond Gulf.

While a considerable portion of the bay's coast had been investigated during 1928, it was in 1929 that the major explorations were carried out. These extended westward from a broad front on the bay side reaching from Eskimo Point to Repulse Bay, entirely across the Barren Lands to Bathurst Inlet and the mouth of the Coppermine River on Coronation Gulf. In this work, an N.A.M.E. 'plane was forced down through lack of gasoline near the Arctic mainland coast, between Baker Lake and Wager Inlet, in August, 1929, and the party was found after about a week of searching by Pat Reid. The lost 'plane was Loening amphibian, G-CATM, piloted by C. A. "Duke" Schiller, with Jack Humble, the mechanic, and Tom Creighton, a prospector, on board. Tom Creighton was the discoverer of Flin Flon, and had lived nearly all his life in the north, having spent years at The Pas. After being refuelled, the aircraft with its passengers was flown back to its base at Baker Lake by Duke Schiller.

Air navigation was difficult along the west coast of Hudson Bay, above the 60th parallel or so of North Latitude. The compass varied greatly, owing to the nearness of the North Magnetic Pole, and the landmarks, except on the coast line, were few. The country was a maze of small lakes and its surface was very often bare rock. There was no adequate map of the district at the time. Several lakes more than 100 miles long were seen from the air which were not shown on any map. The rivers also had little relation to their charted courses or positions.

In this region, too, much difficulty was

met in landing prospectors and finding safe anchorages for the 'planes. This was especially true on the coast. The shore was littered with large boulders, exposed at low tide, but hard to locate when the tide was in. In 1929 very high winds were encountered almost all summer; these, accompanied by heavy seas on the bay and inland lakes, required most careful navigation and increased the difficulties of taking off and landing with heavy loads.

Northern Aerial Minerals Exploration Limited sold a good portion of its aerial equipment to Canadian Airways in February, 1932. After that, the company began to fade away during the early depressed thirties, until finally the company's charter was surrendered on March 6, 1936. However, during these years the company was revived briefly in the minds of the shareholders, upon the distribution of some Pickle Crow Gold Mines' stock in 1935 to the company's shareholders. The production of gold at Pickle Crow Gold Mines began in April, 1935, under Jack E. Hammell, and in less than twelve months a dividend of five cents per share was declared.

Northern Aerial Minerals Exploration flew prospectors to the Pickle Crow area in 1928, and it was this company that first discovered gold in that area. Winter transportation to Pickle Crow was by way of Savant Lake, or by air from Allanwater or Hudson. The company had spent $100,000 in the early development of Pickle Crow, while Jack Hammell, himself, had put up $115,000 for additional work.

Doc Oaks left Northern Aerial Minerals Exploration to establish Oaks Airways Limited in April, 1931, and became its President. The company's base was at Sioux Lookout. They operated two aircraft. A Fairchild KR-34 with a J-6-5 engine was used entirely on mining reconnaissance. A Junkers W-34 with an SC1 Wasp engine was used on general freight and passenger carrying in the

Patricia mining district in Ontario, and up into the God's Lake area in Manitoba.

The longest freight haul performed by Oaks Airways during the year was from Collins, Ontario, on the C.N.R. main line, to Big Trout Lake, a distance of 540 miles return. Approximately 50 tons of freight were moved into this point in March and April for the Hudson's Bay Company.

In April, 1935, Oaks Airways Limited sold its Junkers W-34 to Canadian Airways and subsequently confined its operations to mining exploration with Fairchild KR-34, CF-AWO. All flying was done in Ontario and Manitoba, which totalled some 315 hours and 15 minutes' flying time. Of this, 100 hours were spent on exploration flying and the rest on transport work. This company's operations were discontinued during World War II, and its charter was surrendered on February 26, 1944.

During World War II, in 1943, Oaks was associated with the Clark Ruse Aircraft Company, Eastern Passage, Halifax, Nova Scotia. Oaks had known J. Clark Ruse since the time when, one day in June, 1916, as a young lad during the Battle of the Somme, Doc arrived up from the base as a reinforcement to be immediately set upon by the company's bully. When Clark Ruse attempted to interfere in a solicitous way, he was told by this seemingly mere boy to keep out of it, as he could handle things himself. The effect was instantaneous and permanent, with the lives of Doc Oaks and Clark Ruse crisscrossing through the years. Clark Ruse was an early pilot and an air engineer, too, having received both licences in 1924. He flew for the Ontario Forestry Service and the Ontario Provincial Air Service for a number of years. J. Clark Ruse lived in Grimsby, Ontario, in the heart of Canada's rich fruit belt, for many years after World War II.

Doc Oaks' next association was with Central Aircraft of London, Ontario, from

Doc Oaks in later years.
Photo courtesy of Doc Oaks.

1944 to 1945. From there he returned to his mining and exploration work at Port Arthur, and in 1952 he moved to Toronto where he continued his active work as a mining engineer. In 1953, he became a consultant to James A. Richardson and Company, Toronto.

To most of his friends, Harold A. Oaks was known as "Doc," a nickname which he was given as his father was a doctor — and through the years he tried to get away from it, but just didn't succeed. Doc Oaks was a man who had courage and integrity, often tested — but never questioned. Although it has been said that the faculty of courage does not exist where there is no sense of humour, Doc's sense of humour stood the test of time. It was the main ingredient in all the good and bad things that had befallen him through the years. Then, when you came to analyze it, you began to realize that this humour was "Doc," himself. Oaks was one of those persons who could be

your loyal friend — and at the same time your most severe critic. In a sense, he might have been considered a sort of rebel. His forwardness as a youth was shot through with streaks of humility as time went by and, blended together with sound perception and reasoning, showed the intellectual power of his mature mind. His rather slight frame of five feet eight inches, his neat white hair, his brown eyes, with his fine physical features, all helped to make up this man known as Doc Oaks.

Oaks' pioneering work as a leader in organizing air transport in Canada in the 1920s made outlying mineral areas more readily accessible to the mining men for a longer period of time during the year, thus greatly advancing the early mining industry. Through the introduction of the use of aircraft to fly men and equipment to these distant mining areas for mining and development work, he helped two great industries, aviation and mining, to

thrive by working together. Today, mineral areas can be located through the use of airborne scintillometers for locating radio-active ore bodies, and airborne electro-magnetometers for locating ore bodies. These early efforts of Doc Oaks and his interest in the mining industry have helped add substantially to Canada's industrial progress.

Harold A. "Doc" Oaks, D.F.C., B.A.Sc., P.Eng., M.E.I.C., was living in Toronto, Ontario, at the time of his death on July 21, 1968, at the age of 71 years. He was married and had four children; three sons and one daughter. (Ann, B.A., M.A., Ph.D.; Stephen, graduate of R.M.C. and a civil engineer; Anthony, University of Toronto, Arts; and Richard, University of Toronto, mathematics and physics.)

Doc Oaks was named a member of Canada's Aviation Hall of Fame in 1973. He was made a Companion of the Order of Flight (City of Edmonton).

1928

Punch Dickins, 1934-35.
Photo courtesy of Punch Dickins.

Clennell H. "Punch" Dickins

Citation: in recognition of his work in organizing air services to outlying districts

Captain Clennell H. "Punch" Dickins, O.C., O.B.E., D.F.C., LL.D., Honorary F.C.A.S.I., F.R.C.G.S., while Chief Pilot of Western Canada Airways, Winnipeg, Manitoba, received the second award of the Trans-Canada Trophy for meritorious service in the advancement of aviation in Canada during 1928, "in recognition of his work in organizing air services to outlying districts." The announcement of the award was made by Colonel, the Honourable J. L. Ralston, Minister of National Defence, and conveyed to Captain Dickins on March 14, 1929, by G. J. Desbarats, Deputy Minister of National Defence.

Through the pioneering work of Punch Dickins in his efforts to organize air services to the Far North, and through the exploratory flights which he made in these areas and in western Canada, he helped aviation in its early stages to forge ahead. The possibilities of an air mail service to the north had greatly impressed Punch Dickins for some time as he visualized the opening up of the north country by aircraft for carrying mail, passengers and goods, as well as for aerial surveys and prospecting. He did

The Committee of Award for the Trans-Canada Trophy for the year 1928 consisted of the following members:

Mr. J. A. Wilson, Controller of Civil Aviation, Department of National Defence, Ottawa.
Squadron Leader H. Edwards, Royal Canadian Air Force, Department of National Defence, Ottawa.
Squadron Leader J. H. Tudhope, M.C., Royal Canadian Air Force, Department of National Defence, Ottawa.
Colonel R. H. Mulock, D.S.O., Canadian Vickers Limited, Montreal.

not have too long to wait before all of this came to pass.

In his announcement, the minister also said that Punch Dickins had flown mining and prospecting parties and their equipment throughout northwestern Ontario, thus helping the growth of aviation and the development of Canada's natural resources.

During this one year alone, Punch Dickins flew 1,035 hours, covering some 87,467 miles, both of which were formidable achievements at that time. Much of this time was spent on flying hazardous missions pioneering unknown territory in the inhospitable northern sections of Canada, chiefly from bases where facilities for aircraft on floats and skis were always meagre, to say the least.

Clennell Haggerston Dickins, known to his friends everywhere as "Punch," was born in Portage la Prairie, Manitoba, on January 12, 1899. It was in 1908, when Punch was only nine years old, that his parents moved to Edmonton, Alberta, where he more or less became an Albertan. Upon completing his formal education in Edmonton, he attended the University of Alberta.

In 1917, the youthful Punch Dickins enlisted in the 196th Western Universities' Battalion, Canadian Expeditionary Force, and later transferred to the Royal Flying Corps, receiving a commission as a Second Lieutenant. He arrived in France in April, 1918, and reported for duty with 211 Squadron, R.A.F., near Dunkirk. This was a former R.N.A.S. Squadron attached to the British Third and Fourth Armies. He was credited with the destruction of seven enemy aircraft during World War I. Punch Dickins stayed in France until he was demobilized in March, 1919. He was awarded the Distinguished Flying Cross for gallantry. He returned to Canada in May, 1919.

For a time he was employed with General Motors. Then this former teen-age fighter pilot joined the Canadian Air Force in 1921 and carried out various flying duties.

Punch Dickins was issued Commercial Air Pilot's Certificate No. 161, dated November 21, 1921, by the Air Board, and Transport Certificate No. 29, dated July 15, 1936, as well as Air Engineer's Certificate No. A-582, dated January 29, 1931, which superseded Certificate No. 213, dated March 10, 1922.

During the winters of 1925-26 and 1926-27, when Punch Dickins was with the R.C.A.F., he did some winter testing of Siskin fighter aircraft at Edmonton. Siskin aircraft were in the air as late as 1939, when the last of them were replaced by the famous war-time Hurricanes. The aircraft were kept outside at Edmonton, and the personnel had to devise methods of starting and keeping the Jaguar 400 h.p. engines running properly, as well as fitting skis to these aircraft, so that they could operate under winter conditions without full service facilities being available. From 1921 until 1927, his work with the Canadian Air Force, and then with the Royal Canadian Air Force upon its formation in 1924, took him to a number of remote areas in Canada.

During the time that Punch Dickins was testing Siskin aircraft in Edmonton, the city's new municipal airport was opened. Flying Officer Dickins and Flight Lieutenant R. Collis, who commanded No. 2 Squadron at High River, landed their Siskin aircraft at Edmonton's new snow-covered municipal airport on January 8, 1927, a Saturday. The airport was then declared officially open by Mayor A. U. G. Bury, who greeted them on arrival. This was the Blatchford Field site — and was Canada's first municipal airport.

In the course of his flying duties with

the service, Flying Officer Dickins carried out much forestry patrol work and photographic survey work in Alberta and Saskatchewan, thus laying the foundations for his later successful career in commercial flying with which his name was so often associated.

Punch Dickins left the Royal Canadian Air Force in 1927 and joined Western Canada Airways. From January to August, 1928, he flew a number of mining and prospecting parties and their mining equipment throughout the northwest region of Ontario in the Woman Lake, Confederation Lake, Red Lake and Favourable Lake areas.

In late August and early September of the year 1928, at the request of Dominion Explorers of Toronto, Punch Dickins made a pioneering flight across the Barren Lands from Baker Lake to Stony Rapids on the east end of Lake Athabaska, via Dubawnt River, over unmapped and desolate territory. Piloting the historic Fokker Super Universal seaplane, G-CASK, chartered by Dominion Explorers, Punch Dickins flew Colonel C. D. H. MacAlpine, the President, and Mr. Richard Pearce, editor of *The Northern Miner*, Toronto, who were visiting several prospecting parties on the west shore of Hudson Bay and in the area north of Stony Rapids. Air engineer W. B. Nadin was the other crewman on the flight. These prospecting parties had been sent in earlier in the year. The purpose of this trip was primarily to study the possibilities of prospecting by air.

Punch Dickins began his reconnaissance and exploratory flight at Winnipeg on August 28, 1928, when he left for Norway House. He then followed the Nelson River to Jackfish Island, thence to Churchill on Hudson Bay, to Mistake Bay, to Corbet Inlet, to Chesterfield Inlet and west to Baker Lake. The explorers' own description of Chesterfield Inlet was absorbing. It was a magnificent waterway extending 200

miles inland to Baker Lake. Around Chesterfield Inlet and Baker Lake, the country was much more rugged than farther south, and one hill near Baker Lake stood out for miles, a wonderful landmark for pilots.

Here was the real Barren Lands, but apparently it was a prospector's paradise, since the rocks were clear of overburden.

From Baker Lake, Dickins flew G-CASK and his prospecting party west and south over the Barren Lands following the course of the Dubawnt River as far as Wholdaia Lake, then over the height of land to Stony Rapids on Lake Athabaska, and onwards west and north to Fort Smith, Northwest Territories, on the Slave River. Dickins and his prospecting party returned by way of Fort Chipewyan, Stony Rapids, Reindeer Lake, Cold Lake (Manitoba), The Pas and south to Winnipeg. An excerpt from Punch Dickins' own report reads as follows:

On September 3rd, we left Baker Lake and followed up the Thelon River to Aberdeen and Beverly Lake, then south by west up the Dubawnt River to Dubawnt Lake, and on through a chain of lakes to the height of land and to Fond du Lac, 50 miles west of the east end of Lake Athabaska. This was over the real Barren Lands, and from the time we left Baker Lake we never saw a living thing until getting near the tree line again, when a few birds were seen. The tracks of caribou could be seen here also.

The maps I find are fairly accurate of this route to Dubawnt Lake, but from there on practically useless. There is a great maze of lakes all over this country, which would make a good seaplane route. Nearing the height of land the lakes get smaller, but are quite large enough for any machine the size of the Fokker. The height of land is very clear and is a good landmark. I flew by the sun

The MacAlpine party at Dease Point. Left to right: E.A. Boadway, S.R. McMillan, D.A. Goodwin, A.J. Milne, Col. C.H.D. MacAlpine, "Joe" (an eskimo), G.A. Thompson and Maj. R.F. Baker.

Photograph was taken by R. Pearce.

most of the way, as the compass was not reliable due to large deviations in several places, and the last hundred miles the visibility was very poor, owing to smoke. Wholdaia and Selwyn Lakes do not look anything like the map, and both lakes are much larger than marked, with many bays and inlets. The best landmark on this route is the height of land.

This trip by Punch Dickins was heralded as one of the greatest air surveys in Canada's early history, as large areas of the region were mapped en route.

Dickins covered a distance of 3,960 miles in 37 hours' flying time during a period of twelve days, which, by the previous modes of travel by land, would have taken eighteen months — or two seasons' travel with much hardship.

The first experimental flight in connection with the establishment of an air mail service across the Prairies was carried out by Punch Dickins in October, 1928, flying aircraft G-CASK, a Fokker Super Universal, for Western Canada Airways. The route was from Winnipeg to Regina; from Regina to Calgary; from Calgary to Edmonton; from Edmonton to Saskatoon; and from Saskatoon to Winnipeg.

An earlier attempt to make an experimental flight was made by Pilot Buck Buchanan, who had reached Calgary from Winnipeg. However, in taking off from the landing field at Calgary to fly to Edmonton, the de Havilland aircraft hit a fence and burst into flames. It was destroyed but the pilot and his passengers were unhurt.

A temporary air mail service was started late in November, 1928, over a route from Winnipeg to Regina and Calgary; and over another route from Regina to Saskatoon, North Battleford and Edmonton. This air mail service was operated by Western Canada Airways, and Punch Dickins was one of the pilots on the Regina-Saskatoon-Edmonton

section, flying G-CASK; while Pilot Paul Calder flew the aircraft from Edmonton to Saskatoon and Regina. Leigh Brintnell, who was chief pilot and General Manager of Western Canada Airways, also flew a sector of the route. The air mail flown to Regina from both Edmonton and Calgary was merged at Regina, then one aircraft flew the combined mail east to Winnipeg. Similarly, one aircraft operated between Winnipeg and Regina, with one aircraft flying from Regina to Calgary and another from Regina to Saskatoon and Edmonton. Some 35,540 miles were covered. The service was terminated on December 31, 1928, after carrying 2,526 pounds of mail (250,000 letters).

The weather conditions were very bad during the time of these experimental flights. Strong headwinds and fog, an unusual condition on the Prairies, and heavy snowstorms caused forced landings at some places and only three flights were possible over the whole section. It was after these flights that it was decided to carry the mail at nights so that air mail connections would be better.

Then the Minister of National Defence announced in the spring of 1929 that Captain Punch Dickins had won the Trans-Canada Trophy "in recognition of his work in organizing air services to outlying districts."

As Dickins' schedule in the spring of 1929 did not permit him to go to Ottawa to receive the trophy personally, it was forwarded to him at Winnipeg, and the replica for his retention was sent to Edmonton in May, 1929.

In January, 1929, Punch Dickins of Western Canada Airways was detailed to explore the possibilities of establishing a regular air mail service from Edmonton down the Mackenzie River to Aklavik, Northwest Territories. For this purpose a base was established at Edmonton, and one at Fort McMurray, by Western Canada Airways. When the Honourable P. J. Veniot, then Postmaster General, learned that Western Canada Airways

had arranged a schedule of ten winter flights down the Mackenzie River from Waterways to Fort Simpson, he immediately made arrangements for the Post Office to take advantage of this opportunity. Considerable mail had accumulated at Fort McMurray, the end of the railroad line to the north, to be taken north by dog team. However, now authority was given to send in extra mail, including parcels, by air. Flying Fokker Super Universal aircraft G-CASN, and accompanied by air engineer Lew Parmenter and Post Office Inspector T. J. Reilly, Dickins left Waterways for Fort Resolution on January 23, 1929. This was the first exploratory air mail flight down the Mackenzie River to Fort Simpson, Northwest Territories. It took five hours' elapsed time.

On his second landing at Fort Resolution, Punch Dickins ran into rough ice and wiped off the undercarriage of his Fokker. The metal propeller was also badly damaged. Without the ingenuity of the pilot and his mechanic, the ravages of nature would take their toll in the icy cold of winter. However, undaunted, Punch Dickins and Lew Parmenter set to work and rebuilt their landing gear with some pipe obtained at the post, straightened out the propeller, cutting eight inches off of each tip, then flew the aircraft back to Waterways! It took five days to make the repairs. The trip to Aklavik, Northwest Territories, was cancelled for the time being.

A commercial flight was made on March 6, 1929, by Punch Dickins to Fort Good Hope from Fort McMurray in one day, with five stops en route. He carried air mail and one passenger. The flight was for the purpose of collecting furs for Northern Traders Limited of Winnipeg. Incidentally, this was the first delivery of furs by air. Also, Punch Dickins was the first commercial pilot to cross the Arctic Circle on the Mackenzie River.

A short press item is quoted as being typical of Punch Dickins' work in

First mail flown from Waterways to Fort Resolution on January 23, 1929, by Punch Dickins of Western Canada Airways in G-CASN, a Fokker Super Universal.
Photo courtesy of Punch Dickins.

developing the air service:

An auction sale of $75,000.00 worth of furs in Winnipeg on March 14th was interesting, in view of the fact that the furs had left Fort Good Hope, 1,600 miles north of Edmonton and on the rim of the Arctic Circle only four days previously. Pilot Dickins of Western Canada Airways, who was recently awarded a trophy as the pilot who had done the most for aviation in Canada in 1928, made the trip from Waterways, at the end of the rails in northern Alberta, to Fort Good Hope and return, on behalf of the Winnipeg Fur Trading Company, calling at the various trading posts along the way. On the trip north he carried 950 pounds of mail and a passenger. The flight was made under difficult conditions, the thermometer dropping to 64° below zero F. at times. The value of this method of transportation may be appreciated from the fact that furs from the northern Mackenzie River District would not ordinarily reach Winnipeg until late August, once each year.

Mail which previously took weeks to reach the lonely posts in the Mackenzie Basin District is now delivered promptly within a day or two, while travellers may reach their destination with ease and comfort instead of "mushing" for weeks behind a dog team.

There were times, though, when this "comfort" meant sitting on an oil can during the trip!

On July 1, 1929, Punch Dickins flew in to Aklavik with a load of air mail, a distance of some 1,676 miles. Pioneer Pilot Dickins was the first person ever to reach Aklavik in an aircraft. Hardly had he landed when a number of the local Eskimos, none of whom had ever seen an aircraft before, were clamouring for a ride in it.

However, it was said by Richard Finnie, a writer, that one old woman was

skeptical of the aircraft and said, "I don't believe it — the wings don't flap."

These pre-inaugural and exploratory flights made by Punch Dickins laid the foundation for future air mail routes and were the forerunner to the air mail contract service awarded to Commercial Airways on November 1, 1929.

In July, 1929, Punch Dickins made a pioneering flight to Great Bear Lake for Western Canada Airways, carrying a prospecting party for a mining company from the United States. Several other flights were made later that summer too, taking prospectors to the area.

Then in late September, 1929, Punch Dickins flew in to Great Bear Lake to bring out Gilbert LaBine, the discoverer of pitchblende, the ore containing both radium and uranium, and his partner. It was on the way out that Gilbert LaBine spotted the heavily mineralized area on the southeast shore of Great Slave Lake for which he had been looking.

Pilot G. A. "Tommy" Thompson, flying G-CASK, a Fokker Super Universal on floats belonging to Western Canada Airways, left Baker Lake, Northwest Territories, on September 8, 1929, to fly to Aklavik, via Bathurst Inlet, Coppermine, Great Bear Lake and Fort Norman. G-CASK was chartered by Dominion Explorers, Toronto, for a prospecting expedition to the Arctic under the direction of Colonel C. H. D. MacAlpine, the 43-year-old President of the company, along with a party of seven others, and a float-equipped Fairchild aircraft, owned by Dominion Explorers, and flown by Stan McMillan. On the first lap of their journey they were to visit parties prospecting for copper deposits on the Coppermine River. Tommy Thompson, the captain of the expedition, in his mid-thirties, was also the Superintendent of The Pas District for Western Canada Airways. It was from the company's base at The Pas that the two aircraft left for Baker Lake, reaching there safely.

When the two aircraft from Baker Lake, which is some 800 miles north of The Pas, failed to arrive at Bathurst Inlet within ten days, a search was instituted immediately between Baker Lake and Bathurst Inlet. In the beginning it was agreed that no search would be made for the MacAlpine party until ten days had elapsed, in the event that they happened to be unreported or overdue on the flight. General D. M. Hogarth of Toronto, along with five others, including Guy Blanchet of the Department of the Interior who had spent some time in the Arctic and Thayer Lindsley, Vice-President of Dominion Explorers, arrived in Winnipeg on September 25, 1929, to organize a search for Colonel MacAlpine and his men.

Western Canada Airways, Dominion Explorers, Northern Aerial Minerals Exploration and the Consolidated Mining and Smelting Company contributed from their resources. Four aircraft belonging to Western Canada Airways were amongst those chosen for duty with the search organization. They were Fokker Super Universals: G-CASM, piloted by Punch Dickins; G-CASQ, piloted by A. D. "Andy" Cruickshank; G-CASO, piloted by F. Roy Brown; G-CASL, piloted by Herbert "Bertie" Hollick-Kenyon. J. D. "Jimmy" Vance flew G-CARK, an aircraft belonging to Northern Aerial Minerals Exploration Company. They were later joined by Bill Spence and Charles Sutton flying two aircraft belonging to Dominion Explorers. Pat Reid, Andy Cruickshank and Jimmy Vance flew in supplies for the first four search pilots. Stony Rapids, east of Lake Athabaska, was selected as a base for their search operations, and in October the base was moved to Baker Lake.

Colonel MacAlpine's party consisted of Major Robert Baker of Port Colborne, Ontario, who was the camp manager for Dominion Explorers at Burnside River on Bathurst Inlet and had joined the party at Baker Lake; E. A. Boadway, a mining

G-CASN, a Fokker Super Universal on Great Bear Lake, 1929, with Pilot Punch Dickins in the cockpit, after flying in a prospecting party.
Photo courtesy of Punch Dickins.

engineer and pilot from Ann Harbor, Michigan, about 28 years of age; Richard Pearce, editor of *The Northern Miner*, Toronto, somewhere in his mid-thirties; pilots Tommy Thompson and Stan McMillan; Don Goodwin, a 24-year-old air engineer with Western Canada Airways; and Alex Milne, a 28-year-old air engineer with Dominion Explorers.

Punch Dickins flew aircraft G-CASM to Coppermine, A Dominion Explorers' searched along the Arctic coast between September 28 and 30th. Air engineer Lew Parmenter accompanied him. From Coppermine, a Dominion Explorers' party of four prospectors who had been left stranded in the rough country on the Coppermine River was picked up by Dickins and flown out to Fort Smith. Punch Dickins also made another flight over the Barren areas northeast from Fort Smith to Fort Reliance and to Bathurst Inlet, returning to Great Slave Lake via the Thelon River, until the freeze-up period halted seaplane flying from October 9, 1929, to October 25, 1929, when it was not advisable to make aerial searches. However, during the freeze-up period Jimmy Vance, Andy Cruickshank and Bertie Hollick-Kenyon, accompanied by their mechanics, with their aircraft still on pontoons, flew from Stony Rapids, Saskatchewan, to Baker Lake. This now made five aircraft based at Baker Lake for the search.

After much anxiety and much searching, word was received on November 4, 1929, from a wireless operator of the Hudson's Bay Company at Cambridge Bay saying that the party of eight was safe. They had walked fifty miles across the treacherous ice of Dease Strait from Dease Point, guided by Eskimos whom they had met.

They were forced to make a landing on Dease Point on the Arctic coast, west of Ellice River, near Melbourne Island (104° 30′ West Longitude) on September 9, 1929, due to strong headwinds and a heavy snowstorm, and because neither

machine had sufficient gasoline to reach the nearest Hudson's Bay post. The men remained near the aircraft until Dease Strait froze over, living in a cold, damp make-shift shelter using the wings of the Fairchild aircraft as a "roof" for their home.

As the days passed by, they had less and less food, and were showing the results of hunger. They had made several attempts to cross the ice of Dease Strait to Cambridge Bay, but they had met with many hardships and difficulties. Besides, walking over ice hummocks was hard on strong men in top physical condition, let alone men weakened through lack of food. In addition, there was still water in the strait preventing them from making a direct crossing from Melbourne Island. Finally, on November 3, 1929, after some ten days of walking and stumbling across the ice in the face of bitter winds and the hummocky, crackling ice, they reached the Hudson's Bay Company's post at Cambridge Bay on the southern shore of Victoria Island about 4:30 P.M., where they were fed and cared for after their ordeal. Without the assistance and guidance of the Eskimos, it is hard to say if the men would have reached Cambridge Bay.

A few days later, three rescue 'planes flew from Bathurst Inlet to Cambridge Bay to pick up the party. The aircraft were flown by Bill Spence, Roy Brown and Bertie Hollick-Kenyon. The MacAlpine party was then flown to Bathurst Inlet. They reached The Pas a few days later; and on December 8, 1929, they reached Winnipeg — three months from the date of their landing at Dease Point. In this search, three rescue aircraft were lost and several were damaged. Don Goodwin, the air engineer, whose feet were frozen earlier, had to have a couple of toes amputated at the hospital in Winnipeg. The ravages of nature had taken their toll on the men and the aircraft.

A most important person in this rescue

mission was Tommy Siers, Chief Engineer for Western Canada Airways, ably assisted by air engineers and mechanics. The superhuman work carried out by Tommy Siers and his men in repairing broken undercarriages and other aircraft parts to keep the aircraft serviceable for flying on their rescue mission was a great story in itself, which is told briefly later on in this book.

There were other problems, too, and troubles to be overcome in connection with the rescue of the MacAlpine party. For instance, Bill Spence and Bertie Hollick-Kenyon, two of the pilots flying the aircraft to Fort Reliance carrying the rescued members of the MacAlpine Expedition, were forced down by fog on Musk Ox Lake for two days. Bill Spence's aircraft was damaged somewhat when it ran into heavy drifts of snow while attempting to take off, so his passengers were then transferred to another aircraft. Tommy Siers and Graham Longley, the air engineer flying with Bill Spence, then made the repairs. Roy Brown and two mechanics flying to their assistance two days later met with a mishap, breaking a wing, when they were forced down on Aylmer Lake, about fifteen miles south — where they were stranded for fifteen days, with little food, before they were eventually rescued by Andy Cruickshank and flown to Fort Reliance. So there were many cases where the rescuers had to be rescued — including even on the final rescue mission.

The search occupied some ten weeks and involved some fifteen pilots before the party was found and flown to Winnipeg on December 8, 1929. Of course, owing to freeze-up conditions in the Arctic, operations were greatly hindered and the search considerably delayed. Some 29,144 miles were flown on the search for the members of the MacAlpine Expedition in 305 hours' flying time, costing Dominion Explorers close to half a million dollars.

Pilot Punch Dickins of Canadian Airways, shown at extreme left, at Coppermine on August 12, 1935, after having flown his party there in Fairchild CF-ATZ. Bill Sunderland is third from the left and Dr. Camsell is wearing the fedora.
Photo courtesy of Dan McLean.

The Fokker Super Universal G-CASK remained on the shore at Dease Point for a whole year until August, 1930, when it was rescued and flown back to Fort McMurray by Buck Buchanan — just before Walter Gilbert flew it on an unexpected flight to the North Magnetic Pole. The Fairchild, the other aircraft, however, had found its last resting place on the shore. So the MacAlpine rescue mission had ended — for the most part.

During 1929, Punch Dickins put in some 1,000 hours' flying time which, at that time, was a distinctive record.

Some of the pilots who flew early air mail flights for Western Canada Airways were: Punch Dickins, Leigh Brintnell, Tommy Thompson, Roy Brown, Andy Cruickshank, Herbert Hollick-Kenyon, Donald MacLaren, Jack Moar, Paul Calder, Buck Buchanan, Con Farrell, Norm Forrester, Harold Farrington, Ted Stull, A. E. "Jock" Jarvis, Pat Holden, Milt Ashton, Bill Holland, Joe E. Crosson, amongst others.

It was largely as a result of James A. Richardson's vision and efforts that the Prairie section of a proposed trans-Canada air mail service was inaugurated on March 3, 1930 — a four-year government contract having been awarded to Western Canada Airways to operate a nightly Prairie Air Mail Service. The route was from Winnipeg to Regina, Moose Jaw, Medicine Hat and Calgary (later via Lethbridge and Calgary); with a branch line from Regina to Saskatoon, North Battleford and Edmonton. Stamps designed by Western Canada Airways and sanctioned by the Post Office were placed on the mail.

Night lighting facilities along the route, such as beacons, were ready by the end of January, 1930. Then weather became a problem which only time could solve. Attempts to get the service under way had been made, but it was not until March 3, 1930, that inaugural flights of the Prairie Air Mail Service were made covering the three sectors. Punch Dickins made the first official air mail flight from Regina to Edmonton; while Con Farrell was making the first official air mail flight from Edmonton to Regina. The aircraft were flown without the aid of radio voice equipment, directional facilities or accurate weather data.

In the late spring and early summer of 1930, Western Canada Airways sent Punch Dickins and Walter Gilbert to Gilbert LaBine's radium deposits in the area of Great Bear Lake for commercial transportation purposes. The first commercial flight was made in aircraft G-CASK, which had made so many flights through the northern skies.

However, several prospecting parties had been flown to Great Bear Lake during 1929 and early 1930. Gilbert LaBine's famous radium strike took place on May 16, 1930, near Great Bear Lake. It became known as Eldorado in the days to come.

Western Canada's business connections were taken over by Canadian Airways on November 25, 1930, and Punch Dickins, who had played so prominent a role in the development of air transportation and air mail services in the Mackenzie district, was appointed Superintendent of the Mackenzie district for Canadian Airways at Edmonton at the same time.

Punch Dickins, whose name has become synonymous with bush flying, with air engineer Lew Parmenter, flying CF-AJC, a Fokker Super Universal, was to do much flying for Canadian Airways. Also based at Fort McMurray, the railhead base and the starting point for flights by Canadian Airways Limited to the whole of northwestern Canada, were pilot Walter Gilbert, and air engineer Stan Knight. Here, too, was based the historic Fokker Super Universal G-CASK that had been rescued from Dease Point, about which many an epic tale could be told.

On March 31, 1932, the contract for the Prairie Air Mail Service was cancelled by the government as an economy measure during the Depression Era. This caused great loss to Canadian Airways.

Canadian Airways were employing 44 pilots by 1932, 50 air engineers and 47 unlicensed mechanics; while they were flying 72 aircraft.

Through the years Punch Dickins had made many other trips to the uranium deposits at Great Bear Lake and one in 1935 when he was Superintendent of Northern Operations for Canadian Airways. On this return trip to Edmonton he brought out J. G. Halbert and A. J. Rooney, mining men from Toronto.

Punch Dickins in later years.
Photo courtesy of Punch Dickins.

On an exploratory flight to the north during 1935, Dickins was at the controls of Canadian Airways' Fairchild seaplane CF-ATZ. He carried Dr. Charles Camsell, Mr. A. D. "Dan" McLean, Superintendent of Airways, Ottawa, and air engineer William H. Sunderland as passengers on the flight.

Dr. Charles Camsell, C.M.G., B.A., LL.D., F.R.S.C., F.G.S.A., was Deputy Minister of Mines and Resources for Canada and a member of the Council of the Northwest Territories. He made a study of conditions in the north and inspected some of the field parties created by the million-dollar mineral exploration scheme. A. D. "Dan" McLean was Superintendent of Airways and Airports for the Department of National Defence for Canada, who was to carry out an investigation and survey for a northwest airways' system through northwestern Canada into Alaska and of the facilities and routes along the Mackenzie to Coppermine and in the Yukon. Much of this territory was photographed from the air by Dan McLean and Bill Sunderland.

Pilot Punch Dickins, Dan McLean and Bill Sunderland left Fort McMurray on July 16, and flew to Fort Chipewyan, Fort Fitzgerald, Fort Smith, Fort Resolution, Hay River, Fort Providence, Fort Simpson, Fort Norman, Fort Good Hope, Arctic Red River, Fort McPherson, Aklavik, Mayo, Mayo Lake, Dawson, Selkirk, Carmacks, Whitehorse,

Skagway, Carcross, Atlin, Juneau, Telegraph Creek, Hazelton, arriving at Prince Rupert on July 29, 1935. Here they picked up Dr. Camsell and left Prince Rupert on July 31, 1935, and went on to Wrangell, Dease Lake, McDame's Creek, Fort Liard, Hot Springs, Fort Liard, Nahanni, Fort Simpson, Fort Norman and Cameron Bay. Continuing their journey, they went to Contact Lake, Cameron Bay, Coppermine, Cameron Bay, Fort Rae, Fort Smith, Beaverlodge, returning to Fort McMurray on August 16, 1935. During Punch Dickins' trip, he covered some 8,400 miles in 81 hours and 35 minutes' flying time. This was the first flight made from the Pacific to the Mackenzie at Simpson via the Liard River.

Punch Dickins and his party, also accompanied by Fred Camsell, post manager for the Hudson's Bay Company, arrived at Imperial Oil's Discovery Well, fifty miles below Fort Norman on August 5, 1935, to have a look at the refinery which was supplying 700 tons of fuel oil to the Eldorado Gold Mines at Great Bear Lake during the 1935 season.

A flight was made over the Bear River Rapids to photograph the swift water and the portage, known as the Franklin Road, which was nearing completion under the direction of Colonel T. Newcomen.

From Fort Norman, Dickins flew his party to Great Bear Lake, north of the Coppermine, then flew over Yellowknife, Northwest Territories, where, under the guidance of Major Lauchlan T. "Lauchie" Burwash, the noted Arctic explorer, a sensational gold strike was made in September, 1934. The party then flew to the Beaverlodge field on the north shore of Lake Athabaska.

It was a fine tribute to Punch Dickins that Dr. Camsell and Dan McLean should have chosen him to usher them through the northland. This distinguished war-time pilot and pioneer of the northern realm was becoming well known to many Canadians for his exploits.

During the latter part of 1935, Punch Dickins, Superintendent of the Mackenzie District for Canadian Airways Limited at Edmonton, was promoted to General Superintendent of Northern Operations, with headquarters in Winnipeg. G. A. "Tommy" Thompson, General Manager of the company, and an aviation pioneer, stated in announcing the promotion that, due to the continued expansion of Canadian Airways' operations during the past two years, it has been considered advisable to appoint Mr. Dickins as General Superintendent. He was to maintain closer co-operation between the base superintendents, and was to direct his efforts towards co-ordination of services throughout the Dominion.

Canadian Airways maintained their own wireless system throughout the north. Their Edmonton office was in constant touch with every one of its stations between Fort McMurray, Aklavik and Coppermine on the Arctic Ocean. Data concerning the arrival and departure of aircraft, weather reports and other instructions concerning freight or passengers were received constantly. Orders were then sent out to their aircraft to go to this or that place, and do thus and so. In this way, passengers, express and freight were moved from point to point in a matter of a few hours over distances that previously would have taken months.

It was this same year, 1935, that Punch Dickins was made an Officer of the Order of the British Empire.

During the summer of 1939, Punch Dickins made a tour of the north from Edmonton to Port Radium and throughout the Mackenzie River area. On the southward flight he visited Goldfields on Lake Athabaska, and was present at the ceremony for the pouring of the first gold ingot at the Consolidated Mining and Smelting Company's mine at Goldfields.

In February, 1941, Punch Dickins was appointed Manager of the Canadian

Western Canada Airways airmail stamp, 1929.

Pacific Railway Company (Air Services) to organize flight delivery of service aircraft from Canada and the United States across the Atlantic, which was handed over to the Royal Air Force Transport Command in 1942. On January 19, 1942, he was made Assistant to L. B. Unwin, Vice-President of the Canadian Pacific Railway Company (Air Services, Financial) and, on May 1, 1942, he was appointed Vice-President and General Manager of Canadian Pacific Air Lines Limited, Montreal.

In January, 1947, Punch Dickins joined The de Havilland Aircraft Company of Canada, Limited, Toronto, in the capacity of Sales Director; then he became Vice-President of Sales in 1948, and Executive Vice-President in 1964. As Sales Director, Punch Dickins was largely responsible for the successful marketing of the famous Beaver and Otter aircraft. His energetic and dynamic marketing methods made possible the sale of aircraft on a world-wide basis, as well as in Canada.

Punch Dickins retired from The de Havilland Aircraft Company on June 1, 1966.

He is a past president of the Air Industries and Transport Association. He was awarded an honorary degree of Doctor of Laws by the University of Western Ontario in 1964.

On June 6, 1967, he became an Honorary Fellow of the Canadian Aeronautics and Space Institute, which is the highest honour the institute can bestow, and is reserved for exceptional and sustained contribution to aeronautical work or space research.

Punch Dickins is endowed with the qualities of great courage and the intrepid spirit of the explorer. He has a keen active mind. His career has been singularly devoted to aviation and the acquisition of a great fund of knowledge which has proved of inestimable value to the organizations which he has served through the years. He has a fine sense of humour and is always ready to make a speech whenever he is called upon to do so. He enjoys the limelight.

During Punch Dickins' distinguished career, he was credited with many firsts in northern flying in Canada. He opened Canada's first municipal airport at Edmonton in January, 1927. He made the pioneer flight over the Barren Lands of the Northwest Territories in September, 1928, flying the historic aircraft G-CASK, a Fokker Super Universal, with Colonel MacAlpine. It was he who first delivered fur by air in March, 1929. He was the first commercial pilot to cross the Arctic Circle on the Mackenzie River in Canada in March, 1929. He pioneered the first air mail route between Edmonton and Aklavik on the Arctic coast in the summer of 1929. The Barren Lands were his familiar stamping grounds for years. He pioneered many arduous bush routes in northern Canada. Along with others, he played a leading role in the development of Canadian aviation.

Punch Dickins has had a long and illustrious career in both the operational and industrial sides of Canadian aviation.

Alberta named a lake after him in 1954, called "Dickins Lake," in recognition of services to his home province.

Mr. C. H. "Punch" Dickins, O.C., O.B.E., D.F.C., LL.D., Honorary F.C.A.S.I., F.R.C.G.S., moved from Toronto to Victoria, British Columbia, in 1970, where he lives today. Mr. and Mrs. Dickins have two sons and one daughter.

He is President and a director of Canada's Aviation Hall of Fame. He was named a member of Canada's Aviation Hall of Fame in 1973. He is a Companion of the Order of Icarus (Hall of Fame), and a Companion of the Order of Flight (City of Edmonton). He was made an Officer of the Order of Canada.

1929

Wop May, 1929.
Photo courtesy of Wop May.

Wilfrid Reid "Wop" May

Citation: in recognition of his work in organizing air services to outlying districts

Captain Wilfrid Reid "Wop" May, O.B.E., D.F.C., while Chief Pilot of Commercial Airways of Edmonton was awarded the Trans-Canada Trophy for meritorious service in the advancement of aviation in Canada during 1929, "in recognition of his work in organizing air services to outlying districts." The announcement of the award by the Minister of National Defence was conveyed to "Wop" May on May 1, 1930, by Mr. G. J. Desbarats, Deputy Minister.

Captain May's outstanding achievement during 1929 was in connection with the inauguration of Commercial Airways' air mail route extending for 1,676 miles over the remote territory of northwestern Canada, following the Mackenzie River from Fort McMurray, Alberta, to Aklavik, Northwest Territories. More than five tons of mail were carried in the four aircraft on the inaugural flight — and in temperatures

The Committee of Award for the year 1929 consisted of the following members:

J. A. Wilson, Controller of Civil Aviation, Department of National Defence, Ottawa.

Squadron Leader A. E. Godfrey, M.C., A.F.C., Royal Canadian Air Force, Department of National Defence, Ottawa.

Squadron Leader H. Edwards, Royal Canadian Air Force, Department of National Defence, Ottawa.

Squadron Leader A. T. N. Cowley, Royal Canadian Air Force, Department of National Defence, Ottawa.

No presentation of the trophy was ever made to Wop May, as there seemed to be no suitable time that was convenient to both him and the Department of National Defence.

down to -60° F.

Wilfrid Reid "Wop" May was born in Carberry, Manitoba, on March 20, 1896. He moved to Alberta with his parents in 1903. He attended Western Canada College in Calgary, and the University of Alberta for a while.

Wop May joined Great West Motors in August, 1914, and received his early training as a mechanic with them.

Then on January 16, 1916, he enlisted in the Canadian Expeditionary Force and became a machine gun instructor at their Machine Gun School. By February, 1917, Wop May was attached to the 202nd City of Edmonton Battalion and went overseas as a Staff Sergeant. Upon arrival in England he applied for a transfer to the Royal Flying Corps, but his transfer did not materialize until he reached Étaples, France, then a famed infantry training base. In addition to his flying instruction, he also qualified for a commission and became a Second Lieutenant in the Royal Flying Corps on July 10, 1917. In March, 1918, he crossed the English Channel with the Royal Flying Corps and reported to the 209th Squadron as a fighter pilot. On his first combat flight he shot down an enemy aircraft, and on returning home with his guns jammed he was chased by the German ace, Baron Manfred von Richthofen, who was shot down during the chase by Captain Roy Brown of Carleton Place, Ontario, an old school chum of Wop's.

Wop May continued to serve with the Royal Air Force with the rank of Lieutenant upon its formation on April 1, 1918. After that, May fought on every part of the British front in France and Belgium until the big Amiens battle in August, 1918, when he was shot in the face and arms with flak while engaged in strafing enemy troops from a low

Wop May barnstorming in G-CAEN in the early twenties.
Photo courtesy of Wop May.

altitude. Wop May was successful in safely bringing down his Camel scout 'plane even though it was seriously damaged. Returning to France with No. 9 Naval Service, he was promoted to Flight Commander with the rank of Captain on September 12, 1918, and retained his flight of five Camels until armistice was signed.

Captain May was awarded the Distinguished Flying Cross for gallantry in disregarding personal danger and destroying seven enemy aircraft. At the end of the war, he was credited with destroying twelve enemy aircraft.

He returned to Canada after the war, and relinquished his commission on May 8, 1919. Captain May had 790 hours of flying to his credit overseas.

Wop May returned to Edmonton and started a commercial aviation company, which was formed on May 19, 1919. It was called May Airplanes Limited, Edmonton, and Wop May was the senior member, pilot and mechanic with the company.

Then a re-organization of May Airplanes Limited took place, and May-Gorman Airplanes Limited, Edmonton, came into existence on March 18, 1920. Besides Wop May, the other two members of the company were his brother, Court, and George W. Gorman. The company was engaged in extensive barnstorming throughout Alberta and Saskatchewan at places such as Edmonton, Calgary, Saskatoon, Brandon and Regina, mostly at exhibitions and rodeos. The company also operated a flying school at Edmonton using Curtiss aircraft, which had been used previously for training purposes. During this period Wop May spent two hundred hours doing this type of flying. At this time flying was not readily accepted by the people and this early venture was, perhaps, in advance of its day, and so its demand faded away.

Wop May then joined Imperial Oil Limited as a pilot in November, 1920.

He and his brother, Court, were responsible in the first instance for persuading Imperial Oil Company's officials of the feasibility of purchasing aircraft to use in transporting men and equipment into their experimental oil field at Discovery Well on Bear Island. This renowned oil field about 50 miles north of Fort Norman was discovered by Dr. Theodore Link, a geologist with Imperial Oil Limited, in the summer of 1920. When Imperial Oil decided that they would purchase Junkers aircraft for this purpose, pilots Wop May and George Gorman, and air engineer Pete Derbyshire, went to New York around the end of November, 1920, to ferry back two Junkers aircraft (G-CADP and G-CADQ), all-metal monoplanes, to Edmonton for Imperial Oil Limited. Each aircraft was powered with a B.M.W. engine, 185 b.h.p., and had a maximum speed of around 110 m.p.h. On wheels each would carry about one ton of freight. In flying Junkers aircraft G-CADQ to Edmonton, George Gorman had to land at Brandon, Manitoba, due to very stormy weather, causing minor damage to the aircraft. He was delayed at Brandon for several weeks until his aircraft was repaired. Wop May reached Edmonton safely on January 5, 1921, in G-CADP, having also flown home through blustery sub-zero weather, but fortune and his skill had been kinder to him.

Captain May was granted a commission with the Canadian Air Force on March 15, 1921; and he completed a refresher course of one month at Camp Borden on April 19, 1921.

Then, in March, 1921, Wop May severed his connections with Imperial Oil Limited after a winter's pioneering efforts in the north to carry on his own commercial flying venture during the summer months, known as May-Gorman Airplanes Limited. During the winter months Wop May worked as a mechanic. When his brother, Court, died on May 21,

1922, through a non-flying accident, this hit Wop very hard as he and Court were very close to each other. When the summer of 1923 arrived, Wop May decided to sell his interests in his company to Great Northern Services Limited. He then worked as a mechanic with this company for a time.

When May of 1924 dawned, Wop May decided to go on some barnstorming tours again, making flights at exhibitions, rodeos, and so on. He flew G-CAEN, a Standard J.1 aircraft belonging to L. Harry Adair of Lake Saskatoon, Alberta. His base was at Peace River. Sunoco Motor Oil sponsored some of his flights. He continued barnstorming during the summer and fall, and in November he was married and left for Dayton, Ohio. Here he was employed as a mechanical inspector with the National Cash Register Company.

May returned to Edmonton from Dayton in the spring of 1926, where he continued to work for the National Cash Register Company, first in Edmonton and then in Calgary.

During 1927 the Department of National Defence planned to inaugurate a scheme in an endeavour to arouse interest in aviation by forming flying clubs throughout Canada. Mr. K. Blatchford, M.P. for East Edmonton took a special interest in this aviation project and called a meeting on August 27, 1927, in the McDonald Hotel, Edmonton, with a view to forming a flying club for Edmonton. Of those invited, 45 people attended. They decided to call their club "The Edmonton and Northern Alberta Aero Club." May was amongst those who attended this gathering and assisted in organizing the club. He was elected President at this meeting; S. A. Yorke was elected first Vice-President and J. Syde became second Vice-President. As no machines were to be distributed by the government until the spring, the club made preparations to run a ground school during the fall and winter months. S. A.

Yorke also acted as instructor. The lectures were well attended. Wop May was absent from the club in Edmonton during the winter months, as his business with the National Cash Register Company took him to Calgary. Therefore, a new election of officers took place. Charles "Cy" Becker then became President and Jimmy Bell, Vice-President.

The interest of the members of the club continued to be kept alive during the spring of 1928 by the ground school until the aircraft would arrive. In the meantime, the club's executive entered into negotiations with the city for the use of Blatchford Field, the City of Edmonton's airfield, for the newly formed flying club. This airfield was originally acquired by the city at the suggestion of Mr. Blatchford, while Mayor of Edmonton, Wop May and City Engineer A. W. Haddow. Blatchford Field, which was named after the Mayor, first consisted of an area of land about 1,000 yards by 800 yards, partly natural prairie and partly brush, willow and poplar. Under the guidance of the R.C.A.F., the city cleared air strips.

For a while the club was unable to obtain a flying instructor and had to stand back and watch other clubs get their machines before they did. However, Wop May solved this problem. He received leave of absence from the National Cash Register Company in Calgary for the summer to become flying instructor. He was given permission by the Controller of Civil Aviation, Mr. J. A. Wilson, to take a special course as a flying instructor at Moose Jaw in May, 1928, instead of having to go to Camp Borden, as was the custom. The club received its first government-sponsored aircraft on June 23 and flying instruction was under way. Not long after Wop May began his instruction, his hand became badly poisoned, so severely that it prevented him from flying. Therefore, it was decided to overhaul the club's first aircraft, G-CAKJ, a D.H. 60X Moth. It was not until July 19 that flying in-

struction was under way again, with a class of about fifteen pupils. The club received its second machine, G-CALB, on August 19, 1928.

A general meeting of the club's officers was held on August 24 to review its activities. Due to a number of personnel changes as a result of the club's growth, a third re-organization of the executive became necessary. In this re-organization of the Edmonton and Northern Alberta Aero Club in August, 1928, Cy Becker was elected President; Jimmy Bell, Vice-President; S. A. Yorke, Secretary-Treasurer and Wop May, flying instructor and air engineer. As the club decided that the increase in flying instruction was too much for one instructor, Cy Becker, the new President of the Club, was given permission by the Controller of Civil Aviation, Mr. J. A. Wilson, to also assist as instructor, and he gave these services without remuneration. J. "Vic" Horner was an officer of the club.

The club's first machine made an unscheduled landing in a grain field not far from the edge of one of the air strips on August 29, 1928, requiring extensive repairs to both wings and the undercarriage!

On September 7 and 8, 1928, Flight Lieutenant Walsh from High River Station came to Edmonton and gave the club's first applicants their tests for their private pilot's licences, amongst whom were R. F. Brinkman, A. L. Clark, R. P. Owen and Art Rankin.

It was a sub-zero day in December, 1928, that Dr. Hamman, the Indian settlement doctor at Fort Vermilion, Alberta, sent an urgent message for help to Peace River by dog sled — a distance of 280 miles — to be wired immediately to Dr. M. R. Bow, Deputy Minister of the Department of Health, Edmonton. They had no means of telegraphing the message from Fort Vermilion. Dr. Hamman's urgent message, which Dr. Bow received on December 31, 1928, said that an epidemic of diphtheria had

broken out at Fort Vermilion and Little Red River — and they had no diphtheria antitoxin to prevent the spreading of the epidemic. Could some antitoxin be sent to them immediately somehow?

If it was to be effective, it was necessary that this diphtheria antitoxin be delivered immediately. From Fort McMurray, the end of steel, the only means of transportation at this time of the year was by dog sled. As travel by dog sled would be much too slow, Dr. Bow asked Wop May if he would fly the diphtheria antitoxin to Fort Vermilion. The factor at Fort Vermilion was already dead.

On New Year's Day, January 1, 1929, with the temperature hovering around −40° F, Wop May, accompanied by his friend and pilot Vic Horner, took off from Blatchford Field, Edmonton, in their little silver two-seater Avro Avian aircraft G-CAVB, on wheels, as they had no skis for it, to deliver their precious life-saving cargo of antitoxin to Fort Vermilion. In addition, the aircraft had an open cockpit! Vic Horner had purchased this Avro Avian aircraft, with a 75 h.p. engine, from England about six months prior to this time. The nearest cabin aircraft were at Winnipeg and it would take too long to fly them to Edmonton. Only aircraft with open cockpits were available in Edmonton, and they were all put up for the winter season. Besides, none of them had any skis, either.

They had to cover a distance of some 600 miles over trackless wastes and sparsely inhabited country through cold Arctic blustery weather. They covered the 320 miles to Peace River and landed to gas up, as well as thaw out, before continuing the 280-mile lap of their flight onward to Fort Vermilion. On the way to Fort Vermilion it started to snow and blow, and the storm gathered such momentum that its blizzard-like squalls forced them to land at McLennan and spend the night there. The next day they arrived at Fort Vermilion so numb from

G-CAVB used on January 1, 1929 to fly a cargo of anti-toxin to Fort Vermilion, Alta. The 'plane had a 75 h.p. engine. Note the open cockpit!

the bitterly intense cold and chilled through by the dampness that they had to be physically taken from their little silver Avro Avian open cockpit aircraft. The intense cold had told on them — they were suffering from frost-bite, and their faces had been whipped by the cold biting winds and were bleeding from the cuts. A fast dog team was on hand at Fort Vermilion to take the antitoxin the 50 miles to Little Red River. Wop May and Vic Horner returned to Peace River on January 5, 1929, in the sub-zero weather, again so cold and numb that they had to be helped out of the aircraft — their faces still sore from the cold whipping winds. The following day, January 6, they arrived in Edmonton during a blustery snowstorm to be heartily welcomed by about 5,000 or so people of Edmonton, as they exuberantly expressed their gratitude and appreciation to Wop May and Vic Horner. They were glad to be back in Edmonton again where it was not so cold, and thankful that this job had been completed successfully.

This life-saving and truly arduous flight by Wop May and Vic Horner was successful in every sense of the word — as the antitoxin was effective, the epidemic subsided and the patients recovered.

Wop May, Vic Horner and Cy Becker organized Commercial Airways of Edmonton in February, 1929. Wop May was chief pilot; Cy Becker was General Manager and secretary-treasurer and Vic Horner was President. All three were directors.

It was with Commercial Airways that Captain May carried out his outstanding work in the Peace River district and the north country; and it was Commercial Airways that was to receive the first air mail contract in the Mackenzie River district on November 1, 1929.

Commercial Airways started off in 1929 with only one little silver two-seater Avro Avian aircraft, G-CAVB, which had

an open cockpit. It had a 75 h.p. engine. The company decided that a more modern type of aircraft would be necessary for its operation. So Wop May and Vic Horner left immediately for Burbank, California, where they purchased a Lockheed-Vega from the Lockheed Aircraft Corporation. This Lockheed-Vega, CF-AAL, with its closed-in cabin, was considered to be one of the first modern aircraft of that time. After a 2,000-mile flight from Burbank, they arrived back in Edmonton on February 10, 1929. The company operated throughout the summer months with these two aircraft.

In February, 1929, flying their newly purchased Lockheed-Vega aircraft, CF-AAL, May made another life-saving flight to Westlock, Alberta, from Edmonton, and during the following month, in March, another similar flight was made to Waterhole from Edmonton carrying diphtheria antitoxin in both instances. Roads were drifted in with snow and, in the latter case, infrequency of train service made air transport imperative if the antitoxin was to be available in time to be effective in saving life and preventing an epidemic.

Wop May left Blatchford Field on April 21, 1929, and made the inaugural air mail flight to Grande Prairie, Alberta. He flew CF-AAL, Commercial Airways Lockheed-Vega aircraft, and made the flight in three hours and ten minutes. This particular flight was made in summer-like weather with the sun shining, unlike many of his flights.

Some other memorable and emergency flights which Wop May made during 1929 in his Lockheed-Vega mercy ship were:
to Alberta Beach from Edmonton to carry a tank of oxygen for a patient seriously ill with pneumonia;
to Carcajou to bring out to the hospital in Edmonton a mentally deranged woman and her newly born baby, as well as the doctor in attendance; and a trip to

Keg River for a similar purpose;
to Vegreville from Edmonton to bring out a patient suffering from a broken back.

All of these rescue flights required resolute endurance, which Wop May possessed. The flights were carried out at the request of the Alberta Provincial Department of Health at Edmonton. Indeed, all of his life Wop May was helping people in one way or another. Is it any wonder he was so well thought of and respected, especially in the north country?

Then he made the first non-stop flight from Edmonton to Winnipeg in 1929 in Lockheed-Vega CF-AAL, in seven hours, covering some 800 miles, averaging 112 miles per hour.

However, Commercial Airways was looking into the future, and had an eye on the contract for air mail services down the Mackenzie River. For this specific purpose alone, more aircraft were required. Therefore, in the fall of 1929, with this foremost in mind, Wop May and George Hoskins, who was associated with Rutledge Air Service of Calgary, left for the east to purchase three more aircraft. In September, 1929, Commercial Airways became associated with Rutledge Air Service, Calgary, under certain financial arrangements to take care of a government-sponsored air mail service from Edmonton to Aklavik, which they were hoping to fly that fall. In New York they purchased three new Bellanca six-seater aircraft with closed-in cabins, in preparation for their northern flights. They bore the registration markings: CF-AJQ, CF-AJR and CF-AKI. With their Lockheed-Vega, CF-AAL, Commercial Airways now had four closed-in cabin monoplanes for its use. The company was employing five pilots and five air engineers.

During the month of December, 1929, Wop May flew a total of 4,862 miles over the Slave River-Mackenzie River route between Fort McMurray and

The first Bellanca aircraft of Commercial Airways to arrive at Aklavik, N.W.T. on the inaugural air mail run — December 26, 1929.
Photo courtesy of Wop May and Commander Frederick B. Watt.

Aklavik — to open up a new era of flying in the north — for the convenience of trappers, fur traders, prospectors and commerce in general. He flew to Fort McMurray in November in his Bellanca ski-equipped aircraft to make advance preparations for the inaugural air mail service to Aklavik. As the contract with the Post Office Department was awarded on November 1, 1929, rather late in the year, May had only time enough to fly over the route as far as Fort Simpson before freeze-up. Equipping the Bellanca aircraft with skis, etc., for the first time for the Arctic operation was no easy task.

Wop May made Fort McMurray his headquarters this same fall, from which to carry on this 1,676-mile northern air mail service — which was the farthest north and the longest air mail route in the world for many years. This was to be Wop May's headquarters for a long time to come. Here a slipway, a shop and a hangar were built for their aircraft. Sub-bases and caches were established at Fort Fitzgerald, Fort Resolution, Fort Simpson and Aklavik. On December 9, 1929, when weather conditions improved, the other three pilots, who were to go on the inaugural air mail flight, flew in from Edmonton with their aircraft. The other three pilots on the inaugural flight were Cy Becker, Moss Burbridge, who was on loan from the Edmonton and Northern Alberta Aero Club, and Idris Glyn-Roberts, a former R.A.F. pilot who was employed by Commercial Airways.

December 10, 1929, was the historic day that marked the inauguration of the first contract for an air mail service "down north" via the Mackenzie River to Aklavik beyond the Arctic Circle. In addition to piloting one of the three Bellanca aircraft to and from Aklavik, Wop May was responsible for having the aircraft in readiness for the flight, and for the entire organization and supervision of the complete air mail operation north of Fort McMurray to Aklavik on the Arctic

Ocean — an exacting and onerous job. Moss Burbidge flew the Lockheed-Vega, CF-AAL, and left the fleet at Fort Resolution after completing his part of the journey. Cy Becker flew one of the Bellancas and went as far as Fort Simpson, while Wop May and Idris Glyn-Roberts went through to Aklavik, their destination, in their Bellancas. The sacks of mail were piled sky-high for the flight. There were 120,000 or so philatelists' letters alone.

Starting from Fort McMurray, stops were made along the route to Aklavik at Fort Chipewyan, Fort Fitzgerald, Fort Smith, Fort Resolution, Hay River, Fort Providence, Fort Simpson, Wrigley, Fort Norman, Fort Good Hope, where they, including their two air engineers, Tim Sims and C. Van der Linden, spent a cold and forlorn Christmas Day; then on to Arctic Red River, Fort McPherson and Aklavik — a 1,676-mile route — arriving on December 26, 1929. They were delighted and satisfied with having successfully completed their northern mission.

Leaving Aklavik on December 30, 1929, for their homeward journey, they arrived back at Fort McMurray on January 3, 1930 — with the inaugural trip of many cold days and much hard work behind them.

Frederick B. Watt, a reporter attached to the *Edmonton Journal* at the time, flew with Wop May in his red Bellanca aircraft, the *Lady Edmonton*, on this inaugural flight to Aklavik. In his vivid description of the flight in the June, 1930 issue of *Canadian Aviation*, he says:

The lengthy and arduous outward trip was attributable to a number of reasons. The bulk of the cargo was the chief of these. It was necessary to ferry the entire shipment ahead from post to post, with the result that when the two ships finally reached Aklavik they had each flown nearly 5,000 miles in covering the 1,676-mile route for the air mail.

It was a case of flying into darkness as well. From Fort Simpson north the hours of daylight dwindled with breathtaking rapidity. Beyond Good Hope there was no sun at all, nor would there be for a matter of two weeks. The perpetual Arctic twilight, added to the perils of unknown landings, had cut the flying days decidedly short. On the return journey, going into the light and over territory that was no longer strange to the pilot, the 500-mile jaunt from Arctic Red River to Fort Wrigley was accomplished in one day by flying at 120 miles an hour from dawn to dusk. It was a close enough race, even with a speedy machine. Farther south, hopping from Fort Simpson to Fort McMurray, 720 miles was a cinch compared to that northern 500. Adverse weather played its part in making the initiation to the Arctic regions a real one. Fort Chipewyan on Lake Athabasca remembers the afternoon that three red ships with "Royal Mails" on their flanks swept out of a blinding snowstorm over the lake and sank gracefully to the smooth ice before the post. Fort Simpson recalls the day that Wop May droned through 150 miles of falling snow from Wrigley, while Idris Glyn-Roberts, pilot of the second Aklavik-bound Bellanca, came through the same storm from Fort Resolution. These were but instances. Extremely cold weather was almost welcome, inasmuch as it usually brought an atmosphere clear of everything except the constant Arctic mist. It was 60° below zero F. at Fort Good Hope when we staged our Stag Christmas dinner in the Hudson's Bay Post. It was 54° below zero F. when we took off the next morning and crossed the Arctic Circle into territory never before seen from the air in winter. The actual flying wasn't so bad, but the business of preparing the ships for the night and the heating of engines in the morning contained few elements

This picture was taken at Aklavik, N.W.T., after the Mad Trapper had been found. From left to right: E.A. Broadway, S.R. McMillan, D.A. Jack Bowen, Air Engineer Frank Hartley, Mash Neery, Constable Carter and Wop May.
Photo courtesy of Wop May.

of humour. Frost-bitten hands and faces became too common to attract any attention. On two occasions Tim Sims and C. Van der Linden, guardian of the motors, worked until after midnight in 45° below zero F. temperatures to ensure dawn take-offs. One of these occasions was Christmas Eve and both of them occurred on the naked face of the Mackenzie with no hangar facilities and only the light of an electric torch to work by.

Colonel Walter Hale of the Post Office Department in Edmonton also accompanied this flight to Aklavik, flying with Idris Glyn-Roberts.

The measure of success which attended this practical and pioneering effort was acclaimed by the Post Office Department of Canada. These were the first aircraft ever to have flown to Aklavik on the Arctic coast during any winter up to that time. The contract called for a weekly service between Fort McMurray and Fort Resolution; a monthly service between Fort McMurray and Fort Simpson; and six times a year between Fort McMurray and Aklavik.

The opening up of this air mail service meant that it was possible to reach Aklavik from Fort McMurray in three or four days in winter — as compared with two months or more by dog team. In the midwinter season, only about two and a half hours of flying was possible each day in the Far North.

Then the Minister of National Defence announced in May, 1930, that Wop May had won the Trans-Canada Trophy for the year 1929 "in recognition of his work in organizing air services to outlying districts."

In May, 1930, Wop May and Archie McMullen went east and purchased two new Bellanca aircraft with closed-in cabins, as their northern operations were continuing to expand. They quietly passed through Ottawa on their way from New York. They landed at Rockcliffe Airport to refuel. Their visit to

Ottawa was just a short while after the announcement had been made that Wop May was the recipient of the Trans-Canada Trophy for 1929. And he was greeted with the good news!

While with Commercial Airways, Wop May made flights to Baillie Island, Herschel Island, the Nahanni River, Great Bear Lake, Hunter Bay, Franklin, Reliance and Stony Rapids during 1930, and in December of that year a mercy flight was made to Letty Harbour to fly out a sick trapper. One morning at 6:00 A.M., Wop May took off in a Bellanca from Fort McMurray and arrived at Aklavik the following morning at 3:00 A.M. — making the complete trip during the hours of daylight — and mail was left at each post along the way. Prospectors, engineers and mining supplies were transported into various mineral areas of the Northwest Territories for several mining exploration companies. Trips were also made to the lead-zinc properties on the south shore of Great Slave Lake; the copper finds on the east shore of Great Bear Lake and the copper showing at Yellowknife and Rae. Mining personnel and drilling machinery were taken in and periodic visits were made to bring in supplies of food. They flew aircraft to the gypsum deposits on the Peace River carrying Dr. Wallace, President of the University of Alberta, and members of his engineering faculty. During their summer season a party of big game hunters from New York was flown into the Nahanni River district and succeeded in obtaining a number of excellent specimens of a new kind of sheep. Tourists were also carried to these northern areas. The R.C.M.P., the Department of the Interior, the National Research Council and a Hydrographic Survey party also used these aircraft for their special needs.

Commercial Airways was absorbed by Canadian Airways Limited on May 1, 1931. At the same time, Canadian Airways took over the Fort McMurray to

Aklavik air mail contract, as well as operating a passenger and express service along this 1,676-mile route. Commercial Airways was now operating two Bellanca CH300's, two Bellanca Pacemakers and one Lockheed-Vega. This equipment was also bought by Canadian Airways. They had five pilots and five engineers in their employ. Commercial Airways had been most active in transporting prospectors to the Great Bear Lake mining fields and to the gold fields in the Island Lake district. Other operating activities of Commercial Airways were taken over by Western Canada Airways, a subsidiary of Canadian Airways. Commercial Airways now ceased to exist, and Wop May immediately went on the payroll of Canadian Airways Limited.

In February, 1932, at the request of Punch Dickins, Superintendent of the Mackenzie River District for Canadian Airways at Edmonton, Wop May flew Bellanca aircraft CF-AKI to assist the R.C.M.P. officers in their pursuit of Albert Johnson, known as the Mad Trapper of Rat River. He had been terrorizing the natives of the Arctic. The search for the Mad Trapper had been under way since early January, 1932, when he had shot Constable Alfred King who had gone to Johnson's cabin to question him about some of his activities, such as tearing up the traps of the Loucheux Indians along the Rat River, about 1300 miles northwest of Edmonton.

Wop May flew in supplies, including some dynamite and members of the posse, to Aklavik, and helped in searching for the tracks of the Mad Trapper. This was the first Arctic manhunt by air. Flying his ski-equipped Bellanca CF-AKI, with his air engineer, Jack Bowen, and Constable Carter, en route to the R.C.M.P. camp through the cold Arctic skies, they reached the Rat River area. Below them in the snow they spotted some figures of men huddled in a camp

— but no Mad Trapper or tracks could they see. Landing, they left Constable Carter at the camp and picked up the frozen body of Constable Edgar Millen who was shot and killed by the Mad Trapper. Wop May returned to Aklavik with the constable's body in his Bellanca, and then went back to the area to spend much time searching for Albert Johnson's tracks from the air to assist the R.C.M.P. This he was able to do and he saved the posse several days' travel on one occasion, as the Mad Trapper possessed the skill of a veteran when it came to doubling and backtracking to elude his pursuers. However, this precise skill was to be the means of his capture a little later.

From the beginning the Mad Trapper had plodded tirelessly on to evade his pursuers and did a good job too, in spite of the sub-zero weather, even though he was improperly equipped for this kind of Arctic travel. To cover his tracks on one occasion he even removed his snowshoes and followed a hard-crusted caribou trail. On what was to be Wop May's final search flight for Albert Johnson on February 17, he observed a lone figure below him on the ice of Eagle River in the Yukon surrounded by others at a distance, which he took to be the posse. The battle was finishing when he arrived. Flying low over the scene, May realized, from appearances, that the Mad Trapper must be dead. He and Jack Bowen then landed and picked up a seriously wounded constable and flew him back to Aklavik for urgent medical attention — as another half-hour would have been too late to save his life. So this fugitive from justice, known only as Albert Johnson, and had shot three men, killing one, died without pity — the way he had lived at the last. Wop May flew Johnson's body, carrying some $2,000 in cash on it, as well as some gold teeth, back to Aklavik.

Wop May and Sammy Tomlinson, air engineer, made a three weeks' flight for Canadian Airways from Fort McMurray to Aklavik, covering a distance of approximately 4,300 miles, for the purpose of transporting Mr. A. L. Sawle, Comptroller of Northern Traders Limited, to the company's trading posts — the first time that this company had made a winter trip by air to their trading posts. This trip showed still more the ever-increasing scope for aircraft for business transport in the north country. While this trip was carried out, the temperatures ranged from -20° to -60° F.! On Tuesday morning, December 27, 1932, the party left Edmonton by railway for Fort McMurray, then the end of steel, and on Thursday morning, December 29, left by aircraft for their northern posts. They stopped at various trading posts along the way at Fort Smith, Fort Resolution, Hay River, Fort Providence and Fort Simpson, where they spent New Year's Eve. They continued on to Fort Norman, Fort Good Hope, Arctic Red River, Fort McPherson and Aklavik, where they spent two nights and a day. Aklavik was well within the Arctic Circle, and the sun was not visible at this time of year. The inhabitants did not expect to see it again until January 9, 1933, when only a portion would be visible for a short period during the day. Therefore, lights were necessary until about noon, when they were turned out for an hour or so. Daylight lasted from about ten in the morning until two in the afternoon.[1]

Wop May and his party started their southward journey on Saturday, January 7, 1933. They climbed to 8,000 feet in the clear, cold air and had a wonderful view of the Mackenzie Delta, which is more than 100 miles long and almost 100 miles wide. The several large channels from the Mackenzie River are joined by thousands of small islands of alluvial deposit of various sizes and shapes. In the Mackenzie Delta nature has laid out a pattern of scenic wonder displaying her waterways. They returned to Fort McMurray, their starting point of

the flight, and Mr. A. L. Sawle arrived back in Edmonton on Tuesday, January 17, 1933, just three weeks after leaving Edmonton for his northern journey.[2]

In the fall of 1933, Wop May flew Mr. Sawle on another trip to visit the trading posts of Northern Traders Limited in the Arctic regions. A. L. Sawle said that one would expect the pilot and engineer would be glad of a rest in the evenings after a day's travelling under Arctic winter conditions, but this was not the case as they were never idle. When Wop May arrived at whatever house furnished accommodation for him during his stay, he peeled off the outer couple of layers of his clothes and looked around for a gun that did not function properly and, in no time, whenever he found one, had it apart and adjusted and reassembled, ready for bigger and better caribou. He invariably found a gun needing attention and ended each day in peace and happiness. The air engineer, Rudy Heuss, would spend his evenings visiting. He always visited homes with a radio and, at the least sign of faulty reception, he pulled out his screwdriver and in a short time had the radio spread out over the floor. No youngster ever took a Christmas toy apart faster than Rudy did radios. However, he always managed to replace all the pieces and usually the radios were improved in tone when he was finished with them. Such was the way these crews spent their spare time in the north.[3]

One day in 1933 Wop May landed an aircraft successfully on one ski, through necessity of course, as he had lost the other one. It might be said that he was lucky; but it was really his skill.

On a January day in 1934, May, flying Canadian Airways Bellanca CF-AKI, turned days into minutes (two minutes to the day) on a 150-mile hop from South Nahanni to McLeod Creek, British Columbia. His time was 75 minutes in and 90 minutes back. By dog team, the only alternative means of travel, 42 days

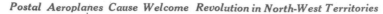

Postal Aeroplanes Cause Welcome Revolution in North-West Territories

"The recent inauguration of a regular air mail route to Aklavik in the Mackenzie delta near the western Arctic Ocean, has revolutionized life for trappers, prospectors and other residents of the Northwest Territories. The map: (1) shows the route followed by mail, it being transported by train from Edmonton to McMurray and there transferred to 'planes. (2) is Kittigazuit on the Mackenzie River delta, one of the Arctic settlements profiting by the new service. (3) is Capt. W.R. (Wop) May of Edmonton, senior pilot on the inaugural mail trip, while (4) are auxiliary supply schooners operated by the Hudson's Bay Co. on the northern Mackenzie. Around the border of the layout are the air mail cachets prepared by the post-office department to commemorate the inauguration of this northern postal service."

The Leader, Regina, Wednesday, February 19, 1930.

1935. Another first!

He was created an Officer of the Order of the British Empire in 1935 "for numerous mercy flights to outlying points in northwestern Canada." Wop May believed that civil aviation in Canada held a great destiny.

In March, 1936, this man with the great pioneering spirit was appointed Superintendent of the Mackenzie River District for Canadian Airways and was transferred to Edmonton from Fort McMurray. He succeeded Punch Dickins who was appointed Superintendent of Northern Operations at Winnipeg. Wop May did little flying after he took over this administrative post. The following year, in 1937, he had an operation performed on his right eye, having it removed, due to a freak accident which he had when he was working in Dayton, Ohio. In 1942 Canadian Pacific Air Lines was to absorb Canadian Airways, along with a number of other companies.

Wop May was elected President of the Edmonton and Northern Alberta Aero Club early in 1939, succeeding Cy Becker, who had been President of the club during the previous two years and had now become Vice-President. At the end of the club's year (1938), a total of 1,102 hours had been flown and 2,205 flights were made. The club had 60 active members and a total membership of 175. This was a very successful year.

Shortly after World War II broke out, the British Commonwealth Air Training Plan came into existence in Canada, and various training schools were established. Canadian Pacific Air Lines was operating some of these schools. Wop May was appointed District Supervisor of Western Schools for Canadian Pacific Air Lines at Edmonton. He next became General Manager of all the Air Observers Schools operated by Canadian Pacific Air Lines for the R.C.A.F.'s Northern and Western Commands.

In 1943 he organized an Aerial Rescue School to train first-aid parachute crews

would have been required for the one-way journey alone![4]

Flying this same aircraft, CF-AKI, on another occasion, May went from Cameron Bay on Great Bear Lake, Northwest Territories, the scene of mining activity for radio-active ore and silver, to Fort McMurray, Alberta, a distance of some 800 miles, on February 13, 1934, in record time. He covered the distance in seven hours and fifteen minutes elapsed time, with a stop-over for refuelling at Fort Resolution. He was also carrying a full load of passengers, mail and furs.

Pilots who fly in far distant territories away from the regular routes have to be prepared for all emergencies and, on occasions, for strange missions. One of the latter, unique in Canadian flying history, was given to Wop May on March 15, 1934, when he was invested with the authority of a sheriff's bailiff by Sheriff John Rae of Edmonton, and commanded to arrest a motorship locked in the ice of the Athabasca River, 90 miles north of Fort McMurray. Wop May's authority was contained in two legal documents, a writ of summons; and a warrant of

arrest, issued under admiralty law, which he was instructed to nail to the mast of the motorship *Mabel,* whose owners were being sued for wages by the master and the crew. Under admiralty court procedure, the ship itself is sued and arrested, and the writ of summons corresponds to the statement of claim issued in civil litigation, while the order for arrest is the counterpart of a writ of seizure under civil law. Wop flew a Bellanca Pacemaker, CF-AKI, one he so often flew, to do this job.[5]

On another day in 1934, May left Norway House, at the north end of Lake Winnipeg, about 8:00 A.M., flew to Island Lake, and returned to Norway House, a round trip of 300 miles — and then took off for Winnipeg, 275 miles south, after including a stop at Berens River. He reached his destination about 4:00 P.M.

During 1935, Wop May was appointed Commissioner of Oaths for the Saskatchewan Government to help the prospectors with their business of recording and transferring mining claims.

Wop also flew the first air mail to Goldfields, Saskatchewan, in August,

44   CANADA'S AVIATION PIONEERS

— a plan he had thought about for years and hoped to see materialize. He was convinced that pilots who crashed in remote areas would survive if given early treatment and attention. The following is the citation of the award, which was presented by Brigadier-General Dale V. Gaffney, Commanding General, Alaskan Division, United States Air Transport Command, when Wop was presented with the Medal of Freedom, Bronze Palm, in connection with the Air Rescue Squad, organized by Canadian Pacific Air Lines who operated No. 2 Air Observers School in Edmonton:

Mr. Wilfrid Reid May, Canadian civilian, performed meritorious services for the United States Army Air Forces from January, 1942, to January, 1946. Mr. May, serving in the capacity of General Manager of the Air Observers School at Edmonton Municipal Airport and later as Director of Northern Development of Canadian Pacific Air Lines, voluntarily loaned the personnel and the facilities of his school to assure the delivery of aircraft to the Aleutians and Alaska without delay. He conceived the idea of aerial rescue crews for rescue of fliers in the bush area, and after developing a trained parachute squad he furnished a rescue service indiscriminately to Americans and Canadians, thus saving the lives of many of our fliers. In so doing, he fulfilled the highest traditions of the Dominion of Canada.

Wop May, O.B.E., D.F.C., became Director of Northern Development with Canadian Pacific Air Lines, Edmonton, in 1946. The company's offices were transferred from Edmonton to Vancouver in the fall of 1949, at which time he became Director of Development. Wop May was transferred to Calgary in March, 1951, as Manager of the Repair Depot there for Canadian Pacific Air Lines.

He was issued Commercial Air Pilot's Certificate No. 7, dated July 31, 1920, and Air Engineer's Certificate No. A-726, dated December 15, 1931, which superseded Certificate No. 364 of September 1928, also superseding Certificate No. 92, issued by the Air Board in January, 1921.

Wop May was christened "Wop" by a young cousin whose home he so often visited — as "Wop" was the closest she could come to saying "Wilfrid." Wop May stood six feet in height, was broad-shouldered, of a reddish-fair complexion with blue eyes, and wore a tattoo on his left arm. During his many colourful years of bush flying and commercial flying — from his pioneering exploits, his many mercy flights and his search and rescue flights in the Far North to his latter day responsibilities — he always remained undaunted.

Yet one day, the one who went on so many other search and rescue flights was, himself, to be the object of such a search. May was once thought to be lost when he was overdue for one whole week in returning from a flight which he had made into the Nahannies with some prospectors. They had gone in search of the Lost McLeod Mine — and located it, never to find it again!

This famous bush pilot of the north through whose cold frigid skies he so often flew was climbing a hill in Timpanogos Cave National Park, near Provo, Utah, while on vacation when suddenly he collapsed on June 21, 1952. His death was attributed to a heart attack. He was vacationing with his son Denny, who was then 17 years of age. He was married, and had one son and one daughter.

Wop May was named a member of Canada's Aviation Hall of Fame in 1973. He was made a Companion of the Order of Flight (City of Edmonton).

NOTES

[1] A. L. Sawle, of *Canadian Aviation*, March 1933.
[2] *Canadian Aviation*, March 1934.
[3] *Canadian Aviation*, May 1934.
[4] *Canadian Aviation*, April 1934.
[5] *Canadian Aviation*, April 1934.

Wop May, 1949.

1930

"Tuddy" in 1930.

John Henry "Tuddy" Tudhope

Citation: in recognition of his outstanding work in carrying out airway surveys preliminary to the inauguration of an air mail service in Canada

Squadron Leader John Henry Tudhope, M.C., while Superintendent of Airways with the Civil Aviation Branch of the Department of National Defence, was awarded the Trans-Canada Trophy for meritorious service in the advancement of aviation in Canada during 1930, "in recognition of his outstanding work in carrying out airway surveys preliminary to the inauguration of an air mail service in Canada." The announcement of the award was made on March 3, 1931, by Colonel, The Honourable Donald M. Sutherland, D.S.O., Minister of National Defence.

Squadron Leader Tudhope pioneered the east and west air mail routes from the Atlantic to the Pacific during 1930, said the Minister, by carrying out preliminary aerial reconnaissances.

He made a preliminary aerial reconnaissance of the Rocky Mountain route early in 1930. After several exploratory aerial reconnaissances of a number of passes through the Rockies from Lethbridge to Vancouver, Squadron Leader Tudhope recommended the southern route through British Columbia, known as the Crow's Nest Pass. Most of

his flying on this route was carried out in a Stearman aircraft, under variable weather conditions.

His flying duties during the year took him by air from Sydney, Cape Breton, to Victoria, British Columbia, over some very hazardous territory at times. These he accomplished successfully — without untoward incident or accident other than an occasional frost-bite.

John Henry Tudhope was born in Johannesburg, South Africa, on April 17, 1891, where his father, Frank Selwyn Tudhope, was resident director of the Robinson Gold Mines near Johannesburg. He was educated in the public school at Johannesburg and matriculated at Tunbridge School in Kent, England. Returning to Africa, he took a job for a short while, prior to joining the South African Army.

Tudhope joined the Imperial Light Horse of the South African Defence Forces as a machine gunner on August 28, 1914, serving under General Brink. He served throughout the German Southwest African Campaign until the force was disbanded in September, 1915. Shortly after this he went to England where he joined the Royal Flying Corps as a cadet in January, 1916. He was granted a commission on April 13, 1917, and took preliminary training at Netheravon and advanced training at Terne Hill, obtaining his wings as a pilot in May, 1917. He was promoted to Flight Commander on November 18, 1917.

Tudhope was then posted to France with No. 40 Squadron, Royal Flying Corps, where he served from June, 1917, to May, 1918. Mannock, the famous ace, was also with the unit. Tudhope was awarded both the Military Cross and Bar for conspicuous gallantry and devotion to duty in attacking enemy aeroplanes and

The Committee of Award for the year 1930 consisted of the following members:

Squadron Leader A. T. N. Cowley, R.C.A.F., acting for the Controller of Civil Aviation, Department of National Defence, Ottawa.

Squadron Leader L. F. Stevenson, R.C.A.F., (C.G.A.S.), Department of National Defence, Ottawa.

with advice and assistance from

George Herring, Superintendent of Air Mail Service, Post Office Department, Ottawa.

carrying out numerous reconnaissances.

When the Royal Air Force was formed on April 1, 1918, Tudhope was promoted to the rank of Flight Lieutenant. In May, 1918, he became instructor and Officer Commanding of the Training Group at Shotwich, England, where he served until he left for Canada. He retired from the service with the rank of Major.

Upon his arrival in Canada in November, 1919, he went to Lumby, British Columbia, where he farmed. Eventually, however, he returned to flying and joined the Canadian Air Force and was granted a Commission as a Flight Lieutenant on October 4, 1920. He served as an instructor at Camp Borden until August 31, 1921, when he joined the Air Board and was employed as an air pilot navigator at High River Station until February 28, 1923. He also took a special course in seaplane training at Vancouver during February, 1923.

Major Tudhope became known to his friends everywhere in Canada as "Tuddy" — and "Tuddy" he was wherever he went.

Tuddy was employed with Laurentide Air Service as a pilot from June, 1923, until September 30, 1923, during the time that the company was taking over the forestry patrols from the Air Board in the Province of Quebec.

On October 1, 1923, Tuddy returned to the Canadian Air Force. When the R.C.A.F. was organized on April 1, 1924, he was posted to Dartmouth as Commanding Officer of the R.C.A.F. Station there, and held this position until he was posted to Jericho Beach Air Station, Vancouver, in November, 1924. He was appointed Commanding Officer of this station on December 8, 1924. The following month, on January 1, 1925, he was promoted to the rank of Squadron Leader. Tuddy remained at Jericho Beach Air Station until he became Superintendent of Airways with the Department of National Defence on

July 1, 1927.

In 1927 the Post Office authorities requested that experimental air mail flights be made to hasten the delivery of incoming and outgoing transatlantic mail by their delivery at Father Point (Rimouski) during the summer season of navigation on the St. Lawrence, and then to Montreal by air. One of Tuddy's first jobs with the Department of National Defence was to make some preliminary experimental flights for an air mail service. A lack of sheltered air harbours along the St. Lawrence prevented the organization of a reliable seaplane service. However, several experimental flights were made in September.

The first experimental flight was made by Tuddy on September 9, 1927, when he went out to meet the incoming *Empress of France* in a seaplane. Due to the roughness of the water and other factors, the Vanessa seaplane capsized and Tuddy was fortunate to get away himself. This Vanessa seaplane was built by Canadian Vickers as an experimental 'craft.

Other experimental flights were made on September 12, 1927, to meet the outgoing *Doric*; on September 16 to meet the incoming *Empress of Australia*; on September 21 to meet the outgoing *Empress of Scotland*; on October 2 to meet the incoming *Montroyal*; on October 26 to meet the outgoing *Empress of Scotland*; on October 27 to meet the incoming *Montroyal*; on October 29 to meet the outgoing *Regina*; on November 5 to meet the outgoing *Megantic* by Tuddy who made the flight in an aircraft on wheels; and on November 11 to meet the incoming *Montnairn* by Tuddy, who made the flight in an aircraft on wheels again. For these last two flights, arrangements were made for Tuddy to use an aerodrome at Rimouski, from where a regular service by aeroplane was to be run to St. Hubert aerodrome at Montreal.

The following year, 1928, the Ottawa-

Montreal-Rimouski air mail service was operated by Canadian Transcontinental Airways Limited, Quebec (on a contract basis) during the open navigation season of the St. Lawrence River so that transatlantic mail might be carried by air throughout the year. The first trip was made on May 5, 1928. The flights were to coincide with the incoming and outgoing steamships which came and went from Rimouski.

It was in 1928, under J. A. Wilson's direction, that a decision was made for the survey and construction of aerodromes across Canada for the Trans-Canada Airway over which an air mail service was to be operated. Aerodromes were coming into existence at the larger centres across Canada since the government had decided to assist the flying clubs in their activities in 1927. Now, intermediate aerodromes were to be built between these larger centres. The selection of sites for Western Canada was to be made by A. D. "Dan" McLean, while the selection of sites from Winnipeg east to Halifax was to be done by Major Robert "Bob" Dodds, Major Tudhope and George Wakeman. It was initially planned to have the airway in operation by July 1, 1937.

Eastern Canada, in this instance, included that section from Winnipeg east to Halifax. It was over most of this section that Tuddy made the preliminary aerial reconnaissances and some detailed selection of sites. Bob Dodds chose the sites from Winnipeg to Kapuskasing, while Tuddy chose those between Kapuskasing and Montreal; and George Wakeman chose the sites on the route from Montreal to the Maritimes, carrying out the detailed selection of these sites.

Some work began in 1927 with the Montreal-Rimouski section to speed overseas delivery of the mail. The Prairie section was not started until 1929. The most difficult section for locating sites was in northern Ontario, particularly between Cochrane and the Manitoba

boundary. Some 22 fields had to be selected in this district. It was all bush country from Ottawa to Cobalt. There was fairly good country from there to Englehart, then rough country around Kirkland Lake to Ramore, and good farming land from Ramore to Hearst. From Hearst to the Manitoba boundary, there was nothing but rock, spruce and muskeg. That part of the route ran from a point almost directly north of Sault Ste Marie to approximately 110 miles east of Winnipeg.

In March, 1928, Tuddy made a test flight to Halifax and inspected several possible sites for aerodromes in the Maritimes. At this time, Halifax did not have an airport either.

Tuddy carried out a preliminary aerial survey between Ottawa and Winnipeg during August, 1928, for the purpose of obtaining information that would assist in selecting the best route for a regular air mail service.

On his way west, he followed the Canadian Pacific Railway line from Ottawa to North Bay, then he followed the Canadian National Railway line from North Bay to Brereton, Manitoba, via Cochrane. On his way east, Tuddy followed the Canadian Pacific Railway line from Minaki to Fort William, Port Arthur and Nipigon, then the Canadian National Railway line from Orient Bay, Sudbury, North Bay to Ottawa. In all, some 2,237 miles were covered in 28 hours' flying time.

Tuddy found the country heavily timbered and rocky. There were many lakes, and landing areas for seaplanes were good. However, there were few ready sites for aerodromes. Tuddy flew a Fairchild FC2 seaplane with a 200 h.p. Wright engine.

A second flight was made from Ottawa to Halifax for a similar purpose and Tuddy made preliminary aerial reconnaissances of air harbours and possible air routes along the way.

A series of flights was carried out

between Montreal and Toronto for the purpose of investigating an aerial route between these two cities in connection with the carrying of air mail. Nine return trips were flown in two periods of ten days each.

Another series of flights was undertaken for the same purpose between Toronto and Buffalo. Six return trips were flown between these points.

In 1929 further surveys and development of air routes were undertaken between Toronto-Buffalo; and Toronto-Windsor. The new route from Hamilton to Windsor was lighted for night flying. Twenty-four-inch rotating beacons of 2,000,000 candle power were installed at the main centres, while beacons of 5,000 candle power were erected at intervals of twelve to fifteen miles along the route.

Aerial surveys were continued to the Maritime Provinces in 1929, too, to develop an air route from Montreal east to Saint John, Halifax and Moncton.

During the month of March, 1930, Tuddy made a preliminary aerial survey of an air mail route all the way from the Prairies through the Rocky Mountains to Vancouver.

Three flights were made from High River as far as Fernie in January. Tuddy made the first flight on January 21, 1930, in Pitcairn Mailwing G-CAXJ. The second and third flights were made on January 23, with Tuddy and Squadron Leader Leitch each flying an aircraft. The landing strip at Fernie was only partly developed at this time. The Pitcairn aircraft which Tuddy was flying was not equipped for winter flying, hence the reason for Squadron Leader Leitch making the one flight. It was on this second flight on January 23 that Tuddy froze his hands while flying the Pitcairn near Cranbrook.

Tuddy flew a D. H. Moth on an air survey flight from Winnipeg to Regina, Medicine Hat, Calgary, Vernon, Kamloops, Princeton to Vancouver

between March 17 and 23, 1930. He left Vancouver the same day and returned to Moose Jaw, reaching there on March 27, 1930. He spent almost forty hours in the air. Then he hopped off to Wichita, Kansas, to pick up a Stearman aircraft on April 21, 1930. He flew back to Medicine Hat and this was the aircraft that he flew when he made the other survey flights east of the Rockies before returning to Ottawa.

Later on in 1930, Tuddy made a preliminary aerial survey of the northern route from Edmonton via the Yellowhead Pass; while Dan McLean surveyed the central route from Vancouver to Calgary, following the main C.P.R. line. Together they made a preliminary flight of the southern route through the Crow's Nest Pass to Vancouver from Lethbridge. This southern route was through southern British Columbia via Coleman, Fernie, Cranbrook, Creston, Trail, Grand Forks and Princeton to Vancouver. After a number of surveys, Dan McLean chose this southern route through the Crow's Nest Pass, as the way was shorter and the climate was better. The construction of aerodromes on this route would not be as difficult as those on the alternative routes through either the Yellowhead or Kicking Horse Passes. However, there was only one aerodrome at Grand Forks between the Prairies and Vancouver. By observing the topographical features, landing grounds and meteorological conditions, much valuable data was obtained. A distance of some 3,000 miles was covered by air during this preliminary aerial survey by Tuddy.

The ultimate aim of the development of an airway was a complete transcontinental airway system, with feeder routes to serve all important communities in Canada. It was hoped that this would be completed by July 1, 1937. The program outlined by the Post Office Department for 1930 in the way of air mail services included the completion of the Prairie Airways, the extension of

First survey part of R.C.E.'s leaving on T. & N.O. Railroad for a site at Diver, Ontario, to drive the "first" spike on the Trans-Canada Airway. To the extreme right is Capt. W.E. Bostock, and standing next to him is Bob Dodds.

Photo courtesy of Capt. N. Elliott Rogers.

airways through the Rocky Mountains to Vancouver and the linking of Montreal with the Maritime Provinces. However, part of this program had to be put aside due to financial restrictions.

To give efficient airmail connections, night flying became necessary over some of the airways. This then meant more expense in lighting the intermediate aerodromes, and providing radio, meteorological and communication services. Ground staffs were required to do this work, and then maintain the airways.

During 1930, on the route from Windsor to Toronto, three intermediate aerodromes were constructed at Tilbury, Northwood and Strathburn, each equipped with one 2,500,000 candle power beacon, boundary and obstruction lights suitable for night flying. This 190-mile route had five municipal airports, three intermediate aerodromes, seven revolving beacons, one stationary electric beacon and ten acetylene range lanterns.

An intensive survey was made of the Montreal-Saint John-Moncton route by air and by ground. Thirteen intermediate sites were selected, including four in the Province of Quebec, five in the State of Maine and four in New Brunswick. The Canadian sites were at St. Eugene, Windsor Mills, Bishopton and Megantic in Quebec; and Upper Brockway, Blissville, Havelock and Stanley, near Halifax. On the site at Upper Brockway, near McAdam, New Brunswick, two landing strips were cleared for the convenience of winter traffic.

Then one day in March, 1931, the Minister of National Defence, Colonel Donald M. Sutherland, announced that Squadron Leader Tudhope had won the Trans-Canada Trophy "in recognition of his outstanding work in carrying out airway surveys preliminary to the inauguration of an air mail service in Canada."

At the time of this award, he had logged over some 3,000 hours. During 1930, his flying time was 234 hours, mostly while using a Stearman aircraft, either CF-CCG or CF-CCH. Some of this time was flown at night on air mail route investigation work so that the Prairie Air Mail Service, which went into operation on March 3, 1930, might be extended from coast to coast.

The presentation of the Trans-Canada Trophy to Squadron Leader Tudhope took place at the annual meeting of the Aviation League of Canada which was held at the Chateau Laurier in Ottawa in March, 1931. On March 26, the evening of the League's annual banquet, which was a gala climax to the third annual meeting of the Aviation League, Colonel Donald M. Sutherland, Minister of National Defence, presented the trophy to Squadron Leader Tudhope. This gathering took the form of the first official reunion of war-time pilots since the 1918 armistice.

Tuddy held Canadian Commercial Air Pilot's Certificate No. 148, issued on October 3, 1921, and, on April 1, 1936, he was issued Transport Certificate No. 7. He also held Air Engineer's Certificate No. A-647, dated June 18, 1931, which superseded Certificate No. 170, dated October 3, 1921, issued by the Air Board.

As a result of still further economies in 1931, no extensions were made to any of the existing airways. The only work undertaken was completing the details in connection with surveys from Lethbridge to Vancouver; further preliminary investigation of an air route through northern Ontario; and extensions to surveys already made in the Maritimes.

Tuddy resigned as Superintendent of Airways on June 30, 1931, to become associated with Coastal Airways of B.C., until September, 1931. He became chief pilot for the newly-formed company. His task was to organize flying routes. However, he remained with this company for only three months, as it went broke.

Tuddy returned to the R.C.A.F. in September, 1931, as an Inspector of Airways. On March 31, 1932, as an economy measure, the government discontinued inter-city air mail services. However, to assist in relieving the unemployment situation which existed and, at J. A. Wilson's insistence, further site selection and surveys of aerodromes were carried out in British Columbia, Ontario, Quebec and the Maritime Provinces.

For a number of years Tuddy worked along with Bob Dodds, who had joined the Department of National Defence in June, 1930, as an Inspector of Airways and Airports. Tuddy and he travelled thousands of miles by air, rail and — all too often — on foot to chart the most suitable route for aerodromes and airports. The most difficult stretch was the one through northern Ontario (the Winnipeg-North Bay route), and the site selection finally arrived at was something of a classic achievement.

In 1932 Bob Dodds, George Wakeman and Tuddy chose the locations for the construction of aerodromes on the Trans-Canada Airway between Winnipeg and Ottawa, and between Montreal and Moncton. This included anything from preliminary aerial surveys to on-the-ground survey work. The installation of airway facilities and organization and maintenance of ground services on the system throughout Canada were also equally important items.

Tuddy and Bob Dodds set out on June 2, 1932, in a Fairchild FC2 "Razorback" aircraft, "YV", on an extensive survey of several alternate routes from Winnipeg to Toronto, via North Bay, to investigate those sections of territory not previously surveyed by the Airways Branch, such as Toronto-North Bay; Toronto-Sudbury; Sudbury-Gogama-Nakina; and Port Arthur-Sioux Lookout. Also they were to check certain information obtained on previous surveys which had been made during the winter periods, and to see about the possibility of establishing intermediate aerodromes at intervals of 25 to 30 miles. Two main alternate routes were to be compared — the one via Port Arthur and Sudbury on the C.P.R., and the other one via Sioux Lookout and Cochrane on the C.N.R.

This survey by Tuddy and Bob Dodds was made from the air and on the ground, and took them from June 2, 1932, to July 28, 1932. Aerial photographs were taken of areas which had been located and investigated on the ground and wherever possible still photos were taken of properties which were sufficiently cleared and developed. As no survey had previously been carried out by the Airways Branch of the Department of National Defence of the Toronto-North Bay section, this route was flown over from Orillia to North Bay on the first three days of the survey period. Detailed ground surveys were made at Gravenhurst, Bracebridge, Powassan and North Bay and, with the exception of Gravenhurst, good sites were available at these places. The plotted course of this airway followed closely the Canadian National Railways and the main highway from Toronto to North Bay, so that communications and ground transportation were well established. The main disadvantage of this route was the prevalence of early morning and evening mists in the vicinity of Lake Simcoe and the Muskoka Lakes, and the fact that the radio beam from Toronto to the north was directly across Lake Simcoe at its widest point from Morton Park on the south shore to Eight Mile Point on the north shore, a distance of 15 miles. The terrain was generally undulating, but there were some well-developed farms providing suitable ground conditions for the operation of small wheel-type aircraft.

The alternate route from Toronto to Sudbury was flown over from Sudbury as far south as the Muskoka Lakes via French River and Parry Sound. This route was essentially a seaplane route, the terrain being mainly bare rock with

long narrow lakes, except for a short distance south of Sudbury to Burwash where there were several well-developed farms. The proximity of this route to the Georgian Bay shores made it undesirable from a meteorological point of view, as fog conditions were bad during the fall and spring periods.

The route from Sudbury-Gogama-Nakina was investigated in the first week of the survey period to see if this section might provide better facilities for the provision of intermediate aerodromes than either of the two main alternate routes of the C.N.R. and C.P.R. This route was found to be essentially a seaplane route with very few locations suitable for intermediate aerodrome development. Locations for intermediate aerodromes were found at: Nandair, Hutton Township; Raphoe; Wigwam Lake; Ostron; Gogama and Foleyet. An old survey line from Nipigon due west to Raith was investigated as an alternative to following the north shore of Lake Superior from Nipigon down to Port Arthur. It was unsuitable as the terrain was extremely rough and it had no communication whatsoever, and for the small mileage saved it was not considered worthwhile.

The section from Port Arthur-Sioux Lookout was surveyed only from the air. Northwest of Linko this route afforded excellent facilities for establishing intermediate aerodromes at the desired intervals, there being numerous jack pine sand flats right into Superior Junction, at which point it met the northern, or Canadian National, route a few miles east of Sioux Lookout. Regardless of whichever route was developed it was considered desirable that these two points should be linked up.

Information gathered on previous surveys which were made chiefly during the winter months was closely checked from the air and on the ground, with the exception of the gravel pits, which it was thought at first might be turned into

landing strips. Most of the gravel pits which were looked at were unsuitable for runways without entering into heavy expenditures.

As it had been decided to establish intermediate aerodromes at intervals of 25 to 30 miles, 36 sites were investigated on the C.P.R. route between Rennie and Sudbury and 27 sites on the C.N.R. route between Rennie and Hearst. Properties which were cleared of timber, or nearly so, were surveyed, and sketches, photos and detailed reports were made up on them.

The greatest difficulty in establishing intermediate aerodromes without entering into costly construction was found to be on the sections from Lewis to Quibell, a distance of 130 miles; Sioux Lookout to Armstrong, a distance of 140 miles; New Liskeard to North Bay, a distance of 90 miles; between Upsala and Flett, a distance of 50 miles; and between Sultan and Forks, a distance of 60 miles on the C.P.R. route.

Considering the existing ground facilities, cleared lands and settlement, the southern route afforded better opportunity for flying between Sudbury and Winnipeg, but then meteorological conditions on the southern route were known to be generally very much worse than conditions on the northern route, especially in the vicinity of Lake Superior where fogs were frequent both in summer and winter. There was little settlement on the northern route, but the average altitude and the nature of the terrain made it far more desirable for a transcontinental route.

The construction of intermediate aerodromes over the northern route would be more expensive on account of the heavy clay soil covered with heavy timber and moss from eighteen inches to three feet in depth. Clearing would be heavy, removal of moss would be a problem and, to provide a satisfactory all-year-round landing ground, it would be necessary to carry out extensive drainage

Tuddy on a survey trip in Ontario in the early '30s.

and surfacing, and gravel the inter-mediate aerodromes. This was to be compensated for partially in the cost of radio beacons for the two routes, four installations being required on the northern route and six on the southern route to cover each one efficiently. This was because the northern route followed a more direct line and there were no variations in courses such as would be necessary on the southern route in order to follow lines of communications. If the northern route was selected for development, the forced-landing facilities afforded by the new highway, then under construction on the southern route, would not likely be equalled on the northern route for many years to come.

Another consideration was the supply of power in the north. West of Kapuskasing on the northern route there was no power available other than that which might be procured at divisional points on the Canadian National Railways, so it would be necessary to install automatic power plants at each intermediate aerodrome. This would, in turn, require the services of a caretaker and, where sufficient land could be acquired, additional areas could be cleared and turned over to the caretaker for future development.

Locations surveyed on the C.N.R. route from Winnipeg to Hearst were: Rennie, Malachi, Wade, Redditt, Quibell, Amesdale, Richan, Sioux Lookout, Baldhead Lake, Tempest Lake, Collins Lake, Armstrong (which was located on an old glacial moraine), Ferland, Tashota, Kowkash, Cavell, Nakina, Grant, Jobrin, from which the country seemed to be an endless tract of green timber, Pagwa, Savoff, Nagogami, Amos and Hearst. At Hearst, they used the Ontario Provincial Forestry Branch's speeder following the railway tracks in the area. From Hearst to Cochrane, the country adjacent to the railroad was partially timbered and there were some cleared areas which were settled; also some areas which were

slashed and on which only the stumps remained. The terrain was generally flat with little variation in altitude and the highway engineers said there should be no difficulty in establishing aerodromes wherever they might be required on this section, provided adequate drainage was installed.

The following sites along the C.P.R. route from Winnipeg to North Bay were surveyed: Rennie, Hertz Lake; from Kenora to Vermilion Bay was typical lake country, heavily timbered and very rocky; Dryden, Dyment, Ignace, Martin, Upsala, Horne, Pearl, Ouimet, Dorion, Black Sturgeon River, Nipigon, Gravel Bay, Pays Flat, Selim, Schreiber, Jackfish, in country which was extremely hilly and rough, with a number of good jack pine sand flats; Heron Bay, Mobert, Denison, White River where there were several jack pine areas, Amyot, around which the terrain was badly burned over; Franz, Dalton, Chapleau and Sudbury. From Chapleau to Woman River the route was heavily timbered and very undulating. From Woman River to Metagama, after they cruised the height of land, typical lake country was in evidence. From Sudbury to North Bay, there were good farming districts where intermediate aerodromes could be established.

On one occasion when Tuddy and Bob Dodds were travelling by air making these airport site selections in northern Ontario, they were forced to alight on a mosquito-infested swamp near a railroad not far from White River, due to engine trouble. They prepared to spend the night there in their Fairchild FC2 "Razor-back" aircraft, "YV". After it became dark, Bob Dodds heard a train coming and, wrapping about him a mosquito bar (a large tentlike affair made out of white mosquito netting), ran struggling through the bush to the railway track — hoping he might flag the train and get a ride to the next settlement. The train did not stop — but he was obviously seen, as the trainmen later mentioned having seen

"a wild figure plunging out of the bush on to the right-of-way adorned with a long white flowing veil." So a rumour was started then about a "Wendigo" or some other evil spirit being in the vicinity. It is not recorded that Bob Dodds ever made any determined effort to counteract the rumour. However, the next day he and Tuddy had better luck and were taken on board a freight train for White River.

Finding the best route through northern Ontario's thousand miles of forests, lakes and rocks was a difficult task for them. The aerodromes were to be built as closely as possible along the route of the old National Transcontinental Railway line from Winnipeg to Cochrane, then on to North Bay, Ottawa and Montreal, as this way the rough terrain was less difficult to conquer. This route would also serve the mining districts in northern Ontario and Quebec. Locations for suitable sites for aerodromes in the Laurentian area at 35-mile intervals were not easy to find. The clearing, stumping and grading of sites provided work under the Unemployment Relief Scheme.

This site selection was something of a classic achievement. It involved careful examination of possible aerodrome sites from the air, getting to the sites on the ground, and then the hard slugging through the bush and muskeg, and over rocks under the vicious attention of black flies and mosquitos, making notes, planning engineering surveys and, finally, construction at the places which were chosen. A truly great amount of hard work was involved, and the aerodromes were brought into existence quickly. They served a purpose in the initial stage of cross-country flying, and some of them continue to serve even now, though in a smaller way, in these days of long-range aircraft with more reliable navigation aids.

After the survey of the route from Winnipeg-Toronto-Montreal was completed by Tuddy and Bob Dodds in the summer of 1932, the decision was made to select the route from Winnipeg-Sioux Lookout-Cochrane-North Bay to Toronto and Montreal.

In the fall of 1932 survey parties were sent in to the field to define the boundaries of eleven properties on this route for the purpose of establishing relief camps for unemployed men. These eleven sites were located at Vermilion Bay, Amesdale, Sioux Lookout, Wagaming, Camp Creek, Kowkash, Nakina, Pagwa, Nagogami, Gillies and Diver. Camps were organized and clearing commenced at Diver, Nakina and Wagaming.

During 1933 airway lighting equipment on the Windsor-Toronto and Prairie routes was laid up for economic reasons, but the intermediate aerodromes on which this equipment had been installed were maintained. Surveys for the acquisition of property selected for intermediate aerodromes on the Montreal-Moncton airway were completed, and relief camps were established at Bishopton, Megantic, Upper Brockway and Fredericton Junction.

When June 26, 1934, came along, Tuddy left Ottawa to take a quick look at the progress being made on the intermediate aerodromes on the Trans-Canada Airway in the North Bay and Madawaska Group. Tuddy joined Bob Dodds on June 30, and together they toured the sites at Tudhope (named after Tuddy), Porquis Junction, Ramore, Round Lake, Gillies, Diver, South River, Emsdale and Reay. Bob Dodds had been in the field since May 18, and stayed until October 17. Tuddy and Bob Dodds also looked at the sites at Madawaska and Lake of Two Rivers before Tuddy returned to Ottawa on July 10. They were both pleased with the excellent progress being made.

Tuddy made an aerial inspection of the intermediate landing fields in the North Bay Group from August 7 to August 15, 1934. Then, joining Bob Dodds again, they made an aerial reconnaissance of those sites on the eastern end of the

Nakina Group for the purpose of locating suitable sites for development at Calstock (Kabina) and Lowther. They found it somewhat difficult to make a decision at the latter place owing to the dense foliage on the new poplar growth and at Kabina there appeared to be several possibilities. A decision was left until later when a ground survey would be made.

Photographs were taken of all the fields in the North Bay Group, two projects in the Madawaska Group and the projects in the Nakina Group from Kapuskasing to Nakina.

In locating each air route, a preliminary aerial reconnaissance was made to locate the route, then it was decided just what fields would be chosen. The next step was to fly over the country at low altitude to get an idea of the ground conditions. Alternative routes were pinpointed on a map, and then a ground survey was commenced. Where highway or road facilities did not exist, a landing was made on the nearest lake and the party went to the site on foot, or by freight train, or gasoline speeder on the railway tracks, to make a ground survey. The land was measured up and a plan to scale was made on which was shown the dimensions, all growth and formations, that is, whether rock, muskeg, etc. If the site met the requirements after a ground survey had been made, the next step was to get information about the timber rights, pulp concessions, and so on; if it was provincial Crown land, from the Crown timber agent; and if it was a mining district to obtain mining information from the Mining Recorder and make application to the Department of Lands and Forests of the province for the transfer of the property to the Dominion Government. If it was privately owned property an option to purchase was obtained from the owner.

The whole of the area was thoroughly covered on foot and roughly measured. In some cases where the growth was very heavy a timber cruiser was used to get

more specific information of what was on the property. Where the timber was not so thick, in some cases, lanes were cut across the site every 200 feet to allow a thorough ground survey of the property.

Recommendations were then sent to the Department of National Defence headquarters and, if approved, the property was purchased or transferred and work on the project was started. Also, a legal survey was made of the land, and a camp erected on high ground, as near as possible to the source of water supply, communications, transportation, and so on.

Supplies were then brought in and a fire-guard was cut around the camp to prevent fires. Cutting was usually started wherever the most suitable firewood seemed to be until a supply had been cut. Then work was concentrated on the most suitable area of the site. On some sites where the bush growth was not heavy and easily cleared, the cutting, stumping and grading were all done in one operation, but where the growth was very heavy and the timber was saleable it was cut, piled and disposed of to the best advantage. Stumping had to be done by tractors or horses. On other sites where fires had gone through some years before, the areas were covered by deadfall with second growth poplar, such as at Nakina, for instance. Actually the heaviest deadfall, with little second growth, was at Wagaming. On several sites where there was muskeg, these areas had to be ditched and drained so that the muskeg could be removed. Then it was piled and burned, and the area usually filled with gravel. Draining was usually done in districts where the weather was wet, as in dry seasons muskeg could be burned without draining. Burning could only be done at certain times of the year with the approval of the Ontario Forestry Branch so this took up a lot of time.

Muskeg is a formation of dead vegetation, old roots, etc., accumulated over many years in low areas where water does not drain away. In some places this muskeg was eight or ten feet deep without any sign of clay or rock underneath.

There were a few areas in northern Ontario where sand and clay ridges had been formed by glacier action and these areas were very desirable had they been large enough for airport development, as the soil was much easier to work and drainage conditions were easier.

After a site had been cleared and stumped, the best portions of the field to develop could be seen more clearly. Sometimes it was necessary to resort to landing strip development and site the strips around rock outcrops, muskeg or small lakes. A detailed survey was made and levels taken and landing strips 3,000 feet long by 600 feet wide were staked out, and the primary development to 300 feet in width was carried out.

All-way aerodromes were the ultimate objective but, where it was necessary to have only landing strips, every effort was made to meet these dimensions. Runways were laid out and developed in the following order: runway No. 1 would be laid out so as to run into the prevailing wind; No. 2 into the secondary wind; and finally any additional runways required.

On some fields green timber was cut during the winter and the stumps removed and burned during the summer in readiness for grading. On several fields in British Columbia it was necessary to remove the large cedar, pine and fir stumps; on two fields, one in British

Columbia and one in Alberta, thickly strewn boulders varying in size up to three feet in diameter were removed leaving only a thin layer of soil for preparing the surface; and in a few instances several hundred tons of solid rock outcrops had to be removed. However, every effort was made to select sites which would be easy to develop and the variation in size and shape of the aerodromes was the result of avoiding difficult sections whenever this was possible.

During the first year practically all the work was done by hand with a few teams of horses when these were available and, of course, stumping powder was often used where the stumps were large, and dynamite for solid rock. Whole aerodromes were completed and made level as billiard tables in British Columbia using a few teams of horses and wheelbarrows for grading. In the final stages, on some of the larger fields, power machinery was used where the nature of the work was beyond being

done by hand. The use of this equipment was much more economical and saved the men from doing so much back-breaking work.

The landing strips were developed and graded so as not to exceed 1-1/2 per cent. On some sites where the runways or landing strips met or crossed, it was necessary to make deep cuts to make the grade constant throughout. After the landing strips were graded and levelled they were sown to grass.

Next came the provision of facilities for the aerodrome. At the main fields where aircraft had to land or refuel, there were to be hangars, caretaker's quarters, meteorological and refuelling facilities, and at some places radio broadcasting, beacon and communication stations. At the intermediate landing fields there were to be only caretaker's quarters and eventually lighting and communication facilities. The caretaker's duties were to assist any aircraft which was forced to land on the field and to service lights and the beacon on the field.

During the summer of 1932 when Tuddy and Bob Dodds were surveying sites for aerodromes for the Trans-Canada Airway between Winnipeg and Ottawa, Tuddy took time off from his work for an impromptu bath, hanging his clothes on the struts of "YV", their Fairchild FC2 "Razorback" seaplane moored on Encamp Lake.
Photo courtesy of Bob Dodds.

For lighting the fields, there was to be a revolving electric beacon having around two million candle power, and where no commercial power was available a small electric generating plant or, in some instances, gas or acetylene beacons, at intervals of five to ten miles, were to be installed. Obstruction lights were to mark all obstacles on areas surrounding the field or on the field. Ground approach lights marked the approaches to the runway and white boundary lights indicated the perimeter of the field or landing area. A pilot flying the route would not be more than 12 or 15 miles away from a beacon at any time.

Most beacons were visible on a clear night for over 50 miles. A beacon located on the field, displaying a green flash, along with the white flash, indicated that the field was suitable on which to land. Where the beacon was located off the field on higher ground, displaying a red flash, along with the white flash, it indicated that the area near the beacon was not suitable for landing. In this case there would be a directional light pointing to the landing area.

Radio beacon stations were equipped to transmit beams which were received in the aircraft by equipment which provided either a visual or aural signal so that a pilot could use the system. Also, radio broadcasting stations were used for collecting and disseminating weather reports, and from the time the pilot left the ground he received radio reports at fifteen-minute intervals.

In November, 1934, Tuddy took the train from Ottawa for Moncton and other places in the Maritimes to survey aerodrome sites on the ground. The sites had been chosen from the air earlier.

Since the sites in northern Ontario were first chosen in 1932 to form part of the chain of aerodromes on the Trans-Canada Airway system, many surveys had been made, both from the air and on the ground. Options on property were taken. Clearing of trees and brush from

the area had to be done. Brush had to be burned. Stumps had to be removed, and the area grubbed. The area for the aerodrome had to be ploughed in many cases, and then harrowed and smoothed. Rocks and boulders had to be removed from rock outcrops. Grading had to be carried out. Runway layouts had to be staked and marked, taking full advantage of the most suitable ground for the preliminary development. When this survey inspection trip was made of the aerodrome sites from Winnipeg to Ottawa and Montreal, the aerodromes were in various stages of development.

On May 4, 1935, Bob Dodds took the train from Ottawa to go to Winnipeg to start his survey work. This job was to take all summer, right up until September 4, 1935, when the last site was inspected. The first part of this survey was carried out by Bob Dodds, then he was joined by Tuddy at Porquis Junction on June 6 and together they continued the surveys of the sites.

Bob Dodds left Winnipeg for Kenora by train on May 9 with Brigadier J. Lindsay Gordon and Colonel F. Logie Armstrong. From Kenora they went by C.P.R. track car to Vermilion Bay to inspect the runway layout and returned to Kenora and Winnipeg the same way. All three drove to Whitemouth to check over the runway layouts. Rock outcrops had to be removed and a slough filled in. Grubbing had to be done at Vivian, and little grading was required. Brigadier Gordon arranged to have an engineer survey and stake out the runways. Another survey had to be done at Caddy Lake to clearly define the boundaries of the site. Bob Dodds returned to Caddy Lake by train two days later with Lieutenant A. B. Connelly, of the Royal Canadian Engineers, and Mr. McGibbon to stake out the runways. They next visited Lac du Bonnet by road to make an on-the-ground inspection. Bob Dodds also made an aerial survey of Lac du Bonnet in an R.C.A.F. Vedette flown by

Flight Lieutenant Dave Harding. Returning to Winnipeg, they met Squadron Leader A. T. Cowley, Superintendent of Air Regulations, Ottawa, and T. M. Shields, District Inspector of Air Regulations at Winnipeg.

Arriving at Sioux Lookout on May 25, Bob Dodds with Mr. Stewart and Mr. G. Hill, the foreman, looked over the site to see what progress had been made on it. Satisfied with the work being done, Bob Dodds left Sioux Lookout for Sunstrum two days later in a "caboose hop." With Foreman Alex Monroe, they checked another runway layout. Bob Dodds then took the afternoon freight train for Amesdale, arriving an hour and a half later. From there he returned to Sioux Lookout, which was his temporary headquarters. With J. McInnes, road-master, they went by gas car to Allanwater early the next morning. Bob Dodds met R. McDonald, the foreman, who went along with him doing his usual job of checking the runway layouts. Going to Armstrong, Bob Dodds checked the work there with F. L. Davis, the foreman. He was then met by a D.N.D. track car and left for Lamaune where he and Engineer Ole Nelson looked over the runway layout which was recently staked by Engineer O. L. Colborne. Continuing to Kowkash, he looked over the work under way with Ole Nelson and T. Dwyer, the foreman. Then he went to Nakina where he spent the day checking the plans with W. Harry and Ole Nelson. The No. 1 strip was moved to shorten the distance across the muskeg area, and still the approach would be over an unobstructed area. He went over the project with Ole Nelson and F. Peterson, the foreman, and visited the radio beacon station site. He met W. B. Swanton, Superintendent of the Nakina Group and discussed projects and future plans. With Ole Nelson, Bob Dodds left Nakina by track car for Pagwa to line up the runway for the new foreman, Ed Glenn. Next they went to the sites at Grant, Ogahalla,

Nagogami, Hearst and a site near Ameson Station, returning to Hearst and Kapuskasing late that night. Kapuskasing, now a thriving town in Northern Ontario, is the headquarters of the Spruce Falls Power and Paper Company Limited. One strip had been filled in and the other was ready for ploughing at Kapuskasing. The foundation for a hangar was laid. Major W. L. Laurie and H. D. Wethley, Royal Canadian Signals, and G. L. McGee from the North Bay Group, met Bob Dodds there. A couple of days later, Bob Dodds left for Tudhope and then he went on to Porquis where he met Tuddy, who had just flown in from Ottawa in Stearman CF-CCH on June 6, 1935, to join him on the survey.

Together, Tuddy and Bob Dodds drove to Ramore to look over the site there from the ground. Then they made an aerial reconnaissance of Ramore and the vicinity of Cochrane in Tuddy's aircraft. The following day they made an aerial reconnaissance of the route from Cochrane through to Nagogami.

They drove to South Porcupine to look at the hangar and seaplane port of the Algoma Air Transport Company. Following this, they made ground reconnaissances of sites around Cochrane. As it rained heavily they were unable to see the site at Lowther, so they returned to Kapuskasing and helped with a survey of the Kapuskasing site. They checked over the runway layout and grading operations with Mr. Jordan. A few days later, Tuddy and Bob Dodds left by car for Lowther where they completed the survey. Driving to Cochrane, Bob Dodds looked over the sites there. Leaving their base at Kapuskasing, Tuddy and Bob Dodds drove to Hearst, and travelled from there in a gas car to visit sites at Ameson and at White River. On June 21, 1935, they made an aerial reconnaissance in Stearman CF-CCH of sites from Lowther to Cochrane. The following day they

drove to Cochrane, then Ramore before returning to Iroquois Falls. There was much rain during these weeks which impeded their inspection of these sites.

The following week they made a ground reconnaissance of an area at Cochrane, and aerial reconnaissances of Earlton, Gillies, Diver, South River, North Bay, Emsdale and Reay. Then they went to Nakina where, with Ole Nelson, they checked the new runway proposal. Bob Dodds returned to Winnipeg on June 29 while Tuddy returned to Ottawa. After attending to some business in Winnipeg, Bob Dodds drove to Vivian, Kenora and Vermilion Bay, returning to Kenora, from where he was called back to Ottawa, arriving on July 11, 1935.

After a little more than a month in Ottawa, Tuddy and Bob Dodds were off again to take another look at the sites. They left Rockcliffe aerodrome by air in Stearman CF-CCH on August 19, with Tuddy at the controls. Their first stop was at Emsdale, then Kapuskasing, Tudhope and North Bay, where they picked up G. L. McGee and took him along. Returning to Kapuskasing they next drove to Hearst. G. Hill, assistant engineer, inspected Hearst with them. Nakina was next on their list, then Grant, Ogahalla and Pagwa. They returned to Nakina. Bob Dodds travelled to and from Kowkash by gas car and by C.N.R. to Armstrong, and by gas car to and from Allanwater.

On August 26, Bob Dodds waited all day at Allanwater for transportation to go to Sioux Lookout, and had to walk a considerable distance to the Town of Allanwater to make arrangements for a freight to pick him up. This was due to a railway wreck involving fourteen cars which blocked the C.N.R. main line. With W. Harry, he left by freight train for Amesdale. There, as at many other sites, he checked over the aerodrome and radio station sites and looked over a proposed road to the aerodrome and radio station sites. Bob Dodds returned to Winnipeg

to discuss the aerodromes in the Winnipeg group with Major Sherwood and Lieutenant Connelly. The Vivian and Whitemouth projects were inspected again. Then Bob Dodds drove to Kenora where a further inspection was carried out, and to Vermilion Bay and Caddy Lake to wind up this survey inspection before returning to Winnipeg. He then returned to Ottawa by train, arriving on September 7 after a long summer's work in the bush.

A number of sites were selected in 1935 for radio beacon and communication stations. Buildings were erected for radio beacon stations by unemployment relief personnel at Dane, Emsdale and Ottawa in Ontario; and St. Hubert, Quebec. Equipment was installed at Ottawa and St. Hubert. The St. Hubert station supplied communications for the Montreal-Albany Airway, both point-to-point and aircraft services. Lighting equipment on the Windsor-Toronto route had been in operation between Windsor and Hamilton throughout the year, this airway being used by air lines flying between Detroit and Buffalo.

The following year, 1936, survey inspections were made similar to those which were carried out in 1935. On May 14, Bob Dodds left for Winnipeg, and from there he went to Caddy Lake, the seaplane base at Lac du Bonnet, Kenora, Whitemouth and Kenora again, Vermilion Bay and Vivian. His next inspection took him to Sioux Lookout and Sunstrum, and by freight train to Amesdale, Savant Lake and Allanwater, returning to Sioux Lookout. There he visited a number of air services and continued to Armstrong, Lamaune, Kowkash and Nakina, Grant, Ogahalla, Pagwa, Hearst and Kapuskasing. Tuddy flew Engineer G. L. McGee and Engineer G. W. Smith from the North Bay office to Kapuskasing on June 4 to meet Bob Dodds and make a short inspection.

When the Department of Transport

was organized in November, 1936, and took over the Civil Aviation functions, Tuddy was seconded to the new department where he was employed as an Inspector of Airways until his retirement from the R.C.A.F. in 1938.

Tuddy, piloting a Fairchild aircraft, flew the Right Honourable C. D. Howe, newly appointed Minister of Transport; Senator N. Lambert and J. A. Wilson, Controller of Civil Aviation, on a brief inspection tour of the Ottawa-Winnipeg section of the Trans-Canada Airway on July 10 and 11th, 1936. Bob Dodds went along in Stearman aircaft CF-CCH to carry the baggage, refreshments and the bush and refuelling equipment. The party left Ottawa at 08:45 hours on July 10 and arrived at Kapuskasing at 18:45 hours, after inspecting the intermediate aerodromes along the route at Killaloe, Lake of Two Rivers, Emsdale, Diver, Gillies and Ramore. Leaving Kapuskasing at 07:45 hours by C.N.R. track car on July 11, they arrived at Armstrong at 21:00 hours, inspecting Hearst, Pagwa, Ogahalla, Grant, Nakina, Kowkash, Lamaune and Wagaming. Then Mr. Howe, Senator Lambert and J. A. Wilson left by No. 1 C.N.R. train from Armstrong for Winnipeg.

Several experimental flights were made over the Rocky Mountain section of the proposed trans-Canada air mail route by Air Commodore H. Hollick-Kenyon flying a Lockheed Electra, during the latter months of 1936. He was accompanied by Tuddy. Hollick-Kenyon of Canadian Airways piloted the Electra for Tuddy when he carried out the radio range work until the Department of Transport purchased its own Lockheed 12 aircraft. Later in the year, Inspector W. S. "Bill" Lawson of Regina assisted him in locating these radio range stations.

Tuddy went west in 1937 and was in charge of the calibration of radio ranges through the mountains in preparation for the trans-Canada air services with which

he had been identified so long. He was working between Winnipeg and Vancouver.

On July 8, 1937, shortly after Philip Johnson became Vice-President of Trans-Canada Air Lines, he made a survey by air and on the ground of the entire proposed transcontinental route between Vancouver and Montreal, as well as inspecting all the airway facilities that were available. He was accompanied by his advisory associates, D. B. Colyer and D. R. MacLaren; Dan McLean, Superintendent of Airways, Department of Transport; and Inspector Tudhope of the Department of Transport who piloted the aircraft. Stops on the 2,550-mile tour were made at Princeton, Oliver, Grand Forks and Cranbrook in British Columbia; Edmonton, Calgary, Lethbridge and Coleman in Alberta; Regina, Saskatchewan; Winnipeg, Manitoba; Wagaming, Gillies, Emsdale, Toronto and Ottawa in Ontario; and Montreal, Quebec. Throughout this trip they were accorded the whole-hearted co-operation of the provincial, civic and other officials, and from citizens in general. This trip was made in the Department of Transport's Lockheed aircraft, CF-CCT. Later in the year, Philip Johnson made a survey of the proposed route east of Montreal.[1]

On July 30, 1937, after Philip Johnson completed his inspection tour, the Minister of Transport, Mr. C. D. Howe, made a dawn-to-dusk flight over the route from Montreal to Vancouver, a distance of some 2,550 miles, in 17 hours and 10 minutes' elapsed time, with 14 hours and 10 minutes' actual flying time. The purpose of this trip was to demonstrate that the airway was an entirely practicable proposition — and by no means was it intended to indicate that the route was ready for commercial operations. Aboard the Department of Transport's Lockheed Electra CF-CCT on its transcontinental flight were: Mr.

C. D. Howe, H. J. Symington, Commander C. P. Edwards, Inspector and pilot J. H. Tudhope, co-pilot Jack Hunter and air engineer Lew Parmenter. Stops were made en route for refuelling and weather reports at Gillies, Ontario; Winnipeg, Manitoba; Regina, Saskatchewan; and Lethbridge, Alberta. The flight over the Rocky Mountains presented a magnificent view of nature's grandeur.[2]

Tuddy relinquished his position as Inspector of Airways with the Department of Transport to become Vice-President of the First Canadian Aviation Insurance Group in February, 1938, to assume direction of the business of Canadian Aviation Insurance Managers Limited as its Vice-President. His headquarters was in Montreal. This company served as underwriting managers for the newly formed Canadian Aviation Insurance Group to provide insurance facilities for aviation insurance in the Dominion.

Tuddy became General Manager, Operations, of Trans-Canada Air Lines at Winnipeg in 1943, and helped in the further planning of the transcontinental air route started in 1928, over which Trans-Canada Air Lines commenced operating in 1937.

From the summer of 1948 until the time of his death on October 11, 1956, at the age of 65 years, Tuddy was civil air attaché, and in later years also telecommunications' attaché, at Canada House, London, England. Since 1955 he acted as Canadian representative on the Commonwealth Telecommunications Board. He had been ill about a month.

Tuddy's wife, the former Elsie Marriott of Montreal, continued to live in London until 1959 when she returned to Montreal. Today, she lives in Ottawa.

Major J. H. Tudhope was the donor of the "W. F. Tudhope Memorial Trophy", which he presented to the Royal Canadian Flying Clubs Association in

Bob Dodds (right) and George Banks of the Ontario Forestry Branch with their gas speeder on a siding near Wapiti, Ontario, during an inspection and survey trip of the aerodrome sites for the Trans-Canada Airway in the summer of 1934. The Ontario Forestry Branch provided the transportation here, but often Bob Dodds had to go by foot through the bush with its vicious mosquitoes and black flies.
Photo courtesy of Bob Dodds.

1950, in memory of his son, Pilot Officer William F. Tudhope, D.F.C., who was killed in the Battle of Britain. The trophy was to be awarded annually to a private pilot member of a flying club who was judged to be the best as the result of a national competition.

Tuddy was named a member of Canada's Aviation Hall of Fame in 1973. Also, he was made a Companion of the Order of Flight (City of Edmonton).

So it is "in recognition of his outstanding work in carrying out airway surveys preliminary to the inauguration of an air mail service in Canada" that Tuddy's name shall be remembered through the years. He was known as the most affable of men, and had a wide range of acquaintances across Canada. And in time of war he served his country with valour.

NOTES

[1] *Canadian Aviation*, August 1937.
[2] *Ibid.*

1931

George Phillips in 1949.

George H. R. Phillips

Citation: in recognition of his work for the Provincial Forestry Branch

George H. R. Phillips, while Superintendent of Eastern Flying Operations for the Ontario Provincial Air Service of the Department of Lands and Forests at Sault Ste. Marie, Ontario, was awarded the Trans-Canada Trophy for meritorious service in the advancement of aviation in Canada during 1931, "in recognition of his work for the Provincial Forestry Branch." The award was announced by the Minister of National Defence, Colonel, the Honourable Donald M. Sutherland, D.S.O., on February 23, 1932.

He carried out many hazardous flights during 1931 in the performance of his duties on forestry and fire patrols; he conducted flights for the provincial police services; and took an active part in the training of pilots for the Ontario Provincial Air Service.

George Hector Reid Phillips was born on August 17, 1893, at Laurel (near Orangeville), Ontario, where he attended school and then farmed until 1913. The following year he went to Iroquois Falls, Ontario, where he worked in an engineer's office as an assistant. Then he enlisted as a private in the 2nd Pioneer Battalion of the Canadian Expeditionary

---

The Committee of Award for the year 1931 consisted of the following members:
J.A. Wilson, Controller of Civil Aviation, Ottawa
Squadron Leader H. Edwards, Royal Canadian Air Force, Ottawa
Squadron Leader A. T. N. Cowley, Royal Canadian Air Force, Ottawa
Squadron Leader G. R. Howsam, Royal Canadian Air Force, Ottawa
J. A. D. McCurdy, Curtiss-Reid Aircraft Co., Montreal, Quebec.

Force on October 8, 1915, and served continuously until 1918. He was commissioned as a Lieutenant at Mont St. Eloi, France, on March 19, 1917. This same year he was mentioned in Despatches. He was attached to the R.A.F. on October 24, 1918, where he took an observer's course. He was then posted to the Independent Air Force, France, a few days before armistice was signed in 1918.

Back from World War I, he returned to farming in 1920 and farmed for four years near Laurel, Ontario. He joined the newly formed Canadian Air Force and attended a short course at Camp Borden in February, 1921. Then he entered the Forest Service of the Province of Ontario shortly before the Ontario Provincial Air Service was formed in the spring of 1924, and was employed as an observer.

At this time the principal outlet for flying in Canada was in forest conservation work. The provinces controlled their own natural resources and were vitally interested in forest conservation.

In 1922 the Ontario Forestry Branch, in co-operation with the Canadian Air Board, made aerial surveys of the Algonquin Park area for the purpose of looking into the possibilities of aircraft being used on a large scale in forest fire detection and suppression. The Canadian Air Force transferred personnel and aircraft to the Algonquin Park area for operations and placed them at the disposal of the Provincial Forest Service. Flight Lieutenant C. McEwen was in charge of these operations for the Air Board. Operations were carried out from May to October from a base at Whitney in H.S. 2L flying boats in close co-operation with Mr. W. A. Delahaye, district forester for the Ontario Provincial Government. Up to this time, the

Forestry Service had used a tower system to locate forest fires and George Phillips was to be one of these pioneer observers, prior to becoming a pilot with the service in 1928.

The following item appears in the *Annual Report* of the Honourable James Lyons, Minister of Lands and Forests for the Province of Ontario, for the year ending October 31, 1922: "Aircraft for forest fire detection were used this season for the first time. The operation was carried on in co-operation with the Dominion Air Board, and proved highly satisfactory. Aircraft patrols were carried out from bases established at Whitney in Algonquin Park, and at Parry Sound. A total of 613 hours was flown."

After the formation of the Department of National Defence in January, 1923, the Dominion authorities withdrew their Air Force personnel from the provincial field in eastern Canada, feeling that the need for flying for the Provincial Governments of Ontario and Quebec on a repayment or partial repayment basis in the first experimental stage during the years 1920, 1921 and 1922 had passed. They now wanted to concentrate on their own work, and leave the field open for the few commercial aviation companies struggling to make ends meet. The provincial authorities agreed, and flying was continued in Ontario with the Provincial Forest Service letting commercial contracts for whatever flying was required.

Then, in 1923, flying was done under contract with the Laurentide Air Service Limited, one of the first of Canada's commercial pioneer companies, who carried out a programme of forest protection patrols, forest inventory work and transportation under the direction of the Ontario Provincial Forest Service. Ontario's worst forest fires, up to that time, took place in 1923, with some two million acres of timber having been destroyed.

At the end of the 1923 season of operations, after four years of experimental aerial work, both in forest fire detection and forest mapping, the Honourable James Lyons decided that the Ontario Government should own and operate an air service of its own, as part of the Forestry Branch of the Province of Ontario, Department of Lands and Forests. So the minister asked Captain W. Roy Maxwell, who was then flying for Laurentide Air Service, and also the manager of the company, if he would organize an air service for the Forestry Branch. Roy Maxwell had received his Commercial Pilot's Certificate No. 34, dated May 31, 1920, and was one of the earlier pioneer pilots. So, in December, 1923, he left Laurentide Air Service to form an Ontario Provincial Air Service, which he was later to direct at the invitation of Mr. Lyons.

The Ontario Provincial Air Service was formed in the spring of 1924, and George Phillips was there to observe its birth.

In 1924, Captain Maxwell had before him a number of problems. Three of the biggest were to provide pilots, air engineers and suitable aircraft for this work of forest fire detection and suppression patrols, forest survey, inventory work and transportation to remote districts.

One of Roy Maxwell's first steps was to acquire thirteen H.S. 2L flying boats from the United States, which had been in use in the Naval Service during 1917 and 1918 as U-boat spotters over the North Sea, and still had their gun mountings in them. The flying boats were reconditioned by Laurentide Air Service. The Canadian Air Board was also using a number of these flying boats for their experimental flying, fishery patrols, aerial dusting, transportation, etc., and so were Laurentide Air Service (formed in 1922), Bishop Barker Aeroplanes and Captain H. S. Quigley of Dominion Aerial Explorations Limited (formed in 1923) using them. Besides, no commercial aircraft were available in Canada anyhow. The

H.S. 2L flying boats pioneered any commercial flying in Canada until the Vickers flying boats made their debut. These H.S. 2L flying boats were the early aircraft used in forest conservation work. They had a 78-foot wing spread, with low compression Liberty engines, which had to be changed to high compression by the Ontario Provincial Air Service before putting them into service. Other modifications had to be made, too. Later in the year, another H.S. 2L flying boat and a Loening amphibian were added to the fleet. So from June till the end of October, 1924, the aircraft were flown under the direction of the Ontario Provincial Air Service during the forest fire season.

The facilities of the Ontario Provincial Air Service throughout the whole northern part of the province, as far as 150 miles north of the railway, greatly assisted any air travelling in their areas and on many occasions the R.C.A.F. and others travelling through Ontario made use of the facilities they provided through the courtesy of the Department of Lands and Forests.

Captain James Dalzell McKee, the donor of the Trans-Canada Trophy, and Squadron Leader (now Air Vice-Marshal) A. E. Godfrey, R.C.A.F., made use of the facilities on the first trans-Canada seaplane flight which they made in September, 1926, when they landed at Ramsay Lake and other Ontario Provincial Air Service's bases.

As pilots and others became more familiar with the operations of the Ontario Provincial Air Service, more use was made of their facilities from year to year. In addition to their main purpose of fire detection and suppression patrols, when the fire hazard permitted, transportation was supplied to many who were working in districts away from the railway. Forestry and geological survey parties in the field were kept supplied with provisions and mail by aircraft operating in the district. Inspection work

was also carried out by air with ease and speed throughout the length and breadth of the northern part of the province by the senior officials of the provincial government, who could visit districts which were practically inaccessible before the establishment of the air service owing to the time required to reach them.

When George Phillips was still an observer with the Ontario Provincial Air Service he was receiving elementary instruction in flying, and in the fall of 1927 he was sent to Camp Borden by the Ontario Provincial Air Service where he took advanced instruction in flying from the Royal Canadian Air Force. He received his Commercial Air Pilot's Certificate No. 342, on May 16, 1928, after less than ten hours' solo flying. The Ontario Provincial Air Service then engaged him as a pilot in forestry work. He was to become well known as a pioneer bush pilot.

Meanwhile, Roy Maxwell, Director of the Ontario Provincial Air Service, went to England in 1927 on behalf of the O.P.A.S. to look over the Moth aircraft being manufactured by The de Havilland Aircraft of England. Watching them fly, take off and land, he was greatly impressed with them. When he returned to Canada towards the end of 1927 he went to see the Minister of Lands and Forests in the Ontario Government, explaining to him that the Moth aircraft were what they needed for their fire detection work in Ontario. The Minister of Lands and Forests listened intently about the Moth, and agreed that they would be useful in their forest fire detection work. Thus, an order was placed for the purchase of four Moths, with 80 h.p. Cirrus Mark II engines. They were delivered to the O.P.A.S. that same year. This is how the Moth aircraft were introduced to Canada. The Moth aircraft were the first light aircraft to be equipped with floats. These Moth seaplanes gradually took the place of the H.S. 2L flying boats used by the O.P.A.S., which

were not the most suitable aircraft for fire detection patrol work in any case. With the addition of these Moth aircraft to the fleet for fire detection work, more H.S.2L's were then available for suppression and transportation work.

The Moth aircraft was satisfactory for fire detection work, as well as fire suppression work. With their use the operating costs were greatly reduced as the maintenance and capital costs of the Moth were low. The Moths were also able to get into small lakes to carry pumps, fire hose and other equipment where the larger flying boats could not manoueuver. These aircraft were also being used for light transportation work in Ontario, Manitoba, Saskatchewan, Alberta and British Columbia, in addition to private use and fire detection patrols.

And George Phillips flew one of these Moth aircraft equipped as a seaplane in his forestry operations for the O.P.A.S., since he found it useful in getting into smaller lakes and areas.

Then, in 1928, the O.P.A.S. purchased a D.H. 61 seaplane, G-CAPG, powered with a Bristol Jupiter engine having 500 h.p. This transport-type aircraft could carry eight fire-fighters along with their pumps and equipment.

The O.P.A.S. purchased additional Moths in 1928, and disposed of some H.S. 2L flying boats, until their fleet of 22 aircraft consisted of the following: eleven H.S. 2L flying boats, G-CAOF, G-CAOG, G-CAOI, G-CAOJ, G-CAOK, G-CAOA, G-CAON, G-CAOP, G-CAOQ, G-CAOR and G-CAPE; four D.H. 60X Moths, G-CAOU, G-CAOV, G-CAOW and G-CAOX; six D.H. 60X Moth seaplanes, G-CAOY, G-CAOZ, G-CAPA, G-CAPB, G-CAPC and G-CAPH; and one D.H. 61 seaplane, G-CAPG. They were employing 20 pilots and 20 air engineers that season.

In 1929 almost every phase of flying operations increased. The severity of the fire hazard which existed throughout the season threw a heavy burden on the

entire O.P.A.S., including George Phillips. Light aircraft purchased primarily for detection flights were constantly called on for suppression flights and again showed their adaptability. During the season light aircraft flew 6,089 hours; while the heavier flying boats flew 5,123 hours. The hours flown by H.S. 2L flying boats stationed at Sioux Lookout and Goose Island merited special notation: G-CAOQ, 662 hours; G-CAON, 642 hours; G-CAOK, 626 hours; and G-CAOP, 532 hours. That was during the months of May, June, July, August and September.

A Vickers Vedette amphibian powered with a Wright J. 6 engine was added to the service for use as a photographic and sketching aircraft. Because of the calls made upon this aircraft for suppression work, its time for photographic and sketching work was limited.

The D.H. 61 seaplane was successful with dusting operations, for which this aircraft was well suited because of its excellent payload. A Pratt and Whitney 525 h.p. air-cooled engine was installed in the D.H. 61. Then the 80 h.p. Cirrus engines in the Moth aircraft were replaced by the new 100 h.p. Gypsy engines.

With these new types of aircraft, the pioneering flying boat was fighting a losing battle with the more economical and lighter aircraft for fire detection and even transport work.

The O.P.A.S. operated a school of flying instruction during February and March, 1929, the year after George Phillips received his Commercial Air Pilot's Certificate. Eight pupils were given instruction. Six of the eight pupils received their commercial pilots' licences after further training on floats and boat-type aircraft in the spring. At the time, other than their own pilots, the O.P.A.S. was unable to obtain more experienced commercial pilots or air engineers, so the officials decided to establish a school to instruct their own pilots, at the same time teaching them the kind of flying required for forestry work. Some of the air engineers and personnel from the Forestry Branch took advantage of this course and received their commercial pilots' licences. Also, pilots from other companies came to the O.P.A.S. to receive flying instruction and refresher courses as the days went by. George Phillips was one of those instructors who took an active part in the training of pilots for the O.P.A.S. He excelled in getting into difficult areas and inaccessible spots.

The O.P.A.S. added four new metal Hamilton seaplanes to its fleet in 1930. They were powered with Pratt and Whitney Hornet 575 h.p. engines, having a speed of 120 m.p.h. with a 1,500-pound payload.

George Phillips became Superintendent of Eastern Flying Operations for the Ontario Provincial Air Service in 1931, with his headquarters at Sault Ste. Marie.

The fire hazard in that section of Ontario under his control was unusually high that season and the work was strenuous and continuous. In June, 1931, he flew 126 hours and 15 minutes; in July, flying each day of the month, he flew 203 hours; while in August he flew 161 hours. During 1929, the year after George Phillips received his licence, he flew 560 hours; during 1930, 555 hours; and during 1931, mainly between May and October, 771 hours on mercy flights and fighting fires. This was indeed a remarkable record.

To be successful in fighting forest fires, speed, and the ability to fly fire-fighters and their equipment safely into and out of small lakes, meant the difference between a little fire and a big fire that would spread for miles destroying valuable timber before it could be checked by man or put out by nature. George Phillips knew the art of getting into these places quickly.

While most of his work was in forestry operations during the summer months,

he continued to operate throughout the winter months flying aircraft on skis when required by the Forestry Branch, the Department of Health and the Department of Provincial Police.

George Phillips was also responsible for a considerable amount of the flying instruction given by the Ontario Provincial Air Service to its pilots, having himself taught some of those pilots then in their employ.

The record of efficiency and safety held by the Ontario Provincial Air Service might be credited largely to the devotion to duty of its personnel. Of these, George Phillips was an outstanding exemplar.

A report from W. Roy Maxwell, Director of the Ontario Provincial Air Service, gives a typical account of the work performed by George Phillips in 1931:

"On the evening of August 1st, we received an alarming telephone call from a summer resort at MacGregor Cove on Lake Superior shore, approximately 100 miles north of Sault Ste. Marie. One of the campers became very ill and a friend of his walked from MacGregor Cove, a distance of some 20 miles to the Algoma Central Railroad, to communicate with Sault Ste. Marie. By the time we had information regarding the serious illness it was quite dark.

"Mr. Phillips volunteered to take the doctor in that night. We immediately got in touch with a doctor and, when he learned that Mr. Phillips was going to be the pilot, he, too, volunteered to go in.

"Mr. Phillips flew the doctor in after dark, along the rocky shoreline of Lake Superior, landing him there long before the chap who had gone out to communicate with Sault Ste. Marie had returned to camp. The doctor attended to the sick man, who was later returned to a hospital in Sault Ste. Marie in one of our transport aircraft.

"Mr. Phillips returned to his base the

same night, had his machine serviced and was away again the following morning, August 2nd, on Air Service duty shortly after daybreak."

George Phillips made many rescue flights while with the Ontario Provincial Air Service and took many grateful persons to the hospital for medical attention. This is just one illustration of his mercy flights.

The Ontario Provincial Air Service's fleet had increased to 27 aircraft by 1931, consisting of one D.H. 61, three Hamilton, one Fairchild 71, one Fairchild KR-34, one Vedette, fourteen Moths and six H.S. 2L flying boats. They were employing 33 pilots and 39 air engineers to fly and take care of the aircraft. The Fairchild 71, with a Wasp "B" engine, and the Fairchild KR-34, with a 165 h.p. Wright engine, were purchased in 1931. The Fairchild KR-34 was for the use of the Superintendent of Algonquin Park.

Then one day in February, 1932, the Minister of National Defence announced that George Phillips had been awarded the Trans-Canada Trophy for 1931 in recognition of his work for the Provincial Forestry Branch.

The Trans-Canada Trophy was officially presented to George Phillips by Colonel Donald M. Sutherland, Minister of National Defence, in Ottawa, on April 4, 1932.

In presenting the trophy to George Phillips, Colonel Sutherland took the opportunity of expressing his personal gratification that the excellent record of the Ontario Provincial Air Service had been fittingly recognized in awarding the trophy to one of its officers. "Since its formation in the spring of 1924, it had been a model of efficiency and its operations resulted in an immense saving to the people of the province in the preservation of its forest wealth and played an important part in opening up the more remote areas of the province," he said. He extended his most hearty congratulations to George Phillips per-

G-CAPG, a D.H. 61 seaplane, bought by the O.P.A.S. in 1928. Note the Edo pontoons, with which the Moth was equipped in 1933. For a time its base was at Oba.

sonally, and to the directors and staff of the Ontario Provincial Air Service for their long record of good work.

The Provincial Air Service purchased two more Fairchild 71 aircraft and another D.H. 61 Moth in 1932, which further reduced the number of H.S. 2L flying boats in use. The rest of the H.S.2L flying boats were retired from service when the Department of National Defence issued regulations at the end of 1932 making them all obsolete. The following year, the O.P.A.S. equipped two of their Moth aircraft with Gypsy Mark II engines — and new-type Edo floats.

Feelers were still going out for more suitable aircraft for O.P.A.S. requirements; one that would carry a net payload of 800 pounds, or the weight of a fire-fighting crew fully equipped. In an attempt to meet the needs of the pilots and the foresters, the O.P.A.S. acquired all engineering data and the right to manufacture Buhl aircraft from the Buhl brothers in the United States who had gone out of business. Many modifications were required to meet Canadian standards. Four Buhl aircraft were built at Sault Ste. Marie. They were powered by Pratt and Whitney Wasp (440 h.p.) engines. Two of these aircraft were put in

operation in 1936, and the other two in 1937.

George Phillips was appointed district forester in 1936, with his headquarters at Sault Ste. Marie, Ontario. He was then one of Canada's best-known pioneer bush pilots.

In spite of the fleet which the service had in 1936, they still had to hire more aircraft to help with the work, as the forest fires were so bad that summer. Over some 1,264,430 acres were burned in 1936. Many of the fires were caused by lightning. The peak period for fires that summer was in July. Except for 1923, the year 1936 was Ontario's worst in years for forest fires up to that time.

The O.P.A.S. went into the Stinson aircraft field in 1937 by buying two SR-9 seaplanes built to their requirements. The aircraft were powered with Pratt and Whitney 440 h.p. Wasp engines. In 1938 they bought four more of them. These aircraft could be used both for detection and suppression work.

One of George Phillips' more outstanding flights was made in 1937 when he left Sault Ste. Marie on April 16 in a D.H. 61 Moth, a single-engine aircraft on

floats, to fly to the Moose River Mine in Nova Scotia, carrying a small microphone to lower to the men trapped in the mine. Another aircraft, a Vickers Vedette, flown by A. C. "Joe" Heaven of the O.P.A.S., left Sault Ste. Marie on April 25 carrying a special type of wool to be given to the men trapped in the mine to stuff in their clothing to help keep them warm. Meanwhile, the rescuers were working hard both day and night to reach the trapped men. Of the three men in the mine, two were brought out alive a few days later.

In George Ponsford's[*] report on this episode, he said:

"April 16th to 25th is the break-up period but by reason of the current in the St. Mary's River and the service being located here at Sault Ste. Marie, we have open water much earlier than in any other part of northern Ontario. By this time of the year we usually have many of our ships re-assembled and ready for testing as soon as ice conditions in the river permit. When this emergency call reached us we immediately put the D.H. 61 Moth in the water, completed its test flying and

[*] Roy Maxwell remained Director of the Ontario Provincial Air Service until he resigned in 1934, when George Ponsord was appointed to the position.

George Phillips standing in front of G-CAPC, a D.H. 60X Moth seaplane, owned by the O.P.A.S. in 1931 and flown by him in the course of his duties.
Photo courtesy of George Phillips.

it was off for Toronto the same day. Phillips, I believe, had to dodge floating ice in order to carry out his test flight and subsequent take-off.

"When a few days later, the second call came for another ship, we were not so fortunate. We had nothing actually ready, but we put a crew at work day and night until the Vedette was finally ready. Heaven also had to dodge ice in getting under way."

When war broke out in 1939, many of the pilots and others left to join the R.C.A.F. and other services, some of whom never returned. George Phillips was one of those who resigned his position late in 1939 to join the R.C.A.F., and in February, 1940, he took a refresher course in flying at Trenton, upon the completion of which he became a flying instructor at Camp Borden where he instructed for two and one-half years; then became restless. In 1942 he was loaned to the R.A.F. Transport Command to ferry 'planes across the Atlantic. On his very first flight with the R.A.F.T.C. he ferried a Hudson bomber to North Africa, along with navigator William G. Campbell of Port Elgin, Ontario, and a wireless operator. Leaving West Palm Beach in October, 1942, his route took him to Trinidad, Georgetown, Belem, Natal, Ascension Island to Accra on the Gold Coast of Africa.

His trip went well until he had almost reached his destination when his radio went dead, and it was getting dark. To land at Accra after dark meant that they would have to give a half-hour's notice by radio — or risk being shot down. With his radio inoperative, George Phillips decided against landing at Accra and flew along the coast until he came to an unlighted landing strip in French West Africa at Cotonou. Seeing a strip he went in to land in the dusk — to find at the last minute that the strip had steel rails placed across it. The landing caused the tires to fly off and the bomber, fortunately not carrying bombs, came to a

standstill on its belly on land under the control of "Vichy" France. And that was how George Phillips and his crew came to be interned by the "Vichy" French forces for ten full weeks during World War II — until the Allied forces took Casablanca in December, 1942.

When Phillips returned to Canada again, he became a flying instructor at Camp Borden, and was later posted to Natal, Brazil. After a second ferry trip to Africa he was appointed Commanding Officer of the unit at Natal where he remained until May, 1944. Again he was returned to Camp Borden, became a Squadron Leader, then for a time took command of the R.C.A.F. base at Edenvale, Ontario. He retired from the Service with the rank of Squadron Leader.

Early in 1945 he returned to the Department of Lands and Forests, and became Superintendent of Algonquin Park in Ontario.

During the early part of his sojourn with the Services, the O.P.A.S. had not purchased any new aircraft. In any case, the aircraft manufacturing plants were busy building machines for war purposes. The O.P.A.S. bought two used Stinson aircraft in 1940 and two more in 1941, and still another one in 1944. They also picked up a Waco in 1943, which had a 330 h.p. Jacobs engine.

In 1945 the O.P.A.S. bought four new Noorduyn Norseman aircraft, each powered with a 550 h.p. Pratt and Whitney Wasp engine. One of these was CF-OBG, the first Mark V Norseman, purchased in June, 1945. CF-OBI, Mark V, was purchased in July, 1945; while

CF-OBJ, Mark V, was purchased in August, 1945. With the purchase of these Norseman, the O.P.A.S. disposed of their two Hamilton aircraft.

The Norseman, an all-Canadian designed 'plane, was outstanding amongst Canadian-produced aircraft. R. B. "Bob" Noorduyn started to build the Norseman in 1934. The Norseman was a heavier aircraft for transport work. It was used in bush work and flew during the war on many missions. The Norseman was manufactured by Noorduyn Aircraft Company at Cartierville for ten years, from 1935 to 1945. In April, 1946, the rights were sold to the Canadian Car and Foundry Company of Montreal.

On March 26th, 1948, the O.P.A.S. bought their first Beaver aircraft. This aircraft was the first one produced by The de Havilland Aircraft of Canada. By the end of 1948 the Ontario Department of Lands and Forests had a fleet of seventeen Beavers. George Phillips flew one of these Beavers while Superintendent of Algonquin Park. In 1955 the O.P.A.S. bought their first Otter aircraft. These aircraft were used for fire detection, fire suppression and patrol work, as well as transportation and other purposes.

Early in 1957 the first of a test series took place on a new method of water dropping. The test was made in an Otter seaplane, with water tanks on the top of each float. The testing was over a concrete runway against the wind, with the wind, and cross wind at different wind speeds. Five drops were made in each case. With each water drop, some 160 gallons of water were released. The

CF-OAQ, a Buhl CA-6 floatplane built by the Ontario Provincial Air Service at Sault Ste Marie, was flown to the Ottawa Air Station in October, 1935, for a test flight for its Certificate of Airworthiness. The Buhl had a Vickers' type float with Edo rudders, a Pratt and Whitney Wasp Jr. engine and a Hamilton Standard propeller.

Photo courtesy of the R.C.A.F.

officials of the Forestry Division were delighted with this experiment, so much so that they decided to equip their thirty-nine Beavers and six Otters with these float tanks for the 1958 season. The success achieved in 1958 from this method of water dropping helped to quench many fires in the early stages, thus saving from destruction much of Ontario's woodlands that might otherwise have been destroyed or ravaged.

Originally, the O.P.A.S. was established for the specific purpose of detecting forest fires and suppressing them for forest conservation purposes. Today, they sketch the area concerned and provide transportation by flying fire fighting crews and their equipment where they are needed. They also make many special transportation flights, game detection flights, photography, sketching of infected forested areas and dusting, mercy flights, flights for other government departments, flying instruction for their own personnel, and many other activities which help make up the day's work.

As Superintendent of Algonquin Park, George Phillips made the rounds of the park at the controls of his Beaver aircraft. With the short take-off characteristics of the Beaver seaplane, he could land in small areas in the park, do his work, and then fly off to the next job. He had been flying a Beaver since September, 1948. He enjoyed his work at Algonquin Park, especially because it allowed him to keep his hand in the flying business while covering the great open areas of the park; and this was as important to him as his forest conservation work. The loss of his pilot's licence in 1957 for medical reasons was keenly felt by him because his heart was in his flying and he loved every minute of it. After being Superintendent of Algonquin Park for fourteen years, George Phillips retired to his farm at Orangeville in the fall of 1959 with 14,000 flying hours to his credit.

Maurice Giles reported in the *Imperial Oil Review* of October, 1957:

"Good pilot that he is, Phillips has had his share of airborne mishaps. His first was at the Sault when he tried too close a spot-landing on a frozen lake in a ski-equipped Gypsy Moth. At low speed on a turn one wing dipped and when he put the nose down to straighten it out, he hit the lake. "I almost got screwed into the ice," he recalls. Ten stitches closed a gash over one eye, but otherwise he was undamaged. Caught in a snowstorm on another occasion he decided to land his plane on a lake which proved to be only 450 yards long. The skis sank into soft snow, one broke and the plane flipped up on its back. Phillips' safety strap broke and he was catapulted out into the snow, the plane coming to rest gently on his chest. He was unhurt but the plane had to be dismantled and shipped out by freight. "A few years ago he was taking off with a canoe lashed atop one of his floats, destined for a gang of firefighters in the bush. The front end of the canoe broke loose when he was about one thousand feet above the water, the canoe whirled sideways like a sail and two feet were sheared off by the whirling propeller. But he kept in the air long enough to circle the lake and come down for a safe landing. Phillips modestly says he was saved only by the extra straps on the canoe which his air engineer, Red McCrea, forced him to put on. On another take-off the cockpit seat broke and he rolled onto his back on the cabin floor, but managed to scramble back to the controls just as the plane was roaring off the water."

Mr. and Mrs. George Phillips had three children; two sons, Jack and Allan, and one daughter, Margaret, who is married to Robert H. "Bob" Fowler, Chief Engineering Test Pilot for The de Havilland Aircraft of Canada, Limited, Downsview, Ontario, who is also a winner of the Trans-Canada Trophy. Allan is with Air Canada in Montreal; while Jack, a former R.C.A.F. jet pilot, amongst other things, retired as a Lieutenant-Colonel and lives in Ottawa.

He was named a member of Canada's Aviation Hall of Fame in 1973. He was made a Companion of the Order of Flight (City of Edmonton).

George Phillips lived in Orangeville, Ontario, until the time of his death on July 20, 1977, at 84 years of age.

He was a most popular member of the Ontario Provincial Air Service, and he had a legendary career as a pioneer bush pilot with the O.P.A.S. in forestry work and rescue missions. All his life he had a keep-fit programme to which he adhered. He enjoyed the outdoor life.

The Ontario Provincial Air Service of the Department of Lands and Forests for Ontario has grown through the years until today it owns and operates the largest forest fire-fighting organization in Canada. And, with it, George Phillips made many contributions, both known and unknown, to help this great organization; in so doing, conserving our forests, our animal life, our natural wealth — and perhaps, in part, our way of life.

1932

Moss Burbidge, 1932.
Photo courtesy of Moss Burbidge.

Maurice "Moss" Burbidge

Citation: in recognition of his work as Club Instructor

Captain Maurice "Moss" Burbidge, while Instructor of the Edmonton and Northern Alberta Aero Club, Edmonton, Alberta, was awarded the Trans-Canada Trophy for meritorious service in the advancement of aviation in Canada during 1932, "in recognition of his work as Club Instructor." The announcement of the award by Colonel, the Honourable Donald M. Sutherland, D.S.O., Minister of National Defence, was conveyed to Captain Burbidge on March 21, 1933.

In his announcement, Colonel Sutherland said that the Club had been outstanding in its work and organization each year of its existence. The Club had had no accidents of any kind. The number of pilots trained and hours flown since 1929 are shown on the following page.

The Edmonton and Northern Alberta Aero Club had been a model in every respect, continued the announcement. It had the strong support of the municipal authorities and the community in which it operated, as well as that of the commercial operators in the district, most of

The Committee of Award for the Trans-Canada Trophy for 1932 consisted of the following members:
J. A. Wilson, Controller of Civil Aviation, Department of National Defence, Ottawa.
H. M. Pasmore, General Manager, Fairchild Aircraft Ltd., Longueuil.
Wing Commander N. R. Anderson, Royal Canadian Air Force, Department of National Defence, Ottawa.
Squadron Leader A. T. N. Cowley, Superintendent of Air Regulations, Department of National Defence, Ottawa.
Squadron Leader L. F. Stevenson, Royal Canadian Air Force, Department of National Defence, Ottawa.

whose pilots were members of the organization. The success of the Club was principally due to its Instructor, Moss Burbidge. The leadership, initiative and discipline which he had shown in this difficult work merited the recognition accorded to him.

Maurice "Moss" Burbidge was born on April 15, 1896, at Brough, Yorkshire, England. He attended the Pocklington School.

He joined the Royal Flying Corps in 1915 at the actual age of 19 years, serving part of the time as an instructor, and later piloting Handley-Page night bombers. He was commissioned as a Captain. Upon the formation of the Royal Air Force in the spring of 1918, he was posted to Bomber Squadron No. 115 with which he served until the end of the war. He served in France at the same time as Captain James Bell, former Manager of the Edmonton Airport. They went on dawn patrols together. Years later, Maurice Burbidge was to come to Canada and live in Edmonton for a number of years, where he became the Club's Instructor. Captain Burbidge later served two years in India with a bomber squadron.

While in India, Maurice Burbidge was in command of the Rajkot Aerodrome from 1919 to 1920, when it was opened to receive the first air mail from Bombay to Karachi. It was operated by the Royal Air Force.

On his return to England, he took an instructor's course at the Central Flying School in 1922, and another one in 1925. In 1925 the first class of officer pilots of the Fleet Air Arm of the Royal Navy was posted to No. 1 Flying Training School, R.A.F., Netheravon, England. This class was trained and soloed by Maurice Burbidge. He was an instructor with the Central Flying School for a while in 1928. He had flown some

Two of the 'planes of the inaugural air mail flight from Fort McMurray to Aklavik, N.W.T., on the frozen Mackenzie River. This photo was taken in the mid-day twilight of the Arctic in December, 1929.

Photo courtesy of Frederick B. Watt.

| YEAR | PILOTS TRAINED | | AB INITIO | DUAL INSTRUCTION | HOURS FLOWN |
	PRIVATE	COMM.	SOLOISTS	(HRS.)	
1929	22	4	26	493.15	1,080.20
1930	29	5	43	510.55	1,777.15
1931	15	5	19	436.40	1,300.45
1932	22	3	22	286.40	809.25
	88	17	110	1,727.30	4,967.45

sixty-eight types of aircraft, and accumulated a considerable number of hours of flying.

Captain Burbidge came to Canada early in 1929. In lieu of his British Air Ministry Certificate No. 1712, he was issued Commercial Air Pilot's Certificate No. 428, dated March 13, 1929.

In March, 1929, Moss Burbidge became Instructor of the Edmonton and Northern Alberta Aero Club. Prior to this, Wop May had been the Instructor, but he had left to form Commercial Airways, along with Vic Horner and Cy Becker.

Burbidge was loaned to Commercial Airways Limited in December, 1929, to assist the company in connection with the inauguration of the Mackenzie River air mail service, and made three pioneer flights into the north. Wop May flew to Fort McMurray from Edmonton in November, 1929, in his Bellanca ski-equipped aircraft to make advance preparations for the inaugural air mail service to Aklavik, Northwest Territories. As the contract with the Post Office Department was awarded on November 1, 1929, rather late in the year, Wop May had only time enough to fly over the route as far as Fort Simpson before freeze-up. Equipping their Bellanca aircraft with skis, and other necessities, for the first time for Arctic operations, was no easy task.

Wop May made Fort McMurray his headquarters this same fall from which to carry on this 1,676-mile northern air mail service. A slipway, a shop and a hangar were built for their aircraft at Fort McMurray. Sub-bases and caches were

established at Fort Fitzgerald, Fort Resolution, Fort Simpson and Aklavik. On December 9, 1929, when weather conditions improved, the other three pilots who were to go on the inaugural air mail flight flew in from Edmonton with their aircraft. They were Cy Becker, Moss Burbidge, who was on loan from the Edmonton and Northern Alberta Aero Club, and Idris Glyn-Roberts, a former R.A.F. pilot who was employed by Commercial Airways.

December 10, 1929, was the historic day that marked the inauguration of the first contract for an air mail service down the Mackenzie River to Aklavik beyond the Arctic Circle. Wop May was responsible for having the aircraft in readiness for the flight, and for the entire organization and supervision of the complete air mail operation north of Fort McMurray to Aklavik. Moss Burbidge flew Lockheed-Vega CF-AAL and left the fleet at Fort Resolution after completing his part of the journey. Cy Becker flew one of the Bellancas and went as far as Fort Simpson, while Wop May and Idris Glyn-Roberts went through to Aklavik, their destination, in their Bellancas. The sacks of mail were piled extremely high for the flight.

Starting from Fort McMurray, stops were made along the route to Aklavik at Fort Chipewyan, Fort Fitzgerald, Fort Smith, Fort Resolution, Hay River, Fort Providence, Fort Simpson, Wrigley, Fort Norman, Fort Good Hope, where they (Wop May and Idris Glyn-Roberts), as well as their two air engineers, Tim Sims and C. Van der Linden, spent Christmas Day; then they went on to Arctic Red

River, Fort McPherson and Aklavik — a 1,676-mile route — reaching there on December 26, 1929. They were delighted and satisfied with the successful completion of their northern mission. Leaving Aklavik on December 30 for their homeward journey, they arrived back at Fort McMurray on January 3, 1930, with the inaugural trip of many cold days and much hard work behind them.

More than 600 students (including those soloed by Moss Burbidge while with the Fleet Air Arm and the Royal Navy) had made their first solo flight under Captain Burbidge's instruction by the end of 1932, and, of these, not one was hurt or injured in any way while under his supervision. There had been only minor damage to aircraft. Most of the flying instruction in Canada was carried out on Cirrus Moths with wooden fuselages. Two of these were G-CAKJ and G-CALB. By the end of 1932 each of the three had flown an average of 1,453 hours each. The Edmonton and Northern Alberta Aero Club had always been at or near the top of the list of Canadian flying clubs, both in its record of hours flown and for efficient operation. Too, Grant McConachie, winner of the Trans-Canada Trophy for 1945, later President of Canadian Pacific Air Lines, learned to fly in 1929 at the Edmonton and Northern Alberta Aero Club under Moss Burbidge's instruction.

Then an announcement was made in March, 1933, by Colonel Donald M. Sutherland, Minister of National Defence, that Captain Maurice Burbidge had been awarded the Trans-Canada Trophy for 1932 in recognition of his work as

The three Bellancas on the inaugural air mail run shown on the ice of Great Slave Lake, N.W.T., near Fort Resolution, in December, 1929.
Photo courtesy of Wop May and Commander Frederick B. Watt.

Club Instructor.

As no official presentation ceremony took place, the trophy and the replica were forwarded to Moss Burbidge in Edmonton in April, 1933.

Moss Burbidge went to England on a three months' holiday in the spring of 1933. While there he completed an aerobatic course with Air Service Training Limited of Hamble. Upon his return to Canada, he was given an instructor's categorization test by Flight Lieutenant Elmer Fullerton in July, 1933. Flight Lieutenant Fullerton was also a winner of the Trans-Canada Trophy. The categorization of civil flying instructors was something quite new at the time, but the Department of National Defence was of the opinion that this policy was necessary in the interests of safety.

Moss Burbidge took a special instrument flying course at Camp Borden, Ontario, in the spring of 1936, under the instruction of Mr. H. Wilson.

Moss Burbidge resigned his nine-year term of office as Instructor of the Edmonton and Northern Alberta Aero Club at the end of April, 1938, to become associated with Trans-Canada Air Lines in Winnipeg. He joined the ground staff of the company and took a special training course, later spending some time at each of the western terminals of the company to familiarize himself with the details of the operation.

However, he was not to remain with Trans-Canada Air Lines for very long. In

December, 1939, he took a refresher course for flying club instructors at the R.C.A.F. Station at Camp Borden between November 6 and December 2, 1939, and then was reappointed as Instructor of the Edmonton and Northern Alberta Aero Club.

He became Airport Manager of the Lethbridge Airport on January 1, 1942, and remained in this position until he resigned on August 1, 1943.

At a later date, Moss Burbidge was a master at St. Michael's Boys School, Vancouver Island, for some six years.

He was named a member of Canada's Aviation Hall of Fame in 1973. He was made a Companion of the Order of Flight (City of Edmonton). He is a member of the Pacific Club, Victoria, British Columbia.

Today, Mr. and Mrs. Burbidge live in Victoria.

Moss Burbidge was a born instructor with a knack for gaining a student's entire confidence in the first few minutes. It was said of him that he could fly anywhere with his eyes shut, but couldn't find his way around the streets of Edmonton.

Many were the pilots trained by Moss Burbidge during his time at the Edmonton and Northern Alberta Aero Club. As an Instructor, he always considered the welfare of his students. In the field of instruction, Moss Burbidge rendered a great service to Canada's flying fraternity.

Moss Burbidge, 1949.
Photo courtesy of Moss Burbidge.

1933

Walter Gilbert, at time of award, dressed for northern flying.
Photo courtesy of Walter Gilbert.

Walter E. Gilbert

Citation: in recognition of his exploratory flights in northern Canada

Walter E. Gilbert, F.R.G.S., F.R.C.G.S., while a pilot and Assistant District Superintendent for Canadian Airways Limited at Fort McMurray, Alberta, was awarded the Trans-Canada Trophy for meritorious service in the advancement of aviation in Canada during 1933, "in recognition of his exploratory flights in northern Canada." The announcement of the award was made on March 1st, 1934, by Colonel, the Honourable Donald M. Sutherland, D.S.O., Minister of National Defence.

Walter Gilbert's services to aviation had been brought to the minister's attention as a candidate for the trophy each year since 1930. In making this award to Walter Gilbert, the minister felt that it was a fitting tribute to a pilot with sound judgment, lots of enthusiasm, and a fine and continuous record of arduous work well done under even the most rugged conditions.

During 1933, Walter Gilbert carried out flying in connection with bush freighting

---

The Committee of Award for the Trans-Canada Trophy for 1933 consisted of the following members:
J. A. Wilson, Controller of Civil Aviation, Department of National Defence, Ottawa.
W. J. Sanderson, President, Fleet Aircraft of Canada Ltd., Fort Erie, Ontario.
'Wing Commander N. R. Anderson, Royal Canadian Air Force, Department of National Defence, Ottawa.
Squadron Leader A. T. N. Cowley, Superintendent of Air Regulations, Department of National Defence, Ottawa.
Squadron Leader L. F. Stevenson, Royal Canadian Air Force, Department of National Defence, Ottawa.

and a mail run which was operated on an average of one trip per week. He started the year by flying a cargo of equipment and supplies for the Eldorado Gold Mines from Resolution to Great Bear Lake. His longest non-stop flight during the year was on April 8 when he piloted a Fokker from Fort McMurray to Winnipeg — a distance of approximately 800 miles. Also, he logged 523 hours and 30 minutes during 1933. His total flying time at the time of the award amounted to 3,179 hours.

Walter Edwin Gilbert was born on March 8, 1899, at Cardinal, Ontario, which lies along the sparkling waters of the St. Lawrence River. Here, too, he received his education. When he was eleven years of age, his family took him to Canada's first "aviation meet" which was held at the Lakeside Race Track, near Dorval (west of Montreal), in 1910, where the aeroplane was introduced to the people. Another aviation meet was held that same summer at Weston, Ontario, near Toronto. Actually, attending the aviation meet was Walter Gilbert's own idea. He enjoyed immensely the demonstration of the flying machines.

Walter Gilbert left school to join the Army. At first he worked as a junior inspector of shrapnel time-fuses for the Imperial Munitions Board at International Munitions in Montreal East. At the time, the British Recruiting Mission of the Royal Flying Corps was established in New York City. When a representative was sent to Montreal, Walter Gilbert applied for service with the Royal Flying Corps, and was accepted as a cadet at the age of 18. He received some early training in an open cockpit Curtiss 'plane at Camp Mohawk (near Deseronto), Camp Rathbun and Camp Borden from May to August, 1917.

After receiving his initial training, he left for England on August 17, 1917, for

Walter Gilbert of Western Canada Airways flew G-CASK The Wonder Ship of the North, from Coppermine to the North Magnetic Pole, and back to Edmonton, during the summer of 1930. Shown from left to right: Stanley Knight, air engineer; Richard Finnie, a writer; Walter Gilbert, the pilot; and Major Lauchie Burwash.
Photo courtesy of Walter Gilbert.

further training at the Central Flying School at Upavon, Wiltshire. Next, he took a short course at the School of Aerial Gunnery at Turnberry and the School of Aerial Fighting at Ayr. Returning to London, now a Flying Officer, he was immediately posted to France with No. 32 R.A.F. Squadron, where he served from April 7, 1918, until September 26, 1918, when he caught influenza. Then he was returned to England in December, and to Canada in April, 1919, where he was demobilized.

Walter Gilbert took a refresher course in flying at Camp Borden in 1920, with the newly formed Canadian Air Force, along with a number of other pilots of the First World War.

He spent some twenty-six months working for the Department of Railways and Canals in Ottawa. This was at the time that the initial survey for the "flood contour" was being done to establish areas to be evacuated for what is now the St. Lawrence Seaway. Walter Gilbert was doing field work between Lachine and Valleyfield on the east and Iroquois on the west. However, his interest lay in other fields. He went to Vancouver in September, 1922, and joined a topographical survey party of the Geological Survey in British Columbia in the fall of 1922, so he was engaged in both survey and mining work. He was sent to Vancouver Island and then to the Kimberley area for a couple of months. Walter Gilbert then joined the Britannia Mining and Smelting Company and worked in the mines for a year before surveying claims for the company.

However, flying got a strong hold on him again and he received his commission as a Flying Officer in the non-permanent R.C.A.F. on April 21, 1927. Then he was employed as a pilot on forestry patrol operations in the Cormorant Lake area in northern Manitoba for the R.C.A.F. During the summer of 1928 he was a pilot for a photographic survey flight which photographed some

27,000 square miles mostly in the Reindeer Lake area between Saskatchewan and Manitoba, as well as in northern Ontario.

In November, 1928, he joined Western Canada Airways as a commercial pilot. During the winter of 1928-29 he flew out of The Pas and Cranberry Portage, Manitoba, along with Roy Brown. Tommy Thompson was the company's Superintendent of The Pas district at the time, which included all the northern Manitoba area over to Hudson Bay. The flying business in northern Manitoba was quite good in those years, mostly coming from the mining areas. Then, in March, 1929, Walter Gilbert was sent to British Columbia by Western Canada Airways to fly on fishery patrol work. He remained in British Columbia until January, 1930, and from time to time made other photographic survey flights for the B.C. Electric Co., and the Power Corporation of Canada. Also, he made exploratory flights during the summer and autumn of 1929, and flew freight to a new gold-bearing area on the Unuk River in the mountainous area in Alaska. He always enjoyed flying over the mountains and seemed to get so much satisfaction in just seeing nature's own rugged splendour. In fact, since he first saw the mountains of British Columbia in 1920, he has never voluntarily been out of sight of them.

Walter Gilbert made his first flight north of Stewart, British Columbia, in the Portland Canal area in 1929. It was while he was in this area that H. C. Hughes, Superintendent of the Emerald Mine, owned by the Consolidated Mining and Smelting Company at Ootsa Lake in central British Columbia, was badly mauled by a grizzly bear. His condition became critical owing to infection, requiring hospital treatment. So Walter Gilbert of Western Canada Airways, who had a contract with the Consolidated Mining and Smelting Company, flew the Boeing flying boat, CF-ABB, from

Stewart to Burns Lake, British Columbia, on the afternoon of September 10, 1929, a distance of some 280 miles in two hours and ten minutes. The following morning, Mr. Hughes and an attendant were put on board the flying boat at Ootsa Lake and flown to Vancouver via Quesnel and Bridge River.

Then in January, 1930, Western Canada Airways transferred Walter Gilbert to Fort McMurray, Alberta, where he arrived on New Year's Day, January 1, on a cold stormy day. This was his first glimpse of Fort McMurray where he was to be based for a number of years. Also, it was from Fort McMurray that he made many historic flights, and enjoyed new experiences in his flying along the Mackenzie River route. So it was here in the dead of the subarctic winter that he and his wife took up residence in a two-room "wooden shack" and started their pioneer living in the north. Punch Dickins and Harold Farrington, also pilots with Western Canada Airways, were stationed at Fort McMurray at the time.

It was late in June, 1930, when Western Canada Airways sent Walter Gilbert and Punch Dickins to Gilbert LaBine's radium deposits in the area of Great Bear Lake, Northwest Territories, for commercial transportation purposes. Flying Fokker Super Universal aircraft G-CASK they made the first commercial flight to Great Bear Lake where the greatest mineral strike of the north had taken place on May 16, 1930.

Walter Gilbert left Fort McMurray on June 28, 1930, to make his first flight "down north" to Aklavik, Northwest Territories, near the Arctic coast. This was the first time that he had flown all the way down the Mackenzie River, and so most of the country was new to him.

While Walter Gilbert was in Aklavik, he made the first commercial flight to Herschel Island on July 1, 1930, taking along Bishop Geddes to visit the Anglican Church Mission there. The aircraft was chartered for the 140-mile

This photo was taken on the occasion of Col. Lindbergh's visit to Aklavik in August, 1931. Walter Gilbert acted as a reception committee for Canadian Airways; while Lewis Parmenter serviced his aircraft. From left to right: Col. Charles A. Lindbergh, Walter Gilbert and air engineer Lewis Parmenter. Photo courtesy of the Edmonton Journal.

flight by five persons who had just arrived in Aklavik on the first steamer that year.

On a flight to Aklavik in August, 1930, Walter Gilbert and air engineer Lew Parmenter made a three-hour flight across the mountains to Fort Yukon in Alaska to pick up two American tourists from Los Angeles. They had arrived at Fort Yukon from Seattle by boat, and were flown to Aklavik so that they could travel by boat over the Mackenzie River from Aklavik to Fort McMurray, thus comparing these two transportation systems.

After having just returned to Fort McMurray from a trip to Fort Simpson, Walter Gilbert received an assignment from Western Canada Airways to fly Major Lauchie T. Burwash, M.E., F.R.G.S., a noted Canadian Government explorer, to the west coast of King William Island in the late summer of 1930. Stanley Knight of Western Canada Airways was the air engineer (mechanic) on this flight. The trip was chartered by the Dominion Government and was an exploratory one to investigate reports that had been received by Canadian authorities that the remains of the ill-fated Franklin Expedition of 1845-1848 had been found; and to photograph the Arctic coast, including the area of the North Magnetic Pole.

Sir John Franklin, with 128 officers and men, had left England in 1845 with two ships, the *Erebus* and the *Terror*, to search for the Northwest Passage to the Orient. Two months later, they were seen by whalers in Baffin Bay with whom they sent back messages that all was going well. Then no word was ever heard from them again, and many expeditions had been sent out in search of them.

The route of this historic aerial expedition was from Fort McMurray, by way of the Athabasca, the Slave and the Mackenzie Rivers for 1,000 miles to Fort Norman, then east 400 miles across Great Bear Lake to the Arctic Coast at the mouth of the Coppermine River. Walter Gilbert flew Fokker Super Universal G-CASM to Coppermine. They carried a portable radio, powered from a motor-driven generator of its own, and a special Fairchild aerial camera for taking photographs. Walter Gilbert made a few stops along the way so that Major Burwash could make some inspections. Their first stop was at Fort Norman. Crossing Great Bear Lake they met Punch Dickins at Hunter Bay who had flown in from Fort Rae in another Fokker Super Universal. With him was W. J. "Buck" Buchanan, another of Western Canada Airways' pilots, who was being flown to Dease Point to fly out the abandoned Fokker Super Universal G-CASK, which had been left there a year earlier when it ran out of gas while on a mission for the MacAlpine Expedition.

Walter Gilbert continued his flight to Coppermine with Major Burwash, while Punch Dickins flew on to Coppermine. Leaving Buck Buchanan there, Punch Dickins returned to Fort McMurray the next day. While awaiting the arrival of the *Bay Chimo* from Vancouver, a supply ship belonging to the Hudson's Bay Company, Walter Gilbert flew the 400 miles east to Dease Point with Buck Buchanan and Stanley Knight to see what condition G-CASK was in and if it could be salvaged. Major Burwash had work to do at Coppermine in the meantime. So, taking along a supply of gas and oil, they set out to find G-CASK, and found it quite undamaged, having withstood well the rigours of the north with its Arctic gales, shifting tides, summer winds and other forces of nature for one whole year without shelter, from the summer of 1929 to the summer of 1930. After refuelling the aircraft, removing the engine cover, priming the engine, cranking the starter, the engine started — much to their surprise. Then it was taxied out to the bay and moored for the night. As it was late in the day, they decided to spend the night on Dease Point.

Meantime, the Eskimos who had been "assigned" the job of "guarding" the aircraft the previous year arrived and returned the key to the cabin of the aircraft which had been entrusted to them by members of the MacAlpine Expedition. The next day both aircraft left Dease Lake and were flown to Cambridge Bay on Victoria Island, where they landed and refuelled from gasoline left there a year earlier, and then flew on to Coppermine, arriving on August 17. G-CASK was flown back to Fort McMurray by Buck Buchanan.

Back at Coppermine, Major Burwash had just completed his work there. The supply boat, *Bay Chimo,* had arrived and unloaded the annual supplies for Coppermine in preparation for its long journey to Cambridge Bay. Richard Finnie, a writer, also arrived at Coppermine on the *Bay Chimo* in August, and was to join the flight at Coppermine to fly to the North Magnetic Pole.

G-CASM, piloted by Walter Gilbert, was checked over and ready to leave on the morning of August 18, 1930, on its long rugged flight over the little-charted areas. Richard Finnie was standing on the shore at the time ready to take photographs as it was being taxied on a take-off test flight. Richard Finnie says in *Canadian Aviation,* October, 1936: "He watched it manoeuvre into the wind, gain speed as the motor roared and the pontoons were rocked, then make a frantic effort to "get on the step" and into the air. Then it failed, and another attempt was made, and this time a long column of dark vapour poured from the exhaust pipe. G-CASM puttered back to the beach with a blown-out piston!" They had no spare parts with them, and besides there were no facilities available to repair this kind of damage. Meantime, Richard Finnie, fearing that the trip was off for the year, lost no time and got aboard the *Bay Chimo* which was

Canadian Airways' base at Cameron Bay, Great Bear Lake. Photo was taken at 12:00 midnight on June 13, 1933, by the light of the midnight sun.
Photo by Walter Gilbert.

heading for Cambridge Bay. Then he changed from the *Bay Chimo* to another smaller schooner and went the rest of the way to Peterson Bay (Gjoa Haven), on King William Island, their final base. It took him two weeks to reach Peterson Bay on the schooner which brought in the annual supplies and provisions for the trading post. Then she left on September 4 for her return voyage, cutting the trading post off from ground communication to the south for another year.

Meanwhile back at Coppermine, in response to a message which Walter Gilbert had sent to Western Canada Airways' Winnipeg office over the *Bay Chimo's* wireless before she left Coppermine, a replacement aircraft for G-CASM had arrived there. This replacement aircraft was none other than G-CASK, with a new set of control cables — the aircraft which had just been flown to Fort McMurray from Dease Point about a week earlier. When Walter Gilbert assisted in salvaging this aircraft, he never expected for a moment that he, himself, would be flying it to the Arctic before his assignment was completed. This aircraft was one of two left there a year earlier, in 1929, by the MacAlpine Expedition when they had been blown north of their course and had landed on Dease Point when they ran short of gas. So this was the aircraft that was now being readied to carry Major Burwash on the historic flight to the North Magnetic Pole.

They left Coppermine (Fort Hearne) on August 25, 1930, now in G-CASK, without the aircraft's wireless set as it was not working properly, to fly to King William Island. But if they wanted to get the assignment done that season, they had to take such chances. Their flight took them to Bernard Harbour on Dolphin and Union Strait, 80 miles north of Coppermine, where they sought shelter because of a bad storm. They were stranded at Bernard Harbour for a whole week until the gale blew itself out.

Meantime, September had arrived in the Arctic, heralding the soon-coming of winter. A survey was made of Bernard Harbour while they were there and then they flew on and crossed over to the south coast of Victoria Island photographing the coast line all the way to Cambridge Bay on Victoria Island where they landed after a four-hour flight and spent the night near the place where Amundsen's schooner *Maud* was lying. That evening they were entertained by the Hudson's Bay Company's staff. The following day, they flew on to Peterson Bay (Gjoa Haven), an isolated trading post on King William Island, where they landed on September 5 at 6:30 P.M. and remained overnight. They had photographed the terrain all along the way.

Picking up Richard Finnie the next morning, they flew up the east coast of King William Island across James Ross Strait, flying over the outer fringe of the Great Polar Ice Pack to the area of the North Magnetic Pole, near Cape Adelaide on Boothia Peninsula, reaching the Pole on September 6, 1930. They climaxed their historic flight by actually photographing the site of the North Magnetic Pole itself. They were the first to fly over the area of the North Magnetic Pole where compasses become erratic and point in every and all directions at the same time — well, almost! They did not land in this desolate area due to poor visibility, mist, fog and clouds. On the return flight from Boothia Peninsula they landed on a small lake at Victory Point near the top of King William Island, after flying over an ice-choked sea. They stayed overnight at Victory Point to look for relics or other evidence of the Franklin Expedition. Everyone took part in the search the first afternoon and evening. While all were properly dressed for the rigours of the north, the Eskimo summer "water boots" which Walter Gilbert and Stanley Knight were wearing could not take the extremely sharp rocks under foot, so only

Major Burwash and Richard Finnie searched the next day. Walter Gilbert was quite a stickler for proper attire and usually carried even the extras, but this time they had eliminated all extra weight — including their stout boots of the south. Then G-CASK took off from the lake on which ice was starting to form along its edges. The lake was just barely long enough for the aircraft to get off the water, and Walter Gilbert did a superb job of piloting. They reached Peterson Bay (Gjoa Haven), King William Island, at dusk, where they remained overnight — and where Richard Finnie remained to spend the winter in the Arctic. They completely encircled King William Island, photographing the coast line and making aerial surveys as they flew along. The North Magnetic Pole, which is always on the move, was on the northern tip of Prince of Wales Island at that time.

As it was beginning to snow, they took off from Peterson Bay and flew along the south shore of Victoria Island to Cambridge Bay and thence along the south shore of Dease Strait and Coronation Gulf. Coppermine (Fort Hearne) was reached that afternoon, September 8. The entire length of coast line which they followed was mapped photographically. Edmonton was reached on September 29, 1930, via Fort Smith, covering a total distance of some 5,000 miles on the flight. Some 1,800 miles of the coast line were photographed, which, in itself, was a great task.

Major Burwash discovered some very interesting relics of the Franklin Expedition, but not what he expected from the reports which had been received by the government. New camp sites and new graves of the Franklin Expedition were found on the west coast of King William Island.

For Walter Gilbert's survey and photographic work, as well as his flying on this trip to the North Magnetic Pole, he was honoured with a Fellowship in the Royal Geographical Society in 1932. He was, it is believed, the first Canadian pilot to have this honour bestowed on him. Dr. S. C. Ells, M.E., F.R.G.S., and Major Lauchie Burwash recommended him for this honour.

While based at Fort McMurray during the early thirties, Walter Gilbert made many flights between Fort McMurray and Aklavik for Canadian Airways. He also made many flights to the uranium area of Eldorado Gold Mines at Great Bear Lake during the early thirties, carrying mail, freight and passengers. Often he flew G-CASK. Walter Gilbert even flew out to Fort McMurray the press photographs of Colonel Charles A. Lindbergh's visit to Aklavik when he was en route to the Orient from New York between July 29 and August 26, 1931. His route took him through Churchill and Coppermine. Flying G-CASK, Walter Gilbert made the trip in one day, on August 9, 1931, leaving Aklavik at 5:00 A.M. and arriving at Fort McMurray at 9:00 P.M. that evening. He refuelled at Fort Norman and Hay River, covering the distance of 1,465 miles in 11 hours and 55 minutes in his faithful old G-CASK.

Canadian Airways started operating on November 25, 1930, and Western Canada Airways became a part of it.

Through the years, Walter Gilbert took part in many searches for lost aircraft and their crews, as most pilots did in the north. One of these searches was for Andy Cruickshank and his two mechanics, Horace W. Torrie and Henry Jones, in 1932, on a flight from Great Bear Lake to Fort Rae. However, it was Con Farrell who discovered the wreckage near Fort Rae. All had been killed in the crash, and Walter Gilbert flew the bodies back to Edmonton. Then in January, 1933, he took part in another search for G-CATL flown by Paul B. Calder and Bill Nadin, his air engineer. The wreckage was located south of Cambridge Bay by Wop May, and the bodies were flown out to Edmonton by Walter Gilbert. These, and many other rescue missions, were all

a part of flying in the north. Perhaps it could well be said that Walter Gilbert held some sort of record for bringing out so many bodies by air throughout his years in the north.

Then there was the time when Walter Gilbert was flying the mail to Aklavik during the first week of June, 1932, and flew the new Bishop of the Arctic on the same flight. He was on an inspection tour of his missions from Fort McMurray to Aklavik and also at Shingle Point, which is halfway to Herschel Island. Walter Gilbert flew G-CASK, one of the two 'planes on the trip, while Wop May flew the other one, a Bellanca. They stayed overnight at Fort Simpson. The next day, due to a heavy snowstorm, they were forced to land at Thunder River, a small trading post, for a short while. Then they flew on to Aklavik where they found the country covered with eight inches of snow, and remained for the night. On June 2, in their pontoon-equipped aircraft, they set out for ice-locked Shingle Point with the mail. As there was nowhere for them to land, they dropped the sacks of mail from the 'plane. Lew Parmenter who was the Air Engineer on this flight had the task of dropping the mail sacks. As Walter Gilbert flew the 'plane as close as possible to the mission, Lew Parmenter dropped the two sacks of mail. Then Walter Gilbert looking over his shoulder saw what he thought was one of the mail sacks, and told Lew Parmenter to drop that one, too. Lew Parmenter dropped the "other sack," too, without asking the whys and wherefores. Walter Gilbert later learned that the "other sack" contained, not mail, but the padre's clothes and other personal items!

Walter Gilbert also flew some Hudson's Bay Company officials on an inspection of the company's posts in the north in 1932. The party was headed by Mr. P. Ashley-Cooper, Governor of the Hudson's Bay Company. This was the first trip ever made to the Northwest

Territories by a governor of the company, and it was believed to be his first official inspection trip of their posts in Canada. Mr. P. A. Chester, General Manager of the company for Canada; Mr. Ralph Parsons, the Fur Commissioner; and Mr. William Bartleman, the District Manager for the Mackenzie-Athabaska area also accompanied the party. They inspected the Hudson's Bay Company's posts at Fort McMurray, Fort Chipewyan, Fort Fitzgerald and Fort Smith.

G-CASK was destroyed by fire while being refuelled at the base at Fort McMurray on the morning of March 31, 1933. The aircraft was being prepared for a freighting trip from Fort McMurray to Great Bear Lake on Friday morning, March 31, 1933. A load of freight was laying beside the aircraft ready for loading. The pilot was to be Walter Gilbert; and the air engineer was to be Lew Parmenter. While the aircraft was being refuelled, the refuelling hose, which had been made up from two sections joined together with a "nipple" of galvanized gas pipe, came apart near the funnel, and the hose, streaming gasoline, fell to the ground. Suddenly the whole side of the engine cover burst into flames. Within a few seconds, the whole front of the engine was engulfed in flames and within five minutes the entire aircraft was destroyed with all its equipment. However, none of the freight was damaged as it was on the ground. It was almost impossible to determine just what caused the fire in the first place, as all precautions had been taken. The log books of G-CASK listing all the historic and rugged flights that it had made were also destroyed.

Walter Gilbert describes the passing of G-CASK in his book, *Arctic Pilot* (1939). He says:
"It was one of those perfect mornings in the early spring when long hours of daylight and splendid take-off conditions for the ski-equipped 'planes made everything seem right with the

world. From the pilot's viewpoint it was truly the perfect season of all the year. We had six 'planes at work on the 820-mile "through" express haul from Fort McMurray to Great Bear Lake, and every pilot was making a daily one-way trip. In one day and back the next, with not a "bump" in the sky, and nothing to do but loll over the joystick while the sturdy motors drummed away the miles.

"On this particular morning we were loading mixed freight for the lake. We had just completed "heating up" the engine of SK (a short and simple procedure on these mild spring-like mornings), and Lew had turned out his heating-torches and climbed to the top of the wing to remove the engine-cover.

"The sliding's pretty good this morning," he said. "How about giving her a few more gallons of gas so we won't have to take so much at Fort Fitzgerald?" (Fitzgerald was our next refuelling stop on the Great Bear Lake route.)

"Okay," I answered, and passed up the hose. Lew removed the tank covers and signalled for the fuel pump to be started. The next thing we knew was the gas-hose gushing raw fuel over the engine cover (a defective joint in the line had given way). Reaching forward to retrieve the hose, we were hurled back by a muffled explosion and the whole front end of the 'plane burst into flames. Something — static electricity probably — had ignited the gas as the broken hose slid across the engine cover. With lightning rapidity the flames spread to the already uncovered tanks, and Lew was barely able to slide from the rear edge of the wing before their 160 gallons of fuel were sending two roaring geysers of flame far into the still air. It was fortunate that the tank covers had been removed, for this at least prevented an explosion.

"No cargo was in SK. We were to have carried dynamite in cases, and such freight is never loaded until the pre-heating job is finished.

"But other aircraft were near at hand. Seeing that it was already too late to do anything to save this veteran of the northern airways, all efforts were concentrated upon getting the rest of the fleet away from the danger zone. "The air was absolutely still. Most of the ships were covered with a slight film of wet snow that had fallen during the night. So luck was partly with us, and we were able to save the rest of the 'planes from damage.

"When the worst of the fire was over, and old SK lay, a crumpled skeleton of steel tubing, in the middle of the small lake she had melted for herself in the ice of the river, I had time to begin to realize what had happened.

"The first feeling was one of unreality, as though I expected momentarily to awake from an unfriendly dream. Then gradually the significance of the tragedy dawned upon me. And I may truly say that the sense of loss, when realized, was quite as great as that felt when a tried and trusted friend "passes."

"It will probably be difficult for the layman to realize the depth of affection which may be built up between the crew of an aircraft and the ship itself, after tens of thousands of miles of flight together over the far places of the world. Many times I have remarked the inability of the casual reader to comprehend the genuine affection of the typical pioneering pilot for the companion of his adventures.

"So passed the "wonder ship" of the North.

"One of an identical pair of two Super Fokker 'planes built in 1928 in the United States, she logged barely 150,000 miles of flight in her short life — less than half the total of her sister ship. Yet in half the mileage, SK took part in more outstanding flights than any other two 'planes in Canada. Her "life" was cut short by an untimely end,

but her record remained unstained."

After G-CASK's passing, the aircraft used by Canadian Airways on the run from Fort McMurray to Great Bear Lake were: CF-AKI, a Bellanca Pacemaker; CF-AIA, a Bellanca CH300; CF-AMZ and CF-ARI, Junkers W-34; CF-ATZ, a Fairchild 71C; and CF-AKY, a Fairchild F.71. They were flown by pilots Walter Gilbert, Wop May, Archie McMullen, Con Farrell, John B. Bythell and B. Hollick-Kenyon. Later in the year Norm Forrester joined the company. The air engineers on this run were Bill Tall, Frank Kelly, Al Parker, Lew Parmenter and Don Goodwin, Fred Little and Sammy Tomlinson, Rudy Heuss and Tom Caddick.

Walter Gilbert logged 776 hours and 21 minutes in 1930; 567 hours and 40 minutes in 1931; 663 hours and 50 minutes in 1932; and 523 hours and 30 minutes in 1933. Most of this flying was carried out in the Northwest Territories — much of it inside the Arctic Circle in unmapped and unexplored territory where the most rigorous conditions prevail.

As the years went by, Gilbert continued to make valuable sketches of water routes, islands and terrain, along with his flying duties, particularly when flying over poorly mapped or virgin territory.

His company, Canadian Airways, was expanding, too, in its mail, freight and express service. During the year 1933 that Walter Gilbert won the Trans-Canada Trophy, Canadian Airways carried 328,618 pounds of mail and 2,522,233 pounds of freight and express; compared with 299,066 pounds of mail and 1,870,136 pounds of freight and express in 1932; and 459,458 pounds of mail and 764,449 pounds of freight and express in 1931.

Walter Gilbert became Assistant District Superintendent for Canadian Airways at Fort McMurray, Alta., in 1933.

CF-ARI at Fort Smith being unloaded on the shore, where drums of gasoline were transferred to barges to be taken north. This was during the late summer of 1933 when traffic became heavy at the 16-mile portage between Fort Fitzgerald, Alta., and Fort Smith, N.W.T., so that aircraft were used in September to expedite the movement of supplies over this portage. Some 176 barrels of gasoline were moved by aircraft. The photo shows the method of unloading at the north end of the portage. At the south end loading was simplified as the plane was alongside the dock.
Photo courtesy of Walter Gilbert.

Commercial Air Pilot's Certificate No. 389, dated December 4, 1928, and Air Engineer's Certificate No. A-992, dated November 18, 1933, which superseded Certificate No. A-686, dated September 1, 1931, were held by Walter Gilbert.

Then an announcement was made on March 1, 1934, by Colonel Donald M. Sutherland, Minister of National Defence, that Walter Gilbert had been awarded the Trans-Canada Trophy for the year 1933 in recognition of his exploratory flights in northern Canada.

As no official presentation of the trophy was ever made, it was forwarded to Canadian Airways, Montreal, with a replica being sent to Walter Gilbert at Fort McMurray, in April, 1934.

On January 26, 1934, the first scheduled air mail flight was inaugurated to Coppermine River on the Arctic Ocean. When the weather was 50° below zero F., Walter Gilbert, accompanied by Postal Inspector R. W. Hale of Edmonton and air engineer Lew Parmenter, arrived at Coppermine from Cameron Bay, Great Bear Lake, 150 miles away, with 600 pounds of mail and express. This included 4,800 first-flight covers. The flight left Fort McMurray on January 18, 1934, and reached Cameron Bay (Port Radium) and then Coppermine on January 26. They were plagued with blizzard after blizzard on this flight. In addition, the few daylight hours of January made flying time very short each day.

Walter Gilbert and Lew Parmenter of Canadian Airways took off from Fort McMurray on December 7, 1934, in Junkers CF-ARI for Yellowknife River, carrying a load of mining equipment and supplies, and four passengers.

Another noteworthy flight in the north by Walter Gilbert was a fur charter trip for Canadian Airways in a Junkers aircraft on January 10, 1935, from Fort McMurray via Great Bear Lake and Fort Norman for Aklavik. He covered the distance of 1,575 miles in 14:35 flying

hours, arriving on January 13. Then, on January 14, he loaded his aircraft with a cargo of furs and left Aklavik on his return flight by way of Fort McPherson, Arctic Red River, Fort Good Hope, Fort Norman, Fort Simpson, Hay River, Fort Smith, Fort McMurray and on to Edmonton, covering the 1,747 or so miles in 11:25 flying hours, thanks to a good tail wind to speed him along. He reached his destination on January 17. Lew Parmenter, who flew with Walter Gilbert as his air engineer on two-thirds of all his flights — including the toughest ones of all — was also his air engineer on this trip.

On January 31, 1935, Walter Gilbert left Fort McMurray with a full load of mail to fly to Aklavik via Great Bear Lake and other northern points. From Aklavik, he flew to Herschel Island and picked up a consignment of furs for the Northern Whaling and Trading Company of New York. Post Office Inspector R. W. Hale of Edmonton accompanied the flight to Aklavik and Herschel Island. They returned to Fort McMurray on February 6 with their mail and thirty-one bales of furs weighing some 1,200 pounds. The cargo of fur was worth some $35,000. Their flight covered nearly 3,500 miles of territory in just five and one-half days. As the daylight hours in the Far North were so short in the winter, this made the trip a real achievement. Walter Gilbert made hundreds of flights carrying furs throughout the years. Actually, carrying furs was probably the company's mainstay cargo.

Flying CF-ARI, a Junkers aircraft, Walter Gilbert with Air Engineer Lew Parmenter left Fort McMurray in the spring of 1935 for Fort Norman carrying mail, freight and express. In June, 1935, Pilot Gilbert made a four-day flight in a Bellanca from Winnipeg to Berens River, Flin Flon, Island Falls, Pelican Narrows, Nistowiak, Lac la Ronge, Fort McMurray, Beaverlodge, back to Fort McMurray,

then to Ile à la Crosse, Waskesiu Lake and Prince Albert, with four passengers, two of whom were cabinet ministers from Saskatchewan. For the 1,450 miles, he took 20 hours and 30 minutes' flying time, from June 11 to June 15.

When White Eagle Silver Mines ceased their operations for the winter in the fall of 1935, Pilots Gilbert, Heuss and McMullen of Canadian Airways were engaged to fly the men from the mines at Great Bear Lake to Edmonton.

Walter Gilbert continued flying in the north for Canadian Airways through the years and when the company established a base at Prince Albert, Saskatchewan, in the spring of 1937, he was appointed Superintendent of Canadian Airways with his base at Prince Albert. The following year he was transferred to Vancouver where he became Superintendent of Canadian Airways for their British Columbia Division.

During these years, too, Walter Gilbert was putting his pen to paper and wrote a number of stories of life and flying in the north. Also, he wrote the excellent and colourful book *Arctic Pilot* (1939), which tells first-hand about bush flying down north in the Mackenzie district in the early days. Walter Gilbert's more important exploratory flights and experiences in the north are related in this book, along with those of other northern pilots.

Walter Gilbert continued to be associated with Canadian Airways Limited until the company was taken over by Canadian Pacific Air Lines after its formation on January 1, 1942. He then became Superintendent of Canadian Pacific Air Lines' Vancouver district at Vancouver and, later, Superintendent of their Mackenzie district at Edmonton.

At the end of 1945, Walter Gilbert left his work with Canadian Airways and he and Russell Baker started flying commercially from a base at Fort St. James, British Columbia. Their company, incorporated in British Columbia on July 7,

Walter Gilbert hiking to Lindeman Lake, in August 1949, at the time that he was running his unique sport fishing resort there.
Photo courtesy of Northwest Sportsman Magazine.

1945, became known as Central British Columbia Airways Ltd. Walter Gilbert was its President, and Russell Baker was Managing Director of the company.

They started off flying Beechcraft CF-BBB, which was leased from Leigh Brintnell for charter work from Fort St. James under a temporary licence until such time as an operating certificate was issued to the company. The company also flew a Noorduyn Norseman, Mark IV, under lease to assist the British Columbia Government in their urgent requirements in battling forest fires in the province. Both Walter Gilbert and Russell Baker carried out many emergency flights after they acquired Junkers CF-ATF and Junkers CF-ASN. By 1948, Central British Columbia Airways had operating bases at Fort St. James and Prince George, as well. Russell Baker was based at Fort St. James, while J. K. Herriot was based at Prince George. H. S. Quinn was stationed at Kamloops, J. D. Duncan at Castlegar and H. C. Hicks at Cranbrook. Engineer F. W. Coulter was stationed at Fort St. James, while Engineer L. C. Hanratty was at Kamloops.

Walter Gilbert left Central British Columbia Airways in 1949 to develop a unique sport-fishing resort at Chilliwack Lake, British Columbia, which was accessible only by air. For a time, this resort was internationally known as a rendezvous for the flying fraternity. However, after a few years at this beautiful resort, he sold out to a wealthy lawyer from California. He then left Chilliwack Lake and he and his wife moved to Yakima, Washington, U.S.A., where they lived for several years. Then they went to Vancouver where they lived for a time. Today, they live in Point Roberts, Washington, where Walter Gilbert is engaged in the real estate business. His firm is known as Walter Gilbert Realty.

Walter Gilbert is a Fellow of the Royal Geographical Society and a member of the Canadian Geographical Society; a member of the British Guild of Air Pilots; and a member of the Explorers Club (New York); as well as a winner of the Trans-Canada Trophy. He was named a member of Canada's Aviation Hall of Fame in 1973. He was made a Companion of the Order of Icarus (Hall of Fame), and a Companion of the Order of Flight (City of Edmonton).

During the 1920s and 1930s, Walter Gilbert was a member of the British Columbia Mountaineering Club. Climbing mountains was a favourite pastime of his, as was also fishing; while flying was his business, along with terrain sketching, photography, map making and aerial surveying. His method of mapping was to have a large-size map with the available information on the areas already shown on it. Whenever he flew from place to place, he was sketching water routes and terrain, and mapping topographical survey data, making corrections or additions to the map at hand. His sketches and data were then forwarded to the Topographical Survey Branch of Canada, Ottawa, to be included in the latest maps. This information was always greatly welcomed.

His first aerial mapping of unmapped areas was done in 1929, and was one of Canada's earliest air surveys. The area was near the British Columbia-Alaska boundary where there were glaciers at the 7,000 to 8,000-foot level. He flew north from Stewart, British Columbia, at an altitude of 10,000 feet, to reach the area and see this panoramic view.

One of the most notable and greatest of his sketches was of the Thelon River in the Northwest Territories.

Walter Gilbert was a great Canadian artist in every sense of the word, and his talents, aside from flying, contributed so much to pioneering sketching and mapping of Canada's northland by air. This helped in accurately defining Canada's outlying areas.

Yet, throughout Walter Gilbert's extensive flying over a period of thirty years, from 1917 to 1947, he was never involved in any major accident to aircraft, or suffered any injury, got lost, or caused any third party any injury or damage. He had an extraordinary record of safety.

So, in his exploratory, pioneering and regular flights in northern Canada through the years, this great Canadian artist and pilot went quietly about his way sketching, surveying, and recording the unmapped areas of our vast northland by air. His contribution to Canada through making travel to inaccessible areas a matter of hours instead of months did much to develop her natural resources. As well, he brought the benefit of modern medicine within the grasp of northern settlements at that time.

Walter Gilbert shall ever be remembered in the annals of Canadian history for his many contributions to Canada; and for his colourful book, *"Arctic Pilot"*, on bush flying "down north."

1934

Elmer G. Fullerton

Citation: meritorious service in the advancement of aviation in Canada during 1934, and in recognition of his work as Chief Instructor in instrument flying

Group Captain Elmer G. Fullerton, A.F.C., C.D., while a Flight Lieutenant with the Department of National Defence and second-in-Command of the R.C.A.F. Station at Rockcliffe, Ontario, was awarded the Trans-Canada Trophy for "meritorious service in the advancement of aviation in Canada during 1934, and in recognition of his work as Chief Instructor in instrument flying." The announcement was made by the Honourable Grote Stirling, Minister of National Defence, on April 10, 1935.

The announcement said that few officers had had such a wide and varied career and Flight Lieutenant Fullerton's experience as a Flying Instructor was unrivalled in Canada. He had been responsible, while Chief Flying Instructor at Camp Borden, for the introduction of the latest methods of ab initio instruction, instrument flying, air pilotage and night flying. The syllabus used in instrument flying training, both for civil and military pilots, was prepared by him and he was responsible for many im-

The Committee of Award for the year 1934 consisted of the following members:

J. A. Wilson, Controller of Civil Aviation, Department of National Defence, Ottawa.

George M. Ross, Executive Secretary of the Canadian Flying Clubs Association, Ottawa.

Squadron Leader A. T. N. Cowley, Superintendent of Air Regulations, Department of National Defence, Ottawa.

Squadron Leader L. F. Stevenson, Royal Canadian Air Force, Department of National Defence, Ottawa.

provements in the methods and facilities used. The high standard of flying instruction, both in the R.C.A.F. and by all civil instructors, was due, in a large measure, to his instruction and example.

The Minister of National Defence, appreciating the fundamental importance of sound flying training methods in all phases of aviation, both civil and military, stated that he was pleased to see the services of one of the officers of the R.C.A.F. recognized in this way. Also, this was the first time that an active member of the R.C.A.F. had received this award, which was based solely on individual effort — yet it served to draw attention to the advancement in both civil and military aviation, in which the Air Force, as a whole, had played a part.

Elmer Garfield Fullerton was born on October 29, 1894, in Pictou, Nova Scotia. He received his education at Kenora High School, the University of Manitoba, the Royal Naval College, Greenwich, England, and attended courses at the Royal Military College, Kingston.

Elmer Fullerton served overseas with the Royal Canadian Engineers in the Canadian Expeditionary Force during the First World War from June, 1916, to December, 1917. He was then transferred to the Royal Naval Air Service and later to the Royal Air Force serving as a Flying Officer-Pilot and Instructor until July, 1919, when he returned to Canada.

He joined the Canadian Air Force in February, 1920, and was appointed Flying Instructor at Camp Borden.

Elmer Fullerton received Air Engineer's Certificate No. 72, dated December 31, 1920. The following year he received Commercial Air Pilot's Certificate No. 103, dated February 19, 1921. During 1921 he also became a Flight Lieutenant on a non-permanent basis.

He was on leave of absence without pay from the Canadian Air Force during 1921, while he was employed as a pilot with Imperial Oil Limited on their exploratory and pioneering flying expedition to the Far North in connection with the first discoveries of oil near Fort Norman on the Mackenzie River. This expedition was the first to penetrate the lower Mackenzie Basin by air and it was this pioneer effort which preceded the great expansion of air transport in that district in the early thirties. Flight Lieutenant Fullerton was the first pilot to fly into the Northwest Territories, and Imperial Oil Limited was the first company to make an aerial expedition to the Canadian Arctic for commercial purposes.

In those days flying was an especially rugged and dangerous enterprise but Imperial Oil's confidence in its future was shown by their purchase in 1921 of two Junkers J.L. 6, single-engine, six-passenger monoplanes, with which they pioneered flying in Canada's Far North. Their aim — backed by Charles Taylor, Imperial Oil's Edmonton Manager — was to get men and equipment into their experimental oil field at "Discovery Well" on the north shore of the Mackenzie River, about 50 miles north of Fort Norman on the fringe of the Arctic Circle, as quickly as possible. This was later to be the site of Imperial Oil's Norman Wells' refinery.

At the time the only available transportation from Edmonton to the north was a railroad extending a distance of 225 miles from Edmonton to Waterways (Fort McMurray). This was as far north as the railroad went. In the summer time, transportation was by steamboat via the Athabaska River, Lake Athabaska, Slave River, Great Slave Lake and the Mackenzie River to Fort Norman, an approximate distance of 1,200 miles. The navigation season lasted about three months, from June to September. Journeying this way took from two to

three weeks, and included one 18-mile portage from Fort Fitzgerald to Fort Smith, due to the rapids in the Slave River. The steamboat went as far as the south end of the portage (Fort Fitzgerald) where she turned around for the trip back south after discharging northbound cargo and passengers and taking on southbound cargo and passengers. All northbound cargo and passengers at Fort Fitzgerald were then transported by tractor and other vehicles along the 18-mile road to the north end of the portage (Fort Smith) where a rather large paddle-wheel boat, the S.S. Mackenzie, made the remainder of the journey right up to the mouth of the Mackenzie River at Aklavik. Stops were made at all trading posts en route to pick up and discharge cargo and passengers, as necessary. In the winter time, of course, sled dogs were used which took a month or so to cover this route. It was natural, therefore, for Imperial Oil to want a faster and better method of transportation to their new oil field — hence they looked to aviation, which they thought had great possibilities.

Their two Junkers aircraft, each powered with a B.M.W. engine, 185 b.h.p., having a maximum speed of 110 m.p.h., were purchased in New York from Mr. J. L. Larsen. Wop May and George W. Gorman entrained for New York around the end of November, 1920, to purchase these aircraft for Imperial Oil and fly them back to Edmonton. Wop May arrived home in aircraft G-CADP on January 5, 1921, when the weather was 50 degrees below zero F., having braved the capricious snowstorms successfully. George Gorman's aircraft, G-CADQ, was delayed en route for several weeks at Brandon, Manitoba, where he had to make an unexpected landing after storm and icing conditions had forced him down, necessitating some minor repairs to the aircraft.

George Gorman and Elmer Fullerton,

who replaced Wop May in Edmonton to make the flight for Imperial Oil to Fort Norman, were engaged as pilots of these two aircraft. Wop May was wishing to enter a flying venture of his own at the time. Fullerton's aircraft (G-CADP) was christened *Vic*; and George Gorman's aircraft (G-CADQ) was christened *René*. William "Bill" Hill and Peter Derbyshire were the two air engineers engaged to accompany these aircraft and keep them in proper flying condition.

Elmer Fullerton and George Gorman flew north from Edmonton to Peace River Crossing where their air engineers, Bill Hill and Peter Derbyshire, replaced the aircraft's wheels with skis, overhauled the aircraft's engines, and did whatever was necessary for their forthcoming trip to the Far North. Peace River was to be their base of operations. Here they picked up W. W. Waddell, a Dominion Land Surveyor for Imperial Oil, and Sergeant Hubert Thorne of the Royal Canadian Mounted Police, who was stationed at Fort Simpson and was returning there after completing an eight weeks' trek by dog sled from Fort Providence to Edmonton to bring in an Eskimo prisoner. The distance from Peace River to Fort Norman was a little over 800 miles by air.

Elmer Fullerton said in the May, 1934, issue of *Canadian Aviation* that:

"the preliminary fuel-carrying flight to the Upper Hay River was carried out by both aircraft on the 22nd of March, 1921, without incident. The landing was made on the ice of the Upper Hay River. The gasoline which they were ferrying in was contained in 50 four-gallon cans, 25 being carried in each aircraft, in addition to one similar size can of oil. When they were unloading this on the ice a few Indians began to assemble a short distance away. They viewed them with much undisguised awe and wonderment, not unmixed with suspicion. For some reason or other, they showed a definite disin-

Imperial Oil Junkers monoplanes, G-CADP and G-CADQ, at Edmonton, Alberta, February, 1921, before taking off for the north.
Photo courtesy of Imperial Oil Limited.

clination to come close to them or the aircraft, which they afterwards learned from the Factor of the Hudson's Bay Trading Post was because it was the first time they had ever seen an aircraft and they feared they might be evil spirits of some kind. They thought it was rather amusing to watch some of the Indians examining their ski tracks, especially where the skis had first made contact with the snow, pointing to the beginning of the marks, then to the sky — evidently convincing one another that the suspected 'Evil Spirits' had unmistakably come out of the air — and then discussing the mystery in typically Indian fashion, punctuated by frequent gestures. "Through the assistance of the Factor, the party was able to engage a dog team and toboggan, as well as a driver, to transport their gasoline and oil to a suitable cache about 150 yards away, which they had made arrangements to use. After their fuel had been safely stored, they remained only long enough to have some light refreshments and, in a short time, they were in the air again winging their way south to Peace River. The return trip was made without incident, also; the flying time being two hours and twenty minutes for the 190 miles. Inspecting their aircraft later, they noticed two small holes in the fuselage covering of one of the aircraft near the tail. These holes were about half an inch in diameter, one being at the bottom of the fuselage and the other at the top, directly opposite. They were at a loss to account for these holes but, as they resembled bullet holes and were directly opposite, their conclusion was that some of the superstitious Indians had fired at them as they passed over. There was no other damage, and the holes were quickly patched."

Elmer Fullerton, piloting the *Vic*, and George Gorman, piloting the *René*, took off from the aerodrome at Peace River

for their big trip to Fort Norman on March 24, 1921, at 9:00 A.M. on a bright promising morning, with their passengers and emergency equipment and rations for ten days. They followed the Peace River and had good weather for the first 100 miles until they reached the Upper Hay River country. Here the clouds were low and visibility was poor, so they turned east along the Peace River to Fort Vermilion. Within half an hour both aircraft had landed near a trading post belonging to the Hudson's Bay Company, where they stayed for the night as a blizzard was developing. They put their aircraft in the shelter of a barn and moored them there. They refuelled with ordinary gasoline obtained from the trading post, but were unable to leave for Great Slave Lake until two days later, due partly to the stormy weather and partly to the fact that the rather low-grade gasoline did not allow the engines to reach maximum power. Full power was 1,500 r.p.m., whereas with poor gasoline only 1,200 r.p.m. could be obtained. However, by dismantling the carburetors and enlarging the jets slightly this was overcome, and satisfactory power was obtained for take-off. Their route lay over 200 miles of featureless country. After flying for two hours and forty minutes, they reached the mouth of Hay River on Great Slave Lake where they landed their aircraft in thirty inches of snow near another Hudson's Bay Company trading post. Here they spent the night as guests of the Hudson's Bay Company's Factor.

En route there, Elmer Fullerton flew over Hay River Falls, which he thought was one of the great wonders of the north. Although these falls are seldom heard about outside the north, they actually rival Niagara Falls in magnificence and splendour. Here, a beautiful stream, from 300 to 400 feet wide, plunged over a limestone ledge in a sheer drop of 106 feet at the upper falls, known as Alexandra Falls; while a little

farther on it again dropped another 46 feet, known as Louise Falls. At that time of year, the spray from the falls had turned to ice, revealing most beautiful patterns.

They gassed up and left the next morning for Fort Providence on the Mackenzie River. By the time they reached the western end of Great Slave Lake a blizzard had developed, so they landed on the ice of the lake near the Mackenzie until the blizzard had lessened in severity, and also to conserve their fuel supply. In the space of half an hour or so, visibility had slightly improved so they took off again and continued their trip to Fort Providence, landing in a clearing near the settlement.

At Fort Providence the snow was deep also, and they found it difficult to get up sufficient speed to get the aircraft airborne. Twice they failed to become airborne, so all six of them and some of the inhabitants, wearing snowshoes and walking abreast of each other, packed the snow by foot to improvise a runway surface to support the aircraft's skis. On March 28 they took off and headed for Fort Simpson, 140 miles farther along the Mackenzie. En route to Fort Simpson, their visibility was good and they were able to see the lofty mountains in the distance. They reached Fort Simpson in one hour and forty-five minutes, arriving there during a light snowstorm, only to find that a landing on the Mackenzie River was impossible as it was a mass of jagged ice hummocks.

George Gorman, Peter Derbyshire and Sergeant Thorne landed first on a field they chose as suitable near the edge of the settlement. In landing, the *René* struck a hard snow-drift and the machine went up on its nose, breaking the propeller and one ski which broke through the heavy crust of snow, as well as a few other smaller things. This four-foot snowdrift was hard covered in places in a very deceptive way. Fortunately, no one was hurt, but they were slightly shaken up. Elmer Fullerton observed this landing from the air and decided to land a good distance from George Gorman's aircraft where there appeared to be fewer drifts. This he did, although his undercarriage was buried in the deep snow. In his aircraft were Bill Hill, his air engineer, and W. W. Waddell. They hurriedly ran over to George Gorman's aircraft to see what had happened to it. After examining the damage, they decided it would be best that Elmer Fullerton should fly the 250 miles to Fort Norman the following day in his aircraft, the Vic. Bill Hill and Bill Waddell would go with him. However, when the Vic was in flight from the field, where it landed, to the adjacent snye in preparation for the flight to Fort Norman, its engine suddenly developed intermittent pre-ignition knocks due to the low-grade gasoline causing excessive accumulation of carbon. This meant that it was necessary to overhaul the Vic's engine to remove accumulated carbon before it could be flown any distance. In view of the delay that would thus be involved, they decided to transfer the propeller and a ski from Fullerton's Vic to the René, which was then flown by Gorman to the snye (a channel back of Simpson Island) where the Vic was parked, so that the René could be flown to Fort Norman the following day.

The next morning the René was loaded with emergency equipment and, with Pilot George Gorman at the controls, accompanied by Bill Hill and Bill Waddell, the aircraft took off. Shortly after the take-off, however, before the aircraft had barely reached an altitude of 50 feet, it stalled and crashed to the ice. Thus, another propeller, plus one wing and an undercarriage, had had its day! Needless to say, this did not put George Gorman or the others in the best of spirits. Again, beyond being shaken up, no one was hurt. Fortunately! As the Vic's ski was practically undamaged, it was returned to the Vic again. But it was

still without a propeller — and to make a propeller hundreds of miles in the north-land without the proper equipment, and by hand, was considered unthinkable, at first.

Nevertheless, after some discussions, both pro and con, by all the personnel — Elmer Fullerton, George Gorman, Bill Hill and Pete Derbyshire and, in collaboration with Philip Godsell and Walter Johnson of the Hudson's Bay Company at Fort Simpson — they decided that the making of a propeller was worth attempting, to say the least. Otherwise, without this important piece of equipment, they would have to spend about three months or so waiting until the navigation season opened up in July before they could have a new propeller shipped in.

It seemed that upon the shoulders of Bill Hill and Walter Johnson was to fall the task of "manufacturing" the propeller by hand. A further search revealed that the Hudson's Bay Company had a few oak sleigh boards available, about 10 feet long by 7 inches wide, which were originally intended to be made into dog sleds. However, Philip Godsell very kindly handed them over to be made into a propeller. Father Decoux, O.M.I., head of the Roman Catholic Mission, very thoughtfully and kindly made available to them the mission workshop and tools for this task. But, as some of the tools had not been used for years, they were not in the best of condition and showed some effects of rust; not just the kind of tools one would expect to use in doing a job of great precision. From the broken propellers they were able to form a pattern. Now they were all set for their difficult and highly exacting job!

Walter Johnson, a local handyman for the Hudson's Bay Company post, had formerly been an excellent cabinet-maker, and knew the art of it. He, too, knew how to use a good set of tools. The Hudson's Bay Company was glad to assist by making his services available.

The people of Fort Simpson also gave every assistance in their gracious way.

As Bill Hill and Walter Johnson started out on their unique job, they discovered that the seven oak boards were about an inch too narrow, and would have to be "fanned." For laminating they used babiche glue, which was made from moose parchments which the Hudson's Bay Company had on hand. For this work, the mission workshop had to be maintained at a temperature around 80° F. These two men completed their "manufactured" propeller in eight days — an ingenious job of which every one was proud. By the ninth day at noon, the red-painted propeller was dry enough to be fitted to the engine. During the time that this propeller was being made northern-style, by hand, Elmer Fullerton and Peter Derbyshire overhauled the Vic's engine and repaired the damaged ski. As there were no buildings or tents available, this work was done in the open right where the aircraft was parked on the snye. They did have a small tarpaulin to protect the engine while they were working on it.

At the same time, the mission kindly provided a team of oxen to haul the René from the snye to a place of safety and storage on the island, where it would have to remain until an undercarriage, floats, propeller, and other necessary parts could be shipped in by boat in July.

The newly-made propeller was attached to the Vic and it functioned well, being perfectly balanced, with no trace of vibration on the ground — and, when tested for an hour in the air by Elmer Fullerton, he found that the propeller was functioning normally in every way. This was on April 23. Needless to say, Elmer Fullerton was more than delighted, even though he was understandably a bit apprehensive at first.

They all acclaimed Bill Hill and Walter Johnson as the heroes of the hour — as their skill, perseverance and resourcefulness had enabled them to produce a

Bill Hill proudly displays the newly made propeller, April, 1921.
Photo courtesy of Imperial Oil Limited.

piece of highly technical equipment that has remained a monument to them and an inspiration, if not a challenge, to future pioneers of the northern air trails.

This historic propeller has had a place in the National Aeronautical Establishment, Ottawa, through the years. Today it has been given a place in Canada's National Museum of Science and Technology in Ottawa. (Incidentally, and as a matter of interest, a second propeller was made in Fort Simpson for use on the *René,* but it did not function properly and was never used. It, too, was placed in the National Aeronautical Establishment, and now has a place in the National Museum of Science and Technology.)

The date being April 23, 1921, preparations were under way to return to Peace River Crossing as soon as possible. This time of year had caused a new hazard to arise, the spring break-up period which was due any day! As it was not possible to reach Fort Norman in a ski-equipped 'plane, they had no choice but to return to their base at Peace River. A characteristic of the Arctic and subarctic is that, once the spring season commences, it develops very quickly due to the rapidly increasing hours of daylight. During the winter the subarctic nights are extremely long and the days extremely short; and in the summer the reverse conditions exist, especially around June 21 when there is continuous daylight. The short gap between winter and summer, and between summer and winter, is very noticeable. Around June 21 at Fort Simpson, the sun merely dips a short distance below the horizon for about a couple of hours, which is supposed to constitute night. However, there is still enough daylight to read a newspaper, or do almost any work without artificial light.

Arrangements were made to start early the following morning, April 24, as there was not enough daylight left for them to start their long flight that day. Pete Derbyshire, the air engineer, was to remain behind at Fort Simpson to guard the *René* until the spare parts arrived by boat. Elmer Fullerton, George Gorman, Bill Waddell and Bill Hill were to return to Peace River in the *Vic.*

Around 5:00 A.M. just before dawn on the morning of April 24, the pilots and air engineers were awakened by an excited Eskimo, known locally as Henry Lafferty. He told them that the ice of the Mackenzie River was breaking up! Dressing quickly, with a little light from the moon to guide them, they hurriedly snowshoed to the *Vic,* which was parked on the ice of the snye about a mile from the Village of Fort Simpson, hoping to get it off the snye before the ice would demolish it. In the distance they could hear the ominous rumbling of the mass of ice on the Liard River as it was breaking up. This was no consolation to them at all. Fort Simpson is situated on an island in the Mackenzie River at the mouth of the Liard River. The Liard River breaks up earlier than the Mackenzie River in the spring, and this had now happened. An ice jam was forming above the island causing water to rise on the snye.

When Elmer Fullerton first went to the *Vic* there was about 400 yards or so of ice from which he could take off. However, he had to wait until the water and oil for the engine had been pre-heated in cans over a bonfire. In the meantime the take-off distance had dwindled to about 200 yards of ice with open water beyond. It had taken them practically no time at all to remove the tarpaulin cover from the cockpit and engines, to unfasten the mooring ropes and control lashings. Elmer Fullerton decided to fly it to a still-frozen lake about five miles away after removing everything from the aircraft to make it as light as possible for the short take off. He invited Jack Cameron of Fort Simpson, a trapper and guide who had always wanted to fly but had never done so, to accompany him. So Jack Cameron climbed aboard the aircraft, taking with him his snowshoes which would be needed for the return trek. Elmer Fullerton's take-off distance had by now dwindled still more and, as the *Vic* took to the air, the heels of her skis sent up a spray of water before the aircraft finally became fully airborne. Beneath them now lay a mass of heaving ice floes on the Mackenzie River, but the home-made propeller during this precarious moment performed nobly. The *Vic* and its capable and daring pilot landed safely on a small lake of solid ice some five miles to the south.

Wearing snowshoes, Elmer Fullerton and Jack Cameron trekked back to Fort Simpson to get their equipment and to guide their other crew members to where they had flown the aircraft, but not before they had tethered their aircraft and drained the water and oil into cans.

It took them five hours to reach the snye owing to the muskeg condition that existed under the snow throughout the entire return trek. This allowed their snowshoes to partly sink into the slush which lay underneath the soft snow, as they took each step. This slush and snow would then freeze to their snowshoes making them increasingly heavy and unwieldy, necessitating frequent stops to remove this frozen accumulation. For these reasons, it took some five hours to reach the snye — a snowshoe trek that, had it not been for the muskeg, would have taken no more than two hours at the most to cover the five miles. On reaching the snye of the Mackenzie River, which was now covered with floating and moving blocks of ice, and which they had to cross (a distance of some 75 yards), they did so by jumping from one ice-cake to another. This had its hazards for the uninitiated, which included Elmer Fullerton, but Jack Cameron was accustomed to this sort of thing and was quite adept at it.

As the day, by now, was too far spent for the party of four to undertake the trek back to the aircraft, arrangements were made for an early start the following morning, April 24.

The next morning, after saying good-bye to their hosts, Sergeant and Mrs. Thorne of the R.C.M.P., Fort Simpson, also Father Decoux of the Mission, Walter Johnson, Philip Godsell, Factor Camsell of the Hudson's Bay Company, and their other kind friends at Fort Simpson, the trek back to the aircraft began. The party consisted of Elmer Fullerton, George Gorman, Bill Hill and Bill Waddell. Jack Cameron rowed them and their equipment across the snye by boat, as most of the ice jam had cleared away by then. From there, the going was by foot on snowshoes, an arduous journey to say the least. It took them all of five hours to cover the five miles back to the aircraft carrying their equipment on

their backs. As the hours of daylight at this northern latitude were still relatively few, twilight had fallen upon their arrival at the aircraft so they camped beside the *Vic*, and had a roaring hot fire going throughout the night to keep them warm. They left at 8:00 A.M. the next morning, April 25, for Peace River, after enjoying a hearty breakfast cooked over their camp fire.

The next morning, after the usual procedure of pre-heating the water and the oil over the camp fire, and duly warming the engine, the final take off was made without incident, with Elmer Fullerton at the controls. Seated alongside of him to assist in the navigation was Bill Waddell, while in the cabin were George Gorman and Bill Hill.

The return flight had to be made non-stop, directly across uninhabited country (instead of by their previous and normal river route) for four reasons. First, on the flight north, which was via Fort Vermilion, Hay River and Great Slave Lake, they had used up all the gasoline that was available at the trading posts en route. Secondly, as the aircraft was equipped only with skis, and due to the lateness of the season with the river ice all going out and the lake ice melting further south, landing facilities en route for skis would likely be an uncertain and risky undertaking. Thirdly, the direct non-stop route to Peace River would greatly shorten the flying time required of the home-made propeller; and fourthly, with no apparent habitation of any kind along the direct route, there was no point or wisdom in considering an intermediate landing, especially as the fuel endurance of the aircraft was barely enough to complete the flight.

By flying at the most economical cruising speed of the aircraft, which was only 80 miles per hour, and being forced to buck a head wind most of the way, the flight back to Peace River Crossing in the *Vic* took exactly eight hours and ten minutes. This was the longest continuous

time at the controls that Fullerton had had up to that time. There was no snow whatever on their home field at Peace River for a landing with skis and, as all the ice had gone out of the Peace River, Fullerton decided to land on the ice of Little Bear Lake (Cardinal Lake) which was some ten to fifteen miles northwest of their base. So, after dropping a note to their cook-caretaker (Charlie Woodman) at their base headquarters requesting him to take out to the lake ten gallons of gasoline and wheels for the aircraft, Fullerton landed safely on the lake ice. After landing, he decided to drain the tanks to see just how much gasoline actually remained — and there was only enough for a few more minutes' flying! So luck was really with them all the way.

Shortly after Elmer Fullerton and his party landed their aircraft on Little Bear Lake, a Junkers aircraft flew in and landed a safe distance from them on the ice, much to their surprise, as they were unaware of any other Junkers in that part of the north. The owner of this one was Mr. J. L. Larsen of New York, from whom Imperial Oil had purchased their two Junkers aircraft, the *René* and the *Vic*. Mr. Larsen had flown to Peace River to find out how they were getting along with their new aircraft, and at the same time to scout around for a further market for Junkers aircraft. He was talking to Charlie Woodman when the note was dropped at the Peace River Aerodrome. He graciously offered to fly in the ten gallons of gas and the wheels for the aircraft, for which they were most grateful. Carefully inspecting their home-made propeller, they found no indications of weakness or cracks. It had fulfilled its destiny. After replacing the *Vic*'s skis with wheels, they took off for their base at Peace River.

Elmer Fullerton thought that his experience in flying the *Vic* off the snye was decidedly thrilling while it lasted but frankly admitted it was too close a call!

Captain Amundsen in centre, with Elmer Fullerton shown on the right. This was taken in Vancouver in May, 1922.
Photo courtesy of G/Capt. Elmer Fullerton.

Jack Cameron thought it was great fun, and this was his first flight! So ended the first pioneer flight in the Mackenzie River District to explore the possibility of air transport in the Far North. The *René* was eventually returned to its base at Peace River. Its flying days were soon to be over.

But the mission itself had not yet been accomplished. It must be remembered that both aircraft were venturing where no aircraft had ever been before so, in another effort to reach Fort Simpson, laminated wooden pontoons and spare aircraft parts were forwarded to Peace River by boat. On May 27, 1921, piloted by Elmer Fullerton, the *Vic* again took off from Peace River for Fort Simpson, carrying Dr. Theodore Link, geologist for Imperial Oil, W. W. Waddell, Land Surveyor engaged by Imperial Oil, and Bill Hill, air engineer. Conquering minor difficulties this time, such as a burst exhaust pipe and a leaking radiator, the *Vic* was on its final lap from Fort Simpson to Fort Norman on June 2, a hop it made in three hours and twenty-nine minutes, when it shattered a pontoon in landing on the Mackenzie River. A small scow was lashed under the right wing and in this manner the aircraft was steered 50 miles downstream to the site of Discovery Well on Bear Island, 100 miles south of the Arctic Circle. The previous year it had taken the party five weeks by boat to cover this short distance.

Early in August, Elmer Fullerton's machine, the *Vic*, was re-equipped with a new float which had been brought in by George Gorman on the *S.S. Mackenzie*.

Now, in one hour's flight time, Elmer Fullerton flew his party, Dr. Theo Link, Bill Waddell and Bill Hill, over the same territory that Dr. Link's 1920 party had taken the entire season to cover by foot and canoe when they first discovered oil on Bear Island. Thus, in spite of the considerable difficulties encountered which were not uncommon at that time,

the expedition did demonstrate the tremendous usefulness that could be made of aircraft in exploring the north country, and that it actually could be done. However, much planning lay ahead in the future.

During 1922, Elmer Fullerton, still on leave of absence from the Canadian Air Force, was associated with Captain Roald Amundsen, the famous Norwegian polar explorer, on his trans-polar flight, and gained further experience in Arctic flying. Elmer Fullerton accompanied Amundsen's Expedition as far as the northern part of Alaska, where the Schooner *Maud* was later to begin her historic three-year float in the ice floes across the North Pole to the Atlantic Ocean. Here they unloaded the Junkers aircraft, assembled it and made it ready for the flight by the Norwegian Pilot Umdahl (who was to have been Elmer Fullerton's co-pilot), assisted by their Norwegian air engineer.

In the meantime, Captain Amundsen and Elmer Fullerton continued to the shore of Siberia on board the Schooner *Maud* for the purpose of collecting some special Eskimo clothing and certain other items which they planned to take with them on their trans-polar flight. They also wanted to have with them a small team of Eskimo dogs, complete with harness and sled, so that, in the event of a forced landing which might necessitate their having to "walk" out, they would have a better chance of survival by having the dogs to transport their emergency supplies, sleeping-bags and other equipment — as well as having the dogs for possible food, should the ultimate necessity arise. Captain Amundsen preferred the Siberian Eskimo dogs and clothing, rather than that used by the Alaskan Eskimo, because the dogs were hardier, and then the distance across to the Siberian coast, near the Bering Strait, was only some 25 miles.

When they returned to the aircraft a few days later, they were greatly

disappointed to learn that Pilot Umdahl, while flight testing the aircraft, had some misfortune in landing, which resulted in damage of a nature that necessitated the postponement of their projected polar flight until the following year. However, when the time came, Amundsen decided to make the trans-polar flight by airship, instead of by aeroplane and, as history records, this flight was successfully completed in the Italian-built dirigible *Norge* in May, 1926. Elmer Fullerton was not part of this later expedition which was made in the opposite direction from Norway.

In 1923, Elmer Fullerton returned to the Canadian Air Force, and was engaged in customs patrols on flying boats from Vancouver. Early in 1924 he was granted a permanent commission in the R.C.A.F. and was appointed Second-in-Command at the High River Air Station in Alberta, where he also carried out forest fire patrols.

In March, 1925, in view of his high standard of flying and his previous experience as a flying instructor, he was transferred from High River to the R.C.A.F. base at Camp Borden, as Officer Commanding "B" Flight in the Flying Training School.

As a flying instructor at Camp Borden, and being directly associated with the supervision of flying training, Elmer Fullerton felt that his professional knowledge might be enhanced to some extent if he could have the first-hand experience of a parachute jump. It was compulsory for all pilots to wear parachutes when flying, in the event of an emergency, but it was not compulsory for the pilots to carry out a practice parachute jump. Each pilot was issued a parachute and always took the greatest care of it. From an economic standpoint, Elmer Fullerton thought that this policy was justified, as it cost several thousand dollars, with many months of training, to produce a fully qualified military pilot. Under war conditions, when manpower

G/Capt. Fullerton and his pipe band at Centralia, Ontario, in 1944.
Photo courtesy of G/Capt. Elmer Fullerton.

and trained personnel were at a premium, the justification was still greater.

Then Fullerton had a great curiosity to know, from personal experience, what a parachute jump was like. He had been wearing a parachute every day for a long time now, and was lucky enough not to have had an occasion to use it. So, with inspiration from these two sources, he applied for permission to carry out a "premeditated" parachute jump. Of course, he received permission from the R.C.A.F. to make the jump.

One cold morning, early in April, 1926, snow was still covering the ground and there was a frosty touch to the atmosphere, so Fullerton had to wear full winter flying clothes when he climbed into the rear cockpit of a Clerget-Avro two-seater training 'plane. The engine was warm and running. The clouds looked to be from three to four thousand feet high. Fullerton asked the pilot, Squadron Leader A. A. Leitch, to climb as high as possible without actually getting into the clouds, in case he should wish to do a prolonged free fall before opening his parachute.

They climbed to 3,500 feet and levelled off just underneath the clouds. The motor was throttled down and speed was reduced to a minimum to facilitate Fullerton's getting out of the cockpit. Even when the force of this slipstream was reduced to 60 m.p.h., there was sufficient force to make it somewhat difficult to get out of the cockpit on to the step preparatory to jumping while wearing cumbersome flying clothing and two parachutes, including the small emergency chute.

When Elmer Fullerton left the aircraft, his first impression was the sudden tranquillity of everything; the engine noise had ceased and there was no longer any slipstream beating against him. Instead of experiencing a sensation of falling, Fullerton was floating peacefully and comfortably in space! He was fascinated, so fascinated that, instead of pulling the

ripcord after counting the usual one-two-three as he normally should have done, he decided to continue to fall for some distance to learn more about this new and fascinating experience of floating in space. He opened his parachute about 2,000 feet from the ground, so he must have fallen free about 1,500 feet. This, then, is how Flight Lieutenant Fullerton enjoyed his first parachute jump.

In January, 1928, Fullerton went to England to take the Army Co-operation Course at Old Sarum with the Royal Air Force and returned to Camp Borden in May of that same year.

On April 1, 1930, he was appointed Chief Flying Instructor at Camp Borden.

Then, in March, 1931, Fullerton was posted on exchange to the Royal Air Force, where he took the Flying Instructor's Course in their Central Flying School and obtained an A. 1 category. For approximately one year of his service with the Royal Air Force he was employed as an instructor at the Central Flying School. Elmer Fullerton gave such excellent service in that capacity that the Royal Air Force sent him on a series of courses on instrument flying and landing on the deck of aircraft carriers. He was then posted on temporary duty with the Royal Air Force Flying School in Egypt at Abre Sueir for a period of six weeks to carry out categorization tests of the Royal Air Force flying instructors and students stationed there.

Flight Lieutenant Fullerton returned to Canada and was again posted to the R.C.A.F. Flying Training School at Camp Borden in March, 1933, where he was again Chief Flying Instructor.

In July 1933, at the request of Mr. J.A. Wilson, then Controller of Civil Aviation, he proceeded to western Canadian points in a de Havilland Moth training aircraft to test and categorize all civil flying instructors at civil flying schools and flying clubs from Fort William to Vancouver inclusive, while Squadron Leader Brookes went east

from Fort William to the Maritimes for the same purpose.

Fullerton performed aerobatics at a number of air shows. The first time that he took part in an air display was in July, 1934, while Officer Commanding the R.C.A.F. Detachment at Camp Borden, when he took part in the Toronto Centennial Air Display. His perfect handling of his machine in a series of intricate manoeuvres, including "bunts," thrilled the crowds completely. Also, on July 14 of this same year, at Ottawa's Air Force Display, the three highlights of the afternoon were the exhibition of single aerobatics by Elmer Fullerton in a Fleet trainer with a Kinner engine. He executed complicated manoeuvres with superlative skill, and his display brought forth exclamations of admiration from the crowds.

In the fall Fullerton was transferred to Ottawa and appointed Second-in-Command of the R.C.A.F. Station at Rockcliffe, Ontario, in September, 1934. He was promoted to the rank of Squadron Leader on April 1, 1935. Also, this same year, he was appointed Commanding Officer of No. 7 General Purpose Squadron, Rockcliffe.

Then an announcement was made by the Minister of National Defence in April, 1935, that Squadron Leader Elmer Fullerton had been awarded the Trans-Canada Trophy for meritorious service in the advancement of aviation in Canada during 1934, and in recognition of his work as Chief Instructor in instrument flying.

The Trans-Canada Trophy which Elmer Fullerton had won during 1934, along with the replica, were forwarded to him at the R.C.A.F. Station, Rockcliffe, Ontario, on July 2, 1935.

Squadron Leader Elmer Fullerton possessed a great interest in and knowledge of the magnetic compass, and why it did this and that. He wrote several technical articles on the idiosyncrasies of the magnetic compass in 1936. He was

G/Capt. Elmer Fullerton when he was Commanding Officer of No. 9 S.F.T.S., Trenton, Ontario, in 1946.

Photo courtesy of G/Capt. Elmer Fullerton.

of his accomplishments.

Group Captain Elmer G. Fullerton, A.F.C., C.D., lived in Calgary, Alberta, in his retirement years, until the time of his death on March 6, 1968, at the age of 73. He was married and had three daughters, who became registered nurses. They are now married.

He was named a member of Canada's Aviation Hall of Fame in 1973. He was made a Companion of the Order of Flight (City of Edmonton).

Air Staff Officer, M.D. 2, Toronto, from 1936 to 1938.

He became Commanding Officer of No. 1 Fighter Squadron at Trenton, Ontario, in June, 1938, where he served until November, 1939. The squadron was equipped with Siskins and then later with Hurricanes.

During 1940, he served as Senior Air Staff Officer at No. 3 Training Command Headquarters, Montreal, and on May 1 of that year he was promoted to Wing Commander.

In January, 1941, Wing Commander Fullerton was appointed Commanding Officer of No. 9 S.F.T.S. (Service Flying Training School) at Summerside, Prince Edward Island.

Incidentally, while Fullerton was Commanding Officer at Summerside, he conceived the idea of a tartan kilted pipe band for the Royal Canadian Air Force, and, after submitting his ideas and proposals to Air Force Headquarters at Ottawa, he was granted official authority in 1941 to organize and equip a band. He designed the uniform and the special R.C.A.F. tartan for the kilt and the shoulder-shawls. The tartan is made up of the three Air Force colours: light blue, dark blue and red. This tartan was later duly registered by the R.C.A.F. at the College of Heralds, Edinburgh, Scotland. Thus was started the first kilted pipe band in the Air Force which soon became one of the real highlights and

feature attractions, not only of No. 9 S.F.T.S. and the surrounding district, but gradually throughout the entire R.C.A.F. The band was periodically sent on official tours during the Second World War in the interests of recruiting. Since the Second World War a number of similar bands have been formed in the R.C.A.F. and the tartan has become very popular.

When No. 9 S.F.T.S. was moved to Centralia, Ontario, Fullerton remained as Commanding Officer. He was promoted to the rank of Group Captain on October 15, 1941.

Group Captain Fullerton assumed command of the R.C.A.F. Station at Trenton on September 23, 1945, where he served until his retirement on August 9, 1946. At the time of his retirement from the R.C.A.F, he had completed twenty-eight years of service.

He was awarded the Air Force Cross in 1945 "in recognition of his outstanding service in the field of flying training."

Throughout the many years of excellent service that Group Captain Fullerton gave to his country, he continued to advance toward improvement in his genial sincere way in whatever duty may have been assigned to him and as he saw the need for it. Through the years he developed a number of hobbies, such as electronics and cabinet-making. He was a very methodical person, careful in everything, and always very precise. He was an extremely modest person, in spite

1935

William Archibald in 1929.
Photo courtesy of William Archibald.

William Munroe "Roe" Archibald

Citation: in recognition of his work as a pilot and in organizing the flying services of the Consolidated Mining and Smelting Company

William Munroe "Roe" Archibald, B.A.Sc., while Manager of Mines for the Consolidated Mining and Smelting Company, Trail, British Columbia, was awarded the Trans-Canada Trophy for meritorious service in the advancement of aviation in Canada during 1935, "in recognition of his work as a pilot and in organizing the flying services of the Consolidated Mining and Smelting Company." The award was announced by the Honourable Ian Mackenzie, the Minister of National Defence, on March 13, 1936, who expressed his appreciation to him for the service he had rendered to aviation during the past six years.

The announcement also paid tribute to his admirable exploits in the use of aircraft in opening up new fields of endeavour in mining development, thus advancing the cause of aviation in Canada.

The Committee of Award for the year 1935 consisted of the following members:
J. A. Wilson, Controller of Civil Aviation, Department of National Defence, Ottawa.
Squadron Leader A. T. N. Cowley, Superintendent of Air Regulations, Department of National Defence, Ottawa.
Squadron Leader W. A. Curtis, D.S.C., O.C. of No. 10 Squadron, Royal Canadian Air Force, Department of National Defence, Ottawa.
Flight Lieutenant A. L. Morfee, Royal Canadian Air Force, Department of National Defence, Ottawa.
George Ross, Executive Secretary of the Canadian Flying Clubs Association, Ottawa.

William Archibald learned to fly in 1929, when 53 years of age. He had to his credit many transcontinental trips and much of his flying was done under the arduous conditions prevalent in the Rocky Mountains. He had carried out a great deal of pioneer flying, and was one of the first men to fly across the Canadian Rockies from the Prairies to the Coast.

William Munroe "Roe" Archibald was born in Halifax, Nova Scotia, on February 19, 1876. He graduated from McGill University in Montreal in 1897 with a degree in mining engineering, and went west to Rossland, British Columbia, where, in the years to come, he blazed a trail in the use of aircraft for mining development.

He was employed in a mining engineering capacity with the British American Corporation of Rossland for a short time before becoming associated with the Consolidated Mining and Smelting Company of Trail, British Columbia, in 1901.

Canada's first gold ingot was poured at the Trail smelter in 1897 — the year that William Archibald went west.

William Archibald started off early doing considerable travelling for the Consolidated Mining and Smelting Company in the line of duty. On one of his mining trips to California he met Mary Sym and married her in 1901. He continued his travels through the years by train, boat or any method that would take him to where he was going. It was on another of his trips to their mining interests in the Yukon Territory in 1926 that he met Andy Cruickshank, then a member of the North West Mounted Police, who later became a pilot.

By 1929 Mr. Archibald had made up his mind to fly — even though he was 53 years of age. Besides, aircraft were

D.H. 60 Moth aircraft — William Archibald's first aircraft, shown at the old Sea Island Airport, Vancouver.
Photo courtesy of William Archibald.

starting to be used to open up the mining areas in out-of-the-way places, and special efforts were being put forth during 1928 and 1929 by a few exploration companies using aircraft. So Mr. Archibald commenced his flying instruction from Dominion Airways Limited at Lulu Island Airport, near Vancouver, in 1929. Dominion Airways was operated by the Dobbin Brothers. The company's chief instructor was G. S. "Barney" Jones-Evans. Captain E. C. W. "Clair" Dobbin was also an instructor. Both of these men instructed Mr. Archibald from time to time. Clair Dobbin was later stationed in Frobisher where he was associated with the Federal Electric Company during the building of the Distant Early Warning Line. Barney Jones-Evans later went to China to fly and was killed there.

When Mr. Archibald applied for his Private Pilot's Certificate in June, 1929, he had only ten hours' solo flying and thirty hours' dual flying to his credit. As a passenger, he had flown twenty-five hours. However, he completed his tests, and was issued his Private Pilot's Certificate No. 319, dated June 21, 1929, after satisfying the medical people as to his physical fitness. Squadron Leader E. L. Macleod, Commanding Officer of the R.C.A.F. Station at Vancouver, gave him his flight test there.

He had already purchased a D.H. 60M Gipsy Moth aircraft, CF-ADF, from The de Havilland Aircraft of Toronto, through Dominion Airways Limited, who was their Vancouver agent. It had been test flown by Leigh Capreol, who was de Havilland's first test pilot, and later became Airport Manager of the Montreal Airport for the Department of Transport. Mr. Archibald was the first private aircraft owner in British Columbia.

It was also at this time that Cominco (the Consolidated Mining and Smelting Company) sent a number of mechanics to the United States to take courses in motor mechanics, specializing on the engines which they planned to use in

their company's aircraft. Too, it was early in 1929 when Ken Dewar, Carl Gill and Eric Gunner were sent to Portland, Oregon, by Cominco to take a refresher flying course. W. G. "Bill" Jewitt and Bill Dean joined them in February at Vancouver, where the group received commercial pilot's licences. Ben Harrop left the R.C.A.F. to become one of these pioneer pilots with Cominco. For these six airmen, the company had six aircraft, a Fokker, two Fairchild, and three Gypsy Moths. They were put in service at Prince Albert, Saskatchewan, that spring. Bill Jewitt and Bill Dean spent the summer season flying in the bush.

Just after Mr. Archibald received his new Gipsy Moth and his new licence in June, 1929, he decided to make his first cross-country flight from Vancouver (Lulu Island Airport) to his home at Rossland via Princeton. He left on Saturday, June 22, for the interior, accompanied by William Bolton, a newly licensed private pilot with one arm, who was employed with the Aero Club of B.C., as a mechanic. They left Vancouver at 8:15 A.M., followed the Fraser Valley to Hope, and flew over the mountains to Princeton. They reached Princeton at 9:45 A.M. where they stopped for about forty-seven minutes and refuelled, then took off for Rossland, arriving at exactly 12:45 noon. It took them three hours and forty-three minutes to make the entire flight, a record for that time. Mr. Archibald made a perfect landing at the company's farm above the smelter. He was the first amateur pilot to fly to the interior of British Columbia. En route to Rossland, they flew through the Coquihalla Pass at 10,000 feet. The flight through the pass had been made once before in 1921 by G. K. Trim of the Aerial League of Canada.

Shortly after this flight was made, Mr. Archibald planned another one from Vancouver to Trail and then on to Kimberley, about 100 air miles from Trail. Kimberley is located in the interior

mountains of British Columbia. William Bolton of the Aero Club of B.C. also accompanied him on this flight. However, this trip over the mountains was not to be without incident.

With his new Gipsy Moth, CF-ADF, he was forced to make an emergency landing at Hanson's Meadow, Upper Priest River, Idaho, due to a fuel shortage. Mr. Archibald said that, while returning from Kimberley, the aircraft bucked a very heavy head wind. He had been following the Canada-United States boundary line fairly closely after passing Kootenay Lake in order to avoid the cloudy summits to the north and, when near the summit at the head of the Priest River, the marker in the gas tank dropped out of sight so that it seemed advisable to make for some meadows in view rather than endeavour to reach the Salmon River, which would have meant crossing the worst part of the summit. After a normal landing in the first instance, the aircraft was filled up with gas which they were able to get at Priest River about 40 miles away. While taking off, the aircraft went into too steep a bank and turned too close to the trees. This caused the machine to side-slip until a wing caught the ground and turned the aircraft around causing it to hit a fence. Now they had a damaged aircraft on their hands.

This accident was reported to the American Customs at Porthill. Upon paying a $100 fine, they were given permission to remove the aircraft by truck to Trail. This was an experience from which Mr. Archibald learned a lot about flying through the mountains, and used it to advantage in the years ahead when he was to make so many flights through these same mountains.

However, Mr. Archibald did not let this incident deter him in any way from flying from place to place by aircraft. After it was decided not to rebuild the Gipsy Moth, the Consolidated Mining and Smelting Company bought another de

Dragonfly aircraft, CF-AYF, at Creston, B.C., which was flown by William Archibald on some of his trips.
Photo courtesy of William Archibald.

Havilland Gipsy Moth biplane. Mr. Archibald, with Pilot-Instructor Barney Jones-Evans of Dominion Airways, Limited, Vancouver, picked up the new Moth on Saturday, November 2, 1929, at Calgary. They flew to Kimberley in two hours and twenty minutes, a very fast time then. Leaving the 'plane at Kimberley, Mr. Archibald went to his new summer home in Creston for the week-end. Then on Monday, Barney Jones-Evans, with Mr. Kirby of the Consolidated Mining and Smelting Company at Kimberley, flew the aircraft to Mr. Archibald's ranch home at Creston in one hour and twenty-five minutes. On this flight they met strong head winds. In the afternoon they left the ranch at Creston and flew to Trail in two hours' time, again facing strong head winds. Then on November 6, Wednesday, Mr. Archibald and Barney Jones-Evans flew from Trail to Felts Field, Spokane, Washington, in an hour and a quarter. They flew back to Creston later the same day.

Cominco then distributed some half-dozen air cones to various emergency fields between Vancouver and Kimberley. The company had a private landing field on their land near Kimberley, and one at Trail, also on company property. Mr. Archibald was also preparing a landing field on his own ground at Creston, with a landing strip suitable for the Moth.

At this time, Mr. Archibald was Manager of Mines for the Consolidated Mining and Smelting Company and planned on using as a landing field certain ground belonging to the company at Trail, until such time as the Municipality of Trail had a regular aerodrome in operation. The municipal aerodrome became known as "Columbia Gardens," and was built in 1930. It was seven miles east of Trail. It had one strip 2,000 feet long at first. A hanger was built as well.

Mr. Archibald had moved from his Rossland home in the fall of 1929 to his summer home in Creston in the East Kootenays. The fertile Creston Valley was set amongst towering mountains in all directions, which added to its beauty. His landing field was a mile and a half from his home, where he had erected a hangar and put out ground markings.

When the Archibalds first moved to Creston and Mr. Archibald started flying there, the drone of his plane could be heard in the valley every Sunday morning. For a short period there was considerable protest and opposition to his flying on Sundays from the local clergy and some of the people. They wanted it stopped. When he was interviewed by his opposers, he said he'd be glad to stop flying when they stopped people from driving their cars on Sundays.

Mr. Archibald established a flying school at Creston early in 1930 to teach promising engineers to fly. Instruction was given in aircraft equipped with wheels and skis. The class was taken to Kaslo in March, 1930, for instruction in the intricacies of float flying. The instructors were Page McPhee and W. G. "Bill" Jewitt, a World War I pilot. These engineers included Bob Walton, Curly Somerville, Leigh Bladon, Bill Castle, Jim Warren, Mike Finland, Charlie Gordon and Walter Jewitt. Bill Jewitt, who was then Vice-President of Mines for Cominco at Trail, was one of the company's first mining engineers to fly into the north.

In July, 1930, another new aircraft was purchased by Mr. Archibald, and he flew his new D.H. Puss Moth CF-AGT, a three-seater cabin aircraft, west from Toronto to Creston, in about forty-eight hours' elapsed time at the end of July. He was accompanied by Page McPhee. They made three stops en route.

On another occasion Mr. Archibald set out with Page McPhee to fly from Creston to Montreal in February, 1931. When they reached Fort William and landed the wheel-equipped aircraft in a snow-covered field because they could not find the local aerodrome, they were unable to take off. Mr. Archibald just left the aircraft behind and took the train to Montreal the next day.

Mr. Archibald and Page McPhee made the first trans-Canada flight from Vancouver to Halifax in May, 1931, in a Puss Moth aircraft equipped with wheels. Mr. Archibald was on a business trip to Montreal to attend a directors' meeting, and decided to visit his home town, Halifax, for both business and personal reasons. He was the son of Kent Archibald, who years earlier had operated the Salmon River Gold Mines in Halifax County with his brother Edward. From Halifax he flew to Truro, Nova Scotia, and Saint John, New Brunswick, to visit his relatives and friends. He, too, had lived in Truro at one time. His brother, Frank K. Archibald, and his sister, Mrs. W. J. Bird, lived in Truro. When Mr. Archibald arrived in Truro he didn't like the look of the field on which he was to land so, being a very careful pilot, he returned to Halifax and phoned to Truro to give instructions as to how any rough spots on the field should be marked. He suggested white sheets. Then he flew back to Truro and made a perfect landing. His combined business and pleasure trip to Halifax and Truro was short. He arrived in Truro on May 22, on Friday, and left for the west again on Saturday, May 23.

On the occasion of the visit of the Trans-Canada Air Pageant to Grand Forks, British Columbia, while he was en route to Vancouver in July, 1931, Mr. Archibald's flying ability and activities were receiving much attention. He was invited by the Grand Forks' Board of Trade to greet the fliers from the east at a luncheon in Grand Forks. A number of the pilots who were to fly to Vancouver from Grand Forks were somewhat keyed up about flying over the mountains — but not Mr. Archibald, who was quite at ease about the trip, considering it just a commonplace means of transport. Due to the many trips that he had made over such mountainous territory, he had become quite familiar with the mountains — so much so that he felt quite at home flying over them.

During 1931, he and Page McPhee logged some 40,000 air miles in a six-month period, a feat in aviation at that time. Mrs. Archibald often accompanied her husband on the flights, and flew frequently from their home in Creston to Columbia Gardens Airport. Their granddaughter was the youngest aeroplane passenger flown in the interior of British Columbia at the time. That was in October, 1930. The following year, on March 21, 1931, little Carol Ruth Warren at the age of fifteen days, accompanied by her mother, Mrs. James Warren, flew from Spokane, Washington, to Creston in D.H. Puss Moth CF-AGT, owned and piloted by her grandfather, Mr. Archibald, and became the youngest passenger to fly in Canada. It was a quick flight, made in one hour. Mrs. James Warren was Mr. Archibald's daughter, and was the only woman to go along on the Trans-Canada Air Pageant. James F. Warren's father was President of the Consolidated Mining and Smelting Company of Canada during these years. Jim Warren was a pilot with the company and was Mr. Archibald's son-in-law and the father of the two little girls who made the flights. He liked flying the Puss Moth. When he was at home and weather permitted, Mr. Archibald flew from his home in Creston to Trail daily in thirty minutes, going over the mountains. When he had to follow the Kootenay River and Lake route via Nelson it took him fifty-two minutes.

On June 22, 1932, Mr. Archibald, with Page McPhee as his co-pilot, made a record flight from Toronto to Trail in a very quiet way in Puss Moth CF-AGT. They left Toronto at 2:35 hours in the early morning, following a route to the north of the Great Lakes which was hazardous for flying aircraft on wheels.

As no airway was yet established north of the Great Lakes, it was customary for pilots to fly the route south of the Great Lakes, as it was considered safer, though longer than the northern route. They stopped first at Sudbury at 5:00 A.M., then at Fort William at 9:50 A.M., at Winnipeg at 1:35 P.M., at Moose Jaw at 5:10 P.M., and at Lethbridge at 9:30 P.M.. Just before dark, while they were flying from Lethbridge towards Crow's Nest Pass, the aircraft was subjected to strong head winds, almost equal to the speed of the machine, making it imperative that they turn back and find a spot in a field on which to land. This they did near Cowley — successfully and safely. Mr. Archibald said that they could probably have made Creston, but they thought it wiser to turn back to Cowley for the night. On the following day, the 23rd, they reached Creston in time for an early breakfast.

Page McPhee learned to fly in the United States. He was an air engineer also and did all the maintenance work on CF-AGT for Mr. Archibald. He really knew how to take good care of the machine, and spent much extra time on it. The aircraft was dual-controlled and each took turns at flying it, while the other relaxed.

The following morning, Mr. Archibald arrived at his office in Trail, as usual, shortly after nine o'clock, to carry out his duties for the day. This was typical of his matter-of-fact way of doing things. In fact, it had been said that he was partly responsible for the inauguration of the Trans-Canada Airway because he had flown back and forth so often over the "sticks" that it was considered advisable to lay out an airway under him!

Mr. Archibald usually visited the International Nickel Company's smelter in operation at Sudbury when he went east. Flying a wheel-equipped aircraft between Parry Sound and Sudbury, he and Page McPhee, who usually travelled together, felt that, if necessary, they could find the

odd field in which to land. He found a good place at Chapleau in a school ground southeast of the town; in a lumber yard at Dalton where Jim Warren once had to land unexpectedly with the company's Puss Moth. On the other side of Franz, en route to Fort William, there was just nothing on which a landing could be made safely. He found fields at Heron Bay and Jackfish. Fields were scattered all along the way from Nipigon to Fort William. From Fort William to Winnipeg, there were several fields, but they were mostly little fields. But then the Puss Moth only required a little field.

They found that in flying through the Rockies there was much wind but usually no bumps. However, they recalled one rough trip. Commuting from Creston to Trail was about 50 miles over the mountains. They climbed up Cultus Creek, going through a short pass. This trip took forty-five minutes by air, then a twenty-minute drive from the field to the plant. They had been to Vancouver many times. They found a good place to land at Midway, should it ever be necessary. There was an aerodrome at Grand Forks. The Okanagan Valley had a few places on which to land. The Similkameen Valley was usable. They knew of a good place at Keremeos and Princeton, and there was an aerodrome at Belfort. When the aircraft rose above the peaks, there were, strangely enough, a few meadows right on the top on which they could land. Their usual route was by Coalmount.

Mr. Archibald in his many flights had wonderful opportunities to behold the pristine beauty of so much of Canada — her fair countryside, her majestic mountains, the wealth of her mineral resources and her fruit orchards. These reasons help, perhaps, to explain why Mr. Archibald liked to fly, as he would have missed so much inherent satisfaction which all these wonders gave to him. By 1932, he had made two complete trans-Canada trips by air from

CF-AGD, William Archibald's second Gypsy 'plane, at Creston, B.C., which he flew during the winter of 1930-31.

Photo courtesy of William Archibald.

Victoria to Halifax and back. He was very partial to CF-AGT, his Puss Moth, and knew its every heartbeat. They had flown 1,300 hours in this aircraft, and only had to put down once.

By the end of 1932, he had accumulated some 1,300 hours of flying time, and had made many long trips and carried many passengers. He had made many hazardous trips over the Rocky Mountains, so that he considered them of no particular significance.

Mr. Archibald made history in 1934 when he and Page McPhee made the first landing on the newly-built intermediate aerodrome by the Civil Aviation Branch at Salmo, British Columbia, on the morning of April 23. The landing strip was some 2,000 feet or so in length by 200 feet wide, and had been graded and sodded. The aerodrome was on the Vancouver-Lethbridge air route, and was situated some three miles southeast of the town on the east side of the Salmon River. Everything was being done to have the aerodrome in good condition for the expected arrival of Dan McLean, Superintendent of Airways, with the Civil Aviation Branch, in the near future. Meantime, while en route from Creston to Trail one day, Mr. Archibald decided to try out the new aerodrome himself. Seeing what he had in mind as he circled the field, the workers and others quickly ushered the stray cows and horses off the landing strip, and removed the odd wheelbarrow. Sure enough, Mr. Archibald set his aircraft down on the field, looked over its condition, and left a half-hour later for Trail. The work at this field was carried out under the Unemployment Relief Scheme.

Mr. Archibald kept up his good work in aviation, then an announcement was made one day in March, 1936, that he was the recipient of the Trans-Canada Trophy for the year 1935.

This mining executive and pilot was entirely responsible for the inauguration of the extensive air service for the

Consolidated Mining and Smelting Company to assist them in their mining activities in inaccessible regions, particularly in northern Canada. This he did in the early thirties. He inaugurated the first air route in the north to Stewart, British Columbia, and Ketchikan, Alaska, from Trail in 1935. The care that he took in inaugurating and administering the services was evidenced by the fact that, although there had been as many as eleven aircraft in operation with a staff of fourteen pilots and mechanics, they had covered millions of miles, yet there had not been a single fatality. Some of the company's geologists became pilots, too.

It was routine for Mr. Archibald to fly from his home in Creston each morning, over the Nelson Mountain Range to Trail. Each evening, his day's work done, he returned home by 'plane. His broad field of mining interests — which stretched from remote areas on the west coast to the east coast, reaching areas as far north as Great Bear Lake, and south to Idaho — required that he devote considerable time to flying to reach these far-flung regions. During these remarkable flights, he covered a distance of about 1,500 miles a day — and yet this was only a normal day to him.

His total flying time as a pilot at the time of the award amounted to over 2,600 hours. During 1935, he logged 448 hours and 39 minutes' flying time, covering approximately 44,865 miles.

The following long distance flights were also carried out by Mr. Archibald in 1935, largely over mountainous areas:

68 trips —	Creston to Trail
2 trips —	Creston to Wells, Nevada
3 trips —	Creston to Vancouver and return
1 trip —	Creston to Halifax and return through northern Ontario
1 trip —	Creston to Truro, N.S., and return
2 trips —	Creston to Edmonton and return
1 trip —	Creston to Vanderhoof and return
1 trip —	Creston to Edmonton to Vanderhoof via Jasper
1 trip —	Creston to Winnipeg
1 trip —	Creston to Fort St. James.

The official presentation of the trophy itself was made on March 19, 1936, by the Honourable T. A. Crerar, Minister of Mines, acting on behalf of the Honourable Ian Mackenzie, Minister of National Defence, at the annual dinner of the Mining and Metallurgical Institute of Canada which was held in the Chateau Laurier in Ottawa. Mr. Archibald was attending the banquet in any case and flew east for that particular purpose, so advantage was taken of his presence there to present the trophy to him. Any feeling of disappointment on the part of the flying fraternity in not having an opportunity to participate in the presentation of the trophy was, to some extent, offset by the advantage afforded by the occasion to give many of Mr. Archibald's mining friends a better idea of the distinction signified by the award.

The Fifth Annual Roosevelt Goodwill Flight from Long Island, New York, to Montreal, took place in June, 1936, and Mr. Archibald in another new aeroplane, this time a D.H. 90 Dragonfly, flew in from Toronto. This was a five-place twin-motored biplane that had just arrived from England and was for the use of the executives of the Consolidated Mining and Smelting Company at Trail. It was the centre of much interest. With Mr. Archibald were Phil Garratt, then Manager of The de Havilland Aircraft, Toronto, and Page McPhee, who was with Mr. Archibald on so many of his flights. Pilot G. S. Gilmore also accompanied him on occasion in his Dragonfly.

During 1938, the year before Mr. Archibald retired, the company's pilots flew 4,128 hours in their operations, carrying 4,308 passengers and 1,078,250 pounds of freight and express. The

William Archibald's 'plane, CF-AGT, a Puss Moth, at Creston, B.C. in the thirties. Page McPhee (left) and William Archibald.
Photo courtesy of William Archibald.

company's fleet of aircraft consisted of two Fairchild 71's, four Hornet Moths, one Dragon Rapide, two Dragonflys, one Puss Moth and one Gypsy Moth. The principal bases of the company were at Marysville Airport, near the big mines at Kimberley, and at Columbia Gardens, serving the Trail district. Their field bases were at Fort St. James and Burns Lake, for northern British Columbia operations; at Fort McMurray for Alberta and Saskatchewan; at Resolution for the Northwest Territories; at The Pas, Manitoba; at Senneterre, Quebec, for Quebec; and at Sioux Lookout, Ontario, for their Ontario operations.

He had established his own weather-reporting system to receive information about weather conditions at Great Bear Lake, Lake Athabaska and Burns Lake, and tied in this information with various other sources of weather information. This, too, was a fine tribute to his resourcefulness.

Mr. Archibald was colour-blind most of his life. Once he arrived home driving a bright red roadster with red leather upholstery — but his wife never had nerve enough to tell him what colour it was, as he was always so conservative in his other habits. However, his son Donald was more than pleased with his father's flashy choice of colour!

It was the year after Mr. Archibald got his new D.H. Dragonfly that he and his son, Donald, made a flight to Montreal. On that particular flight they flew through Winnipeg, then went south to St. Paul and on to Chicago. Northwest Airlines was using Lockheed Electra aircraft on their routes then. As Mr. Archibald and Donald were approaching the airport at Chicago, one of Northwest Airlines' Lockheed Electras was also approaching the field. Mr. Archibald and Donald were alone, so Mr. Archibald instructed Donald to watch carefully as he wished to land after the Lockheed had done so. They had no radio equipment, so they kept circling the field behind the

Lockheed. After several circuits and fifteen or twenty minutes or so later, it was impossible to tell who was following whom. At this time their gas supply was running low and Mr. Archibald said: "I can't wait any longer; here we go. See if you can see a green light from the tower." Donald had been seeing the green light from the tower for the last ten minutes but his father didn't know it was a green light. Anyhow, they landed with the Lockheed right on their tail. While Mr. Archibald was clearing customs and taking care of the usual formalities, Donald went into the lunch counter and seated himself on a stool beside several air line crew members in uniform. He overheard one of them say that he was fifteen minutes late because the tower instructed him to allow a Canadian 'plane to land first, but the guy must have been sightseeing as he made six circuits before he finally came down!

On this same trip in May, 1937, a rather amusing incident occurred when Mr. Archibald was actually "up in the air" over Sarnia and couldn't land. Mr. Archibald was Supreme Grand Master of Sovereign Great Priory of Canada and sometimes made surprise visits to Masonic gatherings throughout the country. In this instance he flew to Sarnia to attend the installation ceremonies. However, he did not know that Sarnia did not have a landing field until he arrived at Detroit Airport. He was then advised to fly to Marysville and land his 'plane at the Port Huron Airport. It was when he arrived there that he discovered a flock of sheep contentedly grazing on the field. Returning to Detroit, he was finally driven to Sarnia in time to attend the installation ceremonies.

A professional mining engineer, William "Roe" Archibald, was known throughout Canada as "the flying engineer," and had flown from coast to coast in Canada more often than any other pilot. T. M. "Pat" Reid once said: "Why, that Old Man has landed on more airports and

fields than any other pilot in Canada." And it was an indisputable fact that, up until Trans-Canada Air Lines started operating their transcontinental flights, "the Grand Old Man of the air" had crossed the Rockies more times than all the other pilots in Canada.

Although he was very quiet and retiring he was extremely happy to have as his flying friends such men as Pat Reid, Jack Sanderson, Punch Dickins, Wop May, Leigh Brintnell, Romeo Vachon, Geoff O'Brien, amongst many, many others. He was never in such a hurry that he couldn't spend a few minutes talking with anyone as long as the subject was flying.

The Consolidated Mining and Smelting Company of Canada, Limited, known under its abbreviated title as "Cominco", was incorporated in 1906 under Dominion charter in order to consolidate under one ownership the Canadian Smelting Works at Trail, the War Eagle and Centre Star Mines at Rossland, the St. Eugene Mine at Moyie, and certain other companies.

Cominco has two big operations on the shores of Great Slave Lake. One is the Con Gold Mine at Yellowknife. Mr. Archibald was mostly responsible for developing this mine and keeping the mill operating, at first in laborious circumstances. This mine produced the first gold bars in the Northwest Territories. Early in 1953 its thousandth gold ingot was poured.

William "Roe" Archibald was known as "The Father of the Yellowknife Gold Fields" and it was through his insistent efforts, shrewdness and enthusiasm that the properties were developed.

Mr. Archibald retired in 1939 from his position as Vice-President in Charge of Mines with the Consolidated Mining and Smelting Company, Limited, having completed 38 years of service. He continued to live at Creston and to be actively interested in mining and engineering, having his office at 302 Bay Street, Toronto — also spending con-

William Archibald, Creston, B.C.
Photo courtesy of William Archibald.

siderable time there. He was, perhaps, the only Canadian grandfather ever to fly four generations of his own family. But he did not retire from flying until December, 1944, when at the age of 68, due to his physical condition, it was considered best for him if his licence was not renewed. He had been permitted to fly longer than other pilots with similar physical defects because he was accompanied by a pilot in his later years. His company, family or friends, usually saw to this. He was known as "Roe" to his friends, which was short for his second name, "Munroe".

On one of Mr. Archibald's trips to the west coast he had nothing to do so he browsed around, and bought a book on tides which gave all the details of times and heights or elevations. Some months later he wanted to see a Mr. Dunn who lived in Prince Rupert and worked for Cominco. So, he sent him a wire saying he would fly in on a certain day and at a certain time. He did, landing on the beach. He picked up Mr. Dunn and took off again. Somehow or other, word of this beach landing got around and reached officials of the Civil Aviation Branch in Vancouver. As a result, Mr. Archibald received a letter saying that they had not been notified that he had changed his aircraft from wheels to pontoons — and would he please drop in to see them on his next trip to Vancouver. Mr. Archibald called at the Vancouver office several months later. When the purpose of his visit there was broached, Mr. Archibald replied: ". . . . . I landed on wheels and if I'd had that little book on tides sooner I'd sure have saved myself making so many boat trips to Prince Rupert."

Another time while he was on the C.P.R. travelling west from Sudbury to Fort William he noticed a small clearing alongside of the track and, after getting the mile number from the conductor, he went to see the C.P.R. Vice-President at Winnipeg and succeeded in getting him to arrange for the section men of that area to put off a barrel of gas at that point. Later Mr. Archibald began to receive letters from the Civil Aviation Branch to the effect that . . . . . "it is reported on good authority that you flew from Fort William to Sudbury with wheel equipment. If this is so, please advise where and how you landed and refuelled."

Mr. Archibald's son, Donald, also took flying instruction from Barney Jones-Evans of Dominion Airways Limited, Lulu Island, in 1930, and in so doing got in Dutch with his father when he disobeyed Barney's orders about approaching the runway. The approach was over the B.C. Electric Company's line and the railway, as well as being directly over the hangar. When Barney told him he was too low, he held the throttle back as hard as he could and just managed to clear the obstacles. He lost his feeling of smugness in showing off when his instructor posted him for two whole weeks — the entire period for which he was to receive instruction. When his father learned of this, he told Donald in no uncertain terms that an aircraft was a machine to operate between two points in the shortest time and, in Mr. Archibald's own life, there never was a time when he lost sight of this fact. As a matter of fact, the day Mr. Archibald soloed he remained aloft for ninety minutes and everyone thought he was afraid to attempt a landing. Afterwards he said it was such a thrill to be up there all alone that he didn't ever want to come down! It is believed that he never lost that wonderful feeling of joy in flying throughout his whole life. Mr. Archibald worked very hard to be a good pilot and never tired of practising. Whenever he made a bad landing, he would often take off again and make several more landings until he was satisfied that he had corrected the fault. For relaxation at home on a Sunday morning, he would fly the Kootenay River from Kootenay Lake in Canada to Bonness Ferry, Idaho. Mr. Archibald may have thoroughly enjoyed this flying but, on more than one occasion, when Donald couldn't get out of going with him it turned him very green!

At the time of Mr. Archibald's death on Friday, November 10, 1949, following a heart attack while in Toronto, he was 73 years of age. He and Mrs. Archibald had one son, Donald K. Archibald and one daughter, Mrs. F. G. Rutley.

Whenever he flew, in his cordial and quiet way, he made friends for himself, for his company and for aviation in general. Yet he was a man with a strong mind and liked to finish whatever he set out to do. He took a keen interest in the welfare of the Creston valley in all its phases. He disliked any form of publicity.

It can well be said that by his enterprise, initiative and fine example of the practical use of the aeroplane, he rendered a great service to the development of air transport in Canada. In the inauguration of the extensive air services for Cominco, in establishing his own weather-reporting systems in the early days, and in establishing a flying school at Creston, his actions spoke for themselves on the various phases of aviation in Canada, showing forth in their true light. He, who loved seeing the grandeur of the Rockies as he winged his way through them and over them, will be remembered, too, as a pioneer of the great Yellowknife Gold Fields.

He was named a member of Canada's Aviation Hall of Fame in 1973. He was made a Companion of the Order of Flight (City of Edmonton).

1936

Arthur Massey "Matt" Berry

Citation: in recognition of northern transportation flights which he made in Alberta and the Northwest Territories, which included several hazardous flights to the Arctic Coast and some outstanding mercy flights

Arthur Massey "Matt" Berry, while associated with Canadian Airways Limited, Edmonton, was awarded the Trans-Canada Trophy for meritorious service in the advancement of aviation in Canada during 1936, "in recognition of northern transportation flights which he made in Alberta and the Northwest Territories, which included several hazardous flights to the Arctic Coast and some outstanding mercy flights." The announcement of the award was made on March 8, 1937, by Colonel L. R. Laflèche, Deputy Minister of the Department of National Defence, on behalf of the Honourable Ian Mackenzie, the Minister.

In congratulating Mr. Berry, the deputy minister, on behalf of the minister, emphasized his long record of excellent service in the advancement of civil aviation in this country.

Mr. Berry's devotion to duty and his extreme skill as a pilot had not only enhanced the already enviable reputation of Canadian pilots, but had, in addition, been the means of saving several lives.

The Committee of Award for the Trans-Canada Trophy for 1936 consisted of the following members:

J. A. Wilson, Controller of Civil Aviation, Department of Transport, Ottawa.

Air Vice-Marshal W. A. Bishop, V.C., D.S.O., M.C., D.F.C., A.F.C., McColl Frontenac Oil Co. Ltd., Montreal.

Wing Commander A. T. N. Cowley, Superintendent of Air Regulations, Department of Transport, Ottawa.

Squadron Leader C. R. Slemon, Royal Canadian Air Force, Department of National Defence, Ottawa.

His record in 1936 was a brilliant climax to many years of arduous, efficient and skilful service in northern flying, and was the most outstanding year of his career at that time. A most popular pilot in the north country, he was well known in flying circles and well liked and admired by those with whom he was acquainted.

Matt Berry was born on June 19, 1888, in the Township of March, near Ottawa, Ontario. He received his education there. Upon the death of his father, he moved to Guelph, Ontario, where he operated a farm close to the city.

When World War I broke out, Matt Berry enlisted in the 153rd Battalion of the Canadian Expeditionary Force in 1915, and received his commission as a Captain. Then he went overseas. He transferred to the Royal Flying Corps in England. Upon receiving flying instruction, he became a pilot. He was later returned to Canada where he served for a period as a flying instructor with the Royal Flying Corps at Deseronto, Ontario. He transferred to the Royal Air Force on July 24, 1918.

When World War I was over, Captain Matt Berry went to Ottawa where he was employed by the Soldier Settlement Board as District Superintendent of the Ottawa district for a year and a half before going to Alberta and buying a large farm near Rimbey early in 1921. The Depression in the following era was too much for him and his family so they sold the property and moved back to Ottawa in 1925 and Matt Berry went into the grocery business with a brother-in-law. He remained in the grocery business for a few years, and then decided to become a pilot and go into the flying business.

Doc Oaks, who was Director of Aerial Operations and Assistant Manager of Northern Aerial Minerals Exploration Company, had assured Matt Berry a job with the company by June 15, 1928, if he had his commercial licence. So, on April 24, 1928, Matt Berry submitted his application for a licence and took a refresher course in flying with the R.C.A.F. at Camp Borden in May, 1928. He received his Commercial Air Pilot's Certificate No. 330, dated May 25, 1928.

Jack Hammell, a Toronto mining promoter, and Doc Oaks, a mining engineer, were in the process of organizing Northern Aerial Minerals Exploration Limited to open up mining fields in the north. The company received its charter on February 10, 1928.

The Northern Aerial Minerals Exploration Company was one of the first manifestations by the mining industry of its realization that the pioneer flying of 1924, 1925 and 1926 in the Rouyn, Quebec, and the Red Lake, Ontario, districts had demonstrated the superb usefulness of the aeroplane in prospecting and the early development stages of mining.

So, in July, 1928, Matt Berry became associated with Northern Aerial Minerals Exploration Company, Toronto, under President Jack Hammell, and remained with the company for four years. During that time he carried out flying assignments, first in the Sioux Lookout area in northern Ontario, then in Manitoba, Saskatchewan, Alberta and British Columbia, until he reached the then distant, unknown and inhospitable Baker Lake area in the Northwest Territories. His flights were mostly made on mining exploration work.

During the first summer of Northern Aerial Mineral Exploration's operations in 1928, T. M. "Pat" Reid, flying G-CATM, a Loening amphibian, and Matt Berry, flying G-CARK, a Fokker Super Universal, made pioneer flights to carry prospectors along with their equipment

and supplies to various places in the northern Hudson Bay area. The pioneering trip left Winnipeg for The Pas, then went northeast to Fort Churchill, Cape Eskimo, Chesterfield Inlet, on the northwest coast of Hudson Bay, and Baker Lake. There the remaining prospectors and their supplies were left. Matt Berry and Pat Reid separated at Chesterfield Inlet and Pat Reid and C. A. "Duke" Schiller took the Loening amphibian down around James Bay and up the east coast of the bay, while Matt Berry carried on alone from Chesterfield Inlet, Baker Lake and Wager Bay. Matt Berry spent the summer ferrying prospectors around the area, as far away as Wager Bay. He told of heart-rending conditions there — of constant gales and many blizzards, practically no shelter for aircraft, anchors dragging on moored aircraft and having to beach them on the rocky shores.

Coming south in October, just before the freeze-up, Matt Berry landed at Churchill to refuel. Ice was then in the river; it was cold and a gale was starting to blow — and the sea was heavy. In order to get away at all, Matt Berry had to take off as soon as his aircraft was refuelled before the river froze. Taxiing to take off in the heavy seas, a float was damaged and the aircraft had to be beached. Fortunately, no one was injured. This was the only loss of any size in the north in 1928, yet hundreds of hours of flying were carried out by many aircraft.

Pat Reid flew with Matt Berry on his first flight into the Northwest Territories from Churchill to Chesterfield Inlet in 1928, and from that time on took a personal interest in his flying career.

These are some of the aircraft flown by Northern Aerial Minerals Exploration Company during their first year of operations in 1928: G-CARA, G-CARJ, G-CARE and G-CATL, all Fairchild FC2's: G-CARU, a D.H. 60X Moth; G-CARK, a Fokker Super Universal; and

G-CATM, a Loening amphibian.

Matt Berry was given a flying instructor's course by the R.C.A.F. at Camp Borden, Ontario, in November and December, 1929. His instructor was Flight Lieutenant G. R. Howsam.

During 1930 and 1931, Matt Berry made many flights to the Coppermine River and Great Bear Lake areas on mining and transportation work for his company. He flew during both summer and winter in the northern district.

Matt Berry had just become Chief Pilot with Northern Aerial Minerals Exploration Company when, in February, 1932, the company sold most of its aerial equipment to Canadian Airways, so Matt Berry then went along with Canadian Airways. However, shortly afterwards, in two months' time, he joined the staff of the newly formed Mackenzie Air Service, whose President and founder was W. Leigh Brintnell.

While in the employ of Mackenzie Air Service, Matt Berry went on an arduous and venturous flight in the winter of 1933-34 when he and Freddie Hodgins went to Gjoa Haven, King William Land, to bring back a load of furs for the Canalaska Trading Company (The Northern Whaling and Trading Company) and the Hudson's Bay Company. The visibility on this flight was extremely poor due to a frosty haze over Queen Maud Gulf. The sea, itself, appeared very rough and was filled with old ice from the north channel, making it both treacherous and dangerous. This exhausting flight was made when the weather was -45° F., and for navigation a magnetic compass was used, with the magnetic variation ranging up to 50°. The flight was made in CF-ATW, a Fokker Super Universal, bought by Mackenzie Air Service in November, 1932, from General Aviation Manufacturing Corporation, Dundalk, Maryland. The flight by Matt Berry was notable as it was the first one to King William Land that had been made with a commercial aircraft equipped with skis.

Con Farrell of Canadian Airways and his party at Gordon Lake, north of Great Slave Lake, N.W.T., when found by Matt Berry on September 11, 1935. From left to right: Indian interpreter from R.C.M.P., Fort Reliance, Con Farrell, Frank Hartley (Matt Berry's mechanic) and Frank Kelly (Con Farrell's mechanic).
Photo courtesy Matt Berry.

On another occasion when Matt Berry was flying CF-ATW from Wilmot Island to Cambridge Bay, Victoria Island, on the morning of April 4, 1934, he was suddenly encompassed by heavy fog and snow which covered the entire bay. With no landing area in sight, he flew inland hoping to find the trading post. He then flew to Finlayson Island in search of a place to land but saw nothing that looked at all suitable. As his gas was running low, he flew as near as possible to the trading post where the Canalaska Trading Company's buildings were at Cambridge Bay. When his engine cut out, he landed on a small lake behind the residence. He made a perfect landing about the centre of the lake, but while still going very fast the port ski struck a large hidden snow-covered boulder. The ski was carried away, throwing the aircraft on to a gravel ridge to the right where the starboard ski was knocked off and the aircraft slid forward on its fuselage. The left wing was broken off about six feet from the top. Both bottom longerons were broken at the forward undercarriage fittings, and the under-carriage was a complete loss.
However, the engine was undamaged. Air engineer Freddie Hodgins removed the engine and stored it in the Hudson's Bay warehouse. They had one passenger on board, Mr. P. Gibson, inspector for the Hudson's Bay Company. No one was injured.

Matt Berry had landed safely at the same place on March 15 — but this time the well-hidden boulder had to put its ugly head in the way of one of the air-craft's skis and cause so much damage to the aircraft.

It was announced over the radio that Matt Berry and Freddie Hodgins were missing. Stan McMillan of Mackenzie Air Service went in search of them and flew them out from Cambridge Bay to Coppermine on April 19.

The Edmonton and Northern Alberta Aero Club's big annual Air Day Show on

May 24, 1934, featuring spot landings, balloon bursting, bomb dropping and stunting, proved very successful. However, it was cut short about 4:30 P.M. by the tragic crash of Mackenzie Air Service's Fokker 14, CF-AUD, when it nosed into the ground just after take off, causing the death of air engineer Freddie Hodgins, seriously injuring Matt Berry, the pilot, and James Bell, the Airport Manager. It was believed that the controls were crossed in some way during the overhaul, causing the crash.

Matt Berry returned to Canadian Airways Limited in December, 1934, under Punch Dickins, a veteran bush pilot and winner of the Trans-Canada Trophy for 1928. Punch Dickins was happy to see him return to Canadian Airways after his convalescence from the accident he had several months earlier. After the severe shaking up and the serious injuries which Matt Berry had received, Mackenzie Air Service considered he would be unable to fly again and were reluctant about his returning to the company as a pilot. However, Punch Dickins did not share this conviction. Matt Berry carried out transportation flights for Canadian Airways in the Mackenzie River district and the North-west Territories, making many flights in the vicinity of the Coppermine River and Great Bear Lake. Punch Dickins' con-viction proved to be right in the years to come.

When Matt Berry rejoined Canadian Airways he had been away from flying for six or seven months, so he went to Camp Borden, Ontario, to take a refresher course in flying with the R.C.A.F., and at the same time he took an Instrument Flying Course during January and February, 1935. His in-structors at Camp Borden were Dave Harding and Doug Edwards. Dave Harding was well known then both as a flier and a football player. Immediately after the completion of this course, Matt Berry went to the R.C.A.F. Station at

Ottawa for one week's short course in radio beacon flying.

On June 15, 1935, Matt Berry piloted a Fairchild to Cameron Bay and Resolution in the Northwest Territories, a distance of 428 miles, to bring out two sick Indians.

In 1935, Conway Farrell of Canadian Airways and his air engineer, Frank Hartley, were lost for eleven days in the Barrens. They had flown a number of trappers to their northern posts during the month of August. They were en route from Musk Ox Lake to Fort Reliance, about 750 miles north of Edmonton, when a sudden blizzard descended upon them. In an endeavour to escape the storm, they flew west. They made several attempts to land but were unable to do so. Now they were running out of gas, with about five gallons left. They landed their pontoon-equipped aircraft on Gordon Lake, near an island. Con Farrell was carrying a small portable radio amongst the baggage in his aircraft. However, as he was very rusty in its operation, he was slow in sending a message. When he managed to contact Fort Rae, Con Farrell gave their position as close to Fort Reliance, when actually they were on the north end of Gordon Lake, some 150 miles away.

Matt Berry was at Fort Rae at the time the message came through about Con Farrell's predicament. Matt Berry and his air engineer, Frank Kelly, then took off to look for Con Farrell and his party. They did not have a radio set in their aircraft so they had to drop in at Fort Rae from time to time to pick up any additional news that Con Farrell might have sent regarding his position. When no aircraft turned up within a few days, Con Farrell became extremely annoyed because he thought that the rescue 'craft were not looking for them at the position which he gave. So he voiced his annoyance vehemently over his radio to the station at Fort Rae. When Matt Berry and Frank Kelly learned of this, they decided that they would have some fun with Con Farrell, if and when they did find him and his party, and perhaps teach him a lesson in courtesy. Matt Berry and Frank Kelly put in six days of intensive searching before they located the lost party and their Junkers aircraft CF-AMZ on a small island at the north end of Gordon Lake, north of Great Slave Lake, Northwest Territories — 150 miles from Fort Reliance — scarcely the position which Con Farrell gave as his location.

The stranded party had large signal fires burning so that any aircraft in the vicinity could not possibly miss their camp. So, deciding to have some fun with the stranded party, Matt Berry and Frank Kelly flew over their camp at 5,000 feet and gave no indication that they had noticed the signal fires, or even the camp itself. Con Farrell became very concerned at this aircraft passing over, apparently not seeing their fires or their camp. After letting them worry over this for a good half-hour, Matt Berry and Frank Kelly returned to rescue them! After this Con Farrell was careful not to call them unwelcome names over his radio set and was extremely grateful to be picked up, especially since their emergency rations had been nearly all destroyed when a tin of fly-tox was spilled over them. On September 11, 1935, Matt Berry and his party arrived back at Fort McMurray. After having spent eleven days camping out, Con Farrell and his party were none the worse for their experience. Con Farrell later joined Canadian Pacific Air Lines, Vancouver, as Terminal Superintendent.

Two of Matt Berry's many outstanding flights were made to the Arctic in the spring of 1936. Matt Berry, while employed by Canadian Airways, Edmonton, made the annual trip for Canalaska Trading Company to Cambridge Bay to pick up a load of white fox furs; and the other trip was to Read Island (Victoria Island) for the Hudson's Bay Company to pick up another load of white fox furs.

Both flights required great skill as a pilot and thorough knowledge of Arctic coast flying. Navigating through all these white wastes was a tough job, as Matt Berry and Frank Hartley used only a magnetic compass which varied greatly at times. They had no other navigation aids to assist them.

During the winter and spring of 1936, many flights of particular importance for mining and prospecting companies were made by Matt Berry to the Goldfields and Yellowknife areas. Matt Berry and Frank Hartley carried a number of canoes from Fort McMurray to the Yellowknife area for these companies to use, thus making their transportation problems easier. This was done by attaching a canoe under each wing of Junkers aircraft CF-ARI. This method of canoe-carrying was considered superior to any other method of carrying them outside the aircraft.

One day in May, 1936, while Matt Berry was flying CF-ARI for Canadian Airways Limited, he had a complete

engine failure when he was about forty-five minutes' flying time north of Fort McMurray. He landed the aircraft on the Athabaska River with its full load of passengers and freight. When the S.S. Athabaska River came along, CF-ARI surrendered to a more ancient and tedious method of travel, when Captain Alexander of the sternwheeler kindly offered to take the Junkers aircraft in tow and haul it back to Fort McMurray, if it could be done. This towing job was a difficult operation for the sternwheeler. However, by placing the Junkers aircraft to the side of the sternwheeler, the towing operation was accomplished. They arrived back at Fort McMurray before any search 'craft had started out to look for them.

When summer came, Matt Berry was off flying to the Arctic coast again where he visited Burnside Harbour (Bathurst Inlet), Read Island and Victoria Island for the Hudson's Bay Company. On the trip from Coppermine to the mission at Burnside Harbour, Matt Berry flew a

Junkers CF-ARI towed up the Athabaska River by the sternwheeler S.S. Athabaska River *in May, 1936. Matt Berry is shown in photo.*
Photo courtesy Matt Berry.

Matt Berry and Frank Hartley, his mechanic, when they arrived in Edmonton, from Read Island and Coppermine, with a load of white fox furs for the Hudson's Bay Company, in the spring of 1936.
Photo courtesy of Matt Berry.

party, which included the Hudson's Bay Company's manager and his wife, a priest from the Roman Catholic Mission at Coppermine and Dr. Fred Jolliffe of the Geological Survey of Canada. While there, Patsy Klengenberg, a fur trader, was reported overdue in his schooner so, on the return flight, Matt Berry and air engineer Frank Hartley searched the sea from the air and found him temporarily disabled in the lee of an island in Bathurst Inlet. He had lost his propeller in water about thirty feet deep, but in the crystal-clear water it could be clearly seen, and he managed to recover it without assistance.

Matt Berry did most of the flying for Dr. Fred Henderson of the Geological Survey of Canada while he was making a geological survey of the Nenacho Lake area. He had a number of survey parties in the field and this required a lot of flying. Dr. Henderson was particularly pleased and highly complimented Matt Berry on the admirable flying which he did for them on this important work during the summer of 1936. In one day alone, Matt Berry accomplished 25 landings when completing one specific district.

During the early autumn of 1936, Flight Lieutenant Sheldon W. Coleman and his mechanic, Leading Aircraftsman Joseph A. Fortey of the R.C.A.F. became lost somewhere in the Barrens of the Northwest Territories. They had been missing since August 17. Matt Berry was called upon to assist in the rescue. His first job was to fly two floats for a stranded R.C.A.F. Fairchild 71 aircraft to Fort Reliance, Northwest Territories, as aircraft were urgently needed for the search. After considerable difficulty the floats were secured to his aircraft, CF-ARI. This was the first time that an undertaking of this nature had been carried out. Matt Berry took off from Cooking Lake, Alberta, and, in spite of the reduced speed of his aircraft (from 75 to 80 miles per hour) due to the carrying

of these extra floats, he flew the 750 odd miles from Cooking Lake (Edmonton) to Fort Reliance the same day and did not make more than two turns in the air during the flight!

The delivery of these floats meant that three more aircraft could be made available for the search, as the Fairchild 71, which was equipped with the floats which had been flown in, would be able to ferry gas to keep the two Bellancas in operation, as they had been unserviceable due to a shortage of gasoline.

After delivering the floats, Matt Berry was asked to assist further in view of his knowledge of the north country. By this time the two members of the R.C.A.F. had been missing for twenty-five days and freeze-up was rapidly approaching. Five days later, when Matt Berry, in aircraft CF-AAO, a Fairchild, accompanied by air engineer Frank Hartley, found the party in a most unlikely spot in the Point Lake area, 250 miles northwest of Fort Reliance, they were on the point of starvation. Fort Reliance is northeast of Edmonton, some 750 miles.

Flight Lieutenant Sheldon Coleman and Leading Aircraftsman Joseph Fortey left a point 220 miles northeast of Fort Reliance, on August 17, 1936, to fly to Fort Reliance. They had been assisting the crew of a disabled aircraft which had encountered trouble while employed on photographic operations for mapping. When this disabled aircraft was visited by air on August 21, it was learned that Coleman had left for Reliance but had not yet reached there. His aircraft had an adequate supply of fuel for the trip, and a favourable wind. A search was immediately undertaken in an endeavour to locate these men. Six R.C.A.F. aircraft and two chartered civil aircraft took part in the search.[1]

Some 70,000 square miles were covered, and still they had no success. However, on September 12 some trappers in the Lac de Gras area, which is quite far northwest of the route the

missing aircraft was supposed to have taken, told members of the search party that they had observed an unidentified seaplane flying north around the time that Coleman and Fortey had started their flight to Reliance. Now, with this information, the search was extended northward. On September 13, 1936, they found some empty gas drums belonging to the missing aircraft on a lake about 30 miles northwest of Lac de Gras. Attached to one of these was a note from the missing men saying that they had only enough fuel left for one hour's flying — and they were now intending to fly south for thirty minutes and then land.[2]

The search parties were having their own tough time with the stormy weather, and freezing temperatures. Ceilings were low and visibility was very limited. All this hampered the search. Freeze-up was imminent, almost forcing the searchers to withdraw their seaplanes from their temporary base in the Lac de Gras area. They had made every effort to find the men in view of the freezing conditions, and thought that surely they would be located soon.[3]

Sheldon Coleman and Joseph Fortey were found by Matt Berry on September 16, 1936, about 150 miles northwest of Fort Reliance, after a month's anxiety for their safety. Although the rescuers were expecting to find the missing aircraft and crew south of the point where the note was left, they were located northwest of this point, much to everyone's surprise.[4] This was, no doubt, due to their having trouble with their compass. It was so cold when Matt Berry landed that some two inches of ice formed on the floats of the aircraft, the rudder and tail plane, Matt Berry said.

They did have emergency rations for one week, and they had fishing tackle along with them, but no guns. They were glad to see the lights of home again, after Matt Berry flew them back to civilization in blustery weather, just as temperatures were dropping sharply to the freezing point. For Matt Berry's outstanding rescue work, he received recognition from the City of Edmonton in the form of an illuminated address.

Then in December, 1936, the mission schooner, *Our Lady of Lourdes*, was trapped in the ice off the Arctic coast. Bishop Peter Fallaize, two priests and three Eskimo children tramped inland from the schooner and sought shelter at the Roman Catholic Mission at Hornaday River, 50 miles south of Letty Harbour on the Arctic coast. They were in quite serious condition due to lack of food when Matt Berry found them. He left Edmonton on December 3, 1936, in Canadian Airways' Junkers CF-ARI, accompanied by Air Engineer H. R. Terpening, in an endeavour to rescue the party. Matt Berry made the flight from Aklavik to Hornaday River on December 9, and the next day flew to Letty Harbour for a load of supplies for the party. It became necessary to fly some members of the party out, due to the serious shortage of food supplies. They were held at Hornaday River for eleven days on account of the weather and, on December 19, during the return flight Matt Berry was forced down on a small lake half-way between Hornaday River and Aklavik and they had to spend the night in a blizzard, when the weather was 40 degrees below zero F. Matt Berry returned to Edmonton on December 27, 1936, his rescue mission having been accomplished.[5]

The following are extracts from Matt Berry's reports on the trip to Hornaday River. These cover only the days on which he flew, so the condition of the weather on the days when he made no flight can be imagined.

Dec. 3 —Edmonton-McMurray, 280 m., McMurray-Chipewyan, 151 m.
Dec. 4 —Chipewyan-Smith, 105 miles, Smith-Resolution 137 miles. Strong head winds upstairs. At Resolution started to blow a gale as we landed, and remained quite dirty rest of afternoon.
Dec. 5 —Resolution-Rae, 177 miles. Rae-Norman, 385 miles. Beautiful clear day.
Dec. 6 —Norman-Good, Hope, 162 miles. Unable to land on runways at Good Hope due to low-lying fog in river valley. Made three attempts to get on to runway but had to give up as it was too dangerous. Landing on south side of island and was able to taxi round. Very cold -40° F. on the river.
Dec. 7 —Good Hope-Arctic Red River, 208 miles. Arctic Red-Aklavik, 108 miles. -54° F. at Good Hope. Very foggy on the river this morning and we were forced to wait till it cleared somewhat to take off. Heavy fog over river at Thunder River so we could not land at all. Open water about 200 yards from Clark's house so it will be very unlikely we can land there this trip.
Dec. 9 —Aklavik-Mission, 350 miles. Clear all the way over to Darnley Bay but blowing a gale from south when we arrived. Could not see landing marked out for us but we got down okay even though Bay is quite rough. (Priests had marked out landing with sacks of coal.)
Dec. 10 —Mission-Letty, 60 miles; Letty-Mission, 60 miles. Took off 9:35, landed 12:30. Brought back two passengers. Father Griffin and brother. Brought back load of grub for Mission. Got away to an early start hoping to be able to go through to Aklavik today, but light was bad when we returned from Letty Harbour

and weather report from Aklavik was bad so we tied up for day. Quite cloudy to west and south. Radio very poor today.
Dec. 14 —Mission-Mission, 75 miles. Took off 10:15 a.m. with Bishop Fallaize and party, six passengers. Landed 11:00 a.m.
Seemed to be clearing from southwest and we had a good report from Aklavik so took off even though it was still quite dark. Unable to read the instruments in cockpit. Got some place over Darnley Bay but had to turn back as it got too dark to follow anything. Seemed to be overcast and probably snow ahead.
Dec. 19 —Mission-Bishop Lake, 225 miles. Took off 10:15 a.m. with party of six. Landed 12:30.
Clear morning and good report from Aklavik so we pushed off. Got quite hazy later and at Liverpool Bay it was so bad we could not follow coastline at all. Forced to land on small lake off the coast. Visibility nil and light terrible. -28° F. on the ground.
Dec. 20 —Bishop Lake-Aklavik, 200 miles. Took off 10:45 a.m. Clear morning with temperature of -40° F. but got very hazy at bottom of Husky Inlet. Missed Husky Lakes entirely and had to fly compass course across to Campbell Lake. Clear from there in to Aklavik. -50° F. at Aklavik.
Dec. 21 —Aklavik-Arctic Red River, 108 miles; Arctic Red River-Good Hope, 208 miles. -50° F. Aklavik, -60° F. Good Hope.
Dec. 22 —Good Hope-Norman, 162

Matt Barry and Frank Hartley carrying two canoes beneath the wings of their Junkers aircraft, CF-ARI, in the spring of 1936. Note the aircraft is on skis. This method was for winter transport only.
Photo courtesy of Matt Berry.

miles. –60° F. at Good Hope.
Dec. 23 —Norman-Contact Bay, 270 miles. Cameron Bay filled with fog, not able to land there. Came over to Contact Lake.
Dec. 24 —Contact Bay-Rae-Yellowknife-Resolution. 428 miles.
Dec. 25 —Resolution-Smith, 207 miles. Spied a plane in slough 35 miles north of Smith. Could not land with load so went on to Smith, emptied machine and returned. Found Gil MacLaren with disabled engine. Flew MacLaren and engineer to Smith.
Dec. 26 —Smith-McMurray, 256 miles, McMurray-Newbrook, 205 miles. After passing Newbrook storm got so thick visibility so bad was forced to turn back and try a landing. The field near the village looked good and was large enough so I went down. Unfortunately there was a narrow strip of plowing across the stubble and when the skis hit this the left one turned under, breaking the pedestal. Undercarriage was not injured. Made a solid block pedestal that night, ready to take off in the morning.
Dec. 27 —Newbrook-Edmonton, 80 miles. Took off light to test ski and to take load from a small lake west of Newbrook instead of attempting to get out of rough field. New pedestal okay.[6]

During the year that Matt Berry was awarded the Trans-Canada Trophy, he flew various hospital cases under adverse weather conditions — the most outstanding of which was in search of Dr. Lewis who was weather-bound in the Lake Athabaska Delta. Dr. Lewis had been required to attend a very sick woman at Fort Chipewyan. The flight began at 3:00 A.M. during a heavy snowstorm. It took two hours to find the doctor, since his location was unknown as he was obscured from view in one of the numerous channels in the Delta. The trip was successful and the woman's life was saved.

Matt Berry's flying time in 1936 was 691 hours and 40 minutes. His total flying time at the time of the award was about 7,000 hours, carried out mostly on northern transportation work in Alberta and the Northwest Territories, and included the hazardous flights he made to the Arctic.

Through the years Matt Berry had become thoroughly experienced in every phase of flying. Acknowledgement was made of this when he was awarded the Trans-Canada Trophy for 1936. This year was to be long remembered by him in so many ways.

The official presentation of the trophy took place on March 17, 1937, at the annual meeting of the Canadian Institute of Mining and Metallurgy in the Mount Royal Hotel in Montreal and was made by Air Vice-Marshal W. A. "Billy" Bishop, V.C., D.S.O., M.C., D.F.C., A.F.C.

Matt Berry left Canadian Airways early in 1937 to accept the position of General Manager of the Northern Transportation Company, Waterways, a subsidiary of Eldorado Gold Mines, which was then opening up the first radium mine in Canada at Eldorado.

When World War II broke out in 1939, Matt Berry volunteered his services to the R.C.A.F., but due to his age he was not accepted.

Early in 1940 Matt Berry left the Northern Transportation Company, and he and Charles "Cy" Becker opened and operated No. 7 Air Observers School at Portage la Prairie, Manitoba, for Yukon Southern Air Transport. Cy Becker returned to Edmonton when Canadian Pacific Air Lines was organized in 1942, and Matt Berry remained as Civil Manager of the School until Grant McConachie, the President, asked him to return to the Mackenzie River district to start building landing strips, and enlarge those already in existence, along the Athabaska and Mackenzie Rivers to serve the Canol Project (Canadian Oil Line). The United States was in need of additional fuel at the time due to their entry into World War II in December, 1941.

The Canol Project was a joint defence undertaking between Canada and the United States. An agreement on the development of the Canol Project was reached in June, 1942. Under the terms of this agreement, the cost of the project was to be borne by the United States. The project was fourfold: to increase the production of the Norman Wells oil field for the use of the armed forces in north-western Canada; the construction of a pipe line to carry the crude oil from Norman Wells to Whitehorse; the erection of a refinery at Whitehorse to provide aviation gasoline and other petroleum products; and the construction of supplementary pipe lines for the distribution of the petroleum products from the refinery. Canada was also to provide sites and rights of way; while the United States would retain ownership of the pipe line and refinery until the end of the war, when they would be offered for sale. The Canadian Government was to have the first option to purchase them.

The regular means of transporting supplies from Waterways to Norman Wells was by boat down the Athabaska River to Lake Athabaska and thence down the Slave River to Fort Fitzgerald. At this point, a series of rapids on the Slave River necessitated a 16-mile portage by road to Fort Smith. The water route continued from Fort Smith down the Slave River to Great Slave Lake, thence westward across the lake and down the Mackenzie River to Norman Wells. There were also tractor trails in the winter time.

As there were not enough boats and barges on the Mackenzie River to carry the equipment down the river, pre-fabricated barges and diesel tugs were shipped to Waterways where they were assembled in the shipyards built during the latter part of 1942.

As a speedier method of transportation was required, an agreement was reached between the United States and Canada to enlarge the landing strips already in existence and build others along the Athabaska and Mackenzie Rivers so that supplies could be flown in by air to expedite the construction of the Canol Project.

So, early in 1942, Matt Berry was appointed Superintendent of Con-struction for Canadian Pacific Air Lines for the building of the flight strips for aircraft flying men and supplies for the Canol Project. Canadian Pacific Air Lines had finished enlarging the landing strip at Fort McMurray and were just starting to enlarge the one at Fort Smith, when the American troops and civil contractors arrived on the scene in the late summer of 1942 to start work on the Canol Project.

Matt Berry was then loaned by Canadian Pacific Air Lines to the new aerodrome contractors, Bechtel, Price and Callahan of Edmonton, to choose the new sites for flight strips and to superintend their construction, as well as the enlarging of the existing strips at Fort McMurray, the 1,200 ft. strip at Fort Smith and the one at Fort Resolution.

The construction of the 5,000 ft. by 500 ft. landing strips commenced late in August, 1942. The flight strips along the Athabaska River and the Mackenzie River were built at Fort McMurray, Embarras, Fort Smith, Fort Resolution, Hay River, Fort Providence, Fort Simp-son, Wrigley, Norman Wells and Canol Camp, to facilitate bringing in personnel, mail and light freight and supplies for the early construction of the Canol Pipe Line and the Canol Road.

Later on, flight strips were built along the route from Norman Wells to Aklavik,

partly as an alternative air route to the Northwest Staging Route to Alaska, and partly to relieve the traffic situation at the Whitehorse Airport.

On completion of the landing strips along the Mackenzie and Athabaska Rivers, Matt Berry then became associated with the "Marine Operators" of the firm of Cunningham and Keiwit, Contractors, from Omaha, Nebraska. He was Superintendent of their "operation water transportation" from Fort Smith to Norman Wells and Canol Camp until the completion of the Canol Pipe Line and the oil refinery at Whitehorse, Yukon Territory.

Matt Berry's next move upon leaving the Canol Project was to go to Toronto in 1944 and purchase CF-OAE, and then do some contract flying for Canadian Pacific Air Lines.

A contract was awarded by the Department of Transport to A. M. Berry in 1944 to construct a road from the Yellowknife settlement to the airport site, a distance of some four and a half to five miles, and to make minor improvements to the existing landing strip. This work was to be done on a cost-plus-percentage basis.

Matt Berry selected the route for the road himself, and built the road from the Yellowknife settlement to the airport in the fall of 1944, stopping at freeze-up time; while Larry Somerville, an engineer from the Department of Transport, took part in laying out the road.

At that time, the U.S. Army Engineers had just completed the Canol Project and had a lot of surplus equipment on their hands. To move this used equipment out of the country would be expensive. So the larger equipment, including blade graders, trucks, bulldozers and scrapers, was purchased by the Department of Mines and Resources from the United States Government. Then the equipment was made available for Matt Berry's use.

When the spring of 1945 arrived, it was decided by the Department of

Transport, the Department of Mines and Resources and Canadian Pacific Air Lines to build a new 5,000 ft. by 500 ft. landing strip first. Meanwhile, Matt Berry was continuing his work on the five-mile access road. Since they were pleased with Matt Berry's work during 1944, the Department of Transport entered into a similar contract with him in 1945 to put Canadian Pacific Air Lines' existing 3,473 ft. landing strip in shape to take larger aircraft by enlarging it; and also constructing a new gravel landing strip that was planned for Yellowknife Airport.

Then in 1945 he formed A. M. Berry and Company, General Contractors, at Yellowknife, with an office in Edmonton. This was at the time that the Yellowknife Airport was coming into existence as a result of a new gold rush to the area.

Later, other construction work at Yellowknife Airport, amounting to around $700,000, was given to A. M. Berry and Company on a cost-plus-percentage basis and work started on May 13, 1946. This work included building landing strips, installation of a radio range, roads and buildings, and so on.

On August 28, 1947, W. M. Neal, Chairman and President of the Canadian Pacific Railway Company of Montreal, flew in to Yellowknife to officiate at the opening of the N-S runway. This N-S runway replaced Canadian Pacific Air Lines' original landing strip. The N-S runway, as well as the NW-SE runway, had gravel surfaces. After visiting the gold mines in the area, Mr. Neal arrived by 'plane for the ceremony. With him was Grant McConachie, President of Canadian Pacific Air Lines and others. Resident Engineer E. J. Garrett, Fred Fraser, Matt Berry, the contractor, and a number of local people met the party.

The radio range road, site and trans-mitter building were not completed until mid-September, 1947. The site was located three and a half miles due south of the N-S landing strip. The radio range went into operation in November, 1947.

This very same year, 1947, the R.C.A.F., who had been using DC-4's and North Star aircraft from a base at Yellowknife on photographic survey work and re-supply of the Loran stations and other northern outposts, were wanting longer runways, up to 6,000 feet.

Matt Berry was still the prime contractor for the airport construction work during 1947 and 1948, when some half-million dollars was spent on the airport.

After finishing his work at Yellowknife Airport, Matt Berry then became President of Davenport Mining Company Limited of Toronto, Ontario. The company held a temporary operating certificate, dated March 6, 1947, and a temporary A.T.B. Licence, dated February 13, 1947, for approximately a year, approving operation of a contract service based at Yellowknife and Port Radium for the carriage of passengers and goods exclusively within the terms of an agreement, dated June 19, 1946, entered into between the licensee and International Uranium Mining Company Limited. The company used a Fox Moth DH-83C, which was sold to Associated Airways of Edmonton upon completion of their agreement.

Matt Berry conducted a non-scheduled contract commercial service in his own name from October, 1946, to April, 1948, from a seaplane base at Fort Smith, Northwest Territories, to areas in the Northwest Territories and northern Alberta, under Operating Certificate No. 342.

Territories Air Service Limited, of Edmonton, was formed in January, 1949, by Matt Berry, who became President and Manager. This company operated a non scheduled air charter service from a base also at Fort Smith, serving northern areas, including Aklavik, Northwest Territories, under Operating Certificate No. 630, dated January 27, 1949.

Matt Berry had been operating a non-scheduled charter air service in his own name from a base at Fort Smith, under Operating Certificate No. 630, of January 27, 1948. However, this service was absorbed by Territories Air Service upon its formation in January, 1949.

Yellowknife Airways Limited, Yellowknife, N.W.T., was organized and operated by George Pigeon of Montreal, carrying out a non-scheduled charter service from a base at Yellowknife, under Operating Certificate No. 346 of October 24, 1946. They served mostly the Northwest Territories and northern and central Alberta areas. Territories Air Services Limited of Edmonton and Yellowknife absorbed Yellowknife Airways Limited, as well as the bush equipment of Canadian Pacific Air Lines at Yellowknife in November, 1949. Ernie Boffa, a veteran bush pilot, joined Territories Air Service Limited at that time. However, Yellowknife Airways continued to operate under its own name, and Matt Berry became its President then. On November 9, 1950, Yellowknife Airways took over the operation of a scheduled commercial air service from Yellowknife under Operating Certificate No. 971. This service was from Yellowknife to Rocher River, Fort Rae, Indin Lake, Port Radium and Coppermine. In July, 1951, Matt Berry sold Yellowknife Airways Limited to Associated Airways of Edmonton, to be operated as a non-scheduled commercial air service, which also included Hottah Lake, Northwest Territories. This route was subsequently taken over by Pacific Western Airlines (Alberta) Limited on October 18, 1956.

In July, 1951, Matt Berry sold Territories Air Services Limited, as well as Yellowknife Airways Limited, to Associated Airways Limited of Edmonton. The Air Transport Board's approval for this combined transaction was given on August 21, 1951.

So, after being in the flying business for twenty-three years, Matt Berry left aviation when he was 59 years of age. He was often referred to as one of the most illustrious of the pioneer pilots. After 1951 he devoted himself to his oil

F/Lt. Sheldon Coleman (left) and L/A/C. Joseph Fortey (centre) are shown beside their tent just after they were found by Matt Berry (right) of Canadian Airways on September 16, 1936, north of Fort Reliance, N.W.T.
Photo courtesy of Matt Berry.

Matt Berry and Dick Leigh of Canadian Airways attached two large Fairchild floats to Junkers aircraft CF-ARI, to transport them from Cooking Lake to Reliance in the early autumn of 1936. These floats were for the R.C.A.F. 'plane which was damaged. This was the first time that floats were carried in this manner.

Photo courtesy of Matt Berry.

and contracting interests, amongst other things.

Matt Berry later became President of Datlasaka Mines Limited, President of Gateway Gold and Vice-President of Stride Exploration and Development.

Matt Berry was married and had two children, a daughter and a son. He was living in Edmonton, Alberta, at the time of his death on May 12, 1970, at 81 years of age. Mrs. Berry was the former Dorothy Clarke of Edmonton. Their son, Laurie, is a professional engineer; while their daughter, Betty, married M. A. Jackson.

This man of stature, standing five feet eleven inches in height, was known wherever men flew in Canada as one of the older stock of war-trained pilots who learned his flying with the Royal Flying Corps. Although in his whole flying career, Matt Berry was forced down many times, due mostly to weather conditions, yet he said he was never lost, and always did find his way back. He was injured seriously only once, and that was in 1934 when his aircraft nosed into the ground after take-off. Once when Matt Berry was forced down in the northern wilderness with a broken ski on his aircraft, he contrived a radio from a battery, a starter coil and other odds and ends, so he could attract attention.

Aviation in Canada became richer through Matt Berry's many contributions through the years, particularly in helping open up the northern areas, not only to flying but also to mining. He helped to forge the legend of the bush pilot, and was known as "the King of Northern Fliers" for years.

Matt Berry was named a member of Canada's Aviation Hall of Fame in 1973. He was made a Companion of the Order of Flight (City of Edmonton).

NOTES

[1] *Canadian Aviation*, October, 1936.
[2] *Canadian Aviation*, October, 1936.
[3] *Canadian Aviation*, October, 1936.
[4] *Canadian Aviation*, October, 1936.
[5] *Canadian Airways Bulletin* of February, 1937.
[6] *Canadian Airways Bulletin* of February, 1937.

1937

J. P. Romeo Vachon

Citation: in recognition of his work in the operation and development of air services along the north shore of the Gulf of St. Lawrence, without accident

J. P. Romeo Vachon, while District Superintendent of Canadian Airways, Montreal, and Manager of Quebec Airways Limited, Montreal, was awarded the Trans-Canada Trophy for meritorious service in the advancement of aviation in Canada during 1937, "in recognition of his work in the operation and development of air services along the north shore of the Gulf of St. Lawrence, without accident." The announcement of the award was made on April 4, 1938, by the Honourable Ian Mackenzie, Minister of the Department of National Defence.

It was largely attributable to Romeo Vachon's foresight and administrative ability that the air service from Quebec along the north shore of the Gulf of St. Lawrence came into existence. He had been outstanding in his dual capacity as a pilot and an air engineer.

The minister said that Romeo Vachon's qualification for the award was not dependent on any spectacular feat in aviation, but on the more solid basis of years of untiring and painstaking effort, which rightfully earned for him the admiration and high regard of those connected with aviation in Canada. He had logged a total of 3,100 hours' flying time up to the time of this award.

Joseph Pierre Romeo Vachon was born at Ste. Marie de la Beauce, Quebec, on June 29, 1898, and received his education at the Brothers of the Christian Schools' local college.

He joined the R.C.N.V.R. in March, 1918, and saw service in the North Atlantic while serving as an engineer (fourth class) during the last year of World War I. He served until February, 1919.

Romeo Vachon enlisted in the Canadian Air Force as a fitter in Sep-

tember, 1920, and was posted to Camp Borden. Within a few months he became a flight sergeant. However, in February, 1921, he was granted leave of absence from the Canadian Air Force and followed in Roy Maxwell's footsteps and joined the Laurentide Pulp and Paper Company's air service, which operated from a base at Lac à la Tortue, near Grand'Mère, Quebec.

While he was with this company his career as a pilot began, when he learned to fly at Lac à la Tortue, and at Dayton, Ohio, during 1923. Then, when the Laurentide Air Service was formed in 1922, Romeo Vachon flew for the company upon receiving his licence.

Laurentide Air Service actually had its beginning back in the summer of 1919 in the St. Maurice Valley. Ellwood Wilson, Chief Forester of the Laurentide Company, was inspired with the idea that flying boats or seaplanes would be useful in providing assistance in patrolling the forested areas of Quebec and Ontario for fire detection purposes. There was a surplus of aircraft from World War I at the time which were serving no useful purpose. So Ellwood Wilson went ahead and enquired from the Air Board if he might have assistance from them in the form of some surplus flying boats so that he might do his experimental flight test work in patrolling the forested areas. The Province of Quebec assisted by providing a small subsidy, while the Dominion Government (the Air Board) loaned two H.S. 2L flying boats to the Laurentide Company. The flying boats were in storage at Halifax and Sydney.

The Laurentide Company engaged their first pilot, Stuart Graham, and Bill Kahre, as a mechanic. The two flying boats were overhauled before being flown to Lac à la Tortue by Stuart Graham, where a civil

air harbour was established for these civil operations. This air harbour was one of Canada's earliest. During the summer of 1919, Stuart Graham made many flights for the Laurentide Company, and he was actually the first person in Canada to fly aircraft on forest fire patrol operations. In 1920 and 1921 the forested areas were again patrolled by flying boats to locate forest fires. Then it was thought best to form a separate company to do the flying operations, rather than continue with this work as part of the Laurentide Company's activities. So, Laurentide Air Service Limited was incorporated in 1922, having no connection with the Laurentide Company.

Laurentide Air Service Limited then went ahead and obtained contracts for flying, and likewise purchased more flying boats. G. A. "Tommy" Thompson, Roy Maxwell and Roy Grandy were the company's first pilots. Roy Maxwell was Manager of the company, as well. The first year that the company was formed, 1922, they received a large contract from the Provincial Government of Ontario for flying in connection with the preparation of a reconnaissance map which would show the forest types in that part of northern Ontario lying north of the National Transcontinental Railway, between the Ontario-Quebec boundary and the Abitibi River.

Then Laurentide Air Service entered into a contract with the Province of Ontario in the spring of 1923 to do the flying required for forest sketching and fire detection and fire-fighting purposes. Forest type mapping was made the basis of the operations and flying boats were steadily employed on that work. When the fire hazard was high, type mapping was stopped and the flying boats were used in forest fire fighting and patrol work. The company's operations were widespread and reached from the Lake of the Woods' district in western Ontario to Pembroke on the Ottawa River in eastern Ontario; and from the southern limit of

the forested country of Ontario as far north as Moose Factory and Albany Post on James Bay. The main base of their operations was at Sudbury, with subsidiary bases at Trout Lake near North Bay, on Lake Temiskaming, on Lake Nipigon, at Remi Lake, at Bisco, at Como and at Gowgama. Others were established temporarily, if required.

Exploration and reconnaissance work was also carried out from the air for the Temiskaming and Northern Ontario Railway Commission to determine the nature of the country and a preliminary location for the extension of their line northwards to Moose Factory. When the Lieutenant-Governor of Ontario and the prime minister went through the area as far as Moose Factory by canoe in September, 1923, they were met by flying boats of the Laurentide Air Service and were flown back to the railway at Remi Lake, Ontario, which was the base for all operations in the James Bay district.

In the Province of Quebec aerial operations were also carried out for commercial firms, and ten pupils were given flying instruction during 1923 by the company. Experimental flights in connection with the development of wireless telegraphy for fire detection patrols, communication and passenger flying and some photographic flights completed the company's programme for 1923. In this same year, the company was employing ten pilots and ten licensed air engineers, compared with six pilots and five licensed air engineers for the previous year. The company was also using twelve flying boats and aeroplanes in 1923, compared with six in 1922. Their flying time was 1,480 hours in 1923, double the 711 hours for 1922. Some 550 passengers were carried during 1923, and forest sketching and exploratory reconnaissance of 20,000 square miles had been done. There were over 400 fires detected by flying boats and seaplanes during the 1923 season.

The company had acquired nine H.S. 2L flying boats, one Vickers Viking amphibian, one Loening seaplane and one Curtiss JN-4.

J. H. "Tuddy" Tudhope flew as a pilot with Laurentide Air Service from June, 1923, until September 30, 1923, while the company was taking over the forestry patrol work from the Air Board in the Province of Quebec. Romeo Vachon was one of the ten pilots with Laurentide Air Service who did fire prevention and photographic work in the Province of Quebec. Other pilots were: C. S. Caldwell of Lacombe, Alberta (also an air engineer); J. Scott Williams of Montreal; and B. W. Broatch of Haileybury, Ontario. Lieutenant-Colonel J. Scott Williams was Director of Sales for Laurentide Air Service, as well as a pilot.

In the fall of 1923 Laurentide Air Service transferred its main base from Grand'Mère to Three Rivers, as the Grand'Mère base had become too small to house their aeroplanes. Another reason was the late break-up of the ice at the company's Grand'Mère (Lac à la Tortue) base which delayed opening of their operations in Ontario during the spring of 1923. At Three Rivers operations could start early on account of the open water.

In 1923 forestry operations in Quebec were taken over by the Province of Quebec upon the formation of its own air service.

The Government of Ontario established its own air service in the spring of 1924, known as the Ontario Provincial Air Service. Laurentide Air Service then sold part of its equipment to the Province of Ontario; but kept one Vickers Viking amphibian, with a Napier Lion engine, and three H.S. 2L flying boats for their own work.

The company's most important operation during 1924 was the provision of an air mail, passenger and freight service from the end of the railway at Haileybury, Ontario, to the Rouyn gold

Canadian Transcontinental Airways made the inaugural flight of the air mail service from Montreal (Cartierville Flying Field) to Rimouski on April 28, 1928. Romeo Vachon was the pilot of the Fairchild FC2.
Photo courtesy of the Department of the Interior.

fields, when mining development began in the area. This was the first air mail, passenger and freight service to be established on a regular basis in Canada — and it was operated by Laurentide Air Service.

The company started operating this air transport service in June, 1924, and continued the air service without interruption until around the end of November, 1924, when ice formed on the lakes in the interior. Express delivery of telegrams was a feature of the company's service. These could be sent from outside points, delivered to the pilot at either Haileybury or Angliers, flown to the mining camps and a return message brought out to be telegraphed from either point to its destination, all within a few hours. Laurentide Air Service had operated the air mail service free of charge since June, then in August the Post Office Department decided to officially recognize the company as a regular mail carrier, as it had proved its reliability through the summer months.

Therefore, the Post Office Department issued the first sticker on August 30, 1924, and the company was officially authorized to carry mail bearing a special twenty-five-cent stamp which it issued. The first flight carrying the special mail sticker was made on September 11, 1924. After the Laurentide Air Service discontinued operations in 1925, Northern Air Services Limited of Haileybury, Ontario, was formed in the summer of 1925 to continue carrying air mail, freight and passengers from Haileybury to the Rouyn gold fields. B. W. Broatch became Managing Director and Chief Pilot of Northern Air Services and operated the service on a small scale for a while.

When the 1924 season first started, the service operated from Angliers, Quebec, the terminus of the Canadian Pacific Railway line in the district, directly to Lake Osisko, a distance of about 45 miles. It was then found that the railroad connections at Haileybury had improved

since the previous year. The company then transferred their main base to Haileybury. Trips were made from there on the arrival of the through-trains, with one aircraft calling regularly at Angliers to pick up the mail, telegrams, freight, express and passengers en route every day and stopping on its return flight for the same purpose. At the Rouyn end, Lake Osisko was made the main base, though passengers and freight were delivered on the shores of any waterways in the district, as required by individual customers.

The company also carried out several contracts for forest type sketching in conjunction with the James D. Lacey & Company of Canada, the largest of which was in the District of Algoma for the Spanish River Pulp and Paper Company, for which similar work had been done the previous two years. This sketch survey covered an area of 2,000 square miles of forest land. Much similar work was carried out in the Province of Quebec, including an operation in the difficult and mountainous country northeast of the City of Quebec, and another in the Upper Gatineau region. They also contracted to supply the flying required on one of the aerial photographic operations for the Fairchild Aerial Surveys Company in northwestern Quebec.

Late in the fall of 1924 Laurentide Air Service purchased a Westland Limousine six-passenger aeroplane fitted with a Napier Lion engine, and a D.H. 9 Siddeley Puma three-seater. They were both fitted with skis and were used when the lakes were frozen over. The Department of National Defence lent the company a hangar for erection at Larder Lake which was to be their winter base. Mining engineers, prospectors and others wishing to visit the new gold fields used the service as much time and trouble were saved — besides being a more comfortable trip than by steamboat, launch or canoe. These flights also

replaced the cold sleigh rides over rough winter roads. The company carried 1,004 passengers in 1924 — double those carried in 1923. Likewise, the express and freight carried by air weighed over 78,000 pounds, while 15,000 letters and telegrams were carried from June to November. Some 66,000 miles were covered in their operations in 933 hours.

Under an arrangement with Laurentide Air Service during 1925, Lieutenant-Colonel Scott Williams, with C. S. Caldwell as his second pilot and air engineer, carried out an operation during the summer in northern British Columbia and the Yukon Territory to do prospecting and exploration work, using Laurentide Air Service's Vickers Viking Napier Lion amphibian. This amphibian was purchased by Northern Syndicate Limited in 1926.

Although Laurentide Air Service seemed to be doing very well, nevertheless the company was forced to discontinue its operations, and went out of business in 1925. This was, in part, due to the improved ground and water transportation to the area, which reduced the aerial traffic. So when Laurentide Air Service stopped operating, Romeo Vachon joined the Ontario Provincial Air Service in the summer of 1925, where he did forest fire patrol work and sketched terrain from the air.

Towards the end of 1927 Canadian Transcontinental Airways commenced operations and organized an air service along the north shore of the St. Lawrence. Due to Romeo Vachon's knowledge of the north shore of the St. Lawrence, as well as his ability as an engineer and a pilot, his services were sought and obtained by Canadian Transcontinental Airways. These air mail services were operated during the winter months under contract with the Post Office Department. An air mail service from Quebec to Seven Islands was inaugurated on December 15, 1927; while an air mail service from Seven

Romeo Vachon standing beside the Bremen Junkers aircraft on Greenly Island, April, 1928. He took a leading part in a rescue operation of the crew.

Photo courtesy of Romeo Vachon.

Islands to Anticosti Island was inaugurated on December 25, 1927. Then these two air mail services were combined and made into one service from Quebec to Seven Islands and thence over to Anticosti Island in the mouth of the St. Lawrence River, with Romeo Vachon making the first flight on February 3, 1928. He had gained much of his knowledge of conditions along the north shore with Laurentide Air Service when they surveyed a large part of the north shore of the St. Lawrence on behalf of several lumber companies. Fairchild monoplanes with Wasp engines were used on the air mail service. Another air mail service was inaugurated between Montreal and Rimouski on April 28, 1928, by the company, and Romeo Vachon made the inaugural flight.

The activities of Canadian Transcontinental Airways Limited included the carrying of mail, freight and passengers in Quebec and New Brunswick. A contract was obtained from the Canadian Pacific Railway Express Company to carry express on their air mail route. In all, they operated air mail services under contracts with the Post Office Department between Quebec-Seven Islands-Anticosti, and Moncton-Magdalen Islands during the winter months; and a service between Rimouski, Montreal and Ottawa was operated during the 1928 navigation season in the St. Lawrence River in connection with the incoming and outgoing transatlantic mail. Their bases were located at St. Hubert, Lac Ste. Agnès, Pointe au Père, Quebec City and St. Félicien, all in Quebec, to serve the mining centre at Chibougamou. Several trips were made carrying passengers to the Lower St. Lawrence, as far as Godbout on the north shore, and Rimouski and Rivière-du-Loup on the south shore.

Most of Romeo Vachon's operations were carried out in Fairchild monoplane G-CAIP or G-CAIQ, which were both operated by Canadian Transcontinental

Airways. These aircraft were powered by Pratt and Whitney Wasp engines, which were the first engines of that type to be used in commercial work in Canada. C. A. "Duke" Schiller, also employed with Canadian Transcontinental Airways, flew one of the aircraft.

Romeo Vachon took a leading part in a rescue operation of the crew of the *Bremen*, a Junkers aircraft, which made the first east-to-west crossing of the North Atlantic Ocean in 1928. It was flown from Germany to Baldonnel Aerodrome, Ireland, from where the flight left on April 12, 1928. Captain Hermann Koehl, Baron Guenther von Huenefeld and second pilot Captain James Fitzmaurice, an Irishman, made up the crew of the *Bremen* on its planned flight to New York. Captain Koehl and Captain Fitzmaurice were the two pilots. Their aircraft was blown north of its course and ran into fog as they neared Newfoundland. However, they flew on and as they neared the Labrador coast line they ran into a blizzard. As they followed the coast line, although not knowing just what coast line it was, they saw a lighthouse. Then Captain Koehl put the Junkers monoplane down on Greenly Island, off the northwest coast of Newfoundland, just before the aircraft ran out of fuel. Greenly Island was both

barren and rocky. It was in landing the *Bremen* that the aircraft's undercarriage was demolished and the propeller smashed. No one was injured, however. It took thirty-six and a half hours to make this first east-to-west flight across the North Atlantic, a distance of some 2,125 miles.

Word of the landing of the *Bremen* was sent across the ice to the mainland by dog team, where help was sought.

Then the rescue of the crew began. Between April 14 and April 27, twelve aeroplanes, including Ford Trimotor G-CARC of Sky View Lines Ltd., visited Lac Ste. Agnès. Conditions on the lake were such that all aeroplanes could land and take off either on wheels or skis from the ice.

On April 14, 1928, two Fairchild monoplanes belonging to Canadian Transcontinental Airways Limited were sent to the rescue of the crew of the *Bremen*. Greenly Island in the Strait of Belle Isle was some 700 miles from the company's base at Lac Ste. Agnès. The first aircraft, G-CAIQ, piloted by Duke Schiller, with Dr. Louis Cuisinier, left Lac Ste. Agnès on Saturday, April 14, at 10:45 A.M., and spent the night at Seven Islands. Then the next day, Sunday, the 15th, they flew through a heavy snowstorm in the afternoon to reach the

Five seaplanes belonging to Canadian Airways Limited at their base at Oskelaneo, P.Q. They served the Chibougamou and Opemiska areas in the thirties.

transatlantic crew on Greenly Island. The aircraft, equipped with skis, landed on the bay between Greenly Island and Blanc Sablon.

The second aircraft, G-CAIP, piloted by Romeo Vachon, left the base at Lac Ste. Agnès carrying representatives of the American and Canadian press, and also moving picture equipment. On Wednesday, April 18, Duke Schiller returned to his base with Captain James Fitzmaurice and the doctor; and the following day, the 19th, Romeo Vachon returned to Lac Ste. Agnès with the other two members of the crew and the press party, who brought out with them the pictures of the *Bremen*.

Pilots Bernt Balchen and Floyd Bennett hopped off from Detroit on April 20, 1928, in Ford Trimotor G-CARC, having chartered it from the Sky View Lines, Ltd., of Chippawa, Ontario, to fly to Greenly Island, also in an attempt to rescue the crew of the *Bremen*. Floyd Bennett had not been well since his accident a year earlier and he had caught cold on the flight which later developed into pneumonia. They reached Murray Bay but Floyd Bennett could go no farther. He was taken to a hospital in Quebec City where he died from pneumonia on April 25, 1928.

Just two years earlier, on May 9, 1926, Floyd Bennett, a pilot with the United States Navy, had piloted the *Josephine Ford* from Spitzbergen for Commander Richard E. Byrd, a naval officer and Antarctic explorer, in a dash to be the first to reach the North Pole by aircraft, covering a distance of 1,550 miles in about 15-1/2 hours.

Bernt Balchen flew the crew of the *Bremen* from Lac Ste. Agnès to New York where they were fêted. They reached New York on April 24, 1928, in aircraft G-CARC, and ironically went on to Washington to attend Floyd Bennett's funeral, who had died while on a mission of mercy to rescue them!

Today, the *Bremen* is on display in the

Henry Ford Museum in Dearborn, Michigan.

A good percentage of mail carried by air in Canada in the late twenties was carried along the north shore of the St. Lawrence. This ran into thousands of pounds each year. During 1928, for instance, 28,000 pounds of mail, 5,000 pounds of freight and 1,320 passengers were carried by Canadian Transcontinental Airways in their north shore operations along the St. Lawrence. Their total flying time for the year amounted to 544 hours, covering 56,035 miles. The company was using four Fairchild cabin monoplanes, two Loening amphibians and one Stearman aircraft, while they employed six pilots.

When Canadian Transcontinental Airways was taken over by Canadian Airways in 1930, Romeo Vachon remained in their employ and was responsible for the operation from 1928 until 1938, except for the year 1931 when he was employed by Saunders Roe Company as a pilot, and flew the Saro Cloud, CF-ARB, a British aeroplane, which was owned by W. R. G. Holt.

During all of these operations, thousands of pounds of mail were transported safely as well as several thousand passengers. Through the development of air services along the north shore of the St. Lawrence by this company it was made possible to render more and better service to the public. This development also ensured greater safety to the air transportation world as a whole.

From 1928 to 1932, most of the flying by this company was carried out from the ice surface of the St. Lawrence or from a snow landing strip bordering the river. From 1932 onwards, the development of winter landing strips was pursued widely by the company. During the following years, winter landing strips were established at Matane, Forestville, Baie Comeau, Trinity Bay, Shelter Bay, Clark City Bay, Seven Islands, Thunder

River, Havre St. Pierre and Natashquan, all in the Province of Quebec.

In 1932 when a base was established at Rimouski by the company, a repair base was opened there also in order to ensure greater utilization of their aircraft. It was equipped and staffed especially to carry out any maintenance work at night that might be required on any of the company's aircraft, thus enabling the aircraft to be flown as much as possible during the day.

In 1933, Canadian Airways moved their eastern headquarters from Murray Bay to Rimouski, with a sub-base at Forestville, Baie Comeau, and Godbout, all in Quebec, where radio facilities were established, as well as at Seven Islands, Havre St. Pierre and Natashquan. Romeo Vachon was also responsible for the introduction of twin-engine aircraft into the company's service along the north shore of the St. Lawrence.

Upon the formation of Quebec Airways on December 28, 1934, as a subsidiary of Canadian Airways, Romeo Vachon became its first Manager. When Clarke Steamships complained about Canadian Airways operating a mail service over an area for which they had the contract, Quebec Airways was then formed to operate the winter mail service.

However, it was later seen that Winnipeg more nearly represented the geographical centre of the company's transportation, and there was a great concentration of air transportation business in the north country, so the headquarters of Canadian Airways Limited was moved from Montreal to Winnipeg on July 1, 1934. Under the new organization, operations were to be conducted from six bases throughout the Dominion, each under a district superintendent. The six districts under this set-up and their District Superintendents were: Maritime Provinces, with headquarters at Moncton, W. Fowler; Quebec and Eastern Ontario, with headquarters at Montreal, Romeo

Group photo of Canadian Airways Pilots and Engineers taken at St. Hubert Airport in 1930. The mooring tower shown in the background is now dismantled. The aircraft is a Stearman 4EM Mailplane. Back row (left to right): Al Parker, O.C. Wallace, A. Schneider, C. Caverly, George S. Lace, F. Pare, J. Hertle, S. Larder, Alex, Ross, G. Eadie, G. Brignell, R. Heuss and L.H. Power. Centre row (left to right): H. Cook, B. Martin, W.H. "Bill" Irvine, not known, A. Stunden, E. Patreault, P. Ryan, and G. Rose. Front row (left to right): J. Pringle, Scotty Miller, Romeo Vachon, A. Bates, H. Fletcher, J. Douglas, R.H. Mulock, G.C. Drury and A.F. Ingram.

Vachon; Western Ontario, with headquarters at Sioux Lookout, A. Westergaard; Central Manitoba, with headquarters at Norway House and Ilford, H. Hollick-Kenyon; Mackenzie River district, with headquarters at Edmonton, C. H. Dickins; and the Pacific coast, with headquarters at Vancouver, D. R. MacLaren. James A. Richardson was the President; E. W. Beatty, K.C., and S. J. Hungerford, Vice-Presidents. G. A. Thompson was Assistant General Manager in charge of transport operations.

Romeo Vachon was issued Commercial Air Pilot's Certificate No. 182, dated March 7, 1923, and Transport Certificate No. 46, dated January 6, 1937, as well as Air Engineer's Certificate No. A-603, dated March 27, 1931, which superseded Certificate No. 93, dated January 28, 1921.

Then an announcement was made by the Minister of National Defence in April, 1938, that Romeo Vachon had been awarded the Trans-Canada Trophy for the year 1937.

The Committee of Award for the year 1937 consisted of the following members:

Wing Commander A. B. Shearer, Royal Canadian Air Force, Department of National Defence, Ottawa.

J. A. Wilson, Controller of Civil Aviation, Department of Transport, Ottawa.

Squadron Leader C. C. Walker, Royal Canadian Air Force, Department of National Defence, Ottawa.

Flight Lieutenant P. C. Garratt, A.F.C., Royal Canadian Air Force (Aux.), Department of National Defence, Ottawa.

The presentation of the Trans-Canada trophy was made in the minister's office by the Deputy Minister of National Defence, Lieutenant-Colonel L. R. Lafléche, D.S.O., on behalf of the minister, at 9:30 hours on May 5, 1938. At this ceremony Colonel Lafléche reiterated the statement that the minister had made concerning Romeo Vachon's qualifications for the award not being dependent on any spectacular feat in aviation, but on the more solid basis of years of effort. Romeo Vachon had many thrilling experiences as a pilot, though he dismissed them with the assertion, "I was always lucky." In thanking Colonel Lafléche, Vachon said that he started flying in 1922 and that he had enjoyed every minute of it, particularly in Quebec. In those days, he continued, there was no communication by air between many points on the north shore and the rest of Canada. They carried 4,000 passengers between points in that part of the province during the winter of 1937-38. He mentioned that seven airports between Quebec and Natashquan had been established, apart from the fact that the air line operates its own radio stations in the area.

Romeo Vachon left Canadian Airways to become Assistant Superintendent of the Eastern Division of Trans-Canada Air Lines, Montreal, in October, 1938.

From June, 1940, until April, 1941, he was on loan from Trans-Canada Air Lines to the Department of Munitions and Supply, where he shared responsibility for the organization of aircraft overhauls for the British Commonwealth Air Training Plan.

Romeo Vachon became a member of the Air Transport Board, Ottawa, when it was established in September, 1944,

and held this position with distinction until the time of his death on Friday, December 17, 1954. He was 56 years of age.

In his honour, a public park was named the Romeo Vachon Park (Parc Romeo Vachon). It is located at Ste. Foy, a suburb of Quebec City, and was officially dedicated in November, 1957. This park area was formerly an airfield operated by Canadian Pacific Air Lines years ago. This old airfield site was purchased by the League of Pioneer Airmen, headed by André Légendre, who was a former Lieutenant Commander with the Royal Canadian Navy. The park commemorates Romeo Vachon's pioneering activities with the aerial postal services of Canada, and later with the Air Transport Board. In the development of the park, its planners were careful to perpetuate the exact landing field which Romeo Vachon used hundreds of times when he landed to deliver the mail in the early days of the air mail services to Quebec City.

The Romeo Vachon Award is presented annually for outstanding contribution of a practical nature to the art, science and engineering of aeronautics and space in Canada. Mrs. Romeo Vachon donated the trophy to the Canadian Aeronautics and Space Institute in 1969 for annual presentation.

Romeo Vachon was well known for his work in the field of aviation through the years, having spent thirty-four years in aviation up to the time of his death. He and his wife had two sons and twin daughters. Mrs. Vachon continues to live in Ottawa.

Romeo Vachon was named a member of Canada's Aviation Hall of Fame in 1973. He was made a Companion of the Order of Flight (City of Edmonton).

1938

Philip G. Johnson

Citation: in recognition of meritorious service in the inauguration and outstanding progress of Trans-Canada Air Lines during 1938, thereby contributing greatly to the advancement of aviation in Canada

Philip G. Johnson, while Vice-President of Trans-Canada Air Lines, Winnipeg, was awarded the Trans-Canada Trophy, to be held in trust as a group award to the operating personnel of the company, "in recognition of meritorious service in the inauguration and outstanding progress of Trans-Canada Air Lines during 1938, thereby contributing greatly to the advancement of aviation in Canada." The announcement of the award was made by the Honourable Ian A. Mackenzie, Minister of National Defence, in May, 1939.

The announcement said that the most outstanding events in Canadian aviation during 1938 were, undoubtedly, the organization of the air lines' system across Canada and the inauguration of a daily service between Montreal and Vancouver.

The construction of a transcontinental air line to operate efficiently in the short period of two years was recognized as being one of the most remarkable feats in air transport history — but it was the work of the group as a whole and not any one man.

The selection of Philip Johnson as custodian of the trophy on behalf of the operating personnel of the company was symbolic of the important and impressive part he played in successfully bringing the air line service into operation.

The Trans-Canada Air Lines' Act, 1937, under which Trans-Canada Air Lines came into existence, was assented to by Parliament on April 10, 1937. It was covered by Chapter 43 of the Statutes of Canada, 1937. Upon the completion of the Trans-Canada Airway, the government was to award a contract for carrying passengers, mail and freight

to the most suitable company qualified for this work. A number of aviation groups who felt they were in a financial position to operate such a trans-continental service brought considerable pressure to bear upon the government to have the contract awarded to each one. With so many after the contract, this made the selection difficult. After battling these problems out in Parliament, the government was still in a quandary, and decided that the best way out would be to form a new company. So, it was decided that a national company would be the solution to the problem, and this company became known as Trans-Canada Air Lines. The Right Honourable C. D. Howe, Minister of Transport, sponsored the Act in Parliament. It was known as Bill No. 74, and was first introduced to Parliament for a reading on March 22, 1937, by Mr. Howe.

The subsequent debates on the Trans-Canada Air Lines' Act, held on March 25 and 31 and on April 1, did not attract any exceptional attendance in the House of Commons, but there was a high quality of helpful criticism offered by a small body of air-minded members, particularly the remarks made by the Leader of the Opposition, the Right Honourable R. B. Bennett, who discontinued the Prairie Air Mail Service on March 31, 1932. Mr. Bennett protested, not once, but several times, that the cancellation of the Prairie Air Mail Service was "strictly in accordance with the terms of the contract." "We discontinued it," Mr. Bennett said on March 22, "strictly in accordance with the terms of the contract, because with the crop failure in western Canada, and with 300,000 of a population receiving

CF-TCN, a Lockheed 1408, which was one of the types of aircraft used by T.C.A. in their early operations.
Photo courtesy of T.C.A.

some form of relief, there was very little gratification in seeing an aeroplane passing by, day after day, when the unfortunate owner of the soil could hardly see the aeroplane because his crop had gone up in dust."[1]

Throughout the debates in Parliament, in a perfect hail of suggestions, criticisms and questions, most of which were relevant, though some were pretty far-fetched, the Minister of Transport pursued his course to its logical conclusion; here explaining and there accepting gracefully a piece of advice and having it moved in the form of an amendment by his colleague, the Honourable Ian Mackenzie, the Minister of National Defence; reiterating his assertion that the main thing was to get the corporation set up first and then settle the details afterwards.[2]

Mr. Howe told the House of Commons that, at that time (March, 1937), around $7,000,000.00 had been spent on the construction of landing fields to provide for the operation of aircraft on wheels throughout the year. When Mr. Howe was queried in the House as to whether or not Canada had invited private interests to participate in this air service, he countered with: "May I say we did not need to invite them. They came from every part of Canada and the United States, and put on the most persistent lobby in Ottawa that I have ever seen!"[3]

The new company's management was vested in a board of seven directors, four to be elected by the shareholders and three to be appointed by the Governor-in-Council. Trans-Canada Air Lines was created for the operation of an air line service across Canada from coast to coast, and for international main line connections to other countries. This national air service for Canada was to operate over a completely equipped airway.

Trans-Canada Air Lines was to furnish adequate modern aviation equipment, two-way communication service, hangars and other buildings and equipment required for its services. The Department of Transport was to be responsible for the provision, operation and maintenance of emergency landing fields, lighting, radio range systems, meteorological service, and similar essential services and facilities. The Act also provided that the Governor-in-Council might authorize the Postmaster General to enter into a contract with the company for the transportation of mail.

Under legislation, Canadian National Railways was to hold the capital stock of Trans-Canada Air Lines, which was $5,000,000.00, in shares of $100.00 each. The Canadian National Railways was to retain not less than 51% of the stock. While the original proposed draft of the Trans-Canada Air Lines' Act provided for both the Canadian National Railways and the Canadian Pacific Railway to share equally in the organization of the air line company, the Canadian Pacific Railway Company declined to participate. Therefore, the Canadian National Railways assumed complete responsibility for this air line venture.[4]

The three directors were appointed by Order-in-Council, dated May 5, 1937, and a few days later at the first shareholders' meeting the four directors from the Canadian National Railways were elected. Those directors first elected by the Governor-in-Council were: C. P. Edwards, Chief of Air Services, Department of Transport, Ottawa; J. A. Wilson, Controller of Civil Aviation, Department of Transport, Ottawa; and George Herring, Chief Superintendent of Air and Land Mail Services, Post Office Department, Ottawa. Those directors first elected by the shareholders of the Canadian National Railways were: S. J. Hungerford, who was Chairman and President of the Canadian National Railways, Montreal; James Y. Murdoch, K.C., Director of the Canadian National Railways, Toronto; H. J. Symington,

K.C., Director of the Canadian National Railways, Montreal; and Wilfrid Gagnon, Director of the Canadian National Railways, Montreal.

When the directors held their first meeting on May 11, 1937, they had before them the immediate question of selecting a most capable person to organize the operation of Trans-Canada Air Lines. With so many problems that would come to light in the inauguration of a regular scheduled transcontinental service of the type and magnitude contemplated by the Act, it was important to choose the right man. The equipment to be used was to be larger and faster than that regularly operated in Canada; instrument and radio range flying would be required, as contrasted with contact flying; a complete radio communication and despatching system had to be provided; and there were numerous other unforeseen factors which would be encountered along the way. Large-scale operations embracing all of these features had been established in the United States for some years. So, after deliberation, the directors thought that it would be desirable to obtain the services of an experienced United States air line executive, if possible.

Philip Gustav Johnson, a graduate engineer from the University of Washington, had been associated with commercial aviation in the United States since 1917 when he went to work for the Boeing Aircraft plant of Seattle, first as an engineering draftsman, then as Manager of their Production Department in 1918, and as Superintendent of Production in 1919. Philip Johnson became Vice-President and General Manager of the Boeing Aircraft Company in 1922, and President in 1926. He next became President of Boeing Air Transport Company in 1927.

Two years later, in 1929, Philip Johnson became one of the two Vice-Presidents of United Aircraft and Transport Corporation, New York, which

To commemorate the founding in 1937, of Canada's transcontinental air line, the following persons active in its beginning have signed:

Photo courtesy of T.C.A.

was formed early in the year as a holding company for Boeing Airplane Company, Boeing Air Transport Company, Pacific Air Transport Company and Pratt and Whitney Aircraft Company. United Air Lines Inc., was formed on April 1, 1931, with Philip Johnson as President. This company included Varney Air Lines, National Air Transport, Boeing Air Transport and Pacific Air Transport. Philip Johnson was also president of each of these companies.

In July, 1933, Philip Johnson became President of United Aircraft and Transport Corporation, whose head office was in Chicago, and resigned as President of its subsidiaries. He remained as President of United Air Lines, Inc.

Philip Johnson reluctantly resigned these Presidencies, left his problems and frustrations behind him in the United States, then came to Canada and became Vice-President of Operations of Trans-Canada Air Lines in June, 1937. The Directors of Trans-Canada Air Lines considered they were most fortunate in having obtained the services of 43-year-old Philip Johnson. He enhanced his value to Trans-Canada Air Lines by bringing with him Duard Browning Colyer, Oscar Theodore Larson and Oliver West, each an expert in his own field, to help in the organization of Trans-Canada Air Lines.

Donald R. MacLaren, a former Major in World War I, who was Assistant General Manager (Pacific Lines), Canadian Airways Limited, was appointed as Assistant to the Vice-President of Operations during the latter part of April, 1937. He was asked to join the company by Mr. Howe, and was the first person to be taken on strength. D. B. Colyer became Chief Technical Adviser to Philip Johnson at a later date, because of his intimate knowledge of modern air line operation for over twenty years. A one-time school-teacher and former pilot in the United States Army during 1917-18, D. B. Colyer was employed with the

United States Air Mail Service as Assistant Postmaster General. In 1927 he joined Boeing Air Transport Company, as Superintendent of Operations and General Superintendent, before becoming Vice-President of Operations and later Vice-President of Operations with United Air Lines.

Oliver West was appointed technical adviser for maintenance and overhaul, having had eighteen years' experience in aircraft and engine maintenance and construction. He had been Superintendent of Engineering with United Air Lines, Chicago, and President of the Air Lines' Maintenance Association. H. T. "Slim" Lewis was appointed technical adviser for flying. He had behind him twenty years of flying experience, and was formerly chief pilot of United Air Lines, Oakland, California. Oscar "Ted" Larson was appointed technical adviser for meteorology and despatch. He had ten years of aviation and meteorological experience and was assistant chief despatcher with United Air Lines, Chicago. S. S. Stevens was appointed Technical Adviser for Communications. Born in Vancouver, British Columbia, he went to the United States where he became assistant chief of radio with Eastern Airlines, Miami, Florida.

On July 8, 1937, shortly after Philip Johnson became Vice-President of Trans-Canada Air Lines, he made a survey by air and on the ground of the entire proposed transcontinental route between Vancouver and Montreal, as well as inspecting all the airway facilities that were available. He was accompanied by his advisory associates, D. B. Colyer and D. R. MacLaren; Dan McLean, Superintendent of Airways for the Department of Transport, and Inspector J. H. Tudhope, also of the Department of Transport, who piloted the aircraft. Stops on the 2,550-mile tour were made at Princeton, Oliver, Grand Forks and Cranbrook, in British Columbia; Edmonton, Calgary, Lethbridge and

Coleman in Alberta; Regina, Saskatchewan; Winnipeg, Manitoba; Wagaming, Gillies, Emsdale, Toronto and Ottawa in Ontario; and Montreal, Quebec. Throughout this trip they were accorded the whole-hearted co-operation of the provincial, civic and other officials, and from citizens in general. This trip was made in the Department of Transport's Lockheed aircraft CF-CCT. Later in the year, Philip Johnson made a survey of the proposed route east of Montreal. (5)

On July 30, 1937, after Philip Johnson completed his inspection tour, the Minister of Transport, the Right Honourable C. D. Howe, made a dawn-to-dusk flight over the projected route from Montreal to Vancouver, a distance of some 2,550 miles, in 17 hours and 10 minutes' elapsed time, with 14 hours and 10 minutes' actual flying time. The purpose of this trip was to demonstrate that the airway was an entirely practicable proposition — and by no means was it intended to indicate that the route was ready for commercial operations. Six persons were aboard the Department of Transport's Lockheed Electra CF-CCT on its transcontinental flight: — Mr. C. D. Howe, Mr. H. J. Symington, Commander C. P. Edwards, pilot J. H. Tudhope, co-pilot Jack D. Hunter and air engineer Lew Parmenter. Stops were made en route for refuelling and weather reports at Gillies, Ontario; Winnipeg, Manitoba; Regina, Saskatchewan; and Lethbridge, Alberta. Flying over the Rocky Mountains presented a breath-taking array of natural wonders.[6]

The company's head office was to be in Montreal, where Trans-Canada Air Line's first President, S. J. Hungerford, was located. However, it was necessary to have the Vice-President's office located in Winnipeg, as operations could be directed from there more efficiently than in the east. Winnipeg was also to be the centre for the training of personnel. The new instrument and radio range flying, or on-the-beam flying, was carried out under

From left to right: Dan McLean, Supt. of Airways, D.O.T., Philip G. Johnson, Major Don MacLaren; D.B. Colyer, Mayor D.H. Elton of Lethbridge; and S/Ldr. J.H. Tudhope, pilot of Lockheed CF-CCT. This landing was at Kenyon Field, Lethbridge's Municipal Airport, which was later opened by the Lt.-Governor on June 7, 1939.

Photo courtesy of Lethbridge Herald.

the direction of Slim Lewis. Assisting him were pilot-instructors Z. L. "Lewis" Leigh, who joined Trans-Canada Air Lines in August, 1937, and W. A. "Bill" Straith.

Lewis Leigh began flying in 1926. Later he was associated with Southern Alberta Airlines, Leigh Air Services, Explorers' Air Transport, Brandon Aero Association and Canadian Airways, before joining Trans-Canada Air Lines. Incidentally, Lewis Leigh, later a Group Captain, was the first pilot to be taken on strength with Trans-Canada Air Lines. Bill Straith had built his own plane at Winnipeg in the early days and taught himself to fly. He was President of Canadian Aircraft Co. Ltd., Winnipeg, in 1928. He joined Northwest Airlines as a pilot, then was a technician, and later an instructor, before becoming associated with Trans-Canada Air Lines. A Link Trainer had also been set up at Winnipeg for the preliminary training of pilots.

By September, 1937, Trans-Canada Air Lines had four pilots on their payroll. They were Lewis Leigh; E. P. H. "Billy" Wells, who was chief pilot on the Vancouver-Seattle service; Maurice McGregor, formerly President of B.C. Airlines; and George Lothian.

"Careful planning and preparation in all details must be made before actual service can be begun. A policy of making haste slowly will be followed," said Philip Johnson.[7]

Trans-Canada Air Lines' first commercial operation was inaugurated on September 1, 1937, when passengers and mail were carried from Vancouver to Seattle, a 122-mile route. This service was taken over from Canadian Airways Limited, along with their equipment and staff. The equipment consisted of two Lockheed Electra 10A aircraft, CF-BAF and CF-AZY, which were purchased by Canadian Airways Limited late in 1936, and one Stearman single-engine biplane used as a trainer and as a spare for carrying mail. The pilots on this inaugural run were Billy Wells, later Trans-Canada

Air Lines' base manager in Vancouver, and Maurice McGregor. Changing the name "Canadian Airways Limited" to "Trans-Canada Air Lines" on these aircraft was an overnight paint job, as these two pilots had just arrived from Seattle the day before in the employ of Canadian Airways, and the following day made the inaugural flight for the new company, Trans-Canada Air Lines.

During the last few months of 1937 considerable flying for training purposes was done between Winnipeg and the coast. When 1937 ended, Trans-Canada Air Lines' personnel numbered seventy-one and they had five Lockheed Electra 10A aircraft.

In January, 1938, Trans-Canada Air Lines inaugurated a flight training programme. A scheduled training service carrying first-class air mail between Winnipeg and Vancouver became effective on March 1, 1938. Passenger services were not to be operated until all airport and airway facilities had been thoroughly tested and tried under actual operating conditions.

There was progressive development in the company's operation of training flights in western Canada, with an occasional trip across the Rockies, to a regularly operated daily schedule between Montreal and Vancouver with a connecting schedule from Lethbridge to Edmonton.

The principal events during 1938 — the year that Philip Johnson was awarded the Trans-Canada Trophy — were as follows:

February 1 —	Scheduled training service between Winnipeg and Vancouver inaugurated; daylight flights with Lockheed 10A equipment.
March 6 —	First-class mail carried on training schedule between Winnipeg and Vancouver.
April 1 —	Night flying inaugurated in western Canada.
June 20 —	Twice daily schedule established on Vancouver-Seattle service.
July 1 —	Twice-daily training schedule established between Winnipeg and Vancouver; the daylight flight with 10A equipment and the night flying with 14H equipment.
August 15 —	Day schedule between Winnipeg and Vancouver discontinued. Experimental flights east of Winnipeg commenced.
September 7 —	Scheduled training service between Winnipeg and Montreal inaugurated.
September 19 —	Air express service established between Winnipeg and Vancouver.
October 1 —	Regular air mail service established between Winnipeg and Vancouver carrying only mail at surcharged rates, night schedule; air mail and air express service established between Lethbridge and Edmonton, night schedule.
October 17 —	Air express service extended to Montreal and Toronto.
December 1 —	Air mail service extended from Winnipeg to Montreal and Toronto; day schedule. Occasional night flights undertaken east of Winnipeg.

When the eventful year of 1938 came to a close, Trans-Canada Air Lines'

A group of officials shown at St. Hubert Airport, P.Q., on July 30, 1937, prior to the Right Honourable C.D. Howe's dawn-to-dusk flight over the projected route from Montreal to Vancouver. (Left to right) — Don Saunders, Lew Parmenter, F.I. Banghart, W.H. Hobbs, H.J. Symington, Hon. C.D. Howe, Pilot J.H. Tudhope, Cdr. C.P. Edwards, co-pilot J.D. Hunter, J.A. Wilson, G.C. Wakeman and D.R. MacLaren.

Photo courtesy of The Public Archives of Canada.

equipment consisted of nine Lockheed 14H aircraft and five Lockheed 10A aircraft. The first two Lockheed 14 aircraft were received from Burbank, California, by Trans-Canada Air Lines in May, 1938. Pilot Lewis Leigh with co-pilot J. L. "Lindy" Rood; and Pilot Slim Lewis with co-pilot Maurice McGregor made up the two crews who picked up the aircraft in Burbank. The Lockheed 14H aircraft were equipped with two Pratt and Whitney S1E2G Hornet engines of 850 h.p. each, hydromatic full-feathering propellers and Bendix radio equipment. Each aircraft had accommodation for ten passengers and a crew of three. The cargo-carrying capacity was 2,700 pounds. The 14H had a cruising speed of 200 m.p.h., and a cruising range of some 1,575 miles. This 14H equipment was used on the transcontinental services while the 10A equipment was used on the Vancouver-Seattle and Lethbridge-Edmonton services. The Lockheed 10A aircraft were equipped with two Pratt and Whitney super-charged S.B. Wasp Junior engines of 450 h.p. each, with controllable pitch propellers and Western Electric radio equipment (except one aircraft which had Bendix radio equipment). There was passenger accommodation for ten, with a crew of two. Each 10A was capable of carrying 800 pounds of cargo, as well as passengers. Cruising speed for the 10A was 175 m.p.h., with a cruising range of 720 miles.

It was Trans-Canada Air Lines' policy to lease hangar space and other necessary facilities on a rental basis wherever possible, but at some points it

was necessary for them to construct their own hangar accommodation. They designed a hangar which permitted expansion with a minimum of disturbance to the existing structure. Hangars of this type were completed in 1938 at Stevenson Airport, Winnipeg, and at the municipal airport at Lethbridge. Another hangar was completed at Malton Airport in February, 1939.

Arrangements were made with the municipalities for the use of the municipal airports at Winnipeg, Regina, Lethbridge, Edmonton, Vancouver and Seattle, and with the Department of Transport for use of the facilities at Montreal (St. Hubert), Ottawa, North Bay, Kapuskasing and Wagaming.

By the end of 1938, four-course radio range equipment, transmitting on low or medium frequency, provided by the Department of Transport, was in operation at Montreal, Ottawa, Toronto (Malton), North Bay, Kapuskasing, Wagaming, Winnipeg, Regina, Lethbridge, Edmonton and Vancouver, and at the intermediate or 100-mile fields. These facilities were available for the use of all aircraft. Low-frequency four-course radio range equipment was planned by the Department of Transport as early as 1936, and the first installation was made at Vancouver in 1937. Active in this work for the Department of Transport were Harold Walsh, Bill Acton and Iva Shepherd of the Radio Divison, and Gordon Bulger, Superintendent of Aircraft Maintenance for the Civil Aviation Branch.

In the mountain section it was found that better coverage would be afforded if

the radio ranges between Cranbrook and Princeton were on a straight line. So, it was arranged with the Department of Transport to have two new improved radio ranges installed at high locations at Crescent Valley and Carmi. This work was completed in December, 1938, and calibrated in January, 1939.

The Department of Transport installed a very high frequency (VHF) range marker at Maple Ridge, 15 miles east of Vancouver, the approximate point at which the westbound flight commenced its descent after crossing the mountains. The range marker was a ground radio installation transmitting a signal on a very high frequency which was received by the pilot both audibly and visually by means of a special receiver in the aircraft. Knowing the location of the marker, the signal enabled the pilot to check his course and location within very definite limits.

Philip Johnson had stressed the paramount importance of developing a weather-reporting service suitable for the needs of scheduled air line transportation. Arrangements were then made to have the Meteorological Branch, Department of Transport, provide this service on a 24-hour basis from Montreal west.

The personnel of Trans-Canada Air Lines had increased to 332 by the end of 1938. During the month of July, 1938, stewardesses were first engaged for the Vancouver-Seattle service. Only registered nurses were acceptable by Trans-Canada Air Lines. However, the policy of employing only registered nurses as stewardesses was discontinued

Lockheed Electra 10A aircraft, CF-TCA, taking off from Vancouver Airport en route to Seattle, carrying passengers and mail on a regular scheduled trip. This was the first new aircraft that T.C.A. purchased in 1937. It was turned over to the National Museum of Science and Technology, Ottawa in 1968.

Photo courtesy of T.C.A.

in April, 1957.

A traffic department was organized towards the latter part of 1938, and George G. Wakeman was appointed General Traffic Manager at Montreal. District officers were appointed at Winnipeg and Vancouver.

The Right Honourable C. D. Howe introduced in Parliament "The Transport Act, 1938", which placed air transport, including Trans-Canada Air Lines, under the jurisdiction of the Board of Transport Commissioners for Canada in respect to regulation and licensing of air carriers transporting goods or passengers for hire or reward; investigations and surveys respecting operation and development of commercial air services in Canada and other matters relating to public service. These functions ceased to be under the jurisdiction of the Transport Commissioners when they were taken over by the Air Transport Board when it was formed in September, 1944, by an amendment to the Aeronautics Act.

A regular air mail and air express service already established between Montreal, Toronto and Vancouver, and between Lethbridge and Edmonton, on December 1, 1938, on a daylight schedule, was changed on March 1, 1939, to a night schedule providing first morning delivery in Winnipeg and Regina and afternoon delivery in Lethbridge, Calgary, Edmonton, Vancouver and Victoria of mail picked up the previous evening in Montreal, Ottawa and Toronto; also afternoon delivery in Toronto, Ottawa and Montreal of mail picked up the previous evening in western Canada. On February 1, 1939, Calgary became a regular point of call on the Lethbridge-Edmonton service.

February, 1939, saw the completion of a hangar at Malton Airport (Toronto) by Trans-Canada Air Lines. Later in the year one was completed at St. Hubert Airport by the company. Administration buildings were constructed at the municipal airports at Malton, Regina,

Calgary and North Bay, under arrangements made between the Department of Transport and the municipal authorities.

Trans-Canada Air Lines entered into a temporary agreement with Canadian Airways Limited, effective March 1, 1939, under which the company would carry mail between Vancouver and Victoria by seaplane.

On April 1, 1939, a transcontinental passenger, mail and express service was inaugurated between Montreal, Toronto, Winnipeg, Lethbridge and Vancouver, with connections at Lethbridge, from Calgary and Edmonton. This historic flight left St. Hubert Airport at Montreal for Vancouver on April 1, 1939. The ten-passenger Lockheed aircraft was piloted by Captin Kelly Edmison, while First Officer Frank Young was the co-pilot. At Winnipeg, Captain Lewis Leigh, with co-pilot Gil MacLaren, took over the flight on April 2, 1939, and flew from there to Vancouver. Stops en route were made at Toronto, North Bay, Kapuskasing, Winnipeg, Regina and Lethbridge. The flight took 16:05 hours' flying time. Also, at this same time an east-bound flight left Vancouver for Montreal on April 1. Frank Young was captain of the east-bound flight from Winnipeg to Montreal on April 2. It was Captain Gordon Haslett who made the inaugural flight from Edmonton to Calgary and Lethbridge on April 1, 1939.

Then an announcement was made in May, 1939, by the Honourable Ian A. Mackenzie, Minister of National Defence, that Philip Johnson had been awarded the Trans-Canada Trophy in recognition of meritorious service in the inauguration and outstanding progress of Trans-Canada Air Lines during 1938, thereby contributing greatly to the advancement of aviation in Canada. The trophy was to be held in trust as a group award to the operating personnel of the company.

No formal presentation of the trophy was ever made to Philip Johnson, as it

never seemed possible to set a date that was convenient to both him and the Minister of National Defence.

On July 18, 1939, a direct Montreal-Ottawa-Toronto passenger service was established and the air mail service was extended to cover that route. A second daily schedule between those points became effective on November 1, 1939. The lack of complete radio coverage delayed the inauguration of passenger service to Moncton until February 15, 1940.

An air express service which was inaugurated between Montreal, Toronto and Vancouver on October 17, 1938, was extended during the year 1939 to cover the Montreal-Ottawa-Toronto schedules when these were established, and to Moncton when the training schedule was inaugurated to that city on November 1, 1939.

Radio range facilities, transmitting on low or medium frequency, furnished by the Department of Transport, were in operation at all stations along Trans-Canada Air Lines' route from Moncton to Vancouver and at the intermediate or 100-mile landing fields before 1939 came to a close. New ranges were installed at Megantic, Quebec; Blissville, New Brunswick; and Moncton, New Brunswick, on the Montreal-Moncton run; and

---

The Committee of Award for the year 1938 consisted of the following members:

Wing Commander G. R. Howsam, Royal Canadian Air Force, Department of National Defence, Ottawa.

J. A. Wilson, Controller of Civil Aviation, Department of Transport, Ottawa.

Squadron Leader C. C. Walker, Staff Officer in charge of Civil Government Operations, Department of National Defence, Ottawa.

Dr. J. J. Green, representing the Canadian Flying Clubs Association, Ottawa.

T.C.A. Lockheed aircraft at Vancouver Airport in 1938.

at Stirling, Ontario (about 20 miles north of Trenton), on the direct route between Ottawa and Toronto. The first three were in operation in the late fall of 1939 and the Stirling range was in operation by the end of 1939. With the completion of a radio range by the United States authorities at Millinocket, Maine, by the end of January, 1940, there was full radio coverage on the Montreal-Moncton route.

The pilot-training programme was carried on as expeditiously as the provision of flying equipment permitted during 1939. In all, some 2,096 hours were flown in training, and twenty-one candidates successfully completed the training courses and were assigned to duty. Daylight cross-country trips were operated in the Prairie section for the advanced training and familiarization of potential captains.

Philip G. Johnson submitted his resignation as Vice-President of Trans-Canada Air Lines on September 1, 1939, to become President of Boeing Airplane Company. Appreciating his personal reasons, the directors of Trans-Canada Air Lines accepted his resignation with much regret. When Philip Johnson became Vice-President of Trans-Canada Air Lines, he agreed to make his services available only until the basic structure of the air line was completed and operating efficiently, and this was now so. During a difficult period, he had done a good job. In returning to Boeing Airplane, the company with which he had been associated for seventeen years, he returned to his birthplace, Seattle, where he was born on November 5, 1894. Here he remained until the time of his death in 1944. Phil Johnson had, perhaps, a greater interest in the construction and

selling of aircraft, than in flying them. He was a highly qualified engineer, a good salesman, an extrovert and a splendid person.

D. B. Colyer, who was Chief Technical Adviser to Philip Johnson, was then appointed Vice-President of Operations as of September 1, 1939.

NOTES

[1], [2], [3], and [4] — quotes from *Canadian Aviation*, April, 1937.
[5], [6], [7] — quotes from *Canadian Aviation*, August, 1937.

1939

Murton Seymour at Vancouver, B.C., on May 23, 1916, just after being commissioned in the Royal Flying Corps.
Photo courtesy of Murton Seymour.

Murton A. Seymour

Citation: in recognition of the outstanding leadership he gave to the Flying Clubs of Canada that year (1939)

Murton Adams Seymour, O.B.E., Q.C., B.A., while President of the Canadian Flying Clubs Association, Ottawa, was awarded the Trans-Canada Trophy for meritorious service in the advancement of aviation during 1939, "in recognition of the outstanding leadership he gave to the Flying Clubs of Canada that year." The award states "he elevated the Flying Clubs to a position where they could render a great service to Canada." The announcement of the award was made on May 7, 1940, by the Honourable C.G. Power, M.C., Minister of National Defence.

Simultaneously with the outbreak of war in September, 1939, the Canadian Flying Clubs were in uniform. Their years of experience in supervising civil pilot training were applied to the training of provisional pilot officers for the R.C.A.F., and later to the direction of the Elementary Flying Training Schools under the British Commonwealth Air Training Plan.[1]

The Flying Clubs of Canada came into existence in 1927 and 1928 under a subsidy policy established by what was then the Civil Aviation Branch of the Department of National Defence, subsequently taken over by the Department of Transport upon its formation in November, 1936. J. A. Wilson, then Controller of Civil Aviation, had taken a leading part in getting this Light Aeroplane Club or Flying Club Scheme under way. This policy was established following a similar policy in England of creating Light Aeroplane Clubs for the purpose of training civilians to fly so that a reserve of partially trained pilots would be available for defence purposes.[2]

The name *Club* was really a misnomer as they were not clubs in the ordinary social sense, but were essentially flying training schools for civil pilots.[3]

These clubs were practically all organized under the various provincial statutes dealing with non-profit organizations, and no one could receive any remuneration other than, of course, the full-time paid personnel and all revenues, such as they were, were devoted to the training of pilots. The few clubs which were organized on a share capital basis all had by-laws prohibiting the declaration of dividends, payment of directors' fees and, in effect, were also purely voluntary non-profit organizations.[4]

This Flying Club Scheme had three objectives: First, the establishment of aerodromes throughout Canada, as at that time there were practically no airports in existence; secondly, creating air-consciousness amongst Canadians; and thirdly, the main objective, the creation of a reserve of partially trained pilots for defence in the event of war.[5]

The first objective was achieved, and the history of the development of airports prior to the outbreak of war proved not only the wisdom of the plan but indicated that, had it not been for the early establishment of these clubs, municipal airports would not have reached the development they had at the outbreak of the war. In all some twenty-six clubs were established. Twenty-two of these survived the Depression and were active when the war broke out. In most instances, the airports which these clubs used for their early training activities developed into municipal airports.[6]

The second objective was also achieved. No one can reflect upon the development of flying in Canada throughout the years without realizing how Canadians, as a whole, have come

Murton Seymour in an OX-powered Curtiss pusher aeroplane at Minoru Park Race Track, on Lulu Island, B.C., where he learned to fly in 1915.

Photo courtesy of Murton Seymour.

to look upon air transportation as one of the developing forces in Canada. In this respect, the clubs, directly and indirectly, played a very large part by providing airports and training facilities and making available flying instruction at a low cost.[7]

The third objective was never achieved. This was partly due to the influence of peace-seeking international agreements, and also due to the economic depression that struck in 1930 and cut down the money available for development of aviation.[8]

The standard conditions for the Light Aeroplane Club Scheme were laid down by P.C. 1878, dated September 24, 1927 (supplemented by additional assistance under the terms of P.C. 1309, dated June 11, 1930). Briefly, these required each club to:

(a) Provide its own flying field.
(b) Arrange for the services of a qualified instructor and an air engineer.
(c) Have at least thirty members prepared to qualify as pilots.
(d) Have not less than ten members already qualified as pilots.

After the clubs fulfilled these conditions, then the government undertook to give them the following:

(a) Each approved club would receive two aeroplanes and engines as an initial grant.
(b) A further issue annually, for a period of five years, would be made of one aeroplane and engine complete, providing the club purchased an aeroplane of equal value.
(c) The sum of $100 would be granted to each club in respect to each member who qualified as an ab initio pilot.
(d) The sum of two dollars per flying hour, up to 50 hours, would be granted to each club for a club member continuing his training and qualifying for a commercial pilot's certificate (1930 provision).
(e) An issue of closed aircraft in lieu of

open aircraft would be made to clubs graduating at least 25 pilots (1930 provision).
(f) One parachute would be loaned to clubs providing one at their own expense (1930 provision).

In later years these grants were supplemented in various ways, such as by additional aircraft and by grants for the renewal of licences. Other revenue for these clubs was received from flying training, as well as whatever revenue they were able to obtain from local municipal and community assistance. For many years, however, the total revenue received by the clubs was so small that it was only by the dogged determination of the men behind the clubs that they were kept in existence at all during the Depression. Nevertheless, they did acquire, throughout their eleven or twelve years' existence prior to the outbreak of war, substantial elementary and advanced civil flying training experience and a great capacity for the economical maintenance of aircraft under most difficult conditions.[9]

These clubs trained, during their prewar existence, some 3,000 pilots, hundreds of whom found their way into the R.C.A.F. before the war. Others went into commercial and auxiliary service flying and were of great value when the war came.[10]

In 1929 the Civil Aviation Branch of the Department of National Defence realized that, with clubs scattered from Sydney on the Atlantic to Victoria on the Pacific, a central organization was essential in order to bind them together and to act as a liaison between the clubs as a whole and the government.[11]

Out of this grew the Canadian Flying Clubs Association which was organized on November 1, 1929, and has continued as the central organization for the clubs.[12] The association's first annual meeting was held at the Royal Edward Hotel, Fort William, Ontario, on November 1, 1929. Sixteen out of the

twenty clubs were represented.

Murton Seymour, one of the founders, drafted the first constitution and by-laws of this association, which had been supported by an annual grant from the Civil Aviation Branch and by annual fees paid by the club. Its first annual grant of $5,000 was received in June, 1930, and was given on the condition that it appoint a secretary whose qualifications and duties would be acceptable to the Civil Aviation Branch, then under the Department of National Defence, and since November 2, 1936, under the Department of Transport. This additional assistance was authorized under the terms of P.C. 1309, dated June 11, 1930 (supplemental to P.C. 1878, dated September 24, 1927). Its headquarters was established in Ottawa. The annual grant to the Royal Canadian Flying Clubs Association was increased to $10,000 in 1948-49.

Permission was given to the Canadian Flying Clubs Association in 1944 to use the prefix "Royal," in recognition of its contribution to the British Commonwealth Air Training Plan, so that henceforth it would be known as the Royal Canadian Flying Clubs Association.

The first grant, coming just after the association's organization in 1929, was most encouraging to the clubs and helped to stimulate additional groups to organize others. It also proved an incentive to clubs not yet connected with the association to give serious consideration to the benefits to be derived from connection with this national organization of Canadian Flying Clubs.

The Dominion was geographically divided into seven zones for the purposes of administration, and a vice-president presided over the clubs in each zone. These vice-presidents, together with the treasurer and the president, composed the executive of the association. At this time the association had a full-time paid secretary and a very small clerical staff

The OX-powered pusher aeroplane at Minoru Park Race Track on Lulu Island, B.C., in 1915. The aeroplane was built by William Stark about 1912. From left to right: William Gordon McRae, Phillip Scott, William Stark, Phillip H. Smith, Murton A. Seymour and J.V.W. (Vick) Phillips.

Photo courtesy of Murton Seymour.

and, of course, was in itself a purely non-profit organization, its directors and executive being the representatives of the respective clubs. No one on the executive received any remuneration.[13] The association's first President was Flight Lieutenant Jack A. Sully of Winnipeg (later Air Vice-Marshal Sully of Goderich, Ontario).

To stimulate interest in aviation, the association organized and directed the first Trans-Canada Air Pageant, which started from Hamilton, Ontario, on July 1, 1931, Dominion Day. Pat Reid, Trans-Canada Trophy winner for 1942-43, was the tour leader; while George Ross, Executive Secretary of the Canadian Flying Clubs Association, was business manager of the tour. The flight left from Hamilton and went to Vancouver, via the United States and returned to Hamilton, then continued to the Maritimes, from where it returned to Toronto on September 8 where a final show was staged on Aviation Day at the Canadian National Exhibition. Twenty aircraft and a picked flight from the Royal Canadian Air Force comprised the pageant which staged twenty-six performances throughout the tour.

At the end of 1931 the Canadian Flying Clubs Association took over the publication of the magazine *Canadian Aviation*, previously directed by the Aviation League of Canada since its first year of publication in 1929. Since September, 1939, it has been published by the MacLean-Hunter Publishing Company, Toronto.

Murton Seymour was the Association's Treasurer for the years 1931 and 1932. In 1938 he was elected Vice-President of the Central Zone and was elected President of the Canadian Flying Clubs Association in January, 1939, remaining President of the Association until February, 1944.

In February, 1939, the newly elected executive of the association, convinced that the gathering war-clouds meant

trouble for the Commonwealth, decided that the government should be approached with a view to expanding the activities of the clubs in elementary flying training for defence purposes.[14] So, in that same month, the Executive of the Canadian Flying Clubs' Association, led by Murton Seymour, the new President, visited the Honourable Ian Mackenzie, Minister of National Defence, to discuss the situation concerning the defence of our country, should war become inevitable. Out of this visit, came the request that the association have eight of its twenty-two member clubs undertake the elementary flying training instruction of a number of provisional pilot officers for the R.C.A.F. The eight clubs entered into an agreement with the Department of National Defence, which was negotiated by Murton Seymour on behalf of the association, both as its President and as a lawyer. After special refresher courses for the eight club instructors, training of thirty-two provisional pilot officers started on June 5, 1939.

Early in July, 1939, Murton Seymour went on a tour of the flying clubs in Canada to tell them how important it was to strengthen their organizations and prepare for a training programme right away. Squadron Leader A. T. Cowley (later Air Vice-Marshal), then Superintendent of Air Regulations, flew the Beechcraft of the Department of Transport which carried Murton Seymour on this mission of national importance. They visited every club in the West — Fort William, Winnipeg, Portage la Prairie, Regina, Saskatoon, Edmonton, Calgary, Moose Jaw, Vancouver and Victoria. He gave a very inspiring talk to each club he visited and told them about the plans for training pilot personnel and how these flying clubs could help to carry out this training in the national interest.

This opportunity was eagerly grasped by the flying clubs so that upon the outbreak of war in September, 1939, when the association was asked to bring

the remaining clubs into the training programme as quickly as possible, within a month the remaining fourteen clubs were all training pilots for the R.C.A.F. This agreement and the training given by the clubs formed the basis of the civil Elementary Flying Training Schools of the British Commonwealth Air Training Plan.

So, from February, 1939, the elementary stage of flying training of pilots for the Royal Canadian Air Force was entirely in the hands of the flying clubs — and they responded magnificently to this responsibility. During the period that the clubs carried on this training, over 500 provisional pilot officers and leading aircraftsmen were given elementary training.[15] The pilots trained by the clubs in the pre-war period also helped to staff the first squadrons to go overseas, as well as staffing the instructor strength of the R.C.A.F. in its service schools and the Elementary Flying Training Schools.

On Sunday morning, September 3, 1939, at the hour of 8:00 A.M., the telephone rang at Murton Seymour's residence in St. Catharines. Wing Commander George Howsam, later Air Vice-Marshal, Director of Air Training for the R.C.A.F., Ottawa, was at the other end of the line. He said: "The balloon's up, and so on. Come to Ottawa immediately." Within twenty-four hours, by telephone and telegraph, the remaining fourteen clubs were informed and they responded and on September 4 Murton Seymour left for Ottawa, where for the next five weeks he worked as a civilian at a desk in Wing Commander Howsam's office. The preliminary organizing done, he then left to tour the clubs in eastern Canada.

As the Canadian Flying Clubs' Association was convinced that its clubs were capable of carrying out elementary training under the Air Training Plan, Murton Seymour, as President, made earnest representations to the

Honourable Ian Mackenzie, Minister of National Defence, and later to the Honourable Norman Rogers, requesting that the clubs be given the opportunity of continuing and expanding this training as a patriotic effort. The Department of National Defence finally decided to use the training experience of the club's personnel, but required that separate civil companies be formed to operate and manage the Elementary Flying Training Schools.[16]

Where a school was to be established in an area in which a flying club existed, the club would have the first opportunity of sponsoring and organizing the school company. The original plan was to have thirteen Elementary Flying Training Schools but the Association urged that the size of the schools be cut in half and the number doubled, thus giving an opportunity to each one of the twenty-two clubs in the Dominion.[17]*

This suggestion was accepted and, as a result, practically every club sponsored an Elementary Flying Training School. All clubs, except those located where circumstances prevented the establishment of a school in the area in which the club operated, were included. The clubs had behind them the benefit of twelve years of elementary training and felt they could interest, in their respective communities, business and professional men with the highest type of executive ability.[18] This proved to be so.

The clubs were prepared to carry on this training without any desire for financial reward, other than the hope of having something left over at the end of the war with which to revive the post-war training activities of the clubs. The Department of National Defence wisely decided that the school companies should have sufficient capital to assure continuous operation and good management, and this necessitated that the clubs go to the public for money with

which to comply with these requirements.[19]

The whole scheme was new and the idea of elementary training being done for the R.C.A.F. by civil companies was somewhat strange to those who did not know the history and background of the flying clubs and even to many who did. As a result of this, some of the flying clubs had difficulty in getting the required capital, but all eventually succeeded.[20] Murton Seymour raised or helped directly in raising the capital for ten of the schools.

The government programme provided that the school company should pay interest on their capital at a rate not exceeding five per cent. This stipulation raised in the minds of some the question why, if this was to be a patriotic effort, it was necessary to pay any interest. Several of the club-sponsored school companies received their capital in the form of donations or subscriptions to stock, without any strings attached whatsoever. Others found it necessary to undertake to pay the interest authorized by the government.[21]

The directors of these schools served without any remuneration and in most instances without even asking for their out-of-pocket expenses. With the exception of one school established in an area where there had been no club, and no club was near, the school then having to be undertaken by a commercial company, all of the schools were club-sponsored. In such instances, any surplus that remained at the end of the war from the operation of the schools reverted to the sponsoring club which in itself was a non-profit organization.[22]

The president and the executive of the association, consisting of A. M. Alexander, G. R. Ferguson, J. J. Green, W. G. MacKenzie, C. W. Nicholls, Wilfrid A. Stempel and H. A. Yates, met the government, R.C.A.F. officers and the British Mission, in negotiations leading up to the drafting of the contract

under which the Elementary Flying Training Schools subsequently operated.

The government and R.C.A.F. representatives were K. S. Maclachlan, Deputy Minister; Air Commodore L. S. Breadner; Brigadier R. J. Orde, Judge Advocate General; Air Commodore E. W. Stedman and the government's financial adviser for the R.C.A.F., Henry G. Norman.

The British Mission was headed by Lord Riverdale and with him were Sir Robert Brooke-Popham, later General Officer Commanding at Singapore, Sir Christopher Courtney and Group Captain James M. Robb, later Air Chief Marshal Sir James M. Robb, with whom Murton Seymour had trained at Upavon in 1916.

The costs of elementary flying training operation covering a period of many years, as disclosed by the clubs, several of which had the services of chartered accountants, were used as the basis of the remuneration set out in the contract. Mr. H. G. Norman commented that they were the most satisfactory figures of costs of flying training that he had been privileged to examine. Some 41,000 personnel received training at these Elementary Flying Training Schools.

The schools received payment under five headings:

(1) A management fee to cover the salaries of the administrative and clerical staffs. This was a fixed fee every lunar monthly period of four weeks, and any economies effected thereunder belonged to the school company.

(2) There was also an operation or maintenance payment, known as the target price, payable every period, out of which the company was required to pay its instructors, engineering and other operation and maintenance personnel, costs of maintenance of aircraft, including spare parts, maintenance of grounds and buildings, etc.

If any economies were effected which

*see Appendix A

Murton Seymour in the cockpit of an F.E. 8, with the 41st Squadron, Royal Flying Corps, British Expeditionary Force, at Abeele, Belgium, just before taking off on a test flight, in October, 1916.

Photo courtesy of Murton Seymour.

resulted in savings in this figure, the Crown was entitled to 75 per cent thereof and the school company entitled to 25 per cent. Conversely, in the event of a loss, the Crown paid 75 per cent of the loss, and the school company, out of its own funds, paid 25 per cent of the loss. The amount was subject to revision every six periods, based on their experience; the intent being to keep it as close as practicable to actual operating costs. The experience of the schools was that substantial savings were effected under this heading, all of which were held in a reserve fund and invested almost entirely in Dominion non-interest-bearing certificates.

(3) Each company also received a gas and oil allowance and a messing allowance per R.C.A.F. personnel per day, both of which were on a basis of actual cost and from which the company could obtain no benefit.

(4) In addition, the company received a per-flying-hour allowance for what was called a "crash reserve" to provide for crashes of aircraft which were inevitable due to the high pressure of war-time training and the ordinary hazards of training absolutely green personnel. This reserve did not belong to the company but remained the property of the Crown.

(5) The contract also included an allowance per flying hour as profit for the company, something which was not asked for by the association in any of its representations but was inserted by the government in the contract. It was said that this was for the purpose of providing a surplus which, at the end of the war, would be available to the sponsoring clubs for renewing their civil flying training activities. This allowance was later reduced on a sliding scale, depending on the size of the school, at the

voluntary request of the association representing the companies, to as little as one-fifth of the original allowance.[23]

All the training activities of the schools were closely supervised by R.C.A.F. personnel, and also all the financial accounting of the schools was closely supervised.[24]

When the Elementary Flying Training School contracts were completed, the clubs, of their own volition, returned all profits in excess of $5,000 per annum per school to the government. In the over-all picture, this amounted to $4,849,185.

The success of the training provided by these schools was so obvious that it needs no comment, other than that the subcommittee of the Special War Expenditures Committee of the House of Commons, which investigated the contracts and the whole set-up of the civil schools, reported that the training being done by the schools was entirely satisfactory to the Training Directorate of the Royal Canadian Air Force and, as Air Vice-Marshal Robert Leckie stated to the committee, "If the Service had been called upon to assume this training, it would be an intolerable burden upon the Service." The committee also found that the cost of operating the schools was considerably below that originally estimated by the government.[25]

The committee recommended that the capacities of the civil schools be utilized to the full and also made a recommendation, on the suggestion of the president of the association, which was enthusiastically received by the sponsoring clubs, that the clubs all be required to reorganize with uniform charters under the Dominion Companies' Act, providing additional safeguards to ensure that all the benefits which the clubs might receive from the operation of their respective schools would be utilized solely for their post-war training activities.[26]

The combining of civil management in

the elementary schools with service requirements presented many difficulties that needed careful co-operation to overcome, but this was achieved with the result that these schools had all the advantages of civil management, including the ease and flexibility of change in carrying out a syllabus of training provided by the Service. Murton Seymour, until February, 1944, voluntarily provided almost full-time liaison with the government and the R.C.A.F. The final responsibility for assuring adequately and properly trained pilots for operational units, of necessity, rested in the hands of the R.C.A.F. and naturally the methods of training were under Air Force direction; but the achieving of that training by civil instructors, the management and training of administrative and mechanical personnel, the administration of all the details that made up the operation of a training school, were under the direction of the civil companies and benefited from the application of the ordinary business efficiency to service requirements. This combination resulted not only in outstanding efficiency of training and serviceability of aircraft but in economies in personnel and cost of operation that were impossible under service procedure.[27]

The objectives of the civil companies were the training of pilots within the requirements of the syllabus laid down by the R.C.A.F. to a standard of proficiency acceptable to the service and the provision of this training at as low a cost to the government as possible. Judging from the results as evidenced by the report of the subcommittee, both were achieved and the schools could devote their whole attention to improvements in the standard of training and in economies of operation. Thus the assurances of the association were fulfilled and the country received the benefit of the application of the business efficiency to service requirements.[28]

While the primary concern of the association then was elementary school management, it did not lose sight of the fact that these schools were the clubs "in battle dress," so to speak. With the experience of the flying clubs in the past and their added experience of elementary training during the war, they became the basis for the establishment of a comprehensive training programme for the peace-time development of aviation in Canada.[29]

Murton A. Seymour was born in St. Catharines, Ontario, on July 6, 1892. He received his education at Queen's School and King Edward School in Vancouver, British Columbia; the University of Toronto, where he received his B.A. in 1915; and Osgoode Hall, Toronto.

He learned to fly in the "early days", commencing his flying lessons at Lulu Island in the Fraser River Delta near Vancouver and went solo on September 2, 1915. These activities were carried out in an OX-powered Curtiss pusher aeroplane, built about 1911, and owned by William Stark, also an aviation pioneer of British Columbia. Along with a group of eleven other students who purchased the machine from William Stark in 1915, Murton Seymour gained his initial instruction by sitting on the wing of the aircraft and watching the actions of William Stark during ground demonstration flights. Then each pupil practised taxiing along the ground, being given more engine power as he became more proficient until finally the pupil had enough power to make short solo hops of three or four feet from the ground.[30]

Later that year, in 1915, the scene of operations was moved to Sea Island on the very site of the present Sea Island Airport where longer flights were possible. The group was organized as a club in July of 1915 by Murton Seymour. The name "Aero Club of B.C." was chosen. This club, the original Aero Club of B.C., was the first flying club ever established in Canada. Murton Seymour,

at this time a law student with the firm of Gwillam, Crisp and Mackay in Vancouver, drew up its constitution and by-laws.[31] He had the distinction of being the first pilot to be trained by the Aero Club of B.C. when he graduated in November, 1915, under Instructor William Stark.

A few weeks later, Lieutenant Colonel Percy Burke, D.S.O., Commandant of the Central Flying School, Upavon, England, arrived in Vancouver on a tour of Canada to look into the prospects of establishing training schools. He inspected the members of the new Aero Club of B.C. and its OX-powered Curtiss-pusher aeroplane and, though being rather jocular about the whole outfit, promised to recommend two of the group for commissions in the Special Reserve of the Royal Flying Corps.[32]

Much to their surprise, Murton Seymour and Phillip Smith were chosen in May, 1916. They left for England on the 16th of the month. Murton Seymour went overseas as a pilot with the Royal Flying Corps, Special Reserve.[33] He had been attached to the 158th Battalion of the Canadian Expeditionary Force and the 31st B.C. Light Horse.

Commissioned as a Second Lieutenant, he trained at the Central Flying School at Upavon, England. On October 16, he proceeded to France with the 41st Squadron, Royal Flying Corps (single-seater fighters), and was stationed at Abeele, Belgium. Here he remained until early in 1917. However, he was subsequently medically boarded out of flying at high altitudes and he was transferred to administrative work in England.[34] Years later this turned out to be due to a lack of oxygen.

In May, 1917, he was posted to the Royal Air Force, Canada, as a Wing Adjutant. He was promoted to the rank of Captain on July 1, 1917, and to the rank of Major (administrative) on January 5, 1918, being then on the headquarters' staff of the Royal Air Force in Canada[35]

as the officer in charge of all flying and technical training. He had been sent to Texas in September, 1917, in charge of the advance party of three British and four U.S. Signal Corps officers (Aviation Section) to open up three airfields at Fort Worth for 1917-18 winter training. When he was demobilized in 1919, he held the rank of Acting Wing Commander.

Upon the cessation of hostilities, he continued his law studies, and was called to the Bar of British Columbia in 1919, and to the Bar of Ontario in 1919. He then became a member of the Law Society of British Columbia and the Law Society of Upper Canada.

Murton Seymour was associated with the law firm of Ingersoll, Kingstone and Seymour from 1919 to 1932 in St. Catharines. Then in 1933 he formed his own firm of Seymour and Lampard, later Seymour, Lampard, Goldring, Young and Nicholls.

He was the first President of the St. Catharines Flying Club which he organized in 1928, and prepared its constitution and its by-laws. He served as its President for eight years.

In 1934, Murton Seymour was created a King's Counsel. In 1938 he was elected Vice-President of the Central Zone of the Canadian Flying Clubs Association; and President of the Canadian Flying Clubs Association in January, 1939. He held the position of president until 1944.

The Committee of Award for the year 1939 consisted of the following members:

Group Captain A. T. N. Cowley, Royal Canadian Air Force, Department of National Defence, Ottawa.

J. A. Wilson, Controller of Civil Aviation, Department of Transport, Ottawa.

Wing Commander C. C. Walker, Royal Canadian Air Force, Department of National Defence, Ottawa.

Dr. J. J. Green, Executive Member of the Canadian Flying Clubs Association, Ottawa.

Murton A. Seymour (left) who was presented with the Trans-Canada Trophy by the Hon. C.G. Power M.C. on June 5, 1940, in Ottawa.
Photo courtesy of the R.C.A.F.

For his service, par excellence, which he gave to the Canadian Flying Clubs Association and to Canada, in particular during 1939, he was awarded a gold medal by the association. This, too, was the year he was awarded the Trans-Canada Trophy in recognition of the outstanding leadership he gave to the Flying Clubs of Canada during 1939.

The official presentation of the trophy took place at a luncheon in his honour in Ottawa on June 5, 1940, and was made by the Honourable C. G. Power, M.C., Minister of National Defence.

Murton Seymour was created an Officer of the Order of the British Empire in 1943 for organizing the Elementary Flying Training Schools under the British Commonwealth Air Training Plan.

Although never having been engaged professionally in flying, having taken up law as his profession, Murton Seymour had combined aviation and law, being active in both fields through the years. He was Honorary Counsel for the Royal Canadian Flying Clubs Association.

He was President of Industrial Docks and Supplies Limited and Niagara Peninsula Transfer Docks Limited; a director of Davis Forest Products, Ltd., and an honorary life member of the St. Catharines Flying Club. He had been the solicitor for the Corporation of the City of St. Catharines since 1932 and held the appointment for many years. He was

governor and secretary of the St. Catharines General Hospital; a Life Bencher of the Law Society of Upper Canada; a member of the Lincoln County Law Association; a member of the Canadian Bar Association and Delta Upsilon Fraternity; the St. Catharines Club; the Albany Club, Toronto; and the Royal Canadian Military Institute. He was named a member of Canada's Aviation Hall of Fame in 1973. He was made a Companion of the Order of Flight (City of Edmonton). Also, he had invaded the field of writing and was the author of articles on the law of water pollution, municipal expropriation, compensation and injurious affection, and the law of negligence as applied to nurses and hospitals. He and his family resided in St. Catharines, Ontario.

He married Marion Merritt of St. Catharines in Folkestone, England, in 1916, and they had two children: Ann (Mrs. R. P. Rigby) and R. H. M. Seymour, both of St. Catharines. His first wife died in 1947 and in 1948 he married Jean Elizabeth Infield Jenking of Toronto. They had three children. Murton Seymour died on December 27,

1976, in St. Catharines, Ontario. He was 84 years of age.

Murton Seymour, while carrying on with his law practice for many years, much of which concerned aviation and its various legal aspects, continued to be au fait concerning not only the flying clubs, but civil aviation affairs as well. His interest in aviation never waned since the day he first learned to fly, as could be observed by his attendance at various aviation gatherings for so many years. He rendered a great service to our nation. This was especially so when early in 1939, as president of the association, he pursued the course of action he had in mind. This action of his was motivated by what, in his opinion, was the need for expanding the activities of the clubs in elementary flying training for defence purposes. This period, as it later turned out to be, was the immediate pre-war era! Through his prescience, he put the clubs in a position to be of the utmost assistance to Canada at a strategic time. Of his great mental resources and ability, Murton Seymour gave without stint to help keep the freedom of our Canadian way of life.

NOTES

[1] to [29]: article by Murton A. Seymour, *Canadian Aviation*, March, 1942.
[30] [31] [32] [33] [34] and [35]: article on M. A. Seymour, *Canadian Aviation*, March, 1939.

1940

Thomas W. "Tommy" Siers

Citation: in recognition of his outstanding contribution to military and civil aviation in Canada, and indirectly to British aviation, in the development in Canada of the Worth principle of oil dilution for aircraft engines

Thomas W. "Tommy" Siers, while Superintendent of Maintenance, for Canadian Airways Limited, Winnipeg, was awarded the Trans-Canada Trophy for meritorious service in the advancement of aviation during 1940, "in recognition of his outstanding contribution to military and civil aviation in Canada, and indirectly to British aviation, in the development in Canada of the Worth principle of oil dilution for aircraft engines." The announcement of the award was made on August 27, 1941.

In making this award, the importance of ground organization for the servicing and maintenance of aircraft was stressed, as it is an established fact that the backbone of successful air transportation is the ground organization which is carried out by the air engineer. This was substantiated by the splendid work carried out by the air engineers as a whole in the development of northern transportation.

This accomplishment of Tommy Siers was achieved in the face of the gravest difficulties and in a spirit of faith and perseverance. By the use of this oil dilution system, the most difficult problem of starting aero engines without pre-heating them under Arctic winter conditions was solved, thus saving thousands of dollars for northern transport operators and reducing fire hazards which always existed when blowtorch heating methods, or similar methods, were used.

Tommy Siers' work in this field was a distinctive and important contribution to the British Commonwealth war effort and, in addition, greatly simplified civil air operations in all northern climates.

Thomas William "Tommy" Siers was

born on May 13, 1896, in Yorkshire, England. Completing his primary and secondary school education in British schools, he came to Canada and went to Winnipeg living near there. On September 1, 1913, he started working as a machinist's helper at the C.N.R. shops in Winnipeg, where he stayed for some six months. Then he took special courses from the International Correspondence School at Scranton, Pennsylvania, on internal combustion engines. In the fall of 1914 he took up drafting and automobile engineering at the Technical School in Winnipeg, completing the year.

Tommy Siers was 21 when he joined Lord Strathcona's Horse in Winnipeg as a trooper in 1917, and went to England with them, being based at Shorncliffe. Then the Lord Strathcona's Horse and other Canadian Cavalry Regiments joined the 3rd Imperial Cavalry Brigade and went to France during the summer of 1918. He saw action at Arras and Cambrai. That November the armistice was signed, and Tommy Siers returned to Winnipeg in the spring of 1919.

After demobilization, Tommy Siers, still mechanically inclined, started operating tractors and overhauling them in the Otterburn district of Manitoba, south of Winnipeg, on May 1, 1919. The following year, the Canadian Air Force was formed by Order-in-Council No. 395, of February 18, 1920, and that fall, after having a week's holiday from his job, he joined the new service at Camp Borden on October 12, 1920, thus commencing his long and famous career in overhauling and servicing aircraft engines and equipment. With the Wing Repair Section of the Canadian Air Force, Tommy Siers worked on stationary engines and rotary engines until the end of the year. He received his Air Engineer's Certificate, No. 100, dated February 2, 1921.

Tommy Siers left the Canadian Air Force to join Laurentide Air Service at Lac à là Tortue, Quebec, in March, 1923, where he was employed as an aero engine fitter. Laurentide Air Service was federally incorporated on April 24, 1922.

His next association was with Huff-Daland Aircraft Corporation of Ogdensburg, New York, in July, 1923, being in charge of aircraft assembly work. Returning to Canada, he joined the newly formed Ontario Provincial Air Service, Sault Ste. Marie, Ontario, in April, 1924, where he was to remain for three years working on engine and machine overhaul work.

In April, 1927, Tommy Siers joined Western Canada Airways at Winnipeg, as chief mechanic. This was a newly formed company, and Doc Oaks, the first Trans-Canada Trophy winner, was in charge of its flying operations. In March, 1928, Tommy Siers was appointed Superintendent of Maintenance, in charge of overhauling and servicing of engines, aircraft and equipment. When Western Canada Airways and the Aviation Corporation of Canada were merged to form Canadian Airways on June 27, 1930, Tommy Siers continued in the employ of the new company as its Superintendent of Maintenance, while still stationed at Winnipeg. At this time, Tommy Siers had worked on many aircraft, which included Fokker Universal, Fokker F.14, Boeing Boat, Laird Mail, Avro Avian, Fokker Super Universal, Fairchild FC2 and 71, Fleetstar Model 20, Pitcairn Mail, Sikorsky, Fokker F.7 Trimotor, Boeing 40-B-4, Junkers, D.H. 61 and Moth, as well as the following engines: Wright, Pratt and Whitney Wasp Junior, Wasp and Hornet, Cirrus and D.H. Gipsy.

It was mentioned earlier in the book that a most important person in the MacAlpine rescue in the fall of 1929 was Tommy Siers, an engineer for Western Canada Airways, who was in charge of the mechanics and air engineers. It was the responsibility of these men to keep the aircraft serviceable for flying. Tommy Siers' helpers were Bill Nadin, E. Graham Longley, Paul Davis, Pat Semple and Alf Walker. (Later, in 1939, Alf Walker joined the Department of Transport as an aircraft inspector at Winnipeg, retiring in 1958.) Baker Lake was the base used for the change-over from floats to skis. Many were the problems with which they had to contend to keep the aircraft flying, and the bitterly cold weather added to their heavy problems. When Herbert Hollick-Kenyon's G-CASL sank at Stony Rapids, the aircraft was rescued from the lake and put into operation again by Tommy Siers and his men.

Another achievement was the salvaging of Fokker Super Universal G-CASQ, Andy Cruickshank's aircraft, when it broke through the ice at Bathurst Inlet — when the weather was –20° F. When G-CASQ was taxiing, it went through the ice and sank nose first, until the leading edge of the wing touched the ice and its engine and the forward part of the cabin were completely submerged, with only the wings holding the machine from sinking. In spite of the extreme cold, and working in the open with few facilities, Tommy Siers supervised the salvaging of this aircraft; completely overhauled the engine and had it in operation in the short space of ten days. Alf Walker was the air engineer flying with G-CASQ who helped put it in the air again. So efficiently was this work carried out that later this aircraft alone, of the four engaged in the rescue, was serviceable. This, as well as the almost superhuman work carried out by Tommy Siers and his men in the repairing of broken undercarriages and other aircraft parts to keep the aircraft serviceable for flying on this rescue mission, showed the indomitable spirit of the men themselves, and was a great story in itself.

One day when Bill Spence and Herbert Hollick-Kenyon went to assist in the rescue, their aircraft were forced down by fog on Musk Ox Lake for two days. Bill Spence's aircraft was damaged somewhat when it ran into heavy snowdrifts while attempting to take off. His passengers were transferred to another aircraft while Tommy Siers, Chief Engineer for Western Canada Airways, and E. Graham Longley, who was Bill Spence's air engineer, made the repairs. Two days later Roy Brown, while coming to their aid, was forced down on Aylmer Lake, about fifteen miles south, where he and his air engineer were stranded for some fifteen days.

Tommy Siers was issued Air Engineer's Certificate No. A-641, dated May 1, 1931, which superseded Certificate No. 100, dated February 2, 1921.

While with Canadian Airways, Tommy Siers had many opportunities to acquire further knowledge and experience by visiting various aircraft and engine manufacturing plants in the United States, Europe and Canada. He had been to the Junkers aircraft plant in Dessau, Germany, in the fall of 1931, and spent about a month acquainting himself with the Junkers 52 and W33/34 types of aircraft in assembly and repair work, and the Junkers water-cooled engine, as well as the BMW VII engine. He had spent a short while with The de Havilland Aircraft Company in Toronto in 1935 studying the Gipsy Six engine and Dragon Rapide aircraft. The following year, he spent some time with the Noorduyn Aircraft Company in Montreal acquainting himself with the construction of the Norseman. When the winter of 1937 came along, Tommy Siers took instruction from the Department of Civil Engineering, University of Manitoba, Winnipeg, on the strength and testing of materials, as applied to aircraft.

Largely through his efforts, an advanced course was given at the

Photo taken at Povungnituk, Ungava District. A snow shelter was erected around CF-AAT, a Fairchild 71C, to protect the engineers while repairing the undercarriage. Note folded wings. Photo by R.H. Bibby.

University of Manitoba to improve the efficiency of air engineers, particularly in the "C" and "D" categories (for testing and ascertaining strength of materials), a few years before he received the Trans-Canada Trophy.

When Wop May, Superintendent of the Mackenzie Division of Canadian Airways, was flying Junkers CF-ARI on December 12, 1935, he came in for a landing on the ice at Fort Chipewyan, Alberta. While taxiing to the shore, the aircraft went through the ice, immersing the undercarriage and the lower part of the front end of the fuselage. Complete immersion was checked by the low wing structure characteristic of the Junkers aircraft.

Engineers A. Don Goodwin and Frank Kelly were assigned the task of salvaging the machine, a job fraught with much risk and keen discomfort because the ice in the vicinity had become thin from below and each day someone fell in the water, with the result that much time was spent in changing to dry clothes and thawing out. As the water was some twenty feet deep at this spot and the current was swift, ropes were tied around the waists of the air engineers as a precaution against being pulled under the ice.

The first thing they did was erect tripods from which to swing the block and tackle. Owing to the thin ice, it was necessary to lay planks all around the machine and on these the engineers stood as they worked. One tripod was set up at the front end and the other at the tail, the ends of the spruce poles resting on the bed of the lake.

The machine was then gradually hoisted out of the water, but it could not be moved shoreward until the ice thickened. This was a slow process because of the mild weather prevailing, and because of the swift current underneath. At this stage, Tommy Siers, Superintendent of Maintenance, who had come in from Fort McMurray, appeared

on the scene. Examination by him disclosed that the parts damaged by immersion and ice were the rudder, the tail plane, and the trailing edges of the wings, while some damage had been done to the longerons at the rear end of the fuselage during the salvage work.

The use of an empty warehouse was obtained, part of the end of which was removed, and a heater installed. The owner of the local restaurant, a Chinese-Canadian, obligingly loaned a Delco lighting plant and also attended to the physical comforts of the trio. The usual daily procedure at this period of the work was to flood the ice and work on salvage during the daytime, while the evenings were occupied in repairing the dismantled units.

Although the surface was flooded daily, ice formed slowly and, on December 23, 1935, as it was still considered unsafe to attempt to move the aircraft, supplementary skis were improvised from pieces of lumber two inches by eight inches. With the additional bearing surface thus secured, plus a timely drop in temperature to -24° F. on the afternoon of December 24, the men decided to move the machine toward the shore. This was done with the assistance of a team of horses hitched to the shore end of a long rope. That night the wings were removed, and repairs to the rudder and the tail plane were completed.

On Christmas Day the fuselage was moved over to the warehouse, and during the next five days work consisted of thawing the ice from the wings, the fuselage, and the engine, a Pratt and Whitney Wasp, and in repairing the bottom of the fuselage and the wings. On January 3, 1936, new members for the top longerons arrived, and good progress was made until the middle of the afternoon of January 4 when the Delco engine failed because of leaky valves. Several hours had to be spent on grinding the valves before work on the machine could be resumed. The tem-

perature on this day was close to -60° F., and the intense cold hindered the work, as can be imagined.

January 7, 1936, was another bad working day, as it was not until after lunch that the Wasp engine could be started, and then it ran so badly and threw out so much gasoline that the carburetor had to be removed for inspection. There was too much gasoline around the engine to use torches when the carburetor was being removed, with the result that the engineers received severe frostbites on hands and wrists. By 10:00 P.M. the trouble caused by ice in the float chamber had been overcome. By noon the next day, the carburetor had been refitted, the engine had been run up, and the Junkers taxied on to the lake. As the weather was still none too good, the remainder of the day was spent in checking spark plugs and engine preparatory to a test flight.

In the early morning of January 9, 1936, a test flight was made by Pilot Archie McMullen, accompanied by Tommy Siers. The propellor pitch was found to be too coarse, and the air speed indicator was not working. As time pressed, the latter was left for later attention. After reducing the propellor pitch, the aircraft was flown to McMurray with all hands on board, and they arrived there just before noon.

Daylight hours during midwinter days, even at Fort Chipewyan, were only of a few hours' duration, so whatever work was to be done outside had to be done during those few hours of daylight.

While Tommy Siers was with Canadian Airways, commercial air transportation in the Dominion was emerging from the purely experimental phases of development to become a potent factor in the industrial development of northern Canada. During this period, most commercial aircraft in use in Canada were not designed specifically to meet Canadian requirements, and had to be modified in many details to suit

Canada's rugged conditions, particularly in so far as winter flying in the north was concerned. This could not have been done at one stroke, but slowly as experience was acquired. Operations gradually extended northward; yet, despite climatic extremes, reliable air mail, passenger, and express services were maintained all the year round throughout that territory lying north of the transcontinental railways up to the Arctic Ocean.

Tommy Siers had been closely associated with the technical modifications and improvements in construction detail. His work had been accomplished unobtrusively, but the log books of the company's pilots bore witness to its efficacy, the general result being seen in more efficient services and increased comfort to the travelling public. His contribution to the development of skis, ski-pedestals, ski-harness, carburetor hot spots, cabin heaters and methods of warming motors in extreme cold was outstanding. His resourcefulness was demonstrated on many occasions, both at bases where there were facilities and in remote territory. One of these instances was when, under his supervision, he had a new reduction gear manufactured for the BMW IIIA engine in Junkers JU-52 CF-ARM. On two occasions when this aircraft had reduction gear failure in the bush area, this gear enabled the aircraft to be flown out to Winnipeg for permanent repairs. Without this gear, the aircraft would have had to stay in the north for many months facing possible serious damage or deterioration to it.

In the development of accessories and in technical modifications that make for more successful operation of aircraft under the extreme and difficult conditions prevailing in northern Canada, Tommy Siers made an outstanding contribution to aviation in Canada. His experience was unique in that no other Superintendent of Maintenance in the Dominion

had such a large fleet of commercial aircraft under his supervision for such an extended period and under such varying conditions.

Since bush flying came into being, Canadian operators had to heat engines and oil in order to start the engine in sub-zero temperatures. The common method of heating was by using plumber's blowtorches, wood stoves and, wherever electric current was available, electric flat-type heaters. This heating up, especially with blowtorches, might take a man from one to two hours, according to how low the temperature was and to what extent the wind was blowing. Of course, in the case of electric strap heaters, these could be left on all night and, once the engine cover was removed and oil poured into the tank, the engine could be started at once.

All those connected with the maintenance of aircraft and engines in Canada looked forward to the day when someone would develop a means of starting aero engines in sub-zero temperatures without going through the aforementioned procedure. Although the use of light oils, as tested by the R.C.A.F., was pointed out by Squadron Leader A. Ferrier in 1935, commercial operators were reluctant to eliminate the method of heating up engines before starting them.

Tommy Siers believed that the main arguments against the light oils were: An oil that would be satisfactory at –20° F. would be a cause of trouble and annoyance at, say –40° F., and, as no commercial operator had more than two grades of oil in stock at outlying bases, the very thought of providing at least three grades appeared to be unreasonable.

The heating of engines, prior to starting in sub-zero temperatures, made it necessary for personnel to work long hours each day, as the first thing in the morning a man had to light his torches, place them under the engine in the

proper manner and then sit under the engine cover and watch them for fear they might set the engine or aircraft on fire. In addition, the oil had to be warmed either in the tank or in oil containers. This might or might not be done under the engine cover but it all took time and the heating of engines and oil were chores which did not appeal to maintenance personnel. However, even with this strict attention to torches, hoping that no part of the aircraft would catch fire, it seemed that every winter, aircraft and engines were either destroyed or partially so, much to the dissatisfaction of the aircraft operating companies and insurance companies alike.

In December, 1936, it was brought to Tommy Siers' attention that the United States Army Air Corps was thinning out engine oil with gasoline to bring about a low viscosity oil in all sub-zero temperatures, which would do away with the draining of oil and applying heat to engines before starting them. When Tommy Siers first heard of this, he admitted that it appeared to be an extremely foolish idea, in that gasoline mixed with oil would probably result in a fire. However, it was in January, 1937, that Tommy Siers attended a maintenance meeting at Wright Field, Dayton, Ohio. In talking this matter over with the engineers attached to the United States Air Corps, Tommy Siers then thought that the oil dilution system, as developed by the United States Army, was far from being a crazy idea, as he had first thought it to be.

Mr. Weldon Worth, Assistant Mechanical Engineer with the United States Army Air Corps, Dayton, Ohio, was the inventor of this oil dilution system. The U.S. Army Air Corps found that this was the best solution to their problems of starting aircraft engines in cold weather. Therefore, this system underwent extensive tests by the U.S. Army Air Corps which proved very successful during experimental development flight tests conducted in the winters of 1935-36 and 1936-37 by the Air Material Division at Dayton, Ohio, and on flights to localities where colder weather existed.

This system was based upon the established principle that, within practical limits, a cold oil, when diluted to the proper lubricating viscosity by the addition of gasoline, would provide satisfactory lubrication. It was felt that the grease-like viscosity of ordinary oil at sub-zero temperatures was not only a poor lubricant that failed in its basic purpose of reducing friction, but it actually prevented the relative motion of the engine parts when cranking was attempted. The oil dilution system, with a total weight of a very few pounds, provided for thinning the circulating engine oil, prior to stopping. This thinning permitted the engine to be started upon a moment's notice after exposure to sub-zero temperatures for long periods of time. This system assumed that the carburation, priming, ignition and other accessories were functioning properly. When diluting the oil in this manner, no auxiliary apparatus or heat of any kind was used, and the complete equipment was carried in the aircraft at all times. In addition, the oil dilution system provided proper lubrication immediately after starting and did away with the usual long warm-up periods considered necessary in conventional engine and oil systems.

In tests during the winter of 1936-37, the aircraft was placed on the line with no engine covers or protection from the cold, and the start was made by the pilot without the assistance of mechanics or other personnel. After leaving the aircraft outside overnight, a test was made the next morning with a temperature of −10° F. It required less than four minutes from the time the pilot approached the aircraft until a take-off was completed. If necessary, it was believed that the time could be reduced further. With the

refinements in the other accessories, no difficulties were experienced in obtaining starts at the coldest temperatures they encountered, i.e. −20° F.

Tommy Siers, as Superintendent of Maintenance for Canadian Airways, began to investigate the possibility of using the Worth oil dilution system for the cold-weather starting of aircraft engines himself. This was now early 1937. This development by Tommy Siers was to lead to a major contribution to the maintenance problems in northern air transportation, with particular reference to the development of the oil dilution system in Canada for cold-weather flying.

Once the details of the oil dilution system were firmly impressed in Tommy Siers' mind, he could see that Canadian operators could use the system to great advantage and brought the matter to the attention of the General Manager of Canadian Airways, Tommy Thompson, a well-known pioneer pilot himself. Tommy Thompson was quite convinced that the idea was well worth trying out. Incidentally, Tommy Siers and Tommy Thompson had known each other since the spring of 1923 when they both joined Laurentide Air Service.

First of all, Canadian Airways Limited was under the impression that they should go into the research and design of the oil dilution system used by the United States Army Air Corps. However, months went by and nothing was done. Then one day in July, 1937, when Tommy Siers was attending a maintenance meeting in Boston, he made it his business to find out how Canadian operators could use the oil dilution system as developed by the U.S. Army Air Corps, without infringing on patent rights and getting mixed up with red tape.

Tommy Siers was informed that any aircraft manufacturer or competent aeronautical engineer could obtain the manufacturing rights for the oil dilution system from Mr. Weldon Worth of

Dayton, Ohio. So, upon Tommy Siers' return to Montreal, he proposed to one aircraft manufacturer that he take over the rights but, as nothing had been done by December, 1937, Tommy Thompson suggested that Mr. R. J. Moffett of Canadian Vickers look into the oil dilution system and make arrangements with Weldon Worth for the rights to design such a system for use in one of Canadian Airways' aircraft.

It was hoped that Mr. Moffett would be able to rush through one oil tank design and machine installation so the system could be tried out in the spring of 1938, as they had been informed that the United States Army intended to make the oil dilution system standard on all aircraft, other than training machines, which made Tommy Siers and Tommy Thompson more certain than ever that the system had many advantages. So, with the dawn of 1938, Tommy Siers had introduced to Canada the Worth oil dilution system for cold-weather starting of aircraft engines and had started to develop the system invented by Weldon Worth. It was at a Maintenance Committee Meeting of the Air Transport Association of America in Los Angeles, about 1940, that Tommy Siers gave a paper on the oil dilution system showing how he had developed it. After reading it, Mr. Worth said that, although he had thought of the principle of the oil dilution system after he had invented it, it was Tommy Siers who had developed it and made it of practical value. Indeed, Mr. Worth paid Tommy Siers a fine tribute.

Practically the whole of the spring and summer of 1938 was spent in getting the design and first oil dilution system through and the first tank installation ready for one of Canadian Airways' Norseman aircraft. During this time, they received criticism, all of which tended to delay the installation of the system.

In November, 1938, the first oil dilution system was completed and installed in CF-BDC, a Norseman aircraft, by

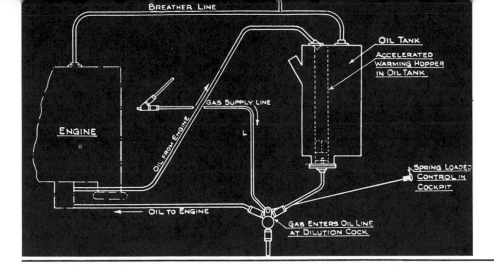

Diagram illustrating the installation of the oil dilution system. It shows the tank within a tank, and the hopper within the main oil tank. When the engine is started, gasoline-diluted oil from this hopper flows through it until it warms up. The gasoline evaporates and oil flows from the main tank as the engine becomes warmer.

Photo courtesy of Tommy Siers.

Canadian Vickers. It was to be tried out under Tommy Siers' personal supervision. However, this aircraft, flown by U. S. Wagner, made a normal landing at Bill Joe Lake, Ontario (Jackson Manion Gold Mines), on December 9, 1938, but, when it was taxiing to the Canadian Airways terminal, the ice gave way submerging the aircraft to the level of the wings. Fortunately, no one was hurt. It was not salvaged until January, 1939. In the meantime, Mr. Moffett of Canadian Vickers had been given an order for designing and making up the oil dilution system for Junkers aircraft CF-AQW. Before this installation was completed, Norseman aircraft CF-BDC was salvaged and flown to Winnipeg for a complete overhaul. As a test, the oil dilution system was tried out before the aircraft was overhauled. The oil dilution valve was pulled at the end of the day's flight and, although the temperature during the night fell to 2° F., the engine started next morning without any difficulty and definitely proved that the oil dilution system installation was satisfactory and that they were on the right track as far as starting engines in cold weather without the use of heat was concerned.

The overhaul and testing of "AQW" was completed towards the end of February, 1939, and it was decided that the oil dilution system installed in this aircraft should be given a thorough test. The engine installed in this aircraft was an "H" Wasp, 6248. This test was to determine whether or not such a system should be installed in other Canadian Airways' aircraft for the next winter's operations. This test was completed by pilot W. E. Catton, and Air Engineers H. Rex Terpening and E. W. Chapman, at Stevenson Field during February, March and April, 1939. Tommy Siers and W. E. Catton both kept independent reports of everything that was done to the aircraft or engine which affected the oil dilution system and starting of the engine in sub-zero temperatures. On March 18, E. W.

Chapman said that the oil dilution system was working quite satisfactorily, the only trouble seeming to be in getting the engine to fire without using too much prime. However, this same day they tried using a special gas machine naphtha. With the temperature –12° F., and using only twelve shots of prime, the engine started immediately. Tommy Siers believed that this gasoline had more tendency to fire under cold weather than ordinary aviation gas. So, upon the completion of all of their tests, their experience showed it to function satisfactorily down to a temperature of –35° F., which they encountered at God's Lake.

Tommy Siers said that many of the methods they tried out in the Junkers were hard to believe now that they have been done, but they had written down everything, no matter how unimportant it was at the time. He said that they had no unusual amount of grief. Canadian Airways was well satisfied with these tests, and for the winter of 1939-40 they planned to have several aircraft equipped with the oil dilution system. The personnel who carried out these tests felt that the oil dilution system was the greatest advance in bush operations during the previous ten years. Tommy Siers was grateful for the assistance he received from Weldon Worth of the U.S. Army Air Corps; R. J. Moffett, Canadian Vickers Limited; Pratt and Whitney Aircraft Company Limited; Canadian Wright Limited; Imperial Oil Limited; Standard Oil of New Jersey; Squadron Leader A. Ferrier, Department of Transport; H. O. West, Trans-Canada Air Lines (for the loan of a direct cranking starter when Canadian Airways had none available for the tests); pilot W. E. Catton and air engineers Rex Terpening and E. W. Chapman.

Tommy Siers' work in this field was a distinctive and important contribution to the British Commonwealth war effort and, in addition, greatly simplified civil air

operations in all northern climates.

The essential parts of the oil dilution system are:

(1) An oil tank in which an internal tank or hopper has been incorporated, having a capacity of approximately one and a half gallons. The design of the hopper tank is such that oil circulating through the engine is kept from the main supply which surrounds the hopper. As the oil in the hopper is used up, oil from the main supply creeps or flows in at the bottom of the hopper and, theoretically at least, keeps the main supply of oil and hopper oil at a constant level. The upper end of the hopper is open and connected with the expansion space of the main oil tank.

(2) The oil return from the engine either goes through or by-passes an oil radiator, after which it enters the upper end of the hopper in such a manner that the oil flow not only has a downward but also a circular path, which assists in separating air from the scavenged oil.

(3) From the bottom or lower end of the hopper, oil is piped to the engine and in this pipe is connected a line from the fuel pressure line through which gasoline flows to dilute the oil entering the engine. In the line from the fuel pressure line is a jet or metering device and a shut-off valve which is operated from the cockpit. The shut-off valve has an internal spring which holds the valve closed and fuel can flow through the valve and line only when the knob of the valve is pulled sufficiently to overcome the spring load. This valve is the only control or movable part in the oil dilution system. When diluting oil, the valve is usually held open for approximately four minutes.

(4) As the heat from the engine distils the gasoline from the oil as it circulates, it is necessary to extend the

engine breather beyond the engine cowl line and away from the exhaust pipes or manifolds. According to the U.S. Army Air Corps, this distillation is completed after thirty minutes' engine operation, and in fact most of the dilution is eliminated in the first ten minutes.

Every aircraft belonging to Canadian Airways having engines capable of using the oil dilution system was equipped with it when it became available, and during the winter of 1940-41 the company had cold starts in weather down to -57° F. on Wasp engines and -37° F. on Rolls-Royce engines. There was no doubt that the Rolls-Royce engines would have started in much colder weather, but the minimum temperature registered during the operation was as stated.

This system resulted in the saving of thousands of dollars to the northern transport operator, as well as a reduction in fire hazards. Also, Tommy Siers was requested to provide full details concerning his development of this oil dilution system to the air services of both Britain and the United States, to the British Air Ministry, to various public bodies throughout the United States, and also to the National Research Council in Canada and the Department of Transport.

The Committee of Award for the Trans-Canada Trophy for the year 1940 consisted of the following members:
Group Captain F. V. Heakes, Royal Canadian Air Force, Department of National Defence, Ottawa.
Mr. J. A. Wilson, Director of Air Services, Department of Transport, Ottawa.
Group Captain W. A. Curtis, Royal Canadian Air Force, Department of National Defence, Ottawa.
Dr. J. J. Green, Executive Member of the Canadian Flying Clubs Association, Ottawa.

In recognition of Tommy Siers' outstanding contribution to military and civil aviation in Canada, and indirectly to British aviation, in the development in Canada of the Worth principle of the oil dilution system for cold-weather starting of aircraft engines, he was awarded the Trans-Canada Trophy for 1940.

The presentation of the trophy to Tommy Siers took place on November 17, 1941, at the banquet which was held in the Yellow Room of the King Edward Hotel, Toronto, by the Air Industries and Transport Association on the occasion of their annual meeting on November 17 and 18, and was made by Air Vice-Marshal E. W. Stedman, O.B.E., on behalf of the Minister of National Defence.

Tommy Siers was loaned to the Department of Munitions and Supply by Canadian Airways in April, 1941, and assumed the position of Supervisor of Aircraft Overhauls for the Air Training Plan, with the Department of Munitions and Supply in Ottawa. While Tommy Siers was on loan to the Department of Munitions and Supply, Canadian Pacific Air Lines came into existence. Upon its formation on January 1, 1942, Canadian Airways, along with nine other companies, was bought out by Canadian Pacific Air Lines.

At this time, Canadian Pacific Air Lines had a contract with the Department of Munitions and Supply to manage five repair plants for the overhaul and repair of aircraft and engines used in the air training schools of the British Commonwealth Air Training Plan and on R.C.A.F. operations. These plants were located at Vancouver, Moose Jaw, Winnipeg (2) and Cap de la Madeleine. The one at Moose Jaw was operated by R. W. "Dick" Ryan of Prairie Airways Limited, who was later Executive Vice-President and Director of Canadian Pacific Air Lines. A major task was the training of employees to do this work, as about 80 per cent of the personnel had

no experience with aircraft work before joining these war plants. At these plants, they overhauled Tiger Moths, Fleets, Cessnas, Norseman, Bolingbrokes, PBY's, Stranraers, Hurricanes, Hampdens and even Kittyhawks. Engines were also overhauled, such as Pratt and Whitney, Cheetah, D.H. Gipsy, Menasco and Ranger types. In addition to the repair and overhaul of aircraft and engines, the plants spent time in modification work of operational aircraft. This included such items as wintering Ansons, modifying wings and tail planes of Cessnas and general modifications to Hampdens. There were times, too, when production was retarded in some of the plants by lack of available spare parts. These plants also performed a number of miscellaneous repair jobs for the R.C.A.F., such as skis, muffs for heaters, repairing tow targets, and so on. Also, Canadian Pacific Air Lines operated a repair base at Calgary for the R.C.A.F.

In February, 1943, Tommy Siers was appointed General Superintendent of Maintenance for Canadian Pacific Air Lines, Montreal, and was responsible for the organization and functioning of the maintenance department on all air line operations.

Later he was appointed General Supervisor of Repair Plants. In September, 1949, Canadian Pacific Air Lines made Vancouver its headquarters, instead of Montreal, and Tommy Siers was then transferred to Vancouver, where he became Maintenance Research Representative that same year. In 1951 he became Assistant to the Director of Maintenance and Engineering. Tommy Siers retired from this position in May, 1961, at the age of 65 years.

Today, he and Mrs. Siers live in Vancouver. They have one son, Donald M. Siers, who also lives in Vancouver. Tommy Siers is a former member of the Canadian Aeronautical Institute and the Society of Automotive Engineers. He is a member of the Quarter Century Club and

Canada's Aviation Hall of Fame. He was made a Companion of the Order of Flight (City of Edmonton).

In addition to Tommy Siers' technical ability, due to the happy faculty possessed by him of never being discouraged in the most trying circumstances — his knowledge of human nature — and his gift for imparting his knowledge to others — he has been of inestimable value in training engineers and imparting to them a true ésprit de corps. It may also be said, fairly, that the high standard of efficiency in the maintenance of aircraft and engines, which are today a well-known characteristic of the Canadian commercial aviation fleet, is largely attributed to the organizing ability and outstanding example provided by him throughout his years of service to Canadian aviation.

The introduction and development of the Worth oil dilution system in Canada for easier starting of aircraft engines in cold weather was a great achievement by Tommy Siers. Perhaps those who appreciated it most were the air engineers. This system permitted the aircraft industry to make major advances in flying operations in the north. In addition, military and civil aircraft operations derived full benefit from this successful endeavour. Indeed, the success of Tommy Siers' work in this particular sphere is in evidence today — wherever aircraft fly in Canada's cold domain, and in northern climates around the world.

1941

A. Daniel "Dan" McLean

Citation: in recognition of the outstanding service in aviation that he rendered for many years

A. Daniel "Dan" McLean, O.B.E., while Controller of Civil Aviation with the Department of Transport, Ottawa, was awarded the Trans-Canada Trophy for 1941, for meritorious service in the advancement of aviation in Canada "in recognition of the outstanding service in aviation that he rendered for many years." The announcement of the award was made on October 30, 1942, by the Minister of National Defence for Air, Major Charles G. Power.

In advising Dan McLean of the award, the Minister said, in part:

"The unanimous decision of the Committee of Award was based on the long and outstanding service that you have rendered to aviation in Canada. Following service in war and peace with the R.C.A.F., you have, since 1929, devoted your talents and managerial ability to the great task of locating, constructing and equipping airports and airways throughout Canada. It was under your direction that there came into existence the civil airways' system of Canada which culminated in the completion of the Trans-Canada Airway in 1937. Since then you have most successfully borne the great responsibility of constructing the aerodromes required under the C.T.E. [Combined Training Establishment]. The Committee of Award is aware, also, that in all circumstances you have displayed a rare ability to maintain harmonious relations with other Services, whether of Canada or of the United States. Your practical knowledge of aviation, your enthusiasm and your thorough comprehension of the broadest aspects of the problems which engage your attention have found tangible expression in the chain of aerodromes extending from coast to coast in Canada — and which embrace all those home war and military outposts of Dominion defence which have contributed incalculably to Canada's national war effort."

Alexander Daniel "Dan" McLean, "the Flying Scotsman," was born on January 31, 1896, at Maxville, Ontario, in Glengarry County. In 1907 he went to Innisfail, Alberta, with his parents, who were both descendants of Scottish pioneers. After graduating from Normal School in Calgary, he taught school for a year and a half but this life was too mild for this rugged, husky Scotsman who was destined for greater things. While helping his equally diligent father in the sale of real estate, insurance, power equipment, automobiles and other successful business ventures, he became enthusiastic about the new means of communication — the telephone. This involvement enabled him to sense the satisfaction of building things that would be of benefit and joy to others, and, before giving it up for another new venture, he was placed in charge of construction and maintenance for three municipal telephone companies in Saskatchewan.

Enlisting in the Royal Flying Corps in Canada in 1917, he took his indoctrinational training at Camp Mohawk, near Toronto, which was one of the first six training camps established in Canada. From there he went to the School of Military Aeronautics at the University of Toronto, from where young Cadet McLean was selected as one out of a special contingent of one hundred chosen to go to England in 1917 to take pilot training. When his flying training course was finished, he was commissioned during World War I as a Second Lieutenant in the Royal Flying Corps, which later became the Royal Air Force. Upon the completion of the Gosport

Stearman CF-CCH, and Stearman CF-CCG (in the background) belonging to the Civil Aviation Branch of the Department of National Defence, which landed on most of the aerodromes and airports across Canada at the time that they were being built for the Trans-Canada Airway. Dan McLean made inspections of these aerodromes and sites under construction from coast to coast in the early 1930s in CF-CCG, his favourite Stearman, while Tuddy usually flew the other one.

Course at Shoreham, he was posted for duty as a flying instructor. Incidentally, he was the first solo pupil of none other than Lieutenant Leigh Forbes Stevenson, later to become an Air Vice-Marshal in the R.C.A.F. in World War II.

Lieutenant McLean returned to Canada on September 29, 1919, and went immediately to the University of Alberta in Edmonton to round out his academic studies by taking a course in electrical engineering. While at university, he joined the Canadian Air Force Reserve of Officers and took a pilot's refresher course at Camp Borden in March, 1921, receiving his Canadian Commercial Air Pilot's Certificate No. 124, dated May 17, 1921, and his Air Engineer's Certificate No. 129, dated April 12, 1921, from the Air Board.

He had been offered a position with Imperial Oil Limited to carry out exploration work in the Mackenzie River area in connection with the discovery of crude oil at Fort Norman, Northwest Territories, but this company's operations in the area were closed down before he could accept the position. Imperial Oil had purchased four Junkers aircraft for their northern expeditions with the hope of establishing more efficient communication to the new oil field from Edmonton. Dan McLean had flown one of the Junkers aircraft. Experimental work had shown that aircraft could play a most important role in transportation to the outlying districts of Canada, but the impact of a number of unfortunate aircraft accidents displaced the venture. However, the advantageous use of aircraft for this activity was later confirmed in such work as forest patrol and exploration, aerial surveys, photography, sketching and other similar work. The knowledge that air transport in the north was a necessity rested for a time in the dreams of those who believed that in the years to come it would be so extensive as to go beyond all expectations.

He then became a partner in business

with his father in Innisfail. However, during 1926 and 1927 the R.C.A.F. was soliciting former pilots to meet their requirements for an expanding aerial programme which included the Hudson Strait Expedition and aerial photography and survey work. So, early in 1927, Dan McLean received a second request from the R.C.A.F. to join the staff at Camp Borden. Lured by the overtures of his old love, he reported to Camp Borden on March 1, 1927, and, following a short refresher course, was assigned to the staff side of this famous air base.

In the fall of 1927, Flying Officer McLean took a seaplane and flying boat course at Vancouver; and in the winter of 1927-28 he took air navigation and aerial photographic courses at Camp Borden. Two operational seasons were spent doing aerial vertical photography in Ontario, Quebec and the Maritimes, and forestry sketching in Cape Breton.

Flying Officer Dan McLean left Ottawa on January 29, 1929, in a ski-equipped Douglas aircraft, "ZG," on the inaugural flight of the special air mail service from Ottawa to Saint John, New Brunswick. Interestingly, this Douglas seaplane was the one that had belonged to J. Dalzell McKee, the donor of the Trans-Canada Trophy. It was flown across Canada in 1926 by Squadron Leader A. E. Godfrey (now Air Vice-Marshal) and Captain McKee when the first trans-Canada seaplane flight was made. After Captain McKee was killed at Lac là Pèche, P.Q., in 1927, his Douglas seaplane was purchased by the Royal Canadian Air Force. The seaplane had a newly installed Pratt and Whitney "Wasp" engine in it — the first of this type ever installed in any aircraft in Canada. The R.C.A.F. converted it from a two-place to a three-place seaplane. It was also the same type of aircraft that the United States Army used in 1924 on their round-the-world flight.

Upon arriving at Saint John Airport in this historic aircraft, McLean was met by

Squadron Leader (later Air Vice-Marshal) T. A. Lawrence in a Fairchild skiplane, who picked up the mail and flew it on to Halifax (Dartmouth Lake).

The lake at Millidgeville served as the landing area for Saint John during the winter time, and maintenance of ice landing strips in those days was almost as primitive as the aircraft. When Dan McLean landed his Douglas skiplane on the ice on the lake, one ski suffered minor damage. It was, nevertheless, to say the least, a bit disconcerting to our intrepid flyer to run afoul of a log, or "dead-head" (known to the Maritimers as a spar buoy), frozen in the ice, and which seemed by some satanic plot to have been hidden from view by the freshly fallen snow. However, by the time that Lawrence had returned to Saint John from Halifax with the mail, a new ski had been put on "ZG." Then on January 31, 1929, Dan McLean left Saint John for Ottawa in "ZG" with first-cover mail from Halifax and Saint John.

During the Saint John-Montreal (St. Hubert Airport) leg of his flight, he had battled the high winds and driving snow for which the Appalachian Mountains of northern Maine are well known. Visibility was reduced to a point where he could make no further use of the "iron compass" (the railway track), and a forced landing on an unknown lake was small comfort and relief. When the storm abated in about half an hour Dan McLean pressed on to St. Hubert Airport for refuelling before leaving on the last leg of the flight, which ordinarily would have been an easy one. However, shortly after he took off, "ZG's" Wasp engine started to give trouble around Lake of Two Mountains. Normally, this should have meant returning to the aerodrome — or making a forced landing. However, Dan McLean had in mind that "the mail must go through," especially on a first flight. When only twenty miles from Ottawa, the willing but tired engine wheezed a last gasp and gave up, and a landing was

Arctic Red River, N.W.T., at the time that CF-ATZ visited there on July 18, 1935, carrying Dr. Camsell and Dan McLean. The view is north-northwest towards the Mackenzie River.

Photo courtesy of "Dan" McLean.

made on the ice of the Ottawa River in the black darkness of night during another stormstorm. The climactic landing was almost completed but was not without insult, as the shrouds of snow and darkness hid from sight the jutting point of trees that, with a piercing shudder, severely damaged one of the wings of the aircraft — but the pilot was unhurt.

After a walk of six miles through the deep snow in the darkness to the Village of Rockland, and a telephone call, Squadron Leader Roy S. Grandy, Commanding Officer of the R.C.A.F. Station at Rockcliffe, drove to Rockland by car. He took George Herring, Superintendent of Air Mail Services, along with him and he personally took the mail to Ottawa — and thus "the mail did go through!"

A number of cars with their lights turned on were lined up along the runway at Rockcliffe Airport to light the way for Dan McLean's delayed return in the dark. A celebration was to be under way just as soon as he arrived with the first-cover mail from Halifax and Saint John. As time went by and he still did not arrive, there was much concern and consternation about his whereabouts for several hours — until the telephone call reached Roy Grandy. A secondary reason for the anticipated celebration was his birthday — since it was January 31!

However, the captain stayed with his ship the next day — until it was towed up the ice of the Ottawa River to the R.C.A.F. repair base at Victoria Island so that the wing might be repaired.

But there was a "dividend." Pratt and Whitney, in one of their efforts to improve an already excellent Wasp engine, had for the first time enclosed the rocker boxes. It was subsequently discovered that the engine failure occurred because ice from condensation had formed in the rocker boxes during refuelling. Modifications to all engines were made immediately, and, no doubt as a result of this discovery, others were saved the

inconvenience of forced landings or of engine failure from this cause.

Dan McLean subsequently took over the experimental air mail service in the Maritimes between Saint John and Halifax from Squadron Leader Lawrence and operated it during the remaining winter months in 1929.

Dan McLean was first appointed to the Civil Aviation Branch of the Department of National Defence on April 1, 1929, as Inspector of Western Airways with his headquarters at Regina. At the time, J.A. Wilson, who was Controller of Civil Aviation, was his chief. While stationed in the west, he constructed the first section of the airways' system in Canada in the Prairie Provinces from Winnipeg to Calgary, and then from Regina to Edmonton, in preparation for the air mail service. On this system, airports were provided at the major centres along the route by the municipalities. Then intermediate aerodromes, which were established at thirty-mile intervals, were required to span the wide gaps between the major centres. The Dominion Government assumed responsibility for the construction of these intermediate aerodromes, as well as the provision of airway and aerodrome lighting for night flying, and radio and weather services. The construction of the aerodromes and facilities for the Prairie Air Mail Service was completed by January, 1930.

Western Canada Airways, which had been operating since 1927, had already received a contract to operate a nightly Prairie Air Mail Service from Winnipeg to Regina, Moose Jaw, Medicine Hat and Calgary (later via Lethbridge and Calgary); with a branch line from Regina to Saskatoon, North Battleford and Edmonton. The inaugural flight was made on March 3, 1930. While it was planned to make the inaugural flight at the end of January, one thing or another, especially the weather , delayed the flight until March. Then on March 31, 1932, the necessity for economies in all public

services forced the government to discontinue the inter-city air mail services. Permission was given by the government to maintain intact those sections of the airway which had been constructed and to continue surveys for its completion.

When construction of the airports on the Prairies was finished, Inspector McLean conducted aerial surveys through the Rocky Mountains to determine the best route to Vancouver from the Prairies. He, himself, surveyed the central route from Vancouver to Calgary, following the main C.P.R. line; while Squadron Leader J.H. Tudhope made a preliminary aerial survey of the northern route from Edmonton via the Yellowhead Pass. Together they made a preliminary aerial survey of the southern route through the Crow's Nest Pass to Vancouver from Lethbridge later on in 1930. After a number of surveys, Dan McLean chose the Crow's Nest Pass route through southern British Columbia via Coleman, Fernie, Cranbrook, Creston, Trail, Grand Forks and Princeton to Vancouver. He determined that it was a shorter route and had a better climate, and at the same time it passed through more settled areas. He also considered that the difficulties of constructing aerodromes on this route would be less than on the alternative routes through either the Yellowhead or the Kicking Horse Passes. At the time there was only one aerodrome at Grand Forks between the Prairies and Vancouver. Even at Vancouver, the race track on Lulu Island was used as an aerodrome.

Then, in 1931, Inspector McLean was transferred to Ottawa as Acting Superintendent of Airways and Airports when J.H. Tudhope resigned from the position to become associated with Coastal Airways of B.C. in Vancouver.

In his new position, Superintendent McLean directed the completion of the surveys and the construction of the airway from Winnipeg through northern Ontario to Montreal and Halifax in

Arrival of Dan McLean's party at Cooking Lake (Edmonton), on August 17, 1935, upon the completion of the 8400 mile exploratory flight throughout the north-west, in Fairchild seaplane 71C, CF-ATZ. From left to right: Bill Sunderland, pilot Puch Dickins, Dan McLean and Dr. Camsell.

Photo courtesy of "Dan" Mclean.

eastern Canada, as well as the aerodromes built under the Unemployment Relief Scheme. These projects were the forerunners of what was to become the Trans-Canada Airway. Under the Unemployment Relief Scheme (U.E.R. Scheme), he made frequent visits and inspections to all the aerodromes and sites under construction from coast to coast wherever possible in his favourite Stearman aircraft, CF-CCG. Some of the aerodromes were not finished at the time; nevertheless, he managed to make three-point landings on many of these fields.

In 1935 funds were made available by Parliament for the Civil Aviation Branch of the Department of National Defence to make an investigation and survey of a possible northwest airways' route through northwestern Canada to Alaska, and of the facilities and routes along the Mackenzie to Coppermine and in the Yukon. The Department of National Defence chose Dan McLean to make this exploration trip.

So, a contract was arranged with Canadian Airways Limited to provide air transportation. Dan McLean chose Punch Dickins, a pilot with the company and an early Trans-Canada Trophy winner, to make the flight, due to his wide knowledge of the north country and of the many flights he had already made in the north. William "Bill" Sunderland was the air engineer with the flight. For the trip, they used a Fairchild seaplane 71C, CF-ATZ. For the outgoing flight from Edmonton to Aklavik and Prince Rupert, the seaplane was chartered from Canadian Airways by the Civil Aviation Branch of the Department of National Defence; and for the return flight, as far north as Coppermine and back to Edmonton, by the Department of Mines and Resources. Much of this territory was photographed from the air by both Dan McLean and Bill Sunderland for the purpose of assembling information with a view to establishing suitable aerodromes

in the north country. Many hundreds of photographs were taken.

Dan McLean started the first phase of his 8,400-mile exploration trip on July 15, 1935, from Edmonton (Cooking Lake), to fly to Fort Smith, and up through the Northwest Territories to Aklavik, near the Arctic Coast. Leaving Cooking Lake in Bellanca aircraft CF-AIA, they reached Fort McMurray in two and one-half hours' time, where they remained for the night. They left Fort McMurray in Fairchild seaplane CF-ATZ, on July 16 for Fort Chipewyan, Fort Fitzgerald, Fort Smith, Fort Resolution, Hay River, Fort Providence, Fort Simpson, Fort Norman, Fort Good Hope, Arctic Red River and Fort McPherson, arriving at Aklavik late in the evening of July 18. The following day they left Aklavik, continuing the flight to the Yukon via the Peel River.

Waterways, lying four miles east-southeast of Fort McMurray, was the end of steel and the beginning of a water route which extended to Aklavik and Cameron Bay, with the exception of the 16 mile portage between Fitzgerald, Alberta, and Fort Smith, Northwest Territories. Dan McLean saw that the country was ideal for seaplanes and skiplanes. Most of the air operations began at Fort McMurray, although many flights during the year before this, in particular, were being extended south to Cooking Lake, the new combined base operated by the City of Edmonton.

Their trip took them through the Yukon Territory and the Alaska Peninsula. Dan McLean and Punch Dickins were first planning on flying from Aklavik to Dawson via Old Crow, Yukon Territory, and Fort Yukon, Alaska, but, as the weather was unfavourable up the Rat River Pass on the 19th, the course was altered to one from Fort McPherson up the Peel and Wind Rivers to Mayo. The flight continued from Mayo to Whitehorse with calls at Mayo Lake, Dawson, Fort Selkirk and Carmacks,

arriving at Whitehorse on July 22.

While Dan McLean was at Whitehorse he made a return flight to Fairbanks, Alaska, in a Lockheed Electra through the courtesy of Pacific Alaska Airways, Whitehorse, on one of the company's regular flights. J.C. Morrison headed up the company. This trip was made to determine the feasibility of an aerial connection from Canada to the Orient. At the time, Pacific Alaska Airways operated a semi-weekly service between Juneau, Whitehorse and Fairbanks using Lockheed aircraft.

The party then flew through northwestern British Columbia and the Alaskan Panhandle. They left Whitehorse on July 25 for Carcross and Skagway, returning to Carcross following the route of the White Pass and Yukon Railway through the White Pass. The next flight was made from Carcross to Prince Rupert via Atlin with a side trip to Juneau, Telegraph Creek and Hazelton. They arrived at Prince Rupert on July 29.

Their route from Carcross to Skagway passed through a rugged mountainous section with a narrow valley at the Skagway end. Skagway, in the Indian language, means "the Home of the North Wind," 'tis said. Skagway lies at the head of the scenic Lynn Canal, at the base of steep mountains. It is exposed to hazardous winds from the south which can attain high velocity with practically no warning.

It was at Prince Rupert that Dr. Charles Camsell, C.M.G., LL.D., F.R.S.C., who was Deputy Minister of Mines and Resources for Canada, and a member of the Council of the Northwest Territories, joined Dan McLean and his party for the rest of the trip.

Dr. Camsell was the author of *Son of the North*, an inspiring story of his life in the rugged north in the early days where he lived and worked for so many years. He was born at Fort Liard when his father was the Hudson's Bay Company's Factor there. Dr. Camsell was a geologist.

Lockheed CF-CCT carrying a D.O.T. inspection party throughout the west in August, 1939 is shown at Swift Current, Sask. The three at the right from left to right, are: Harold Walsh, Bill Fenn, District Radio Inspector and Dan McLean, who was Supt. of Airways. Jack Hunter, the pilot, is fourth from the left, while the co-pilot is on the extreme left.

Dr. Camsell was making a study of conditions in the north and inspected some of the field parties created by the million-dollar mining exploration scheme, which was under way. Mining exploration of the north started in the spring and summer of 1928, and on a larger scale in the spring and summer of 1929, when Northern Aerial Minerals Exploration Company and Dominion Explorers Company and other interests used aircraft to fly men and equipment to the mineral areas of the north.

Dr. Camsell and Dan McLean left Prince Rupert together on July 31, to fly to Fort Liard, Dr. Camsell's birthplace, via Wrangell, the Valley of the Stikine, crossing over the Pacific-Arctic Divide to Dease Lake and McDame's Creek, where they had a rather hazardous landing. Leaving McDame's Creek on August 2, they continued to the Valley of the Upper Liard the following day, going by the Dease River to Lower Post and the Liard River to Fort Liard. The flight which started out from Prince Rupert was the first one that was made from the Pacific to the Mackenzie River at Simpson via the Liard River. From Fort Liard another flight was made up the Liard River as far as the Coal River from which point it turned north along the Coal River about 25 miles, then easterly to the Liard River in the vicinity of LaBiche River, looping back to Fort Liard. On this latter flight they landed on the Liard River about 20 miles above Devil's Portage adjacent to the so-called "Tropical Valley." There were a number of rapids in the Upper Liard River, the longest of which was at the Devil's Portage.

The Tropical Valley was located along the Liard River. In this Tropical Valley were hot springs with temperatures ranging up to 100° F. It was here where Dr. Camsell, Dan McLean and his party landed on August 3, 1935, and took advantage of the opportunity of seeing these fabled hot springs in Canada's northland. (Dr. Camsell had also visited the Tropical Valley in 1898-99 while trying to reach Dawson City during the gold rush to the Klondike.) There were other hot springs on both sides of Devil's Portage, but they did not get a close look at them, as it was not so easy for Punch Dickins to find a suitable place to land the seaplane in this area. When the Alaska Highway was built by the United States Corps of Engineers in 1942-43, its course followed alongside this famous valley. The hot springs were greatly enjoyed for bathing purposes by the men attached to the U.S. Corps of Engineers when the highway was under construction.

There were also hot springs just east of Atlin in a lush green area that showed signs of having been at one time a plush resort.

Dr. Camsell and Dan McLean found a trail in this Tropical Valley and, out of curiosity, followed it to see where it would lead them. Through the woods they followed it until they saw a broken-down cabin. Continuing on the trail, they came upon a large meadow, with luxuriant green vegetation. The grass was seven feet high! So high was it that they could only follow the trail by using their feet to sort of feel the path as they went along. At the other end of the meadow, they entered a beautiful green grove of large spruce and poplar trees, where two other old log cabins with crushed roofs were located. The grove also held tracks of many animals which had come and gone. Nearby flowed a stream of water, crystal clear.

Then Dan McLean, Dr. Camsell, Punch Dickins and Bill Sunderland re-entered the Northwest Territories on the return trip via the Liard River on August 4 and made stops at Fort Liard and South Nahanni. Their next stop was at Fort Simpson, a place Dr. Camsell knew so well. They arrived at Fort Norman on August 5. Dr. Camsell stayed with his brother Fred, who was the Hudson's Bay Company's Factor there. The party flew to Norman Wells, 50 miles below Fort Norman, so that Dr. Camsell could have a look at the Imperial Oil Company's refinery which was supplying 700 tons of fuel oil to the Eldorado Gold Mines at Great Bear Lake that season.

Next they went to Cameron Bay, which is located on the north side of Echo Bay on Great Bear Lake. It was here that Gilbert LaBine, who became famous as a prospector and mining executive, took Dan McLean and Dr. Camsell for a trip in a canoe to show them the location of his radium mine which he had discovered in 1930, and told them the story of how he discovered the mine.

Gilbert LaBine said that he had been looking for silver, not pitchblende, the ore containing radium. In 1929 when he was flying out from the north with Punch Dickins after having had a busy season in the prospecting field, he noticed a mineralized area, and decided to come back again the next year to take a look at it. This he did in 1930 and brought along with him Charles St. Paul, a noted prospector from Ottawa. Then one morning in May, 1930, as Charles St. Paul was suffering from snow blindness, Gilbert LaBine strode out alone to look over the area and came across a strong mineralized zone. Samples of the minerals were sent to the Assay Office in Ottawa. When he received the report telling him that he had discovered pitchblende, he was amazed. This was one of the greatest mineral strikes in the north, and Eldorado Gold Mines became a thriving company.

At this time, three companies were operating regular transportation service to the area; Canadian Airways Limited, Mackenzie Air Service (operated by Leigh Brintnell, a noted pioneer pilot of Edmonton); and United Air Transport (operated by G. W. Grant McConachie of Edmonton). The Consolidated Mining and Smelting Company operated its own aircraft and there were miscellaneous

flights. Aviation was responsible for the rapid investigation and the preliminary development of the mineralized areas in the north and for carrying air mail in these northern areas.

Two major companies were operating boats, the Hudson's Bay Company and the Northern Transportation Company Limited. From Fort Smith these boats made two trips per summer to Aklavik and one trip to Fort Liard. Traffic for Great Bear Lake was trans-shipped at Fort Norman and taken by means of small boats up the Bear River through the Bear Rapids and trans-shipped again on to lake steamers operating on Great Bear Lake. A flight was made over the Bear River Rapids to photograph the swift water and the portage, known as the Franklin Road, which was nearing completion under the direction of Colonel T. Newcomen at the time. This was built with a view to eliminating the hazardous trip required by specially constructed boats carrying small loads.

From the fabulous Eldorado Gold Mines at Great Bear Lake, the party left for Coppermine on August 12. Small evergreen trees were scattered in the vicinity of Cameron Bay and for some little distance north, but from about half-way to Coppermine north there were no trees with the exception of a few small evergreens near the streams. The barrenness of the country was accentuated by a scattering of huge rough boulders on low bare rock hills. They returned to Cameron Bay (Great Bear Lake) from Coppermine, where they remained overnight. The flight south was then resumed the following day calling at Fort Rae, Fort Smith, Beaverlodge and Fort McMurray en route to Cooking Lake. Between Fort Rae and Fort Smith, the flight passed over Yellowknife at the eastern end of Great Slave Lake where a gold strike took place the previous year, in September, 1934, under the direction of Major Lauchlan T. "Lauchie" Burwash, the Arctic explorer.

During this trip, 8,400 miles were covered in 81 hours and 35 minutes' flying time. They reached Cooking Lake on August 17, 1935, after an extensive and memorable trip. Much valuable information was gathered by Dan McLean for the Civil Aviation Branch on this exploratory trip — and for the future development of aviation in Canada. When it was later decided to build aerodromes through the northwest to Alaska, which established the Northwest Staging Route from Edmonton to Whitehorse and Fairbanks, the data which Dan McLean had assembled determined the route. He had covered a large area and got as much information as possible concerning air routes, operating bases, communications, weather, operating conditions and other factors.

With the exception of a flight from Edmonton to Cameron Bay on Great Bear Lake, which was made in four days in 1934 by J. A. Wilson, Controller of Civil Aviation, for the purpose of observing operating conditions for aircraft in the Far North, the trip made by Dan McLean in 1935 was the first flight of any duration to the north, the Northwest Territories and the Yukon by an official of the government.

In the early part of 1936, Dan McLean travelled to Europe to study the system of airports and airways in the United Kingdom, France, Belgium, Holland, Denmark, Germany, Sweden and Switzerland. He had made several trips to the United States to keep in touch with technical advances in aviation in that country from 1929 to 1937.

When the Department of Transport was formed on November 2, 1936, Civil Aviation became a part of that department. Dan McLean then became the first Superintendent of Airways and Airports in the new department. In this position, his duties remained the same, directing the selection, development and operation of airports and air routes in Canada.

From the investigation which Dan McLean made on his trip through northwestern Canada in 1935, a decision was made by the officials of the Civil Aviation Division that the route from Edmonton to Whitehorse via the Valley of the Liard River would be the best one from a weather standpoint, and the easiest one to follow. This route was east and north of the Rocky Mountains in the dry belt where flying conditions were quite good, and were the rule, not just the exception. The route also lay over comparatively low elevations throughout its whole length, through Fort Nelson and Lower Post to Whitehorse. Further, Grant McConachie's pioneering operations in the north were being successfully carried out which showed the Canadian authorities that the route was feasible.

Therefore, the Department of Transport authorized that an aerial survey be made of the northern route in the spring of 1939; and W. S. "Bill" Lawson, District Inspector of Western Airways, Regina, was put in charge of the work; while the ground survey party was headed by R. J. "Bob" Crossley, a pilot and a surveyor. So, in 1939, when the weather permitted, aerodrome sites were to be located at Grande Prairie, Alberta; Fort St. John and Fort Nelson in British Columbia; and Watson Lake, and Whitehorse in the Yukon Territory.

The survey parties spent the summer in the field, and were still there when the war erupted in September, 1939. For a time it was thought advisable to bring them in from the field in case they might be required to help out on the construction of airports across Canada. Upon further thought though, and as there were no specific plans to build other airports across Canada at that time, it was decided to hasten the completion of the survey of aerodromes for the northwest route, as the route through the northwest would be of strategic value in the event of war in the East — and there were ominous rumblings in the Pacific.

When war was declared, it was not unnatural that Dan McLean was made responsible for the selection, survey and development of airports for the British Commonwealth Air Training Plan and for Home War purposes. As a reserve R.C.A.F. Officer (a Squadron Leader), he was called for service duty but served only two weeks when he was re-called to civil duty connected with the war effort. It was during this period that he foresaw the need for and organized a complete airway and airport traffic control system that has expanded to rank high amongst such systems throughout the world. This was only a part of his responsibility for the civil administration, operation and maintenance of all the principal airports on the airways' system in Canada.

One day in the fall of 1940, Dan McLean left for Edmonton and he and Bill Lawson made a quick flight over the route between Edmonton and Whitehorse between October 26 and 31 to get a last minute look at the proposed aerial route to the northwest. They made the flight on a regular scheduled trip of Yukon Southern Air Transport, which was skippered by Grant McConachie, the company's President, due to his knowledge of the route and his experience in operating over it for several years.

They looked at sites at Peace River, Grande Prairie, Dawson Creek, Fort St. John, Fort Nelson, Watson Lake, Teslin and Whitehorse. Grant McConachie explained how the facilities along the route could be improved. And Dan McLean listened carefully to his ideas as he flew as co-pilot on the flight.

One major difficulty foreseen with the development of this aerial highway was the transportation of heavy equipment to isolated points, such as Fort Nelson, Watson Lake and Teslin, since there was no Alaska Highway at that time.

Colonel O.M. Biggar was the Canadian Chairman of the Permanent Joint Board on Defence, and he was aware of the plans that the Department of Transport had for developing the air route from Edmonton to Whitehorse. So, when the Canada-United States Permanent Joint Board on Defence met in Victoria, British Columbia, on November 13, 1940, Dan McLean was the representative of the Civil Aviation Division in attendance at the meeting, since he had made the original survey of the northwest route for the department. Thus, a decision was reached at the meeting to develop the northwest air route which was already laid out from Edmonton to Whitehorse to the Alaska border, leading to Fairbanks, by the Department of Transport as a possible military air route.

As Controller of Civil Aviation, Dan McLean was responsible for the planning and construction of the Trans-Canada Airway, the Northwest Staging Route, and the building of airports for the British

---

Following in the steps of his illustrious predecessors, Dan McLean was appointed Controller of Civil Aviation on July 1, 1941 — the same year that he was awarded the Trans-Canada Trophy. The growth and stability of civil aviation in Canada had been guided throughout the years by the following Controllers of Civil Aviation: Honorary Air Commodore J. Stanley Scott, M.C., A.F.C. (then Lieutenant-Colonel) upon its creation in April, 1920; by Air Marshal L. S. Breadner, C.B., D.S.C., (then Squadron Leader) on March 28, 1922; by Air Vice-Marshal A. T. N. Cowley, C.B.E. (then Squadron Leader) on January 30, 1924; by J. A. Wilson, C.B.E., on July 1, 1927; by A. D. McLean, O.B.E. on July 1, 1941; and by Major R. Dodds, O.B.E., M.C., on July 1, 1950. On November 2, 1956, the title of the position of Controller of Civil Aviation was changed to Director of Civil Aviation.

Commonwealth Air Training Plan during World War II.

Then an announcement was made on October 30, 1942, by the Minister of National Defence for Air, Major Charles G. Power, that Dan McLean had been awarded the Trans-Canada Trophy for 1941 in recognition of the outstanding service in aviation that he rendered for many years.

The presentation of the Trans-Canada Trophy was made on January 19, 1943, at the fourteenth annual dinner of the Canadian Flying Clubs Association at the Chateau Laurier in Ottawa by Air Marshal L.S. Breadner, C.B., D.S.C., Chief of the Air Staff, on behalf of the Minister of National Defence.

In accepting the trophy, Dan McLean modestly said that he felt that the award was not due to his merit alone but to that of all his colleagues in the Civil Aviation Branch.

Dan McLean was one of the Canadian delegates who attended the International Civil Aviation Convention in Chicago in November and December, 1944.

With the coming of VE Day on May 8, 1945, the great flow of aircraft from the United States over the northwest war-time air route to Russia was staunched. During World War II, some 14,000 to 15,000 aircraft, such as Aircobras,

---

The Committee of Award for the year 1941 consisted of the following members:

Air Commodore F.V. Heakes, Royal Canadian Air Force, Department of National Defence, Ottawa.

J.A. Wilson, Director of Air Services, Department of Transport, Ottawa.

Air Commodore E. E. Middleton, Royal Canadian Air Force, Department of National Defence, Ottawa.

Dr. J.J. Green, Executive Member of the Canadian Flying Clubs Association, Ottawa.

Presentation of the Trans-Canada Trophy to Dan McLean by A/M L.S. Breadner on January 19, 1943. Left to right: J.A. Wilson, C.B.E., A.D. "Dan" McLean, O.B.E., A/V/M. A.T.N. Cowley, C.B.E., and A/M L.S. Breadner, C.B., D.S.C.

Photo courtesy of R.C.A.F.

Thunderbolts, Tomahawks and Lightning fighters, and B-24 and B-26 bombers, etc., were flown over the northwest route to Fairbanks where they were picked up by Russian pilots. These pilots had not flown most of these types of aircraft before, but it made no difference; they hopped in the aircraft anyhow, took off, and most of them made it to Russia. Then, too, there were those that didn't even make Fairbanks, and a goodly number landed in "Million Dollar Valley" along the way.

Dan McLean was created an Officer of the Order of the British Empire in 1946 for his services during World War II.

In February, 1947, he attended the South Pacific Regional Air Navigation Conference in Sydney, Australia, representing the Department of Transport. He headed the delegation.

He continued as Controller of Civil Aviation until he was appointed a Member of the Air Transport Board in June, 1950, by Order-in-Council, under the Minister, Mr. Lionel Chevrier. He took up his new duties on May 1, 1950, and remained with the board until he retired in April, 1962.

The Air Transport Board was established in September, 1944, by an amendment to the Aeronautics Act. The board consisted of three members appointed by the Governor-in-Council, and was primarily reponsible for regulation and licensing of air carriers transporting goods or passengers for hire or reward; investigations and surveys respecting operation and developing of commercial air services in Canada and, in view of the board's interest in the economic aspects

of commercial air services, to recommend assistance to these carriers, financial or otherwise.

Dan McLean was issued his Commercial Air Pilot's Certificate No. 124, dated May 18, 1921, by the Air Board, and Transport Certificate No. 105, dated May 16, 1938, as well as Air Engineer's Certificate No. A-1019, dated June 5, 1934, which superseded Certificate No. 129, dated April 12, 1921. Through the years he flew some thirty or more different types of aircraft, including the early D.H. 9a, H.S. 2L and Vedette flying boats, Avro, Douglas, Fairchild, Pitcairn, Siskin, Moth, Lockheed, Stearman, Waco, and others.

A methodical type of person, Dan McLean always planned ahead. He possessed a good sense of humour, typical of his Scottish ancestry. He was a big man in every sense of the word with a ruddy complexion. He and Mrs. McLean resided in Ottawa at the time of his death on Friday, May 16, 1969. He was 73 years of age.

He was a member of the Rideau Club, the Canadian Club, the United Services' Institute, the Arctic Circle, and was active in several fraternal organizations. He was an Honorary Vice-President of the Royal Canadian Flying Clubs Association and was one of the founders of Trans-Canada Air Lines. He was named a member of Canada's Aviation Hall of Fame in 1973; and was made a Companion of the Order of Flight (City of Edmonton), and a member of the Order of Polaris (Government of the Yukon Territory).

Mr. and Mrs. McLean had two

children; a son, Douglas, is a geologist (University of New Brunswick '57) who lives in Toronto with his wife and family; and a daughter, Kathryn, now Mrs. James Lynn, lives in Ottawa. Mrs. McLean continues to reside in Ottawa.

Dan McLean, pioneer pilot, air engineer and able administrator, never failed to peer into the future to have a long-range look at the problems in the aviation world, especially in the projection of air routes, national and international, and the selection of aerodrome sites and their design. He played many leading roles in Canada's early aviation development.

This aviation pioneer was a thorough-going individual, meticulous in his ways and a man of decision. Having built the first section of the airways' system in Canada in the Prairie Provinces, and guided the development of those provided by municipalities; having made aerial surveys through the Rocky Mountains; having built the vast Trans-Canada Airway system; having amassed information on his exploratory flight throughout northwestern Canada in 1935, which was of inestimable value in the building of the Northwest Staging Route, which is a story in itself — he was a busy man who gave so much of his ability and time to the development of aviation in Canada. It was for all this work that he received the Trans-Canada Trophy, and a King's Citation.

1942-43

Pat Reid, 1949.
Photo courtesy of Pat Reid.

Thomas Mayne "Pat" Reid

Citation: in recognition of the whole-hearted and energetic support that he had given to everything worthwhile in aviation in Canada, both in peace and in war, during the past twenty years

Thomas Mayne "Pat" Reid, D.F.M., while Aviation Sales Manager with Imperial Oil Limited, Toronto, was awarded the Trans-Canada Trophy for the combined years 1942 and 1943, for meritorious service in the advancement of aviation in Canada, "in recognition of the whole-hearted and energetic support that he had given to everything worthwhile in aviation in Canada, both in peace and in war, during the past twenty years." In informing him of the award, Major, the Honourable Charles G. Power, Minister of National Defence, said in his letter of April 13, 1944, extending his most cordial congratulations to Mr. Reid, "that you have been awarded the Trans-Canada Trophy for the amalgamated years of 1942 and 1943."

"His very keen interest in the advancement of aviation — his extensive knowledge of all parts of the Dominion and his unbounded belief in the development of aviation in this country — instilled confidence in Canada's future in the aviation world in those with whom he came in touch. During 1942 and 1943, his active and energetic co-operation with the research and manufacturing branches of Imperial Oil Limited made possible the production in Canada of an aviation oil which would meet Canadian conditions and requirements — thus contributing materially to Canada's war effort," continued the Minister in his letter to Pat Reid.

Pat Reid pioneered a route through Canada's northwest by air in 1929 when he flew in an exploration party from Sioux Lookout, Ontario, to Great Bear Lake. His travels to the north were many and he so visualized the opening up of the fascinating north country that he remarked that this unexplored territory and its mass of ice, snow and cold could not, in itself, be a barrier behind which our nation could feel secure from invasion, and that travel via the north by air would soon become a reality. This he lived to see. Pat Reid saw a prosperous future for his company, Imperial Oil, and visualized the aviation industry's future as an expanding one.

This he, too, helped to fulfil and, from Canada's eastern coast to her western coast, Imperial Oil's services increased year by year and served Canada's flying men in her hours of need. This staunch pioneer in Canadian aviation took part in a number of rescue missions in the Far North and in Canada's Arctic lands, as well as Alaska, including playing a leading role in the search for the MacAlpine party in the fall of 1929. One of Pat Reid's jobs in this rescue was to fly in material and supplies for the use of the search party.

At the time of this award, Pat Reid

The Committee of Award for the Trans-Canada Trophy for the combined years 1942 and 1943 consisted of the following members:

Air Commodore K. M. Guthrie, Royal Canadian Air Force, Department of National Defence, Ottawa.

Mr. A. D. McLean, Controller of Civil Aviation, Department of Transport, Ottawa.

Group Captain A. H. K. Russell, Royal Canadian Air Force, Department of National Defence, Ottawa.

Dr. J. J. Green, Executive Member of the Canadian Flying Clubs Association, Ottawa.

Pat Reid at Great Whale River, on the way to Richmond Gulf in January, 1929, to pick up party of prospectors to fly out to Remi Lake.
Photo courtesy of Pat Reid.

had some 4,775 hours of bush flying to his credit.

The official presentation of the trophy to Pat Reid took place on Thursday, June 1, 1944, in the Lisgar Building, Ottawa, at 3:00 P.M., and was made by Air Vice-Marshal J. A. Sully, C.B., A.F.C., for the Chief of Air Staff, on behalf of the Honourable Colin Gibson, Minister of National Defence for Air.

Pat Reid was born in Ballyroney, County Down, Northern Ireland, on August 22, 1895. He received his education there, and his training as an automotive engineer with the Ferguson Automotive Company of Belfast, Northern Ireland. However, before his career as an engineer could materialize, World War I was under way — and co-incidentally Pat Reid's flying career was just in the offing. It began in March, 1915, when he joined the Royal Naval Air Service and the Royal Air Force. He served with them for four years, and his experiences taught him much.

With the Naval Air Arm, he took an active part flying in the Dardanelles' campaign and later in the Salonika, Greece, and Belgium coast campaigns, where he also served as an observer and an air engineer. For the last two years of the war he was stationed at Dunkirk on the French coast on submarine-spotting convoy duties and general reconnaissance. It was during this period that he was taught to fly by the Royal Air Force pilots with whom he flew as a crew member on the flying boats. In 1918 he joined the North Sea patrol. He was awarded the Distinguished Flying Medal for gallantry.

When World War I was over, he joined the Handley-Page Transport Company Limited in 1920, and made the inaugural flight on the London-Paris line, as well as on the Amsterdam-Brussels service. Later, he became Superintendent of Engine Overhaul at Croydon, and was Manager for the Handley-Page Transport Company at Zurich, Switzerland, for one

year, just before he decided to come to Canada and see what it had to offer in the field of flying.

Upon arrival in Canada in 1924, he joined the Ontario Provincial Air Service as a pilot and an air engineer and flew forest fire detection and suppression patrols for three years. He received his Commercial Air Pilot's Certificate No. 234 on May 17, 1927. He received his first Air Engineer's Certificate No. 401 on March 15, 1929, later superseded by No. 2005 on April 7, 1945.

When the Northern Aerial Minerals Exploration Company was organized on February 10, 1928, by H. A. "Doc" Oaks and Jack E. Hammell, Pat Reid was one of those who joined the company as a pilot in charge of remote exploration to do trail-blazing in the north. Northern Aerial Minerals Exploration Company came into existence to embark on a large-scale mine-hunt all over the north country using aircraft for transporting men, equipment, supplies, gas, etc. N.A.M.E. was classified as a commercial operating company but its flying activities were distinct from most commercial operators in that there was no direct revenue from the operation of its aircraft. The company's fleet of aircraft was used solely for more effective prospecting. N.A.M.E. had an operating base at Sioux Lookout, Ontario. The company's mechanics were tops in their field, too, as they had to keep the aircraft serviceable in all kinds of weather and temperatures.

During Northern Aerial Minerals Exploration Company's first summer of operations in the Hudson Bay area in 1928, Pat Reid, flying G-CATM, a Loening amphibian, and Matt Berry, flying G-CARK, a Fokker Super Universal, made pioneer trips to carry prospectors and transport their equipment and supplies to various places in the north. The trip left Winnipeg for The Pas, then went northeast to Fort Churchill, Cape Eskimo, Chesterfield Inlet, on the northwest coast of Hudson

Bay, and Baker Lake. There the remaining prospectors and their supplies were left.

Then Pat Reid, accompanied by C. A. "Duke" Schiller, flew his Loening amphibian south to Moose Factory on Hannah Bay, over to Rupert House, and up the east coast of James Bay and Hudson Bay to Richmond Gulf and Port Harrison. Pat Reid told of the time he had on this trip when he visited Port Harrison on the east coast of Hudson Bay and five stout little Eskimo lads 'piloted' him through stormy seas for three days to get to Richmond Gulf. He remarked on their unusual skill in navigating a boat through such rough water in pitch darkness. On this trip he visited Great Whale River, East Main, Fort George — and Rupert House, the place he was later to be so glad to see after he was blizzard-bound in an aircraft for two whole days on the sea ice about five miles from shore.

Pat Reid did not arrive back at Winnipeg until some time around the middle of September, 1928. On this extended pioneer trip, which took him about a month, he almost completely circled Hudson Bay and James Bay by air.

On December 27, 1928, Doc Oaks and Pat Reid, both pilots with Northern Aerial Minerals Exploration, left Remi Lake on the Canadian National Railways to make a flight up the eastern side of Hudson Bay as far as Richmond Gulf. Each was piloting an aircraft. They were to meet a prospecting party that had been left there the previous summer by schooner, on the understanding that they were to be picked up by 'plane in January, 1929. Doc Oaks and Pat Reid were accompanied by two courageous honeymooners, an Anglican missionary and his wife, who wanted to return to the mission station at Rupert House. By dog team this would have taken six or eight weeks to make the outward journey alone. There were only five settlements

Two N.A.M.E. 'planes at Baker Lake, May, 1929. In the background is the company's wrecked schooner, Patrick and Michael. The 'plane at the right is G-CATM, a Loening amphibian, flown by Duke Schiller, while the one on the left is G-CATL, flown by Pat Reid at the beginning of their exploration trip to Great Bear Lake.

between the railway and Richmond Gulf, and the route lay over several hundred miles of the rocky eastern shore of James Bay and Hudson Bay, fully exposed to the sweep of the Arctic gales over the open areas. An hour after leaving, they arrived at Moose Factory where they left the mail, and continued their trip to Rupert House.

Without warning, while they were crossing Hannah Bay, a blinding snowstorm swept down on them preventing the two pilots from seeing each other. Visibility was zero. They both had flown over Rupert House, but were unable to see it due to the blizzard. About an hour before dusk, and at about the same time, each landed — Doc Oaks on the coast seven miles north and Pat Reid on the ice three miles offshore. Upon landing, Pat Reid froze his skis to the surface of the ice to prevent the aircraft from being blown away, and he and Ken Murray, his mechanic, endeavoured to make themselves as "comfortable as possible" in the cabin of the Fairchild 'plane until the storm subsided.

Doc Oaks, with the honeymooning couple, and Kel Mews, his mechanic, taxied to shore to look for a sheltered spot from the storm where they could spend the night. He then noticed that one of his aircraft's skis was broken. They ate emergency rations for supper, heated over a blowtorch. Then they settled down for the night as best they could.

The weather was no better in the morning. The 'plane was disabled and frozen in — the blizzard was still raging and it was around -40° F. — so Oaks set out on foot to try to find Rupert House. After walking for miles along the coast, he came across a familiar landmark and realized that he was north of the post and not south, so he returned to the aircraft. He then found that an Indian trapper had passed by and taken word of their predicament to Rupert House.

About midnight, on New Year's Eve, a dog team arrived for the newlyweds and took them to the mission.

The following day the weather cleared and repairs were made to the aircraft's broken ski by a blacksmith from the mission station. Pat Reid and Doc Oaks, and their mechanics, then took off to continue their trail-blazing flight to Richmond Gulf, where they were to pick up their party of prospectors. They reached there on January 11, 1929, and between them brought back thirteen men to Remi Lake on the same day, thus completing safely another northern adventure.

According to the records, this flight was the first one that was made to Richmond Gulf during the winter months.

While Pat Reid was a pilot with Northern Aerial Minerals Exploration Company, he and Jim Vance, another pilot with the company, flying Tom Creighton, a prospector, and his party, made a historic flight from Hudson Bay across the Barren Lands of northern Canada to the Arctic coast and Great Bear Lake in 1929 to pioneer a Northwest Passage by air. The Barren Lands were beyond the northern limit of wooded country, a land of tundra, where little wild life existed. However, most important of all, and the reason why man was drawn to such remote areas was because the land had vast resources and was rich in minerals. This mineral wealth was sought by man.

Leaving Northern Aerial Minerals Exploration Company's base at Sioux Lookout, Ontario, in April, 1929, Pat Reid, piloting a Fairchild FC2-W2 aircraft, G-CATL, accompanied at first by Duke Schiller, also a pilot with the company, who was piloting G-CATM, a Loening amphibian on skis, flew to The Pas. At The Pas they picked up the prospecting party which was making this extended six months' exploration trip to Great Bear Lake. From The Pas they flew to Fort Churchill and then to Baker

Lake, near Chesterfield Inlet. This party was under the leadership of Tom Creighton, a prospector and the discoverer of the Flin Flon mine which produced copper, zinc, gold and silver.

On this flight Duke Schiller, at the controls of G-CATM, was carrying Tom Creighton and Jack Humble, the air engineer. Duke Schiller was in the vicinity of Wager Bay in August, 1929, when his aircraft ran out of fuel and he was forced to land in the Barrens. They were not located for two weeks and one day, until Pat Reid, in his Fairchild G-CATL, who was searching for them, found them walking to the Northern Aerial Minerals Exploration Company's base camp at Baker Lake. They had left their aircraft and had decided to try to reach their Baker Lake camp, which was many miles away. When Pat Reid found them, all three were tired and hungry, but otherwise quite well.

In August, 1929, Jim Vance, also flying for Northern Aerial Minerals Exploration Company, arrived at Baker Lake in his Fokker Super Universal aircraft, G-CARK, to take Duke Schiller's place with the party and accompany Pat Reid and Tom Creighton and his party on this extended exploration and prospecting trip.

As soon as it could be arranged, an aircraft flew in gas for Duke Schiller's downed Loening amphibian.

Upon refuelling G-CATM, Duke Schiller flew it to the company's base at the foot of Baker Lake (about 64° N., 94° W.) where the company's vessel *Patrick and Michael* had been wrecked. Duke Schiller remained at Baker Lake to service the prospecting parties which were there.

So, Pat Reid and Jim Vance flew Tom Creighton and his prospecting party of one or two others across the Barren Lands from Baker Lake to Beechey Lake and Bathurst Inlet on August 31, 1929. Then the next day, September 1, the two aircraft were winging their way across

Coronation Gulf on the Arctic coast to Coppermine. They were the first to fly to Coppermine.

Their Arctic exploration flight was climaxed at Great Bear Lake. Then they left Great Bear Lake for Fort Norman to start the return journey to The Pas and Sioux Lookout. They followed the Mackenzie River to Great Slave Lake. From there they flew to Fort Smith, Lake Athabaska, Fort McMurray, Edmonton, Prince Albert and The Pas. Upon arrival at The Pas, Tom Creighton and his prospecting party remained there. Reconnaissance work was undertaken in the various areas for minerals. They also staked gold-bearing areas on their exploration trip. Pat Reid and Jim Vance flew back to their base at Sioux Lookout, via Winnipeg, arriving there early in October, 1929 — completing their six months' exploratory trip across the Barren Lands to the Arctic, as well as pioneering a Northwest Passage by air. Such a trip without trouble to the aircraft spoke well for the mechanic or engineer looking after it and the pilot, as well as its manufacturer. Jim Vance was killed in a flying accident the following year, in 1930, at Great Bear Lake while flying for Dominion Explorers Limited. It was on a similar journey that the MacAlpine party of Dominion Explorers was lost in 1929.

This exploratory flight, also pioneering a Northwest Passage by air, was practically self-sustaining for the whole six months. Pat Reid and Jim Vance covered more than 30,000 miles and penetrated remote areas never before trod by man. All this Pat Reid sketched on paper to provide Canadian map makers with his knowledge of the north, so little of which had been charted before. But on such flights to new territory it was customary for pilots in those days, and even today, to sketch new areas. This was the first time an aircraft had completed such an extensive trip over such hazardous country.

Pat Reid lost his life within a few days

of what would have been the twenty-fifth anniversary of his historic flight to pioneer a Northwest Passage by air.

Then Pat Reid was to lead a rescue expedition in search of Carl Ben Eielson and Frank Dorbandt. Early in November, 1929, Carl Ben Eielson and Frank Dorbandt left Teller, Alaska, each piloting an aircraft, to assist an American fur-trading schooner which had been icebound off North Cape on the Siberian coast in the Bering Sea since September. The schooner, the S.S. Namikesu of Seattle, owned by O. Swenson, a fur trader, was running low on supplies by November and had sent out an S.O.S. The icebound schooner carried a half-million dollars' worth of furs.

Carl Ben Eielson and Frank Dorbandt had answered the schooner's call and gone to her assistance. On their first flight, they returned from the fur-trading schooner with six persons, including the owner O. Swenson and his daughter, Marion. Then, on November 9, 1929, the two pilots left on their second rescue flight to go to the schooner, but on this flight they ran into stormy weather.

Flying through the Rocky Mountains today in single-engined aircraft, even in the summer time, can be often fraught

with danger as well as adventure; but in the winter time when swirling snowstorms suddenly sweep upon you, and you cannot see the way before you, a forced landing usually has to be made to avoid even a greater risk of running into the side of a mountain. Even if a forced landing was safely made, the two great enemies of man — cold and hunger — would be present, if a rescue was not made soon.

Frank Dorbandt returned to Teller after about an hour's flying from his base when the storm increased in intensity. Carl Ben Eielson did not return to Teller, Alaska, nor did he reach the schooner off the Siberian coast. So, rescue expeditions were organized by air and by dog sled to search for him and Earl Borland, his mechanic.

Carl Ben Eielson, a well-to-do American, was flying out of Fairbanks in 1923 and flew the first Alaska air mail run in 1924 from Fairbanks to McGrath, a distance of 350 miles. Eielson was the renowned pilot who accompanied Sir Hubert Wilkins on his two 1927 Arctic flights north of Alaska and on his flight across the North Pole from Point Barrow, Alaska, to Spitzbergen, Norway,

Pat Reid's Fairchild which he landed on a creek bed during the search for Carl Ben Eielson (1929-30).
Photo courtesy of Pat Reid.

Pat Reid and Duke Schiller with the Eskimos at Chesterfield Inlet, September 1930, while stopping over on one of their exploration trips.
Photo courtesy of R.C.A.F.

(via Ellesmere Island) in April, 1928. He was also Sir Hubert Wilkins' pilot on the 1928-29 Wilkins-Hearst Antarctic Expedition. Eielson had always thrived on public acclaim and excitement, and had opened up much of the Arctic to aviation.

Joe Crosson and Harold Gillam, both pilots, were two to search for Eielson and Borland, and reached the schooner on December 23, 1929, flying from Teller, Alaska. Joe Crosson was a well-known Alaskan pilot, and also was co-pilot with Eielson on Sir Hubert Wilkins' Antarctic Expedition of 1928-29. Joe Crosson headed up Pacific Alaska Airways, Seattle, Washington, some years later. Then the Aviation Corporation of New York asked Pat Reid of Northern Aerial Minerals Exploration Company, and air engineer W. "Bill" Hughes, from the Ontario Provincial Air Service, to lead a rescue expedition to search for Eielson. This expedition started from Fairbanks, Alaska, extending to the Siberian Arctic. On this mission Pat Reid was compelled to make a landing with his Fairchild in a valley in the Alaskan mountains between the Yukon River and Nome, due to a sudden heavy snowstorm sweeping through the mountain passes making visibility almost impossible. A quick decision was made to land in the creek bed. In landing the right wing tip of his aircraft was broken and he was delayed a week. After temporary repairs were made to the wing tip of the aircraft, they took off for Analakleet to have permanent repairs made. During this time Pat Reid was reported missing, and he returned to read a factual account of his own obituary in the *Patricia Herald,* one of the northern newspapers. However, he shivered when he thought of how close it had come to being the truth.

An excerpt from Pat Reid's report of his experience reads as follows:

"We ran into a snowstorm after crossing the Endicott Mountains, and because of poor visibility were unable to get back across the mountains to a safe landing on the Yukon River. Hemmed in by the mountains on all sides, we had to attempt a landing on a short narrow stretch of creek bed, the sides of which rose almost perpendicularly for about 200 feet. The creek bed was barely wide enough to accommodate the wing-spread of the 'plane but we managed to get the machine down. Unfortunately, the gap at the end of the stretch was so narrow that it broke off about four feet of wing tip before the machine came to rest, leaving my two companions (Bill Hughes and Jim Hutchins) and myself stranded in the mountains.

"We either had to repair the wing or hike out on snowshoes to an unknown destination, and we decided on the former.

"After sleeping in the 'plane for seven days and nights, and living on emergency rations, we managed to repair the wing tip, took off and reached Analakleet, where we made permanent repairs.

"Getting out of the creek was even more hazardous and difficult than landing, as we had to have sufficient height to clear the gap or we would have torn off a wing section and been completely wrecked. However, we were able to scrape through with just enough height to get out.

"Subsequent to the repairs of the aircraft, the expedition continued to a sorrowful conclusion on the Siberian Arctic Coast where we located the wreckage of the lost aircraft and brought back to the United States the bodies of both Eielson and Borland, who had been killed in the crash."

After permanent repairs had been made to the wing of the Fairchild aircraft at Analakleet, Pat Reid, Bill Hughes and Jim Hutchins continued their search for Eielson along the Siberian coast and out over Bering Strait. During their search, they sighted in the distance what they thought to be the schooner and, while banking the aircraft to have a better view, Pat Reid glimpsed the wing of an aircraft protruding from the glistening white Arctic snow on the frozen lagoon at the mouth of the Anguema River (177-1/2° W.) That was on January 25, 1930. They went on to the schooner, the *S.S. Namikesu,* and returned later with Joe Crosson and some of the schooner's crew to the spot where the wing of the aircraft had been seen in the snow. Eielson's wasp-powered Hamilton aircraft was dug out from beneath about eight feet of snow by a mixed crew. The bodies were found near the aircraft about the middle of February after much digging. Thus was brought to light the dénouement of the fateful disappearance of Carl Ben Eielson and Earl Borland on their ironic rescue flight to assist an icebound schooner, when on their second mission their aircraft was caught in one of those swirling snowstorms. Pat Reid flew both bodies to Fairbanks, Alaska, and later to Seattle, Washington.

Also, sufficient supplies were flown to the American crew of the schooner who would remain with her and her wealthy cargo until spring.

Then the *Stravropol,* a Russian ship, was icebound off Cape North. Pat Reid and Joe Crosson found its location and flew the Russian Captain Milzvzorow to Fairbanks. From there he went to Seattle where he took a ship to Russia to get an ice-breaker to come to the rescue of the *Stravropol.* One did.

Pat Reid was at home in the north, having lived there for various periods at fur-trading posts, mounted police stations and even at Eskimo villages. So it was only natural for him to know these people quite well, and to know the country as much as one could be expected to know it, and its mysteries. He knew all about the lonely existence of the pioneers and how they looked forward to receiving word from the world to the south of them. Many are the stories that

Pat Reid visiting the home of one of his Chukshi friends in Siberia.
Photo courtesy of Imperial Oil Limited.

Pat Reid could tell of happenings about pioneers in the Barren Lands, where he made many friends.

Pat Reid told the story of a sergeant at one of the remote police posts who for years before he went into the north had never had breakfast without a morning paper propped up against the marmalade jar before him. For a whole year after his arrival at the distant outpost he ate his breakfast in misery. Then the supply boat came in on its annual visit and from it there was unloaded for the sergeant several large heavy parcels containing a year's issue of a morning newspaper and a weekly paper. Tenderly the sergeant unwrapped the precious freight and he spent a great part of the night arranging the papers in their proper sequences of publication dates and setting them up in twelve neat piles, each of which contained issues for a month. Beside the breakfast table he placed the pile containing the oldest papers, with the most aged of all on the top. Then he retired for the night, well satisfied with his work. In the morning he lifted the paper from the top of the pile nearest his table. It was more than a year old, but he scanned it from front to back and relished its contents more than his food. Each morning he read a succeeding issue and on Sundays he had the more voluminous weekly paper to while away a more leisurely day. He never "cheated." No matter how mysterious a crime, no matter how engrossing a trial or how intriguing a serial story might be, he never picked up the following issue to see what the developments were until the time came for the next day's breakfast. He kept in touch with the news almost one year after the event.[1]

On one occasion after drifting all night in the open water of James Bay in a seaplane with a damaged wing, Pat Reid was especially glad to see Moose Factory. Then, while close to Winisk River near Churchill one day, he was out of gas for his seaplane and was most

fortunate to have some sent out to him in freighter canoes. Pat Reid also told about the time they rowed out from the edge of the ice floe on Fairway Island to get some duck eggs, and spent hours rowing back against the current only to discover that most of the eggs they'd collected were already half-hatched!

When Pat Reid had wandered around in the air for many hours over the Barren Lands betwen Baker Lake and Bathurst Inlet on one of his trips, he was grateful to see signs of human habitation when he came upon Bathurst Inlet. Once he made a forced landing on the sea ice about seven miles from Nome, Alaska, during a blizzard and spent a three-day imprisonment in his machine until the weather cleared.

During the two years or so that Pat Reid was in charge of remote exploration for Northern Aerial Minerals Exploration, he made pioneer flights to the Arctic coast, Great Bear Lake, the Mackenzie River areas, and the eastern coast of Hudson Bay.

Pat Reid joined Imperial Oil Limited in 1931 as Aviation Manager for their western region.

That same year, 1931, he acted as tour leader of the first Trans-Canada Air Pageant, and flew Imperial Oil's entry, CF-IOL, a de Havilland Puss Moth. The aircraft bore the special shade of green with red insignia which distinguished Imperial Oil's gasoline tanks and pumps. This was a two-way transcontinental flight visiting practically every city in the Dominion where there was a place to land. It was an impressive spectacle conducted under the auspices of the Canadian Flying Clubs Association with the sanction of the Department of National Defence and the endorsement of the Aviation League of Canada.

The tour started at Hamilton, Ontario, on July 1, 1931, Dominion Day, and continued through to September 8, where a final show was staged on Aviation Day at the Canadian National Exhibition,

Toronto. After leaving Hamilton, the Trans-Canada Air Pageant toured Western Ontario and went to the Border Cities where a demonstration was conducted on July 4, Independence Day in the United States.

The tour then went to the United States through Michigan, Indiana, Illinois, Wisconsin and Minnesota to Winnipeg. The flight was timed to arrive at Vancouver after flying over the Rocky Mountains, for the formal opening of the new municipal airport at Vancouver, which had cost $400,000 to build at the time. Some side trips were made en route to Toronto on the return trip.

After winding up the show in Toronto, the second stage of the air tour to the Atlantic coast got under way, and culminated in an official demonstration for the new municipal airport at Halifax, Nova Scotia. Other maritime cities were also visited and special programmes were conducted in co-operation with the local affiliated clubs.

There was no entry fee for this tour and it had no competitive feature, as its purpose was "to promote and stimulate public interest in all branches of aviation in Canada." George M. Ross, Executive Secretary of the Canadian Flying Clubs Association was business manager of the tour, which was to cover an approximate 7,700-mile route. George Ross flew the Gipsy Moth belonging to Major-General Sir J. H. MacBrien, C.B., C.M.G., D.S.O., President of the Aviation League of Canada.

Pat Reid flew company-owned aircraft extensively in connection with his duties and, at the time, was reputed to have flown over more Canadian territory than any other pilot. The distance between Canada's northerly and southerly extremities is approximately 3,000 miles — almost as great as its width. And Pat Reid had covered most of this distance as he flew aircraft in the course of his duties with Imperial Oil, which included the establishment and supervision of the

Presentation of the Trans-Canada Trophy to Pat Reid by A/V/M. J.A. Sully, on June 1, 1944, at Ottawa.
Photo courtesy of Canadian Aviation.

company's aviation policy, arranging supplies and service of aviation products on a Dominion-wide basis and making frequent inspection flights over the various Canadian national and international air routes.

Imperial Oil established its Aviation Sales Department in 1931 to co-ordinate the job of supplying aviation fuels and lubricants on a nation-wide basis. The first Manager of the new department was Pat Reid. In September, 1932, he was appointed Aviation Sales Manager for the company, and later transferred to Toronto. His wide flying experience, his unique knowledge of Canada from an aviation viewpoint and his confidence in the dependability of Imperial products made him particularly suited for his job which brought him into contact with operating companies, engine manufacturers, pilots, mechanics and those people in aviation generally. Pat Reid's experiences in the north helped him admirably when he had to decide where his company should establish refuelling bases as he knew just where they should be. In the early days, many a successful trail-blazing flight went through only because Pat Reid's men underwent hardships and overcame obstacles to establish refuelling bases along the projected route. Pat Reid could be found superintending refuelling arrangements for some special flight, taking off his coat and helping organize a flying meet, or doing any other job that came his way.

The following year he made a one-day flight from Winnipeg to Vancouver, covering the 1,785 miles in a little over thirteen hours. He took part in the British Columbia Air Tour, and also acted as leader of the Manitoba Goodwill Air Tour for Imperial Oil.

When the Italian Air Armada of 24 twin-hulled flying boats, lead by General

Balbo, visited Canada en route to the U.S. World's Fair at Chicago, in the midsummer of 1933, they were welcomed by Pat Reid on behalf of Imperial Oil at Shediac, New Brunswick.

Imperial Oil was the first company to go into the north with its pilots to help pioneer and open the way. While Pat Reid actually was piloting less and less himself, yet he had a fine opportunity before him to further the development of aviation in another most important way. His personal interest in people inspired them, especially those who were starting a career as a pilot, and he was always glad for any opportunity to be helpful. Through Pat Reid himself, too, and through the Imperial Oil Company, many early air line companies and operators in Canada, no matter how small or how large, were assisted, both materially and financially — some serving communities not readily accessible by rail or road.

Pat Reid, D.F.M., was still associated with Imperial Oil Limited, Toronto, as Manager of their Aviation Sales Department, at the time of his tragic death on April 8, 1954, at the age of 58. He and his wife, Marjorie, were killed simultaneously in a mid-air collision, when the Trans-Canada Air Lines' aircraft in which they were flying and an Air Force trainer aircraft collided over Moose Jaw, Saskatchewan, while they were on their way to Victoria, to attend the spring conference of the Air Industries and Transport Association. Thomas Mayne "Pat" Reid had lived in Canada for thirty years. Mr. and Mrs. Reid resided in Toronto, Ontario, prior to their death. Their son, John, served in Canada with an R.C.A.F. jet squadron until early in 1957 when he joined Austin Airways.

As a pilot, Pat Reid did not seem to know fear, and on two different occasions this sturdily-built individual even

read his own obituary in the newspapers when he returned to civilization. He was a somewhat shy person with an Irish brogue. His amiable grin — unhindered by his moustache — warmed the hearts of many. Yet, he ever remained an unassuming person. Pat Reid was known as an imperturbable and efficient Aviation Sales Manager for Imperial Oil, in addition to being an ambassador of goodwill wherever he went and in whatever he did.

Pat Reid had been continuously associated with Canadian aviation for more than thirty years, and had long been a familiar leading figure in Canadian flying. So much did he contribute to the development of aviation in Canada that his name became synonymous with the word "aviation". Pat Reid viewed Canada's future in aviation in the early days as a great thriving industry vibrating with life and energy as it made vast strides across the nation — and to this end he worked objectively. His insight was unquestionably responsible for a great deal of today's growth of civil aviation in Canada — to say nothing of the great part that his company played in this growth. Pat Reid shall always be remembered amongst Canada's pioneers in aviation as one of the really great men of our time.

He was named a member of Canada's Aviation Hall of Fame in 1973, and was made a Companion of the Order of Flight (City of Edmonton).

NOTE

[1] *Imperial Oil Review,* 1934, under "Northern Messages."

1944

John Armitstead "J.A." Wilson

Citation: in recognition of his outstanding contribution to Canadian aviation and his assistance in the development of international aeronautics, as well as his long service, energetic support and whole-hearted efforts in the development of civil aviation in Canada — and for his untiring endeavours on behalf of the R.C.A.F. in the prosecution of Canada's war effort and the development of the British Commonwealth Air Training Plan

John Armitstead "J. A." Wilson, C.B.E., M.E.I.C., while Director of Air Services, Ottawa, was awarded the Trans-Canada Trophy for 1944 for meritorious service in the advancement of aviation in Canada, "in recognition of his outstanding contribution to Canadian aviation and his assistance in the development of international aeronautics, as well as his long service, energetic support and whole-hearted efforts in the development of civil aviation in Canada — and for his untiring endeavours on behalf of the R.C.A.F. in the prosecution of Canada's war effort and the development of the British Commonwealth Air Training Plan." The announcement of the award was made by the Honourable Colin Gibson, Minister of National Defence on March 28, 1945.

John Armitstead Wilson, later known as "J.A.", was born at Broughty Ferry, situated at the mouth of the Firth of Tay in Scotland, on November 2, 1879. He attended Dundee High School and St. Andrews University.

He was an engineer by profession, and came to Canada from Scotland in November, 1905, upon his return from Calcutta, India, in May that year, where he had been employed with the Union Standard Mills of Bird and Company in an engineering capacity for four years.

Upon his arrival in Canada, he was employed as an engineer with the Canada Cement Company, and worked at their plants in Exshaw, Alberta and Hull, Quebec.

Mr. Wilson's interest in aviation began in 1910 when, on July 18 of that year, he joined the newly formed Department of Naval Service as Director of Stores and Contracts.

Then he joined the Governor-General's Foot Guards, Ottawa, in 1912, and later became a Captain. He remained with the regiment until around 1920.

On April 1, 1918, he was appointed Assistant Deputy Minister of the Naval Service, and was made responsible for the organization of the Royal Canadian Naval Air Service, and the construction of naval air bases at Dartmouth and Sydney, Nova Scotia, for anti-submarine patrols off the Atlantic coast.

In February, 1919, at the request of the Minister of Reconstruction, J. A. Wilson drafted the Air Board Act (today superseded by the Aeronautics Act) — the original Canadian legislation on aeronautics — which received Royal Assent on June 6, 1919. Actually, it was J. A. Wilson who had first suggested to the Minister of Reconstruction the possibilities of aviation in Canada, especially the north, but the minister said that "he did not think Canada would ever have need of an air service." However, the minister changed his mind later when the Canadian Pacific Railway Company asked Parliament for an extension of the company's charter to include the operation of aircraft. So J. A. Wilson

J.A. Wilson (left rear) on a flight in an R.C.A.F. flying boat doing aerial survey work during the summer of 1924. He covered some 10,000 miles by air.

was asked to draft the Air Board Act. By the Air Board Act, a Board of Aeronautics was established which had broad powers of control over all forms of aeronautics. This statute provided in detail for the regulation of civil aeronautics and it was framed primarily for this purpose. Powers to deal with military aeronautics were less well defined and were then regarded as a temporary measure pending the reorganization of the defence forces.

The first Air Board was appointed by Order-in-Council, P.C. 1295, dated June 23, 1919. The Honourable A. L. Sifton was Chairman. Colonel O. M. Biggar, K.C., Judge Advocate General, who had acted for Canada on the subcommittee on Air Conventions of the Peace Conference in Paris, was Vice-Chairman. The other members of the board were: the Honourable S. C. Mewburn, Minister of Militia and Defence; the Honourable C. C. Ballantyne, Minister of the Naval

The original Air Board, after completing the preliminary work of organization for which it was appointed, resigned, and on April 19, 1920, the Air Board was re-organized by Order-in-Council No. 826 and a new board was formed under the Chairmanship of the Honourable Hugh Guthrie, Minister of Militia and Defence. Colonel O. M. Biggar, K.C., was re-appointed as Vice-Chairman. The chiefs of the flying and administrative services of the board were appointed as the other five members of the board, namely: Air Vice-Marshal Sir W. Gwatkin, K.C.M.G., C.B., Inspector General of the Canadian Air Force; Lieutenant-Colonel R. Leckie, D.S.O., D.S.C., D.F.C., Director of Flying Operations; Lieutenant-Colonel J. S. Scott, M.C., A.F.C., Controller of Civil Aviation; Captain W. Hose, C.B.E., Director of the Naval Service; and Dr. E. Deville, LL.D., Surveyor General of Canada.

Service; D. R. M. Coulter, C.M.G., the Deputy Postmaster General; E. S. Busby, the Chief Inspector of the Department of Customs and Inland Revenue and Mr. J. A. Wilson, who was the Assistant Deputy Minister of the Naval Service.

From this, four civil branches were created: a Secretary's Branch, dealing with organization, finance, staff and departmental duties generally; a Certificates Branch, dealing with the licensing of aircraft and personnel; a Flying Operations Branch, to conduct any flying operations required for other government services, and a Technical Branch.

The position of Secretary to the Air Board became vacant at this time through the resignation of Major A. M. Shook, on account of ill health, and J. A. Wilson, Assistant Deputy Minister of the Naval Service, and a member of the original Air Board, resigned from his position in April, 1920, to accept the appointment as Secretary. In this position he assumed a distinguished and impressive pioneer role in the organization of the early experimental work done by the Air Board in forest protection, aerial photography in survey work, transportation in the more remote areas of the country, and other similar work.

The Air Board served three primary purposes: the regulation of civil aviation, conducting civil government operations and the early aerial defence of Canada, including the organization and administration of the Canadian Air Force.

In September and October, 1919, Mr. Wilson visited England and Scotland to inspect naval and air establishments, aircraft factories and bases.

The formation of a Canadian Air Force (non-permanent) under the Aeronautics Act was approved by Order-in-Council No. 395, dated February 18, 1920. On January 1, 1923, an Act was proclaimed creating the Department of National Defence. The Air Board now ceased to exist, and its functions were assumed by

the newly established Department of National Defence. Under this department, the Chief of Staff and the Director of the Canadian Air Force were made responsible for the direction of all duties, civil and military, with no recognition of the fact that a large part of the administration of aeronautics dealt with purely civil functions having little relation to the Air Force. The Canadian Air Force was re-organized as of April 1, 1924, and was then called the Royal Canadian Air Force, now a permanent force. In the subsequent reorganization, Mr. Wilson was appointed Assistant Director and Secretary of the Royal Canadian Air Force, responsible for civil aviation functions.

In the summer of 1924, after his appointment as Secretary of the Royal Canadian Air Force, J. A. Wilson made a 10,000-mile trip in an R.C.A.F. flying boat, which was on aerial survey work from Ottawa to Sydney, Nova Scotia, then to Natashquan, Quebec, to Grand'Mère, Biscotasing, Moose Factory, Port Albany, Kenora, God's Lake, Norway House, Port Nelson, Churchill, Brochet, Ile à la Crosse, Prince George, Prince Rupert, Alberni, Vancouver, Calgary, Winnipeg, Port Arthur, Windsor, Toronto and back to Ottawa. This was, no doubt, one of the earliest pioneering trips — and perhaps the longest — made by a flying boat in Canada up to that time. On this 10,000-mile flight in 1924, Mr. Wilson saw not only how mapping from the air could be done, but the marvellous scenic beauties of Canada, her unspoiled natural resources, the grandeur of the Canadian Rockies and her green countryside and forests. At Temagami, J.A. and his party were invited by the newly formed Ontario Provincial Air Service to accompany them in a flying boat to Moose Factory. Upon arrival at Minaki, they left the Ontario Provincial Air Service's flying boat after a fond farewell and met the Royal Canadian Air Force's flying boat

J.A. Wilson standing beside an H.S. 2L flying boat at the O.P.A.S. base at Biscotasing, Ontario, in 1924, during an inspection trip that summer. Those H.S. 2L flying boats still in use were retired from service when regulations were issued by D.N.D. at the end of 1932 making them all obsolete.

which was carrying out mapping and survey work.

For many years, Mr. Wilson was instrumental in advising, directing and assisting many Canadian and British veterans of the Royal Air Force in the formation of small air transportation companies in Canada, following the demobilization period after the First World War. At the same time, through Mr. Wilson's suasion, many Canadian cities and towns became interested in building municipal airports to provide landing facilities for these new services.

Thus, with the rapid growth of aviation in Canada during those years, the following four directorates dividing the aeronautical activities of the department were formed in 1927: the Royal Canadian Air Force; Civil Government Air operations; the Control of Civil Aviation; and Aeronautical Engineering.

J. A. Wilson was appointed Controller of Civil Aviation on July 1, 1927, when the Directorate for the Control of Civil Aviation was organized.

At the Imperial Conference in 1926, the Canadian representatives agreed to participate in the development of an empire system of communications by airship. Mr. Wilson was assigned the important task of organizing the Canadian effort in 1927. An airship base was selected at St. Hubert, near Montreal, and construction work on the mooring tower, hydrogen plant and other facilities required for the reception of the airship was commenced; also the organization of the necessary meteorological and radio services proceeded under his direction. These plans culminated in the successful transatlantic voyage of H.M. Airship R-100 from Cardington, the airship base in the United Kingdom, to St. Hubert, arriving at dawn on July 30, 1930. The airship visited Ottawa, Toronto and the Niagara district, leaving for England on August 13, 1930.

He was also instrumental in promoting the flying club movement in 1927-28 for the training of pilots and in developing public air-mindedness in its support. To meet the demand for flying training facilities, the flying club movement was started with government assistance, and some twenty flying clubs were organized in the principal cities, the municipalities being responsible for providing the airports. The standard conditions were drawn up and approved by Order-in-Council P.C. 1878, dated September 24, 1927. These provided that any community pledging itself to provide the services of an instructor and an air engineer, a licensed aerodrome and adequate accommodation for the housing and maintenance of the machines, would be issued with two light aircraft by the Department of National Defence in the first year and, in each subsequent year, if they supplied from their own resources an aircraft of an approved type, the Department of National Defence would issue one more light aircraft. In addition, the Department of National Defence would pay to the club a grant of one hundred dollars for each ab initio pupil obtaining a private pilot's certificate. In this way, the Department of National Defence encouraged aviation by assisting in the establishing of flying clubs in the principal cities of the Dominion. The Department of National Defence was further assisting by having the instructor for each club trained by the R.C.A.F. at Camp Borden.

Under Mr. Wilson's kind and wise direction arrangements were made for the survey and construction of the Trans-Canada Airway from Vancouver to Halifax, some 3,108 miles, after the government decided to build it in 1928. At this time, a chain of early airports at the major centres was coming into existence from coast to coast as a result of the activities of the flying clubs and the assistance they were receiving from their communities. It was now necessary for intermediate aerodromes to be

constructed to bridge the gap between the main aerodromes. The provision of these aerodromes, as well as lighting for night flying, radio and weather services would be the responsibility of the Dominion Government. Surveys to select suitable aerodrome sites were carried out from coast to coast by the Civil Aviation Branch. The construction of aerodromes in the Prairie Provinces was begun first, since the flatness of the land in the Prairies presented simpler problems. The intermediate aerodromes, leasing and improvements to properties, and the installation of the lighting facilities, radio and meteorological services, were actually completed in January, 1930, and a nightly air mail service was inaugurated on March 3, 1930, between Winnipeg and Edmonton via Calgary, and later via Lethbridge and Calgary. Arrangements were made for surveys to be continued through the Rocky Mountains to determine the best route from the Prairies to Vancouver, and also on the sections east of Winnipeg.

President Coolidge of the United States issued invitations for an International Conference on Air Navigation to be convened in Washington on December 12, 1928, to mark the twenty-fifth anniversary of the first flight of a heavier-than-air flying machine by the Wright Brothers in December, 1903. Mr. Wilson, as Controller of Civil Aviation, was one of the official Canadian delegates who attended. The Canadian delegation was headed by Mr. G. J. Desbarats, Deputy Minister, Department of National Defence. Many interesting papers on all phases of civil aviation, aircraft and engine manufacturers, meteorology, wireless, provision of airways, control of air traffic and other kindred subjects were presented by leading aeronautical authorities from many countries. Mr. Wilson gave a paper on the development of civil aviation in Canada. This conference was attended by delegates from various parts of the world.

R-100 at the Mooring Mast at St. Hubert, P.Q.,
in the early morning of August 1, 1930.
Photo courtesy of the R.C.A.F.

J. A. Wilson, oft referred to as the genial and energetic Controller, as well as "the Father of Civil Aviation in Canada," was here, there and everywhere while he was in aviation. During the first week of June, 1930, he was at the air meets at Ottawa, Kingston and Brantford. And a little thing like being forced down was only an incident in his day's work. Such a happening occurred on the way from Ottawa to Brantford with his daughter, when the machine, piloted by Inspector Doug Joy, was forced down just west of Port Hope. Undaunted, Mr. Wilson and his daughter continued the journey as far as Toronto by road through the courtesy of a passing motorist, then flew from Toronto to Brantford.

On March 31, 1932, the necessity for economies in all public services forced the government to discontinue the inter-city air mail services.

Permission was given to maintain intact those sections of the airway which had been constructed and to continue surveys for its completion. In 1932, to continue this work, and as a measure to assist in the relief of unemployment, J.A. induced the government to construct a chain of aerodromes across Canada. So, by November, 1932, upon arrangements with the Department of Labour, which was responsible for the execution of the Relief Act, the Department of National Defence undertook the organization, and later the administration, of various unemployment relief camps.

In 1933, as an unemployment relief project, work was resumed on the construction of aerodromes in British Columbia, Ontario, Quebec and the Maritime Provinces, which continued until July 1, 1936, when the Civil Aviation Branch of the Department of National Defence continued with the construction work by day labour or by contract.

J. A. Wilson was one of the Canadian Government representatives who attended a conference on transatlantic

flying, which was convened by the Government of Newfoundland and held at St. John's, in July, 1933. This gathering resulted in further conferences on the same subject and, finally, in December, 1935, at the Ottawa Conference, an agreement was reached by the Governments of the United Kingdom, Canada, Eire, and Newfoundland on the establishment of a regular transatlantic service by flying boat. At a further meeting in Washington with the United States Government, arrangements were made for their co-operation in these plans.

J. A. Wilson, who was in a very large way responsible for the building of the Trans-Canada Airway in the beginning, made a ten-day inspection tour of all the sites in Ontario, and as far west as Winnipeg, in July, 1934. Dan McLean, his Superintendent of Airways and Airports, accompanied him to see first-hand the progress being made on the clearing, grading and construction of the landing strips along the airway under the Unemployment Relief Scheme. Mr. Wilson was pleased to see the progress being made. He, Dan McLean and Inspector Robert "Bob" Dodds visited these fields, some 30 miles apart, travelling by motor car, railway gas car and seaplane. They visited some twenty sites then under construction. Five other sites had been chosen, but no work had started on them. The sites they visited were: Gillies, Ramore, Porquis, Tudhope, Kapuskasing, Pagwa, Ogahalla, Nakina, Kowkash, Lamaune, Wagaming (near Armstrong), Allanwater, Savant Lake, Sioux Lookout, Sunstrum, Amesdale, Vermilion Bay, Kenora, Caddy Lake and Whitemouth. They also visited seaplane bases at Haileybury, Sioux Lookout, Hudson, Red Lake and Kenora. Four of these sites were main fields for the airway — Kapuskasing, Nakina, Wagaming and Sioux Lookout.

During August and September, 1934, J. A. Wilson made a coast-to-coast

survey of the aerodromes in Canada, as well as flying conditions generally. His trip took him six weeks, during which he covered some 15,000 miles of territory on his extensive survey from the Atlantic to the Pacific, and north to the Arctic Circle. Nine thousand miles were flown by aeroplane; some 1,500 miles in and out of the Rocky Mountains between Calgary and Vancouver were covered by car, and the rest by train. On August 10, 1934, Mr. Wilson started on his journey by going to the Maritimes to see the projects under development there. While there, he participated in the opening of the new municipal airport at Summerside, Prince Edward Island, which was officially opened on August 14, 1934, by Mayor Lidstone. On his return to St. Hubert Airport he helped to welcome members of the Roosevelt Field Goodwill Flight there.

He left Ottawa by train for Winnipeg later to see the progress being made on the airway development work in northern Ontario, and flying operations in the Little Long Lac area en route. From Winnipeg he went to Lac du Bonnet where he took off in a Fairchild seaplane flown by Inspector Shields to survey the flying activity in the mining districts in northern Manitoba and Saskatchewan. He visited the San Antonio Mine, Berens River, Norway House, Island Lake, God's Lake, Ilford (Mileage 286 on the Hudson Bay Railway), Cormorant Lake, Flin Flon, Lac la Ronge, Ladder Lake (where the Saskatchewan Government Air Service was based) and Prince Albert.

Inspector Howard Ingram of Regina met him at Prince Albert and flew him to Edmonton in a Puss Moth. They stopped at Saskatoon. Also, they flew out to take a look at the landing field being developed at Henry House, near Jasper.

Then, accompanied by Inspector Ingram and Colonel R. Walter Hale, Superintendent of the Post Office Department, Edmonton, Mr. Wilson left Edmonton on August 31, 1934, in a

J.A. Wilson (centre) on an inspection trip of proposed aerodrome sites in 1934, at Allanwater, Ontario.

Canadian Airways 'plane piloted by Walter Gilbert, Trans-Canada Trophy winner for the year 1933. They flew "down north" via the Mackenzie River, stopping at Fort McMurray, Fort Smith, where a winter landing strip was being prepared, Fort Rae, Hottah Lake and Cameron Bay on Great Bear Lake. They left Cameron Bay on September 2, called at the Bear Exploration and Radium (B.E.A.R.) and White Eagle Mines. Their next stops were at Fort Rae and Fort Smith, arriving at Fort McMurray at 17:50 hours the same day. They flew a distance of 800 miles that day, before Pilot Walter Gilbert brought them back.

They next inspected the unemployment relief projects in the Rocky Mountains from Calgary to Vancouver. They left Calgary by car accompanied by the district engineers in charge of the work. It took them six days of intensive driving to cover the 1,500 miles between Calgary and Vancouver to look at the construction projects. They inspected landing fields at Coleman, Fernie, Cranbrook, Yahk, Kitchener, Salmo, Grand Forks, Midway, Rock Creek, Oliver, Keremeos, Princeton, Hope, Boston Bar, Merritt and Lytton. Upon reaching Vancouver, J. A. Wilson flew to Victoria with Inspector R. Carter Guest in a Puss Moth. They left Vancouver very early in the morning of September 14, reaching Regina at 17:30 hours the same day, in spite of a delay at Trail due to weather. Calls were made at Moose Jaw and Brandon en route to Winnipeg. J. A. completed his journey from Winnipeg to Ottawa by train.

Mr. Wilson addressed a number of service clubs and flying clubs on his extensive trip, and spoke, as usual, on the progress of civil flying in Canada since the Depression. He told of the aerodromes with their facilities that were being prepared for a transcontinental air mail route. He spoke, too, of the importance of the aeroplane in the mining fields.

The Trans-Canada Airway was ten-tatively scheduled for completion on July 1, 1936; but later changed to July 1, 1937; and then to July 1, 1938, with certain sections being completed even later. The area in the Prairies had been chosen for the initial activity in 1929 as the Prairie terrain gave the Civil Aviation Branch an opportunity to determine what could be done with scheduled transportation of mail and limited passenger services under the most favourable conditions.

J. A. Wilson and Inspector Bob Dodds were the first two persons to fly in a landplane over the new trans-Canada route between Ottawa and Winnipeg, via Nakina, Armstrong (Wagaming) and Sioux Lookout, later known as Green Airway No. 1. This flight was made in a Stearman aircraft, CF-CCH, piloted by Inspector Dodds. The flight left Ottawa for Winnipeg on September 28, 1935, and returned to Ottawa on October 9. In addition to those mentioned, landings were made at Lake of Two Rivers, Emsdale, Reay, South River, Diver, Gillies, Ramore, Porquis Junction, Kapuskasing, Vermilion Bay and Caddy Lake.

The opening of Petawawa Airport was a big event on June 17, 1936, when J. A. Wilson, Casey Baldwin and Dan McLean flew there for the opening ceremony, to commemorate the first military flights in the British Empire carried out at Petawawa on August 2, 1909. On this date, John McCurdy took the *Silver Dart* for a flight before military officials at Petawawa Military Camp. Petawawa Airport was to be known as Silver Dart Aerodrome at that time. The airport was officially opened by the Chief of the Air Staff.

Inspector J. H. "Tuddy" Tudhope, piloting a Fairchild aircraft, flew the Right Honourable C. D. Howe, later appointed Minister of Transport, Senator N. Lambert, and J. A. Wilson on a brief inspection tour of the Ottawa-Winnipeg section of the Trans-Canada Airway on

July 10 and 11, 1936. Bob Dodds piloted the Stearman aircraft carrying the baggage, refreshments and the bush and refuelling equipment. Leaving Ottawa at 8:45 A.M. on the morning of July 10, they arrived at Kapuskasing at 18:45 hours, after inspecting the intermediate aerodromes along the route at Killaloe, Lake of Two Rivers, Emsdale, Diver, Gillies and Ramore. Leaving Kapuskasing at 07:45 A.M. on July 11 by C.N.R. track car, they arrived at Armstrong at 21:00 hours, inspecting Hearst, Pagwa, Ogahalla, Grant, Nakina, Kowkash, Lamaune and Wagaming. Then Mr. Howe, Senator Lambert and J. A. Wilson left Armstrong by No. 1 C.N.R. train for Winnipeg.

With the passing of the Department of Transport Act (Chapter 34), assented to on June 23, 1936, the Department of Transport came into existence on November 2, 1936. It was the Right Honourable C. D. Howe who introduced the Act during the 1936 Parliamentary Session. This Act was sanctioned by Order-in-Council P.C. 59/2798 of October 29, 1936. All federal transportation and communication services were placed under this newly formed department. This included Civil Aviation, which was formerly under the Department of National Defence. Radio and Meteorological Services were also transferred to the new department. These three services were grouped together in the new department under an Air Services Branch, having one Director of Air Services. Civil Aviation, Radio and Meteorological Services were each headed by a Controller. In addition, an Aeronautical Engineering section was formed under the Civil Aviation Division to look after the civil aircraft aspect. So now, the construction of airports with their facilities, aids to navigation, radio, meteorology, etc., was continuing under a new set-up. C. P. Edwards was Chief of Air Services; while J. A. Wilson continued as Controller of Civil Aviation;

J.A. Wilson (right) on his 15,000 mile survey trip through the Northwest Territories during the summer of 1934. From left to right above: Col. R.W. Hale, Superintendent of the Post Office Department, Edmonton; Inspector Howard Ingram, Regina (since 1929) of the Civil Aviation Branch; and J.A Wilson, Controller of Civil Aviation.

with W. A. Rush, Controller of the Radio Division; and Dr. John Patterson, Controller of the Meteorological Service. The newly-formed Air Services Branch in the newly-formed Department of Transport was under C. D. Howe, the new Minister of Transport.

And so the construction of the Trans-Canada Airway System, which was created under J. A. Wilson's competent administration, was to continue under his direction.

Legislation was passed on April 10, 1937, creating Trans-Canada Air Lines, and in July of that year Mr. Wilson was appointed one of the government directors of the company. Also, he was one of the founders of Trans-Canada Air Lines.

The Right Honourable C. D. Howe not only introduced the Department of Transport Act during the 1936 Parliamentary Session; but he introduced the Trans-Canada Air Lines' Act in 1937; and the Transport Act in 1938. The first made provision for an agency to administer civil aeronautics; the second for the operation of a national air line company in Canada and international main line connections with air carriers of other countries; and the third, the Transport Act, created a judicial body known as the Board of Transport Commissioners to handle the licensing of air routes, their economic aspects, necessity and convenience, tariffs, and so on. This third function was later taken over by the Air Transport Board upon its creation in 1944, by an amendment to the Aeronautics Act.

J.A. Wilson, when Controller of Civil Aviation, flew non-stop from Toronto to Winnipeg on September 1, 1938, in a Lockheed 14 aircraft belonging to Trans-Canada Air Lines. He met J. R. "Robbie" Robertson, Airways Inspector, at Winnipeg, who flew him in a Waco aircraft to Rivers and Broadview so that Mr. Wilson could look at the aerodromes. J. A. then drove on to Moose Jaw and

Saskatoon on September 5, from where he flew to Prince Albert and back to Saskatoon on September 6. The following day he flew to Edmonton via North Battleford. He visited the airports at Calgary and Penhold on the 8th and returned to Edmonton.

Then Grant McConachie, President of United Air Transport, flew J. A. Wilson, Robbie Robertson and Colonel Walter Hale of the Post Office Department to Whitehorse in a Waco seaplane.

With pioneer bush pilot and President Grant McConachie at the controls, the flight left Edmonton at 2:00 P.M. on Friday September 9, 1938, and stopped overnight at Fort St. John. They reached Whitehorse about 6:00 P.M. on Saturday, the next day, after stops at Fort Nelson and Teslin Lake. On Sunday morning, the 11th, Mr. Wilson went to Dawson and Mayo and returned to Whitehorse in the evening; and on Monday the party left to go to Vancouver through central British Columbia by way of Teslin Lake, Lower Post and Fort Nelson to Fort St. John; and on Tuesday left there for Findlay Forks, Prince George and thence to Vancouver on September 14, following the Fraser River as far as Lillooet, Seton and Anderson Lakes, Squamish and Howe Sound.

Mr. Wilson travelled by United Air Transport's Waco seaplane, captained by Grant McConachie, and inspected water bases and examined the Whitehorse Airport in detail and found it to be a remarkably fine field. They flew low over several other fields but did not land on them as time did not permit. United Air Transport, Pan American Airways, Northern Airways and the White Pass and Yukon Railway were the principal users of the Whitehorse Airport.

At Vancouver, Mr. Wilson met Inspector Carter Guest who flew him across the Rockies to Regina, stopping at Nelson, British Columbia, where he attended the meeting of the B.C. Aviation Council on September 16. Mr.

Wilson boarded the train for Winnipeg at Regina. He left Winnipeg on September 20 and reached Toronto on the 22nd, having stopped en route to look at other airports. Pleased and satisfied with the progress he had seen after nearly a month's inspection tour of the Trans-Canada Airway, main commercial routes and branch lines through the northwest to the Yukon, and through the interior route of British Columbia to Vancouver, Mr. Wilson arrived back in Ottawa on September 23, 1938.

Then World War II broke out on September 3, 1939, and Canada was at war with Germany, along with other nations. Canada's whole way of life was to change drastically during the war years from 1939 to 1945. Civil Aviation quickly changed from a civil to a military aviation role.

On October 10, 1939, the Prime Minister, the Right Honourable W. L. Mackenzie King said, in part:

"The Governments of the United Kingdom, Australia, New Zealand and Canada have recently reached agreement upon a development of great importance which they believe is destined to make a most effective contribution to the successful prosecution of the war.

"His Majesty's Government in the United Kingdom put forward in September for the consideration of His Majesty's Governments in Canada, the Commonwealth of Australia and New Zealand, an outline of arrangements for the rapid expansion of air training on a co-operative basis. The arrangements provide a training organization for pilots, observers and air gunners required first for the enlargement and then for the maintenance on an enlarged basis of the Air Forces of the respective countries, this to be combined with an expanded production of aircraft.

"The Governments of Canada, Australia and New Zealand have

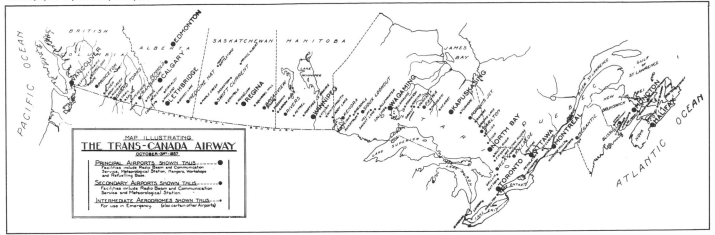

signified their agreement in principle to these arrangements.

"The undertaking is one of great magnitude. Its development would result in a great and rapid increase in the number of training schools, already large, and achieve an increasing output of first line pilots, observers and air gunners which, combined with the output of the United Kingdom, would ensure the greatly increased requirements in trained personnel being fully met. The aim, in short, is to achieve, by co-operative effort, air forces of overwhelming strength."

This then was the beginning of the British Commonwealth Air Training Plan, which was to extend through to March 31, 1945.

On October 15, 1939, the mission from the United Kingdom, headed by Lord Riverdale, arrived in Ottawa, and the British Commonwealth Air Training Plan was about to be shaped.

Then began the working out of the details of this air training plan by the various missions. Canada was represented by Prime Minister W. L. Mackenzie King, and four of his ministers; the Minister of National Defence, the Honourable Norman Rogers; the Minister of Finance, the Honourable J. L. Ralston; the Minister of Transport, the Right Honourable C. D. Howe; and the Minister of Pensions and National Health, the Honourable Ian Mackenzie. Also assisting were many other officials from these departments and the Department of External Affairs.

A joint agreement for large-scale training of air crews was signed by these missions — Canada, Great Britain, Australia and New Zealand — on Sunday, December 17, 1939, the day the agreement was made public by Prime Minister Mackenzie King. This was also the same day that the first contingent of the Canadian Army landed in England.

The Civil Aviation Division of the Department of Transport was officially given the responsibility for the selection, survey and development of suitable sites for aerodromes required under the British Commonwealth Air Training Plan, Home War Establishment, U.S.-Canada Joint Defence Board and by the Department of National Defence for use in the training of airmen, and incidental war requirements.

The decision was made as a result of the experience and knowledge that the Civil Aviation Division had gained in airport development, as at that time it was nearing the completion of a ten-year programme of airport development on the Trans-Canada Airway System, and through this had acquired wide experience and detailed knowledge of all parts of Canada on this work. The Department of National Defence was to be responsible for the construction of hangars and other buildings, since they had greater experience in this field.

More specifically, the work involved the selection, surveying and development of aerodromes and, in co-operation with the Radio Division, radio navigation facilities throughout Canada; aerial investigation of practically every part of Canada, Labrador and Newfoundland; ground investigation for final selection of sites; detailed surveys; preparation of plans and estimates; contracts for development; purchase or lease of properties for aerodromes, radio ranges and similar purposes; estimates for roads, power lines, water line and other service facilities; grading, hard-surfacing of runways and taxi strips; construction of roads; clearing of approaches to aerodromes; installation of lighting equipment, power plants, communication facilities and water and sewage; construction of buildings, including radio range stations and their design, remote control buildings with residences (complete with water and sewerage systems) for the Radio Division; and the calibration and testing of radio aids to air navigation and radio ranges.

This programme also included enlarging and improving airports already constructed in order that they might meet the necessary requirements.

Also, at the commencement of hostilities, arrangements were made for the Department of Transport to take over practically all the larger municipal airports in Canada so that their operation and use might be co-ordinated for civil and military purposes.

Then a Supervisory Committee was formed, and the officials of the Civil Aviation Division worked closely with this committee. J. A. Wilson, in his capacity as Controller of Civil Aviation shouldered much responsibility at this time.

With the experience gained in the construction of aerodromes for the Trans-Canada Airway System, the Civil Aviation Division was in a position to be of invaluable assistance to Canada in her war effort. Even before a final decision had been reached on the details of the British Commonwealth Air Training Plan in the fall of 1939, the Civil Aviation Division was surveying, mapping out and planning the construction of the many aerodromes which were to be constructed for the training of Canadian and Commonwealth youths and men as pilots, navigators, air gunners, bombers and wireless operators. The gigantic task of building over two hundred aerodromes for the British Commonwealth Air Training Plan, and later for Home Defence purposes, was accomplished with precision and celerity, chiefly due to J. A. Wilson's excellent organizing ability and perspicacity, and his personal and broad knowledge of all phases of civil aviation throughout Canada's expansive territory.

Aside from the training of personnel, etc., etc., 148 new airports and aerodromes were constructed for the British Commonwealth Air Training Plan and Western Hemisphere Operations; while 59 were extended and improved, before the British Commonwealth Air

First landing at Watson Lake Airport in CF-DTE, on September 3, 1941. Shown from right to left: Homer Keith, J.A. Wilson, G.L. McGee, W.S. "Bill" Lawson, G.T. "Tommy" Chillcott, the contractor's superintendent, and the other two not known.

Training Plan came to an end on March 31, 1945. Throughout the years of World War II, the civil aspect of aviation had been well in the background.

In the midst of all this war work, J. A. Wilson was appointed Director of Air Services in the Department of Transport, in January, 1941, with jurisdiction over civil aviation, radio and meteorological services.

J. A. Wilson attended a conference in London in the fall of 1942 to arrange for a Canadian Government Trans-Atlantic Air Service, which was later organized and operated by Trans-Canada Air Lines' personnel. In 1943, Trans-Canada Air Lines was given the task of developing a transatlantic air service for the Canadian Government. Under the authority of Order-in-Council P.C. 5742, dated July 19, 1943, Trans-Canada Air Lines was authorized to operate an air service carrying official passengers, goods and mail between Canada and the United Kingdom on behalf of the Canadian Government. The aircraft and all the equipment were owned by the government, and Trans-Canada Air Lines, as a contracting operator, was paid out-of-pocket expenses for operating the service. The need for this arose from the necessity for a better mail service for the Canadian troops overseas. The first flight took place on July 22, 1943, using a modified Lancaster aircraft. Then, on May 1, 1947, Trans-Canada Air Lines (Atlantic) Limited assumed responsibility for the operation previously provided by the Canadian Government Trans-Atlantic Air Service, and operated it as a commercial service.

Mr. Wilson was one of the Canadian delegates who attended the International Civil Aviation Convention in Chicago in November and December, 1944.

In 1944, Mr. Wilson, who drafted many of the early civil air regulations in Canada which are still in existence, was awarded the Julian C. Smith Memorial Medal of the Engineering Institute of

Canada "for achievement in the development of Canada."

Then, one day in the spring of 1945, the Minister of National Defence, the Honourable Colin Gibson, announced that Mr. Wilson had been awarded the Trans-Canada Trophy for 1944 in recognition of his outstanding contribution to Canadian aviation and his assistance in the development of international aeronautics, as well as his long service, energetic support and whole-hearted efforts in the development of civil aviation in Canada — and for his untiring endeavours on behalf of the R.C.A.F. in the prosecution of Canada's war effort and the development of the British Commonwealth Air Training Plan.

The official presentation of the Trans-Canada Trophy was made on July 11, 1945, at 10:00 A.M. in the Air Council Room, Air Force Headquarters, Ottawa, by the Honourable Colin Gibson, Minister of National Defence.

At the invitation of the Governments of Australia and New Zealand, Mr. Wilson visited these two countries in March, April and May, 1945, and had the opportunity to inspect their air bases, aircraft factories and radio and meteorological stations.

J. A. retired from the position of Director of Air Services on July 18,

---

The Committee of Award for the year 1944 consisted of the following members:

Air Commodore J. L. Plant, Royal Canadian Air Force, for Chief of the Air Staff, Department of National Defence, Ottawa.

A.D. McLean, Controller of Civil Aviation, Department of Transport, Ottawa.

Wing Commander M. Lipton, Royal Canadian Air Force, Department of National Defence, Ottawa.

Dr. J. J. Green, representing the Royal Canadian Flying Clubs Association, Ottawa.

1945, after a 35-year career in aviation.

He was created a Commander of the Order of the British Empire "for services in Canada's aviation war effort" in 1946, and he was awarded the "Norwegian Medal of Liberation" in 1948.

J. A. Wilson was, without doubt, one of Canada's greatest pioneer civil aviation historians. Through the years he wrote many papers and articles, many of which were published, and gave many talks, which were usually on the subject of civil aviation. His more important papers and articles are:

"Gentlemen Adventurers of the Air," The National Geographic Magazine, November, 1929.

"Aviation in Canada," March 21, 1937, The Journal of the Engineering Institute of Canada — Semi-Centennial Number, June, 1937.

"Aerodrome Construction for the British Commonwealth Air Training Plan," October 3, 1940, presented to The Montreal Branch of the Engineering Institute of Canada.

"Northwest Passage by Air," December 30, 1942, Canadian Geographical Magazine, March, 1943.

"Air Transportation in Canada," April 6, 1943, The Journal of the Engineering Institute of Canada, May, 1943.

"The Influence of Civil Aviation in the Development of Canada's Air Power," November 3, 1943.

"Report on Visit to New Zealand and Australia, March, April and May, 1945," June 18, 1945.

"The International Civil Aviation Conference — Chicago, November and December, 1944," August 10, 1945, Public Affairs, journal of The Institute of Public Affairs, Dalhousie University, Halifax, Nova Scotia.

"The Development of Civil Aviation in Canada" (1947) Post War Problems.

The Trans-Canada Trophy being presented to J.A. Wilson by the Honourable Colin Gibson, Minister of National Defence, in Ottawa on July 11, 1945. Left to right: A/M. R. Leckie, C.B., D.S.O., D.S.C., D.F.C.; J.A. Wilson and Colin Gibson.
Photo courtesy of the R.C.A.F.

"Aviation in Canada," June 17, 1947, London *Times* Special Canada Issue, October, 1947.

"The Expansion of Aviation into Arctic and Sub-Arctic Canada," 1948, *Encyclopedia Arctica.*

John Armitstead Wilson, C.B.E., M.E.I.C., resided at 178 Rideau Terrace, Ottawa, until the time of his death on October 10, 1954, in his 75th year. Mr. and Mrs. Wilson had two sons and one daughter: Dr. John Tuzo Wilson, William Henry "Peter" Wilson and Mrs. F. A. (Mary Loetitia) Echlin. Dr. Wilson has been Director-General of the Ontario Science Centre in Toronto since 1974.

J. A. had many affiliations during his career and was a very active person. He was a former Vice-President of the Canadian Geographical Society; a Past President of the Ottawa Branch of the Canadian Institute of International Affairs; a member and life member of the Engineering Institute of Canada; a

director of Trans-Canada Air Lines from 1937 to 1946; one of the founders of Trans-Canada Air Lines; a member of the Ottawa Committee of the National Council of Education; and an Honorary President of the Royal Canadian Flying Clubs Association. At the first annual meeting of the Canadian Aeronautical Institute in May, 1954, Mr. Wilson was awarded an Honorary Fellowship in the Institute. He also received the King's Jubilee Medal in 1935 and the Coronation Medal two years later. He was named a member of Canada's Aviation Hall of Fame in 1973, and was made a Companion of the Order of Flight (City of Edmonton).

He attended many goodwill flights, flying club get-togethers, goodwill air tours, officiated at many airport openings and made many first landings on the airports himself, opened air shows and air pageants, attended club banquets and gave many talks and made many speeches on civil aviation topics, con-

ferred with other government departments on the establishment of air mail routes and civil government air operations, issued many reports and presented and wrote many papers and articles on the history of civil aviation, including early civil aviation reports, until they were curtailed at the time of the Depression in 1932. He recorded much aviation history for posterity.

Mr. Wilson was known in aviation circles for many years as "the Father of Civil Aviation in Canada" and was prominently active in all aspects of Canadian aviation. Through his profound knowledge of aviation and his kind and considerate disposition, he contributed substantially to the development of Canadian air transport. This truly great man, yes, truly great, was a grand person. His ways were gracious. He was widely known across Canada and elsewhere in earlier years in civil aviation circles.

1945

George William "Grant" McConachie

Citation: in recognition of long service, energetic support and whole-hearted efforts in the development of civil aviation in Canada, and for his successful endeavours in opening up Canada's vast hinterland in the northwest, especially the area between Edmonton, Alberta and Whitehorse, Yukon Territory

George William "Grant" McConachie, while General Manager, Western Lines, for Canadian Pacific Air Lines, Edmonton, was awarded the Trans-Canada Trophy for meritorious service in the advancement of aviation in Canada during 1945, "in recognition of long service, energetic support and whole-hearted efforts in the development of civil aviation in Canada, and for his successful endeavours in opening up Canada's vast hinterland in the north-west, especially the area between Edmonton, Alberta and Whitehorse, Yukon Territory." The announcement of the award was made on April 17, 1946, when the Honourable Colin Gibson, Minister of National Defence, extended his most cordial congratulations to Grant McConachie by wire.

The minister believed that, through Grant McConachie's exploration and pioneering, both the Alaska Highway and the Canol Project were constructed much earlier than otherwise would have been possible.

His company's aircraft were the first to use radio compass flying in northern Canada, and consequently Grant McConachie established and serviced radio compass stations between Edmonton and Whitehorse for navigational purposes in 1938. These were used until the Department of Transport's radio ranges were installed on this route around the end of 1941. Grant McConachie's company was also the first to use multi-engined aircraft in northern Canada. That was in 1935. Both of these were major factors in promoting safe aerial trans-portation in this pioneering work, the minister said.

Through Grant McConachie's efforts in putting the best operating principles into practice, and advocating the use of aircraft on wheels wherever possible throughout northern Canada, he contributed substantially to the development of air line operation in northwestern Canada to a high standard of efficiency. As a result of his efforts, an air line came into operation between Edmonton-Yellowknife; Edmonton-Norman Wells; Edmonton-Whitehorse-Dawson City; and Edmonton to Vancouver via Fort St. John.

Grant McConachie was one of Canada's youngest aviation executives when he was awarded the Trans-Canada Trophy. He was then familiarizing himself with instrument landing facilities with Northwest Airlines, Minneapolis, Minnesota. Canada had no facilities for instrument landings at this time. However, Grant wished to become familiar with this method of flying, as he was sure that instrument landing facilities would be in use in Canada very soon.

George William "Grant" McConachie was born in Hamilton, Ontario, on April 24, 1909. His parents took him to Edmonton when he was only an infant. Here he grew up and attended the public and high schools in Edmonton, and later the University of Alberta. Being six feet, two inches tall, and having a well-proportioned frame, he was inclined to athletics.

It was at a very early age that flying took his fancy, and Grant was lured

Grant McConachie as a youth.
Photo courtesy of Grant McConachie.

away from following in his father's footsteps with the Canadian National Railways. Meanwhile, he was earning money for his flying lessons. As a young lad, Grant spent a lot of time around Edmonton Airport, and every now and then liked to get a ride with Wop May or Punch Dickins, both early bush pilots and winners of the Trans-Canada Trophy. Grant did odd jobs for them in helping to take care of their aircraft. When he was twenty years of age, he started to receive flying instruction at the Edmonton and Northern Alberta Aero Club, and took his first lesson on October 21, 1929. Maurice Burbidge was his instructor. Grant soloed in a D.H. Moth after seven hours and twenty minutes' instruction, completing and passing his tests for his Private Pilot's Licence on March 23, 1930. However, as his examination papers became misplaced somewhere in the files of the Civil Aviation Branch of the Department of National Defence, he was not to receive his Private Pilot's Licence until February, 1931. He then flew for the club for a while, putting in some sixty hours of solo flying on a D.H. Moth.

In the late summer of 1931, Grant McConachie left for Portland, Oregon, where he took an advanced course in aerobatics from the Paragon Flying Service, flying a Fleet and Bell Pup. When he left Portland on October 10, 1931, he had brought his total hours of solo flying up to eighty-three. He returned to Edmonton and completed his flying tests for his Commercial Licence on November 10, 1931, when he was just 22 years of age.

With his new commercial licence, Grant McConachie set out for Vancouver on what he thought would be the first lap of his trip to China, where he hoped to fly for a Chinese company. Konnie Johannsen was leaving for China at the time to fly for a little company, which later became Chinese National Airways, and wanted Grant to go along with him.

However, when Grant reached Vancouver, he visited his Uncle Harry who, not liking to see him leave Canada, enticed him into staying here by buying him a second-hand Fokker. Shortly after this, a company known as Independent Airways of Edmonton came into existence. It was incorporated on August 12, 1932. His Uncle Harry, Princess L. Galitzine and Grant were shareholders; while Grant was President and General Manager.

The company started off with two standard Fokker Trimotor Universal aircraft, G-CASE and G-CAGD, and a Puss Moth, CF-APE. Grant made his first trip for the company on January 7, 1932, in a Fokker Universal. He flew fish from lakes in northern Saskatchewan and Alberta in a Fokker Universal for A. P. Burwash, a fish broker, in Edmonton. From January 7 to March 12, 1932, he had put in some three-hundred hours' flying to transport fish. The next five months he put in some two-hundred hours flying charter trips, barnstorming and advertising. On September 13, 1932, he took his night flying examination Inspector Howard C. Ingram from the office of the Department of National Defence at Regina was the examiner. He passed the examination successfully, and then went on the Calgary-Edmonton run for his company, Independent Airways, for two months.

Grant McConachie and C. H. "Chris" Green, the company's chief mechanic (air engineer), carried out a mercy flight in November, 1932, to rescue Frank and George Senz, telegraph operators, stationed at the Government Telegraph Station at Pelican Rapids, about 175 miles northeast of Edmonton by air. The two brothers had been badly burned when the station had exploded without warning due to gas seepage. The telegraph apparatus had been blown to small pieces and the two operators were too painfully burned to tap the line, so a runner dashed the nine miles to the

nearest station and word was flashed through to Edmonton to rush an aeroplane to bring in assistance, as the two brothers required urgent medical attention. Assurance was given at once that an aircraft would be sent in. However, with November's ice creeping across the surface of the seaplane base at Cooking Lake near Edmonton, no aeroplane had ventured out — and three days had slipped by. The men were still suffering from their burns, and for a time it seemed as if the wings of mercy had folded.

Then Grant McConachie entered the scene. He said he would risk a flight on wheels if there was a beach wide enough for a landing. So, equipped with bandages and other medical supplies, Grant and Chris Green of Independent Airways took off from the municipal field in the darkness of that early November morning. Flying low over the thin ice of the lake near Pelican Rapids after a quick trip from Edmonton, Grant despaired of landing at first. The beach was not more than sixty feet wide, and part of it was covered with ice while the wing-spread of the Fokker was forty-seven feet. If he landed into the wind, he would be blinded by the morning sun. If he glided in from the opposite direction, visibility would be reduced by smoke from a fire kept burning to mark the "field." Manoeuvring until one wheel skimmed the fragile ice, and the opposite wing grazed the tree line, he settled down for a landing. Suddenly a sharp root pierced the cabin floor, missing the pilot and mechanic by inches and rented the fabric from end to end.

Grant McConachie did his best to bandage the burns of the two brothers, while Chris Green mended the fabric as well as he could. In about an hour, the 'plane was in the air again, flying southwest to Edmonton where the Senz brothers were rushed to the hospital. This was one of the many mercy flights that he made throughout the northwest.

Grant McConachie, Manager-Secretary, Independent Airways, with the company's three aircraft at Edmonton's Municipal Airport in October, 1932. G-CASE and G-CAGD were Fokker Trimotor Universal aircraft; while CF-APE was a Puss Moth.

Photo courtesy of Grant McConachie.

On November 30, 1932, with a total of 580 hours now, Grant McConachie was ready to take off from Edmonton Airport in Fokker Trimotor Universal G-CAGD, with Chris Green as a passenger, to transport equipment to Cold Lake, Alberta, where Independent Airways was hauling fish. Grant had made two un-successful attempts to get off the ground and, on the third attempt, he managed to get in the air after running about three-quarters of the length of the field. But his aircraft failed to climb normally and soon it began to settle. In an effort to avoid some high-tension wires in his path, Grant McConachie tried to turn the aircraft, but it stalled. The port wing tip hit the ground and the aircraft went forward on its nose. Grant was wedged in the cockpit, while Chris Green was thrown against the roof of the cabin and was hit by a spare oil tin, which caused several lacerations to his face. Grant McConachie was extricated from the wreckage and hospitalized with two fractured ankles and a broken right knee, as well as other minor injuries.

Just before the accident took place, Lionel Vines of Independent Airways had made several unsuccessful attempts to take off in Fokker Trimotor Universal G-CASE, so he abandoned the idea. It was later discovered that the pro-peller of C-CASE had a coating of ice on it, preventing him from getting the aircraft into the air. Grant's crash was also due to ice forming on the leading edge of the wings and propeller of the aircraft. The engine had been run up on the ground for about forty minutes. The result of this crash was that the Fokker which his Uncle Harry had given to him had to be written off. Grant's injuries mended rapidly and perfectly under the gentle care of his nurse, Miss Margaret McLean, who later became Mrs. Grant Mc-Conachie. However, it was not until February 28, 1933, that Grant McConachie began flying around the Edmonton Airport again.

On March 27, 1933, Grant started flying commercially again, operating the company's Puss Moth, CF-APE, in northern British Columbia until spring break-up. Then he started barnstorming with a Fokker Universal on floats and later was called to northern British Columbia to fly prospectors out of the central Rockies in a Junkers F-13 owned by Pacific Airways Limited, whose principal work was freighting for Premier Gold Mines, Limited. (Pacific Airways Limited (second company) was in-corporated on January 16, 1933.)

After about two years' operations for Independent Airways, during which another Fokker aircraft was written off, Princess Galitzine grew tired of losing money in aviation ventures and left the company, and so did Grant's Uncle Harry. The other aircraft, the Puss Moth, was seized for hangar rent. That wound up the company's aircraft. (The com-pany's charter was eventually withdrawn on May 15, 1935.)

Undaunted, Grant McConachie got busy and formed another company about August, 1933, known as United Air Transport, Edmonton, in partnership with R. B. "Barney" Phillips, who was a mining engineer with the Two Brothers' Valley Gold Mines. However, this company was not incorporated until August 30, 1934. (Barney Phillips later became Vice-President of Administration for Canadian Pacific Air Lines.) The company purchased two Fokker Universals and started operations in northern British Columbia, out of Burns Lake. During the summer months they flew in northern British Columbia; and in the winter months in northern Saskat-chewan hauling freight and fish by air. Grant was Pilot and General Manager of United Air Transport, while Barney Phillips was Assistant General Manager.

With the arrival of winter, Grant McConachie left on New Year's Day, January 1, 1934, to start hauling fish again in the Fokker Universals belonging to United Air Transport for the McInnish Fish Company from Buffalo Lake to Cheechum, just south of Waterways on the Northern Alberta Railway. By the time March 23 had arrived, Grant had accumulated a total of 1,000 hours. Two days later, he left Edmonton for Whitehorse, Yukon Territory, via Jasper, Prince George, Fort St. James, Dease Lake, Teslin and Carcross, on special charter work into the Upper Liard country for Two Brothers' Valley Gold Mines. Two Fokker Universal aircraft were flown; one by himself, and the other by Ted Field. On this work Grant put in some sixty-seven hours before he returned to Edmonton on April 21, 1934.

Then Grant started freighting from the company's base at Takla Landing, British Columbia, to Two Brothers Lake, British Columbia, on May 24, 1934, using the company's three Fokker Universals, for the Two Brothers' Valley Gold Mines. The company flew in mining equipment and machinery of every kind, including a complete sawmill. United Air Transport had an extremely busy summer season in their flights to the Yukon and throughout northern British Columbia.

While Chief Pilot for United Air Transport, Grant McConachie, along with a number of others, was given a six weeks' Instrument Flying and Night Flying Course by the R.C.A.F. at Camp Bor-den, Ontario. The course commenced on November 1, 1934.

Around the end of January, 1935, Grant McConachie's company purchased an all-metal Ford Trimotor monoplane, G-CARC — the first multi-engined ship to go into service in the north. He flew it from Niagara Falls, Ontario, to Ed-monton, accompanied by his air engineer, Chris Green. The aircraft was purchased from Sky View Lines Ltd., of Chippawa, Ontario, where it was flown by pilots R. H. Bibby and Jack Leach on sight-seeing trips over Niagara Falls. It was the first Ford Trimotor registered in Canada. That was in 1928. G-CARC was con-

verted to skis and Grant test flew the aircraft. Accompanied by Chris Green and Bill Busy, another mechanic, he flew the aircraft to the company's base at Cheechum, where G-CARC completed a fleet of three 'planes for hauling fish for the McInnish Fish Company from Buffalo Lake to the rail line. After finishing this contract for hauling fish, Grant flew G-CARC back to Edmonton, before leaving for Two Brothers' Lake in northern British Columbia on March 18, 1935. An air engineer named Weegan went along with him. G-CARC was the oldest ship in those parts, and had a most interesting past. It was flown by Bernt Balchen and Floyd Bennett when they went to the rescue of the *Bremen* when it crashed on Greenly Island in 1928.

Ford Trimotor CF-BEP joined United Air Transport's fleet in 1935 to be flown through the northern skies on many a jaunt.

On December 15, 1936, the company started a regular run from Edmonton to Peace River and Grande Prairie, leaving Edmonton on Saturdays and returning on Mondays, carrying mail, passengers and freight. Then, early in 1937, Grant McConachie became President and General Manager of United Air Transport, while Barney Phillips took over as Secretary-Treasurer. The company was making good progress under Grant's capable leadership, and through his ingenious ways was reaching into remote areas to transport aerial freight. The company had flown over one million miles by the dawn of 1937, and had a good safety record. The company was operating eight aircraft.

Fort Nelson lay in the heart of a rich trapping and trading centre, and was known as "the wilds" a few years before this time. Its few residents depended on a

river boat that visited them once a year to bring in supplies from the outside. The river boat went from Waterways down the Athabaska and Mackenzie Rivers to Fort Simpson, and then via the Liard River to Fort Nelson. With aircraft coming into use, flights to the trapping areas were made in a matter of hours, taking along their huskies, sleighs, traps and provisions for the winter months. The trappers were put down beside their cabins, and arrangements were made for them to be picked up in the spring of the year. United Air Transport made some seventy charter trips during the winter of 1937 to fly trappers to their scattered trap lines from Fort St. John to Lower Post, and thereabouts. This was a much more economical method than travelling by boat, considering the time that was spent en route.

Briefly, these were the air mail contracts awarded to United Air Transport during these years:

1936 — from Fort St. John to Fort Nelson (winter months only);
1936 — (latter part of the year) from Prince George to Finlay Forks, Fort Grahame and Fort Ware (winter months only);
1937 — from Edmonton to Whitehorse (operating on floats and skis);
1937 — from Prince George to Fort St. James, Manson Creek and Takla Landing;
1938 — from Vancouver to Fort St. John.

Grant McConachie also pioneered the aerial route to the Yukon in July, 1936, in connection with the establishment of an air mail service. On this pioneering flight Grant McConachie flew J. A. Wilson, Controller of Civil Aviation, from Edmonton to Whitehorse, Dawson and Mayo, returning via Fort Nelson to Fort

St. John, thence across the Rockies to Prince George and Vancouver to ascertain the feasibility of a connection from the route to Vancouver, which would be necessary once an air mail service from Edmonton to Whitehorse, Yukon, was established. The flight was made in a Waco seaplane. Mr. Wilson was accompanied by J. Ross "Robbie" Robertson and Colonel Walter Hale.

The Post Office Department, ever ready to extend its service, let a contract to United Air Transport in 1937 for a weekly air mail service, using skis in winter and floats in summer, between Edmonton and Whitehorse via Fort St. John, Fort Nelson and Watson Lake. The air mail contract was awarded by Postmaster General H. J. C. Elliott, and this was actually the first link in an aerial northwest air mail service from Canada to the Orient. It was on July 5, 1937, that Grant and his co-pilot, Ted Field, made the inaugural air mail flight from Edmonton to Whitehorse in Ford Trimotor CF-BEP. The trip was made in sixteen hours and forty minutes. This service also linked the trapping and mining areas in the northwest with a major supply centre. The route via Fort Nelson was through the Liard Pass. The seaplane base at Fort Nelson was near the old trading post at the junction of the Nelson and Muskwa Rivers. They stopped over at Fort St. John, Fort Nelson and Watson Lake, before arriving at Whitehorse. At Whitehorse, the service connected with Pan American Airways operating to Whitehorse from Fairbanks, Alaska. This made it an all-year service, except for freeze-up and break-up periods, until the time when aerodromes would be built.

The following year, 1938, the company was awarded the air mail contract from

Barkley-Grow T8P-1 Transport Yukon Queen *powered by two Pratt and Whitney Wasp Junior engines.*
Photo courtesy of Canadian Aviation.

Vancouver to Fort St. John. This gave the rich Peace River farming country an aerial outlet to the Pacific coast: at the same time Vancouver was linked by air with the Yukon; while Edmonton would have indirect aerial connection with the Pacific Ocean. This was a weekly air service to and from Vancouver. This arrangement was the pacific solution of the intense rivalry which existed between Edmonton and Vancouver for aerial connections with the Yukon and Alaska. As well, placer gold areas north of Prince George were given this means of speedy communication with two major supply centres; while residents of the Peace River area were granted a trade route to the Pacific Coast. To provide this service, United Air Transport of Edmonton merged with a British Columbia company, known as Ginger Coote Airways, Vancouver, operated by R. L. "Ginger" Coote, a well-known coast flier and executive. When the companies merged, Ginger Coote became Vice-President in charge of Vancouver operations.

The inaugural flight of two aircraft carrying air mail and passengers left Sea Island Airport for Fort St. John at 7:00 A.M. one summer morning — August 4, 1938. After an uneventful seven-hour trip, the aircraft arrived at Fort St. John to meet the north-bound Yukon mail from Edmonton. En route to Fort St. John, they made scheduled stops at Williams Lake, Quesnel and Prince George where they were greeted by municipal and Board of Trade officials. Grant McConachie piloted one aircraft, while Ginger Coote piloted the other one, with Sheldon Luck as his co-pilot. Members of the official party included Mayor George C. Miller, Vancouver; J. G. Turgeon, M.P.; and G. H. Clarke, District Inspector of Postal Services.

Almost simultaneously with the inauguration of this service, two-way radio equipment was installed in seven of the company's eleven aircraft, and seven powerful ground stations were established at strategic points on major bush routes so that pilots could be in constant communication with operators on all flights. The company's next move was to install radio compass equipment. United Air Transport was employing nine pilots, all with excellent records, whose names were: Grant McConachie, Ted Field, Ernest Kubicek, Ralph Oakes, Sheldon Luck, Len Waagen, Charles Tweed, Robert Halpenny and Ginger Coote. United Air Transport was not finding it too easy to purchase the type of equipment that the company wanted to operate over these bush routes, particularly twin-engined aircraft, as they were produced only in limited numbers at the time.

In the fall of that year, Grant McConachie picked up a Howard aircraft in eastern Canada and flew it to Edmonton, where it was operated on the company's routes in the northwest. It was put on the Edmonton-Fort Vermilion run first with Ernest Kubicek at the controls.

One day in the late fall of 1938, a United Air Transport aircraft flew a party to Blue Lake, just south of the Yukon border in British Columbia, where a camp was established. The members of the party were Alvin P. Adams, President of Western Air Express (later a Vice-President of Pan American Airways); A. W. Stevenson, Vice-President, Western Air Express (later Western Airlines); Pilot Henry Hollenbeck, Thomas J. O'Connor of Salmon, Idaho, and Grant McConachie. They were enjoying the usual camp life while waiting for a bear to put in an appearance or, for that matter, any other animal — except perhaps the one animal that did come along. This uninvited little guest wearing a white stripe down the centre of his furry back squeezed under the tent's walls around midnight in search of food. A watchdog posted outside had merely sniffed in disdain — but sniffing in disdain did not help the members of the camping party. Hopefully, Pilot Henry Hollenbeck tried wiggling his toes in his sleeping bag, but this just made the curious visitor raise his tail in a threatening gesture. Then Mr. Adams started to talk to the skunk — so 'twas said, smoothly, soothingly, persuasively — and, under the influence of such a flow of velvet oratory, the odour-loaded interloper left peaceably through the front door, and quietly ambled off into the stillness of the night.[1]

Then, too, it was on this same party that the hunters told how Grant McConachie blew the antlers right off a startled bull moose at twenty paces. It was not because he could not shoot as well as the others, as he had bagged his share of moose and caribou. But in this particular instance he was slightly confused, and so was the moose. Rounding a bluff, the hunter expected to find a dead animal. Instead, there it was as large as life pawing the ground just twenty paces off and more than slightly annoyed! Grant's first shot cleared away the antlers, the second threw him flat on his spine, while the third one made sure the job was done![2]

In addition to becoming associated with Ginger Coote Airways in 1938, Grant McConachie also became associated with Cariboo Airways. In the beginning, a company known as Bridge River and Cariboo Airways Limited, Vancouver, was incorporated on October 3, 1933. Its name was changed to Ginger Coote Airways on May 26, 1938 — and this was the company with which United Air Transport became affiliated in 1938. In turn, Ginger Coote Airways was changed to Cariboo Airways on May 25, 1939. Cariboo Airways' charter was withdrawn on June 6, 1940.

Grant McConachie, the President of United Air Transport, was unable to have his company's name registered in the Province of British Columbia, where, to a great extent, his operations were centred. When United Air Transport and Ginger

Barkley-Grow seaplane, CF-BMW Yukon Prince belonging to Yukon Southern Air Transport, which flew survey parties in and out of many sites along the Northwest Staging Route in 1929.

Coote Airways became affiliated in 1938, they continued using their separate company names. This led to confusion. So, early in 1939, United Air Transport was re-named Yukon Southern Air Transport, with offices in Vancouver (Sea Island Airport) and Edmonton. Yukon Southern Air Transport was formerly registered in Canada and known as McConachie Air Transport, Calgary, Alberta; Ginger Coote Airways was to operate independently as of January 1, 1939. McConachie Air Transport was incorporated on January 16, 1937; and Yukon Southern Airways was incorporated on March 6, 1939, with the United Air Transport Company's charter being withdrawn on July 31, 1940.

The same schedules and routes were maintained by Yukon Southern Air Transport. Grant McConachie was its President and General Manager; Barney Phillips was Vice-President and Traffic Manager; and Jack Moar was Operations Manager. The company's operations were on floats and skis. They were operating a weekly service from Vancouver to Whitehorse, connecting with air routes throughout the Yukon and Alaska; from Edmonton to Peace River points; from Prince George to Fort St. James, Manson Creek, Germansen Landing and Takla Landing; a monthly service from Prince George to Fort McLeod, Finlay Forks and Fort Ware; and four times a year from Fort Nelson to Fort Liard.

The company soon decided that it could not economically operate over the route from Edmonton to Whitehorse

using floats in the summer time and skis in the winter time, which it had been doing since 1937. During 1938, United Air Transport carried 178,170 pounds of mail; 356,342 pounds of express and 3,263 passengers in 3,927 flying hours. So, Grant McConachie, being a good organizer and a man of vision, saw the advantages to be derived from year-round operations on wheels at these points, and looked around for aerodrome sites that would be suitable along the route.

There was an airport already at Whitehorse, and also one at Edmonton. But there were no landing strips for aircraft on wheels at Fort St. John, Fort Nelson or Watson Lake.

United Air Transport had established a seaplane base at Fort St. John and one at Fort Nelson for its operations in 1937, and had also erected log cabin buildings for the company's use at these places the same year. United Air Transport first cleared a 3,000 ft. landing strip at Fort St. John and another at Fort Nelson in 1938. The Province of British Columbia had granted $500 to United Air Transport to assist in building the aerodrome at Fort St. John. Too, the company had set up a radio compass station at both Fort St. John and Fort Nelson in 1938 so that it could receive meteorological reports and keep track of its aircraft movements. The aerodrome first established at Fort St. John by Grant McConachie was kept in good condition until 1942, with landings being made on it daily during the early war years by Lockheed 14 and other aircraft. Then,

when the new airport was completed in the fall of 1942 under the Northwest Staging Route programme, all services were moved from the original aerodrome with the grass landing strip built by Grant McConachie to the new airport at Fort St. John. The new airport site at Fort St. John had been chosen in the summer of 1939 as it would provide the longer runways required under the Northwest Staging Route programme. The company used a small-wheeled tractor and a team of horses for clearing at Fort Nelson. H. W. Christensen was the radio operator for United Air Transport at Fort Nelson and with his wife and baby helped to increase the population of Fort Nelson to about fifteen people — a half-dozen of these being seasonal trappers.

After clearing landing strips at Fort St. John and Fort Nelson in 1938, Yukon Southern Air Transport (then United Air Transport) was starting to clear a strip at Watson Lake, but had not gone far when the Department of Transport's survey engineers arrived on the scene in the summer of 1939 to survey airport sites for the construction of airports along the Northwest Staging Route. The area which Yukon Air Transport had chosen at Watson Lake was a good site considering the nature of the terrain in that

Yukon Southern Air Transport's Barkley-Grow seaplane CF-BMW at the dock at Dease Lake, July 18, 1941, flying supplies for the building of the airport at Watson Lake.

part of the country and one on which an airport with reasonably unobstructed approaches could be provided. The landing strip that was being cleared was located one-half mile north of Watson Lake. Early in 1937, United Air Transport had located its original seaplane base at Lower Post, about 16 miles or so from Watson Lake, then the company moved its seaplane base to Watson Lake later in 1937 to a place on the northeast end of the lake, from where it carried out its operations. Here a radio station was set up to receive meteorological reports for the planning of flights. Also, log cabins were built for the company's use and to accommodate any overnight passengers. Watson Lake, like Fort Nelson, was located in an inaccessible wilderness area, and Grant McConachie had to fly in his equipment.

For these northern operations, Yukon Southern Air Transport had purchased a fleet of three twin-engine, all-metal Barkley-Grow aircraft: CF-BLV, *Yukon King* and CF-BMG, *Yukon Queen,* both landplanes; and CF-BMW, *Yukon Prince,* a seaplane; each powered with two 450 h.p. Pratt and Whitney Wasp Junior engines. The *Yukon Queen,* the first Barkley-Grow aircraft received, was equipped with skis, and put on the Fort St. John-Vancouver weekly air mail service in March 1939. Grant McConachie and his chief pilot, Ted Field, flew the aircraft on its inaugural flight to Vancouver. The *Yukon King* was put on the Fort St. John-Whitehorse run late in April, 1939. Ted Field set a record with the *Yukon King* on the Fort St. John-Whitehorse run by flying the 650 miles from Fort St. John to Whitehorse in three hours and thirty minutes.

Ted Field had been flying with Grant McConachie since 1933 in northern British Columbia and the Yukon, and had gone to school with him years earlier in Edmonton. He learned to fly in 1929, flying various types of aircraft through the years, and pioneered commercial flying in

the north with Grant McConachie. He was Manager of Flight Operations for Canadian Pacific Air Lines at the time of his death in January, 1958.

Yukon Southern Air Transport's entire fleet was equipped with two-way radio and radio compass directional instruments at the time. The Barkley-Grow aircraft were purchased from the Canadian Car and Foundry Company, Limited, Montreal, exclusive Canadian distributors for the Barkley-Grow Aircraft Co., of Detroit, Michigan. The Barkley-Grow seaplane was then considered to be the fastest twin-engine seaplane in Canada.

Thus it was that in the fall of 1939 Yukon Southern Air Transport commenced year-round operations on wheels from Edmonton to Whitehorse for the first time. This scheduled service carried both passengers and air mail.

As a result of expanding defence projects in northwestern Canada, Dan McLean, Superintendent of Airways, Ottawa, went to Edmonton late in October, 1940, and he and W. S. "Bill" Lawson, District Inspector of Western Airways, made an aerial inspection of the route from Edmonton to Whitehorse. This route was becoming of particular strategic importance due to the thundering in the Pacific area which was getting louder. Their flight was made on a regular scheduled trip of Yukon Southern Air Transport in an aircraft captained by Grant McConachie, President of the company, due to his great knowledge of the route. Grant also explained where and how facilities along the route could and should be improved. This particular route did not cross the main range of the Rocky Mountains. There were well-timbered areas a good part of the way, and also areas of muskeg.

Yukon Southern Air Transport purchased two Lockheed Lodestars in May, 1941, for use on the Edmonton-Vancouver-Whitehorse run, adding them

to the company's fleet of three Barkley-Grows for this route.

Grant McConachie was made Assistant to the Vice-President of the Canadian Pacific Railway Company (Winnipeg), on November 28, 1941. Following the formation of Canadian Pacific Air Lines on January 1, 1942, his company, Yukon Southern Air Transport, was bought out by them, and he was made responsible for co-ordinating the ten companies which they purchased. This was during the time that the Department of Transport was carrying out extensive development of airports through the whole of the northwest area over which Grant McConachie's company was operating, and which he had pioneered.

The ten companies purchased by this new company were as follows: Arrow Airways Limited, The Pas, Manitoba; Canadian Airways Limited, Montreal, Quebec and Winnipeg, Manitoba; Dominion Skyways Limited, Montreal, Quebec; Ginger Coote Airways, Vancouver; Mackenzie Air Service Limited, Edmonton, Alberta; Prairie Airways Limited, Moose Jaw, Saskatchewan; Quebec Airways Limited, Montreal, Quebec; Starratt Airways and Transportation Limited, Hudson, Ontario; Wings Limited, Winnipeg, Manitoba; and Yukon Southern Air Transport Limited, Edmonton and Vancouver.

On May 1, 1942, C. H. "Punch" Dickins was appointed Vice-President and General Manager of Canadian Pacific Air Lines; while Grant McConachie was appointed General Manager of Western Lines for Canadian Pacific Air Lines at Edmonton, which included all routes west of Fort William. Barney Phillips also joined Canadian Pacific Air Lines at Edmonton as Assistant to the General Superintendent. In December, 1953, he became General Manager of Operations for Canadian Pacific Air Lines; in July, 1956, he was appointed Vice-President of Operations; and in 1959 he became

Lockheed Lodestar purchase by Yukon Southern Air Transport for use on the route from Edmonton to the Yukon. Left to right: Grant McConachie, President and General Manager; Barney Phillips, Asst. General Manager; and Ted Field, Operations Manager.
Photo courtesy of Canadian Aviation.

Vice-President, Administration.

When Canadian Pacific Air Lines acquired these ten companies, including their seventy-seven or so aircraft, along with their different types of equipment, service and maintenance, different types of operation were in existence by the various companies. It was Grant Mc-Conachie's responsibility to mould all of these companies into one smoothly operating unit having the same standards with regard to maintenance, communications, operations, training and personnel, equipment and other related facilities, as well as to co-ordinate bush flying with ground contact on skis and floats, and with the orderly radio-equipped traffic being put into operation upon the installation of the radio ranges by the Department of Transport in northwestern Canada around the end of 1941.

In 1919 the Canadian Pacific Railway received permission from the Dominion Government to own and operate commercial aircraft within and without Canada. Then in 1933 the Canadian Pacific Railway purchased a $50,000 interest in Canadian Airways. When Trans-Canada Air Lines was created in 1937, the other air services were finding it more difficult to get along due to the competition and duplication of some services. Therefore, the Canadian Pacific Railway, which already held a large interest in Canadian Airways, received permission in 1939 to purchase a number of companies. So, on January 1, 1942, Canadian Pacific Air Lines came into existence with the purchase of ten air-craft operating companies. And Grant McConachie's company, Yukon Southern Air Transport, was one of these companies purchased by the Canadian Pacific Railway.

In 1942 Grant McConachie asked Matt Berry to return to the Mackenzie River District to start building landing strips, and enlarge those already in existence along the Athabaska and Mackenzie

Rivers to serve the Canol Project (Canadian Oil Line). So, early in 1942, Matt Berry was appointed Superintendent of Construction for Canadian Pacific Air Lines on this project. The company had finished enlarging the landing field at Fort McMurray and was just starting to enlarge the one at Fort Smith when the American troops and civil contractors arrived in the late summer of 1942 to commence building the Canol Pipe Line from Norman Wells to Whitehorse, and to construct an oil refinery at Whitehorse. The United States was urgently in need of additional fuel at this time due to their entry into World War II in December, 1941.

The regular means of transporting supplies from Fort McMurray to Norman Wells was by boat down the Athabaska and Mackenzie Rivers. As a speedier method of transportation was required along this route, an agreement was reached between Canada and the United States to enlarge the landing strips already in existence, and build others, along the Athabaska and Mackenzie Rivers so that supplies could be flown in by air to expedite the construction of the Canol Project. Matt Berry was then loaned by Canadian Pacific Air Lines to the new aerodrome contractors, Bechtel, Price and Callahan of Edmonton, to choose the new sites for flight strips, and to superintend their construction, as well as enlarge the existing strips. So, flight strips were established along the Mackenzie River route (the Athabaska and Mackenzie Rivers) at Fort McMurray, Embarras, Fort Smith, Fort Resolution, Hay River, Fort Providence, Fort Simpson, Wrigley, Norman Wells and Camp Canol, to facilitate bringing in supplies for the early construction of the Canol Pipe Line and the oil refinery at Whitehorse.

With the completion of the construction of these flight strips, Grant McConachie turned a small bush operation on skis and floats into a major operation on wheels, as he took ad-

vantage of the opportunity which presented itself. Thousands of personnel and hundreds of tons of freight were safely carried from Edmonton to Fort Norman for the Canol Project.

The Minister of National Defence, the Honourable Colin Gibson, announced in April, 1946, that Grant McConachie had won the Trans-Canada Trophy for 1945 in recognition of long service, energetic support and whole-hearted efforts in the development of civil aviation in Canada, and for his successful endeavours in opening up Canada's vast hinterland in the northwest, especially the area between Edmonton, Alberta and Whitehorse, Yukon Territory.

At the time that he was awarded the Trans-Canada Trophy for 1945, he had logged well over 7,000 hours, and during his career had taken various courses in the United States in air line operation in order to keep up with the most modern methods of flying. He had taken courses in air line operation from Pan American Airways, and flew as a member of the crew of Pan American Clipper Ships between New York and Bermuda. This latter training was for the purpose of determining the best methods of operating an air line as Grant McConachie felt at the time that Pan American encountered problems similar to those in Canada. He studied for a month on Western Air Lines and went thoroughly into their despatch, communications, servicing and maintenance systems. He had also taken courses from one to two weeks with American, Eastern and Northwest Airlines and spent a month at Kansas City with Mid-Continental Airlines, then a small airline operating Lodestars.

His zeal led him to prepare for instrument (blind) landings before facilities were available for them in Canada, and before authority was obtained to use instrument landing facilities in Canada. He wanted to familiarize himself with this procedure as he saw its coming into use

CF-CPA a Lockheed 18, en route north over the Rockies.
Photo courtesy of Grant McConachie.

in Canada soon. He took his Instrument Flying Course with Northwest Airlines, Minneapolis.

Grant McConachie held several licences: Private Air Pilot's Certificate No. 788, dated February 20, 1931 (although he qualified a year earlier); Commercial Air Pilot's Certificate No. A-925, dated November 30, 1931; Transport Certificate No. 20, dated April 1, 1936; Air Engineer's Certificate No. A-1091, dated August 24, 1935; Instrument Flight Rating, dated October, 1945; and Airline Transport Pilot's Licence VRA-700, dated July 26, 1953, endorsed with a Class I Instrument Flight Rating.

The official presentation of the Trans Canada Trophy was made in Edmonton on June 25, 1946, by Air Vice-Marshal T. A. Lawrence on behalf of the Minister of National Defence, at the testimonial dinner given by the Government of Alberta.

Grant McConachie became Assistant to the President of Canadian Pacific Air Lines, Montreal, in May, 1946, while C. H. "Punch" Dickins became General Manager of Eastern Lines, Montreal, and R. W. "Dick" Ryan became General Manager of Western Lines, Edmonton. Then, shortly after this, on February 11, 1947, Grant McConachie was appointed as President of the company. The company's head office was moved from

The Committee of Award for 1945 consisted of the following members:
Air Commodore C. R. Dunlap, C.B.E., Royal Canadian Air Force, Department of National Defence, Ottawa.
Mr. A. D. McLean, O.B.E., Controller of Civil Aviation, Department of Transport, Ottawa.
Wing Commander G. A. Hiltz, Royal Canadian Air Force, Department of National Defence, Ottawa.
Dr. J. J. Green, representing the Royal Canadian Flying Clubs Association, Ottawa.

Montreal to Vancouver in September, 1949, and Vancouver became their headquarters.

Under Grant McConachie's direction, Canadian Pacific Air Lines developed from a purely bush-type operation into a major air line operating scheduled domestic, transcontinental and international services. In addition to passenger service, the company also has a mail, express and freight service.

Canadian Pacific Air Lines' polar route as a short cut between continents was envisioned by Grant McConachie in his earliest flying days around Edmonton, and he lived to see his dream become a reality. The certification of the Scandinavian Air Services to start a polar service from Los Angeles to Oslo, via Edmonton, spurred Grant McConachie to renew his efforts to create a Canadian polar route. As it was not possible to fly into London at the time, since permission could not be received from the Department of Transport, the company chose Amsterdam as the European terminus of the line because of its location equidistant between most of the principal cities of Europe and because it was a "free port" where passengers in transit were not required to pass through customs or immigration clearances. A bilateral treaty between Canada and the Netherlands was signed at Ottawa on June 2, 1948, which granted a Canadian air line permission to operate an air service to Amsterdam. The Netherlands exercised their part of the agreement when KLM (Royal Dutch Airlines) started operating a regular service between Amsterdam and Montreal. In flying the polar route, too, the dry polar air provided smooth and storm-free flying conditions.

Canadian Pacific Air Lines entered the field of international flying on July 10, 1949, when it made its inaugural flight from Vancouver via Honolulu and Fiji to Sydney, Australia, using Canadair IV aircraft. Then in September of 1949 the

company started an air line service from Vancouver to Tokyo and Hong Kong. Cold Bay in the Aleutian Islands was the refuelling stop on the west-bound flights, while Anchorage and Fairbanks were alternates for all flights. In December, 1951, the South Pacific service was extended to New Zealand. Two years later, in October, 1953, Canadian Pacific Air Lines started a service from Vancouver down to Mexico and Lima, Peru, using DC-6B aircraft. Within two more years, on June 3, 1955, Grant McConachie's company made the inaugural flight over the polar route or Great Circle route from Vancouver to Amsterdam via Churchill, Manitoba, a 4,900-mile route. The inaugural flight over the polar route was made in a DC-6B aircraft. This route reduced the distance to Amsterdam by 1,000 miles.

In November, 1955, Canadian Pacific Air Lines extended its service from Toronto to Mexico City using DC-6B aircraft, also making a connection with its South American service. Trans-Canada Air Lines had previously been flying from Toronto to Mexico City via Tampa, Florida. Then an agreement was reached between Trans-Canada Air Lines and Canadian Pacific Air Lines in the fall of 1955 whereby Canadian Pacific Air Lines took over Trans-Canada Air Lines' route from Toronto to Mexico City in exchange for all of Canadian Pacific Air Lines' domestic routes in Ontario and Quebec. On June 1, 1956, the South American service was extended from Peru to Buenos Aires, Argentina; and in September, 1957, it was extended over to Santiago, Chile.

In May, 1957, the company inaugurated a service from Toronto to Montreal and Lisbon, which was extended to Madrid, Spain, in July, 1957. Canadian Pacific Air Lines also introduced the 72-passenger, 4-engine, Super DC-6B *Empress* airliners on the Vancouver-Prince George-Fort St. John-Fort Nelson-Watson Lake-Whitehorse route in July, 1957. From Whitehorse to Dawson City, DC-3's were used.

Canadian Pacific Air Lines also made its inaugural flight in February, 1958, in the *Empress of Edmonton*, a DC-6B aircraft, from Vancouver to Amsterdam with a stop at Edmonton to pick up passengers. Prior to that, a stop-over at Edmonton was not allowed to pick up passengers. This was the first Canadian aircraft to carry radar for weather forecasting.

On June 1, 1958, the company started using Bristol Britannias on the Vancouver-Amsterdam polar route. They were powered by four Bristol Proteus engines, and could carry 90 odd passengers. Refuelling points were at Sondestrom, Greenland; Keflavik, Iceland; or Prestwick, Scotland, if weather or other factors required it. Canadian Pacific Air Lines started using Bristol Britannias on its route to the Orient (Tokyo) from Vancouver on August 24, 1948, and to Hong Kong on September 28, 1958, as soon as the new air strip was finished there. With Bristol Britannias in use on the North Pacific it was the first time that commercial turbo-jet aircraft had been put into service on the Pacific.

Canadian Pacific Air Lines inaugurated a Canadian transcontinental service on May 4, 1959, with a flight leaving from both Vancouver and Montreal, each stopping at Toronto and Winnipeg. On these *Canadian Empress* flights, the company used Bristol Britannia, 400 m.p.h., turbojet airliners. These aircraft were all radar equipped. On this service, a daily flight left from Vancouver, while another flight left from Montreal. Both flights stopped at Toronto and Winnipeg for passengers and refuelling.

After Canadian Pacific Air Lines inaugurated its transcontinental service, it relinquished its route in the Mackenzie District to Pacific Western Airlines in June, 1959. Specifically, Pacific Western Airlines took over the scheduled routes

Grant McConachie shown with the Trans-Canada Trophy, which he won in 1945. The trophy was presented to him in Edmonton on June 25, 1946, by A/V.M. T.A. Lawrence.
Photo courtesy of the R.C.A.F.

from Edmonton to Grande Prairie, Peace River, Fort Smith, Fort Vermilion, Hay River, Yellowknife; from Edmonton to Fort McMurray, Uranium City, Fort Smith, Resolution and Yellowknife; as well as the route from Edmonton to Fort McMurray, Fort Smith, Hay River, Providence, Fort Simpson, Wrigley, Norman Wells, Fort Norman, Fort Good Hope, Arctic Red River, Fort McPherson and Inuvik (Aklavik), known as the Mackenzie River Route. Pacific Western Airlines began operating its new service

along the Mackenzie River Route on July 6, 1959.

On December 4, 1959, Canadian Pacific Air Lines inaugurated Bristol Britannias between Winnipeg and Honolulu. On March 4, 1960, Canadian Pacific Air Lines inaugurated a twice-weekly Bristol Britannia service to Rome, Italy, from Toronto and Montreal via Lisbon, Portugal.

Canadian Pacific Air Lines purchased a fleet of four 159-passenger Super DC-8 long-range jet airliners from the Douglas

Aircraft Company of Santa Monica, California, in 1961, and entered the jet age with jet passenger aircraft. The Super DC-8's, costing $6,000,000 each, were powered by four Rolls-Royce Conway bypass engines, Mark 15, developing 18,500 pounds of thrust each.

The first of four Super DC-8's arrived in Edmonton on February 22, 1961, piloted by Captain R. B. Leslie, Director of Flight Operations. The Super DC-8's were to be used on the trans-polar route to Amsterdam, to Rome and to Honolulu, and other routes. The other Super DC-8's arrived over a period of a few months.

The super DC-8 trans-polar jet service between Vancouver - Edmonton and Amsterdam via the polar route was inaugurated on April 30, 1961; and the Super DC-8 went into service on the transcontinental route on May 15, 1961, replacing the Britannias. On May 31, 1961, Canadian Pacific Air Lines inaugurated an extended Super DC-8 service from Amsterdam on to Rome.

The right to fly to London, England, had been sought for a long time by Grant McConachie, and now he was to be given permission. This was a great achievement for him, after so much perseverance. It was on August 15, 1961, that the Minister of Transport, Mr. Leon Balcer, gave permission to Canadian Pacific Air Lines to fly to London, England, by providing an international service on the Vancouver-Edmonton-Gander-London route; and onward to Amsterdam. As well, the company was given permission to fly from Vancouver through Calgary via Gander to London.

Then on October 1, 1961, Canadian Pacific Air Lines inaugurated a trans-atlantic Super DC-8 service from Vancouver via Edmonton and Gander to London, England. The mission had been accomplished.

On May 4, 1962, Canadian Pacific Air Lines began direct jet service from Montreal to Rome; and so the inaugural flights continued in the jet age.

Under Grant McConachie's gifted guiding hand, Canadian Pacific Air Lines continued its programme of expansion at home and abroad through the years.

On June 29, 1965, when Grant McConachie was visiting in the Los Angeles area, he developed chest pains at a Long Beach Hotel and was rushed to the hospital by ambulance. However, he died of an apparent heart attack before he even reached the hospital. He was only 56 years of age. He and Mrs. McConachie resided in Vancouver at the time of his death. They had two sons, Donald and William.

Grant McConachie was a past President of the Vancouver Board of Trade; and a past President of the Air Industries and Transport Association. In 1963 he was named Businessman of the Year by Sales and Marketing Executive Industrial of New York. He was named a member of Canada's Aviation Hall of Fame in 1973. He was made a Companion of the Order of Flight (City of Edmonton).

A plaque was unveiled on October 24, 1968, by Mrs. G. W. G. McConachie in honour of her husband, when an official ceremony was held to name a new highway leading to Vancouver International Airport after Grant McConachie. It was named "McConachie Way" by the Department of Transport. The inscription on the plaque reads: *This roadway is named in memory of G. W. Grant McConachie, pilot, airline president, pioneer of northern flying and innovator of the jet age, whose contribution to Canadian aviation places him in the forefront of memory. 1909-1965.*

Mr. McConachie was a big man and had correspondingly big ideas and great ambitions, with the tremendous energy and the enterprise to realize their achievement. His enthusiasm, combined with an astounding practical knowledge of air transportation, gave him a per-

suasive power that was virtually irresistible. He was known as a man of vision. Although his pilot's licence was still in force in later years, he seldom found time to handle the controls of an aircraft and spent most of his time at his big desk at his Vancouver headquarters, when he wasn't roaming the world's airways in pursuit of C.P.A.L.'s objectives. In later years, his principal hobby was ranching, and he frequently found week-end relaxation at his own ranch in the interior of British Columbia, a far cry from his bush pilot days.

His early wish to go to China in 1932 reached a grand historical climax when he, as President of Canadian Pacific Air Lines, made the inaugural flight to the Orient for the company in September, 1949.

After being awarded the Trans-Canada Trophy for opening up Canada's vast hinterland in the northwest to aviation, Grant McConachie continued to open up further fields to aviation for his ever-expanding company in the inauguration of fifty-odd thousand miles of domestic, transcontinental and global routes while President of the company. In so doing, as President of the seventh largest airline in the world in so far as route mileage was concerned at that time, he brought much recognition and honour to Canada, and, rightly so, since much of the responsibility for this achievement fell on his broad shoulders. He did more to promote Canadian air policies than possibly any other man. In 1946, Grant McConachie began his long battle to win air routes nationally across Canada for his company in an attempt to open up fair markets between the large Canadian and United States cities on an equitable basis. He was truly a legend in his time.

NOTES

[1] Quote from *Canadian Aviation*, November, 1938.
[2] *Ibid.*

1946

Zebulon Lewis Leigh

Citation: in recognition of continuous outstanding performance in his duties as an officer and pilot of the R.C.A.F., coupled with a record of twenty years of exceptional achievement in both civil and military aviation

Group Captain Zebulon Lewis Leigh, O.B.E., E.D., while Commanding Officer of the R.C.A.F. Station at Goose Airport, Labrador, was awarded the Trans-Canada Trophy for 1946, for meritorious service in the advancement of aviation in Canada, "in recognition of continuous outstanding performance in his duties as an officer and pilot of the R.C.A.F., coupled with a record of twenty years of exceptional achievement in both civil and military aviation." On April 30, 1947, the Honourable Brooke Claxton, Minister of National Defence, wrote to Group Captain Leigh expressing his pleasure at his receiving the award.

As Senior Air Staff Officer, No. 9 Transport Group, in 1945, Group Captain Leigh smoothly and efficiently accomplished the transfer of the R.C.A.F. air transport service from a war-time to a peacetime basis, the announcement said. In the latter part of 1946, he was appointed to the position of Commanding Officer of the R.C.A.F. Station at Goose Airport, Labrador, an important western terminal of the North Atlantic air transport route. He remained there until March, 1948.

The announcement added that, in the early days of commercial flying in Canada, Group Captain Leigh was continually in front in the field of newly developed air services. These activities resulted in his participation in flying operations on the Prairies, on the Atlantic Coast, in the Northwest Territories and in the Arctic. This varied experience was to be of great value to his work in later years. Although he was seldom backed by large financial resources, the success of these ventures depended to a large extent on his initiative, energy and unshaken belief in

the future of air travel in Canada.

Zebulon Lewis Leigh was born on June 19, 1906, at Macclesfield, Cheshire, England. He arrived in Canada at the age of three, and was taken to Lethbridge, Alberta, by his parents. There he received his early education. Lewis Leigh was a junior Lieutenant in the 20th Field Battery, Canadian Artillery, a militia unit which received two weeks' summer training each year at Sarcee Camp, just outside Calgary. It was while Lewis Leigh was there that he became intrigued with the occasional aircraft flying overhead for spotting purposes, and determined to try it for himself.

So Lewis Leigh began his flying career at Lethbridge in 1928 under the guidance of Jock Palmer, and with Joe Patton as flying instructor in 1929. Then he spent his time barnstorming and instructing. He gave flying instruction at Lethbridge until August, 1930. When an opportunity presented itself, he hiked off to Medicine Hat, Alberta, where he operated a flying school and barnstorming service under the name of Southern Alberta Airlines Ltd.; and later Leigh Air Services. Here he remained until June, 1931.

Going east was his next step, and he became chief pilot with Maritime and Newfoundland Airways, Sydney, Nova Scotia.

During this period he flew Fokker Standard aircraft on floats which had previously been used by the R.C.A.F. on the Hudson Strait Expedition of 1927, when the government decided to complete the Hudson Bay Railway and terminals in January and required accurate information of the ice conditions. For this purpose they sent in an expedition under Mr. N. B. McLean, with Wing Commander J. L. Gordon, D.F.C.,

Lewis Leigh with his D.H. Moth which he used while operating a flying school and barnstorming service under the name of Southern Alberta Airlines Ltd. in 1929 and 1930. When this company went out of business, Leigh Air Services of Medicine Hat was started, and two aircraft were used for its operation.
Photo courtesy of G/Capt. Z.L. Leigh.

A.D.C., Director of Civil Government Air Operations, who was responsible for the flying operations of the expedition.

While Lewis Leigh was with Maritime and Newfoundland Airways, the Germans started a ship-to-shore mail service from the liners *Bremen* and *Europa*. The pilots were catapulted from the ships about 700 miles at sea. They landed at Sydney, Nova Scotia, for refuelling en route to New York. On one occasion, one of them, Fritz Simon, crash-landed in the Bay of Fundy in fog at night and was lost in its swirling waters. Lewis Leigh was sent out to search for him. After two days' searching in bad weather, he finally found the pilot, Fritz Simon, floating in the water, already dead. They never found his engineer.

Lewis Leigh was issued Commercial Air Pilot's Certificate No. 650, dated March 7, 1930, which was superseded by No. A-944, dated March 1, 1932, as his old one had been lost in a fire at Camp Borden on January 11, 1932. Also, his Air Engineer's Licence No. 586, which he lost in the same fire, was superseded by No. A-741, dated March 1, 1932.

Before the year 1931 had passed, Lewis Leigh was commissioned as a Flying Officer with the R.C.A.F. and was sent to Camp Borden for blind flying and air navigation training. By this time he had accumulated 1,100 hours of flying time. The following year, 1932, the R.C.A.F. strength was drastically cut and he was transferred to the R.C.A.F. Reserve, so he returned to civil flying again.

This time he joined Explorers Air Transport of Sydney, Nova Scotia, and Edmonton, Alberta (incorporated June 2, 1932), as chief pilot, operating Fokker aircraft in the Northwest Territories. These Fokker aircraft were the same ones that Lewis Leigh had flown previously with Maritime and Newfoundland Airways.

Lewis Leigh and George Silke left Camp Borden and the R.C.A.F. behind in April, 1932, and took the train to Sydney. They had arranged with officials of Lewis Leigh's old company, Maritime and Newfoundland Airways, to form a new company to operate in the Northwest Territories. First, they were to overhaul two of the Fokkers, G-CAHJ and G-CAHE, and then fly them out to the northwest where they were to organize a western branch for the company in that area. The new company, based at Edmonton, was to be called Explorers Air Transport Limited.

After their arrival in Sydney, they started overhauling the aircraft. This was a big job and was all the more difficult because of lack of finances, as the country was then in the middle of the Depression. After much work and worry, however, the job was finally done and the aircraft test flown by June 16. But just after completing the test flights, and while standing near an electric grindstone, four pieces of hot steel became embedded in Lewis Leigh's left eye. Dr. Rice, a medical doctor, who was also an official of the company, removed three of these pieces of metal. The fourth piece was much more difficult and required the help of the eye specialist of the Dominion Steel Company before it was finally removed. He was then told, most emphatically, not to remove the bandage from his eye for two weeks. This was a real blow to Lewis Leigh but after discussing the pros and cons and, as their money was low, he and George Silke decided that they would start on their flight anyhow, as Lewis Leigh thought that he could see well enough with one eye to fly the aircraft!

Lewis Leigh and George Silke loaded the cabins of their two Fokker Standard Universal float-equipped aircraft with as many spare parts as they could, in addition to a large, solid iron anchor, and a large coil of rope weighing about 40 pounds for each aircraft. These anchors were very difficult to handle as, when they were needed, it was necessary to climb out of the open cockpit, down the side of the aircraft, duck under the wing struts, climb into the cabin, carry the heavy anchor and rope down to the float, duck under the wing struts again, go to the nose of the float and tie on the anchor, and then throw it overboard. This roundabout method was to be the cause of a touchy but humorous episode later in their travels.

They finally took off from Sydney Harbour on June 21, 1932. The weather was not good at the time due to low clouds and rain, but they didn't expect too much trouble. Their first stop was to be at Saint John, New Brunswick. The weather gradually became worse as they flew along. Soon they were forced to go above the low cloud deck. When their E.T.A. for Saint John was up they could not find a break anywhere in the clouds below. Therefore, they turned back until they found a break and landed at Port Elgin, New Brunswick. By this time their fuel was low. As aviation fuel was not available in Port Elgin, with some trepidation they partly filled their tanks with automobile gasoline, hoping that by mixing it with their remaining aviation fuel the engines would function. A telephone call to Saint John let them know that breaks were appearing in the clouds overhead and that they should arrive as soon as possible before the weather started to close in again.

The take off was successful and they were airborne for Saint John once again. The amount of fuel which they had taken on board at Port Elgin was only enough to take them to Saint John, leaving insufficient gas for them to return if it became necessary. Their engines seemed to be operating satisfactorily with the mixed fuels and they were both undoubtedly relieved until they were forced on top of the clouds again just as they realized that the head wind was getting stronger. When they arrived over where Saint John was supposed to be, they

Lewis Leigh in CF-AOL, a Waco 9, with a Curtiss OX5 engine, also used for flying instruction in 1930.
Photo courtesy of G/Capt. Z.L. Leigh.

found that the breaks in the clouds had disappeared and were solidly undercast. Of course, they had no radio communications in those days, so they waved to each other from their open cockpits and started to circle, looking for a break. In the meantime their fuel was so low that it had ceased to show in their boiler-type fuel gauges.

Suddenly the engine of Lewis Leigh's aircraft stopped and he waved to George and headed down for the cloud. He thanked his lucky stars that they had just finished an R.C.A.F. course in blind flying at Camp Borden, even though at that time they were using the flat turn system. Lewis Leigh went into the cloud, keeping his airspeed up and hoping there were no hills reaching into the clouds. After what seemed like such a very long time he suddenly broke through the clouds and was out over water at a very low altitude. Quickly he flattened out his aircraft and landed. He could then see the City of Saint John not too far away.

In the meantime, after removing his helmet, he could hear George Silke's aircraft circling above. Suddenly George Silke's engine stopped too, and in a minute or so his aircraft popped out of the cloud and landed by some lucky coincidence not too far from his. Boats came out to meet them and towed them in to the dock at Millidgeville, near Saint John. They were a very relieved pair when they stepped ashore. That eventful first day, each flew six hours and thirty minutes.

The next day, June 22, was rainy with low ceilings again, so the day was spent in refuelling and checking over their aircraft in preparation for their departure on the following day.

On June 23, the weather looked better. They got an early take-off in the hope of getting as far as Montreal before nightfall. However, this was not to be as, after passing over Bath, New Brunswick, on the Saint John River, they encountered heavy rain and hail and were forced to turn back to Bath. As senior pilot, it was Lewis Leigh's job to land first. There was little or no wind, the calm before the storm in the Bath area. He made what he considered to be a good approach and landing and taxied to the shore line where people were clustered on the bank. They helped him tie the aircraft when he reached the shore.

In the meantime, George Silke was making his approach from the opposite direction due to the calm conditons. Suddenly, he saw that he was heading towards a high cable stretched across the river. Just in the nick of time he pulled up sharply and missed it, then he continued on and landed. After George Silke pulled in to shore, Lewis Leigh wondered why he had not used the same approach as the one that he had, since he thought his own was a good one. At this point, a local resident spoke up and told Lewis Leigh that he had just missed one or two cables by a matter of only a few feet while he was doing his final approach. Lewis Leigh just couldn't believe it so the man drove them along the river in his car and showed them the cables! Lewis Leigh was astonished, to put it mildly, when he was shown the cables and saw how close he must have been to them. This was, no doubt, partly due to his vision being obscured, as he still had the bandage over his one eye. He and George Silke looked at each other, saw how close Lewis Leigh had come to having a one-way ticket to another plane of existence, laughed rather feebly, and skipped the incident to dwell on more pleasant topics.

On returning to the aircraft they noticed that the rear float struts on one side of George Silke's aircraft were badly out of line. These struts were fastened by a clamp on to the rear wing strut. This clamp had slipped. The rest of the day was spent in correcting this fault, ably assisted by many local townspeople. That day they flew only two hours.

The next day, June 24, showed no improvement in the weather, so they passed the time looking at the town in the company of some of the people they had met after their landings.

As June 25 showed some improvement in weather conditions, they took off again, hoping that they might get as far as Montreal. This was not to be, however. The ceiling gradually dropped and again heavy rain poured down. The visibility became so poor, even though they were flying close to the tree tops, that they had to make a forced landing. What appeared to be a suitable looking lake suddenly appeared so they landed on it. With the shore line looking a bit rough, this meant that their anchoring task would be difficult. When this was completed, two men in a boat appeared alongside the aircraft and offered to take them ashore after their short flight of forty-five minutes that day.

Upon reaching the shore, they were met by a uniformed United States' customs official who said that they had landed inside the United States' border at a town called St. Agathe, Maine. This news came as a surprise. They had not given any official notice of their pending arrival and, of course, they had not been given permission to enter the United States. And they could not take off again because of the weather! So their landing was accepted as an emergency one, and they would leave as soon as the weather cleared up.

It was very early the next morning, on the 26th, when they pulled up their anchors and started their engines. When they took off the weather was fair and everything seemed to be going very well again. They reached the St. Lawrence River, near Rivière du Loup, and headed for Montreal. Lewis Leigh was noticing an occasional fluctuation in his oil pressure so he watched it very closely. After he passed Quebec City, the pressure dropped quickly. He waved to George Silke that he was going to land.

Lewis Leigh with G-CAHE, while flying for Maritime and Newfoundland Airways, operating between Sydney, N.S.; Port-aux-Basques, Nfld.; and the Islands of St. Pierre and Miquelon. G-CAHE is a Fokker Standard aircraft, with a Wright J4B engine, 200 h.p., equipped with Hamilton floats. This was at Sydney, N.S., in 1931.

Photo courtesy of G/Capt. Z. L. Leigh.

George Silke followed him. A landing was made and the aircraft beached at Port Neuf, Quebec, after just two hours and forty-five minutes more of flying.

Much work was required to rectify the oil trouble so it was not until the morning of the 28th that the flight was resumed. They landed on the river near Longueuil close to the Fairchild factory, and tied up safely. This day, they each flew one hour and twenty minutes.

They stayed in Montreal until the morning of June 30 as the weather was unfit for flying until then. While Lewis Leigh was in Montreal, he removed the bandage from his eye and found that he could see fairly well again, much to his great relief.

On the morning of the 30th, the flight left for Trout Mills, near North Bay, Ontario. Apart from fairly strong head winds, this flight was a pleasant one. They tied up at Trout Mills after being in the air for four hours and thirty minutes, and they passed the afternoon obtaining aviation gas, refuelling and getting ready for their next hop.

They were running very short of funds now and, although they had wired Sydney for more money, it had not caught up with them. As the next day was July 1, 1932, Dominion Day, and a holiday, they decided to do some barn-storming to raise money. They flew to Lake Nipissing, near Callander, Ontario. They carried a few passengers, but their finances were not upped appreciably. To fly from Trout Mills to Callander took them thirty minutes.

They took off from Callander for Sault Ste. Marie, Ontario, on the morning of July 2. They bucked strong head winds. When they arrived over the Sault, they found the water conditions very rough due to the wind. Lewis Leigh signalled to George Silke that he would land first. It was very rough when he hit the water, but it was safe enough. He then held his position on the water by using his engine while waiting for George Silke to land

and also whilst waiting for someone to appear on shore to give them a hand in beaching the aircraft.

George Silke landed nearby all right but apparently had decided that the beach was too rough and he would have to use his anchor. Lewis Leigh watched him switch off his engine and then realized what he intended to do. He waved from his cockpit to get him to start his engine again but Silke did not see him. What happened next was serious at the time, but comical in retrospect. George Silke scrambled hurriedly down the side of his aircraft on to the float, as he was drifting fast and rocking heavily. He ducked under the wing struts and disappeared into the cabin. In a moment he backed out again carrying the heavy iron anchor and the coil of rope. Then he had to get under the wing struts of the rolling aircraft again with his heavy load. This he did. Then he staggered on to the nose of the float and, noticing how fast he was drifting, quickly threw the anchor overboard but, in his haste, forgot to tie one end of the rope to the float. The realization of what he had done struck him, but there was no time to tie the rope. He rushed back to the wing struts with the end of the rope. Holding the rope with one hand, he threw the other arm around the front wing strut. The rope quickly became taut. The aircraft turned almost sideways, jerking George Silke off the float. Still holding on to the strut he was pulled right up under the wing to where the struts were connected to the wing spar. There he hung over the water. He realized that there was only one thing to do now, and that was to let go of the anchor rope. Then he slid back down on to the float and the aircraft weather-cocked into the wind. In a moment he drifted, tail first, on to what turned out to be the smoothest part of the beach. At this point, George Phillips, who was with the Ontario Provincial Air Service, arrived at the beach with a helper. He managed to get George Silke's

aircraft tied down and signalled to Lewis Leigh to drift in alongside him, thus ending a three and one-half hour flight. They secured both aircraft. Then George Phillips got a boat and they went out to look for George Silke's anchor and rope, which they found and brought back. George Phillips then arranged to get them some aviation fuel and took them to a hotel.

Difficulties seemed to mount up for the two of them. Now they were completely out of money. They still owed George Phillips for refuelling their aircraft and were going to be faced with hotel expenses. They were in this predicament for six days, and these six days were good flying days. But they were unable to leave as they could not pay their bill. Being rather frantic, they sent collect wires to Sydney for money. In the meantime they were forced to eat expensive meals in the hotel because they could be charged on their bill. On July 7, enough money arrived for them to pay their bill, leaving them some to spare. The next morning they prepared to depart.

Although head winds were strong on the morning of July 8, they decided to leave. Saying "cheerio" to George Phillips who had been most kind and helpful to them, they took off. To save money, they thought they would go directly across the lake. About three-quarters of the way across, Lewis Leigh noticed that George Silke would frequently lose altitude. The aircraft would go down to just above the heavily rolling water, and then would slowly climb again. Lewis Leigh was baffled by what George Silke was doing until he explained to him later that his engine was cutting out and would pick up again just before he had to consider ditching. While getting nearer to Fort William, their destination, bad weather moved in and they lost each other for the first time. Lewis Leigh circled but could not locate George Silke so he continued to Fort William. He landed and tied up to a high dock. As he was very worried

Lewis Leigh (extreme left) upon completion of a test flight of Fokker aircraft, G-CAHJ, just after it had been overhauled before being flown to the Northwest Territories. G-CAHE was also overhauled for the flight. This was in 1932.
Photo courtesy of G/Capt. Z. L. Leigh.

about George Silke he asked someone on the dock if he could get some aviation fuel as his tanks were very low. He told him it would take about an hour to get the fuel. Lewis Leigh felt that he could not wait that long since George Silke had not shown up. He explained to the man what had happened and asked him to get a launch to go out to look for George Silke if he could.

Lewis Leigh then took off with very little fuel in his aircraft, and went out to search for George Silke. He could not find any trace of him so he headed back for Fort William. Just in sight of the city, his engine died from lack of fuel. So he had to make a rough, forced landing. Going into the cabin (via the wing struts) he took out some marine distress flares which he carried. After he fired one or two of these, a launch showed up and towed him in to Fort William. He was feeling very badly as he was sure that George Silke had crashed somewhere. He told this to the members of the boat's crew. They said that just before putting out to help him they had heard that an aircraft similar to his had landed near Port Arthur, a little farther along the lake shore. After tying up his aircraft, Lewis Leigh took a taxi to Port Arthur and, sure enough, there was George Silke's aircraft tied to a dock. He found George trying to get some aviation fuel to go out and look for him! George Silke thought he had landed at Fort William and, since Lewis Leigh had not arrived, he was sure that his aircraft was down somewhere. They celebrated their reunion by having a few beers, in spite of their financial worries. This hectic trip took them five hours and fifteen minutes.

After refuelling their aircraft the next morning, July 9, they were again out of money. Their next planned stop was at Lac du Bonnet, Manitoba. They took off from where they had landed at Fort William and Port Arthur, and joined each other in the air. Then they headed towards the west.

As they flew along, the head winds increased in strength and then they ran into heavy rain. As visibility gradually became worse they landed at Kenora, Ontario, and tied up their aircraft after another three hours and twenty minutes in the air. One of the first persons to come to the dock was Alvin "Shorty" Keith, whom Lewis Leigh and George Silke knew as Flying Officer Alvin Keith of the R.C.A.F. at Camp Borden. Shorty Keith had also been transferred to the Reserve of Officers after the big Air Force cut of 1932. He was flying a special aircraft for a large food-processing firm and had flown the top executive of the firm to Kenora. After explaining to Shorty Keith that they were out of cash he arranged that they stay with him in quarters rented by his company, which was a big help.

When July 10 dawned, it was a good day for flying. They said good-bye and thanks to Shorty Keith (who was killed later in an aircraft crash) and took off for Lac du Bonnet, Manitoba. On arrival there they tied up to some buoys at the R.C.A.F. base and two friends drove them to Winnipeg, where they decided to get a short airlifting job for their aircraft in order to raise some money. This was a short flying day for them, as they spent only one hour and ten minutes in the air.

They spent the next six days in Winnipeg. They had wired Sydney for more money and also were making the rounds of the existing aviation companies trying to get a small contract for some kind of flying work. The Depression was at its peak and, as a result, they were unable to get even the smallest job. The day was saved, however, when some more money arrived from Sydney. They paid their bills and planned their next flight north to The Pas, Manitoba, in order to follow what was called the water route to Edmonton. This was necessary as they were unable to cross the Prairies on float-equipped aircraft.

They took off from Lac du Bonnet on

July 16 and headed north. This four-hour and fifteen-minute flight was uneventful. They landed and tied up at a dock at The Pas.

The next day, July 17, they took off for a three-hour and fifteen-minute flight to the R.C.A.F. base at Ladder Lake, Saskatchewan. After taking on fuel they decided to push on. Forty-five minutes later they ran into severe electrical storms which necessitated a landing on a reed-encircled lake at Spiritwood, Saskatchewan. The people there were kind in looking after them the way they did and helped to secure their aircraft.

When they took off from the lake and headed west on July 18, 1932, the day was nice and clear. After three hours and a half of flying, they reached Cooking Lake, just east of Edmonton. This was to be the southern base for their operations into the Far North.

The first part of their long tedious job, that is, flying the aircraft from Sydney to Edmonton on floats, was now completed. They spent twenty-seven days en route, each having flown forty-three hours and twenty minutes.

The second part of their job was now in sight, to organize the new western branch for their company, arrange flying contracts, establish extensive fuel caches in the Far North and start operations. All this they had to do with very little money and in the middle of the Depression.

These Standard Universal Fokkers had open pilot cockpits which were extremely cold in the winter time. Lewis Leigh readily recalls flying from Edmonton to Great Bear Lake during the winter of 1932-33 when the temperatures were −30° F to −50° F, and he was so stiff with the cold that he had to be assisted from the cockpit. A flight in an open cockpit aircraft had not been made as far north as Great Bear Lake in the winter time before.

When July, 1933, came along, Lewis Leigh was re-checked as a flying instructor at Edmonton by Flight Lieutenant Elmer

Fullerton of the R.C.A.F. After this, Lewis Leigh became Chief Instructor of the Brandon Flying Club (then known as the Brandon Aero Association).

When December of 1933 dawned, Lewis Leigh thought that flying for Canadian Airways Limited looked quite good, so he joined the company as a pilot. He was based at Fort McMurray. Most of the flying he did was carried out in the Northwest Territories and the Barren Lands.

In the summer of 1934, Lewis Leigh and Archie McMullen, another of Canadian Airways' pilots stationed at Fort McMurray, both flying Fairchild aircraft, brought out one ton of pitchblende from the claims of E. Hargreaves at Hottah Lake, near Great Bear Lake, to Waterways. A rich discovery had been made the previous winter. The ore was consigned to the refinery at Port Hope. The value of the radium and by-products derived from the ton of pitchblende was said to amount to more than $100,000, at the time. He also made many flights to Cameron Bay for Canadian Airways to the famous radium fields of Eldorado.

Lewis Leigh flew Colonel J.K. Cornwall, D.S.O., and his party to the eastern end of Great Slave Lake, where they spent the summer of 1934 prospecting. J.P. Dolan, a mining engineer, went in with Colonel Cornwall.

The discovery of gold in 1934 near Beaverlodge Lake on the north shore of Lake Athabaska caused a lot of excitement, and a number of prospectors wanted to be flown to the new area. Lewis Leigh made many flights to this area during the gold rush.

Lewis Leigh tells of the time in 1934 when he flew two trappers, known as the Bell brothers, to their trap line. After four unsuccessful attempts to take off from the river at Fort Fitzgerald, he felt something was amiss somewhere, so he had all the baggage and supplies removed and carefully weighed. The load had been weighed and checked by the agent at Fort Fitzgerald when the Bell brothers had arrived with their equipment. However, bit by bit the load had been increased to the tune of 233 pounds, all unknown to the pilot. The brothers apparently did not realize that an aircraft could be overloaded, nor that they were flirting with danger in other ways. Eventually they reached their cabin in the Northwest Territories, but not before selling some of their cherished supplies.

In the fall of 1934, Lewis Leigh and Wop May were sent to northern Manitoba by Canadian Airways to operate from there to assist in heavy freighting to the Island Lake Mine. After freeze-up they returned to Fort McMurray.

With temperatures hovering anywhere from 50° to 55° F below zero, Lewis Leigh and Air Engineer Sammy Tomlinson picked up Johnny Baker, a mining engineer and prospector from New York, and his three men at Fort McMurray. That was on December 9, 1934. It was the first time that prospectors had been flown into the Yellowknife area. They were flown to Yellowknife along with their equipment and put ashore to do prospecting and staking, something rather unusual in the winter. They were to be picked up in two or three weeks' time. When Lewis Leigh and Sammy Tomlinson returned to pick them up on January 4, 1935, they each had one side of their face frozen while helping to get camp supplies out of the bush and into the aircraft.

Flying Fairchild aircraft CF-ATZ, Lewis Leigh made the first flight of the season into the Northwest Territories carrying mail. He arrived at Fort Fitzgerald on May 20, 1935, and then flew north to Fort Resolution. The next day he flew Howard Price and four other trappers who were on their way out of the Barren Lands to Edmonton.

During heavy floods in the month of July, 1935, the roadbed of the Northern Alberta Railway's lines to Peace River and Waterways was washed out. Northerners heading for northern British Columbia, the Peace River country, Lake Athabaska, Great Bear Lake, or points down the Mackenzie had to fly directly from Edmonton by air, or have their freight and express shipped by air from there. Lewis Leigh made the first trip with overdue mail to the flood-isolated district of Grande Prairie. With him went Post Office Inspector T.J. Reilly of Edmonton. Several other flights were made to the Peace River area carrying passengers and freight too, by Matt Berry and other pilots.

Lewis Leigh was required to make an emergency flight to Lake Athabaska, taking with him Sergeant Vernon of the R.C.M.P. John Harms, a trapper at Singed Dog Island on the north shore of Lake Athabaska, shot and killed his partner in a quarrel and shot at other trapper families in the area. Lewis Leigh and the sergeant were to bring out Harms, who was considered to be a "mad" trapper. So, in December, 1935, they took him quietly, fortunately, and flew him outside where he was later hanged. For this, Lewis Leigh received a letter of commendation from Major-General Sir J.H. MacBrien, the Commissioner of the R.C.M.P.

Canadian Airways sent Lewis Leigh to the Boeing School of Aeronautics, Oakland, California, for a special course in air line instrument flying during the first three months of 1936. Here he flew Boeing 40B2's and Boeing 203's. While in Oakland, Lewis Leigh became acquainted with Phil Johnson, who was later to be Trans-Canada Air Lines' Vice-President, and H.T. "Slim" Lewis, who was also to join Trans-Canada Air Lines. When Lewis Leigh returned in April, he commenced instructing pilots of Canadian Airways in modern, banked turn instrument flying, and was chief instructor of the school in Winnipeg. He started with a class of five.

Then Lewis Leigh received Transport

Three aircraft lined up beside the hangar at Edmonton Airport in the early thirties. G-CAHJ, the Fokker Universal in the foreground, was bought by the Department of Marine and Fisheries for use in the Hudson Strait Expedition in 1927, along with G-CAHE. G-CAHJ was bought by Explorers Air Transport Ltd. of Sydney, N.S., in June, 1932. This was the aircraft flown by Z. Lewis Leigh from Sydney to Great Bear Lake. G-CAHJ, along with G-CAHE, were sold to B. Phillips of Edmonton late in 1933 and were operated in B.C. Then in December, 1938, they were sold to Fleet Aircraft of Canada and finally to Peace River Airways, in July, 1938.
Photo by William Kensit, Edmonton.

Certificate No. 24, dated May 7, 1936. Also, he was the first pilot in Canada to have a United States' airline instrument rating — and was, in fact, the only person in Canada with one at the time.

In addition to the instruction in instrument flying which Lewis Leigh had given in Winnipeg, he later spent some two months instructing the company's pilots in Vancouver. In the fall he left for Prince Edward Island and Montreal, piloting the company's Laird training 'plane, to do similar work. During the first year, some 24 pilots received instruction in instrument and night flying, costing the company about $20,000. Twenty-two of these received their transport pilots' licences. Many of them later held senior positions with Canadian Pacific Air Lines and Trans-Canada Air Lines.

During the winter of 1936-37, Lewis Leigh made flights for Canadian Airways from Winnipeg to Red Lake in Lockheed Electra 10A, CF-BAF, on skis. The Lockheed Electra was a twin-engined aircraft, the first modern airliner to be flown into Canada's mining fields. So, on February 18, 1937, a new era dawned in the history of air transport when this airliner invaded the bush areas. Lewis Leigh and Herbert Hollick-Kenyon were the two pilots on this run. They flew passengers, mail, freight, most anything really. Incidentally, it was this aircraft and CF-AZY, another Lockheed Electra, which Trans-Canada Air Lines used on the inaugural operation of their first route between Vancouver and Seattle on September 1, 1937. These two aircraft had been in use on this route by Canadian Airways and were merely taken over by Trans-Canada Air Lines, along

with the equipment and staff, including pilots Billy Wells and Maurice McGregor, and co-pilot Gordon Haslett, who had just returned from a regular run for Canadian Airways the day before. Overnight the painters got busy on the aircraft and painted out the words "Canadian Airways" and inserted "Trans-Canada Air Lines."

When Trans-Canada Air Lines was formed on April 10, 1937, Lewis Leigh was the first pilot to be taken on strength by the company. That was in August, 1937, at Winnipeg. However, Donald R. MacLaren, Assistant to the Vice-President, who joined the company in the latter part of April, 1937, was the first person to be taken on strength. Philip Johnson was appointed Vice-President of Operations in June, 1937, and personally chose Lewis Leigh as senior pilot, and asked him to start the company's flying operations. Besides, he was the only person in Canada with the required experience. Mr. Johnson was familiar with Lewis Leigh's qualifications for this position, having met him in Oakland the previous year. The company's centre for the training of personnel was to be in Winnipeg. H.T. Lewis was technical adviser for flying, and Lewis Leigh and Bill Straith were pilot-instructors.

This school for the training of pilots in

the use of instrument flying, or on-the-beam flying, was under the direction of H.T. Lewis. A link trainer was also set up at Winnipeg for the preliminary training of pilots. The training and knowledge which Lewis Leigh, as pilot and instructor, imparted to the newly appointed aircraft captains contributed in no small way to the outstanding safety record which the company enjoyed.

Lewis Leigh's first flight with Trans-Canada Air Lines in August, 1937, was in the Department of Transport's Lockheed 12, CF-CCT, piloted by J.H. "Tuddy" Tudhope. J.R. "Ross" Robertson of the Civil Aviation Division and A.K. Bailey of the Radio Division from the Department of Transport also went along. First they flew and then drove over the western section of Canada, primarily to determine the location of the radio ranges to give proper instrument approaches to the field, as well as to take a look at the aerodromes which had been recently constructed. This survey took most of the month of August, 1937.

During May, 1938, pilot Lewis Leigh with co-pilot Lindy Rood, and pilot H.T. "Slim" Lewis with co-pilot Maurice McGregor, went to Burbank, California, to fly back Trans-Canada Air Lines' first two Lockheed 14's to Winnipeg.

Lewis Leigh made many flights during

Lewis Leigh of Canadian Airways, in CF-ATZ, making the first trip to Grande Prairie, with Post Office Inspector T. J. Reilly of Edmonton, during the July, 1935, floods. Much overdue mail was carried.

Photo courtesy of G/Capt. Z. L. Leigh.

1938 for training purposes carrying ordinary mail and non-paying government passengers. As senior captain, he flew the first official paying passenger flight from Winnipeg to Vancouver between April 2 and 4, 1939. Gil MacLaren was co-pilot on this flight. Frank Young flew the flight east from Winnipeg to Montreal at this same time. Lewis Leigh also made a number of prior survey and training flights from Winnipeg to Montreal.

When World War II came along, Lewis Leigh joined the R.C.A.F. early in 1940 as a Flying Officer. He was promoted to Flight Lieutenant and carried out anti-submarine flying operations on both east and west coasts. He was a pilot in No. 5 (B.R.) Squadron and then he became a Flight Commander in No. 11 Bomber Squadron, Dartmouth, Nova Scotia. In 1941 he was posted to Patricia Bay, British Columbia, as Flight Commander and later Commanding Officer of No. 13 Squadron.

While Lewis Leigh, now a Wing Commander, was at R.C.A.F. Headquarters in Ottawa in 1942, he was responsible for organizing the Air Transport Services for the R.C.A.F. He became Director of Air Transport Command with the R.C.A.F. in 1943 with operations in all overseas and domestic theatres of war, and was the executive and operational leader of this undertaking.

As the overall commander of all the squadrons, it was his job to give them their assignments; ensure that they were carried out; plan the creation of any new units and allocate the distribution of aircraft and personnel. Often he left his desk in Ottawa and flew to visit the various squadrons to see how they were doing. Often, too, he flew with them in the course of their duties to their various areas to see the jobs they were doing to keep his finger on the very pulse of things. So it was only natural, therefore, that so much initiative, interest, ability and just plain hard work would carry him

to the top in transport operations; and much of the credit for their success should be attributed to him. It was during these periods, too, that he was associated either directly as senior pilot or in an executive capacity with many important transport flights carried out by the R.C.A.F.

It was to meet the immediate need of transporting personnel and freight for the construction of Goose Bay that No. 164 Transport Squadron was born. So urgent was the need that the official order constituting the squadron was not issued from Air Force Headquarters until nine days after its crews had started operations. The Home War Target Programme for 1942-43, which had been approved by the War Cabinet, had made provision for such a unit, and No. 164 (T) Squadron was to form at Moncton, New Brunswick, "effective forthwith." It was to be under the control of Lewis Leigh's office at Air Force Headquarters for operations and under the Air Officer Commanding Eastern Air Command for all other purposes.

No. 168 Heavy Transport Squadron began operations in December, 1943, on the Ottawa-Prestwick-Gibraltar-Cairo route. The first two Flying Fortress crews included Wing Commander Bruce Middleton, Flight Lieutenant Smith and Flight Lieutenant Niles, all 164 Squadron alumni. Wing Commander Leigh, Director of Air Transport Command, made the inaugural flight with Wing Commander Bruce Middleton.

When the R.C.A.F. was given the commitment of establishing an air mail service for the Canadian Armed Forces overseas, Wing Commander Leigh shouldered the heaviest responsibility. The only aircraft equipment available for this task consisted of old B.17 heavy bombers which required a considerable amount of modification to make them suitable for transport work. In a month's time, the over-all organization was completed by Wing Commander Leigh,

and the first group of personnel was trained by Wing Commander Bruce Middleton for the first crossing to be made in December, 1943.

It was intended to commence operation of the squadron's regular overseas mail service on December 14, 1943, but, due to aircraft unserviceability, Fortress 9204 did not take off until 14:22 hours the next day, December 15, on the first trip. It was loaded with 189 bags of mail, weighing 5,502 pounds. The crew for this inaugural flight was captained by Wing Commander Bruce Middleton with Squadron Leader B.G. Smith as co-pilot; and Wing Commander Leigh as the relief one.

Fortress 9204 was followed by a second Fortress, 9203, at 08:35 hours on December 16, piloted by Squadron Leader Ron Knowles. Both aircraft put down at Dorval for checking before starting on the overseas run. Leaving Dorval on the 17th, the two aircraft landed at Gander where fuel line trouble in one of the Fortresses delayed them until the morning of the 20th. They departed from Gander shortly after 05:00 hours that morning and completed the transatlantic flight in nine hours. No. 9204 with Middleton and Leigh landed at St. Angelo in Northern Ireland. However, they almost had to ditch in the Atlantic due to failure of the fuel lines from the long-range tanks which were installed in the outer sections of the wings. Fortunately, they managed to extend their flight to a forced landing at St. Angelo on the west coast of Ireland. The second Fortress, piloted by Squadron Leader Ron Knowles, carried on to the scheduled destination of Prestwick. The next day, Middleton and Leigh continued on to Prestwick, where they were met by Colonel Ted Underwood of the Canadian Post Office, who was in charge of Canadian mail overseas.

They transferred to Fortress 9203, leaving 9204 to be repaired, and left Prestwick on December 25 to continue

Just before the departure of the crew of Fortress 9204 from Rockcliffe Airport on December 15, 1943, on the inaugural "Mailcan" flight to Prestwick. The flight from No. 168 Squadron was captained by W/Cdr. Bruce Middleton with W/Cdr. Lewis Leigh as one of the co-pilots. Those present for the take-off flight were from left to right: G/Capt. James A. Sharpe, A/V/M. K. G. Nairn, P. T. Coolican, A/M. R. Leckie, W/Cdr. D. D. Findlay (Commanding Officer of the Mail Squadron's Home Station), W/Cdr. Bruce Middleton, Air Minister C. G. Power, and W/Cdr. Lewis Leigh.
Photo courtesy of the R.C.A.F.

their assignment of carrying the mail to the service men overseas, surveying the entire route through North Africa, Egypt and Italy, getting the service in operation. Staging through Rabat Sale, Algiers, Tunis, Catania, Foggia, Naples and Tripoli, they arrived at Cairo on January 3, 1944. The return flight to Prestwick was made between January 6 and 11, with stops en route to pick up mail from service men in Malta, Italy, Sicily and North Africa.

The first return flight to Canada was made by another Fortress which left Rockcliffe on December 22, 1943, with 5,493 pounds of mail, and returned to base on January 11, 1944, completing the round trip as far east as Cairo in 81:45 hours' flying time. An estimated 1,400,000 letters were carried on the flight.

On January 1, 1944, in the New Year's Honours List, Lewis Leigh was awarded the Order of the British Empire for his work in establishing overseas services. Also, it was as a direct result of his outstanding work in organizing these services that he was promoted to the rank of Group Captain early in 1944.

Lewis Leigh, now a Group Captain, and Flight Lieutenant Bill Lavery returned to Rockcliffe on February 8, 1944, with a

load of 257 bags (6,467 pounds) of mail, again in Fortress 9204 which had undergone repairs in the United Kingdom. The fuel trouble showed up again, but they made Goose Bay from Iceland by the skin of their teeth.

Group Captain Leigh was appointed R.C.A.F. adviser to the Canadian member of the Provisional International Civil Aviation Organization in 1945. In this position, his advice had on many occasions been invaluable in the deliberations of that committee.

Then No. 9 Group, replacing the old Directorate of Air Transport Command, came into existence on February 5, 1945, at Rockcliffe Airport under the command of Group Captain Lewis Leigh.

As Officer Commanding the R.C.A.F.'s No. 9 Transport Group in 1945, it was Group Captain Leigh's duty to give executive direction to the transportation of the R.C.A.F. Air Transport Service from a war-time to a peace-time basis. The large war-time Air Transport Command was to be reduced to the

status of a Group, which meant a reduction of about two-thirds, and it was necessary to make the new No. 9 Group as efficient as possible for its size. This he accomplished smoothly and efficiently. On June 1, 1945, Air Commodore J.L. Plant, O.B.E., A.F.C., succeeded him in command. On April 1, 1948, the No. 9 (T) Group again became the Air Transport Command, under the Air Officer Commanding, Air Commodore Larry E. Wray, O.B.E., A.F.C.

When Field Marshal Montgomery visited Canada and the United States in 1946, Lewis Leigh was in command of the air tour. Instructions for the air tour included arriving and departing at each point on the split second, regardless of the weather. This was accomplished, at times with difficulty due to adverse weather, at every point on the tour except at West Point, New York, where they were two and one-half minutes late! On that particular day, the weather was beastly.

Then around the latter part of 1946

Lewis Leigh was appointed Commanding Officer of the R.C.A.F. Station at Goose Bay, Labrador, an important western terminal of the North Atlantic air transport route. While there, he carried out a number of search and rescue operations on a minor scale.

Then in the spring of 1947 the Honourable Brooke Claxton, Minister of National Defence, announced that Group Captain Lewis Leigh had won the Trans-Canada Trophy for the year 1946 "in recognition of continuous outstanding performance in his duties as an officer and pilot of the R.C.A.F., coupled with a record of twenty years of exceptional achievement in both civil and military aviation."

The official presentation of the trophy took place at 16:30 hours on June 14, 1947, at the R.C.A.F. Station, Rockcliffe, and was made by Mr. Brooke Claxton, Minister of National Defence. This special occasion was a part of the ceremonies for the first Air Force Day.

Group Captain Lewis Leigh was posted to Vancouver, from Goose Bay Airport, Labrador, in March, 1948, as Group Commander of No. 12 Group of the R.C.A.F.

During the months of May and June, 1948, the Fraser River overflowed its

---

The Committee of Award for the year 1946 consisted of the following members:

Air Commodore J.G. Kerr, C.B.E., A.F.C., Royal Canadian Air Force, Department of National Defence, Ottawa.

A.D. McLean, O.B.E., Controller of Civil Aviation, Department of Transport, Ottawa.

Wing Commander G.A. McKenna, D.F.C., Royal Canadian Air Force, Department of National Defence, Ottawa.

D.L. Buchanan, D.F.C., Secretary-Treasurer of the Royal Canadian Flying Clubs Association, Ottawa.

---

banks covering thousands of square miles and causing heavy damage. A committee was appointed by the Premier of British Columbia to take charge of the disaster. The three heads of the Services in British Columbia, of which Group Captain Leigh was the Senior R.C.A.F. Officer, as well as certain local officials, were on the committee. Lewis Leigh's job was to control flying of all kinds, including the dropping of sandbags from the air and moving people to places where they were required. Large numbers of sandbags were dropped at danger points for the ground crews to build dykes. This job was known as Operation Overflow.

While Group Commander of No. 12, Lewis Leigh was also Searchmaster of Operation Attaché, conducting a search and rescue operation for a missing United States Embassy aircraft near The Pas, Manitoba. It was towards the end of the 1948 season when some thirty-five American and Canadian aircraft took part in a widespread search for the crew of a United States Navy Beechcraft which disappeared on a flight from Churchill to The Pas on September 12. It was the most extensive aerial search carried out in Canada up to that time. A Lancaster of No. 12 Group, piloted by Flying Officer René Lemieux, finally spotted the aircraft and crew down in the wilderness of northern Saskatchewan. Then a Canso from No. 413 Squadron, captained by Flight Lieutenant R.V. Virr, took over the rescue from there. They landed on a small lake nearby and the next day flew the men back to The Pas. "Thanks to God and the R.C.A.F.," was their heart-felt remark at the end of their thirteen-day nightmare. The men included the United States Naval Attaché in Ottawa, the Royal Navy adviser to the United Kingdom High Commissioner in Ottawa, two United States' Navy personnel and one United States' soldier. For Group Captain Lewis Leigh's role in this search operation, he was awarded the United States Legion of Merit — Degree

of Officer in 1949. The announcement of the award was made on February 25, 1949. Air Commodore Martin Costello, Flying Officer René Lemieux and Flight Lieutenant R.V. Virr were the other R.C.A.F. Officers likewise decorated. The investiture took place in the home of the United States Ambassador, Laurence A. Steinhardt, on March 18, 1949, when all four were decorated by the Ambassador. (Not long after this Ambassador Steinhardt was killed in an aircraft crash just outside of Ottawa.) The citation of the award reads:

"For exceptionally meritorious conduct in the performance of outstanding services to the Government of the United States as Commanding Officer of the Search and Rescue Group at The Pas, Manitoba, from the 12th of September to the 25th of September, 1948. Through his keen judgment and insight into the tremendous problems at hand, Group Captain Leigh was able to plan, co-ordinate and personally direct the search carried out by thirty-five Canadian and United States' aircraft for the personnel lost in a United States Navy Beechcraft on the 12th of September, 1948. Constant and untiring in his efforts throughout the twelve-day search in the wilds of Manitoba and Saskatchewan, Group Captain Leigh by his skill and devotion to duty was instrumental in bringing to a successful termination the largest and one of the most difficult searches ever conducted in Canada and in saving the lives of four United States and one British personnel. This conduct reflects great credit on Group Captain Leigh and the Royal Canadian Air Force."

Group Captain Leigh relinquished his Command of No. 12 Group at Vancouver on September 1, 1949, to attend the National Defence College at Kingston, Ontario. Upon the completion of this course the following year, he returned to Ottawa as Director of Air Operations, at Air Force Headquarters,

The Trans-Canada Trophy was officially presented to G/Capt. Leigh by Brooke Claxton, Minister of National Defence, on June 14, 1947, at Rockcliffe Air Station. The presentation formed part of the ceremonies for the first Air Force Day. From left to right: A/M. R. Leckie, Mr. Claxton and G/Capt. Z. L. Leigh. At this time, Leigh was Commanding Officer of the R.C.A.F. Station at Goose Bay, Labrador.
Photo courtesy of the R.C.A.F.

where he remained for eighteen months.

In 1952, Leigh was appointed Chief Staff Officer, Air Transport Command.

While Group Captain Leigh was Chief Staff Officer of Air Transport Command at Lachine, he and Wing Commander W.H. Lewis of Montreal and Squadron Leader J.A. Anderson of Winnipeg, also with the Air Transport Command, went to England in May, 1953, in a North Star belonging to Trans-Canada Air Lines. They spent about a week checking over the performance in the air and on the ground of The de Havilland Jet Comet, which the R.C.A.F. had ordered for their 412 (T) Squadron, the R.C.A.F.'s V.I.P. Squadron.

On May 29, 1953, the first R.C.A.F. jet transport, the Comet, arrived at Ottawa Airport, flown by a crew which had been taking conversion training in England since September, 1952. At this time the Comet was the only commercial-type jet airliner in operation in North America, and the R.C.A.F. was the first Air Force in the world to have jet transports.

Group Captain Leigh was appointed Acting Air Officer Commanding the Air Transport Command at Lachine, in December, 1953, replacing Air Commodore R.C. Ripley, who was posted overseas. He remained there until September, 1954. It was during the period from 1952 to September, 1954, while Leigh was with the Air Transport Command, first as Chief Staff Officer and later as Acting Air Officer Commanding, that they operated the Korean airlift to carry supplies and personnel from Montreal to Korea and return. Leigh personally spent a period in Korea and Japan during that time to see how well the operation was going and also to gain

some knowledge of the United States' air operations. During this period, the record of work was high, which is apparent from the following figures: 34,000 hours were flown, 6,000,000 miles were covered, 600 round trips were made across the Pacific carrying 15,000 personnel and 7,000,000 pounds of freight and mail, all without loss or a serious mishap of any kind.

In addition, during this same period, the Air Transport Command operated into and resupplied the far northern weather stations in Canada, from Resolute Bay on Cornwallis Island to the most northerly Alert Bay on Ellesmere Island. The amount of freight and personnel carried on this job was huge, also. Lewis Leigh also went into these bases a number of times. The command flew North Stars, Dakotas, C-119's, light Beechcraft Expediters, and other types.

When Lewis Leigh left Lachine in September, 1954, the command was taken over by Air Commodore H.M. Carscallen. In 1959, headquarters for the Air Transport Command was moved to Trenton, Ontario. A new R.C.A.F. overseas terminal for the Air Transport Command at Trenton was opened in January, 1960.

Leigh was then transferred to Toronto as Group Commander of the No. 2 Group in September, 1954.

Group Captain Lewis Leigh, O.B.E., E.D., retired from the Royal Canadian Air Force in February, 1957. Then, that same year, he accepted the position of Director of Operations for the Canadian International Air Show at the Canadian National Exhibition in Toronto, under the chairmanship of Frank I. Young, and directed the air show operations from 1957 to 1966.

Today, Group Captain and Mrs. Leigh live in Grimsby, Ontario, where they have a hobby fruit farm in one of Canada's delightful places. In addition to his O.B.E., E.D., United States Legion of Merit and the Trans-Canada Trophy, he is a member of Canada's Aviation Hall of Fame, as well as a director. He is a Companion of the Order of Icarus (Hall of Fame), a Companion of the Order of Flight (City of Edmonton), a member of the Brotherhood of the Silver Wings (Government of the Northwest Territories), a member of the Order of Polaris (Government of the Yukon Territory) and he holds the Veterans Cross (France).

Lewis Leigh is quick of mind, knows what he wants to do — and does it. As a pilot, he was serious minded. Yet when he wrinkles his nose before he speaks you can expect a humorous remark, or even a joke. He wore the cloak of responsibility well.

The work which Group Captain Leigh did while in the service of the R.C.A.F. in the organization of air transport services and in the establishment of an air mail service for the Canadian Armed Forces overseas during World War II was of infinite value to Canada and her people. Then when peace time came again, he ably put in motion the transition of the R.C.A.F. air transport services from a war-time basis to a peace-time basis, completing this task in his own effective way. The experience which this early bush pilot gleaned from his pioneering days of flying in Canada helped to serve him well, and to give him the assurance and courage he required when he needed it most for his country.

1947

Bernard A. "Barney" Rawson

Citation: in recognition of his outstanding contribution to advancement in the field of aviation, backed by an excellent record of achievement during a 22-year period of association with aviation development in general

Captain Bernard A. "Barney" Rawson, while Director of Flight Development, Trans-Canada Air Lines, Winnipeg, was awarded the Trans-Canada Trophy for 1947, for meritorious service in the advancement of aviation in Canada, "in recognition of his outstanding contribution to advancement in the field of aviation, backed by an excellent record of achievement during a 22-year period of association with aviation development in general." The announcement of the award was made on May 10, 1948, by the Honourable Brooke Claxton, Minister of National Defence.

Captain Rawson had been widely known in aviation circles for many years, both for his ability as a pilot and his technical contributions to safe and efficient flight operations.

His contributions to aviation in Canada during 1947 more than upheld his previous record, and particular reference was made to his "excellent liaison" with various organizations in Canada and the United States and the preparatory groundwork he performed prior to the inauguration of the Great Lakes Airway. This airway resulted in a vastly improved air service for Canadians. The many details which received his personal attention with respect to the technical flight aspects, which involved the co-ordination of American and Canadian federal authorities, were directly attributable to his abilities as an organizer and co-ordinator, the minister said.

Bernard Anderson "Barney" Rawson was born on October 27, 1907, at Fort William, Ontario, where he received his early education, and then went on to attend the University of Toronto.

He first learned to fly at the Dungan School of Aviation in Cleveland, Ohio, in 1927, when he was twenty years of age, and graduated as a commercial pilot. Then, like many other pilots of this period, he started off barnstorming and doing some charter flying. At one time he was chief instructor of the Cleveland School of Aeronautics, and then chief pilot for a small air line operating between Detroit and Sault Ste. Marie, Michigan. For two years, Barney Rawson flew open cockpit biplanes for the United States Department of Commerce Weather Bureau taking daily upper air observations. Without oxygen or cockpit heat, he climbed regularly to the cold and rarefied regions above 18,000 feet each morning on these pioneering flights. The information collected was used to assist the national weather services in compiling a mass air analysis permitting daily and extended weather forecasting.

During his colourful barnstorming career, Barney Rawson encountered emergencies almost as a daily routine. An example of the type of situation which frequently arose to test his skill and judgment was an engine failure at night over Florida. He was flying a single-engine Stearman biplane, with his parachute jumper in the front cockpit, when the engine stopped suddenly. Aided by the dim light of the moon, Barney Rawson was able to execute a remarkably successful "dead-stick" landing in an orange grove. He was able to manoeuvre the fuselage between the rows of orange trees. The wings were shattered, but the fuselage was almost unscratched and the propeller was not even bent in the landing. Both occupants survived unharmed although they and their aircraft were drenched in orange juice.

On another occasion, while flying six

passengers on a charter trip in a Stinson Detroiter, Barney Rawson was suddenly confronted with the alarming fact that not only had his engine quit, but his fabric-covered aircraft was on fire. He managed to divert the flames from the wings by skilfully side-slipping and then pancaked the aircraft into a field and got all the passengers clear seconds before the gas tanks exploded and the aircraft was reduced to a heap of ashes.

As a result of the investigation into this accident, it was recommended that the rigid fuel lines, standard at that time, be replaced by flexible hose. Thus, indirectly, this accident contributed to the safety of flight.

The daily weather flights which Barney Rawson flew consistently for two years represented a very important advance in the understanding of high-altitude weather and particularly icing conditions. At that time very little was known about the high-altitude winds and Barney Rawson, then as now, an enthusiastic radio ham, equipped his aircraft with two-way radio, one of the first of its kind to have this equipment. During his weather flights he radioed reports to the ground stations and this vital information was flashed to the air lines. Indicative of the relatively primitive stage of engine-reliability at that time was the fact that during this period Barney Rawson had eighteen forced landings with dead engines in a two-year period.

When 1933 came along, Barney Rawson was successful in getting a job as a pilot with American Airlines, Inc., and covered the routes from Cleveland to New York, and from Cleveland to Memphis, flying mostly DC-2's, Curtiss-Condors, Stinson Trimotors and Stearman mail 'planes. He remained with this company for five years.

Trans-Canada Air Lines came into existence in 1937 and Barney Rawson joined the company early in 1938 as a Captain. He had some 3,981 hours of flying to his credit at the time, some of

which was on instruments. He became chief pilot in 1939, and Superintendent of the Eastern Division in 1940. During these early years, Barney Rawson played a leading role in pilot training, route development and the establishment of navigation facilities. When he became Superintendent of Flight Operations in 1942, he was responsible for the movement of all flights by Trans-Canada Air Lines; the employment and training of all pilot personnel; the establishment of flight procedures and the technique to be employed by flight crews, and the maintenance of an up-to-date operations manual for flight personnel.

Captain Rawson became Director of Flight Development in 1945. In this position he supervised and controlled the establishment of flight procedures and techniques, consistent with their advancement; the evaluation of new aircraft which could be considered for Trans-Canada Air Lines; the development of cockpit instruments and controls for new aircraft or modifications considered necessary in their aircraft; the surveying of new routes in respect to airports; navigation facilities and the maintenance of close liaison with the Department of Transport in the development of radio and visual aids for air navigation.

With this appointment, too, he was technical flight representative to the Provisional International Civil Aviation Organization for Trans-Canada Air Lines, and later a technical adviser to the Canadian representative of the Permanent Body of the International Civil Aviation Organization.

At the time of the award of the Trans-Canada Trophy, he was an adviser to the Canadian delegates on rules of the air, air traffic control, air operations and personnel licensing. Prior to 1947, he was also a member of the International Air Transport Association and played a large part towards the eventual unification and acceptance of operational flight standards and practices. Much of

his direct research and experimental flying in the early development stages of approach lighting led to international acceptance of the existing cross-bar systems.

During the 1940's the regular route which Trans-Canada Air Lines followed from Toronto to Winnipeg was north of the Great Lakes through Kapuskasing and Armstrong. It seemed that trans-continental flight time could be reduced considerably by a more direct route from Toronto, which would cross over the Great Lakes and go through Sault Ste. Marie and the Lakehead (Fort William-Port Arthur) to Winnipeg. As Trans-Canada Air Lines was flying DC-3 aircraft at the time, this meant that additional airports would be required at approximately 100-mile intervals, as well as the installation of complementary lighting and navigation aids.

With a view to seeing what could be done about having a route over the Great Lakes, W. F. "Bill" English, Vice-President of Trans-Canada Air Lines called to see A. D. "Dan" McLean, Controller of Civil Aviation, Department of Transport, Ottawa, on May 2, 1946, to tell him about the company's proposal. The idea, itself, for this short-cut airway was conceived by Barney Rawson. With the support of Bill English, Barney Rawson was provided with an aircraft to demonstrate the superiority of the short-cut airway in terms of weather and operational merit. On the basis of the factual evidence he was able to compile, T.C.A. decided to see what could be done to bring Barney Rawson's idea to life.

As this proposed airway fell within Trans-Canada Air Lines' central region's headquarters at Toronto, the company assigned to Captain Frank Young, its Operations Manager, Toronto, the task of being Canada's representative for Trans-Canada Air Lines to assist in any negotiating arrangements. As his technical assistant, Frank Young chose

Some winners of the Trans-Canada Trophy and James Mollison and A/Cdr. John Fauquier who attended the official presentation of the trophy to Barney Rawson at the Fort Garry Hotel, Winnipeg, on October 2, 1948. Barney Rawson (extreme left) is being congratulated by James Mollison. First row behind Mr. Mollison: Punch Dickins, J. A. Wilson, Romeo Vachon, Pat Reid, Moss Burbidge and Murton Seymour. Second row: A/Cdr. John Fauquier, D.S.O. with two Bars, D.F.C., G/Capt. Lewis Leigh, Dan McLean, Doc Oaks, George Phillips, Tommy Siers and Wop May.

Photo by Gordon Roberts of The Winnipeg Tribune.

Barney Rawson, Director of Flight Development for T.C.A. It was partly as a result of Barney Rawson's splendid work and the "excellent liaison" work with the various agencies with which he had to deal in the establishment of this route that he was awarded the Trans-Canada Trophy for 1947.

Trans-Canada Air Lines originally made a proposal to fly a direct route from Toronto to Winnipeg, through Sault Ste. Marie and Fort William. However, the Department of Transport required that, with the DC-3 equipment the company was using, emergency airfields must be located at 100-mile intervals over the route they would be flying. In Canada, the best route between Sault Ste. Marie and Fort William, which would even come close to meeting this requirement, was on Caribou Island. Then, when a survey was made of this island, the construction of an aerodrome on it was found to be impractical. Also, the distance from Caribou Island to the Lakehead was 180 miles, and it was not possible to build another airport anywhere on the route as it crossed over a lake. This was the prelude to approaching T. P. Wright, Administrator of the Civil Aeronautics Administration, Washington, D.C., concerning the establishment of a route on the south side of Lake Superior in United States' territory.

It was on May 6, 1946, that the first general meeting of a route for a Great Lakes Airway took place in the office of Dan McLean, Controller of Civil Aviation, to discuss the possibility of a shorter route for Trans-Canada Air Lines to follow from Toronto to Winnipeg, in an effort to eliminate the necessity of spending extra time flying the circuitous route north of the Great Lakes through Kapuskasing and Armstrong. So, in view of the high cost to develop a northern route passing through Caribou Island, and the fact that the Atikokan site was not available for development, a southern

route over United States' territory was being pondered.

In attendance at this meeting were three representatives of Trans-Canada Air Lines, Barney Rawson, Paul Davoud and C. Proudfoot; and a number from the Department of Transport, including G. C. W. Browne, Acting Controller of Radio, and F. Gordon Nixon, Sr. Radio Engineer; Major Robert Dodds, Superintendent of Airways and J. R. Robertson, Chief Inspector of Airways; H. Ainsworth, Illuminating Engineer; F. C. Jewett, Gordon Scott and Theo Ward, Engineers with the Civil Aviation Division. O. Lee Britney, Radio Engineer, acted as secretary of the meeting.

Barney Rawson explained to the committee that he had made an aerial survey of the alternative route between Sault Ste. Marie and Fort William, crossing United States territory on the south shore of Lake Superior, on May 3, 1946, using a T.C.A. Lockheed aircraft. He was accompanied by other members of Trans-Canada Air Lines, as well as members of the Department of Transport, who were J. R. "Robbie" Robertson, Chief Inspector of Airways; Sam Foley, District Inspector of Southern Airways, Hamilton; and George Smith, District Airway Engineer, Hamilton. The safest and most practical route to be followed was from the Lakehead across the relatively narrow arm of Lake Superior to the Keweenaw Peninsula, Michigan, and thence directly to Kinross Field, Sault Ste. Marie, Michigan. Besides, the southern route over United States territory was across relatively flat land, compared with the rocky topography on the Canadian side, so naturally Trans-Canada Air Lines favoured this southern route through northern Michigan as being more suitable.

The Michigan State Department of Aeronautics was to undertake the survey and supervise the development of the landing fields and radio ranges at Houghton and Grand Marais, Michigan,

on behalf of Canada.

The Department of Transport also built intermediate aerodromes between Sault Ste. Marie and Toronto at Gore Bay on Manitoulin Island and at Wiarton, near Owen Sound; while west of Fort William the aerodrome at Graham was enlarged. Also, radio range facilities were established at these three places.

As the installation of the facilities along the southern route at Houghton, Grand Marais, Kinross, Gore Bay and Wiarton had progressed so well by the time June, 1947, had arrived, an inspection of the route took place on June 1 and 2. The inspection was carried out in a T.C.A. Lockheed Lodestar, captained by Barney Rawson. On this inspection trip were A. B. Parrott, third regional officer, Civil Aeronautics Administration, Chicago; Colonel G. R. Richardson; Barney Rawson and Frank Young from T.C.A.; and Dan McLean, Gordon McDowell, Sam Foley and George Smith from the D.O.T.

So, by the time July 1, 1947, had dawned, the installation of the facilities at Houghton and Grand Marais, including the radio ranges, had reached the stage where the direct route from Toronto through Sault Ste. Marie and the Lakehead to Winnipeg could be placed in operation, and Trans-Canada Air Lines made their inaugural flight over the Great Lakes Airway, providing the cities along the Canadian route with their first main line air service. T.C.A. was granted emergency landing rights at Kinross Airport, Sault Ste. Marie, Michigan, as a point of call for passengers and traffic originating from and travelling to Sault Ste. Marie, Ontario.

An impressive international ceremony took place on September 11, 1948, when Houghton County Memorial Airport, Michigan, was dedicated as a memorial to those who served their country. Part of the afternoon ceremony included the unveiling of a plaque, on which the inscription gave recognition to the contribution made by the Canadian Government to the development of the airport.

In attendance on this historic occasion were Governor Kim Sigler of Michigan; United States Senator Homer Ferguson of Michigan; Major General Emmett O'Connell, air member of the Permanent Joint Board on Defence for the United States and Canada; General Ralph Royce of the U.S.A.A.F.; Colonel W.T. Hudnell, U.S.A.F., Commanding General of Selfridge Field; Carl F. Winkler, county highway engineer, Hancock, Michigan; Colonel Floyd Evans; Colonel G.R. Richardson; M.J. VandeBunte of the Michigan Department of Aeronautics, Lansing; and many others. Those from Canada included: Bill English, and Captains Frank Young and Barney Rawson from T.C.A.; and Dan McLean, Harold J. Connolly, J.R. Robertson, George Smith and Gordon McDowell from the Department of Transport.

Captain Herbert W. Seagrim, T.C.A.'s Director of Flight Operations (later Vice-President of Operations) and Captain Barney Rawson made a non-stop flight in a Mark II North Star from Vancouver to Montreal in 1947 in the record time of 6 hours and 52 minutes. They flew at an average speed of 342 m.p.h. at an altitude of 21,000 feet. Captains Seagrim and Rawson were congratulated by the Right Honourable C.D. Howe on the termination of the flight at Montreal. Passengers on the flight were Mr. Howe, H.J. Symington, President of T.C.A., Walter Thompson, Director of Public Relations for the C.N.R. and the stewardess, Phyllis Harding.

An announcement was made in May, 1948, by the Honourable Brooke Claxton, Minister of National Defence, that Captain Barney Rawson was awarded the Trans-Canada Trophy in recognition of his outstanding contribution to advancement in the field of aviation, backed by an excellent record of achievement during a 22-year period of

association with aviation development in general.

The official presentation of the trophy took place in Winnipeg on October 2, 1948, at six o'clock at the Fort Garry Hotel, at the suggestion of W.F. "Bill" English, and was made by Air Vice-Marshal K.M. Guthrie, C.B., C.B.E., on behalf of the Minister of National Defence.

On the occasion of the presentation of the trophy to Barney Rawson in Winnipeg, all former winners were invited to be present, which is the usual custom. The following attended: Doc Oaks, 1927; Punch Dickins, 1928; Wop May, 1929; George Phillips, 1931; Moss Burbidge, 1932; Romeo Vachon, 1937; Bill English (representing Trans-Canada Air Lines), 1938; Murton Seymour, 1939; Tommy Siers, 1940; Dan McLean, 1941; Pat Reid, 1942-43; J.A. Wilson, 1944; and Group Captain Lewis Leigh, 1946.

Barney Rawson received his United States Commercial Pilot's License in 1928; and Canadian Transport Pilot's Certificate No. 119, dated July 6, 1938, which was superseded by his Airline Transport Licence No. AT-527, dated April 22, 1953.

When Trans-Canada Air Lines moved their main offices from Winnipeg to

---

The Committee of Award for the year 1947 consisted of the following members:

Air Commodore J.G. Kerr, C.B.E., A.F.C., Royal Canadian Air Force, Department of National Defence, Ottawa.

A.D. McLean, O.B.E., Controller of Civil Aviation, Department of Transport, Ottawa.

Group Captain J.B. Harvey, A.F.C., Royal Canadian Air Force, Department of National Defence, Ottawa.

Gordon Henderson, representing the Royal Canadian Flying Clubs Association, Ottawa.

Montreal in October, 1949, Barney Rawson's desk went along, too.

It was at the end of April, 1953, that Barney Rawson resigned from his position with Trans-Canada Air Lines and went to work for Canadian Pacific Air Lines in Vancouver, as Director of Flight Operations. In this position he was responsible for flight operations' procedures for the company, including the selection of pilots for training and the establishment and maintenance of flight standards for overseas and domestic flying. He was also a check pilot for the company, conducting instrument flight tests.

He has flown Constellation aircraft, DC-4M2's, DC-3's, DC-6B's, Convairs, DC-2's, Lockheed 1408's-1808's, Ford Trimotors, Boeing 247's, Consolidated PBY-5A's, DC-4's, and other aircraft, over routes in Canada, the United Kingdom, the United States, the Caribbean area and South America.

Barney Rawson became a member of the Airlines Advisory Group on North Atlantic Air Traffic Co-ordination in 1957.

Three top-flight executives from Canadian Pacific Air Lines left Vancouver on March 8, 1957, to attend a nine-week pilot's technical ground course in Bristol, England. Captain Barney Rawson, Director of Flight Development; H.H. Johnstone, chief pilot, overseas lines; and his assistant W.S. Roxborough were those selected for the course. The main purpose of this course was to have these personnel qualify as instructors for the flight-training aspects of the Bristol Britannia's operations. Upon their return to Vancouver, they set up a pilot's training school on Bristol Britannias. Also they assisted in the preparation of operating manuals, visual aids and training publications for use in the school.

With the signing of a contract with the Canadian Aviation Electronics Company in January, 1957, for the manufacturing

Presentation of the Trans-Canada Trophy to Barney Rawson by A/V.M. K. M. Guthrie at the Fort Garry Hotel, Winnipeg, on October 2, 1948. Barney Rawson (left) being congratulated by A/V.M. K. M. Guthrie, C.B., C.B.E.

Photo courtesy of Barney Rawson.

of a flight simulator, Canadian Pacific Air Lines became the first Canadian air line to acquire a full flight simulator. This was an important step forward for Canada's air transport industry. At the same time, it was the first commercial simulator built in Canada, a striking comment on the achievement of Canadian Aviation Electronics in one of the newest and most intricate areas of electronic engineering.

The Canadian Aviation Electronics Company DC-6B flight simulator was installed in a special training centre at the Vancouver Airport headquarters of Canadian Pacific Air Lines and provided a continuous training programme for all flight crews of the company, and a degree of proficiency for pilots unattainable heretofore.

This flight simulator, employing precision analogue computer techniques, accurately reproduced the characteristics of the DC 6B in flight and on the ground of its power plant, fuel, electrical and radio systems, its instruments and propellers. It also realistically reproduced the appropriate sounds for the various aircraft manoeuvres. This project was instigated and developed to its completion by Barney Rawson.

At the time that the DC-6B simulator was taking shape, Barney Rawson was also able to gain approval from Canadian Pacific Air Lines for the construction of a Bristol Britannia simulator. Redifone Limited of London, England, was chosen to manufacture this simulator. It provided for the necessary conversion and refresher training for pilots assigned to Canadian Pacific Air Lines' Bristol Britannia fleet. The simulator was installed alongside the DC-6B simulator in an air-conditioned, temperature-controlled, sound-proofed building at Vancouver International Airport. Captain H. Hollick-Kenyon was Director of the department, with Captain W.H. Rolfe as Assistant Director. The manuals for this ground training course for pilots were written by Canadian Pacific Air Lines, who also developed the visual aids. Technical instructors for this course on the Britannia's giant turboprops were: C.W. Cole, electric systems; C.V. Colson, power plant; L.T. Coddington, airframes; and R. Greening, electronics.

In December, 1958, Barney Rawson joined Radio Corporation of America of Camden, New Jersey, as Director of Custom Aviation Products. In 1960, Radio Corporation of America named him their government service division Administrator to the National Aeronautics and Space Administration and the Federal Aeronautics Administration.

As Director of Airline Marketing for Fairchild Hiller Corporation for six years, he conducted marketing research for regional air line type aircraft for acceptable design parameters.

The sales success of de Havilland Aircraft's Twin Otter short take-off and landing aircraft with commuter air lines in the United States was due to his forcefulness as Vice-President of Miami Aviation Corporation, the American distributors.

Then, in 1973, Barney Rawson was named Aviation Director of Flood & Associates, Inc., consulting engineers, at Jacksonville, Florida. He holds this position today.

Barney Rawson was named a member of Canada's Aviation Hall of Fame in 1973; and in 1976 was elected a Companion of the Order of Icarus (Hall of Fame). He was made a member of the Order of Polaris (Government of the Yukon Territory), and a Companion of the Order of Flight (City of Edmonton). He is also a member of the Brotherhood of the Silver Wings (Government of the Northwest Territories).

During a fifty-year career as a professional pilot, Barney Rawson captained more than one-hundred types of aircraft, from the smallest trainer to giant passenger jets, logging more than 22,000 hours without injury to passengers or crew. He was the first non-military pilot in Canada to fly a jet aircraft. He, along with Frank I. Young, originated the National Air Show in 1953 which is held annually at the Canadian National Exhibition in Toronto, Ontario.

His long experience and knowledge applied in the many fields of flight development have contributed in no small measure to the efficiency and safety of the operation of both Trans-Canada Air Lines (now Air Canada) and Canadian Pacific Air Lines. Flight development techniques to cope with today's advanced airliners are of prime importance.

Barney Rawson certainly has to be categorized as "one of the most unusual characters I have ever met" — being at one and the same time one of the best aeroplane pilots with fine weather sense in North America, said Mr. Bill Bryant, Executive Vice-President of Flood & Associates. The amazing thing is that, despite this remarkable capacity, he works diligently and constantly to improve his proficiency in both areas.

Barney's sense of humour, his poise and sophistication, his obvious capability and self-assurance have been the greatest source of comfort to those who work and fly with him. None of us at Flood & Associates, Inc., can visualize how we would possibly operate without Barney, Mr. Bryant added.

1948

Ron West during World War II.
Photo courtesy of S/Ldr. Ron West.

Roland B. West

Citation: in recognition of his outstanding contribution to advancement in the field of aviation in search and rescue operations during the year 1948

Squadron Leader Roland B. West, D.F.C., A.F.C., C.D., while a Flying Officer with the R.C.A.F., employed on east coast operations with No. 103 Search and Rescue Flight, R.C.A.F. Station, Dartmouth, and later Greenwood, Nova Scotia, from the end of World War II until February, 1949, was awarded the Trans-Canada Trophy for meritorious service in the advancement of aviation in Canada "in recognition of his outstanding contribution to advancement in the field of aviation in search and rescue operations during the year 1948." The announcement of the award was made on May 12, 1949.

Roland Burgess "Ron" West was born at Medford, Nova Scotia, on January 25, 1919. Medford is a farming area just outside of the Town of Canning, and it was here that Ron grew up on his father's farm. Here, too, and at Canning, he received his education.

Ron West enlisted in the R.C.A.F. in August, 1941, and received his training as a pilot at No. 3 Initial Training School at Victoriaville, Quebec; No. 21 Elementary Flying Training School at Chatham, New Brunswick; and No. 16 Service Flying Training School at Hagersville, Ontario. Having received his wings, he was then posted to the Ground Reconnaissance School at Charlottetown, Prince Edward Island.

His war-time service included a tour of duty with the Royal Air Force's No. 111 Operational Training Unit at Nassau, Bahamas, as a student in operational training from late 1942 until the spring of 1943. He then went on an operational tour of duty with No. 116 Catalina Squadron which was operating on the east coast of Canada. He was flying with this Squadron when the war ended in 1945. During the first part of his tour

with No. 116 Squadron at Botwood, Newfoundland, he flew Catalinas on convoy escorts and anti-submarine searches, sweeps and patrols; then about the end of 1943 No. 116 Squadron converted to Cansos. Ron West and No. 116 Squadron were doing most of this flying off the water near Botwood, Newfoundland, in amphibians. Often these missions meant flying eighteen, nineteen or up to twenty-two hours at a stretch. However, in spite of these lengthy hours during his tour of operations on the east coast, Ron West, flying as second pilot, was quickly gaining experience and knowledge of flying boat operations. Like everything else, such whole-hearted application of his ability was a stepping-stone in the post-war era which proved to be invaluable to him and was mainly responsible for his success on the many hazardous and arduous rescue missions and mercy flights that he was to make in the future.

During the winter of 1943-44, they used the runways at the newly-built airport at Goose, Labrador, and the airport at Gander, Nfld., instead of the water for their Canso operations.

Ron West was with No. 116 Squadron for two years, rising from Sergeant to Flight Sergeant, and then to Warrant Officer, second class. His commission as a Pilot Officer was effective from February, 1944. Soon afterwards he became a Flying Officer. While Ron West was with No. 116 Squadron he made the first of what was to be a long series of mercy flights for which he was later to receive much recognition. He was second pilot of a Canso which went on a mercy flight from Gander to Westport, Newfoundland, on April 29, 1944, to evacuate a seriously ill patient to the hospital in Gander. Then, exactly a year

Completion of a successful mercy flight by F/O. Ron West and the crew of Canso 11033, January 4, 1947. The man at the extreme right is a doctor from Halifax, and immediately in front of him are two crew members of the aircraft, L/A/C. George Wilks, Flight Engineer, and L/A/C. Joe Couturier, Para. Rescue, respectively, from right to left.

Photo courtesy of S/Ldr. Ron West.

later, on April 29, 1945, he made another mercy flight from Sydney to Harmon Field, Stephenville, Newfoundland, to bring a badly injured airman to the hospital at Dartmouth, Nova Scotia.

In June, 1944, No. 116 Squadron moved to Sydney, Nova Scotia, and in August Ron West became Captain of his own crew.

While at Sydney the squadron equipped its Cansos with "Leigh" lights, permitting night operations to be carried out against enemy submarines. With these new lights, they flew mostly at night — a situation which continued until the end of the war. A "Leigh" light was a searchlight about three feet in diameter hanging under the starboard wing of the aircraft, which was controlled from the nose of the aircraft. This light was several million candle power and was used to light up the U-boats. The light was turned on at an altitude of 200 feet when the aircraft was about three-quarters of a mile from the target. The pilot then let the aircraft down to 50 feet above the water and when the navigator called, "target in sight", the pilot went visual and either continued the attack or pulled up — depending on what his target was. Detachments of this squadron also operated out of Seven Islands for a time. No. 116 Squadron was disbanded on June 20, 1945.

For having given such splendid and efficient service over a period of two years with No. 116 Squadron, Flying Officer West received the Distinguished Flying Cross in July, 1945.

On the cessation of hostilities in 1945, Ron West was posted to the Communications Flight at Dartmouth, Nova Scotia, and whilst with this unit performed other mercy flights along the east coast. Often he was required to land at tiny villages, or outposts, along the rugged and rough coasts of eastern Quebec, Labrador and in Arctic areas where no aircraft had previously landed.

Upon the formation of No. 103 Search

and Rescue Flight at Dartmouth, Nova Scotia, on April 1, 1947, Ron West was one of the original members of the flight and served for some time as its Operation Officer. As a Captain, he had flown approximately 2,000 hours on search and rescue work. Wing Commander Turner and Wing Commander Smith were two of the officers commanding the No. 103 Search and Rescue Flight during this time. Squadron Leader Grant Nelson and Squadron Leader Mike Dooker flew with Ron West on several trips.

In October, 1947, No. 103 Search and Rescue Flight moved to Greenwood, Nova Scotia. Just before leaving Dartmouth, Ron West made one more flight in a series of mercy flights which marked his service with that unit. From October 6 to 9, 1947, he flew a Canso under very trying conditions from Dartmouth to Ivuguvik, near Cape Wolstenholme in northern Quebec, to bring out a wounded Eskimo to the hospital at Goose Bay.

Flying Officer West's flying operations included so many outstanding examples of personal skill and initiative that it is possible to write about only a few of the one hundred or so rescue missions which he made in 1948. He showed a great human interest in every mission.

One day in early January, 1948, he flew on a mercy mission from Halifax to Harrington Harbour to bring out a seriously ill woman. During this flight, he encountered snow, fog and severe icing but Ron West overcame the elements and brought his patient safely to Goose Bay, Labrador.

While he was at Goose Bay, Ron West was detailed to fly to Mutton Bay, Quebec, to bring out another seriously ill woman. Extremely poor weather prevailed throughout the flight but, in spite of this and the very rough sea conditions existing in the confined harbour at Mutton Bay, he brought his Canso in to a safe landing, and brought the patient aboard the amphibian.

Because of such violent weather and stormy sea conditons, the Canso was badly damaged; nevertheless Ron West made a skilful take-off and delivered his patient to the hospital authorities in Halifax.

In recognition of these two outstanding search and rescue flights he was awarded the Air Force Cross in July, 1948. The citation for the decoration made particular reference to the rescue of Mrs. Alexander Munge from Mutton Bay (in January, 1948) despite heavy clouds, fog, driving snow and adverse sea conditions. The citation said that during two years on search and rescue work, Flying Officer West "displayed utmost keenness, efficiency, leadership and high devotion to duty."

By that time, Ron West had made many flights to rescue people and to perform errands of mercy for over a period of four years.

From time to time he made trips to Sable Island to rescue crews of wrecked ships or personnel from the island who were ill. Sable Island is known as "the graveyard of the Atlantic." During the years that Ron West was on the coast

Canso taking off from the R.C.A.F. Station, Dartmouth, on March 24, 1947. F/O. Ron West piloted the Canso, while Cliff Brown was co-pilot. Dave Parker was the navigator, while Vacanaugh and Short were the engineers.

Photo courtesy of R.C.A.F.

This is the crew of the Lancaster aircraft stationed at North Bay that went on a most successful "Rain-making Operation" on June 22, 1948. From left to right: F/O. Ron West, the captain, F/Lt. Blair Russell, F/O. Ed Johnson, Phil Rhynas of the Ontario Lands and Forests Branch, F/Lt. Slim Barclay and a D.O.T. meteorological forecaster.
Photo courtesy of the Ontario Department of Lands and Forests.

the odd ship was wrecked there, too. In the middle of this barren and desolate island is a "lagoon," just large enough for a Canso flying boat "to put into." When the water in this lagoon becomes very shallow during the late summer, it presents a challenge to the pilot of an amphibian, especially if he has a very heavy load. Ron West was to meet this challenge on several occasions. But the island could be useful, too. After taking off from the lagoon with a heavy load, he would find, upon arrival at home base with his aircraft, that the bottom of his aircraft was all bright and shiny from scraping over the sands of the lagoon on lonely Sable Island.

Then another time, while on a particular operation, he landed at Cartwright, Labrador — only to find that the sea was so rough that the patient could not be brought aboard the aircraft.

In addition to his search and rescue operations, Ron West was captain of an aircraft on special flying operations in the Far North during 1948. Many of his flights were to landing strips in the eastern Arctic where he acquired much knowledge in the various phases of northern flying operations. These flights, using Lancasters, went to Churchill, Coral Harbour and Frobisher. The aircraft were fitted with long-range tanks for the lengthy trips over the Arctic areas. Various scientific personnel were carried on these trips. Flights in a Canso amphibian were also made from Fort Chimo and Coral Harbour to other northern areas.

During Operation Overflow in May and June, 1948, when the Fraser River overflowed its banks in British Columbia, Ron West flew many long hours carrying sandbags and other essential materials across the Rockies into British Columbia. From Greenwood, Nova Scotia, he flew to Calgary, and was temporarily based there while flying two and three round trips a day to Vancouver. All flying at this time was done under the control of

Group Captain Lewis Leigh, including dropping sandbags from the air. Large numbers of sandbags were dropped from the air at the "right" places, and then the men on the ground put them where they were required to form dykes to hold back the floods.

Later in June, 1948, Ron West was chosen to perform the first large-scale Rain-making Operation in Canada, which turned out to be unusually successful in producing large quantities of rain over the forest fire area north of Sault Ste. Marie, Ontario.

The Rain-making Operation was rather novel as it was the first real effort made in Canada using a large Lancaster aircraft with heavy loads of dry ice to "seed" the tops of clouds at a high altitude. The purpose of this effort was, it was hoped, to put out the forest fires, which had been out of control for approximately two weeks and had burned a large area of timber when the Ontario Lands and Forests Branch called on the R.C.A.F. for assistance. As the area that Ron West and his crew were "seeding" was a long distance from North Bay, no results could be observed from the city; and their efforts caused many laughs around the town. Then one day when they were returning from the fire area on a perfectly clear day, one small cumulus cloud was seen just south of the Town of North Bay — so the "rain-makers" decided to fly over the top of this little cloud and "seed" it. As might be expected, this turned out to be a very big mistake on that particular day! Within minutes of seeding the little cloud, it turned very black and ugly looking and spread rapidly over the area for many miles — even to their own surprise. They had just landed at North Bay when very heavy drops of rain pelted against the pavement on the airport. The raindrops were bouncing like mad, and the storm turned into a heavy downpour which lasted for several hours! To top it off, this all happened on a week-end when many hundreds, or

perhaps thousands, of people were out on the lakes and beaches enjoying the pleasant sunshine. Needless to say, the skipper and crew of the R.C.A.F. Lancaster remained in hiding away from the wrath of the citizens for the duration of their stay in North Bay. Ron West was, of course, the captain of the aircraft, and Flying Officer Ed Johnson was his co-pilot. His crew were Flight Lieutenant Blair Russell, Flight Lieutenant "Slim" Barclay and Sergeant Don Short.

Ron West received special mention in 1948 when he was awarded the Trans-Canada Trophy in recognition of his outstanding contribution to advancement in the field of aviation in search and rescue operations during the year 1948.

The Minister of National Defence, the Honourable Brooke Claxton, officially presented the trophy to Flying Officer West on Air Force Day, Saturday, June 11, 1949, at three o'clock, at Rockcliffe Airport, Ottawa. The presentation of the Trans-Canada Trophy formed a part of the Air Force Day ceremonies. In making the presentation, Mr. Claxton said that Flying Officer West had developed new methods now used in search and rescue operations and told the audience that West was typical of the men who make up the Air Force of today. In reply, Ron West said that it

The Committee of Award for the year 1948 consisted of the following members:

Air Commodore J.G. Kerr, C.B.E., A.F.C., Royal Canadian Air Force, Department of National Defence, Ottawa.

A.D. McLean, O.B.E., Controller of Civil Aviation, Department of Transport, Ottawa.

Wing Commander D.E. Galloway, Royal Canadian Air Force, Department of National Defence, Ottawa.

Gordon F. Henderson, representing the Royal Canadian Flying Clubs Association, Ottawa.

Patient being brought aboard the aircraft on a mercy flight to Old Fort Bay on the Labrador Coast on the Strait of Belle Isle, December, 1948..

Photo courtesy of S/Ldr. R. B. West.

was a great privilege for him to receive the honour as a member of the R.C.A.F., but he gave great credit to his crews and to all the others who contributed to the winning of the award. "I personally believe it is to them that the honour should go," he said.

Ron West often displayed a great desire to pass on to other aircrew all the information he acquired as a result of his various flying operations. Unlike many others who are experts in their field, this patient and competent flying instructor delighted in taking along inexperienced co-pilots on such flights, in order that they might benefit from his knowledge and instruction. He was also responsible for converting many new pilots to using Lancaster, Canso and Dakota aircraft. It has been said that he felt prouder of the results of some of his former co-pilots, when they later became captains, than he did of the many well-deserved honours he received.

Ron West was transferred from No. 103 Search and Rescue Flight at the R.C.A.F. Station at Greenwood, Nova Scotia, to serve with the R.C.A.F. at their Recruiting Unit at Brandon, Manitoba, in February, 1949.

As time passed by, he rose in rank to Flight Lieutenant and, on January 1, 1953, to Squadron Leader. In July, 1953, he was transferred to the R.C.A.F. Station at Goose Bay, Labrador, as Chief Operations Officer.

He took a course as a jet pilot in 1956. In July, 1957, Ron West was transferred from Goose Bay to St. Hubert as Squadron Commander of No. 416 All-Weather Squadron, flying CF-100's. The CF-100, Canuck, was a Canadian 'plane, having been designed and manufactured by A.V. Roe, Canada, Limited, Malton, Ontario, to meet R.C.A.F. requirements. The CF-100, first powered with Rolls-Royce Avon engines, made its test flight on January 19, 1950, at Malton Airport. It was test flown by Squadron Leader W.A. "Bill" Waterton, who was formerly Chief Test Pilot for Gloster Aircraft Company in the United Kingdom. The CF-100, Mark 2, was powered with Orenda engines, and was first flown on June 20, 1951. Four months later the first all-Canadian jet interceptor was delivered to the R.C.A.F. Then during the summer of 1953, 70 Mark 3's, equipped with machine guns, were delivered to the R.C.A.F. This same year, the Mark 4's

were being turned out with the more powerful Orenda 9 and 11 engines. By 1956 the Mark 5 model of the CF-100 was in the air. The last CF-100 rolled off the assembly line at the A.V. Roe plant at Malton on December 4, 1958. In all, some 692 CF-100 aircraft were produced.

The twin-engined CF-100 was a two-seater, long range, all-weather jet interceptor then in service with the nine home-based squadrons of the R.C.A.F., which, at that time, were located at Bagotville and St. Hubert, Quebec; Ottawa and North Bay, Ontario; and Comox, British Columbia. Each station had two squadrons, except Comox. General George R. Pearkes, V.C., Minister of the Department of National Defence said, on July 2, 1959: "We are maintaining nine squadrons of CF-100 all-weather interceptors and are making arrangements so that United States interceptors can operate in Candian air space, and consideration is being given to providing facilities so that United States' aircraft may be able to operate from Canadian airfields. . . ." Yet, by the end of 1961, four of these fighter squadrons in Canada were disbanded.

In its role, No. 416 Squadron was at that time one of the nine squadrons controlled by the R.C.A.F.'s Air Defence Command at St. Hubert for the defence of North America under NORAD at Colorado Springs. The R.C.A.F.'s Air Defence Command at St. Hubert shouldered all operational responsibility for Canada's air defence, and it was from St. Hubert that the jet fighter squadrons were directed. The fighter squadrons, which formed the striking part of the air defence system, were equipped with the best aircraft Canada had available at that

Ron West was Squadron Commander of No. 416 All-Weather Squadron, based at St. Hubert, flying CF-100s.

Photo courtesy of S/Ldr. R. B. West.

Presentation of the Trans-Canada Trophy to F/O R. B. West, D.F.C., A.F.C., on June 11, 1949, by Brooke Claxton, Minister of National Defence, at Rockcliffe Airport, Ottawa, Ontario.
Photo courtesy of the R.C.A.F.

time; and they made up the most spectacular part of the Air Defence Command. Of equal importance was the early warning radar and ground control system, along with the Ground Observer Corps. Without an early warning system to detect invading aircraft or missiles, the interceptor squadrons would not serve their intended purpose.

So, as indicated by its name, the No. 416 All-Weather Squadron remained in readiness at that time to fly in all kinds of weather every day of the year on a 24-hour basis. And this was the squadron that Ron West commanded.

This post led to a transfer to C.A.R.D.E. (Canadian Army Research and Development Establishment) in Ancienne Lorette, near Quebec City, in the spring of 1960. C.A.R.D.E. was the Research Arm of the Department of National Defence, and Ron West found it a most interesting place to work. He specialized in infra-red research.

Then in 1961, Squadron Leader West was transferred to Patrick Air Force Base (now known as Cape Kennedy), Florida, as Commander of the Canadian research contingent, working with N.A.S.A. (National Aeronautics and Space Ad-

ministration) and the U.S.A.F. in infra-red and ultra-violet research, namely boost phase and re-entry of I.C.B.M.'s (intercontinental ballistic missiles) and satellites. His unit served three years in this capacity. They had some very interesting adventures there. For instance, Ron West's jet was the first one to land on Eleuthera in the Bahamas and his 'plane was welcomed by an islander astride a donkey with his large family walking behind him!

Squadron Leader West returned to Canada in the summer of 1964 as Operations Officer of the R.C.A.F. base at Rockcliffe. It was from this position that he retired from the R.C.A.F. in the summer of 1966, at the early age of 47 years, the mandatory retirement age at that time.

Shortly after his retirement from the R.C.A.F., Ron West and his family went to Milton, Vermont, and, since then, he has been Manager of Merriam Graves Corporation, a welding supply and oxygen supply business.

Ron West is married, and he and his wife have two children. They and their family live in Milton, Vermont (near Burlington), today. Sailing, hunting,

fishing and the outdoor life in general are Ron's hobbies, when time permits. To each of these in season, he devotes an intense loyalty and an outstanding interest.

He was named a member of Canada's Aviation Hall of Fame in 1973, and was inducted in July of that year in Edmonton, Alberta. He was made a Companion of the Order of Flight (City of Edmonton).

Ron West is known as an excellent organizer, both on the ground and in the air. He has always been very enthusiastic about any activity in which he took part — and quickly passed on to others this same feeling. Not easily turned aside from achieving a desired goal, as a leader he comes as close to perfection as is humanly possible.

Through making these flights, together with many other search and rescue operations, Squadron Leader Ron West made a commendable contribution towards the attainment of the excellent reputation the Search and Rescue Organization holds today. In addition, as a Flight Commander with No. 416 Squadron at St. Hubert, he played a key role in our nation's defence.

1949

Dennis K. Yorath

Citation: in recognition of his outstanding contribution to advancement in the field of aviation

Dennis K. Yorath, M.B.E., LL.D., while President of the Royal Canadian Flying Clubs Association, Ottawa, was awarded the Trans-Canada Trophy for meritorious service in the advancement of aviation in Canada during 1949 "in recognition of his outstanding contribution to advancement in the field of aviation." The announcement of the award was made on May 13, 1950, by the Honourable Brooke Claxton, Minister of National Defence.

In his letter of May 15, 1950, to Dennis Yorath, Mr. Claxton said that the unanimous decision of the Committee of Award was based on recognition of his faithful and tireless efforts in the advancement of aviation, not only during the period of the award but also for many years.

The minister also said that Dennis Yorath, during his term as president, from 1947 to 1949 inclusive, served the Royal Canadian Flying Clubs Association as one of its most able and energetic chief executives.

On Dennis Yorath's initiative, the announcement said, the association carried out several very successful projects designed to enhance the development of aviation in Canada. Foremost of these were the revival of the Webster Memorial Trophy Competition in 1947, which was open to all eligible contestants regardless of whether or not they had any affiliation with flying clubs; the National Flying Club Week, which had become a regular part of the association's yearly programme and was mainly a publicity undertaking aimed at increasing personal participation in flying and awakening public consciousness of Canada's vital need for adequate preparedness in the air; the organization and establishment of the Model Aeronautics Association of Canada in

1948; and also instituting the Safe Flying Campaign among the Royal Canadian Flying Clubs Association's member clubs in 1948, which continued from year to year and had contributed to a substantially lower accident rate.

Dennis Kestell Yorath was born in London, England, on April 30, 1905. He attended primary school in London. Then he came to Canada with his parents and went to Saskatoon, Saskatchewan, where he attended public and high schools, and later the University Military School, Victoria, British Columbia.

Dennis Yorath went into business in public utilities in 1924, and four years later his career in aviation started to take shape. He was one of the charter members of the Calgary Flying Club and, upon its formation, he helped to organize it as a government-sponsored flying club by providing the aerodrome facilities and staff required. The Department of National Defence loaned the club two D.H. 60X Moth aircraft for instruction purposes, under the Scheme of Assistance for flying clubs which had just come into existence. These aircraft were G-CALA and G-CAKQ.

In January, 1929, he became Vice-President of the Calgary Flying Club, holding this office for four years. On March 12, 1929, he was granted his Private Pilot's Licence No. 242. His instructor was W. L. Rutledge of the Calgary Flying Club. His flying tests were taken in G-CALA, and given by Howard Ingram of the district office of the Department of National Defence.

Shortly after this the Calgary Flying Club was experiencing some difficulty and Dennis Yorath was called upon to handle the situation. Under his chairmanship, the Calgary Flying Club conducted a membership campaign in 1930 and got over 1,000 members. He continued active flying as a hobby and recreational sport until the summer of 1933.

He was re-elected Vice-President of the club in January, 1939, and held this office until the spring of 1944 when he was elected President. In 1940, Dennis Yorath was appointed Managing Director of the Lethbridge Flying Training School Limited operating No. 5 Elementary Flying Training School at Lethbridge. In June, 1941, this school was moved to High River, Alberta, and became the High River Flying Training School Limited. Dennis Yorath remained with the school as its Managing Director until it was closed at the conclusion of the British Commonwealth Air Training Plan in May, 1945. No. 5 E.F.T.S. was one of the outstanding elementary schools in Canada, noted for its efficiency of administration and operation.

For his work in directing this school, Dennis Yorath was awarded the M.B.E. in 1946. It was during these years, too, that he was appointed to the Civilian Advisory Committee of the Department of National Defence for Air concerned with elementary flying training.

In January, 1941, at the annual meeting of the Canadian Flying Clubs Association, the first committee of the Elementary Flying Training School Managers was appointed and Dennis Yorath was included in this committee as the representative from Alberta. In the fall of 1943, this association-appointed committee was disbanded and the government appointed its own advisory committee, of which Dennis Yorath was also a member.

In September 1944, Dennis Yorath was elected Alberta Zone Director of the Royal Canadian Flying Clubs Association. In January, 1946, he was elected Vice-President of the association, and in January, 1947, became its President. He held this office until January, 1950. During this time he worked unceasingly towards the bet-

terment of private flying conditions in Canada. Largely through the efforts of the Royal Canadian Flying Clubs Association, a subsidized flying training programme for private pilots was introduced by the Department of Transport on July 1, 1949. It was for the efforts which Dennis Yorath put into this work during these years that he was to receive special recognition.

As Zone Director, Vice-President and President of the Royal Canadian Flying Clubs Association, Dennis Yorath closely observed and analyzed the trends in private flying in Canada, including the costs of operation and the revenue which was received. Aside from a very brief boom following the resumption of civil flying at the end of the Second World War, his observations clearly indicated a declining interest in training, sporting and recreational flying. Rapidly rising costs of living were leaving less and less in individual pay envelopes for activities such as flying. In spite of the fact that the flying clubs and commercial flying training schools generally held hourly charges for flying close to pre-war levels, and did not increase them in line with the general rise in the costs of operation, interest in private flying was waning. Operating losses were considerable and could not be continued for any length of time.

Dennis Yorath was certain that the experience of the flying clubs was indicative of what was happening at the commercial schools, and saw in this trend the development of a very dangerous situation. The tremendous reserve of pilots trained in Canada during the war years was steadily drying up and he was fully persuaded that, if a pool of young pilots was to be maintained against the need of any future emergency, and to help meet the requirements of commercial aviation, this situation would have to be relieved.

In midsummer, 1947, he informed the executive of the association that he was perfectly confident that it would be

necessary in the very near future to ask the government to reinstate some form of financial assistance to flying training, and he determined that the first step was to properly acquaint the minister in charge of civil aviation and the Minister of National Defence with the true facts of the situation, and keep them informed as to future trends and developments.

At his direction, the association prepared progress reports for the Right Honourable C. D. Howe and the Honourable Brooke Claxton. In his annual report to the association for 1947, Dennis Yorath strongly urged immediate action to secure a reinstatement of a system of pilots' grants. At the annual meeting in January, 1948, when this report was presented, he received a clear mandate from the members and directors of the organization to proceed. With this beginning, and becoming more and more convinced of the necessity of government assistance, he personally planned and directed the organization and timing of representations made by the Royal Canadian Flying Clubs Association to the government until his project was fully achieved — the securing of federal grants to flying clubs to aid in flying training.

At this same time, Dennis Yorath wrote the Prime Minister and the Minister of Finance enclosing copies of his letters to Mr. Howe and Mr. Claxton, giving reasons for the association's action and the urgency and importance of the request. Sure that this matter would be discussed by Parliament, Dennis Yorath was anxious that every member of the House of Commons should be thoroughly acquainted with the background of experience and developments leading up to the request for government assistance. Under his supervision the association's office sent a letter to each Member of Parliament reviewing the activities of the flying clubs in peace and in war, and the operational difficulties experienced by them since re-

Dennis Yorath and his instructor, W. Rutledge (left), 1929. The aircraft was a D.H. 60X Moth on loan to the Calgary Flying Club.
Photo courtesy of Dennis Yorath.

establishment in the post-war period. This letter also mentioned the association's request made jointly to the minister in charge of civil aviation and the Minister of National Defence. Dennis Yorath directed all member flying clubs in the association to make their own representations to their Members of Parliament so that all of them would be in a position to discuss the matter intelligently on the floor of the House.

On May 3, 1948, Dennis Yorath called on Mr. Howe at his office and, after considerable discussion with him, it was arranged that a delegation from the Executive Committee of the Association should meet with him and Mr. Claxton on May 7, 1948. On May 4, keeping an appointment previously made by Dennis Yorath, the Executive Committee of the Association was received by Mr. Claxton and the whole matter of government assistance to flying training was discussed at length. Immediately following this meeting, Dennis Yorath sent memoranda to both Mr. Howe and Mr. Claxton suggesting amounts of grants to be paid to graduate pilots, giving reasons for these recommendations and what might be the results of such a program.

On May 7, 1948, an association delegation of three, led by Dennis Yorath, met Mr. Howe and Mr. Claxton at Mr. Howe's office in the Parliament Buildings, at which time Mr. Howe gave definite assurance that he would recommend certain measures of assistance to flying training, and that these measures would apply in all cases to both flying clubs and commercial flying schools. At this time the portfolio of minister in charge of civil aviation was being transferred to Mr. Lionel Chevrier, and Mr. Howe made it clear that he would make the necessary arrangements with Mr. Chevrier to take over this matter. During this visit to Ottawa, Dennis Yorath talked with Air Vice-Marshal A. T. Cowley, Director of Air

Services and Air Commodore J. G. Kerr of the R.C.A.F. Training Directorate about proposals for government aid.

The officials of the Department of Transport then made a thorough and extensive investigation embracing such matters as the present and future personnel requirements of commercial airlines, the need to generally educate the public in the importance and necessity of building up an air industry which would yield immeasurably to the development of the country and its internal and external trade, the operational costs of organizations engaged in flying instruction at that time and tuition costs of students.

Studies by the department's officials perspicuously demonstrated that, in order to furnish the proper encouragement and to ensure a standard of flying adequate for public safety, steps should be taken to reintroduce the plan of government assistance.

Insofar as the extent of the required financial help was concerned, the adoption on January 1, 1949, of an international standard of training of aviation personnel approved by the International Civil Aviation Organization led to a very tangible increase in training costs, both to the student and to the instructing body. Therefore, this "Scheme of Assistance" was timely.

On September 3, 1948, Dennis Yorath of Edmonton received a long distance telephone call from Air Vice-Marshal A.T. Cowley in which the proposed programme of pilot grants, as approved by the Ministers of Transport and National Defence, was outlined, and Dennis Yorath's comments and approval were invited before submitting the plan to the Cabinet. On October 5, 1948, it was officially announced that a plan of government assistance for flying training would be inaugurated on January 1, 1949.

This Scheme of Assistance for private pilot training, authorized by Order-in-

Council P.C. 5518, dated November 30, 1948, permitted payment of certain grants to "ab initio" private pilot applicants who were eligible to take the course, and to operators authorized to conduct an approved course of pilot training, upon the satisfactory completion of this course and the issuance of a licence. This resulted in direct material benefit to flying training operators in Canada and indirectly to the benefit of the whole aviation industry, and was an undertaking that, undoubtedly, was of great value to both military and civil aviation for many years to come.

A few months' experience by the flying clubs and the commercial flying schools with the plan of assistance adopted, and the conditions of training imposed, had indicated by the early summer of 1949 that certain modifications were needed. The association was asked by the Department of Transport to make recommendations for modification and, at Dennis Yorath's direction and under his careful personal guidance, a brief was prepared and submitted to the Director of Air Services, detailing recommended changes in the conditions and syllabus of training, documentation of pupils and written examinations for private pilots. Most of these recommendations were adopted by the Department of Transport and went into effect on July 1, 1949. They contributed to a marked improvement in results obtained under the plan of assistance and increased greatly the number of new trainees participating. The standard of both air and ground training was raised, as was also the cost of obtaining a private pilot's licence. This scheme was also to assist those in the manufacturing and maintenance of aircraft. The flying training operator would also benefit from the grant and in the increase in flying hours.

The text of Order-in-Council P.C. 5518, dated November 30, 1948, amended by P.C. No. 5132, dated October 11, 1949, and P.C. No. 1756,

Dennis Yorath upon completion of his first solo flight in 1929.
Photo courtesy of Dennis Yorath.

dated April 12, 1950, for the granting of financial assistance toward the instruction of flying training students and to approved flying clubs and schools in respect to such training, was as follows:

(i) $100.00 to a flying club or school for each citizen of Canada or of any other Commonwealth country granted a Private Pilot's Licence obtained "ab initio" at the club or school;

(ii) $100.00 to each citizen of Canada or of any other Commonwealth country who obtains a Private Pilot's Licence in the manner above mentioned;

(iii) $100.00 additional to each individual who qualifies for the grant mentioned in (i) above, provided he is a male British subject who is qualified to aircrew standards and is accepted for entry into the Air Component of either the Active Reserve or Regular Force of any of the three services.

Order-in-Council P.C. 5518, dated November 30, 1948, was revised from time to time through the years until the benefits which were originally granted under the Order-in-Council gradually lessened, and then faded away completely by 1968.

Dennis Yorath also lent his energy and support to the preparation by the association of a new *Manual of Ground School Training,* a thoroughly up-to-date and complete text which was published in 1950 and made available to all flying schools and clubs as well as the general public. Upon Dennis Yorath's suggestion, the association in 1949 instituted the practice of holding an annual conference of the club instructor-managers in

conjunction with the annual meeting, and at the same time established an Instructor-Managers' Advisory Committee which provided the machinery for bringing the recommendations of experienced, practical operators in the field to the association's board of directors, and through them to the Department of Transport.

Within the Royal Canadian Flying Clubs Association, Dennis Yorath, being a practical business man, always worked towards the goal of getting the flying clubs established on a sound operating basis as specialists in flying training, and offering a consistently high standard of ground and air instruction right across the country. He worked, and with success, to provide sound financing for the association. While President, Dennis Yorath always took the stand that it was better for the flying clubs' organization to be made up of a smaller number of strong, active clubs than a large number of clubs, some of which were weak and poorly administered. He always fostered the policy of eliminating clubs from the association that were not a credit to it with the objective of maintaining an organization in which government departments could place confidence.

In spite of Dennis Yorath's extensive work on behalf of the Royal Canadian Flying Clubs Association, he found time, often with sacrifice of his own business interests, to participate in many worthwhile aviation activities. He was a strong advocate of properly organized educational air shows as a means of increasing public interest and participation in flying and has always argued strongly against foolhardy exhibitions at Canadian air shows. In 1947 and 1948 he was Chairman of the Calgary Air Show and largely responsible for the excellent organization of this successful

undertaking. By the example of his own club, and with much helpful advice, he encouraged many clubs to stage air shows as annual events.

At the Twelfth International Convention of the Northwest Aviation Planning Council in 1948, Dennis Yorath gave an address on private flying training operations in Canada.

At Dennis Yorath's instigation, the Royal Canadian Flying Clubs Association took associate membership in 1948 in the Air Industries and Transport Association, and this step inaugurated a new phase of close liaison and co-operation between the two organizations.

In September, 1949, he headed the Royal Canadian Flying Clubs Association's delegation to the 42nd World Conference of the Fédération Aéronautique Internationale at Cleveland and took a leading part in the annual deliberations of this world governing body of sporting aviation.

He was a keen promoter of the association's undertaking to encourage international goodwill flying visits between amateur Canadian flying clubs and amateur flying groups in the United States.

For several years Dennis Yorath was a member of the Alberta Provincial Executive of the Air Cadet League of Canada and had, on several occasions, spear-headed successful financial drives for that organization in his home province.

He prepared a number of articles and guest articles for the aviation press on subjects relating to safety in flying.

The tremendous effort, the keen personal interest and leadership, and the vast amount of time given without remuneration by Dennis Yorath during his three-year term of office as Chief Executive of the Royal Canadian Flying Clubs Association, in negotiating with the Canadian Government the approved scheme of subsidized flying training, produced a profound direct benefit to flying training school operators and raised the standards for training pilots throughout the country.

The standards for training pilots were to be: the completion of forty hours of flight time with at least ten hours' solo, or with thirty hours of flight time with at least eight hours' solo, plus a minimum course of ten hours at a ground training school, approved for this training by the Department of Transport, and three hours of cross-country solo flight time. Also, the $100 grant helped to take care of some of the pilot's expenses. The licence fee was then five dollars. Then, when the pilot received his licence, he was entitled to carry passengers, but not for hire or reward.

In the spring of 1950, an announcement was made by the Minister of National Defence, the Honourable Brooke Claxton, that Dennis Yorath had been awarded the Trans-Canada Trophy in recognition of his outstanding contribution to advancement in the field of aviation during 1949.

The official presentation of the Trans-Canada Trophy to Dennis Yorath took

---

The Committee of Award for the year 1949 consisted of the following members:

Air Commodore J. G. Kerr, C.B.E., A.F.C., Royal Canadian Air Force, Department of National Defence, Ottawa.

A. D. McLean, O.B.E., Controller of Civil Aviation, Department of Transport, Ottawa.

Gordon F. Henderson, representing the Royal Canadian Flying Clubs Association, Ottawa.

H. C. Cotterell, President, Air Industries and Transport Association of Canada, Ottawa.

Wing Commander D. E. Galloway, Royal Canadian Air Force, Department of National Defence, Ottawa.

place on the evening of June 16, 1950, at the Chateau Laurier, Ottawa, on the occasion of a dinner given in his honour by the Royal Canadian Flying Clubs Association on their Twenty-First Anniversary. Air Vice-Marshal F. R. Miller, C.B.E., C.D., Air Member for Operations and Training, made the presentation on behalf of the Minister of National Defence. The dinner was attended by seven of the former winners of the trophy: Wop May, 1929; Romeo Vachon, 1937; Murton Seymour, 1939; Dan McLean, 1941; J. A. Wilson, 1944; Grant McConachie, 1945; and Barney Rawson, 1947.

At this twenty-first annual meeting of the Royal Canadian Flying Clubs Association, the "coming of age" of the flying clubs was celebrated. The association's first president, Air Vice-Marshal J. A. Sully, spoke to the gathering at the annual banquet. Of the thirty-three flying clubs, twenty-four were represented. Dennis Yorath, the retiring President of the Association, was acclaimed for his contributions to the flying club cause. (He was succeeded as President by Gordon F. Henderson of Ottawa; while E. R. MacFarland of Lethbridge became Vice-President.) In Air Vice-Marshal Sully's talk, he reminisced about the early days of the clubs when they were trying to get along. He spoke, too, of the way that J. A. Wilson, Air Vice-Marshal Tom Cowley and Major-General Sir James H. MacBrien helped them in the beginning. This was when the government gave each approved club two aircraft and the sum of $100 for each member who qualified as an ab initio pilot, upon the club's fulfilment of certain conditions, such as providing its own field, the service of an instructor and an air engineer. A large number of those of the auxiliary squadrons in the 1939-1945 war period received their early training at these flying clubs, making hundreds of club-trained pilots available to join the R.C.A.F. when the war broke

out, Air Vice-Marshal Sully said. He appreciated that the clubs should not be entirely dependent on government subsidy, as they must retain their independence and vitality. While the next war might never duplicate the Air Training Plan, yet it might be necessary to concentrate on fewer but more highly trained personnel. Thus the auxiliary forces were still very important and the clubs were still important as a reservoir for the squadrons. The Air Vice-Marshal ended his colourful talk by saying that there was a great challenge and a great opportunity for the clubs to prepare young men to serve their country.

While still President of the Royal Canadian Flying Clubs Association in 1950, Dennis Yorath donated a trophy — the Yorath Trophy — to the association to stimulate active competition of the clubs at the management level. The trophy is an annual award to the instructor-manager of one of the R.C.F.C.A. member clubs who has used his club's facilities to the best advantage. The award is based upon a club's statistical record for the year, considering the use that has been made of the aircraft, total number of revenue hours that were flown, the increase in revenue hours over the preceding year, night flying hours carried out, the accident record for the year and the number of pilots who graduated. All of this accounts for 75 per cent of the marks for the award; while the other 25 per cent is based on any confidential reports received from the manager's own president and zone director. All club managers enter the competition for this trophy automatically.

The trophy is retained by the winner for one year only. However, as a permanent memento of his achievement, the winner receives an engraved stein and an honorarium of one hundred dollars. The runner-up in the competition also receives an engraved stein and an honorarium of fifty dollars. Maury Fallow of the Edmonton Flying Club was the first club

Dennis Yorath (left) receiving the Trans-Canada Trophy from A/V/M. F. R. Miller, C.B.E., C.D. (centre), Air Member for Operations and Training, D.N.S., on June 16, 1950, at a dinner given in his honour by the Royal Canadian Flying Clubs Association at the Chateau Laurier, Ottawa.
Photo courtesy of Dennis Yorath.

manager to receive the Yorath Trophy for 1950.

Dennis Yorath joined Northwestern Utilities Limited of Edmonton in 1924, then went to Calgary with the Canadian Western Natural Gas Co. Ltd., where he spent the next twenty-five years serving in various departments of this company. He was elected a director in 1940, and became secretary in 1945. He served as secretary of Canadian Utilities Limited from 1935 to 1939. He was appointed general manager and director of Northwestern Utilities Limited in May, 1949; and became President of Northwestern and Canadian Western in April, 1956. He was Chairman of both companies from 1962 to 1969. Then he was elected a director of International Utilities Corporation in September, 1957, and was Vice-President from 1961 until 1972; Chairman of the Executive Committee from July, 1969, to May,

1973; and Vice-Chairman from May, 1973 to 1976. The corporation's name was changed to IU International Corporation in May, 1973.

He is an honorary director of the IU International Corporation of Edmonton, Alberta; and an honorary director of Northwestern Utilities Limited, Canadian Western Natural Gas Co. Ltd., Canadian Utilities Limited, Alberta Power Limited, and the International Utilities Petroleum Corporation.

Dennis Yorath is a past president, honorary president and life member of the Calgary Flying Club; and an honorary life member of the Edmonton Flying Club. He is a past president of the Royal Canadian Flying Clubs Association; and a member of the Alberta Advisory Council of the Air Cadet League of Canada. He was awarded the Trans-Canada Trophy in 1949. He was named a member of Canada's Aviation Hall of

Fame in 1973. He was made a Companion of the Order of Flight (City of Edmonton). He received an Honorary Degree of Doctor of Laws from the University of Alberta on May 31, 1974.

Mr. and Mrs. Dennis Yorath reside in Edmonton, Alberta. They have two children.

His understanding of the weighty problems associated with private flying and his serious and well-informed representations to the ministers concerned were all prime factors in effecting the inauguration of a program of assistance which influenced the development of aviation in Canada. This brought needed support to many branches of the industry, as well as developing and maintaining a pool of pilots for a time. Those who were acquainted with him over the years had unqualified admiration for his accomplishments in the field of aviation.

1950

Carl relaxing for a moment's rest at one of the campsites.
Photo courtesy of Carl Agar.

Carl C. Agar

Citation: outstanding contribution to advancement in the field of aviation in Canada during the year 1950, particularly in the use of rotary-wing aircraft over mountainous terrain

Carl C. Agar, A.F.C., while Manager of Okanagan Air Services Limited, Vancouver International Airport, Vancouver, British Columbia, was awarded the Trans-Canada Trophy in recognition of his "outstanding contribution to advancement in the field of aviation in Canada during the year 1950, particularly in the use of rotary-wing aircraft over mountainous terrain." The announcement of the award was made on May 14, 1951, by the Minister of National Defence, then the Honourable Brooke Claxton.

In making the announcement, the minister said that Carl Agar pioneered the use of the helicopter and proved its merit in the rugged mountainous terrain of British Columbia which was suited to no other type of aircraft. In so doing, he developed the special techniques required for this type of operation. The value of his work lay in the helicopter's ability to reach points entirely inaccessible to any other form of transportation. The practicability and necessity for using helicopters in areas of this kind were becoming only too evident. This pioneering work involved a great deal of risk to Carl Agar — but through it all he made milestones in rotary wing progress.

The effort that Carl Agar put into learning how to fly a helicopter at altitude under the turbulent conditions existing in the coastal ranges cannot be too highly lauded, and it was in this particular phase of operating the helicopter, with its far-reaching results, where Carl Agar's fame lay.

Carl Clare Agar was born at Lion's Head, Ontario, in the Bruce Peninsula, on November 28, 1901, where he attended school.

He obtained his Private Pilot's Licence

No. 408, dated November 4, 1929, and his Limited Commercial Pilot's Licence No. C. 2557, dated December 8, 1945, which was superseded by his Senior Commercial Pilot's Certificate No. SC-82, dated April 5, 1950.

Carl Agar first became interested in aviation in 1929 when, at the invitation of Wop May, he made his first flight in a fixed-wing aircraft. Under the supervision of Moss Burbidge, who was Chief Flying Instructor of the Edmonton and Northern Alberta Aero Club at that time, Carl Agar obtained his private pilot's licence. However, that was the end of flying for the moment, and he resumed his occupation of farming, southwest of Edmonton. He returned to the airport only twice during the years from 1929 to

Carl, slightly bushed and bewhiskered, drilling a hold in granite rock for a brass plug while on a topographical survey west of the Nass River.
Photo courtesy of Carl Agar.

Carl completing a helicopter landing on one of the mountain sites.
Photo courtesy of Carl Agar.

1940. Then, upon the organization of the British Commonwealth Air Training Plan shortly after the outbreak of World War II, he enlisted in the R.C.A.F. as an AC-2 in January, 1941, and trained at Moose Jaw and Trenton. He became an instructor for the Elementary Flying Training Schools. During the years to follow, his working hours were spent patiently guiding exuberant youngsters through the elementary phases of piloting aircraft, and aviation became his great interest in life.

Carl Agar served at No. 16 Elementary Flying Training School until it was closed, and was then transferred to No. 5 at High River where he remained until July, 1943. He was then posted to No. 3 Service Flying Training School at Calgary to take a refresher course, at the end of which he hoped to go overseas. However, an overseas posting was refused him because of his age, and instead he was posted to No. 24 Elementary Flying Training School at Abbotsford, British Columbia. There he organized the new testing flight system that was being inaugurated in Elementary Flying Training Schools, and remained at Abbotsford until the school was closed to make way for an Operational Training Unit. He was transferred back to High River under Dennis Yorath and took over the test flight there, where he remained until the closing of the training plan. Carl Agar was awarded the Air Force Cross "for devotion to duty in the field of air training" in 1944.

In the early part of 1945, Carl Agar received his discharge as a Flight Lieutenant in Vancouver after four years' service in the R.C.A.F. With a desire to remain in some form of aviation, he entered a commercial flying venture with three other veterans by forming a flying school known as Okanagan Air Service at Kelowna and Penticton, in the Okanagan Valley of British Columbia. Carl Agar was Manager of this company, the other partners being Alfred Stringer,

A. H. "Barney" Bent and Andrew Duncan.

One day in October, 1946, the partners heard that there were helicopters crop-spraying in the State of Washington, and that very night they drove down to their base at Yakima. Here they saw their first helicopter, a Bell 47 B3, which model was the first helicopter in the world to receive commercial certification. Carl Agar took his first helicopter flight and, envisioning the versatility associated with the flying characteristics of the helicopters, was sold on the value of what could be a revolutionary method of transportation. From the Yakima crop-dusters, Carl Agar learned what was then known about flying helicopters and his firm decided to enter the helicopter flying business.

During 1947, with the support of the fruit farmers in the Okanagan Valley of British Columbia, a helicopter was purchased, and the spraying and dusting of orchards in the valley was begun by the newly-formed Okanagan Air Services Limited, with Carl Agar as pilot. The company was financially backed by Douglas Dewar, C.B.E., of Vancouver and O. St. P. Aitkens, M.C., of Kelowna. However, because of the small size of the orchards and other technical factors associated with this type of flying operation, the little company soon realized that if it were to become financially sound it would have to seek business in some other field. They felt that, because of its flying characteristics, the helicopter could well become the "packhorse of the air," supplying transportation to the various types of explorers and surveyors who worked in the mountainous regions of British Columbia. With this end in view, the helicopter was taken into rough country where Carl Agar could gain practical experience in its handling in the mountains.

He had learned to fly a helicopter in Yakima, Washington, under very favourable conditions; he could take off

from flat ground at sea level, climb, fly around and land on the same flat ground with the proficiency that such an operation required; but what confronted him in the mountains was drastically different. He found that mountain flying presented problems that required altogether different techniques; in effect, he had to learn to fly all over again, only this time it was without the comforting guidance of an experienced instructor.

Very little flying with helicopters had been done in the mountains before and, although the British Columbia mountains were breathtakingly beautiful, they were also awesomely rugged. Obviously, flying amongst them required altogether different techniques from those required when flying over relatively flat terrain at practically sea level. For example, it was necessary to learn how to land a helicopter on a small shelf of rock at altitude. This proved to be much more difficult than landing the helicopter on a prepared spot at sea level. And again, Carl Agar found he had to contend with updrafts and downdrafts which would change at a moment's notice. Moreover, he found that the helicopter performed quite differently in the thinner air at altitude.

In effect, Carl Agar embarked on what may well be called a self-imposed familiarization course. This time it consisted of looking for and evaluating landing sites in the mountains, learning how to approach to land on them, and how to take off, all the while coping with the variable conditions presented by the vagaries of mountain winds. In the beginning, many times he had to muster sufficient courage to attempt a landing that could well have been the final one, if his judgment should have erred.

Carl Agar had been told that the helicopter could fly at 4,500 feet. However, on one occasion while flying in the precipitous Coastal Range, he managed to land on the top of a cliff at the 7,500-foot level. Before him was a

A Bell taking off from one of the tower sites. The landing site has been levelled and a tarpaulin laid down to reduce the dust hazard.
Photo courtesy of Bell Aircraft Corporation, Fort Worth, Texas.

2,000-foot drop. The thin atmosphere at that altitude did not permit a normal take off with the Bell helicopter of that era. So, using full power, Carl Agar managed to get the helicopter a few feet off the ground and, as it hovered momentarily, literally dumped the ship over the side of the cliff. Imagine his feelings as the ship dropped 500 feet before the helicopter gained sufficient forward speed to permit the blades to take hold — but they did, and the helicopter began to perform in a normal manner.

With determination and skill, he learned the intricacies of flying rotary-wing aircraft and developed techniques that were eventually handed on to all the pilots trained by him and by his firm. In fact, these very skills were later sought by our military, industry and by foreign countries — and were imparted at Okanagan's own training school.

Carl Agar became known as an authority on mountain helicopter flying and in that capacity, in the spring of 1954, he was called on by the Government of Dutch New Guinea to assess a helicopter project for them.

Gradually, however, Carl Agar was called on to perform work with the helicopter that gave the little company an entrance into the field of natural resources, which had been its goal. In the spring of 1949, they received a request from the Forestry Branch of the British Columbia Government to conduct spraying operations in the Fraser Valley in order to destroy mosquitoes that resulted from heavy flood conditions. Another spraying operation was undertaken in the Windermere Valley where 11,000 acres were sprayed with DDT to destroy the false hemlock looper which was threatening the Christmas tree preserve there. The park entrance at Radium Hot Springs was also sprayed, and the helicopter was flown to Banff, Alberta, where a test was carried out for the Dominion Government to combat other forest infestations.

Carl Agar still maintained his vision of the "aerial packhorse" and he attempted to "sell" this service to the Topographic Division of the British Columbia Department of Lands and Forests. Finally, he was given an assignment which required a landing to be made on the top of Walach Mountain. To make certain that this could be done successfully, he first performed the landing alone, then returned and flew in his passenger, an engineer, thus safely conducting the first helicopter operation at altitude in British Columbia. Carl Agar's work on this operation proved to the Topographic Division that the helicopter could do what he claimed it could, and since that time this branch of the British Columbia Lands and Forests' Department has used helicopters every summer in its field work, when necessary. As a result of the success of this particular operation, men in other fields of endeavour began to realize the practicability of the helicopter, and requests for its services began coming in from various sources.

A successful timber cruise was carried out in the wilds of British Columbia, one-hundred and seventy-five miles northwest of Vancouver, at the head of Knight Inlet, adjacent to the Kleenakleni Ice Fields.

The season of 1949 commenced with a freight haul to a mountain ridge on the west coast of Vancouver Island. A complete diamond drill unit with all the requirements for a camp and the crew were airlifted to a mountain ridge 3,500 feet above sea level. It was impossible to get in on foot at that season of the year (April), but by means of an Okanagan helicopter over 28,000 pounds of materials were carried in during this operation.

The Greater Vancouver Water District requested the services of an Okanagan helicopter to assist in the building of a water-storage dam, the Palisade Lake Dam, and it was found that this particular project was large enough to require the services of a second helicopter and another machine was purchased. Approximately 400,000 pounds of material were transported by the helicopters to a spot 3,000 feet above sea level. Every single piece of material needed on the project was carried in by helicopter: cement, sand, gravel, donkey engine, concrete mixers, dynamite, wheelbarrows, windows, doors, lumber, five-ply sheets, reinforcing structural steel, food supplies, personnel, and so on. The operation required over a thousand trips. The dam stands there today as one of the monuments to the pioneering work of Carl Agar. He, himself, made two-hundred and fifty trips on this one operation, and substantial savings were realized in time and money by using helicopters as the mode of transportation.

The mining world began to see in the helicopter an answer to some of their problems. Jobs such as the reopening of the Rico Copper Mines Limited, on the majestic but extremely rugged Cheam Range, were accomplished in record time with the assistance of the helicopter. Attempts to reach the property by road had previously been abandoned because of the high cost involved but, in a matter of forty-five minutes, one of the Okanagan helicopters reached the area and, in the course of its work there, all the materials necessary for the proving of this property, including materials for the construction of a two-storey bunkhouse, were hauled in. A total of two-hundred and forty-six landings was made between 6,000 and 6,200 feet on the initial operation. In two years of similar operations, over 500,000 pounds of freight of all descriptions were transported by the small Bell helicopter to areas inaccessible to other forms of transportation.

Prospecting by helicopter became popular. In 1949, Carl Agar pioneered

Unloading supplies at the east end of the tunnel at Tahtsa Lake for the Kemano project.
Photo courtesy of Carl Agar.

this type of helicopter operation for a geologist and a mining engineer, who took movies of the project. Prospecting via helicopter was a revelation to these men and made such an impression that one mining engineer, after hearing a version of this particular operation, purchased his own helicopter.

The Surveys and Mapping Branch of the British Columbia Department of Lands and Forests conducted a survey using an Okanagan helicopter, 600 miles northwest of Vancouver, beyond Hazelton, on the old Telegraph Trail. The helicopter moved the men and their equipment to mountain peaks and removed them when the work was done. It also moved into the actual "fly camps" and stayed up top several days at a time. Gas was moved to the mountain peaks in 12 1/2-gallon drums for use when the machine was not returning to its base camp at nights. The method of the helicopter remaining in the top camps speeded up the work tremendously — there being as many as three parties on the move at once, the helicopter rotating from one to the other in turn, thus eliminating practically all of the walking. On this project, one hundred and eighty-eight mountain landings were made above the 4,000-foot level, 66 per cent of them being between the 5,000 and 6,000-foot level, although in many cases density altitudes were considerably higher. No peaks were occupied that the helicopter failed to serve.

Further work was done for the same department in the Kitimat area south of Terrace, British Columbia, when, to quote the party chief, Mr. E. McMinn: "One-third of all the work accomplished this season was done by the helicopter in three days." The party had been in the area three months before the helicopter arrived. Carl Agar was on this operation alone for seven weeks, during which time the helicopter showed not only how much more rapidly the ground could be covered, but that its use was

economically and operationally sound. So pleased was the department with this operation that the Surveys and Mapping Branch at Victoria placed a display in the lobby of the Provincial Parliament Buildings showing the old method "on foot" and the new method "by helicopter"; in other words, the aerial packhorse had arrived. The work accomplished was of enormous importance. Not only did the British Columbia Provincial Government repeat the operation in 1950 on a larger scale, but also the Dominion Government, especially the Department of National Defence and the Department of Mines and Technical Surveys.

In 1950 the construction world called on the helicopter to assist in conducting the survey of a power route for the British Columbia International Engineering Company of Vancouver, who were doing the planning and engineering investigation for the huge hydro-electric project under construction by the Aluminum Company of Canada in the Tweedsmuir Park area in British Columbia. With Professor W. G. Heslop

of the University of British Columbia as the engineer, Carl Agar piloted the helicopter through fifteen mountain passes, and as many routes were examined from the helicopter in order to ascertain which one was most suitable to carry the transmission line from the power-house site on the Kemano River to the site of the proposed Aluminum City at the head of Kitimat Arm on Douglas Channel (40 miles south of Terrace). Although this work was done in very rugged terrain, data of sufficient accuracy was supplied to enable the engineers to select the best route for the power line — and this was done in six consecutive days, with only twenty hours of flying time. It would have taken a ground party several years to cover the same routes and bring back similar data. This survey was only the beginning of the Aluminum Company's world-famous project in the mountains of British Columbia. The little company originally formed by Carl Agar, Alf Stringer, Barney Bent and Andy Duncan, named Okanagan Helicopters Limited since October, 1952, operated the fleet of helicopters and assisted in the

Carl at the controls of a helicopter at Camp 5, Kemano.
Photo courtesy of Carl Agar.

FZX, with Carl at the controls, down on the landing patch at the dam site. Note the rugged area.
Photo courtesy of Carl Agar.

construction of this vast project. Then, the actual construction completed, helicopters remained to patrol the Alcan transmission line, looking for possible damage (from snow slides, leaks and ice), bringing in repair crews when necessary and assisting with any auxiliary construction that might be required.

On May 14, 1951, the Minister of National Defence announced that Carl Agar had won the Trans-Canada Trophy for outstanding contribution to advancement in the field of aviation in Canada during the year 1950, particularly in the use of rotary-wing aircraft over mountainous terrain. By this time Carl Agar had established an international reputation for himself as an authority on helicopter flying in mountainous regions, and had demonstrated great skill and courage as a helicopter pilot. Thus Carl Agar brought revolutionary changes in a new form of air transport to new fields.

The official presentation of the Trans-Canada Trophy to Carl Agar took place on Tuesday evening, October 30, 1951, at the Seigniory Club at Montebello, Quebec, on the occasion of a dinner given in his honour by the Air Industries

The Committee of Award for the year 1950 consisted of the following members:
Group Captain Z. L. Leigh, O.B.E., E.D., Royal Canadian Air Force, Department of National Defence, Ottawa.
Mr. H. C. Cotterell, representing the Air Industries and Transport Association, Ottawa.
Major R. Dodds, O.B.E., M.C., Controller of Civil Aviation, Department of Transport, Ottawa.
Mr. D. L. Buchanan, D.F.C., Royal Canadian Flying Clubs Association, Ottawa.
Wing Commander W. G. Welstead, Royal Canadian Air Force, Department of National Defence, Ottawa.

and Transport Association. Air Vice-Marshal F. R. Miller, C.B.E., C.D., of the R.C.A.F., acting for the Minister of National Defence, made the presentation. The following former trophy winners were in attendance: Punch Dickins (1928); Wop May (1929); George Phillips (1931); Romeo Vachon (1937); Trans-Canada Air Lines (1938), represented by Gordon McGregor; Murton Seymour (1939); Tommy Siers (1940); Dan McLean (1941); Pat Reid (1942-43); J. A. Wilson (1944); and Grant McConachie (1945).

The year 1953 saw one of Okanagan's helicopters in uranium exploration work using an airborne scintillometer. This recording instrument was used for the express purpose of locating radio-active ore deposits. A magnetometer was also employed to assist geologists in locating possible oil-bearing formations, and an electro-magnetometer (EM) for locating ore bodies.

During the year 1955 Okanagan Helicopters spent a four-month period in Canada's Arctic Islands transporting men, dog teams, sleds and other equipment for the Department of Mines and Technical Surveys, who were conducting a geological survey to ascertain the oil and mineral wealth of the north. This was known as the "Franklin Project." The two S-55's operated from bases at Resolute Bay and Eureka, acting as supply and communication aircraft.

Okanagan Helicopters undertook an important forest survey in British Columbia for the first time during 1955.

The Okanagan group set up a subsidiary, Copter Cabs Limited, having in mind the developing of an executive travel service between the airport, head offices, branch offices and plants of major companies in the lower B.C. mainland area. One of the major difficulties which delayed passenger service by helicopter was the Department of Transport's regulations banning flying over built-up areas in a helicopter, which

necessitated following open routes, and increased flying time. With the twin-engine Omega helicopter, and its ability to fly on either engine, Okanagan was allowed to fly over built-up areas. The Omega was powered by two 310 h.p. air-cooled Lycoming engines. It could be equipped either with landing gear for heliport operation or with floats for operation over water. Its rotor was a four-blade design. Its cruising speed was 80 m.p.h. with a payload of 1,000 pounds (or four passengers and the pilot).

Many innovations incorporated in the Omega SB-12D came as a result of advice by Carl Agar and Alf Stringer. Carl Agar worked closely with Bernard Sznycer, President of Omega Aircraft Corporation, on operational requirements, both as to flying characteristics and maintenance, while Alf Stringer offered advice on basic engineering design. Bernard Sznycer's work was well known in Canada. In 1951, he designed and built in Montreal the first helicopter to be certificated in the British Commonwealth. Production of this helicopter was held up for financing, and Mr. Sznycer moved to the United States where he worked on the Omega helicopter. The Omega was certificated by the F.A.A. (Federal Aeronautics Administration) early in 1960, and shortly thereafter by the Canadian Department of Transport.

Carl Agar was awarded the Captain William J. Kossler Award of the American Helicopter Society for 1954. It is awarded annually for "the greatest achievement in practical application and operation of rotary-winged aircraft, the value of which has been clearly demonstrated in actual service during the preceding year." This was the first time that the award was given to anyone outside of the United States. The presentation of the award to Carl Agar was made by Frederick B. Lee, Administrator of the Civil Aeronautics

Carl Agar being presented with the Trans-Canada Trophy in 1951 by A/V/M. F. R. Miller, C.B.E., C.D. Grant McConachie, then President of Canadian Pacific Air Lines, is shown in the centre.

Photo courtesy of Canadian Pacific Railway.

Authority at the Eleventh Annual Honours Night Dinner of the American Helicopter Society in Washington, D.C., late in April, 1955.

The name of Carl Agar and the pioneering of mountain helicopter flying are synonymous and, although Carl Agar gradually left active flying after his work on the Aluminum Company's project, he transferred his attention to helicopter pilot training, and maintained an ever-watchful eye on the work conducted by the group in this field. Okanagan Helicopters also ran a school to train helicopter pilots for those agencies requiring them, such as the R.C.A.F., the Canadian Army, the Department of Transport, the United States Air Force, and others. No one knew better than Carl Agar what mountain flying entailed and there was a story behind every bit of knowledge acquired and every technique evolved. He provided the impetus that sped helicopters on their way to opening a new era.

From November, 1955 to 1962, Carl Agar was Vice-President for Research and Training for Okanagan Helicopters and its various subsidiaries. During 1956 he was President of the Helicopter Association of America, and later a member of the American Helicopter Society. He was also a director of the Okanagan Group. At the beginning of 1962, Carl Agar gave up his Vice-Presidency because of ill health for the

less demanding role of a consultant, though he continued as a director of the company.

Early in 1963, Carl Agar and Alf Stringer, co-founders of Okanagan Helicopters, resigned from the company over a policy disagreement and joined forces with Vancouver Island Helicopters Ltd., with Carl Agar in the role of a consultant and a director.

Some time later, in July, 1965, Carl Agar rejoined the Board of Okanagan Helicopters Ltd., as a director and Honorary Chairman.

Okanagan Helicopters is one of the world's largest commercial helicopter operators today. They also engage in search and rescue work. All of this started from a small commercial flying venture known as Okanagan Air Service, at Kelowna and Penticton in the Okanagan Valley of British Columbia, with Carl Agar as Manager of the company, and his partners Alfred Stringer, Barney Bent and Andrew Duncan. This was back in 1945 when Carl Agar received his discharge from the R.C.A.F. Much could be written about the work performed by the ships and crews of the Okanagan Group of companies through the years.

Carl Clare Agar, A.F.C., known as Canada's "Mr. Helicopter", died of a lung disorder on January 26, 1968, in the Royal Jubilee Hospital, Victoria, at the age of 67. He and Mrs. Agar lived in

Victoria prior to his death.

Carl Agar, the father of helicopter mountain operations, was not a big man physically, but like all notable men he had a stature that resulted from his innate characteristics. He often startled visitors by the whack of one of his large hands on his desk, as he drove home a point. Although usually serious-looking, the merry twinkle that lighted up his blue eyes was never far away and he considered a good laugh the elixir of life. He was a very determined person and, when interested in a project, he would let nothing stand in his way nor would he leave any stone unturned if it would assist him in gaining his objective. Carl Agar enjoyed people and had always encouraged friendly relations amongst the employees of the Okanagan Group, and the resulting ésprit de corps was very noticeable to those who visited them.

The distinction of being known as Canada's "Mr. Helicopter" can aptly be given to Carl Agar for the effort that he put into learning how to fly a helicopter at altitude over mountainous terrain and for developing the special techniques necessary for this effort. He had pioneered the development of now standard techniques used by civil and military operators all over the world.

He was named a member of Canada's Aviation Hall of Fame in 1973, and was made a Companion of the Order of Flight (City of Edmonton).

1951

Philip C. Garratt

Citation: in recognition of his outstanding contribution to the advancement of Canadian aviation during 1951

Philip C. Garratt, A.F.C., while Vice-President and Managing Director of The de Havilland Aircraft of Canada, Limited, Toronto, Ontario, was awarded the Trans-Canada Trophy for the year 1951, "in recognition of his outstanding contribution to the advancement of Canadian aviation during 1951." The announcement of the award was made on May 21, 1952, by the Honourable Brooke Claxton, Minister of National Defence.

The design and manufacture of the Beaver aircraft in 1947 by The de Havilland Aircraft Company under Philip Garratt's direction and guidance was a very substantial contribution to the advancement of Canadian aviation in general. However, Mr. Garratt had a much more ambitious project of a "Big Beaver" crystallizing in his mind. This was the production of an aircraft with the performance of the Beaver — but with almost double its payload. Under his watchful eye, the design was begun in January, 1951, and on December 12 of this same year the DHC-3 "Otter" prototype was rolled out on the runway at Downsview, to make its first official public demonstration — and it took off just like a Beaver, under the hand of Chief Test Pilot George Neal! As fully expected, its performance exceeded that of the Beaver, even to the 600 foot runway it used.

The DHC-3 Otter — landplane, seaplane, skiplane and amphibian — possessing fine qualities of performance, embodied novel features in its design. Some of these features were a spacious cabin area of 345 cubic feet for carrying cargo; a high-lift wing and provision of full-span double-slotted flaps; an exhaust ejector cooling system; a three-bladed propeller; a large dorsal fin to ensure

directional stability; and fuel tanks in the belly making filler caps readily accessible at ground level.

To facilitate flying, and for float or ski operation in the north country, the Otter met the rigid requirements of those who wanted an aircraft that would prove its value in the northland by giving exceptional performance in quick take-off, a high rate of climb, with good flying qualities, especially in those areas where landing and take-off space was restricted. The Otter was designed to operate under tropic or Arctic conditions in temperatures ranging from plus 140° F. to minus 60° F. or thereabouts.

The Otter was the first single-engine aircraft to qualify for approval to the exacting ICAO (International Civil Aviation Organization) category "D" airworthiness requirements, and was eligible for certification in any country in the world where ICAO standards were recognized.

From a humble beginning in the field of creative engineering effort had developed the team that was to be responsible for three remarkably successful all-Canadian designs — the Chipmunk, the Beaver and the Otter.

Too, it was fitting that one of the world's best aircraft in its class should be made — from the drawing board to the finished product — here in the country that produced the finest bush pilots. In this respect, it was natural that the Otter should come into being in Canada, because behind its design was the vast knowledge and experience in wilderness flying possessed by that romantic band of bush pilots who did so much to open up Canada.

In the spring of 1951, Phil Garratt entered the Beaver in a competition held by both the United States Air Force and

Phil Garratt is shown in the cockpit of the first L-20 Beaver at the official ceremony on November 13, 1951, when three of these aircraft were handed over to the U.S. Government.
Photo courtesy of The de Havilland Aircraft of Canada Ltd.

the United States Army for a liaison aircraft at Wright Field, Dayton, Ohio, and at Fort Bragg, North Carolina. Competing with six other types, it won the competition by a wide margin. The United States Air Force designated it the L-20A. A large contract was placed with The de Havilland Aircraft of Canada by the United States defence authorities for this aircraft. Although the specified delivery schedule left little time for tooling, expansion and provisioning for such a heavy production program, Philip Garratt's organization delivered the first one on schedule to the split second.

A formal ceremony took place on November 13, 1951, at Downsview Airport, near Toronto, when three Beaver aircraft were officially handed over to the United States Government. This was the first of a long production run of L-20's to be delivered to the U.S.A.F. and the United States Army. Phil Garratt's dream 'plane had made history! It was the first aircraft ever to be purchased by the American defence authorities from sources beyond the borders of the United States of America in peace time. It had earned this signal distinction on its own merits. Some of those in attendance on this occasion, besides Phil Garratt, were: Major-General Mark E. Bradley, Jr., representing the U.S.A.F. Air Materiel Command; the Right Honourable C. D. Howe, Minister of Defence Production; Air Vice-Marshal Frank McGill, Director of Aircraft Division, Department of Defence Production, and Air Vice-Marshal C. Roy Slemon, Air Officer Commanding the R.C.A.F. Training Command at Trenton, Ontario.

The take off, landing and flying performance of the Beaver was demonstrated by de Havilland's test pilot George Neal, who flew the aircraft.

Such excellent contributions to Canada's national development added substantially to the volume of Canada's foreign trade.

These two outstanding historical events

ranked high in news value throughout the entire aviation world, and placed the mantle of high achievement, which Mr. Garratt so richly deserved, on his broad shoulders.

Philip Clarke Garratt was born in Toronto on July 13, 1894. He received his education at Jarvis Collegiate and the University of Toronto.

He soloed an ancient Jenny at the Curtiss Flying School, Toronto, in 1915. Then in the autumn of this same year, Phil Garratt left university and joined the Royal Flying Corps, and was later sent overseas. He received flying instruction at Catterick Bridge, Yorkshire, England, with the Royal Flying Corps. Having received his wings on May 21, 1916, he spent the summer and fall flying in France as a fighter pilot with the 70th Squadron. He was then brought back to England where he served as a flying instructor at the well-known Gosport School of Flying for the duration of the war. Phil Garratt also took his instructor's course at the Gosport School of Flying. He returned to Canada after the war in 1919.

Phil Garratt was one of those who joined the circle of visionaries in 1920 who first aspired to pioneer aviation in this country. With aeroplanes obtained from the surplus lots of World War I, he threw in his lot with Bishop Barker Aeroplanes in the hope of establishing flying in the public mind via the barnstorming route. Later that year, and during 1921, he served as a flying instructor with the Canadian Air Force at Camp Borden.

During 1928 Phil Garratt did some test flying for the struggling young de Havilland Company at Toronto, mostly just for the pleasure of it. He frequently volunteered to ferry new planes for de Havilland, simply because he loved to fly.

Phil Garratt managed his own chemical firm, first known as Allardyce and Garratt, and later P. C. Garratt and Company, from 1923 to 1936. He

wound up the affairs of this company in 1936 when he was offered the management of The de Havilland Aircraft of Canada, Limited. Phil Garratt succeeded Lee Murray and was the first Canadian to hold this position. (R. A. "Bob" Loader from England was the first General Manager of the company, followed by Lee Murray in 1933.)

Phil Garratt became Vice-President and Managing Director of the company on May 22, 1936, and remained with the company until he retired. During these years he directed the "Canadianization" of a number of de Havilland's aircraft.

Phil Garratt applied all his energy to the business of planning, building and flying aircraft, which to him was a labour of love that was to shape the pattern for a highly successful career.

He was quick to recognize the need in Canada for aeroplanes that could operate on floats and skis in order to exploit the vast resources that awaited development in Canada's northland. To the work that had already been accomplished by the company in adapting the Moth 60, D.H. 61 and the Fox Moth to floats, he added his pilot's "know-how". Under his direction the Dragonfly and Dragon Rapide underwent extensive modifications and emerged as "beefed-up" bushplanes, which were both sturdy and rugged. They included many features which would add to their usefulness in the Canadian north, and they could be operated economically.

In 1937, the need for aggressive rearmament became apparent to Phil Garratt. The de Havilland Tiger Moth had been developed into a highly successful training 'plane and had been extensively modified by its Canadian organization to meet the special requirements of the Royal Canadian Air Force. Mr. Garratt maintained that he headed up an organization particularly well-qualified to supply the pressing need for training 'planes and with his typical tenacity journeyed frequently to Ottawa

The Beaver in flight over the countryside.
Photo courtesy of The de Havilland Aircraft of Canada Ltd.

to get his ideas across to the Department of National Defence, and in this he was successful. In 1937, he received an order for 25 Tiger Moths from the R.C.A.F. and the next year an order for 200 from the British Government. By the time the war broke out in 1939, he had delivered all the Tiger Moths on order and found himself in the ironical position of having an idle aeroplane factory on his hands at a time when the world situation was growing darker and darker.

By retrenchment of his working force, he managed to hang on financially during a trying six-month period. Meanwhile he continually endeavoured to put de Havilland on a full-out war production basis, risking possible financial ruin in doing this. His persistent efforts were finally rewarded in February, 1940, with an order from the Joint Air Training Command for 404 Tiger Moths. The foresight he had shown enabled deliveries to commence almost immediately.

Also, under his direction and guidance, many British-designed aircraft were modified to meet Canadian requirements. This work culminated in an aircraft known as the DH-82C — the Tiger Moth with major Canadian modifications, and which was used widely during the Second World War by the R.C.A.F. as a primary trainer.

The C attested the fact that the aircraft had undergone sufficient modification by The de Havilland Aircraft of Canada to establish its Canadian citizenship. It had acquired float and ski fittings, a coupé top, a cockpit heater, a newly designed engine cowling, a tail wheel and an increase in power. The suffix C symbolized the coming of age of The de Havilland Aircraft of Canada.

The demand for war-time training aircraft kept de Havilland's going at top speed on the Tiger Moth production program. Altogether, a total of 1,548 was produced. In 1940 the company received a contract to assemble Ansons, 375 of which rolled out of the Toronto

plant. Canada, assuming the full responsibilities of a world power, became one of the main sources of supply from which vital war material required by the Allies could be obtained. Pressure was brought to bear on the aircraft industry at this time for production — and still more production. Phil Garratt was faced with Herculean problems of expansion. From a payroll of less than fifty people when the first Tiger Moth contract reached his desk, he built the war-time organization up to a maximum of nearly 8,000 persons at its peak.

In 1941 the company tooled up to produce the world-famous DH-98 Mosquito. W.D. Hunter of the British company came to Canada to help organize the Mosquito production program, and remained in Canada as Director of Engineering. Within a year, in September, 1942, the first Canadian-built Mosquito rolled off the production lines. Ralph Spradbrow was the test pilot who flew it. It was to be the forerunner of more than a thousand of these machines that were turned out by Phil Garratt's organization before the end of the war.

In the post-war period, he guided de Havilland Aircraft through the transition period from war to peace in its production of civil aircraft, with all its associated problems. First of these was the Fox Moth, which was fabricated to a large extent from surplus Tiger Moth components. In all, some fifty of these useful little bush aeroplanes were sold. Most of them found their way into the mining areas of the north. Many of today's successful bush operators got their start with these inexpensive little bushplanes when they went into business after World War II.

In May, 1946, Wing Commander Russell Bannock, D.S.O., D.F.C., joined the company as chief test pilot and Military Sales Manager. During World War II he had a distinguished war record. In 1950, he was appointed to the board as Director of Operations.

Meanwhile, the engineering staff concentrated their efforts on a new all-Canadian designed aircraft, the DHC-1 Chipmunk. The Chipmunk made its first flight in May, 1946. This was an all-metal, two-seater, low-wing monoplane, which was to be the successor to the well-known Tiger Moth. The Chipmunk was used by the R.C.A.F. for pilot training until March, 1958, when, for economic reasons, this type of training was discontinued. The Chipmunk was used by the flying clubs for training sometimes. The Canadian-designed Chipmunk immediately was accepted by the air forces in many parts of the world and Chipmunks were exported to England, Australia, New Zealand, South Africa, South America, India, Iraq, Thailand, Egypt and other lands. By December, 1951, the manufacture of Chipmunks in Canada was discontinued so that de Havilland might make all their production facilities available to complete United States defence orders for Otters. Adopted by the R.A.F. for reserve officer training, it was produced in large quantities by the parent de Havilland Company in England under licence from The de Havilland Aircraft of Canada. Over 1,000 Chipmunks were delivered. The Chipmunk was the aircraft which the Duke of Edinburgh chose for his flying instruction.

With the construction of the Chipmunk, The de Havilland Aircraft of Canada was accepted as a member in the Society of British Aircraft Constructors. It is believed that this was the first and only Canadian company to receive this honour up to that time. The Chipmunk was Phil Garratt's choice of a name for this aircraft — perhaps because there were so many tame little chipmunks around his summer residence.

For many years Phil Garratt had visualized an ideal bushplane — one that would be specifically designed to meet the need of Canadian bush operations. Bush aeroplanes in the past had been

Chipmunk aircraft in flight.
Photo courtesy of The de Havilland Aircraft of Canada Ltd.

imported products, modified to some extent to meet Canadian requirements, but leaving much to be desired from the north country operator's point of view. Some eight-five Canadian bush operators were canvassed from coast to coast and invited to submit their recommendations for a type of aircraft which would be suitable for their work. These ideas tallied very closely with the company's own thinking and, with characteristic thoroughness, they were incorporated into a composite specification. So, in 1947, de Havilland Aircraft began to manufacture the Beaver. It was an all-metal 'plane operating as a landplane, skiplane, seaplane or amphibian. In August, 1947, the prototype Beaver, DHC-2, made its initial flight, flown by de Havilland's chief test pilot, Russ Bannock. The first production Beaver was delivered to the Ontario Department of Lands and Forests on March 26, 1948. By the end of the year 1948, the Lands and Forests' fleet, built up of Beavers, had reached seventeen. In all, twenty-nine aircraft were delivered to Canadian operators and one went to South Africa. In addition to the hundreds of Beavers flying in Canada today, they are operating in many other countries and states throughout the world. Altogether, some 1,600 Beavers were built.

Phil Garratt had his own Beaver, Serial No. 1,000, which he used for business and pleasure purposes. His Beaver's registration markings were CF-PCG — his own initials.

While on a visit to England in 1947, he flew a Vampire Jet Fighter, and thereby became the first grandfather on record in Canada to qualify as a jet pilot.

In May, 1952, the Minister of National Defence, the Honourable Brooke Claxton, announced that Philip Garratt had won the Trans-Canada Trophy in recognition of his outstanding contribution to the advancement of Canadian aviation during 1951.

The official presentation of the Trans-

Canada Trophy to Phil Garratt took place on the evening of November 11, 1952, at the Seigniory Club at Montebello, Quebec, on the occasion of a dinner given in his honour by the Air Industries and Transport Association. Air Marshal W.A. Curtis, C.B., C.B.E., D.S.C., LL.D., E.D., Chief of the Air Staff, acting for the Minister of National Defence, made the presentation.

Phil Garratt was issued Commercial Pilot's Licence No. 42, dated July 30, 1920, superseded by Commercial Pilot's Licence No. C. 5751, dated July 20, 1951, as well as Air Engineer's Licence No. 78, dated December 3, 1920, re-issued on September 1, 1936, under Licence No. 1154, and superseded by Aircraft Maintenance Licence No. YZM-127 dated July 25, 1951.

After more than a quarter-century of progress, The de Havilland Aircraft of Canada officially celebrated the opening of its new eight-million-dollar plant on September 29, 1954. Beavers and Otters were being assembled at the plant at the time; and a number of Grumman S2F components were in one of the plant bays.

The Right Honourable C.D. Howe, Minister of Defence Production, took part

---

The Committee of Award for the year 1951 consisted of the following members:
Air Commodore H.M. Carscallen, D.F.C.,C.D., Royal Canadian Air Force, Department of National Defence, Ottawa.
G.F. Henderson, Royal Canadian Flying Clubs Association, Ottawa.
R.N. Redmayne, Air Industries and Transport Association, Ottawa.
Major R.Dodds, O.B.E., M.C., Controller of Civil Aviation, Department of Transport, Ottawa.
Group Captain A.M. Cameron, Royal Canadian Air Force, Department of National Defence, Ottawa.

in the official opening. In attendance were some 800 leading industrialists and military leaders from the United States, the United Kingdom and Canada. Also present on the speaker's platform were: W.D. Hunter, DHC Engineering Director; the Honourable George Marler, Minister of Transport; Sir Geoffrey de Havilland, President of DHC and Technical Director of The de Havilland Aircraft Ltd.; Francis T. Hearle, retired Chairman of The de Havilland Aircraft Ltd. (Hatfield); Major F.B. Halford, Chairman and technical director of The de Havilland Engine Co. Ltd.; Lieutenant-General Guy G. Simonds, Chief of the General Staff of the Canadian Army; Air Marshal C. Roy Slemon, Chief of the Air Staff, R.C.A.F.; Major-General Fred R. Dent, Jr., Commander of the Mobile Air Materiel Area for the U.S.A.F.'s Air Materiel Command; and Vice-Admiral E.R. Mainguy, Chief of the Naval Staff, R.C.N. Not the least important of these was the master of ceremonies for the occasion, Phil Garratt, Vice-President and Managing Director of The de Havilland Aircraft of Canada.

Also, during this time, a full range of overhaul operations were carried out on such turbojets as the J-47, the Orenda, the Goblin and the Ghost, as well as on the de Havilland Gypsy piston engines for Chipmunks, Doves and Herons.

The de Havilland Aircraft established a Guided Missile Division in 1953. It was set up originally to take part in Canada's first missile program, the R.C.A.F. Velvet Glove air-to-air missile. On January 1, 1960, this division became known as the Special Products Division. In changing the name the company had in mind to diversify its activities in the non-defence field, while continuing to provide specialized equipment for defence requirements. Major activities of the Special Products Division were concentrated in the field of infrared systems, static transistorized power supplies, thermionic and other advanced power

The Otter seaplane in flight.
Photo courtesy of The de Havilland Aircraft of Canada Ltd.

developments, instrumentation, pneumatic, hydraulic and electrical control systems.

In the spring of 1955, the first six of an order of 95 Otter aircraft were turned over to the United States Army at a ceremony in Toronto on Monday, March 14. Major-General Lewis W. Prentiss, Commanding General of the Engineers Center at Fort Belvoir, Virginia, accepted the aircraft on behalf of General Matthew B. Ridgeway, United States Chief of Staff. The United States Corps of Engineers planned on using them for mapping and topographic survey work in Alaska and the Panama Canal areas. The same year, in July, the Otter went to the Antarctic with the United States Navy on "Operation Deep-freeze." The Otter became known as the U-1.A. in 1955. Of the eleven national expeditions participating in the International Geophysical Year (I.G.Y.) Antarctic activities in 1958, seven were equipped with Beavers and Otters. Also, in 1958, the British Commonwealth Trans-Antarctic Otter made a coast-to-coast flight across the ice continent at the Pole to accomplish a "first" for single-engine aircraft.

The de Havilland Aircraft started building Otters for the R.C.A.F. in 1953. They were used mainly for Arctic search and rescue work at the time — but, like the versatile Beaver which is flying in so many countries today, were also doing many other useful chores. The R.C.A.F. placed an order for 27 Otters for 1960. An announcement was made in the British House of Commons on December 17, 1959, that the government would purchase 36 Beavers for the British Army. During 1959 alone, 100 Beavers and 35 Otters were delivered to the United States Army. Otters are now operating in many countries.

In 1955 The de Havilland Aircraft tooled up to build the Grumman CS2F-1 Tracker for the Royal Canadian Navy. The decision to produce this aircraft in Canada was made a number of years earlier. The CS2F-1 Tracker was a twin-engine, high-wing aircraft, built in Canada by The de Havilland Aircraft of Canada Limited, under licence from Grumman Aircraft Engineering Corporation, Bethpage, Long Island. Production of this carrier-based, anti-submarine patrol aircraft commenced in the spring of 1956. The first production model was flown on July 19, 1956, by Test Pilot George Neal. The first one was officially turned over to the Royal Canadian Navy on October 12, 1956. The Tracker was equipped to detect, identify, track and destroy an underwater foe. It could operate from land bases, or a carrier deck. It took off with or without the aid of a catapult. A carrier landing was made with the assistance of its arresting gear.

By 1960 a large number of these aircraft had been delivered to the Royal Canadian Navy. The de Havilland Aircraft of Canada was the prime contractor on the project and was responsible for the engineering and scheduling of the whole program, plus the building of the forward fuselage and pilot compartment, and undertaking the complete assembly of the aircraft, wiring installation of all instruments and electronic gear, for acceptance by the Royal Canadian Navy. The engine and propellers were produced in Canada by the Canadian Pratt and Whitney Aircraft Company.

When the R.C.A.F. wanted Chipmunks for training their pilots in 1955, de Havilland Aircraft of Canada again started to manufacture Chipmunks. They had turned over the producing of these little Chipmunks to the parent company in England in 1951, so as to complete orders for Otters for the United States defence authorities.

The de Havilland Aircraft has always maintained extensive overhaul and repair facilities to keep up with their production of aircraft.

The company also completed the design and manufacture of retractable skis which, together with amphibious gear, assured year-round operation under all conditions for the Beaver. Amphibious float gear for the Otter was first tested in June, 1956, and was later approved by the Department of Transport. It has been in production since 1957.

The de Havilland Aircraft of Canada Ltd. has pioneered the development of STOL (short take-off and landing) aircraft since 1947. The development of the Caribou was under consideration by de Havilland of Canada for over two years before the decision was made to go ahead in January, 1957. During this time intensive design studies were undertaken by the DHC design team. The prototype aircraft ordered by the Canadian Government was used for extensive evaluation trials to validate its certification. The DHC-4 twin-engine Caribou made its debut in September, 1958.

The Caribou was the first aircraft in its weight category in the world to be designed primarily for short field take-off and landing, and for use as an "army vehicle" for close military support to forward areas. With STOL characteristics, it is useful to civil operators working out of limited areas. The original concept was a utility aircraft designed to initiate regular daily scheduled air services into the undeveloped areas of the world where airports were practically unknown and maintenance facilities were few and far between. Like the jetliner pioneers in the field of high-speed transport aircraft development, de Havilland of Canada's engineers met some unusual problems in the unexplored realm of control and manoeuvrability of such a large aircraft as the Caribou at low speeds. Three years of intensive design studies, prototype construction and experimental development went into the Caribou before the type certificate was granted in August, 1959, by the Department of Transport.

The Caribou STOL aircraft, CF-LAN-X, in flight in the spring of 1959.
Photo courtesy of The de Havilland Aircraft of Canada Ltd.

The de Havilland of Canada's original thinking on the Caribou was based on the idea of a "twin-engine Otter," designed around the Otter's two 600 b.h.p. engines, having a fixed landing gear and a gross weight of around 13,000 pounds. This concept failed while it was still on paper because, when CAR-4B requirements had to be realized, it was found that the twin-engine Otter could not carry a payload appreciably larger than that of its single-engine counterpart. The necessity for substantially larger payloads pushed the weight up to 22,000 pounds and the power plants to 1,200 b.h.p. Subsequent design studies increased the weight to 24,000 pounds and finally to 26,000 pounds. Power requirements increased from the original 600 b.h.p. to 1,200 and eventually finalized in the selection of two 1,450 b.h.p. Pratt and Whitney R-2000's. These were considered to be minimum requirements for a twin-engine transport aircraft that could meet CAR-4B requirements for single-engine operation and still achieve better than average operating economy. The cruising speed of the Otter at 7,500 feet was 185 m.p.h. and its stalling speed was 59 m.p.h.

The Caribou "workhorse" was unique in its ability to take off and land in a distance of less than 500 feet. Basically, the DHC-4 Caribou is an all-weather utility transport aircraft. The primary purpose of the aircraft is to serve as a commercial vehicle designed to offer low-cost transportation of passengers or cargo, or combinations of both, over the world air routes, particularly in undeveloped areas. In the design and development of the aircraft, the requirements of the feeder air line operator were kept constantly in mind. During the early formative stages of development, however, it was apparent that a STOL transport aircraft of this type would prove ideally suitable as a close support 'plane for armies in the field. Ideas were exchanged with military experts both at home and abroad. In the end, military requirements exerted a considerable influence on the final configuration of the Caribou. The final decision to go ahead with the production of the Caribou was triggered by an offer from the Canadian Army to contribute $2,500,000 towards its development. The order for five aircraft for evaluation placed by the United States Army in March, 1957, was an "off-the-shelf" order. Military thinking, nevertheless, played a large part in the production of an aircraft that was tailor-made to the new rapid mobility requirements of armies in the field.

The first Caribou STOL transport aircraft was delivered to Lieutenant-General Arthur G. Trudeau, Chief of Research and Development, with the United States Army, by The de Havilland Aircraft of Canada on October 8, 1959, along with two others during a ceremony at Downsview Airport, near Toronto, Ontario. Phil Garratt said at the ceremony that the Caribou program had originally got under way with the assistance of a $2,500,000 grant from the Canadian Army. At the end of 1959 the project had cost some $25,000,000. Two more aircraft were delivered in November, 1959, completing an order for five aircraft for evaluation purposes placed by the United States Army with The de Havilland Aircraft of Canada. Further orders were placed by the United States Army.

The civil Caribou will seat thirty passengers with baggage in the utility version, or twenty-six passengers deluxe style. The Caribou freighter will carry up to three and a half tons and the high, wide, rear loading door facilitates efficient loading and unloading of bulky items, such as mining and oil drilling equipment. It can operate from unpaved runways. The military version will carry thirty combat troops, or three tons of cargo or two fully-loaded jeeps. Its cargo payload will vary from 6,000 pounds with fuel for 600 miles, to 7,320 pounds with a 200-mile range. The ultimate range, with full standard tanks, is approximately 1,200 miles.

Then came the Buffalo, the Turbo-Beaver and the Twin-Otter under Phil Garratt's management.

Phil Garratt, A.F.C., an outstanding figure in Canadian flying and in the aircraft manufacturing world for many years, continued as Vice-President and Managing Director of The de Havilland Aircraft of Canada in Toronto, until his retirement on December 31, 1965, at the

Phil Garratt receiving the Trans-Canada Trophy from A/V.M. W. A. Curtis, C.B., C.B.E., D.S.C., E.D., Chief of the Air Staff, on November 11, 1952, at Montebello, P.Q.

Photo courtesy of The de Havilland Aircraft of Canada Ltd.

age of 71. He held this position for thirty years. For twenty-two years he was also Chairman of the company. He continued as a director of the company until 1971.

At the time of his retirement, the company was employing 7,800 people, and had a world-wide reputation as a designer and builder of rugged utility aircraft. Nearly 1,600 Beavers were flying throughout the world.

Under his management, six STOL-type utility transport aircraft were designed, and in production. Also, under his management, the company grew from an aircraft assembly operation to an internationally recognized leader in STOL aircraft designs.

Phil Garratt received the McCurdy Medal for 1960, which is the premier award in the scientific and engineering fields. In 1962 he was named an Honorary Fellow of the Canadian Aeronautics and Space Institute. He was also the first Chairman of the newly-formed Air Industries Association in 1962; and became honorary director at the association's meeting late in 1965. He was also the first winner of the C.D. Howe Award, which was presented by the Canadian Aeronautics and Space Institute at their annual dinner on May 3, 1966. He was awarded the Trans-Canada Trophy for 1951, and selected by the Honourable Paul Hellyer as an honorary winner of the trophy for 1966. He was awarded the Canada Medal in 1971; and named a member of Canada's Aviation Hall of Fame in 1973. He was made a Companion of the Order of Flight (City of Edmonton).

Phil Garratt died on November 16, 1974, at the age of 80, at Toronto, Ontario, where he and Mrs. Garratt resided. They had two sons and one daughter, who are married.

Phil Garratt possessed unusual tenacity of purpose in his endeavours. He had a perpetual sense of good humour and fair play. He was well respected by the aviation fraternity as an outstanding leader and for his wise counsel. This descendant of the United Empire Loyalists, endowed with a statuesque six-foot figure, was sometimes referred to as the "Dean" of Canadian aircraft manufacturers.

In a lifetime devoted to aviation, Phil Garratt set an enviable record of Canadian achievement in the aviation manufacturing world. With his invincible determination, he kept the Canadian company, which he managed, solvent through good and bad times. Under his dynamic leadership, and with his business foresight, The de Havilland Aircraft of Canada became a national institution that made many valuable contributions to Canadian civil and military aviation and also established a world-wide reputation for Canadian aircraft abroad.

1952

Keith R. Greenaway

Citation: in recognition of his development of new methods of aerial navigation in the Arctic regions

Brigadier-General Keith R. Greenaway, C.M., C.D., J.M.N., F.C.A.S.I., while a Squadron Leader with the Royal Canadian Air Force, Ottawa, was awarded the Trans-Canada Trophy for meritorious service in the advancement of aviation in Canada during 1952, "in recognition of his development of new methods of aerial navigation in the Arctic regions." The announcement of the award was made on Friday, May 22, 1953, by the Honourable Brooke Claxton, Minister of National Defence.

The twilight computer, perfected in 1951, came into operational use in 1952. The twilight computer had been adopted by the R.C.A.F. and the R.A.F. as standard equipment for crews engaged in northern flying.

Keith Rogers Greenaway is the son of Mr. and Mrs. W.E. Greenaway of Woodville, Ontario, and was born on a farm in the Township of Mariposa on April 8, 1916. He received his primary education in Mariposa, Ontario, and from 1929 until 1934 he attended Malvern Collegiate in Toronto where he matriculated.

He was employed in the Canadian office of the United Provinces of India from 1934 to 1935 to assist with a display of cottage industries at the Canadian National Exhibition. Then, in 1936, Keith Greenaway joined the Cambray Telephone Co. of Cambray, Ontario, and remained with this company on full and part-time employment until 1939. Next, he took a course in radio and electronics with the Canadian Electronics Institute, graduating in 1940.

Keith Greenaway enlisted in the R.C.A.F. on May 7, 1940, and went to No. 1 Manning Depot in Toronto for his basic training. Then he was sent to the #1 Wireless School, Montreal, where he completed the course and became a

wireless instructor with the flying squadron based at St. Hubert Airport. He attained the rank of Sergeant at this time. In August, 1943, he remustered to a navigator-wireless operator and went to #4 Wireless School at Guelph, where he graduated in December of the same year obtaining the highest mark for air operating ever given by the Wireless School up to that time. From Guelph he was sent to #8 A.O.S. (Air Observers School), Ancienne Lorette, Quebec, for navigational training where he attended the first Navigator-Wireless Course for Canadians, graduating in May, 1944, at the head of his class. On graduation he was commissioned as a Pilot Officer, and went to #1 A.G.T.S. (Aircrew Graduate's Training School), Maitland, Nova Scotia, where he took an Aircrew Conditioning Course.

In July, 1944, Keith Greenaway was promoted to Flying Officer and posted to #1 C.N.S. (Central Navigation School), Rivers, Manitoba, and was staff navigation instructor at the school for three months. From September, 1944, until March, 1945, he was navigation instructor at #6 A.O.S., Ancienne Lorette. Then he returned to #1 C.N.S. at Rivers, Manitoba, where he remained until August. For the next five months he instructed wireless navigators who were taking refresher courses. During this period he became Officer Commanding of the refresher courses, and in May was transferred to the Specialists Squadron to instruct navigation instructors and to aid in compiling a Navigation Work Book.

Keith Greenaway, now a Flying Officer, was transferred to #1 R. & N.S. (Reconnaissance and Navigation School), Summerside, Prince Edward Island, in December, 1945, with the Specialists Squadron from Rivers where he in-structed on the SNIN (Short Navigation

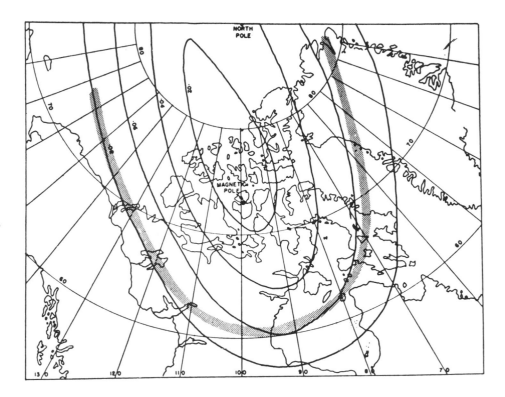

Map showing approximate lines of equal horizontal magnetic force, with the boundary (shaded area) inside of which the directional gyro is normally used for maintaining heading.
Courtesy of Keith Greenaway.

Instructor-Navigator) Courses. While at Summerside he completed the Navigation Work Book as well. From here he was transferred with the A.N.S. (Air Navigation School) to Greenwood, Nova Scotia, in December, 1945.

Then he was seconded by the R.C.A.F. to fly as a navigator with the United States Navy on their aerologation flights over eastern Canada and the North Atlantic which were made in the winter of 1946 on development work in pressure pattern flying. Also, it was in February, 1946, that he prepared a joint report on "the use of pressure data in estimating aircraft drift and its various applications in air navigation." He received a letter of commendation from the United States Navy for his work.

He returned to the Air Navigation School at Summerside in March, 1946, to continue his work as navigation instructor. The following month, Keith Greenaway was promoted to Flight Lieutenant, and was assigned to the U.S.A.A.F. B-29 Detachment of the Low Frequency LORAN Flight Test Program, Edmonton, Alberta. He became officer in charge of the Canadian section of the U.S.A.A.F. B-29 Detachment engaged in the test programme.

During this period, Keith Greenaway assisted with fashioning what are now accepted in Canada as the navigation techniques for flying in the high latitudes of the north. Together, with Lieutenant Colthorpe of the U.S.A.F., he wrote "An Aerial Reconnaissance of the North American Arctic." While on these missions, he made his first polar flights in 1946 and was one of the navigators of the crew of the first U.S.A.F. aircraft, a B-29 Superfortress, to fly over the North Geographic Pole. The flight originated from Fairbanks, Alaska, flew to Cape Columbia, Ellesmere Island, then went to the Pole, and returned directly to Edmonton. The flight was made in twenty-two hours and twenty minutes.

In April, 1947, Keith Greenaway, flying in a B-29 with the U.S.A.F., discovered T-3, a floating island of ice in the Arctic Ocean, several years before a U.S.A.F. crew spotted it while flying out of Fairbanks. T-3 had drifted to a point about 150 miles northwest of Ellef Ringnes Island off the Canadian Arctic Archipelago at the time.

While Keith Greenaway was with the B-29 Detachment, he made numerous flights over the polar regions, extending from Nome, Alaska, in the west, to the North Pole and as far east as Greenland. Also, he prepared eleven reports on the flight testing of Low Frequency LORAN in high altitudes, and on reconnaissance observations. During this time, he helped develop polar navigation techniques, particularly in the use of the directional gyroscope for maintaining a heading in areas where the magnetic compass is unreliable.

It was in 1947, in association with Mr. J.W. Cox, a Defence Research Board scientist, that he developed the R.C.A.F.'s High Latitude Twilight Computer, which is a navigation aid for use in high latitudes.

Then, in October, 1948, Keith Greenaway was transferred from Edmonton to Air Force Headquarters, Ottawa, where he was seconded to the Defence Research Board, and quite naturally was employed in the Arctic Section as a navigation specialist to work on high-latitude navigation and associated problems. During the next six years, many experimental and reconnaissance flights were made throughout the polar regions, many extending to the Pole.

He was a senior observer on a series of reconnaissance flights which he co-ordinated to determine the freeze-up and break-up of ice in Hudson Bay.

His interest and insight were not confined to navigational matters but also to related subjects, such as delivering a paper on "Experiences with Arctic Flying Weather" to the Canadian Branch of the Royal Meteorological Society in November, 1950. For this Greenaway received the President's Prize, an annual award made by the society for "the best scientific paper presented before the Branch during the year." His paper was one amongst thirty others which were presented by professional meteorologists.

Keith Greenaway received his appointment as a Squadron Leader in July, 1951. That same year he was awarded the Thurlow Trophy. This is an annual award made on an international basis by the United States Institute of Navigation to the person making "the most outstanding scientific and practical contribution to navigation during the year."

Then he took part in R.A.F. and U.S.A.F. flights in 1951 to test the radar doppler principle as an aid to navigation in the polar regions.

He received recognition for his work in polar navigation in 1952 when he was awarded the Trans-Canada Trophy.

Brigadier-General Keith Greenaway is recognized as one of the world's leading authorities on Arctic air navigation, and has made many notable contributions to

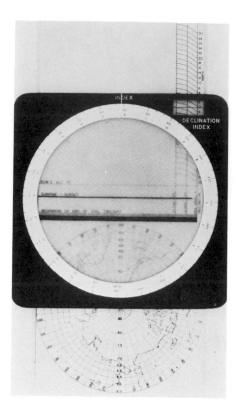

High Latitude Twilight Computer.
Photo courtesy of Keith Greenaway.

aviation, particularly in Arctic flying. His development of grid techniques is of paramount importance in the flying field today, as they are basic to many of the automatic devices used in modern high-speed aircraft. His twilight computer, developed in 1947, perfected in 1951, came into operational use in 1952. The twilight computer has been adopted by the R.C.A.F. and R.A.F. as standard equipment for crews engaged in northern flying. "Previous to this development," he said, "the only method of calculating the duration of twilight on a high latitude flight was by plotting the track and determining twilight conditions at various points along the route. This method, while requiring considerable time, was tedious and still failed to give a complete picture of twilight conditions." In Brigadier-General Keith Greenaway's words, "the computer compounds the speed and flight direction of the aircraft with the earth's rotation, and the aircraft's track in space is presented in graphical form and is shown in relation to the twilight belt."

The primary problems of polar navigation are the convergence of the meridians at the poles, and the convergence of the isogonic lines at the geographic and magnetic poles. When flying in the vicinity of the pole, any track, except a north-south track, will cross a great number of meridians, and consequently the true heading changes frequently. To avoid this, a special meridian is selected as the standard meridian, and a grid net superimposed on the plotting chart with grid meridians parallel to the reference meridian. Maintaining a desired bearing with reference to this meridian is called "grid navigation."

The original concept of "grid" direction dates back to 1928 when Admiral Tonta of the Italian Navy suggested it for polar use. In 1941 it was devised independently by Group Captain Ken C. Maclure of the R.C.A.F., and in 1945 it

was tested by the R.A.F. on their first polar flight. The next year Brigadier-General Keith Greenaway and the B-29 Detachment at Edmonton used it, but changed the orientation — at the same time introducing the technique of steering by gyro, which is now standard for all high latitude flights.

As many polar flights start and end outside the polar regions, the conventional methods of navigation in use necessitate a transfer from one method of navigation to another and more complicated one during a flight. Such a transfer during flight may cause problems, especially if bad weather or twilight is encountered when the transfer is about to take place, as navigators normally wish to check the heading with a celestial bearing at this time.

In the vicinity of the Magnetic Pole, magnetic compasses are of little use due to the weakness of the horizontal component of the earth's magnetic field. Also, aurora borealis and magnetic storms induce large errors in magnetic compasses, rendering them unreliable. Magnetic compasses should not be trusted within an approximate distance of 500 miles of the Magnetic Pole. To steer accurate courses then, some means independent of magnetic influences must be used.

The average directional gyro was not satisfactory for trans-polar flights because of its high rate of precession (wander).

Owing to the lack of reliable radio aids and the difficulty of map reading in the polar regions, and where magnetic compasses are unreliable, celestial observations are the most important aid to navigation. During the twilight period the use of an astro compass and sextant is limited but, by planning a flight in advance, it is sometimes possible to avoid flying in prolonged periods of twilight or, at least, to cut twilight flying to a minimum. Usually one navigator takes altitude and azimuth bearings on a celestial body at regular intervals while

the other plots them, using a gyro to maintain direction. When calculating the duration of the twilight period, it is necessary to consider the speed at which the aircraft is travelling and the direction in which it is going.

Brigadier-General Keith Greenaway explains that

"difficulty arises from the necessity to compound the factors of speed and direction of flight with the easterly drift in space caused by the earth's rotation, since the aircraft's track in space is not the same as its track in relation to the earth's surface, and it is this track in space that must be compared with the position of the twilight belt. To an observer in outer space the twilight belt will, over a period of a day or so, appear fixed, with the earth rotating behind it, while the observed motion of an aircraft will consist of its movement in relation to the earth's surface, combined with a steady drift to the east at a rate of 15° per hour. For example, if the observer is over the North Pole and the aircraft flying due north, its track will appear as a spiral to the left which, in 24 hours, will make a complete revolution."

Then one day in May, 1953, an announcement was made that Brigadier-General Keith Greenaway, then a Squadron Leader, was awarded the Trans-Canada Trophy for 1952 in recognition of his development of new methods of aerial navigation in the Arctic

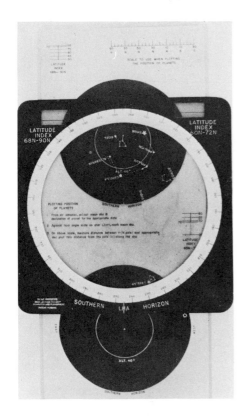

High Latitude Plainsphere. Reverse side of the Twilight Computer.
Photo courtesy of Keith Greenaway.

regions. His achievement had been recognized.

The official presentation of the trophy to Brigadier-General Greenaway took place on the evening of Tuesday, October 27, 1953, at the Chateau Laurier, Ottawa, on the occasion of a dinner held in his honour by the Air Industries and Transport Association at their annual banquet. The Honourable Brooke Claxton, Minister of National Defence, in presenting the trophy said: "I now have the honour to present the Trans-Canada Trophy for distinguished work in aviation

---

The Committee of Award for the year 1952 consisted of the following members:

Chairman: Air Commodore H. M. Carscallen, Royal Canadian Air Force, Department of National Defence, Ottawa.

Members: E. R. MacFarland, President, Royal Canadian Flying Clubs Association, Ottawa.

R. N. Redmayne, Air Industries and Transport Association, Ottawa.

Major R. Dodds, Controller of Civil Aviation, Department of Transport, Ottawa.

Secretary: Group Captain A. M. Cameron, Royal Canadian Air Force, Department of National Defence, Ottawa.

George C. Hurren, Royal Canadian Flying Clubs Association, Ottawa (in attendance).

in 1952 to one who has earned the trophy by his accomplishments in the field of research and development, exploration and flight." Brigadier-General Greenaway graciously replied: "I would like to feel that this is an award to Canadian aviation which has played such a major role in the development of navigation techniques in the polar regions." This dinner was also attended by twelve of the former winners of the trophy: Punch Dickins, 1928; George Phillips, 1931; Romeo Vachon, 1937; Bill English, 1938; Murton Seymour, 1939; Dan McLean, 1941; Pat Reid, 1942-43; J. A. Wilson, 1944; Group Captain Lewis Leigh, 1946; Squadron Leader Ron West, 1948; Carl Agar, 1950; and Phil Garratt, 1951.

Brigadier-General Greenaway planned and took part as senior navigator in a flight for the National Research Council to the North Geographic Pole to measure the ozone content in the atmosphere in January, 1953.

He attained the rank of Wing Commander in June, 1954, and for years made two or three trips a year to the north to gain still further data in Arctic navigation techniques and procedures.

During the six years he was with the Defence Research Board he gave lectures to the R.C.A.F. Staff College, the Department of National Defence Staff, the National Defence College, the United States Institute of Navigation and other organizations and professional groups on polar navigation and associated topics.

Keith Greenaway completed a two-year exchange posting with the U.S.A.F. Strategic Air Command, from September 1, 1954 to October, 1956. He was stationed first at MacDill Air Force Base at Tampa, Florida, and, in 1955, was transferred to Castle Air Force Base, California. His duties were to assist American bomber-navigators in high latitude navigational problems in their flights in B-47 and B-52 jet bombers across the roof of the world and the

covering of great distances exactly on schedule and on target. He made many flights as a crew member in both the B-47 and B-52 aircraft to test equipment and development navigation techniques.

The Boeing B-52 Stratofortress was an eight-jet, swept-wing, long-range heavy bomber built for the U.S.A.F. by Boeing Airplane Company of Seattle, Washington, and Wichita, Kansas. The eight-jet engines were mounted in pairs on sharply raked forward pods under the thin, high-speed wing. The B-52's had a range of 6,000 miles plus, without refuelling, and had a speed of 650 m.p.h. plus. They had a service ceiling of 50,000 feet plus. The B-52's were powered by Pratt and Whitney J.57 turbojet engines, each in the 10,000-pound thrust class. The bomber weighed over 400,000 pounds. The strategic roles of the B-52 were many.

Shortly after reporting to the 6th Air Division at Tampa, Florida, Brigadier-General Greenaway went to Mather Field, Sacramento, California, to take a short course on the equipment in the B-47 Stratojet, the type that they flew at MacDill. The Boeing B-47 Stratojet was a six-jet engine, swept-wing, medium bomber built for the U.S.A.F. Strategic Air Command by Boeing Airplane Company of Wichita, Kansas, and Seattle, Washington. It was in the 600 m.p.h. class, capable of carrying nuclear devices. It had a service ceiling of 40,000 feet. The B-47's gross weight was around 230,000 pounds, with a range of more than 3,000 miles at the time. Orenda Engines, Ltd., of Toronto, also used a Stratojet type for testing its Iroquois jet engine, attaching it to the rear of the fuselage.

Then Keith Greenaway did some work on earth-chart convergency relationship problems associated with the use of the directional gyro on the primary steering device in high-speed aircraft.

During this time, he developed a daylight-twilight-darkness computer for

S/Ldr. Keith Greenaway receiving the Trans-Canada Trophy from Brooke Claxton, Minister of National Defence, on October 27, 1953, at a dinner held in his honour by the Air Industries and Transport Associätion at the Chateau Laurier, Ottawa.
Photo courtesy of Marvin Flatt.

flight planning. This was a further development of the R.C.A.F. twilight computer which he originally developed in 1947, perfected in 1951 and became operational in 1952.

He returned to Ottawa in October, 1956, after two years with the U.S.A.F. Strategic Air Command, to resume duties as a staff officer in the Directorate of Plans and Programmes at R.C.A.F. Headquarters to work on R.C.A.F. programmes.

Greenaway was loaned to the United States Navy in August, 1958, to assist in navigating a U.S.N. airship, ZPG-2, on an experimental flight to Ice Island, T-3, in the polar regions, which he had discovered in April, 1947. It was the last airship to visit the Arctic Ocean. The flight originated from N.A.S. South Weymouth, Massachusetts. The flight from Resolute Bay to Ice Island, T-3, in the Arctic Ocean, returned to South Weymouth, and was made non-stop in seventy-eight hours and twenty minutes.

Then in August, 1959, he was posted to Winnipeg as Officer Commanding of the Central Navigation School there. While at the school he developed the

Aerospace Systems Course currently conducted by the Canadian Armed Forces. He also developed and perfected the "Earth Convergency Grid Technique" for measuring direction in the polar regions. The system is used by the Scandinavian Airline System (SAS) on their flights and by many crews of the Canadian Forces on long-range flights.

Keith Greenaway was promoted to Group Captain in August, 1963, and appointed Commanding Officer of the R.C.A.F. Station at Clinton, Ontario. Then in July, 1967, he was promoted to Air Commodore. However, this rank was changed to Brigadier-General in 1968 upon the unification of the Canadian Armed Forces.

Brigadier-General Greenaway was again seconded to the Department of External Affairs in October, 1967, and then appointed Air Adviser to the Chief of the Air Staff of the Royal Malaysian Air Force. In this position he advised on organization and management and on training for the R.M.A.F. and assisted in a wide variety of matters. He did not return from Malaysia until May, 1970.

He retired from the Canadian Armed

Forces on March 7, 1971, with the rank of Brigadier-General; and became a consultant with the Advisory Committee on Northern Development, which position he held until 1973. Also, during this period, he drafted guidelines and priorities for federally sponsored scientific activities in the north.

He then became a consultant with the Department of Indian Affairs and Northern Development on northern scientific matters in October, 1973; and was appointed senior science adviser to the department in January, 1975.

Brigadier-General Greenaway is the author of a number of publications on air navigation. He is co-author of *An Aerial Reconnaissance of Arctic North America*, published in 1948; author of *Arctic Air Navigation*, published in 1951 and used as a text by a number of air forces as well as commercial air lines; co-author of *Arctic Canada from the Air*, an aerial geography of the Canadian Far North, published in 1956; contributor to *Science, History and Hudson Bay*, published in 1968; and editor of *Science and the North*, published in 1973. Also, he has written over twenty papers on navigation and other topics particularly in relation to northern Canada and the polar regions, which were published in various professional journals.

During a 31-year career directly associated with aviation, he accumulated about 8,000 hours' flying time. A little over 6,000 hours were flown as a crew member on experimental, tests and exploratory flights. He qualified as a navigator and flew as a crew member on twenty-six types of aircraft ranging in size from the twin-engine Dakota (C-47) to the eight-engine B-52, including an airship.

Brigadier-General Greenaway has received numerous awards and decorations, such as: the President's Prize, which was given by the Royal Meteorological Society, Canadian Branch, for the most outstanding meteorological paper presented to the Branch in 1950; the Thurlow Award, which was from the United States Institute of Navigation in 1951 for contributions to the science of navigation; the Trans-Canada Trophy, in recognition of his development of new methods of aerial navigation in the Arctic regions; the Coronation Medal, awarded on June 2, 1953; the Massey Medal, which was awarded in 1960 for outstanding personal achievement; the Centennial Medal, awarded on July 1, 1967; the Johan Mangku Negara (JMN) decoration, awarded by the Government of Malaysia; the Canadian Decoration (CD) in 1952 and Clasp in 1962; named a member of Canada's Aviation Hall of Fame in 1973; appointed to the Order of Icarus (Companion) in 1975; and made a member of the Order of Canada in 1976. Also, he was made a Companion of the Order of Flight (City of Edmonton).

He is a Fellow of the Canadian Aeronautics and Space Institute; a Fellow of the Royal Institute of Navigation (British); a Fellow of the Arctic Institute of North America, and is on the Board of Governors; a member of the Institute of Navigation (US); a member of the Canadian Meteorological Society; a member of the Explorers Club, New York; a member of the Arctic Circle Club, Ottawa, and a past President; a member of the Royal Canadian Geographical Society. Also, in May, 1977, he was elected President of the Canadian Aeronautics and Space Institute for 1977-78.

Brigadier-General Keith Greenaway is married and has two daughters, Brenda and Linda. He and Mrs. Greenaway reside in Ottawa.

He is an internationally recognized authority on aerial navigation, with particular reference to polar flying. General Greenaway has been guest lecturer at a number of professional organizations and universities, including the Technical University of West Berlin.

It has been said that Keith Greenaway is one of the greatest polar air navigators in the world today. Not only is he extremely modest about his navigational achievements, but he likes to speak of the contributions of others with whom he was associated, and those with whom he worked from day to day. He is held in high regard and esteem by those who know him.

In research and achievement in this wonderful world of ours, he has opened up new fields in polar navigation. He has been closely associated with all forms of Arctic operations since they were conducted on an organized basis. As he is one of Canada's foremost lecturers on northern and Arctic aviation subjects, his services for years, and still today, are constantly being sought to brief Army, Navy and Air Force personnel and others on aviation and navigation problems in the Canadian Arctic.

1953

Captain Frank Young.
Photo courtesy of Trans-Canada Air Lines.

Franklin I. "Frank" Young

Citation: in recognition of his outstanding contribution through his production of the National Air Show at Toronto that year (1953)

Captain Franklin I. "Frank" Young, Operations Manager, Central Region, Trans-Canada Air Lines, Toronto, was awarded the Trans-Canada Trophy for meritorious service in the advancement of aviation in Canada during 1953, "in recognition of his outstanding contribution through his production of the National Air Show at Toronto that year." Captain Frank Young received news of the award on Tuesday, August 17, 1954, in a telegram from the Honourable Ralph Campney, Minister of National Defence.

Captain Young made a tremendous contribution to Canadian aviation through organizing the National Air Show at Toronto in 1953, which was held on September 19. Frank Young was Chairman of the 1953 National Air Show, which was sponsored by the Toronto Flying Club under the auspices of the City of Toronto. It was first organized along these lines in 1952, and visualized as an annual event to increase in significance from year to year. The citation referred to Captain Young's "great drive and leadership," in aiming for a national air platform for the presentation of industry and defence to the public. Frank Young designated the site for the National Air Show as the water front of Lake Ontario off Exhibition Park, the home of the Canadian National Exhibition. This site was chosen in the interest of safety for both spectators and participants, and arrangements were made with officials of the City of Toronto and the Canadian National Exhibition to hold the first Canadian National Air Show on September 20, 1952. Both of these shows were unqualified successes.

Frank Young's campaign, approved by the Royal Canadian Flying Clubs Association, soon gained official and industrial recognition for the National Air Show. In past years, air shows had been held in the Toronto area at various airports but they lacked recognition as a National Air Show. In 1953, through Frank Young's efforts, the National Air Show associated itself with the Canadian International Trade Fair and the show became a joint venture. To a large extent the Air Show helped to draw exhibitors to the Canadian International Trade Fair, and gave it greater value and wider scope. This broader participation on the part of the aviation industry was for the mutual benefit of both the Air Show and the Trade Fair, and would contribute to consolidating the position of Canada, already a leader in the field of aviation.

A great deal of credit for the development and progress of the National Air Show was due to the foresight and activities of Frank Young, who made a great contribution to Canadian aviation.

When Frank Young became a director of the Royal Canadian Flying Clubs Association in 1951, and when President of the Toronto Flying Club for 1951-52 and 1952-53, he developed a keen interest in producing a National Air Show for Canada. At this time a national board of honorary directors was set up, composed of leading exponents of aviation throughout Canada. This was largely accomplished through the efforts of Frank Young. He believed, with approximately one billion dollars being spent yearly by the taxpayer on air defence, with 60,000 people employed by Canadian air industries — a greater number than those engaged in the automobile industry — and Canada ranking as a major air power in the world, that this progress should be made apparent to the man on the street, without whom all this could not be accomplished.

Each year, up to 1953, some 100,000

people attended the National Air Show and this, in Frank Young's opinion, was the best answer concerning the merits of such a colourful occasion. Great interest was taken by the people in the static display as well.

There were two main parts to the National Air Show: the flying display over the water front of Lake Ontario; and the static display in some of the Canadian National Exhibition buildings.

The flying display for the 1953 Air Show which took place along the water front of Lake Ontario, opposite the Canadian National Exhibition Grounds, covered a period of three hours and ten minutes. This display included the Governor General's Cup Race, and a grand performance by the Royal Canadian Air Force.

The Governor General's Cup Race, patterned after the King's Cup Race in England, was open to any licensed Canadian pilot with an aircraft of Canadian registry weighing not more than 4,000 pounds at take-off, and with an average cruising minimum altitude of not under 500 feet, except for take-off and the dive-past finish. The method of handicapping the aircraft was in accordance with the estimated performance of the aircraft at full throttle. The race was held over a closed course covering a distance of between fifty and sixty miles. The aircraft which participated in this event were based at Toronto's Malton and Island Airports.

While the Governor General's Cup Race was in progress, The de Havilland Aircraft of Canada presented a flypast of several of their aircraft. Their Otter seaplane made two dramatic landings and take-offs in the breakwater off Exhibition Park. The exceptional performance of Canada's Otter in take-off, climb and landing was apparent by its ease of manoeuverability. This adaptable, sturdy, single-engine aircraft was especially designed to operate in difficult or restricted areas under tropic or Arctic

conditions. De Havilland's Beaver land-plane, Executive Dove and Heron, Mark I, flying beautifully, graced the skies in their turn during the show to leave the spectators enthralled with their fine qualities.

The Royal Canadian Air Force carried out a magnificent programme of flight performance covering a forty-five minute period, as well as a twenty-five minute period with the Army during which anti-aircraft firing took place. Wing Commander J. D. Mitchener was the R.C.A.F. co-ordinator for the Air Show.

The R.C.A.F. show opened with an excellent formation flypast of twelve Avro Canada's CF-100's, all-weather fighter aircraft, powered by twin-Orenda jets, augustly silhouetted against the afternoon sky. The CF-100 was especially designed for the vast spaces and rigorous climates of the Canadian north. The superb all-Canadian Chipmunk performed gracefully in a solo aerobatics display. This all-metal, two-seater, low wing monoplane was designed and constructed by The de Havilland Aircraft of Canada. Next, six P-51 Mustangs took to the air and carried out a spectacular rocket-firing display. A formation of six T-33's, known as "Silver Stars," made a great impression on the crowd with their manoeuvres, and a single "Silver Star" which carried out a solo aerobatics display was equally the centre of attraction. The name "Silver Star" was a combination of Canada's first aircraft, the "Silver Dart", and United States Lockheed's "Shooting Star", which was given to the aircraft on the occasion of the R.C.A.F.'s acceptance of the first production model from Canadair. The T-33A, the Canadian version of Lockheed's Shooting Star, was a two-place advanced jet trainer in the R.C.A.F.'s training programme, bridging the gap between primary aircraft and the more advanced operational jet fighters. Canadair's Silver Stars were the backbone of Canada's training facilities for jet pilots of the

R.C.A.F. and NATO countries. A Canso amphibian, a Consolidated PBY5A, made a very impressive jet-assisted take-off. Thrilling and inspiring as all of these demonstrations were, then came the shining Comet, Mark II, sleek and powerful, presenting a graceful form and elegant appearance as it made its speedy flypast to carry out its part in the show. Not to be outdone was the display put on by the Canadian Harvard trainer aircraft, NA-AT6, manufactured by the Canadian Car and Foundry Co. Ltd. The show ended with a Lockheed Ventura, P.V.1, demonstrating a towing drogue for the Army anti-aircraft firing show. The R.C.A.F. aircraft flew in from their base at Trenton, Ontario, to carry out their brilliant performance.

The absorbing and entrancing display carried out by the Royal Canadian Air Force resulted from their precise training, and their co-ordinated efforts in all phases of their performances added rich colour to their skill in their mastery of the skies.

Frank Young arranged for the static display utilizing some of the fine buildings of the Canadian National Exhibition at Exhibition Park. The main exhibit building of the Coliseum cost fifty million dollars to build. The exhibits were to be part of the Canadian International Trade Fair for the first time in 1954.

Ten thousand square feet of space was set aside in the west annex of the Coliseum for the static display of the Air Show, with a reserve of 25,000 square feet, if required. Also, there was ample space for displaying aircraft and other exhibits outside the Coliseum.

Frank Young, by his visualization of a National Air Show in all its splendour, had sown the seed for future air shows that could become an international meeting ground in aviation progress, particularly between the United Kingdom and the North American market. It would, of course, be a while before the full stature of the National Air Show was

realized but Frank Young, in originating this event, helped to fix in the minds of Canadians, and people from all over the world, the fact that Canada was second to none when it came to designing, developing and constructing aircraft, and flying them.

This show window of Canadian aviation helped to forward the education of our youth in this, the Air Age. It helped to focus the attention of the air-minded world not only on Toronto but on Canada as the fifth nation in the world to feature such an event.

Those concerned with the National Air Show did not receive remuneration of any kind, but they had the satisfaction that they were doing a job that was well worthwhile. Surplus revenues, other than reserve, were distributed in the form of scholarships to members of the Air Cadet League of Canada by a committee created for that purpose under the Chairmanship of Air Marshal W. A. Curtis at that time.

Frank Young's superlative efforts in the promotion of a National Air Show, which he opined should rightly be called the Canadian International Air Show as it telescoped the international aviation world, were warmly appreciated and received. This would be a real tribute to any country, but it was a special tribute to Canada when one considers the vastness of the country. His perseverance in achieving this end, which was still only in its early beginnings, deserved commendation from the industrial and aviation worlds.

Franklin Inglee Young was born on August 7, 1909, at Toronto, Ontario. It was during the latter part of World War I that Frank Young's interest in flying was awakened, when he was only eight years of age, when his father took him to the Military Flying School at Long Branch, near Toronto, where he saw many aircraft on the ground and in the air. Much later on, he was to learn that these aircraft were Curtiss JN-4's.

When Frank Young was only fourteen his father died accidentally, so he left school to assist his mother to augment the family income. In spite of his youth, he realized the need of specialized training in some field, if his ambition was ever to be served. On his sixteenth birthday, in the year 1925, he was with his mother and family on a picnic at Burlington Beach, Hamilton, Ontario, where they noticed an aircraft landing and taking off from a very small field on the Beach Road. Because it was his birthday, his mother decided to satisfy his yearning by letting him have a flight as a birthday present. This experience helped Frank to cherish a desire to become a pilot, and nothing else would do from then on. The 'plane he flew in belonged to the Elliott Air Service, Hamilton, owned and operated by Jack V. Elliott.

The aircraft being used were Curtiss JN-4's. Jack V. Elliott, who had been in the music business two or three years before, had taken possession of two crated JN-4's, which were surplus from World War I, as payment on money owing to him, and with one of these aircraft visited the Air Force at Camp Borden, Ontario, where he learned to fly. It was the practice at that time for the Air Force to teach anyone to fly who owned an aircraft, as there were no schools of a commercial nature in existence. Jack V. Elliott, in turn, purchased several more JN-4's and literally hundreds of World War I surplus propellers for a few cents a piece, and from the crates in which these propellers were packed there was sufficient lumber to build a large hangar. Thus was established the Elliott Air Service in 1924, largely for the purpose of barnstorming, flying training and aerial photography. The aircraft used for aerial photography was a Fokker two-seater with the gun triggers still on the joystick, scalloped trailing edge, and the gas tank between the undercarriage wheels faired

as an auxiliary wing section.

Frank Young began his flying instruction at this school in 1927, at the age of eighteen. Lessons in those days cost one dollar per minute. The school operated from the small field on the Beach Road in the summer and from off the ice at Burlington Beach in the winter, with its base of operations at the foot of McNab Street in Hamilton. Upon the completion of his course of instruction he had to wait a year, until he was twenty, before the government would grant him a licence.

All the students at this school wore a type of military uniform with puttees. Many of these graduates have been successful in aviation in many different countries. Here in Canada, to name a few, were Captain G. Edwards, later Assistant Director of Flight Operations, Trans-Canada Air Lines; Captain Walter Fowler, later Executive Assistant to the President, Trans-Canada Air Lines; Captain Ron George, later with K.L.M. Airlines; Captain E. McKay, later with Colonial Air Lines; and others. Jack V. Elliott, himself, lived in Houston, Texas, in later years, where he ran a trailer court.

International Airways Limited of Hamilton, Ontario, acquired the business of Elliott Air Service on May 1, 1928. It was formed under the leadership of Major-General Sir J. H. MacBrien, C.B., C.M.G., D.S.O., a former Commissioner of the R.C.M.P. The company had branch offices at Toronto and Ottawa in Ontario, and at Montreal and Sherbrooke in Quebec. Flying schools were conducted in Hamilton, Toronto, Montreal and Sherbrooke, with an aerial survey division at Ottawa. International Airways engaged in aerial surveys and air photography for commercial advertising, timber cruising, forest sketching, transportation and taxi services. The company was operating twenty-six aircraft by the end of 1928.

Not having had the opportunity of much formal education, Frank Young

Frank Young (left), "Red" Murray (centre) and G. C. W. "Bill' Dingwall (right) in 1932 when employed by Century Airways Ltd.
Photo courtesy of Frank Young.

found his studies relating to theory of flight, and other pertinent subjects, very difficult, and decided he should receive further schooling. As it was necessary for him to continue working also, that meant evening classes, and so he visited the Principal of the Central Technical School in Toronto. The principal suggested that he should interest himself in a profession with a future, such as electrical engineering, and that, at any rate, his school did not have facilities for Frank Young's purpose. Today, the subject of aviation in all its phases is being taught at this school, and aviation is its largest department. Frank Young thought with certainty that there must be a lesson here in faith versus logic.

Having finished his training and tests for his Commercial Pilot's Certificate, No. 368, which he received on October 31, 1929, he, as well as all the others, had no alternative, due to very few flying jobs being available, but to continue working and barnstorming on week-ends. Hence he joined a barnstorming group of pilots who toured the country giving public exhibitions.

For a short period during the latter part of 1929 and for a while the following year, Frank Young was associated with Aircraft Limited, Dufferin Street, Toronto. This company commenced operations in August, 1928, conducting a Flying Training School.

Early in 1930, Frank Young began flying for Century Airways Limited at Barker Field and National Air Transport at Barker Field, Toronto, as a flying instructor. This was before special licences for this purpose were being issued. Century Airways Limited began its operations at Barker Field in 1928. The company was formed by Allan Lamport, who was Vice-President and General Manager and in later years Mayor of Toronto. Mostly, however, Frank Young made his living from barnstorming.

In 1931 Frank Young submitted his application to the Department of National Defence. He, along with approximately thirty other commercial pilots in Canada, was successful in being selected by the R.C.A.F. to join the first group to attend a course at Camp Borden from January to May, 1932, specializing in instrument and night flying and navigation. The instructor for this course at Camp Borden was Flight Lieutenant C. Roy Slemon, later Air Marshal. At that time this special course was not considered as a requirement to obtain a licence. This course was terminated several months later by the government in the interests of economy, due to the Depression. When Frank Young completed his course, he returned to his former work with Century Airways and National Air Transport, at Barker Field, and also continued his barnstorming. Later in 1932 he revived the Brant-Norfolk Aero Club at Brantford, with the assistance of James J. Hurley, who was later associated with Canada's Department of External Affairs, and the late Wing Commander Eardley Wilmot of Brantford. Frank Young was its Chief Flying Instructor for 1932 and 1933. Also, he worked on other jobs on the side to help get enough money to live.

In 1933 he joined Dominion Skyways, based at Rouyn, Quebec, with two other bases at Senneterre, Quebec, and a base at Oskelaneo, Quebec, and for a while specialized in bush flying in northern Ontario, Quebec and Labrador. Mostly, he was engaged in flying prospectors and supplies, provincial survey parties and their supplies, and carrying furs from remote outposts to civilization. In between such flights, interesting side trips, but less profitable, would be transporting Indian and Eskimo families from one camp site to another, the load including, apart from parents, children and personal goods, their dogs also. Navigation was a little more difficult then than now as photographic survey was in its infancy and large areas of maps of these north-

ern areas were simply a blank. Whenever anyone flew into these areas whatever was observed was pencilled in, and these rough sketches of uncharted lakes and rivers were reversed as a guide to follow on the return flight. Bush pilots had many extra-curricular responsibilities in those days. Frank Young was also usually a Justice of the Peace, a game warden, or whatever he was required to be at the time, performing functions related to these offices in far-flung places; for example, refusing permission for a tribe of Indians afflicted with smallpox to move their camp site near a settled village, certifying deaths and births. As the bush pilot then travelled to more remote places than most others, it was practical to give him wide powers. Those were the days when Canada led the world in tons of freight carried by air, which reflected the energy our nation directed to the expansion of its economy ever farther north.

In 1935 and 1936 Frank Young flew the first scheduled air service for Dominion Skyways linking Montreal, Val d'Or and Rouyn using, by the way, CF-AYO, the first Norseman built by Bob Noorduyn, in Montreal. On this service, he also flew Fairchilds, Wacos and Bellanca Pacemakers. Other pilots engaged by the company at this time were W. Woollett, R. M. Smith, G. R. Spradbrow, G. E. Hollinsworth, M. Gauthier and D. F. MacDonald. A. G. "Tim" Sims was chief pilot of Newfoundland Airways, an associate company of Dominion Skyways.

In 1937 Parliament passed an act creating Trans-Canada Air Lines, and in the fall of that year Frank Young applied for a position as a pilot with this company and he was accepted. He joined Trans-Canada Air Lines in January, 1938. After training in Winnipeg, then the headquarters for Trans-Canada Air Lines, in the technique associated with this type of flying, he began flying mail between Winnipeg and Vancouver for training purposes, in all-weather conditions, prior to flying passengers. The same procedure was followed east of Winnipeg to Toronto and Montreal later in 1938. Frank Young received Transport Pilot's Certificate No. 112, dated May 27, 1938, superseded by Commercial Pilot's Licence C-6797, dated May 21, 1953. In 1939, Trans-Canada Air Lines was flying to the Maritimes and later to Newfoundland. It was Frank Young's pleasure to fly many of the first official flights made by Trans-Canada Air Lines. He was Captain of Trans-Canada Air Lines' first transcontinental flight east from Winnipeg to Montreal on April 2, 1939.

In this year Canada declared war on Germany, and many of Trans-Canada Air Lines' pilots were commandeered for the ferrying of bombers to Europe, delivering aircraft from manufacturers in the United States to the Royal Canadian Air Force, and training pilots for the Atlantic Ferry Command. Frank Young played a substantial part in this, too.

He also piloted Trans-Canada Air Lines' first official flight from Toronto to New York on May 10, 1941. In the latter part of this year he was appointed chief pilot and carried out the responsibilities of that office in checking Captains, promoting First Officers to Captains, as well as carrying on with responsibilities in relation to the war effort.

In 1943, Frank Young was promoted to Superintendent of Operations for Trans-Canada Air Lines' Eastern Region at Moncton, New Brunswick. In 1945, he was appointed Operations Manager for the Central Region of Trans-Canada Air Lines at Toronto.

Through the years, Frank Young flew as air line captain, check pilot, chief pilot and instructor in accumulating his flying time of over 5,000 hours with Trans-Canada Air Lines.

In 1946 it was decided by the Department of Transport and Trans-Canada Air Lines' authorities to reduce transcontinental flight times by eliminating the circuitous course around the Great Lakes to the north through Kapuskasing and Armstrong, Ontario, by having a more direct route crossing the Great Lakes. This route would pass through Sault Ste. Marie and the Lakehead to Winnipeg. At this time, Trans-Canada Air Lines was flying DC-3 aircraft. To fly the shorter route over the Great Lakes, it would be necessary to construct additional airports and install lighting and navigation aids. Trans-Canada Air Lines was requested by the government to assist in negotiating any arrangements with the State of Michigan. The company, in turn, due to this airway being within the Central Region, assigned to Frank Young the task of being Canada's representative for Trans-Canada Air Lines for this purpose. As his technical assistant, Frank Young chose Captain Barney A. Rawson, Director of Flight Development for the company.

To develop a northern route over the rocky topography on the Canadian side would be expensive, even if suitable sites could be found, so it was thought that possibly sites could be constructed on the United States' side, due to its relatively flat land.

Barney Rawon made the first aerial survey of the alternative route between Sault Ste. Marie and Fort William on May 3, 1946. Accompanying him were members of Trans-Canada Air Lines and the Department of Transport. The safest and most practical route to be followed was from the Lakehead across the Keweenaw Peninsula, Michigan, directly to Kinross Field, Sault Ste. Marie, Michigan. It was natural, therefore, for Trans-Canada Air Lines to favour this southern route.

Negotiations were undertaken, surveys made, aerodromes developed, and facilities installed in good time. By June, 1947, the installation of facilities had progressed so well that an inspection was made of the new route, known as the Great Lakes Airway. Those on this inspection trip were A. B. Parrott, Third Regional Officer with the C.A.A. (Civil Aeronautics Authority) at Chicago; Colonel G. R. Richardson; Frank Young and Barney Rawson from Trans-Canada Air Lines; Dan McLean, Gordon McDowell, Sam Foley and George Smith from the Department of Transport. This inspection was carried out in a Lockheed Lodestar piloted by Barney Rawson. This inspection trip gave those from the United States and Canada an opportune occasion to see the progress being made along the whole route in both countries. Also, later in June, Frank Young and Barney Rawson flew over the route with two inspectors from the C.A.A. Captain G. C. Edwards of Trans-Canada Air Lines piloted the aircraft. Trans-Canada Air Lines made its inaugural flight over the Great Lakes Airway from Toronto to Winnipeg on July 1, 1947.

The Toronto-Winnipeg flight time over the Great Lakes Airway was not only greatly reduced, but the weather along this route was much better. Trans-Canada Air Lines then instituted a local service to northern Ontario between Toronto, North Bay, Porquis (Earlton) and Kapuskasing. However, the service to Kapuskasing was discontinued by the company in January, 1958, when Austin Airways took over the route from Timmins to Kapuskasing. Then in March, 1959, the service from Timmins to Kapuskasing was discontinued by Austin Airways as so few persons were using it.

About 1950, as the air line's initial exploring and rapid expansion had somewhat subsided, more personal opportunities became available to Frank Young as outlets for his interests and energy. As his background had left him keenly desirous of opportunities to help Canadian youth, he developed more than just an interest in the Royal Canadian Flying Clubs Association when he became a director of their central zone in 1951.

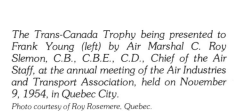

The Trans-Canada Trophy being presented to Frank Young (left) by Air Marshal C. Roy Slemon, C.B., C.B.E., C.D., Chief of the Air Staff, at the annual meeting of the Air Industries and Transport Association, held on November 9, 1954, in Quebec City.

Photo courtesy of Roy Rosemere, Quebec.

Frank Young put a lot of time and energy into organizing the National Air Show in Toronto, too. Canada could really be proud of his endeavours to establish such a worthwhile event. For this achievement, he was awarded the Trans-Canada Trophy for 1953. The announcement was made on August 17, 1954, by the Honourable Ralph Campney, Minister of National Defence.

The presentation of the award was made to Captain Frank Young at the Chateau Frontenac in Quebec City on

The Committee of Award for the year 1953 consisted of the following members:

Air Commodore F. S. Carpenter, Royal Canadian Air Force, Department of National Defence, Ottawa (Chairman).

Group Captain A. M. Cameron, Royal Canadian Air Force, Department of National Defence, Ottawa.

Major R. Dodds, Controller of Civil Aviation, Department of Transport, Ottawa.

Gordon F. Henderson, Royal Canadian Flying Clubs Association, Ottawa.

T. P. Fox, Air Industries and Transport Association, Ottawa.

R. N. Redmayne, Air Industries and Transport Association, Ottawa. (in attendance)

George C. Hurren, Royal Canadian Flying Clubs Association, Ottawa (in attendance).

the evening of Tuesday, November 9, 1954, by Air Marshal C. Roy Slemon, C.B. C.B.E., C.D., Chief of the Air Staff, on behalf of the Minister of National Defence. At the presentation ceremony, Air Marshal Slemon reminisced about a flight which he and another officer of the R.C.A.F. had made in two Vickers Vedette flying boats from Ottawa to Winnipeg in 1926 at the same time as Squadron Leader Earl Godfrey, M.C., A.F.C., now Air Vice-Marshal, was piloting Dalzell McKee across Canada. He spoke of eleven forced landings which they had made, seven of which were due to stone-cold engine failures, and said that in spite of this they arrived at Winnipeg ahead of Mr. McKee. Frank Young, in expressing his appreciation for the trophy, emphasized that he was of the opinion that in future the National Air Show should be called the Canadian International Air Show. In attendance at the dinner were ten of the former winners of the Trans-Canada Trophy: Punch Dickins (1928); Walter Gilbert (1933); Romeo Vachon (1937); Gordon McGregor, representing Trans-Canada Air Lines (1938); Murton Seymour (1939); Tommy Siers (1940); Group Captain Lewis Leigh (1946); Barney Rawson (1947); Squadron Leader Ron West (1948); and Philip Garratt (1951).

Frank Young was Chairman of the Canadian International Air Show for 1954, 1955, and for several subsequent years. He was also President of the Toronto Flying Club for 1954-55, and a member of the Exhibitor Committee of the Canadian International Trade Fair for 1955. He was an honorary member of the Canadian Air Line Pilots' Association; and a member of the Goodfellowship Club of Toronto. He was a former director of the Royal Canadian Flying Clubs Association and a former director of the Canadian International Trade Fair. He was also Chairman of the Canadian National Exhibition Aviation Committee.

Following a company re-organization, Frank Young was appointed General Manager, Eastern Region early in 1968, serving as the senior representative for the air line in the Toronto area. As General Manager, Frank Young continued to have the company's interest at heart just as much as ever, and kept his eye alerted for innovations and improvements in the company's operations.

After a long and distinguished career in aviation, Frank Young retired from the air line in 1970.

Then for a short while he was the Canadian representative for the Business Jets Division of Pan American Airways, with his headquarters still in Toronto. Next, he was appointed a member of the Toronto Transit Commission, of which he later became Chairman. He held this position until retiring in June, 1973.

Franklin Inglee Young, for many years a bush pilot and air line pilot and executive, died on October 11, 1973, in Toronto, after a short illness, at the age of 64. He was married and had a daughter and two sons.

Frank Young was slight of stature. Generally of a quiet manner, he could be most forceful when the occasion demanded it; yet he was tolerant and considerate. He possessed a keen, imaginative mind; and was happiest in the creation and development of ideas, but was impatient with detail. Inactivity made him restless. Frank Young was keenly alert to world problems; but his main interest was in aviation and in the development of our knowledge of space. He was most conscious of the need for encouraging and assisting the education of Canadian youth in the aviation sciences. As he enjoyed reading, he found time to do it, and liked to keep up on various subjects. His interests also included music and the theatre.

He was named a member of Canada's Aviation Hall of Fame in 1973. He was made a Companion of the Order of Flight (City of Edmonton).

1954

W/Cdr. Jerauld G. Wright holding R-Theta Navigation Computer Unit, which is comprised of five major parts and one minor part.
Photo courtesy of PSC Applied Research.

Jerauld G. "Jerry" Wright

Citation: in recognition of his outstanding contribution to advancement in the field of aviation in Canada that year (1954), through the invention of the R-Theta Navigation Computer System

Wing Commander Jerauld G. "Jerry" Wright, D.F.C., C.D., while in charge of the Navigation Instrument Development Branch under the Air Member for Technical Services of the Royal Canadian Air Force, Department of National Defence, Ottawa, was awarded the Trans-Canada Trophy for the year 1954, "in recognition of his outstanding contribution to advancement in the field of aviation in Canada that year, through the invention of the R-Theta Navigation Computer System." Wing Commander Wright received the good news that he was chosen to receive the trophy on May 11, 1955, in a telegram from the Honourable Ralph Campney, Minister of National Defence.

Wing Commander Wright's invention of the R-Theta Navigation Computer System was termed "a significant and outstanding contribution to the science of air navigation." This technical achievement by Wing Commander Wright, a most outstanding navigation specialist, contributed to furthering Canadian aviation by greatly simplifying and improving the operation of long-range, high-speed aircraft. It contributed significantly to flight safety, since it relieved the navigator from burdensome and time-consuming navigation calculations which would detract from the efficient operation of the aircraft. This R-Theta instrument, adopted for use by the R.C.A.F. in 1955, gave the pilot of an aircraft the direction to steer and the distance to go to any position set into the device. It was independent of radio transmission for its operation, making it entirely immune from "jamming" or radio interference. Additional outstanding features to enhance its value were its small size and lightness, most desirable

qualities for equipment in modern jet aircraft, and thought to be impossible of achievement in those pre-transistor days. In plain words, the R-Theta Computer, automatically and continuously, without the usual radio or radar links with base, told the pilot how many straight-line miles he was from his base or his target, and what direction or compass heading he had to fly to arrive there. In the event of hostilities, this computer served yet another purpose, that of showing the pilot how many miles he had to fly to intercept an unfriendly or hostile aircraft and what direction he should fly.

This computer, in addition to having far-reaching effects on air navigation, profoundly influenced military, ground and sea navigation. The computer system consisted of a ground speed and interception computer, integrator and amplifier unit, R-Theta Computer and R-Theta repeater unit (for a pilot in a two-place aircraft).

While this instrument was designed primarily for use in long-range, high-speed aircraft, it operated with equal efficiency in short-range, slower aircraft. This, too, was of great value to pilots of small single-engine aircraft, whether in cross-country flights or following an established airway. The R-Theta Navigation Computer was, however, mostly for military use, although it set the pattern for all the military and civil systems that were to follow.

The R-Theta Navigation Computer system could be installed in army tanks also, which were tested for this purpose both in Canada and the United States. In this role, it gave rise to a new era in vehicle navigation and, as in air, the pattern was set for the systems which followed.

While Jerry Wright designed and invented the computer, the device itself was developed and produced for the R.C.A.F. after three years of study and effort by PSC Applied Research Ltd., of Toronto, who also designed much of the internal circuitry work and devised its packaging. Their project engineers were Mr. W.F. "Bill" Haehnel, Mr. Jack L. McKelvie and Mr. Doug S.L. Durie. The five major parts and one minor part of the packaged R-Theta Computer Unit fit together perfectly into one compact unit.

A later navigational device, the Position and Homing Indicator, based on the same general principles as the R-Theta Computer, was produced and developed under contract from the R.C.A.F. using the original ideas of Mr. J. Stuart Parsons, Chief Engineer for Computing Devices of Canada, Ltd., in Ottawa. It differs from Wing Commander Wright's invention in that names of pre-selected positions are indicated on push-buttons mounted in the instrument, and homing indications to any of these positions may be obtained by simply pushing the button carrying the name of the base, and in that it computes in X, Y co-ordinates and converts data to R and Theta.

The problems which led to the pressing requirement for a compact automatic navigation system were the ever-advancing complexities of modern aircraft operation and the necessity for aerial navigation under combat conditions without requiring radio aids. With the advent of high-speed jet planes, greater distances were covered much more quickly — but, with the use of the R-Theta Computer, the time factor to handle so many important and essential navigation details was lessened. For example, a 1,500 mile flight which normally required a total of seven hours' work was shortened to minutes by using the R-Theta Computer. There was neither time nor space in jet aircraft to do "dead-reckoning" plotting, nor was it feasible for military planes to fly the constant headings required to perform accurate "dead-reckoning" navigation.

Work on automatic navigation systems began in various countries as early as 1935. Research went on in two directions, one intent on solving the problem by developing a "dead-reckoning" instrument, capable of giving the navigator an approximate position, and the other concentrating on radio aids to navigation.

Development of automatic navigation equipment culminated early in the Second World War with the introduction of the British designed Air Position Indicator. This device automatically computed the air position of the aircraft from the heading and airspeed of the aircraft being fed into it. To obtain the actual geographic position, wind speed and direction had to be applied manually to the air position. Its great advantage was that the pilot regained his tactical freedom, and no longer had to fly in a series of straight lines so that the navigator could carry on with conventional navigation. Towards the end of the Second World War, an instrument known as the Ground Position Indicator was devised. To this equipment, wind speed and direction could be added mechanically to project the aircraft's ground position as a spot of light on the appropriate map.

Aids to navigation, such as direction finding, the radio range, Gee, Loran, Decca and search radar were some of the developments of those who attempted to solve the pressing requirement for an automatic navigation system by concentrating on radio. These systems were reliable and time-tested, but suffered from two distinct disadvantages, apart from uncertainties of radio propagation.

The main disadvantage of these systems was the enormous expense of the large ground stations required for radio navigation. The second disadvantage was their dependence on radio transmissions for operation, which in the event of war could be of great advantage to the enemy.

All of the automatic deduced reckoning systems were basically the same. They all sensed the direction and distance that the aircraft had gone, broke down this information into north-south, east-west components, and indicated the aircraft's present position as latitude and longitude.

Although the aircraft's present position can be valuable information for the navigator, he usually requires this information to compute the direction to go to reach his destination and the time required to get there. For this reason it is much more valuable to find a means of expressing position as a distance and bearing from a given point.

Jerry Wright reasoned that, if an automatic machine were devised to calculate how far, and in what direction the aircraft had moved from its starting point, no matter how much it wandered, it would only be necessary to steer the reciprocal of the direction and go back the indicated distance to reach the starting point. Furthermore, he reasoned, if the device were equipped with a set of gears and electrical circuits, it would be able to compute the distance and bearing to any desired position. Simply, that is what the R-Theta does. It computes automatically the combined effect of the aircraft's changing headings and airspeeds and adds to this the distance the aircraft will be blown by the wind, expressing the resultant directly as a distance and bearing, rather than latitude and longtitude, as the bearing and distance between two sets of latitude and longitude.

In addition, the 32-pound, compact navigation instrument can be set to compute the distance and bearing of any other position desired, within the range limit of the device. Translated into terms of a human navigator, it is an automatic plotter and navigation computer.

Calculations in the R-Theta Computer are performed automatically, entirely independent of radio transmissions. A single arrow in the display panel indicates the aircraft's track over the ground. When the pilot turns so as to bring the single arrow over the double one, he is flying towards his destination. Should the pilot wish to return to base, all he need do is lift a small lever marked "Vector-Add," and the double arrow swings around to the direction of the base from him. Distance and bearing of an alternate base or target can be set into the device by turning two knobs and depressing a switch, whereupon distance is indicated on a counter in the face of the instrument, and direction is shown by a double arrow. In this manner any number of vectors can be added one after the other.

One of the most interesting features of the instrument is what is referred to as its "memory," which remembers the aircraft's heading and speed during the time the navigator is adding or subtracting vectors.

The name "R-Theta" is derived from Wing Commander Wright's concept of calculating in polar co-ordinates, rather than "Cartesian" co-ordinates. The new concept required calculating and displaying position in bearing and distance. As explained by the navigation specialist, this can be illustrated by a man standing on a plank and flying a model aircraft on the end of a string. The man represents the Pole. The position of the aircraft at any time during its flight can be expressed by the length of the string (the radius "R"), and the angle between the string and the plank (direction) (the angle "Theta"). A computer indicating position in "R" and "Theta" co-ordinates was naturally called an "R-Theta Computer", by Jerry Wright.

Wing Commander Wright became interested in developing a computer of this type about 1944, but he first put his ideas down on paper in the spring of 1946. He used these ideas as material for a thesis on a specialist's navigation

course at the R.A.F.'s Specialist Navigation School at Shawbury in England.

This inventor was born on August 31, 1917, in Liverpool, Nova Scotia, where he received his education. Jerauld George "Jerry" Wright worked for about five years as a pharmacist in Liverpool, while he studied pharmacy at Dalhousie University, before joining the R.C.A.F. on May 10, 1940, as an aircraftsman. Then, on October 28, 1940, he was promoted to Sergeant.

After receiving his navigator wings at the Air Navigation School at Winnipeg, he was sent overseas in December, 1940, where he served as a navigator flying out of England and India with No. 240 R.A.F. Squadron, and was employed on coastal operations until 1944.

During his operations with No. 240 Squadron he participated in missions to Spitzbergen, Russia, and over the Indian Ocean, completing more than 1,200 flying hours of operations on flying boats, or two tours of operations. For his gallantry while engaged on operational duties, which included sorties to Spitzbergen and Russia, during his two tours, Wright, then a Pilot Officer, was awarded the Distinguished Flying Cross and a mention in Despatches. He had been commissioned as a Pilot Officer on February 4, 1942.

The citation covering the award of his D.F.C. states: "As an air observer, Pilot Officer Wright showed great powers of endurance and outstanding performance in carrying out a mission which involved over 23 hours of continuous flying, 2,000 miles of which was across the sea. Despite adverse weather and intense cold, the success of the flight can be attributed, in part, to the brilliant navigation of Pilot Officer Wright."

He was promoted to Flying Officer on October 1, 1942; and to Flight Lieutenant on January 14, 1943, while still overseas.

In 1945 he was sent to the Empire Air

Navigation School (Test and Development Wing) at Shawbury, Shropshire, England, where he was engaged in test and development work related to aerial navigation. While at Shawbury, Wing Commander Wright (then a Flight Lieutenant) completed the advanced Specialist Navigation Course and in 1946 was posted to the Test and Development Establishment (now the Central Experimental and Proving Establishment) at the R.C.A.F. Station, Rockcliffe, near Ottawa. In the latter part of 1946, he was transferred to the test and development section of the R.C.A.F.'s Air Navigation School at Summerside, Prince Edward Island, (now at Winnipeg, Manitoba) to continue work in the navigation development field. Here at Summerside he developed the Synchronous Astro Compass.

He was promoted to Squadron Leader on January 1, 1949. He remained at Summerside until August, 1949, when he was posted to Air Force Headquarters to be in charge of the Navigation Instrument Development Branch of the Air Member for Technical Services Division.

Jerry Wright was promoted to Wing Commander on January 1, 1954.

He became a national figure in the aviation world by being awarded the Trans-Canada Trophy in recognition of his outstanding contribution to advancement in the field of aviation in Canada that year (1954), through the invention of the R-Theta Navigation Computer system.

So, since first he put his pen to paper in the spring of 1946 in the form of a thesis for his navigation course at Shawbury in England, eight years were to flow by before he was to be honoured in this fashion. The R.C.A.F. can with good reason be proud of him as an understanding person who possessed the "stick-to-it-ive-ness" until his goal was achieved in the face of adversities, when he knew his solution would work and serve mankind by easing the onerous

The 32-lb. R-Theta Navigation Computer System assembled, showing Ground Speed and Interception Computer Unit (top left), R-Theta Computer (top right), pilot's repeater (bottom left) with the amplifier shown at the right. From left to right: J. M. "Monty" Bridgman, Jack McKelvie, W/Cdr. J. G. Wright, Bill Haehnel and Manly Haines.
Photo courtesy of PSC Applied Research.

burdens man already carries.

The trophy was presented to Wing Commander Jerry Wright on the evening of June 3, 1955, at the annual dinner of the Aviation Writers' Association Convention, held in the Crystal Ballroom of the King Edward Hotel, Toronto. The Honourable Ralph O. Campney, Minister of National Defence, delivered the presentation address and said:

"Tonight we honour a man who, by his inventive genius, has performed an inestimable service to aerial navigation and thus to the whole field of aviation. Wing Commander Wright's introduction of the R-Theta concept of navigation and his invention of an automatic navigation computer will, I am sure, rank among the outstanding achievements in the history of aeronautics. Having done my flying in the days when you steered by the compass and the stars, and never having studied the esoteric subject of higher mathematics, I cannot claim to comprehend the intricacies of the R-Theta Computer. But I understand that, using a system of co-ordinates involving a radius (R) and an angle (Theta), the little apparatus works out and indicates to the pilot how far he

The Committee of Award for the year 1954 consisted of the following members:
Air Commodore F.S. Carpenter, Royal Canadian Air Force, Department of National Defence, Ottawa (Chairman).
Major R. Dodds, Controller of Civil Aviation, Department of Transport, Ottawa.
G.C. Hurren, Royal Canadian Flying Clubs Association, Ottawa.
D. Pickering, representing the Air Industries and Transport Association, Ottawa.
Group Captain R.D.P. Blagrave, Royal Canadian Air Force, Department of National Defence, Ottawa (Secretary).

is from his base and what direction he must fly to get there. This remarkable device is proving of great value to Royal Canadian Air Force pilots. "There are other devices for calculating position automatically and thus freeing the pilot from the necessity of flying in straight lines, but the great advantage of the R-Theta Computer, besides its small size, is that it does not rely on radio transmission. . . . This device was not developed in a day or even in a year, but it is the fruit of a decade of effort, and I do not intend to recount here the story of Wing Commander Wright's problems and difficulties in reaching his goal, but I have read the story and it is an inspiring one. . . . the apparatus became a reality because our honoured guest had intelligence, persistence, faith and skill, all of which he exercised to such good purpose. He conceived a brilliant idea and he worked it out cleverly. He kept after his objective even though others, some of them his superiors at that time, forgot about it. When skeptics scoffed at his idea, he refused to believe that it was impossible of achievement. He encountered obstacle after obstacle in working out details but he solved all the problems which he met. I heartily commend Wing Commander Wright for his patience, his skill and his determination. I am proud that he is an Officer of the Royal Canadian Air Force."

The Minister gratefully and frankly expressed his deep appreciation to the personnel of Photo Survey Corporation Applied Research Limited who engineered and developed the system.

In reply, Wing Commander Wright said:

"I am appreciative of this honour which has come my way, and I find it difficult to find words with which to express my thanks. Partly because I am deeply moved for, as the Honourable Mr. Campney has said, it has been a long

road — and partly because I am somewhat embarrassed that so much attention should be focussed upon myself when all of us must know that in this day and age things of this sort can only be done by teamwork. Human nature is strange, is it not? There was a time when I was somewhat concerned that my part in this effort might have been overlooked, and dismissed as routine — which it never was to me — now I find myself very much more concerned that the work of all the others who did so much might be overlooked. I am proud of my service and grateful for the opportunities it has given me. Perhaps, since we share a common interest in aviation, I should try to tell you what these odd Greek letters are all about. Basically, it's not as difficult as it might sound. 'R' and 'Theta', of course, are the Greek letters used to refer to distance and bearing. Now ordinary latitude and longitude navigation is distance and bearing really — distance and bearing from the North Pole. The only trouble is that normally the North Pole is so far away that the grid is badly distorted as we see it because of the curvature of the earth. Allowing for this curvature causes the engineers who make computers a lot of extra trouble and adds weight to their devices. In the R-Theta concept we move the Pole about to suit ourselves and usually locate it at our base. Now we are able to forget about the curvature of the earth and thus get a much simpler computer. A lot of other advantages come as well. Position expressed as distance and bearing tells us also how to go home without requiring another presentation. This again saves space and weight. Further, since we have already shifted the Pole once, there is no reason why we cannot do it at will and thus get the distance and bearing to any place we like while in the air. These are the

The experimental Bras d'Or hydrofoil, the FHE-400, a deterrent to the missile carrying submarine, because of its speed and its grip on the water. The hydrofoil was designed by Mr. M. C. Eames of the Defence Research Establishment Atlantic, Dartmouth, N.S.
Photo courtesy of Mr. M. C. Eames, Defence Research Establishment Atlantic, Dartmouth, N.S.

three basic advantages the R-Theta philosophy offers."

Jerry Wright emphasized the contribution made by industry to the development of this philosophy. He said:

". . . it was not a one-man show — but to name all the people would be impossible. Engineers, draughtsmen and even accountants all played a part. But I leaned most heavily on six people who played a fundamental part in turning this philosophy and these ideas into equipment. If I were to have my way, their names would be inscribed on this trophy, and the least I can do is to tell you who they are. There is Mr. J.S. Parsons of Computing Devices of Canada, the inventor of the Position and Homing Indicator — a system in its own right; then there are Mr. E.E. Wall and Mr. D.S.L. Durie, who are now with de Havilland Aircraft, but formerly with the R-Theta Computer project, and the two men to whom the R-Theta Computer owes most — Mr. W.F. Haehnel and Mr. J. McKelvie of PSC Applied Research Ltd."

He extended his sincere thanks, on their behalf as well as his own, for this recognition which they were given.

In attendance at this dinner were five of the former winners of the Trans-Canada Trophy: Murton Seymour, 1939; Dan McLean, 1941; Group Captain Lewis Leigh, 1946; Philip Garratt, 1951; and Frank Young, 1953.

A new streamlined version of Canada's renowned R-Theta Navigation and Interception Computer was shown publicly for the first time at the Institute of Radio Engineers' Convention in Toronto on October 2, 3 and 4, 1956. It was then being produced in quantity for the R.C.A.F. by PSC Applied Research Limited of Toronto. This Mark II version of the R-Theta featured increased accuracy and decreased weight and volume over the Mark I version invented by Jerry Wright. By using transistors instead of

tubes, the weight was decreased by a few pounds to about twenty-eight. Its accuracy had been improved to the point where an aircraft fitted with it might come within two miles of its destination for every 100 miles of flight, instead of three miles as previously.

By 1958 the CF-100 all-weather fighter aircraft of the Belgian and Canadian Air Forces with NATO were equipped with the R-Theta Navigation Computer system, installed as standard equipment.

In addition, Wing Commander Wright designed and invented the synchronous astro compass; the high-speed Air Position Indicator; the Air Navigation and Tactical Control Systems (ANTAC 1 and 2) for Argus aircraft, which are navigation and anti-submarine plotting and tracking devices; the JGW Compass System standardized by the R.C.A.F.; the C2-CL2 Compass System used in many R.C.A.F. aircraft; and also the Mark 3 Position and Homing Indicator; and others. The ANTAC 1 System and the PHI System are still in squadron use today (1977), after nearly 20 years of good service.

As a sequel to Jerry Wright's invention of the R-Theta Navigation and Interception Computer, he received two cash awards which amounted to $11,944. Air Marshal Hugh Campbell made the presentation to Wing Commander Wright at Air Force Headquarters in Ottawa in September, 1959. These were the largest cash awards ever presented to a member of Canada's Armed Forces for an invention. One award was the result of the R.C.A.F. adopting his invention for use in its CF-100 all-weather fighter aircraft; the other being his share of royalties received by the Crown for the commercial exploitation of the invention. He also has received a part of the more than one million dollars in royalties collected by the Crown on his PHI System and ANTAC patents.

Wright was chosen by the R.C.A.F. to

take a Staff College Course at the R.C.A.F. Staff College, Toronto (Armour Heights) during 1957-58, to give advanced staff training.

However, instead of keeping Jerry Wright on the staff of the R.C.A.F. Staff College at Toronto, as had been planned, it was eventually decided to send him to Dartmouth, Nova Scotia, in July, 1958, as Liaison Officer with the Naval Research Establishment of the Defence Research Board there, where he could carry on with his research and development work — his first love. This he enjoyed. His work involved studies of underwater radar detection devices, research on sonar programs and the feasibility of hydrofoil operations.

Wing Commander Wright, Bill Dingle and Commander Ted Clayards were assigned the task of studying the Naval Research Establishment's hydrofoil project of some year's standing, known as "the Bras d'Or," to recommend whether or not it be continued. Up to this time, it had been, more or less, a research object. The project was a technical challenge, but it had no clear-cut military role, that is, coastal patrol work. Jerry Wright began to see that the project had the potential to be the only real deterrent to the missile-carrying submarine, because of its speed and its grip on the water. Actually, nothing could shake it off once it was "locked on." There were lots of problems involved, but no insurmountable ones, and they could be overcome.

So, instead of recommending the cancellation of the Bras d'Or hydrofoil project, as had been expected, they recommended building a "try-it-and-see" 200-ton prototype. This was done and it did all that was expected of it as to speed and sea-keeping capability, but the corresponding necessary work on the "lock-on" systems was not done; so it became a football to those who were committed to the old favourites: that is, ships, helicopters and aircraft. Also, the

Bras d'Or became something of a political football. It met so many delays and accidents that one might be forgiven for suspecting foul play. In any case, it was mothballed, and any minute now will be dropped to the bottom of some deep ocean, or given to some museum, untried in its real role, and Canada still has no effective counter to the submarine menace, now more menacing than ever, says Jerry Wright, this genius of the invention world.

Then an article by John Best appeared in the Ottawa Journal on Friday, August 5, 1977. It said:

"The navy's experimental hydrofoil Bras d'Or, developed at a cost of $52,000,000, could end up as a museum piece.

"Defence Minister Barney Danson said in an interview, Thursday, he would look 'with favour' on the idea of giving the vessel to the Alexander Graham Bell Museum at Baddeck, Nova Scotia, or some other museum.

"Bell, the inventor of the telephone, did pioneering work on hydrofoil craft at Baddeck on Cape Breton Island.

"The Bras d'Or has been mothballed at Halifax, at an annual maintenance cost of $30,000 since the government halted work on it at an advanced stage of development five years ago.

"Product of several years of design and development work by Canadian scientists, engineers and naval architects, it became the fastest vessel of its kind afloat, clocking better than 70 miles an hour in a test run in the Atlantic.

"It was damaged in a fire, and developed hairline cracks in its foils — the runners on which it rode after its hull lifted out of the water under speed. This problem could have been corrected, say naval experts.

"Nevertheless the government decided against putting the vessel into production for surveillance and control of Canada's coastal waters. The main reason was Canada's failure to sell it to other NATO countries; offshore sales were deemed necessary to lower the per-unit cost.

"Danson said he hoped to make a final decision on Bras d'Or when his department's plan for a *multi-billion dollar ship replacement program* goes before cabinet in the fall!"

So, after this, Jerry Wright was taken out of the Naval Research Establishment at Dartmouth, and sent to London, England, in the early part of 1961 to attend the Joint Services Staff College. While there, he stunned the British with his ability on the typewriter and the pipe organ! He typed all of his course exercises, and played the pipe organ at the chapel week about! At the end, he says he received the dubious accolade, "It wouldn't have been the same without you!"

Then, in October, 1961, Jerry Wright was transferred back to research and development work again at Air Force Headquarters, Ottawa, with the Directorate of Airborne Instruments and Telecommunications, which involved anti-submarine warfare systems for R.C.A.F. aircraft.

During the period he spent in Dartmouth, he had been working up his "general theory of relativity," that is, how to make a common flight and navigation system for all planes, using a building block approach. This led to a rash of inventions and subsequent patents with such strange names as:

the automatic master heading control (AMHC),
the integrated display of situations (IDS),
the integrated display of attitude (IDA),
the integrated command system (ICS),
the tactical display system (TDS),
etc., and so forth, deep into Acronym Land. This, with other bits and pieces, all added up to a wonderful system, ANTAC 2, which co-ordinates all the main and standby functions of the flight and navigation system for a wide variety of aircraft, and copes without change of mode or the need of special-area training from pole to pole.

But the red tape was something terrible, and more and more layers of control were piled on Jerry Wright and his inventions, particularly ANTAC 2, although ANTAC 1 stood proven as a great success by this time. Contracts took years to get through bureaucratic argument and red tape, causing the limits of the system to fall out of phase time-wise. Finally, July 1966 arrived — the time to retire, and production still had not started. The system was now some six years late and falling behind its life span in the fast-moving world of technology. Furthermore, its installation in the Argus might have precluded getting a replacement for that steady old warrior.

And then, of course, there were even darker areas.

At any rate the word went out to kill ANTAC 2. As a result, very few people ever flew this system or learned much about the advanced things that it did, albeit its machinery was by now becoming out of date. And, although the system was produced in full quantity for the Argus and the Neptune, it was canned, all twenty million dollars worth of it! There was little that could be done, although Jerry Wright asked for and was given a study which enabled him to fly on the only system ever installed. The concept, design and fabrication turned out to be sound, he discovered, but the funds to correct the inevitable small snags were not forthcoming, so the system was panned. Finally, after so much time had gone by, the powers that be decided it would cost too much to install the system on an old aircraft! And that was the end of ANTAC 2 — the navigation and anti-submarine plotting and tracking device!

Many of the standard components could and should have been used — many have not been matched to this day — but the mood was to throw the baby

W/Cdr. J. G. Wright being presented with the Trans-Canada Trophy by the Honourable Ralph Campney, Minister of National Defence, on June 3, 1955, at the annual dinner of the Aviation Writers' Association.

Photo courtesy of The de Havilland Aircraft of Canada Ltd.

out with the bath water, and so they did, except for a few of the sub-systems which live on in the CF 5, the Falcon and the Buffalo aircraft.

As the CF 5 started to force its presence upon us, Jerry Wright turned his attention to automatic map displays. This was during the so-called year's transition period of retirement, from July, 1966 to June, 1967.

Upon his retirement from the R.C.A.F. on June 18, 1967, at the early age of 49, Jerry Wright decided to set up his own little atelier, a consulting business (Systems Design Consultants), which he called JGW Systems of Ottawa.

Now, without government money behind him, he invented such things as slide rule gadgets, and light aircraft compasses. In his consulting role, this genius dreamed bigger dreams, and

invented the solid-state horizontal situation indicator called HIAC (Horizontal Indicator and Control), and a radically different projected map display using a five-inch wide transparency instead of the conventional 35-mm spool.

But Jerry Wright says that money was scarce for big developments such as these, and little came of them, except some stimulation for the engineers, so he drifted into interesting off-shoots.

In the map system, one of the problems was how to keep the image of the current over-flown area on your screen. If you unrolled a narrow strip you could run off of it if you moved left or right. If you have individual "slides" as it were, how do you find the next one, since it is always one of the four that are adjacent?

This took him into card retrieval

systems, where he invented three new themes. All developed from the old needle-and-card sorter still used by some libraries, but with retrieval capability increased by several orders of magnitude, and with positive simultaneous search capabilities. These things go by such names as DARACS (direct action random access card sorter) and are invaluable for small businesses, associations, libraries, and so forth.

Jerry Wright's world of inventions led him into furniture, of all things. There's no telling where this great inventor might break out.

It seems his daughter needed a hide-a-bed in a little garret where one wouldn't go. So he was invited to invent a knock-down version. This he did, and it grew to take quite a bit of his time and money. But now it's attracting lots of attention and looks very good. In a word, it looks like other hide-a-beds, but you can carry it around in the trunk of your compact car, and you can re-upholster it yourself for less than $100. As a bed, it looks like a bed should, with a head-board and all — and it's much cheaper than a hide-a-bed.

So here we are, up-to-date as of now in the JGW World of Inventions and Gadgets. This great inventor, this ingenious person still has lots of other ideas simmering on the back burner of his mind! Sooner or later they'll reach the light of day.

In addition to being awarded the Trans-Canada Trophy for 1954, Jerry Wright was awarded the Distinguished Flying Cross; 1939-45 Star; Atlantic Star; Africa Star; Burma Star; Defence Medal; Canadian Volunteer Service Medal and Clasp; War Medal 1939-45; Canadian Forces' Decoration with 1st Clasp; Operational Wings and Bar; Air Observer's Badge; and was mentioned in Despatches. He was named a member of Canada's Aviation Hall of Fame in 1973. He is a Companion of the Order of Flight (City of Edmonton) and a member of the Order of Polaris (Government of the Yukon Territory). He is a Fellow of the Canadian Aeronautics and Space Institute, an Associate Fellow of the American Institute of Aeronautics and Astronautics, and a senior member of several of our learned societies.

Wing Commander Wright is married, and he and Mrs. Wright live in Ottawa. They have four children.

He has many hobbies. He plays the piano, the pipe organ, the cornet and the trombone. He is interested in photography, research work and inventions.

Jerry Wright is a rather easy-going person who wears a ready smile with his pleasant manner, yet he is frequently deep in thought, as he goes about his many inventive tasks from day to day. He is one who gets things done. Over thirty patents have resulted from his inventions through the years, and perhaps there were other inventions which could have been patented as well. He gave many lectures on his research work, and wrote over fifty papers covering his work.

While many of his inventions were put to worthwhile uses, no doubt others could have been similarly used had there been less red tape; less bureaucracy in high places; and less delays or accidents and/or foul play to prevent some of his inventions from being used successfully in the national interest. The inventions were successful in themselves, and did the job they were designed to do when they were invented.

Jerry Wright has gained international acknowledgement and acclaim for himself as well as for the R.C.A.F. for his work in the invention of the R-Theta Navigation Computer — a truly ingenious automatic instrument for navigational use by the R.C.A.F. in their long-range, high-speed aircraft. In addition, he designed and invented the synchronous astro compass; the Air Navigation and Tactical Control (ANTAC 1 and 2) systems for Argus aircraft, which are navigating and anti-submarine tracking devices; the JGW Compass System standardized by the R.C.A.F.; the C2-CL2 Compass System used in many R.C.A.F. aircraft; and also the Mark 3 Position and Homing Indicator, to name but a few. As a result of these inventions, Canada has become a leading exporter of much navigation equipment. Thus, through his assiduous efforts, he has received great inner satisfaction, since he first started his navigation research and development work in 1946.

1955

Captain G. L. "Jerry" MacInnis.
Photo courtesy of Captain G. L. MacInnis.

Gerald Lester "Jerry" MacInnis

Citation: in recognition of his contribution towards the success of the Distant Early Warning Line operations in the Canadian Eastern Arctic

Captain Gerald Lester "Jerry" MacInnis, while an air line transport pilot with Maritime Central Airways, flying out of Mont Joli, Quebec, was awarded the Trans-Canada Trophy for 1955 for meritorious service in the advancement of aviation in Canada, "in recognition of his contribution towards the success of the Distant Early Warning Line operations in the Canadian Eastern Arctic." The announcement of the award was made on June 19, 1956, by the Honourable Ralph Campney, Minister of National Defence.

Captain Jerry MacInnis was the commander of the DC-3 aircraft that made the initial landings at most of the sites on the eastern sector of the Distant Early Warning Line, enabling camps to be set up preparatory to the commencement of construction work. These jobs were carried out by Jerry MacInnis and his crew in spite of formidable difficulties, without accident of any kind. This area, from the eastern-most tip of Baffin Island across Foxe Basin and several hundred miles farther west, was over the most rugged part of Baffin Island where the mountains rise to some 9,000 feet seemingly straight out of the ocean; where the fiords and the glaciers intermingle with the clouds; and where air navigation is most difficult and radio aids very limited.

Baffin Island is the largest of the islands in the Canadian Arctic. It has an area of some 200,000 square miles, about the same size as the Province of Manitoba. Various topographic features are found in such a large area, some presenting the most spectacular scenery in eastern Canada. For instance, along the eastern coast of the island, from Cumberland Sound on the south to Lancaster Sound on the north, and

including Bylot Island, a high, rugged mountain range of Precambrian age rises to altitudes of about 10,000 feet in places, and averages 5,000 to 7,000 feet. These mountains and those of northern Ellesmere Island are the highest ranges in eastern North America. Jagged peaks and serrated ridges are partially buried under permanent snow fields and Ice Caps in some areas. Long, twisting glaciers fill many valleys and empty into the sea at several places. The whole coast, with its indentations and fiords, rises abruptly from the water, presenting a formidable barrier of rugged grandeur towards Davis Strait and Baffin Bay.

It was after a careful study of the best maps of the Arctic areas that were available, and thousands of aerial survey photographs, that the actual selection of the route and the sites was made for the Distant Early Warning Line, (known as the DEW Line). Even the best maps that were available were highly inaccurate, making the job that much more difficult. The location of the Distant Early Warning Line and tentative sites were established by a location study group comprised of U.S.A.F., R.C.A.F. and Western Electric Company personnel. The task of locating the site points was a complicated problem in itself. From the moment approval was given for the construction of the Distant Early Warning Line, an almost insurmountable problem faced the building contractor. It was necessary to establish camps at these previously pinpointed locations. Even though the sites had been previously identified on a map, there were few, if any, geographical features to enable these points to be identified from the air, particularly as it was necessary to establish these camps during the cold Arctic winter months when the initial operations were to be carried out.

Jerry MacInnis' first task in the eastern Arctic was to hedge-hop over the terrain, locate those spots on the ground, then circle the point long enough to allow the engineers to assess whether or not it would be a practical place to establish the pioneer construction camps and landing areas — to go back and find the points again, which is quickly said but very difficult to do, and, finally, when the site was agreed upon to land on it with the first advance party.

For the initial flights, navigation aids were limited to the identification of terrain features and, of course, ground transportation of any form was completely out of the question.

Maritime Central Airways was selected as the airlift contractor for the eastern sector of the Distant Early Warning Line. The company was responsible for the flying involved in locating the sites. Captain MacInnis, being a most experienced and highly skilled pilot for this exacting and rugged type of northern flying, was chosen by Maritime Central Airways to be responsible for landing the original pioneer advance parties at each of the sites which were chosen in this eastern sector, which extended over an area of more than 900 miles across the frozen face of the eastern Arctic. All initial landings, except at one site, were carried out by Jerry MacInnis, flying CF-GKZ, a Douglas DC-3 aircraft, equipped with both skis and wheels. Dave Hoyt of Moncton was his co-pilot, and Roy Jones of Moncton was his engineer.

Cold Arctic winds and drifting snow, as well as reduced visibility, were constant hazards in this cold, bleak, barren country. This made the problem of locating the advance party on the second or third flight to each point almost as difficult as spotting the original site in the first instance. Landing was a particular problem with which Captain MacInnis had to contend, as the snow surfaces in the area were almost always extremely rough and hard, making conditions treacherous for the aircraft, with damage to the skis ever a possibility. However, at no time did Jerry MacInnis ever fail to become airborne again. These early flights were all made without local radio aids of any kind.

General reconnaissance flights were made in the early days of February, 1955, when the hours of daylight were about three out of every twenty-four, and flights were anywhere from six to eight hours' duration, and where the weather conditions at the location for which they were looking were never known until they arrived there. The Foundation Company of Canada made its first aerial survey flight to Baffin Island on February 1, 1955, in CF-GKZ from Montreal. Various V.I.P.'s from the U.S.A.F., the R.C.A.F., the U.S. Navy, the Western Electric Company, New York, and the Foundation Company of Canada, Montreal, were flown on these reconnaissance flights.

Some of those who were on these first aerial survey flights and the flights making initial site landings, as well as those who were members of the advance party, were R. F. Shaw, Vice-President of the Foundation Company of Canada; G. C. Finlayson, who was Project Manager for the Foundation Company of Canada; N. S. Novikoff, Assistant General Superintendent for the Foundation Company; Lieutenant-Commander J. P. Croal of the Royal Canadian Navy, on loan to the Foundation Company of Canada; T. H. Manning, Ottawa; E. M. Cline from Western Electric; Jack Laurie, Superintendent of the Foundation Company of Canada; Charles Hoyt, Foundation Company of Canada; Corporal R. P. Van Norman of the R.C.M.P., Frobisher, who was also responsible for certain activities of the Department of Northern Affairs, and who spoke the dialects of the Eskimo people on the Baffin coast as well; and R. P. Shaw and Terry Coghlan, both of Spartan Air Services, Ottawa.

Flying his DC-3 ski-equipped aircraft, Captain Jerry MacInnis, with co-pilot Dave Hoyt and Engineer Roy Jones, carrying Mr. R. F. Shaw, made the first flight to Frobisher from Montreal for the eastern sector of the DEW Line on February 1, 1955. Surveys along the proposed line were conducted from Frobisher, and later from Coral Harbour, while the first landing with the advance party was made at a DEW Line site on February 14, 1955. The job progressed from then until April 23, 1955, when the final site was established. However, at one proposed site, the pioneering team was withdrawn due to the irregular terrain that prevented the economic construction of an installation there. Later that summer, when the sea ice melted, a more suitable site was selected and occupied by a team transported to this location by a Canso aircraft.

With each advance party, the Foundation Company's policy was to send in at least one man with Arctic experience. Lieutenant-Commander J. P. Croal and Tom Manning took an active part in this phase of the work, both having had much Arctic experience.

Lieutenant-Commander J. P. Croal, R.C.N., served as an Officer on *H.M.C.S. Labrador*. In early February, 1955, he was given leave of absence from his ship to join the Foundation Company of Canada, as an Arctic consultant in charge of putting in advance camps and of carrying out beach surveys for the sealift. These he completed in the spring of 1955. Commander Croal had spent most of his life in Canada's north land.

In those few weeks, one of the toughest jobs of Arctic flying in the history of Canadian aviation was taking place. Due to the distances involved and the lack of alternate bases, it was necessary to leave the main bases on almost every flight with full tanks. This reduced the payload and made the overall job that much more difficult in that, although the "pinpoint" might be located on the first flight and the advance party landed, it required a second and sometimes a third flight to the same site to deliver sufficient supplies and equipment and set up navigation aids by means of putting a radio beacon on the air for further flights.

When Jerry MacInnis made the original landing in Maritime Central Airways' DC-3, CF-GKZ, followed by landings at the rest of the seventeen sites on the eastern sector, all of this pioneering work was done with a competence and a nonchalance which never failed to amaze his associates and co-workers. It was said that his reputation grew until those, uneasy about an Arctic adventure and the hazards of flying over the Arctic wastes, became reassured when they were told that MacInnis, "the Arctic Fox," was doing the driving! His ability to co-operate with the engineers in the initial surveys was exemplified by one instance when, having circled a rather rough proposed site for some time assessing the availability of gravel and water and its suitability as an air strip, as well as the general practicality of the proposed location, one of the engineers looked down and said: "I wish I knew the precise height of that peak." Whereupon, Jerry MacInnis made a diving pass, went screaming across the site and, pointing to the altimeter, said: "Take 50 feet off of that!" Not only had Jerry set the example of many hours of accident-free flying on this project, doing many of the toughest jobs himself, but by his judgment, skill and planning he contributed to the safety of the operations of the other captains. He was the one who decided whether or not strips were suitable for heavy aircraft, whether or not the approach was safe, and established the limits for safe operations.

J. A. Bowman, then Assistant Project Manager of Engineering for Western Electric Company, New York, said that

during the early phase of the DEW Line project he had several occasions to fly with Jerry MacInnis over some rather forbidding terrain. In looking back at his reactions on those journeys he can now realize the complete confidence he had in Jerry MacInnis' abilities as an airman. He can also now appreciate how much Jerry's organizing abilities, leadership and guidance of others meant to the success of a job where air transport under very difficult circumstances was a major requisite.

Jerry MacInnis says that in the embryo stages of the DEW Line project there were many incidents — both amusing and otherwise. Many of them had operated in the north before, but never on the scale they were now attempting, and certainly never when there was such urgency. Everyone took his problems in stride and the lift was on — no strips — no navigation aids along the proposed line — the dead of winter — sub-zero temperatures almost continually — drifting snow and extremely rough snow surfaces. There were times when the 80-odd mile-per-hour cold Arctic winds would drift in a strip that had been cleared, or partially do so — and then the work had to be done all over again. He says that these were simply day-to-day problems with which they were all faced.

Then there was the time that they had been trying to get down at one of the proposed sites for several days and were having difficulty in locating a suitable area. After several unsuccessful trips, according to Jerry MacInnis, they finally chose a spot that looked safe. The snow surface appeared smooth through the field glasses but, when the skis touched the surface, they realized the snow was anything but smooth and before they stopped they knew they had a broken ski. While the drifts were not high, hardly more than a foot, the damage was caused by a combination of the extreme hardness of the snow and the 50° below zero (F) temperature crystallizing the

metal in their skis. After landing they could hardly distinguish the tracks of the skis on the snow. Norm Novikoff of the Foundation Company was one of those who went on this flight with Jerry MacInnis. Their solicitous engineer, Roy Jones, remarked that they should go south and practise on railway ties for they must be smoother! Jerry MacInnis recalls that it was this same wit who said that "Life begins at —," as this was the number of the site they were trying to establish!

Jerry MacInnis says that, combined with this work, they were also doing soundings at the proposed beach sites for the Navy and he is sure there is one thing their northern friend, the Eskimo, will never understand about the white man, and that is why he spends several hours cutting through eight feet of ice and then does not fish! This was at the time that they were carrying out beach surveys in the spring of 1955. Commander Croal made the beach surveys.

For those who have never lived in the north, it must be hard to credit the density to which the continual action of the wind pounds the snow. At one site they arrived with an Oliver tractor on board. Another ski-equipped aircraft had the planks for unloading this tractor, but it had been delayed. After drinking several pots of tea and waiting for an hour with their aircraft engines running, they decided, in the interest of saving gasoline, which you just do not and must not waste in the Arctic, to attempt unloading without the planks. They chose a spot where the snow was hard and proceeded to build a ramp of snow blocks. There was a certain amount of doubt amongst them as to the success of this venture — but something had to be done. When the ramp was ready, everyone crossed their fingers while the driver backed the tractor out the door and down the ramp — with no trouble at all! Everyone gave a sigh of relief, as another load was delivered safely to the

View of a complete DEW Line Station.
Photo courtesy of the U.S. Air Force by Western Electric Company.

DEW Line. However, the Oliver tractor later proved to be useless in the hard snow.

When one stops to consider and think about the number of sites across a distance of 3,000 miles or so, with air strips, radio beacons, communications and all the other equipment involved in air line operation and construction work over trackless wastes of white snow and ice, it is only then that the immensity of this project takes on its true perspective.

In reply to a comment by an engineer from Western Electric in regard to this stupendous task, Colonel W. A. Trippet, when Chairman of the DEW Line Location Study Group, spoke these famous words: "Nobody said it was going to be easy."

Arctic conditions usually call for a different type of approach and Jerry MacInnis finds a good policy to follow is to plan as carefully as you can — "Hope for the best, but always be prepared for the worst" — as a good Maritimer would express it! It will be found that just when you think you have everything under control, and seemingly nothing could possibly go wrong, something new comes up and you are in trouble, often serious trouble, too — like the time their site was lost.

To establish a basic camp, the Foundation Company sent in three or four men for the first trip until shelter and supplies could be built up. Therefore, only these men were carried, plus two tents (two in case of fire — and they had one!), two oil stoves, tools, a shovel, an axe, a water pail, food for two weeks, and oil and naphtha gas for the same period. This, along with other odds and ends, like some lumber for tent bottoms and sides, sleeping bags, a lantern or two and emergency survival equipment, was absolutely all they had until a second and third trip could be made — not a very elaborate or luxurious camp, but it was all they could carry on the first trip.

Therefore, it was imperative that they

return to the site with the least possible delay. Can you imagine the feelings and thoughts of these men who were left behind after they took off? Norm Novikoff, later Project Superintendent for the Foundation Company at Atikokan, Ontario, and Commander J. P. Croal of the Royal Canadian Navy were two of those left behind on some of these trips. Norm Novikoff tells of the very lost feeling they had as they watched the aircraft take off and disappear into the Arctic dusk — knowing that there were no navigation aids to speed their return, but only the skill and ability of the pilot to map-read his way back to them in some three or four days when they were as "settled" as they could be in the circumstances. It was comforting to them to know that Jerry MacInnis was doing the "driving," until heavy Caterpillar tractors could be parachuted in for the construction of strips for aircraft on wheels only for the continuing airlift, and until the radio beacons were installed.

These heavy Caterpillar tractors were disassembled into five pieces in the case of the D-8's (the D-4's were dropped assembled) and were flown in by heavy aircraft, then parachuted to the sites, and reassembled by the men on the site for the construction of snow/ice runways, so that wheeled aircraft could follow the ski-equipped DC-3's.

The first attempted drop of a D-4 Caterpillar tractor was at the first site put in on February 14, 1955, about a month after the site was established. Unfortunately, the U.S.A.F. was using nylon shroud lines on the parachutes which, of course, became very brittle in extreme cold. Yet, during the hundreds of drops on the Pinetree Line by civil operators in midwinter, it was known that silk shrouds must be used in cold weather. Naturally, the nylon shrouds snapped as soon as the parachutes opened and the

D-4 Caterpillar tractor went straight through eight feet of ice. Thereafter, hundreds of parachutes using silk shrouds were successfully used in dropping Caterpillar tractors.

To help the pilots find them on a return trip, Norm Novikoff says that they resorted to the use of "ice-paint," and black crosses painted on the tents, plus smoke flares to aid the pilots to spot their little camps. Probably their best marker, which proved to be a valuable one later on, was the "MacInnis Mark." Once when Jerry MacInnis landed at a site on one of their preliminary surveys, he laid out the only possible landing strip using a caribou skin, as that was all they had in the aircraft, and a 10-gallon fuel drum. On a later flight, says Norm Novikoff, this marker served to help them set down their advance party with a minimum of flying time. This only dark spot within miles showed up vividly in a land with almost no contrast; in a land without shadows at times, where you could walk into a snow-white wall without seeing it.

From the very beginning, one of their biggest worries was landing a camp in the broad white expanse of the Arctic winter — and not be able to find it again. This actually did happen and, to all intents and purposes, the site had disappeared. Where everything is white, and even the travelling Eskimos must dig into the snow to tell whether they are on land or ice, it becomes very easy to make a mistake with an aircraft. Fortunately, before dropping the men and their equipment at this camp, Jerry MacInnis suspected something like this could happen due to the location of the site and other spots in the area having the same topographical features, so he had drawn a map of the site showing landmarks from low level that would not change too much with future storms.

Top-of-the-world map showing approximate location of the DEW line.
Photo courtesy of the U.S. Air Force by Western Electric Company.

There were anxious moments for a lot of people for a couple of weeks until they had made their second and following landings and the camp could be seen from the air.

Flying with Jerry MacInnis, Norm Novikoff landed with nine of the initial parties at the various sites.

Primarily, the American Telephone and Telegraph Company of the United States was selected by the U.S. Department of Defense with the Air Research and Development Command of the Air Force to direct the vast assignment of constructing the DEW Line. In the final analysis, the American Telephone and Telegraph Company's subsidiary, Western Electric Company, Inc., of New York, was the prime contractor for this project. The responsibility for control of the project was handed over to the U.S.A.F. Air Materiel Command in March, 1955.

The Western Electric Company's first Project Manager was Vernon B. Bagnall, until January, 1956. W. E. Burke, later Vice-President of the company, assumed Mr. Bagnall's task, followed by Hardy G. Ross in May, 1956. Upon Mr. Ross' promotion to the position of Works Manager of the Western Electric Company at their Indianapolis Plant, H. D. Lohman became Project Manager.

The Western Electric Company issued various subcontracts and supervised the purchasing of material. For the entire project, more than 4,650 subcontractors and suppliers were involved. The Foundation Company of Canada, Ltd., of Montreal, received the contract for the eastern sector of the DEW Line. The Northern Construction Company and J.W. Stewart Company Ltd. of Vancouver, were awarded the contract for the central sector. The Puget Sound Bridge and Dredging Company and Johnson, Drake and Piper, Inc., of Seattle, Washington, accepted the contract for the western sector.

Spartan Air Services Limited, Ottawa, received a contract from Western Electric Company to do aerial survey work on the Canadian portion of the DEW Line, as well as provide the siting crews. The company spent some three months doing this work.

Maritime Central Airways, in turn, received a contract from the Foundation Company of Canada, Montreal, to fly in equipment and materials to the sites. And this was the company for whom Jerry MacInnis was flying.

Wing Commander J. A. Wiseman, A.F.C., was the R.C.A.F. Project Liaison Officer at the DEW Line's project office in New York, to co-ordinate with the U.S.A.F. and the Western Electric Company, A.F.H.Q., and the Canadian government departments involved in the construction of the DEW Line.

Then, too, the Arctic presented another problem to the construction engineers — permafrost. The Arctic terrain is eternally frozen, but in the summer time a few feet of the top layer of the terrain melts sufficiently to permit the growth of some small vegetation. Steam drills were used to put pilings deep into the frozen silty soil to provide footings for larger buildings in Alaska and the Mackenzie River Delta areas. It was necessary to have the buildings insulated from the ground in all cases by either providing an open-air space or a gravel pad of various depths. This same insulation process was applied to the building of roads, air strips, and so on, to prevent them from sinking.

A main site has forty modules, which are prefabricated units each 16 feet wide by 28 feet long by 10 feet high. While each module is a separate unit they are placed next to each other, end to end, making one long building, a sort of city in itself. The modules were constructed at the base camp and hauled to the permanent site on large sleds towed by Caterpillar tractors. At the site each module was placed about four feet above the ground on a piling-and-crib arrangement over a pad of gravel to prevent the heat inside the module from

Baffin Island Mountains above the clouds. A DEW line Station is located on top of a distant peak.

Photo courtesy of the U.S. Air Force by Western Electric Company.

melting the permafrost beneath. This little "city" contained a theatre, a gymnasium, a hospital, sleeping quarters, a mess hall, diesel generators, modern lavatories and laundry facilities, fire-fighting equipment, office space, a water system, a dark room, a hobby room, a room for mail and freight, a telephone system and a navigation-communications' room complete with teletypes and weather maps. Then there are modules to house the electronic equipment. Rising up into the sky, too, is the huge dome that houses the radar antennae which scan the skies; and the large steel radio towers that were erected with spartan efforts in the sub-zero cold. These huge domes, which came to life at the various stations along the DEW Line, resemble a golf ball on a tee.

The United States assumed the full cost of building the DEW Line, which was originally estimated to cost somewhere around $250,000,000 — but eventually approached $500,000,000. This radar network lies generally along the 69th parallel of North Latitude, reaching from Alaska across Canada to Baffin Island. This line was about 3,000 miles long; it was made up of some three-score electronic watchtowers, about 50 miles apart on the average, when it was built. However, Mr. Paul Hellyer, Minister of National Defence, announced in the House of Commons on July 15, 1963, that twenty-eight of the smaller DEW Line radar stations would be closed; twenty in the Canadian Arctic and eight in Alaska. The purpose of this electronic fence is to track and locate aircraft both in peace and war. This radar network is integrated with other electronic and communication systems, some of which are manned and some are semi-automatic, and operate at a speed that gives instant warning of the approach of aircraft. To give complete coverage from Alaska to Baffin Island, the stations are integrated as a complete line. A development known as

tropospheric scatter, a form of ultra-high frequency radio, is the bouncing of signals off the troposphere so that lateral contact may be made with the various DEW Line bases.

This electronic network was one of the three lines of defence for North America in the fifties and sixties — the other two being the Mid-Canada Line, lying along the 55th parallel of North Latitude, and the Pinetree Line, which roughly follows the Canada-United States' border, or the 49th parallel of North Latitude.

The first of the three lines of defence to be built in Canada was the Pinetree Line, which was backed up by bases equipped with interceptor and fighter aircraft. It ties in with the other defence systems of North America. The United States paid two-thirds of its cost, while Canada paid one-third. The total cost of the Pinetree Line amounted to around $525,000,000. Its construction started in 1950, and it was in operation about 1953.

Because of the proximity of the Pinetree Line to the so-called target areas, together with the development of faster aircraft and more powerful bombs, it was decided to push the defence system farther north to increase earlier warning time. So the Mid-Canada Line came into existence in 1954 on paper, with construction commencing in July of that year. It was in operation by 1957. Canada paid the total cost of this line, which amounted to around $240,000,000, and maintained and manned this defence line until it was closed down completely on March 31, 1965.

On the airlift to the DEW Line were Canadian civil and military air carriers and United States' civil and military air carriers. The civil pilots on the DEW Line came from various countries, but were mostly from Canada and the United States.

Jerry MacInnis believed that the airlift for the construction of the DEW and

Mid-Canada Warning Systems would go down in history as one of the world's greatest, and each one will be justifiably proud of the part he played. He has the greatest admiration for the construction companies and their personnel — both Canadian and American — who undertook this gigantic project, knowing that every day of every month they would be faced with problems that no existing text book could solve, and ticklish problems which would require the utmost ingenuity to overcome, and co-operation of the highest degree. He felt that the main assets required for Arctic construction, for air line operation and for living in the country, in addition to the ordinary skills, were to keep an open mind, to have the ability to think in large terms and, above all, to be able to live and co-operate with your fellow man.

Many types of aircraft were used to carry freight to the DEW Line. In this gigantic airlift, the very large equipment was carried by the United States Air Force (Tactical Air Command's 18th Air Force, Greensborough, South Carolina, and Alaska Air Transport Command) with their four squadrons of Douglas C-124 Globemasters, C-119 Packets, and so forth, as no other aircraft were large enough to take this equipment. Sometimes as much as 50,000 pounds were carried in a Globemaster. However, the usual load was around 43,000 or 44,000 pounds. The United States Air Force did a tremendous job in landing outsized equipment, supplying air and sea rescue operations and, in general, co-operating and assisting to the extent of their ability. Large cargo-type aircraft of the R.C.A.F. were also on the job. This also applied to the Canadian Army and Navy, and the United States Army and Navy for their wonderful sealift and landings at the coastal sites, to the Department of Transport meteorological and associated services and the many other services, both military and civil, too often both unheard and unseen, but nevertheless all part of the team which made the whole operation possible.

Occasionally, parts were interchanged or loaned until replacements could be obtained, and runways were kept open for round-the-clock operation as the days grew longer. In fact, Jerry MacInnis recalls one R.C.A.F. Sergeant, A. E. Bernard, acting as the commanding officer at Coral Harbour who, in the initial stages, with three men, maintained the strip, the lighting on the runway, refuelling trucks, and so on, by his sheer personality, intestinal fortitude and ingenuity — and it takes will power of the highest degree to operate tractors, graders, trucks and various other types of equipment outside in unprotected areas when the temperature is 50° below zero (F) with a cold stinging Arctic wind howling.

Then there were C-47's, C-46's, DC-3's, DC-4's, Yorks, Bristol Freighters, etc., etc., used to fly in the not-quite-so-large stuff. For a long period after the sites were chosen, there were no radio or radio navigation facilities available, and both Canadian civil and U.S.A.F. freighter aircraft had to return to their bases sometimes because they simply couldn't find the place where they were supposed to land.

Piasecki H-21B helicopters were flown in from Stewart Air Force Base in Tennessee in C-124's by the U.S.A.F., where they were reassembled for lateral airlifting of electronic equipment to sites not readily accessible to large aircraft. The equipment to be carried was attached beneath the helicopters by cable slings.

It was Maritime Central Airways who received the contract from the Foundation Company of Canada, Montreal, to fly the equipment and materials to the sites on the eastern sector of the DEW Line. The company operated from railhead bases at Mont Joli and Churchill, and from advance bases at Frobisher and Coral Harbour, Southampton Island. The

advance bases provided the assembly points for the distribution of men and equipment to the individual sites 300 miles farther north and to the vital refuelling bases necessary for such an airlift. The headquarters of Maritime Central Airways still remained at Charlottetown, Prince Edward Island. Carl F. Burke was Vice-President and Managing Director of the company.

Other bases from which DEW Line operations were carried out were Point Barrow, Fairbanks, Yellowknife, Edmonton, Fort Nelson and Churchill.

The story is also told of the C-46 pilot who radioed Frobisher that he was unable to locate the beacon which was to guide him in to a new radar site. Upon landing, he discovered the beacon, crated, aboard his own aircraft!

Landing strips for the larger aircraft were 6,000 feet long by 200 feet wide. Too, many strips were smoothed out on frozen lakes, or bays, where the ice was around five to eight feet thick.

Some 142,000 tons of freight were airlifted to the DEW Line during the twenty-nine months that it was under construction. On the eastern sector, R.F. Shaw, then Vice-President of the Foundation Company of Canada, Limited, said that 72,000 tons of freight were airlifted.

Of prime importance on all of these operations were the repairs and servicing that had to be done to the aircraft by the maintenance and flight engineers. Their duties were never-ending, and meant the safety and success of any air operation, or its failure. Their work had to be done outside in sub-zero weather usually — as there were no facilities to do this work at the DEW Line sites, and not much more at any of the key points from which the flights were made.

Often it meant rising at 4:00 A.M. to warm and start the engine of the aircraft. Then it had to be loaded and ready for take-off by dawn's early light. This was a

great hardship on both the pilots and engineers, as there was no heated hangar space and the servicing and warming up had to be done on the ramps, with temperatures anywhere from 50° below zero (F).

Preparations were made early for the great sealift to take place during the summer of 1955 when the Arctic sea lanes would be open to the ships — or, perhaps, it would be more correct to say were opened to the ships by the icebreakers on many occasions. Equipment and men to unload these ships had to be flown in and be in readiness for their arrival at the various coastal bases.

Originally, the United States Military Sea Transportation Service (M.S.T.S.), commanded by Vice-Admiral John M. Will, was assigned the three-year job of delivering construction materials and supplies to the entire DEW Line network. The cargo ships for the sealift were supplied by M.S.T.S. Each spring the M.S.T.S. Atlantic and Pacific Task Forces, comprising of ships of the U.S. Navy, U.S. Army, U.S. Coast Guard, Royal Canadian Navy and commercially operated United States merchant-type ships of the Merchant Marine carried supplies to the sites in the Arctic while personnel of the U.S. Army Transportation Corps unloaded them. Some of these ships were reinforced with a special heavy thickness of steel to help protect them from the onslaught of crushing ice. The 1957 M.S.T.S. sealift was the third and last season of massive sealifts of the construction and supply materials delivered to the DEW Line stations. Waterways, Alberta, had its own sealift, too, with the Northern Transportation Company using boats and barges to freight supplies down the Mackenzie River to Aklavik for the DEW Line. The Northern Transportation Company, a Canadian Crown company, had supplied the DEW Line sites in the Mackenzie River Delta area using boats

A DEW Line Station in the Baffin Island area.
Photo courtesy of the U.S. Air Force by Western Electric Company.

and barges since operations first began in 1955.

The number of ships used each year to resupply the DEW Line declined as construction and equipping of the bases were being completed. In 1955, the year of the biggest sealift, about 125 ships took part in the operation during the construction period. In 1956, the number of ships was about 122; while there were 96 ships in 1957.

The R.C.A.F. has been in operational control of the DEW Line stations in Canada since February 1, 1959.

On Tuesday morning, August 13, 1957, the DEW Line facilities were officially turned over to the U.S.A.F. in a historic dedication ceremony at Point Barrow. On this occasion the United States was represented by Brigadier General Stanley T. Wray, Chief of the U.S.A.F. Air Materiel Command's Electronics' Defence Systems Division, who accepted the system for the U.S.A.F. from William E. Burke, Vice-President of the Western Electric Company.

In the construction of the DEW Line, there were some 4,651 suppliers, of which 2,491 were Canadian firms.

The total contract commitments were $347,000,000 of which $198,151,000 or 57.1 per cent, was spent in Canada. This involved 66,295 separate orders on Canadian suppliers out of a total of 113,432 supply orders issued. This included the subcontractors for the three major construction companies.

Over 20,000 men were employed by the three major construction contractors during the DEW Line work. The peak number at any one date inside the Arctic was about 7,500 men, exclusive of back-up forces.

Some facts help one to realize the vastness of this whole undertaking. The air strips cover about 625 acres, or some 26,700,000 surface feet. A total of 9,600,000 cubic yards of gravel was produced, laid down, and graded for

roads, air strips and building insulation pads. This would build two replicas of the Great Pyramid, seven Empire State Buildings, or a gravel road (18 feet wide, 1 foot deep) from Montreal to Edmonton!

The civil, or commercial (non-military) portion of the DEW Line airlift involved 50 Canadian and 31 Alaskan and United States air lines in making 55,000 flights, carrying 121,528 tons, an average distance of 720 miles per flight, which rolled up 86,400,000 ton-miles in thirty-two months.

A total of 22,000 tons of food was delivered in the Arctic in over 1,000,000 containers.

Early survey teams flew 1,000,000 air miles and took 80,000 photos during the period of selecting DEW Line sites.

When Project No. 572 was completed, some twenty-five persons, both military and civil, had given their lives to construct it, and some sixty aircraft were written off.

In the year 1952 a group of outstanding science personnel was summoned by the Department of Defense in Washington to Lincoln Laboratory in the Massachusetts Institute of Technology, Lexington, Massachusetts, to work on an electronic system which they hoped would be successful in giving additional warning to North America in the event of enemy aerial attack. They were known as the Summer Study Group. Not too many months were spent on the development of this electronic system. In its development, the advice of many others who excelled in the field of electronics was sought.

Upon its development, the electronic system was first tried out at Barter Island, Alaska, some 240 miles north of the Arctic Circle. Here the first installation was made. If the system was a success, other installations were to be made.

An agreement was reached between Canada and the United States in November, 1954, to build the defence

warning system as far north as possible, and this meant the construction of the Distant Early Warning Line, known as the DEW Line, and also as Project No. 572. This system is a radar network completely without fighter aircraft support. There are three types of stations on the line — the main, the auxiliary and the intermediate (gap fillers), to give complete coverage of the line. Actual construction work on this project was started in February, 1955. Portions of the line were completed by January, 1957, and the entire line became fully operative on July 31, 1957. The Distant Early Warning Radar Line was to be manned and operated by an American civil contractor, who would provide the men required to operate and maintain it, of whom 80 per cent were originally to be Canadians in the central and eastern sectors by 1958; while, by mid-1959, the percentage of Canadians on the line had risen to 97 per cent. The Federal Electric Company of Paramus, New Jersey, a subsidiary of International Telephone and Telegraph Corporation, was given this contract, starting from January 1, 1957.

Jerry MacInnis was born on June 2, 1914, in Amherst, Nova Scotia, and it was here, as well as in Montreal and Prince Edward Island, that he received his education. During the years from 1936 to 1941, while he was taking an extramural course in civil engineering, Jerry MacInnis was Superintendent of a fur farm at Port Meunier on Anticosti Island, which was owned by the Consolidated Paper Corporation. It was closed down in 1940. He had completed the second year of the curriculum which was interrupted by the war, and he enlisted in the R.C.A.F. as an AC-2 on March 10, 1941. He was chosen for observer training. He then completed his Observer's Course in January, 1942, and was commissioned as a Pilot Officer.

He was posted to No. 116 Squadron attached to the Eastern Air Command to carry out anti-submarine operations from

H.M.C.S. LABRADOR passing "Cathedral" Iceberg in 1956.
Photo courtesy of the Department of National Defence.

the east coast in the North Atlantic. This particular duty was one of the more difficult navigation tasks which were done during the war. Inasmuch as the navigation aids were very limited with radio silence being observed most of the time, and much of the flying done close to the water and below cloud, the navigation accuracy required to locate individual ships or convoys was of a high order. So Jerry MacInnis started out in a tough school. After completing this tour of operations as a navigator, putting in some 1,056 flying hours, he decided to convert to a pilot. He was promoted to Flying Officer in July. In November, 1942, he started to train as a pilot at St. Eugene, Ontario.

Completing his pilot's course, mostly flying Fleet and Anson aircraft, at Moncton S.F.T.S. (Service Flying Training School), he received his wings in June, 1943, at which time he was one of the very few R.C.A.F. members who held both Observer's and Pilot's Wings. He was then posted to No. 117 Squadron of Eastern Air Command, flying Cansos and PBY flying boats, and carried out anti-submarine patrol duties until the squadron was disbanded at the end of 1943. Thus he improved his acquaintance with the Atlantic fog and icing and all the nasty problems of long flights over the North Atlantic. After delivering the squadron's aircraft to the Pacific coast at the end of 1943, he was posted overseas with the R.A.F. Ferry Command, flying a PBY flying boat. After a short time in England, he was posted to the Royal Air Force Transport Command for ferry operations.

In 1944 he was with the Royal Air Force Transport Command on ferry duty to the United Kingdom and the Middle East. He was also an instructor on flying boats. In July, 1944, Jerry MacInnis was promoted to Flight Lieutenant. In December, 1944, he was seconded to the British Overseas Airways Corporation and stationed at Baltimore, Maryland, as

an instrument flight instructor for their North Atlantic run, where he flew Cansos, twin-Beechcraft, Ansons, and other aircraft. On September 7, 1945, he was discharged from the R.C.A.F., but still remained with the British Overseas Airways Corporation as their instrument flight instructor, command and route check pilot on the North Atlantic.

When 1946 dawned, Jerry MacInnis was transferred to Montreal with British Overseas Airways Corporation's operations and was employed as an instructor on various types of aircraft, including Lockheed Constellations and Liberators, and the training of North Atlantic crews.

Then, on January 1, 1949, Jerry MacInnis went to Bristol, England, with British Overseas Airways Corporation where he flew Constellations, DC-3's, Doves, etc. Also, he continued as instructor on the various British Overseas Airways Corporation's routes, including their North and South Atlantic and Caribbean routes. He remained with them until September, 1950, when he resigned and returned to Canada, where he owned Dunflyne Farm at Murray River, Prince Edward Island. So farming became his business with flying temporarily taking a rest.

But Jerry MacInnis could not remain away from flying for very long. Now a veteran R.C.A.F. and commercial pilot, he joined Maritime Central Airways Limited in 1951 as Captain to carry out various flying duties on many different types of aircraft with the Pinetree Line project which had just come into existence. In general, many of the tougher assignments on northern flying were in the Labrador and Baffin Island areas. Many such an assignment was received by Jerry MacInnis.

So, in January, 1955, the decision was made to appoint Maritime Central Airways as contractor for the eastern sector of the airlift for the Distant Early Warning Line. Jerry MacInnis was still an

Airline Transport Captain flying for Maritime Central Airways, and had now logged some 12,000 accident-free flying hours. Being very highly skilled and finely trained before he turned his attention to the problem of flying in the Canadian Arctic, he was able to bring to bear upon the new problem all of his experience and knowledge, plus a scientific engineering approach, and it was for his work on the DEW Line that he was awarded the Trans-Canada Trophy for 1955. The announcement of the award was made in June, 1956, by the Minister of National Defence, the Honourable Ralph Campney, and was in recognition of his contribution towards the success of the Distant Early Warning Line operations in the Canadian Eastern Arctic. Jerry MacInnis had spent over 3,000 hours on instrument instruction on the latest aids, training captains for route flying and check pilots on the same routes.

Jerry MacInnis held Airline Transport Licence No. 98, dated April 20, 1951; British Airline Transport Licence No. 25405 with an Instrument Rating and type examiner; American Commercial Pilot's Licence No. 535520 with his Instrument Rating (endorsed for all multi-engine aircraft) and type examiner; British

The Committee of Award for the year 1956 consisted of the following members:

Chairman: Air Commodore F. S. Carpenter, Royal Canadian Air Force, Department of National Defence, Ottawa.

Members: Major R. Dodds, Controller of Civil Aviation, Department of Transport, Ottawa.

W.P. Paris, Royal Canadian Flying Clubs Association, Ottawa.

R.N. Redmayne, Air Industries and Transport Association, Ottawa.

Secretary: Group Captain W.B. Hodgson, Royal Canadian Air Force, Department of National Defence, Ottawa.

First-Class Navigator's Licence No. 1683; R.A.F. Navigation Warrant No. 1273 and Restricted Radio Licence No. 2621.

The presentation of the award to Jerry MacInnis was made on the evening of October 31, 1956, at the annual banquet of the Air Industries and Transport Association, held in the Ballroom of the Chateau Frontenac in Quebec City. The trophy was presented by Air Vice-Marshal M. M. Hendricks of the R.C.A.F. on behalf of the Minister of National Defence. Air Vice-Marshal Hendricks, in presenting the trophy to Jerry MacInnis, said, in part:

"Tonight the award is of double significance; not only does it honour a colourful, distinguished and popular aviator, but in so doing it put the spotlight upon one of the most significant and important breakthroughs in the development of civil aviation since the establishment of scheduled trans-continental flight. The DEW Line airlift in 1955 is now history but, in writing that history, it has rolled back the northern frontier in the short space of one year or so to an extent which staggers the imagination. Important as may be the tonnages carried and the flights made — what is most significant for the future is that there now exists across the entire northern rim of Canada a complete air route with air strips, radio beacons, air-to-ground communication and weather reporting. Whereas, two years ago an air trip into the Arctic, unless it was going to Resolute Bay, Frobisher or Coral Harbour, was an adventure, an extraordinary trip into the blue, but now a trip anywhere along the DEW Line is hardly more difficult than flying any other air route in Canada — the Arctic frontier has been rolled right back to the Arctic Ocean.

"This has been, of course, the work of many people, many organizations, and, as in many other breakthroughs in development and technology, has been inspired by the pressing needs of the military for the air defence of this continent — but among the individuals who can be pointed out as contributing significantly to this rapid development, the name of Captain Gerald Lester MacInnis deserves special mention.

"If Jerry MacInnis can point to 12,000 flying hours and to five years of aerial activity in the Arctic with a perfect safety record it is not because he is lucky, it is because he is smart. He has demonstrated the simple axiom which all operators should remember, that the essence of safety is not to get into trouble — and you do that by figuring out ahead of time what kind of trouble you might get into.

"When the DEW Line airlift came along, Jerry MacInnis was one of the planners of the airlift and he and his slide rule were familiar figures at the preliminary conferences that decided what should be done and how. Then, like any good commander, he jumped into his flying suit and went out and proved that the plan was right.

"On behalf of the Minister and speaking for all your friends and associates here assembled, may I present to you, Captain Jerry MacInnis, this symbol of the Trans-Canada Trophy for 1955 — and with it our collective and heartiest congratulations!"

In thanking Air Vice Marshal M. M. Hendricks, Jerry MacInnis replied, in part:

"It is indeed a great honour and privilege to be here with you tonight. When I think of the illustrious list of past winners of this valued trophy I wonder if someone has not made a mistake this year. I am just one of the many pilots who flew on the DEW Line and in accepting the McKee Trophy I do so more as a tribute to aviation as a whole — this organization and my company, in particular, rather than myself as an individual. Certainly, without the whole-hearted co-operation of many, many people, both within and outside our aviation industry, the exploits with which I am credited in your wonderful introduction would not have been possible. As a matter of fact I would like to take issue with the word "exploits." Many of the aircrew members flying on either the DEW Line or Mid-Canada Line have completed jobs just as rigorous as the ones I am credited with and, like myself, would like to feel that it was just a job of work to be done, rather than an "exploit."

"On behalf of all the people who flew on the DEW Line, all those whom I have had the pleasure to work with and to those who made the presentation of this highly prized trophy possible, my sincere thanks."

Eleven former winners of the Trans-Canada Trophy attended this banquet in honour of Jerry MacInnis. They were as follows: Punch Dickins, 1928; George Phillips, 1931; Gordon McGregor, 1938; Murton Seymour, 1939; Dan McLean, 1941; Group Captain Lewis Leigh, 1946; Barney Rawson, 1947; Carl Agar, 1950; Philip Garratt, 1951; Frank Young, 1953; and Wing Commander Jerauld Wright, 1954.

Jerry MacInnis continued to fly with Maritime Central Airways from their base at Mont Joli on northern and other work associated with the company, until July, 1957, when he was transferred to Montreal. While Jerry MacInnis was stationed at Mont Joli, he spent a good bit of his time in Frobisher. In Montreal, Jerry MacInnis was concerned with transatlantic and other charter work and, in 1958, when Maritime Central Airways decided to cancel their charter operations, he was transferred to Charlottetown, Prince Edward Island, where he flew scheduled flight operations.

Jerry MacInnis joined the Civil Aviation Branch of the Department of Transport as Senior Air Carrier Inspector in the

Captain G. L. MacInnis receiving the Trans-Canada Trophy from A/V/M. M. M. Hendricks, who presented it on behalf of the Minister of National Defence.
Photo courtesy of Air Industries & Transport Association.

Ontario region in February, 1959. He was based at Toronto, Ontario.

He was transferred to Ottawa in July, 1965, where he took up his duties in the training and flight checking of the Department of Transport's Civil Aeronautics Inspector pilots. Then, in January, 1974, he was promoted to Chief of Flight Operations for the Department of Transport. He holds this position today.

Jerry MacInnis is married. Mr. and Mrs. MacInnis have seven children. He was named a member of Canada's Aviation Hall of Fame in 1973. He is a Companion of the Order of Icarus and a member of the Canadian Aviation Historical Society. He was made a Companion of the Order of Flight (City of Edmonton).

Jerry MacInnis is not a big man, yet the force of his personality makes him appear so. He is rather slight of build; and his speech is sharp and crisp, giving the impression of a quick, keen mind. He was known as the type of person who knew what he was looking for. Up and down the DEW Line, the words "Arctic Fox" were heard in connection with his name. It was said, too, that Jerry MacInnis was a source of inspiration to other pilots on the DEW Line, who soon depended on his judgment and experience.

The pioneer flying which Jerry MacInnis did to help in the building of the Distant Early Warning Line for the protection of North America was of great value to Canada in troublous times. In doing this pioneering in Canada's Arctic lands, his name will go down in the annals of Canadian history as one who contributed of his talents and skill towards the construction of this vast assignment — THE DISTANT EARLY WARNING LINE.

1956

W/Cdr. Robert T. Heaslip, A.F.C., C.D.
Photo courtesy of W/Cdr. Robert T. Heaslip.

Robert T. "Bob" Heaslip

Citation: in recognition of his contribution to helicopter operations during the construction of the Mid-Canada Line

Wing Commander Robert T. "Bob" Heaslip, A.F.C., C.D., while a Squadron Leader and Officer Commanding of the R.C.A.F.'s 108 Communications Flight of the Air Transport Command, based at Rockcliffe, was awarded the Trans-Canada Trophy for meritorious service in the advancement of aviation in Canada during 1956, "in recognition of his contribution to helicopter operations during the construction of the Mid-Canada Line." The announcement of the award was made on April 11, 1957, by the Honourable Ralph Campney, Minister of National Defence.

In extending his congratulations, the minister said that Wing Commander Heaslip's great contribution to the success of the construction of the Mid-Canada Line and his energetic development and direction of helicopter operations were outstanding contributions to the advancement of Canadian aviation.

Beginning on February 1, 1956, Wing Commander Heaslip's helicopter unit carried out the major part of the airlift during the construction of the Mid-Canada Line. Six H-34 Sikorsky, six H-21 Piasecki and ten H-19 Sikorsky helicopters were used to airlift the material from the lakehead sites to the main sites to build and furnish the Mid-Canada Line installations. During 1956, approximately 9,000 helicopter hours were flown by the helicopter unit. This time was far in excess of expectations in view of the rugged conditions which had to be encountered. More than 10,000 tons of construction and electronic equipment and close to 14,000 personnel were airlifted safely by the unit.

These operations were often made under hazardous conditions over rugged terrain. Their success was largely at-

tributed to Wing Commander Heaslip's direction of the helicopter activities. He flew extensively on these operations and evolved unique techniques for airlifting a large variety of loads, including bulky antennae assemblies, large diesel engines, steel towers and other equipment relating to this operation. In addition, he was responsible for the perfection of helicopter cold-weather operating techniques which permitted the project to proceed smoothly under extreme climatic conditions in the field.

The Mid-Canada Line was an electronic warning network with no tracking facilities. It was built along the 55th parallel of North Latitude and consisted of a series of main stations with intermediate stations linked by a multi-channel communications' network at intervals along the system. The electronic device sent a beam straight up to detect any aircraft flying through the electronic "fence." The system was designed to detect all types of airborne objects from ground level to heights above the ceiling of any bombers of that day. Main stations maintained operational control of certain numbers of intermediate stations on each side of them, as well as serving as bases for logistic and maintenance support. They received, disseminated and evaluated all alarms received from the intermediate stations.[1]

The line consisted of 102 separate sites, seven of which were major bases, extended from Hopedale, Labrador, on the east coast, through Knob Lake to Great Whale River, Winisk, Cranberry Portage, Stony Mountain and on to Dawson Creek, British Columbia, a distance of some 3,000 miles. The sites were spaced about 30 miles apart.

The unit detector stations used equipment originally devised by an electronics research team sponsored jointly by the Defence Research Board and McGill University in Montreal — hence the name "McGill Fence." This equipment required a minimum of attention in its operation and was supposed to be less expensive than other known types.

The Mid-Canada Line was intended to receive electronic warnings from the Distant Early Warning Line, confirming the direction of any attack. The Distant Early Warning Line would give approximately two hours' warning to the closest North American targets against any bombers flying at speeds up to 700 m.p.h. In addition to confirming reports of the Distant Early Warning Line, the Mid-Canada Line would give a minimum of sixty minutes' warning, and the Pinetree Line, along the Canada-United States border, would control the interceptor forces. The Mid-Canada Line was not a radar warning unit, and it had no tracking system.

It was on April 8, 1954, that the Canadian Government and the United States Government jointly announced plans to establish the Mid-Canada Line, ostensibly for continental defence purposes, and work on the Line began in July, 1954. This system had been in the planning stage for six years or so. From this planning emerged four main links in a joint Canada-United States warning network for continental air defence. The northern link was known as the Distant Early Warning Line. The second link was the Mid-Canada Line. The third link was known as the Pinetree Line. The fourth link was the man-made radar islands, known as the "Texas Towers," which extend down both flanks of North America to prevent outflanking of the transcontinental network by hostile aircraft.

One of the first steps in the organization of the airlift was to appoint an on-the-site co-ordinator at Knob Lake. Gordon E. Hollinsworth, a veteran bush pilot since 1934, was chosen for the job. He soon found himself in need of ten hands, seven-league boots and the patience of Job. No sooner had he arrived at the marshalling area than he was off into the bush. He surveyed all the potential landing sites, charting underwater reefs and shoals on the unmapped lakes to make sure that none of the aircraft would come to grief. He then made sketches of the landing areas and distributed them to the pilots. By June 1, 1955, the airlift was ready to get off the ground.[2]

Wheeler Airlines supplied three Cansos; Northern Wings, two; Eastern Provincial, Quebecair, Mont Laurier, Dorval Air Transport, Central Northern (Transair), Austin Airways, and Arctic Wings (Transair) each contributed one. By October 7, 1955, the aircraft had logged a total of more than 3,000 hours in the air and flown over 380,000 miles. In airlifting close to 3,000 tons of supplies to the lakehead sites for helicopter distribution, they made a total of 2,230 landings. In addition, they ferried 695 passengers from the southern cities to the marshalling points.[3]

When the summer airlift was completed, and the ice moved in over the lakehead sites, Gordon Hollinsworth was sent to check its thickness. At least twenty inches of ice were needed before it was safe to bring in a Dakota. Mr. Hollinsworth asked for twenty-two inches and the pilots didn't fly until there was twenty-two inches![4]

The final location of each site was determined by detailed examination of large-scale maps and by on-the-spot surveys by ground parties flown in by helicopter aircraft. To make an accurate survey of the area concerned by the fastest possible means, the use of SHORAN (Short Range Navigation) was employed.

Selecting the sites for the hundreds of Mid-Canada warning stations was almost as gigantic a task as building the line,

said Group Captain E. C. Poole of the R.C.A.F. Systems Engineering Group. To satisfy this demand, aircraft and crews of the R.C.A.F.'s 408 Photo Squadron, based at the R.C.A.F. Station, Rockcliffe, near Ottawa, with assistance from civil operators, completed nearly 8,000 miles of aerial photography along the intended route. In accomplishing this task, the squadron, flying its four-engined Lancaster aircraft, flew some 17,500 miles, or nearly four-fifths the distance around the world.

Maps of approximately one inch to the mile resulted from the aerial photo operations during 1954 and 1955, employing photographic and mapping facilities of the R.C.A.F. and Canadian Army Survey Branch.

Construction of the line involved many difficulties, which varied with the nature of the terrain through which it passed. Many lakes, rivers and streams, rocky areas, wooded areas, hilly areas, mountainous areas and spongy muskeg country were typical of the country extending from the Labrador coast through the Hudson Bay area, sweeping westward to the Rocky Mountains. In addition, the whole region was infested with black flies and mosquitoes during the summer and fall months. But by far the greatest problem was that of transporting the construction material into this sparsely inhabited region.

In the western provinces, where a limited degree of settlement had taken place near the vicinity of the warning chain, advantage was taken of the existing transportation facilities. These included such railways as the Northern Alberta Railway from Edmonton to Dawson Creek, located near the Alberta-British Columbia border; the airfield at Fort St. John, British Columbia; and the Alaska Highway leading to the Yukon Territory from Dawson Creek.

In the Hudson Bay and James Bay areas, the railways to Fort Churchill in northern Manitoba and Moosonee in

Great Whale River, shown here in this aerial photograph, was a centre of activity from the early days of the construction of the Mid-Canada line, and was a marshalling area during that period. It is located on the eastern shore of Hudson Bay.
Photo courtesy of the R.C.A.F.

northeastern Ontario were used for transportation purposes. Much use was made of existing water transport during the short summer months. However, this was the muskeg area, and the only practicable means of transportation from the rail and lakeheads to individual detection sites along the Mid-Canada Line was by tractor train.

These tractor trains, operating only during the winter months when rivers and lakes were frozen over, consisted of one or two heavy Caterpillar diesel tractors pulling up to twelve large sleds called *wannigans*. A tractor train must carry its own sleeping and feeding facilities, as well as workshops and fuel supplies for the tractors, thus cutting down considerably the tonnage of freight on each trip. At a speed of about two miles an hour, travelling over ice and snow, tractor train journeys were long, tedious operations.

Tractor train operations were hazardous, especially when snow-insulated lakes and rivers across northern Manitoba and Ontario turned to slush. During the winter of 1955-56 heavy snowfalls early in the season, piled on lake and river ice, prevented a good freeze-up, thus endangering the heavy tractor trains crossing over them. In advance of the trains, and travelling in snowmobiles, experienced crews drilled

holes in the ice to test its thickness so that the equipment for the Mid-Canada Line could be moved into the site locations. Tractor trains began operating during the winter of 1954-55 and were repeated in the winters of 1955-56 and 1956-57.

Owned by Hudson Bay Freight Forwarders Ltd., tractor trains snaked out of Moosonee on James Bay and Gillam, Manitoba, for a distance of close to 300 miles, to points near the warning chain to meet other tractor trains operated by another northern hauling firm, the Patricia Transportation Company. This firm then carried the electronic gear and material east and west along the network to the individual installations. In the Hudson Bay and James Bay areas, some 19,000 tons of supplies were carried by tractor trains.

Bob Heaslip, then a Squadron Leader, was assigned the task of forming the first all-helicopter operational unit for the express purpose of providing the airlift to the Mid-Canada Line sites. This unit, designated the 108 Communications Flight, came into existence on June 1, 1954, and was placed under the command of Wing Commander Heaslip in July, 1954. The unit was based at Bagotville, Quebec, and contained three different types of helicopters. The flight took delivery of the first of ten Sikorsky

H-19 helicopters in August, 1954, and eventually had a fleet of twenty-five helicopters. This included ten H-19, nine Vertol H-21 and six Sikorsky H-34 helicopters.

Wing Commander Heaslip's first task was to train pilots and ground crews to the exacting standards required for operation in the bush under all kinds of weather conditions. Special techniques were developed for lifting the various components to be moved by the helicopters to the Mid-Canada Line sites.[5]

He built the 200-man unit into an efficiently trained organization from a small nucleus of factory-trained pilots and aircraftsmen.

Bob Heaslip explained that, since many pieces of equipment would not go inside the helicopters, external lifting techniques were evolved. To provide a realistic training programme, several items, such as fuel tanks and sections of tower steel, were obtained from the contractors and used for the training of pilots in handling external loads. Courses at the plants of the helicopter manufacturers produced a nucleus of ground crew instructors who, in turn, set up a training facility within the unit.[6]

Aircraft and personnel of 108 Communications Flight began their first Mid-Canada Line operations on June 1, 1955. Six H-19 helicopters left Bagotville, their base, for Knob Lake to begin the location and survey of the proposed sites. This involved flying surveyors to a

108 Communications Flight helicopter carrying out a typical operation early in the propagation phase of building the Mid-Canada Line.
Photo courtesy of the Department of National Defence and W/Cdr. Robert Heaslip.

location previously selected from an aerial photograph, which was no mean task. Fuel was available in caches left by ski-equipped Dakotas the previous winter on the shores of various isolated lakes in the area.[7]

The next task was known as the "propagation phase." This was the transporting of electronics' personnel to the sites where they set up temporary towers to test the suitability of the location with regard to signals broadcast from adjacent sites. The leapfrogging of crews and equipment across the entire length of the Mid-Canada Line was involved.[8]

During this period, 108 Flight Helicopters, commanded by Wing Commander Heaslip, were spread from the Atlantic Ocean to the Rocky Mountains. The logistic and maintenance problems created called for the utmost in organization and ingenuity. An example of the problems faced and overcome by the unit was an occasion when an engine failed on an H-19 in a remote spot in the Hudson Bay area. No air strip existed in the area, but the aircraft was near the mouth of a fair-sized river. This river was not deep enough for an aircraft to land on it but a suitable spot was located some eight miles upstream. A new engine was airlifted by Canso to this spot in the river and then floated eight miles downstream on a raft. The engine change was accomplished and the helicopter was back at work within three days.[9]

Operations in the north were never without their problems. The lack of navigation aids created one big headache which could only be overcome by careful

map-reading training. The problem gradually diminished as pilots became familiar with the area. But map reading was always difficult for the helicopter pilot over featureless terrain because of the low level at which he normally operated. Inability of the machine to fly hands-off was no help. Refolding a map with one hand in a relatively cramped cockpit called for real sleight-of-hand.[10]

A most obvious problem associated with these helicopter operations was the intense cold. H-34 and H-21 aircraft used by the unit, although winterized, provided many a challenge to the pilots and engineers alike. To ensure that men camped on a remote hilltop were supplied with food and fuel, Bob Heaslip's helicopters had to get through even though the temperature might drop to 55° below zero F.

At these temperatures, engine oil lines developed a habit of freezing up, resulting in the venting of engine oil. Transmission oil lines also froze, and cylinder head temperatures refused to come up to approved take-off minimums. Every problem was met and conquered in turn. The result was that, during the winter of 1956-57, the helicopters of 108 Flight operated routinely in temperatures down to 50° below zero F.[11]

The unsung hero of winter operations on the Mid-Canada Line was the crewman. It was his task to hook up external loads when a helicopter was engaged in slinging operations. His job

was to get under a hovering helicopter with its attendant downward blast of cold air to hook up the load to the aircraft sling. In freezing temperatures, noses would freeze in seconds and eyelids would freeze shut almost as fast.[12]

Whatever the conditions, freight had to be moved to maintain the schedules. This meant that external load work was carried on in temperatures down to 30° below zero F. But beyond this the blast became unbearable.[13]

Serious frost-bite was avoided by rotating the duties of the crewmen. All personnel watched each other closely to give immediate warning of tell-tale white spots.[14]

Pilot fatigue was another problem. It was particularly urgent in this type of operation, in view of the fact that each 'copter had only one pilot. Sling-type operations required a high degree of precision flying and were most tiring. Since a pilot generally operated alone in the aircraft during these operations, he was not able to gauge accurately the degree of fatigue encountered. So Wing Commander Heaslip restricted pilots to a total of six hours' flying daily on sling operations and eight hours on routine flying. There was also an overall restriction of a total of 35 hours weekly and 100 hours monthly. Experience showed that these restrictions were wise.[15]

Using heavy transport aircraft and R.C.A.F. helicopters, under the command of Bob Heaslip, materials were flown to advance bases set up at Knob Lake, about 700 miles north of Quebec City, and to another one built near the western shore of Hudson Bay on Great Whale River. Rail facilities running from Sept Iles on the St. Lawrence River to Knob Lake were used. The hundreds of tons of equipment taken in to these advance bases were flown by fixed-wing aircraft to crude ice strips located on the many lakes near the detection stations. From these temporary landing fields in the hinterland, the equipment was moved by R.C.A.F. helicopters into the actual sites, landing on helicopter pads set up by advance parties working during the summer of 1955. Also, some temporary air strips were built on a number of eskars, glacial deposits of sand rising out of the muskeg on the edge of a bay.

Airlift, other than by helicopter, was handled by commercial air operators. Where commercial operators were unable to handle fixed-wing aircraft, the R.C.A.F.'s Air Transport Command supported them, using Dakota aircraft from 408 Squadron equipped with a combination ski-wheel landing gear for year-round operation, fitted with JATO units for assisted take-offs from the short lakehead landing strips.

It was recognized early that air transportation must be available in the Hudson Bay area, so in the fall of 1954 an air strip was built at Great Whale River, and during 1955 a strip was built at Winisk, with a second one at Great Whale River. Thus, these points were available to heavy aircraft, as well as shipping. Across northern Quebec, camps were established at the lakes closest to the intermediate stations, supplied by a continuous airlift out of Knob Lake, except for the fall and spring break-up periods.

Planning of supplies to the assembly points at Knob Lake, Great Whale River, Cranberry Portage and Dawson Creek was the key to the whole operation.

Should the weather rule out flying, and that happened, some other means of transportation was used, as forgotten supplies could hold up the job for days, even weeks in some parts. Tractor trains, for instance, took ten days and ten nights in one stretch from their starting point to their destination. [16]

During the winter of 1954-55, C-119 aircraft from the R.C.A.F.'s Air Transport Command airlifted more than 800,000 pounds of material and equipment to the eastern shores of Hudson Bay so that a suitable landing strip and an advance base could be built. This tonnage included heavy equipment belonging to the R.C.A.F.'s Construction and Maintenance Unit based at Calgary, which built the airfield and facilities in good time. In addition, "Flying Boxcars" of 436 Transport Squadron based at Dorval carried thousands of pounds of equipment to sites along the eastern portion of the warning network during March and April, 1956.

Detection equipment and supplies, ferried by Daktoa, C-46 and C-119 aircraft to the main bases and the many temporary lakehead strips, were airlifted by helicopters of the R.C.A.F.'s No. 108 Communications Flight, under Bob Heaslip's direction.

The role of the helicopter in the construction of the Mid-Canada Line was all-important and, to meet the heavy commitments, the R.C.A.F. used Sikorsky H-19's, H-21 Vertols and Sikorsky H-34 helicopters, commanded by Heaslip. To keep the Mid-Canada Line project on schedule, on two occasions U.S.A.F. helicopters and crews assisted the R.C.A.F. and, on one occasion, helicopters and crews from the Royal Canadian Navy participated in the programme.

There were three phases of helicopter operations in connection with the Mid-Canada Line construction. The first two, completed during 1955, included a survey of the entire area through which the

warning network runs, and site testing for radio propagation. These operations involved two complete trans-Canada runs along the line. The third phase was the actual ferrying of equipment and construction material to the detection sites.

External cargo slings were placed on the helicopters to pick up loads without landing and these loads were released at the detection sites, again without landing. To do this, helicopters carried full fuel loads, cutting the payload of the Sikorsky H-19 to 1,200 pounds for each trip, and to approximately 3,600 pounds on the larger H-21 types and Sikorsky H-34's. During the stepped-up winter operations in the Quebec-Labrador region, more than 12,000,000 pounds of freight were moved by fixed-wing aircraft and helicopters into the network's detection sites. At the western end of the line, approximately 36,000,000 pounds of equipment were moved into the sites by tractor train, rail and road and by air.

During 1956, the helicopters of 108 Communications Flight flew approximately 9,000 hours, a total considerably in excess of what it was thought could be accomplished under the rugged conditions encountered. Heaslip's unit airlifted along the line by helicopter more than 10,000 tons of construction and electronic equipment and close to 14,000 personnel. This was carried out without loss of life.

Recognition of the part played by the R.C.A.F.'s helicopters came early in 1957 when the award of the Trans-Canada Trophy for 1956 was announced. It went to Wing Commander Robert T. Heaslip of Oshawa, Ontario, Officer Commanding 108 Communications Flight.

The question of foundations for buildings along the warning network presented many problems. In some areas along the 55th parallel ideal foundations for structures were provided by solid plateaus of rock of the Precambrian Age. At such building sites, which were usually in the Quebec-Labrador region, very little concrete for foundations was needed, lessening the burden of the contractor, and lightening the load of material to be airlifted. In other areas where the top soil was deep, and was subject to freeze-up and prolonged thawing, ordinary construction procedure was entirely ineffective. This was the permafrost region where pile construction was used, with piles sunk in deep holes made by high-pressure steam jets. Similar techniques were required for anchoring the high towers, an essential part of a detection site. Towers, themselves, were provided with special de-icing equipment to withstand the rigours of the climate prevalent in the area.

Construction of the Mid-Canada warning system required new and carefully worked out logistic planning. Caches of fuel oil and lubricants, stores of food and large quantities of building material had to be taken to the points where they were required well in advance of the time when they were to be used and, in some cases, during the very short period when transportation was possible. Also, Canso amphibian aircraft built up supplies of fuel oil and lubricants, as well as other material, at caches along the eastern sector of the line during operations in the summer of 1955.

Some of the construction obstacles were less technical. At one location in the Hudson Bay region in August, 1955, a field party on survey duties found so many polar bears occupying the proposed detection site that work had to be stopped until the animals decided, in their own good time, to retire from the scene.

A typical main station consisted of an administration and operations building, accommodation for personnel, supply buildings, boiler and power plants, housing for inflammable stores, and a garage and a hangar. All stations, including the unit detection sites, had landing facilities for helicopters which were used for supply purposes and

maintenance of the entire network.

Actually, the overall construction of the Mid-Canada Line was the responsibility of the R.C.A.F. Systems Engineering Group under the command of Group Captain E. C. Poole. The Trans-Canada Telephone System of Montreal was appointed Management Contractor for implementation of the line and, in turn, appointed the Special Contract Department of the Bell Telephone Company as project agent. Alex G. Lester of Montreal was General Manager of this department and had the main responsibility for all factors affecting the operation. [17]
The principal contractors on the Mid-Canada Line were: Deschamps & Belanger, Montreal: H. J. O'Connell Ltd., Montreal; Fraser Brace Engineering Company Ltd., Montreal; Carter Construction Ltd., Toronto; Hill Clark Francis Ltd., New Liskeard; Claydon Construction, Winnipeg; Wells Construction, Saskatoon; Mannix Company, Calgary; and General Construction Company, Vancouver.

Throughout the full extent of the Mid-Canada Line, a vast multi-channel communications network had been set up which included air-ground-air communications facilities.

Of the actual electronic equipment, there were 370 towers and radio masts of various sizes, many of which were over 350 feet high; 16 large scatter dishes and 322 diesel alternator units. There were 264 permanent buildings erected, each of which needed a permanent foundation sunk into permafrost. In addition, two major and ten minor air strips were constructed, most of which are still in use.

The main phase of the construction of the Mid-Canada Line was completed early in 1957. The maintenance of the western section of the warning line was taken over by Canadian Aviation Electronics. The eastern section of the line was to be maintained by Canadian

Marconi. The cost of maintaining the line was estimated at $22,000,000 per year. The overall cost of the Mid-Canada Line was some $240,000,000 and was a job of considerable magnitude with many difficulties and problems, accompanied by a great deal of hardship and discomfort for those engaged in the task. The line was originally estimated to cost $100,000,000. The Mid-Canada Line was built and financed by Canada, and was operated by Canada for a period. The Honourable Paul Hellyer, Minister of National Defence, announced in the House of Commons on April 13, 1965, that "the balance of the Mid-Canada Line ceased operations on March 31, 1965." The western half of the line was shut down in January, 1964; while the eastern half from Hudson Bay to Labrador ceased operations on March 31, 1965. Mr. Hellyer said, on April 2, 1965, that the closing down of the entire line was in keeping with a recent examination by the Canadian and United States defence departments of resources committed to anti-bomber defences. Further, Mr. Hellyer said that improvements to the Pinetree Line to the south had made the additional coverage provided by the Mid-Canada Line no longer necessary. It was estimated that, in shutting down this line, the annual savings would be some $13,000,000.

The line was built on the theory that an attack would be launched across the north by conventional bombers. Nuclear weapons, advances in radar-jamming methods, warning devices and air-to-ground missiles, and so on, made the system obsolete.

Thus, the highly controversial Mid-Canada Line was laid to rest.

Robert Thomas "Bob" Heaslip was born at Uxbridge, Ontario, on June 23, 1919. He attended Oshawa Collegiate. Upon graduation in 1936, he took a job with the *Oshawa Times-Gazette*.

In August, 1940, just after the outbreak of World War II, he enlisted as a

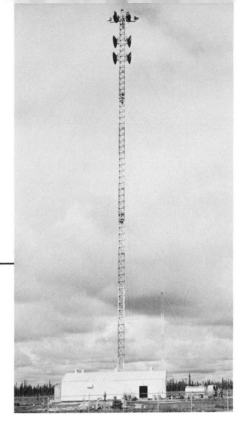

The tower of an intermediate station on the Mid-Canada Line stood sentinel-like on the Northern Manitoba flatlands. Its antennae were about 350 feet above the ground.
Photo courtesy of the Department of National Defence.

private in the 2nd Battalion Ontario Regiment (Tank Brigade). He joined the R.C.A.F. in February, 1941, and received training as a pilot. Then he was posted to No. 122 Communications Squadron at Patricia Bay, British Columbia. In 1943, he was assigned to No. 166 Communications Squadron at Sea Island, British Columbia. He made many rescue flights as a transport pilot with these squadrons. Then, in 1945, he was awarded the Air Force Cross in recognition of his rescue missions.

When World War II ended, he went to Summerside, Prince Edward Island, and took the first pilot/navigator course given by the R.C.A.F. He was promoted to Flight Lieutenant in 1946.* This same year he joined a detachment of No. 435 Transport Squadron in Winnipeg, Manitoba, and later served with No. 112 Transport Flight in Winnipeg and Rivers, Manitoba.

He was one of the first R.C.A.F. pilots to be trained in helicopter flying, commencing in August, 1947. He received his training at Trenton, Ontario. He then went to Rivers, Manitoba, where he was placed in command of the helicopter section of the Light Aircraft School. Here

The Committee of Award of the Trans-Canada Trophy for the year 1956 consisted of the following members:
Chairman: Air Commodore W. R. MacBrien, Chief of Operations, Royal Canadian Air Force, Ottawa.
Members: Major R. Dodds, Director of Civil Aviation, Department of Transport, Ottawa.
Mr. Gordon Henderson, representing the Royal Canadian Flying Clubs Association, Ottawa.
Mr. R.N. Redmayne, General Manager of the Air Industries and Transport Association, Ottawa.
Secretary: Group Captain W. L. Gillespie, Assistant to the Chief of the Air Staff, Department of National Defence, Ottawa.

he instructed pilots to fly helicopters. He remained here until he was appointed Commanding Officer of the R.C.A.F. recruiting centre at Fort William, Ontario, in 1951. Then he was promoted to Squadron Leader in 1952, and went to Hamilton, Ontario, to command the recruiting centre there.

Bob Heaslip formed the first all-helicopter operational unit, designated the 108 Communications Flight, which came into existence on June 1, 1954, and was placed under his command in July, 1954. The Flight began its first operations on the Mid-Canada Line on June 1, 1955.

In 1956, No. 108 Communications Flight outgrew the accommodation that was available at Bagotville, and it was moved to Rockcliffe, Ontario, where it remained until being disbanded upon completion of the Mid-Canada Line operations.

Then, one day in April, 1957, the Honourable Ralph Campney, Minister of National Defence, announced that Wing Commander Heaslip had won the Trans-Canada Trophy in recognition of his contribution to helicopter operations during the construction of the Mid-Canada Line.

General G. R. Pearkes, V.C., Minister of National Defence, presented the Trans-Canada Trophy to Bob Heaslip on November 6, 1957, at the annual banquet held by the Air Industries and Transport Association in Quebec City.

He took a one-year course at the R.C.A.F. Staff College at Toronto, Ontario, in 1957. Upon completion of the course, he was chosen as a member of the Staff College, where he remained for three years.

He was promoted to Wing Commander in 1961, and posted to Trenton as a Senior Staff Officer. His duties there were to supervise a staff to develop military plans concerning transport operations.

Because of his extensive background experience, he was sent to Lahore, West

Pakistan, in 1965, where he was Commanding Officer of No. 117 Air Transport Unit. These operations were associated with the United Nations. The No. 117 Air Transport Unit consisted of 100 men.

Upon his return to Canada in 1966, Heaslip became Base Operations Officer at Trenton, Ontario.

He left the service in 1968 to join The de Havilland Aircraft of Canada Limited of Downsview, Ontario, as Military Marketing Manager, which position he holds today. He and Mrs. Heaslip have three sons.

He was named a member of Canada's Aviation Hall of Fame in 1973. He was made a Companion of the Order of Flight (City of Edmonton).

Bob Heaslip shall be remembered for his exceptional role in developing special techniques for lifting various components to be moved by helicopter to the Mid-Canada Line sites; and for his training of helicopter pilots and ground crew to the exacting standards required for the operation of the helicopter unit — under all kinds of weather conditions.

NOTES
[1]. Frank Reilly article, *Engineering and Contract Record.*
[2]. "Building a Burglar Alarm," *Aircraft,* November 1956.
[3]. *Aircraft,* November 1956.
[4]. *Ibid. Aircraft,* November 1956.
[5]. Squadron Leader R. T. Heaslip, article, *Canadian Aviation,* October 1957.
[6] to [15], *Ibid.*
[16]. Frank Reilly article, *Engineering and Contract Record.*
[17]. *Ibid.*

1957

W/Cdr. J. G. "Jack" Showler, A.F.C., C.D.
Photo courtesy of W/Cdr. J. G. Showler.

John G. "Jack" Showler

Citation: in recognition of his contribution to mapping of the Arctic

Wing Commander J. G. "Jack" Showler, A.F.C., C.D., while commanding the R.C.A.F.'s No. 408 Photo Squadron, based at Rockcliffe, Ontario, was awarded the Trans-Canada Trophy for meritorious service in the advancement of aviation in Canada during 1957, "in recognition of his contribution to mapping of the Arctic." The announcement of the award was made on June 6, 1958, by General, the Honourable George R. Pearkes, V.C., Minister of National Defence.

In making the announcement, General Pearkes said:

"Wing Commander Showler's personal drive and enthusiasm and his ability to accurately assess the capabilities of his men and equipment were largely instrumental in the success of the SHORAN programme and the completion of the Geodetic Survey of the whole of Canada. . . . Wing Commander Showler planned and executed the particularly difficult operation under extreme Arctic weather conditions. To do this, he called on his extensive northern experience and employed techniques developed by squadron personnel under his direction."

John Gavin Showler was born in Winnipeg, Manitoba, on June 15, 1912, where he received his early education. He attended the University of Manitoba, Arts and Science. Then he joined the Hudson Bay Mining and Smelting Company at Flin Flon, Manitoba, as a chemist in 1935.

In his early twenties he had a yearning to fly, so he took flying lessons with the Regina Flying Club, Regina, Saskatchewan, in 1936, while still working as a chemist. One day when he was flying an aircraft at Flin Flon, he was injured in an accident. But this did not discourage him, as he was taking flying lessons again in

1939, this time with the Winnipeg Flying Club.

He enlisted in the R.C.A.F. in May, 1940, at the outbreak of World War II. He was given flying instruction by the R.C.A.F., and graduated as a pilot in November, 1940. Then he became a Pilot Officer in December, 1941. After this, he was sent to the R.C.A.F. Stations at Summerside, Prince Edward Island, and then to Trenton, Ontario, where he served as an R.C.A.F. Flying Instructor. He was promoted to Flight Lieutenant in 1942.

He toured all R.C.A.F. flying schools during 1943 to re-categorize R.C.A.F. flying instructors. He was then transferred to No. 164 Transport Squadron, R.C.A.F., at Moncton, New Brunswick. While there he took a transport pilot's course in 1943. Then he became a transport pilot, and was promoted to Squadron Leader.

He then served at various northern stations, such as Whitehorse, Fort St. John and Goose Bay. As Commander of the Goose Bay Squadron, Labrador, he carried out operations to Greenland and Iceland. For his devotion to duty during

A typical SHORAN Installation scene.
Photo courtesy of W/Cdr. J. G. Showler.

Installation of a SHORAN site on Banks Island. Note the "monument" just below the port wing leading edge of the aircraft.
Photo courtesy of W/Cdr. J. G. Showler.

operations, he was awarded the Air Force Cross in 1944. He was promoted to Wing Commander in 1945.

Wing Commander Showler was involved in "Exercise Musk-Ox," which began at Churchill on February 15, 1946, and ended at Edmonton on May 6, 1946. Three squadrons of R.C.A.F. Dakotas under his command helped fly in supplies to the Army's mobile force at Norman Wells and Yellowknife. "Exercise Musk-Ox" was a joint effort by the Canadian Army and the R.C.A.F. to test the possibilities of moving men and motorized transportation across the Canadian Arctic during the winter and spring of 1946. The moving force was supplied by air during its 3,000-mile journey from bases at Churchill, Yellowknife and Norman Wells. Landings were made by Dakota aircraft at these bases and on the sea ice at various points along the route. On one occasion eight and one-half tons of supplies were dropped by parachute at Perry River on the Arctic coast in an hour by six Dakotas, four from Churchill and two from Yellowknife.

Wing Commander Showler served as Commanding Officer of the R.C.A.F. Station at Fort St. John, British Columbia, from 1947 until 1948. Prior to his transfer to R.C.A.F. Headquarters, Ottawa, in June, 1949, he took a Staff College Course at the Air University of the United States Air Force at Maxwell Field, Montgomery, Alabama.

In January, 1952, Showler was assigned to the R.C.A.F. Station at Goose Bay as Chief Administrative Officer, where he remained until March, 1954.

Then, in April, 1954, he was appointed Commanding Officer of No. 408 Photo Squadron, R.C.A.F., at Rockcliffe, Ontario. This was the largest squadron in the R.C.A.F., consisting of 27 aircraft and 550 personnel, with four aircraft types modified, in many instances, for the very diversified role of the squadron.

Lancasters, ski-wheel Dakotas, amphibious Cansos and ski-wheel and float Otters were employed.

Although the main task of the squadron was the SHORAN (Short Range Navigation) survey and photography of Canada, the versatility of the squadron was utilized for a host of tasks, including selections of some sites and airlift support for the planning and construction of the Mid-Canada Line, assisting the Department of Northern Affairs in re-locating Eskimos in more suitable hunting grounds, fighting forest fires, assisting groups, conducting ice thickness tests for heavy transport airlift along the Arctic coast, in addition to certain important classified operations. The role of the squadron dictated that, throughout the year, it operate small individual detachments from advanced northern bases where facilities were few. It was while with this squadron that Wing Commander Showler planned and carried out this particularly difficult mapping operation under extreme Arctic weather conditions.

During 1956, Showler completed the largest SHORAN programme yet undertaken. Over the three-month period, from May to July, 2,900 flying hours were logged, 20 SHORAN points were established, and an area of one-half million square miles was surveyed. The area encompassed that portion of the Canadian Arctic Archipelago from the north shore of the Canadian mainland up to the 75th parallel of North Latitude.

The SHORAN operation was unique in that 8,000-pound completely self-sustaining stations were airlifted to pre-selected sites which were simply convenient points on the map. Flying was over long distances with few navigational aids and the destination was a snow-swept lake or on ice-covered sea strips where landing conditions had to be assessed accurately from the air. Wing Commander Showler personally selected, by on-the-spot checking, many of the

sites used for installations during the 1956-57 operations. He planned and executed this particularly difficult operation which extended over the 1956 spring break-up period. Instances occurred when personnel were evacuated from isolated ground stations only by landing on ice in the centre of a lake, and shuttling from ice to land in a rubber dinghy.

Jack Showler's painstaking devotion to duty and his ability to accurately assess the capabilities of his men and equipment were largely instrumental in the successful completion of many pioneering endeavours by 408 Photo Squadron and, in particular, the 1956 Arctic SHORAN programme. In 1957, armed with the expert knowledge gained during 1956, he led 408 Squadron back to the Arctic Islands where he completed the last remaining gap in the SHORAN coverage of Canada.

In addition, aside from this obvious contribution to the accurate mapping of Canada, 408 Photo Squadron, under Wing Commander Showler's leadership, significantly added to our still limited knowledge of the Canadian Arctic Archipelago. It can be confidently expected that a wide dissemination of the information on 408 Squadron's successful operational techniques and experiences will stimulate greater aviation activity in the area, thereby materially assisting Canadian Arctic development.

The 1957 SHORAN programme required precise planning as early as 1955 to ensure that every piece of the thousands of pounds of equipment needed was pre-positioned by sea or aircraft. During the 1957 SHORAN programme, more than 100,000 pounds of equipment and over 250 personnel were airlifted to Thule, Greenland, and Resolute Bay on Cornwallis Island, where the main and advanced bases were located. Dakota and Lancaster aircraft flew over 1,700 hours during the operation. Nearly all of this flying was

W/Cdr. Jack Showler, second from left, wearing fur hat, locating bases for final SHORAN for Resolute — Thule — Alert, on the northern tip of Ellesmere Island. Angus Hamilton, Chief Engineer of Geodetic Survey is shown on far right. This was taken at Resolute on Cornwallis Island on April 18, 1956.
Photo courtesy of W/Cdr. Jack Showler.

done north of 75° North Latitude.

The SHORAN (acronym of SHORT RANGE NAVIGATION) device used to conduct the survey was developed by the British during the latter part of the Second World War as a navigation aid for pinpoint bombing of Germany under instrument conditions, in or above the clouds. The bomber generated a radar pulse which was amplified and reflected back from the two widely separated ground stations in the United Kingdom. The time of travel in milliseconds gave the distance to the stations to .001 mile, thus fixing the position of the aircraft.

Essentially an electronic distance-measuring device, SHORAN consists of both airborne radar and ground radar equipment. Through its use, points of unknown positions can be established accurately. SHORAN is a very complex matter.

With the end of the war approaching, Mr. J. E. R. Ross, Dominion Geodesist, decided that the system could be adapted to geodetic survey, thus providing a means of extending the survey of Canada to the Far North, where tedious ground survey was impractical. The equipment was modified and refined so that the aircraft flew half-way between stations, and the read-out was the total distance between the two, thus measuring the exact distance between the stations. By repetitious and painstaking measurements, modified by adjustments for meteorological effects, measurements were produced with sufficient accuracy for survey work and it was possible to fix the position of a network of ground stations by trilateration.

The actual equipment was modified by the National Research Council in Ottawa and was available for use by the R.C.A.F. in 1949. In that year a small SHORAN programme began which grew each year until, in 1954, when Jack Showler took command of 408 Photo Reconnaissance Squadron, it was a major part of the squadron's work.

Geodetic survey is the basis of all other forms of survey. It provides a grid of known points from which measurements may be taken. In 1949 the coasts of the Arctic Islands and the Arctic coast of the mainland were sketched in, but there were large areas on the mainland and the interior of the islands that could not be mapped, even with aerial photographs available, for lack of geodetic reference points.

When Wing Commander Showler took command of the squadron in the spring of 1954, it was the largest in the Air Force, consisting of 550 personnel and 27 aircraft. Ten of these were Lancasters with all armament removed. They had extra fuel tanks in the bomb bays and were fitted for reconnaissance, aerial photography and SHORAN. The remainder of the aircraft were Canso flying boats, Otter seaplanes and ski-equipped Dakotas, which were used for the installation of ground SHORAN stations. The squadron maintained surveillance of the Arctic and carried out varied aerial photo assignments throughout the country, including, as a major portion of its activities, the continuing aerial photo survey of the north. These activities were operated from the home base at Rockcliffe, Ottawa, via a succession of mobile detachments at various northern points, such as Churchill, Goose Bay, Yellowknife, Whitehorse, Norman Wells, Cambridge Bay, Frobisher, Resolute and Thule (Greenland).

In addition, the major commitment each year was the SHORAN Survey, which took about half the squadron's personnel and aircraft for a period of four to five months. It was the practice for the SHORAN detachment to move to a northern base under the personal command of the Commanding Officer, Wing Commander Showler, with the remainder of the squadron's activities continuing under his second-in-command at home base. Thus, in 1954, work was

carried out in the northeast from bases at Goose Bay, with a secondary base at Knob Lake. In 1955, work was carried out in the northwest from bases at Whitehorse and Churchill. In 1956 the survey was carried through the southern Arctic Islands to Lancaster Sound, approximately 75° North Latitude. Churchill, Fox Base on the Distant Early Warning Line, and Cambridge Bay were their bases. In 1957 Thule and Resolute Bay were used as bases, and they surveyed the northern Arctic Islands to the northern tip of Ellesmere, thus completing all of Canada. The SHORAN survey covered a total of five and one-half million square miles.

The technique used was to place the SHORAN stations in a grid about 250 miles apart. They had to be on high ground because the high-frequency radar waves were line of sight, and maximum altitude for the Lancaster was 26,000 feet, thus imposing a horizon limitation. Each station comprised three airmen of the squadron, all technicians, their shelter, housekeeping gear, fuel, SHORAN and radio equipment, generators and the 60-foot SHORAN mast topped by a large bedspring-like antenna. Depending on the position in the grid, the SHORAN crew remained on the site from three weeks to four months. Each station weighed about four tons and had to be frequently resupplied with food and fuel.

The stations were emplaced by the squadron support aircraft: Canso amphibious flying boats, when the lakes were large enough; Otters on floats, when the lakes were small; and Dakotas on skis, when winter operations were in order. During 1954 and 1955 the work was done in the summer to avoid snow cover for the concurrent photo operations, therefore, the emplacements were mainly made with waterborne aircraft. By the time they had pushed north of the Arctic coast, the summer season was too short so they emplaced

George Hees, Minister of Transport, presenting the Trans-Canada Trophy and replica to W/Cdr. Jack Showler on November 5, 1958.
Photo courtesy of Canadian Pacific.

the stations by ski-equipped aircraft before break-up and completed the Lancaster SHORAN transits through the spring and summer, retrieving the men and SHORAN gear in the late summer by waterborne aircraft. In 1957, in the High Arctic, it was entirely a ski-aircraft operation, being completed between March and June, before the spring break-up.

The sites were selected one year in advance by on-the-spot inspection by Wing Commander Showler and the Chief Engineer of the Geodetic Survey detachment, Mr. Angus Hamilton. The location of the sites was vital to the whole operation, and was a major factor in the safety of both the ground parties and the aircrew landing at the locations chosen. Thus this task was too important to be delegated to others.

Mr. Hamilton indicated, by providing longitude and latitude references, the approximate position in the unmapped territory where he would like a station. On navigating to the area, an aerial inspection would be made of high ground with an adjacent possible landing area, and one or more landings would be made to take surface sights by level and transit, until finally a choice was made. Several of these were so difficult of access that, during the actual installation, only two landings were made, one to put in the men and electronic equipment and the other to take them out again. The remainder of the material was dropped to them by parachute. In Ellesmere Island some of the stations were located high on glaciers, in order to get the SHORAN lines over the mountains. They also had a station on the Greenland Ice Cap, north of Thule.

As a result of the far-sightedness of some of our senior civil servants after the war in getting the SHORAN programme started immediately, and the work of the Air Force in carrying it out, the geodetic survey of the whole country was completed in 1957, thus permitting topographical maps to be prepared and paving the way for geological, hydrographic and magnetometer surveys which, in turn, have led to the development of oil resources in the Arctic, amongst other developments.

Thus, this SHORAN programme completed the geodetic survey of the whole of Canada, that began in 1949 and ended in 1957.

An announcement was made in June, 1958, by General George Pearkes, then Minister of National Defence, that Wing Commander J. G. Showler, A.F.C., C.D., was awarded the Trans-Canada Trophy for meritorious service in the advancement of aviation in Canada during 1957, "in recognition of his contribution to mapping of the Arctic."

The presentation of the Trans-Canada Trophy to Wing Commander Showler was made by the Honourable George Hees, Minister of Transport, on November 5, 1958, at the annual banquet of the Air Industries and Transport Association held in the Queen Elizabeth Hotel, Montreal.

Jack Showler became Director of Transport and Reconnaissance Operations in Ottawa in July, 1957, where he remained until 1961 when he retired from the R.C.A.F.

He then went to Portland, Ontario, where he ran a tourist business. Upon leaving this business in 1973, he went to

Brentwood Bay, British Columbia, where he lives today. Wing Commander and Mrs. Showler have three sons and one daughter.

He was named a member of Canada's Aviation Hall of Fame in 1973. He was made a Companion of the Order of Flight (City of Edmonton).

Wing Commander Showler was known as a very resourceful person who possessed rare qualities of leadership throughout his career, and particularly so during the mapping of the Arctic. In this work, his wise guidance, his precise planning, his boundless enthusiasm, his expert knowledge of the Arctic, and his extensive experience in carrying out such a tremendous task were of the highest order and served Canada well.

The Committee of Award for the year 1957 consisted of the following members:

Chairman: Air Commodore W. R. MacBrien, Chief of Operations, Royal Canadian Air Force, Department of National Defence, Ottawa.

Members: Mr. M. M. Fleming, Controller, Civil Air Operations and Regulations, Department of Transport, Ottawa.

Mr. G. C. Hurren, Vice-President, Royal Canadian Flying Clubs Association, Ottawa.

Mr. R. N. Redmayne, General Manager, Air Industries and Transport Association, Ottawa.

Secretary: Group Captain W. L. Gillespie, Assistant to the Chief of the Air Staff, Department of National Defence, Ottawa.

1958

Jan Zurakowski

Citation: in recognition of his outstanding contribution to experimental test flying of jet aircraft in Canada, and for his outstanding contribution to world recognition of Canadian aeronautical achievements

Squadron Leader Jan Zurakowski, while Chief Development Test Pilot for Avro Aircraft Limited of Toronto, Ontario, was awarded the Trans-Canada Trophy for meritorious service in the advancement of aviation in Canada during 1958, "in recognition of his outstanding contribution to experimental test flying of jet aircraft in Canada, and for his outstanding contribution to world recognition of Canadian aeronautical achievements." The announcement of the award was made on April 15, 1959, by General, the Honourable George R. Pearkes, V.C., Minister of National Defence.

In making the announcement, the minister said that the success of the initial "Arrow" flights was largely due to Jan Zurakowski's untiring efforts to familiarize himself with the aircraft, together with his high degree of skill and judgment.

Janusz Zurakowski was born on September 12, 1914, in Ryzawka, Russia. Then he moved to Garwolin, Poland, with his parents when he was seven years old. He was educated there and at Lublin, which is 110 miles south of Warsaw.

As a youth he learned to fly gliders in high school. He first flew in 1929, when he was fifteen years of age. His first flight was in a Lublin LkL-5, an old single-engine trainer. Six years later, in 1935, he joined the Polish Air Force, and attended a school for officers at Deblin, Poland, from 1935 to 1937. Upon completion of his two-year course, he was promoted to sub-lieutenant and attached to No. 161 Fighter Squadron at Lwow, Poland.

Prior to the outbreak of World War II, he had become an instructor at the Central Flying School in Deblin. He continued the work of instruction until the Polish Army was defeated by Germany. Then he escaped to England, along with other Polish pilots, and joined the Royal Air Force. From 1940 to 1945 he served with Fighter Squadrons Nos. 234, 306, 315, 316 and 609. He flew in the Battle of Britain. During this period he was credited with destroying three enemy aircraft. He was shot down twice himself.

He was promoted to Flight Lieutenant in April, 1942, and became Commander of No. 316 Polish Fighter Squadron later that year. In 1943, he became deputy wing leader of the Northold Wing.

Jan Zurakowski was decorated with the Polish Virtuti Militari, Poland's highest medal, and the Polish Cross of Valour, with two Bars. He was mentioned in Despatches on three occasions for distinguished service.

Jan Zurakowski attended the Empire Test Pilots' School in 1944; and from 1945 to 1947 he was a Test Pilot with the Aircraft and Armament Experimental Establishment at Boscombe Down, England, where he tested most of the Royal Air Force fighters, Fleet Air Arm aircraft and American Navy fighters.

He retired from the Royal Air Force as a Squadron Leader in 1947. Then he joined the Gloster Aircraft Company, England, as Chief Experimental Test Pilot, flying Meteor twin-jet interceptor aircraft, bringing them through their development stages.

It was in 1950 that he set an international speed record between London-Copenhagen-London flying a Meteor 8 aircraft for the Gloster Aircraft Company.

CF-100, all-weather jet fighter aircraft.
Photo courtesy of the Department of National Defence.

While flying a Gloster Meteor in 1951 at the Farnborough Air Show in England, this world-famous expert aerobatic flyer demonstrated a new aerobatic manoeuvre, known as the "Zurabatic Cartwheel." He worked this manoeuvre out with a slide rule and graphs first, as usual. This jet manoeuvre was the first new aerobatic in 20 years.

Then in November, 1951, he flew a prototype of the Javelin aircraft for the Gloster Aircraft Company. It had delta-type wings, but a conventional tail. There were many problems associated with the development of this aircraft.

These years of experimental testing of aircraft taught Jan Zurakowski not to accept much at its face value, to doubt nearly everything until proven, and to respect evidence and the importance of collecting flight test information by special instrumentation.

The following year, he decided to leave the Gloster Aircraft Company, and he came to Canada in April, 1952, and he went to work for Avro Aircraft Limited of Toronto, Ontario, as a test pilot. His job was to fly the CF-100, the first jet interceptor aircraft designed and built in Canada. The aircraft was powered by Orenda engines.

Jan Zurakowski was the first pilot to fly a Canadian-designed aircraft, the CF-100, Mark IV, a jet interceptor, faster than the speed of sound. That was on December 18, 1952. The thunderclap rattled windows seconds later in Malton. This was a notable achievement for the CF-100, a Canadian-designed aircraft. Jan Zurakowski brought the CF-100 through its early stages of development. He is credited with being the first to fly beyond the speed of sound in a straight-winged production aircraft. It was designed and built to meet R.C.A.F. requirements and was an all-weather jet interceptor.

Men like Jan Zurakowski are faced with many problems and risk unknown dangers each time they fly to ensure that fighter aircraft will be safe for the R.C.A.F. pilots who fly them. These test pilots are a special breed of men responsible for eliminating the snags in development before each aircraft enters squadron service. Jan Zurakowski was a special kind of person who knew how to use a slide rule and graphs for development purposes. Likewise, he had the sharp and agile brain of a test pilot, and a sense of humour. Yet he was publicity-shy, and very reticent. He was small and balding and it was said that he looked like anything but a test pilot.

At the Farnborough Air Show in 1955, Jan Zurakowski again attracted world attention by putting the CF-100, Mark IV, through a series of delicate manoeuvres, including the "falling leaf," which thrilled the huge crowd. These manoeuvres were in sharp contrast to what was expected from the heavily-armed long-range aircraft. His display did much to advance Canada's reputation in the field of aircraft design and manufacture.

It was on March 25, 1958, that Jan Zurakowski took the Avro "Arrow" prototype on its first flight at Malton Airport, Ontario. He flew the Avro Arrow supersonic jet interceptor aircraft, the CF-105, on all of its initial flights during 1958.

Jan Zurakowski continued to test fly the CF-105 Arrow supersonic jet interceptor until October 1, 1958, when he retired as Chief Development Test Pilot for Avro Aircraft Limited, which had designed and built the Arrow and the CF-100 jet interceptors. Then on October 1, 1958, he became liaison engineer with Avro Aircraft. He held this position for a few months, until the Arrow programme was cancelled by the government on February 20, 1959.

The Mark I, CF-105, Arrow had a needle-like nose, twin engines, and delta wings. It was a supersonic, delta-wing, all-weather jet interceptor that had a supersonic appearance. It weighed about 34 tons. It was 77 feet 9.65 inches in length, with a wing span of 50 feet from delta tip to tip. With its wheels on the ground, it had a height of 21 feet 3 inches to the top of the vertical stabilizer. In 1958, it was the largest known interceptor aircraft.

Dowty Equipment Ltd., of Canada designed the main undercarriage.

The first five Arrow aircraft were fitted with Pratt and Whitney J. 75 engines, each with a thrust of more than 15,000 pounds, while the sixth aircraft was the first Mark II with an Orenda "Iroquois" engine, built by Orenda Engines. Five of the six completed Arrows had already been test flown. But the sixth aircraft, equipped with the Canadian-made Iroquois engine, which was expected to give the CF-105 greater speed and range, was to have been the next aircraft to take to the air, and set a few records. But the sixth aircraft (Mark II), expected to fly at the end of February, 1959, was never flown. The Iroquois engine incorporated an afterburner which was built as an integral part of the basic engine. The afterburner operation was fully automatic, the engine having a modulated final nozzle to produce the desired thrust-to-temperature relationship at the selected power lever setting.

However, it would be interesting to know what would have been the results of the performance of the Arrow, powered by the more powerful Iroquois engines. Had the cancellation of the Arrow been delayed for about ten days or so, these results would possibly have been known, and could have been startling, in view of the outstanding performance of the Arrow equipped with the less powerful Pratt and Whitney engines.

A very sophisticated weapons system was incorporated in the Arrow, which consisted of an integrated airborne system for electronic weapons, navigation and communications. It provided automatic flight control, airborne radar,

telecommunications and navigation, and special instrumentation and pilot displays, and could operate in either fully automatic, semi-automatic, or manual environment. This system was designated the "Astra I" and was the prime responsibility of Radio Corporation of America, in association with the Aeronautical Division of Minneapolis-Honeywell. The Canadian firms of R.C.A. Victor Co. of Canada, Honeywell Controls Ltd., and Computing Devices of Canada Ltd., received subcontracts for engineering services.

The decision was made, therefore, jointly among Avro Aircraft Limited, the R.C.A.F. and the Canadian Government to proceed from the outset with a number of development aircraft on the basis of a production type drawing release. In other words, it was decided to take the technical risks involved to save time on the programme.[1]

It was in July, 1953, that the government authorized Avro Aircraft Limited to develop a twin-engined delta aircraft that would carry a crew of two men and, at the same time, incorporate in it a weapons system that would carry armament with missiles and rockets. The accepted proposal was later designated Project No. CF-105.

This proposal took into account changes in R.C.A.F. requirements which called for an increase in operating altitude. Early proposals, design studies and tests, which later resulted in the basic CF-105 configuration, were largely the responsibility of the Preliminary Design Office, run by Jim Chamberlain, under J. C. Floyd, Chief Engineer (later Vice-President of Engineering).

The first wind tunnel tests were made in September, 1953.

The development of the supersonic jet interceptor which began in 1953 was scheduled to be ready for use by the Department of National Defence in late 1961. This made a very tight schedule from the time of the initial design to

delivery to the R.C.A.F. for squadron use. Preliminary design of the Arrow was completed by the summer of 1954.

Early in March, 1958, the time came to test fly the Arrow. Those were anxious days, to say the least. The flight was made by Jan Zurakowski on March 25, 1958. He took off at precisely 9:51 A.M. The Arrow did not exceed a height of 10,000 feet; and it reached only a fraction of its estimated top speed. It was a 35-minute flight, in which the test pilot made gentle turns and let-downs, and checked the landing gear by moving it up and down to get the feel of the aircraft on approach. Mechanisms were checked and instrument readings noted, and then the Arrow came down and landed with the aid of a drag parachute, well before the end of the runway without using the brakes. It was a good flight. Soft-spoken Jan Zurakowski simply said: "It handled very nicely." He had made the flight for which he had been preparing for eighteen months.

He had two chase planes on this flight. One was a CF-100, flown by "Spud" Potocki; the other a Sabre jet, flown by Flight Lieutenant Jack Woodman of the R.C.A.F. Avro photographer, Hugh Mackechnie, accompanied Spud Potocki.

Upon landing, Jan Zurakowski was cheered by Avro Aircraft workers who gave him a tremendous ovation as he climbed out of the Arrow's cockpit. Ten thousand Avro people had assembled to see the culmination of four and one-half years of research and development unprecedented in Canada's aeronautical history.

The first engine-running in the aircraft took place on December 4, 1957; taxi tests were made on Christmas Eve, 1957; while the first flight was made on March 25, 1958. The first two flights were for pilot familiarization, while the aircraft flew supersonic (Mach 1.4) on the third flight on April 3, 1958, at a height of 40,000 feet. On the seventh flight on August 23, 1958, the Arrow reached a

speed well over 1,000 m.p.h. at an altitude of 50,000 feet in a climb while still accelerating.[2] Jan Zurakowski also flew the second prototype in August, 1958; and the third prototype in September, 1958, which exceeded the speed of sound on its first flight! Spud Potocki also made the first flight on two more Arrows.

Years of research into performance, stability and control problems about which there was no data when the project began, the preparation of 17,000 drawings and the expenditure of a vast sum of money had been, hopefully, vindicated by the success of the Arrow.

But, it was on September 23, 1958, that the Prime Minister, the Right Honourable John G. Diefenbaker, made a five-page announcement to the press. He said, in part, that, in recent weeks the government had fully reviewed the Canadian air defence programme in the light of the rapid development that had taken place during the past year in missiles for both defence and attack.

The highlights of the text were carried by the *Financial Post* of September 27, 1958, and are as follows:

"As a result, the government had concluded that missiles should be introduced into the Canadian air defence system, and that the number of supersonic interceptor aircraft required for the R.C.A.F. Air Defence Command would be substantially less than could have been foreseen a few years ago, if, in fact, aircraft would be required at all in the 1960's, because of the rapid strides being made in missiles by both the United States and the U.S.S.R.

"The development of the Canadian supersonic interceptor — the CF-105, or the Arrow — began in 1953, and, even in the best of circumstances, it would not be available for use in R.C.A.F. squadrons until late in 1961. Since the project began, the government said, revolutionary changes had taken place which required a review of the

AVRO ARROW, CF-105 in flight.

Photo courtesy of Aviation and Space Division, National Museum of Science and Technology, Ottawa.

programme in the light of anticipated conditions when the aircraft would come into use.

"Therefore, the government had decided to introduce the Bomarc guided missile (built by *BO*eing, powered by *MARQ*uardt engines) into the Canadian air defence system which would be used against hostile bombers.

"With the introduction of missiles into Canada's air defence system, and the reduction in the expected need for manned supersonic interceptor aircraft, the government had decided that it would not be advisable at that time to put the CF-105 into production.

"The government believed, however, that, to discontinue abruptly the development of the Arrow and its engine, would be unwise because of its consequent effects upon industry, in particular, and because of the tense international situation.

"Therefore, the government decided that the development programme for the Arrow aircraft and the Iroquois engine should be continued until March, 1959, when the situation would be reviewed again.

"Although both the Arrow aircraft and the Iroquois engine appeared likely to be better than any alternatives expected to be ready by 1961, it was questionable whether their margin of superiority was worth the very high cost of producing them, as only small numbers were likely to be required.

"As a further consequence, the government decided that it would be clearly unwise to proceed with the development of a special flight and fire control system for the CF-105 aircraft, known as the "Astra", and of a special air-to-air missile to be used as its armament, known as the "Sparrow". The contracts for the development of the Astra fire control system and of the Sparrow missile were to be terminated at once.

"In the meantime, modifications to the CF-105 would be made during its development to permit the use of a fire control system and weapon already in production for use in United States' aircraft engaged in North American defence.

"The important savings achieved by cancelling the Astra and Sparrow programmes, and substituting the alternatives already in production, would amount to roughly $330,000,000 for a completed programme of 100 aircraft.

"The total cost to the Canadian Government of developing the Arrow aircraft, and its associated elements, up to the beginning of September, 1958, was $303,000,000. To finish the development of the CF-105, and its components, including the Astra and the Sparrow, and to produce enough for 100 aircraft for squadron use, would cost about another billion and a quarter dollars, approximately $12,500,000 per usable aircraft. By substituting the alternative fire control system and missile for the Astra and Sparrow, the cost would be reduced to about $9,000,000 each."

Further, the Prime Minister said in his press conference statement on September 23, 1958:

"Canadians are proud of what the Canadian aircraft industry has accomplished for defence. The Arrow supersonic plane has already thrilled us with its performance, its promise and its proof of ability in design and technology. The Iroquois engine, too, is a fine technical achievement and its development had led to many industrial advances. Excellent scientific and technical teams had been created for these projects.

"However, it will be recognized, I believe, that as the age of missiles appears certain to lead to a major reduction in the need for fighter aircraft, Canada cannot expect to support a large industry developing and producing aircraft solely for diminishing defence requirements.

"The government deeply regrets the unemployment that will be involved in the termination of the Astra and Sparrow projects and in the Avro plant at Malton. It is hoped that our defence industry will be able to share effectively with the United States industry in one part or another of the major programmes in the air defence of the North American continent and thereby provide alternative employment in the field of missiles and electronics.

"In common with Canadians, the government recognizes the accomplishments and technical quality of the work done, but to continue vast expenditures on aircraft and equipment which military and other expert opinion does not support as the best way to achieve the defence essential to our security would not only be wasteful but unjustifiable.

"It is regrettable that, in Canada's contribution to a full and effective part in the air defence of the North American continent, adaptation to changing techniques and the nature of potential threat to this continent makes necessary from time to time changes in the requirements of deterrent power."

Meanwhile, a decision was pending.

Then on February 20, 1959, the Right Honourable John G. Diefenbaker, Prime Minister of Canada, announced his decision in the House of Commons. He said:

"The government has carefully examined and re-examined the probable need for the Arrow aircraft and Iroquois engine known as the CF-105, the development of which has been continued pending a final decision. It has made a thorough examination in the light of all the information available concerning the probable nature of the threats to North America in future years, the alternative means of defence against such threats, and the estimated costs

Photo shows F/Lt. Jack Woodman (left) holding model of the Arrow, CF-105, while Jan Zurakowski is seated in the replica of the Silver Dart in 1958. (National Exhibition, Toronto).
Photo courtesy of Avro Aircraft Ltd., Malton, Ontario.

thereof. The conclusion arrived at is that the development of the Arrow aircraft and the Iroquois engine should be terminated now.

"Formal notice of termination is being given now to the contractors. All outstanding commitments will of course be settled equitably.

"Having regard to the information and advice we have received, however, there is no other feasible or justifiable course open to us. We must not abdicate our responsibility to assure that the huge sums which it is our duty to ask Parliament to provide for defence are being expended in the most effective way to achieve that purpose."

On February 23, 1959, General, the Honourable G. R. Pearkes, V.C., Minister of National Defence, explained:

"During 1958, when it was becoming obvious that neither the United States nor the United Kingdom would be interested in purchasing the CF-105, very extensive studies were carried out to see what alternatives might be adopted, how many of the CF-105's we could possibly afford to purchase and how many would be required to meet the diminishing threat.

"There was some concern at that time about the range of the CF-105. We had been informed then that the ranges were 238 nautical miles flying supersonically and 347 nautical miles flying subsonically."

Then, in March, 1977, it was reported in the press that the Department of National Defence was searching for a new fighter 'plane, and producers of six supersonic aircraft were being asked to submit proposals to sell from 130 to 150

aircraft to Canada. The cost was estimated at more than two billion dollars. The announcement said it was hoped that the aircraft could be in use by 1981, almost twenty years after the cancellation of the Arrow programme. And where have all the missiles gone?

After the lay-off of the 13,000 employees, more or less, in February, 1959, some 4,000 were re-hired within a few weeks for work on other projects handled by Avro Aircraft Limited and Orenda Engines Limited. Some of these workers were given the task of cutting up the six completed Arrows, and the three on the

The Committee of Award for the year 1958 consisted of the following members:

Chairman: Air Commodore M. Lipton, Chief of Operations, Air Force Headquarters, Department of National Defence, Ottawa.

Members: Mr. M. M. Fleming, Controller, Civil Air Operations and Regulations, Department of Transport, Ottawa.

Mr. G. C. Hurren, Vice-President, Royal Canadian Flying Clubs Association, Ottawa.

Mr. R. N. Redmayne, General Manager, Air Industries and Transport Association, Ottawa.

Captain G. C. Edwards, Deputy to Assistant Chief of Naval Staff (Air and Warfare), Naval Headquarters, Department of National Defence, Ottawa.

Secretary: Group Captain G. F. Jacobsen, Assistant to the Chief of the Air Staff, Air Force Headquarters, Department of National Defence, Ottawa.

production line! Not one of the Arrows was kept as a work of art for a Canadian museum. Not one of the Arrows was kept to show its magnificent design. Not one of these six Arrows was to remain intact. Blueprints, brochures, reports and photographs were all reduced to ashes. Why, one asks? What a pity!

So this man, Jan Zurakowski, with the sharp and agile brain of a test pilot, was awarded the Trans-Canada Trophy for 1958 for his outstanding contribution to experimental test flying of jet aircraft in Canada, and for his outstanding contribution to world recognition of Canadian aeronautical achievements.

The presentation of the award of the Trans-Canada Trophy to Jan Zurakowski took place on October 28, 1959, at the annual convention of the Air Industries and Transport Association held in Montreal. The presentation of the trophy was made by the Honourable Pierre Sevigny, Associate Minister of National Defence.

Jan Zurakowski was named a member of Canada's Aviation Hall of Fame in 1973. He was made a Companion of the Order of Flight (City of Edmonton).

Today, Squadron Leader Jan Zurakowski resides in Barry's Bay, Ontario, where he runs a tourist resort. Mr. and Mrs. Zurakowski have two children.

NOTES

[1]. J.C. Floyd, *Hawker Siddeley Review*, December 1958.
[2]. *Ibid.*

1959

John A. D. McCurdy

Citation: in recognition of his meritorious service in the cause of Canadian aviation during the past fifty years, and for his outstanding contribution to the success of the 50th Anniversary of Powered Flight Observances during 1959

The Honourable John A. D. McCurdy, D.Cn.L., M.B.E., M.E., D.Eng., LL.D., Honorary F.C.A.I., was awarded the Trans-Canada Trophy for meritorious service in the advancement of aviation in Canada during 1959, "in recognition of his meritorious service in the cause of Canadian aviation during the past fifty years, and for his outstanding con- tribution to the success of the 50th Anniversary of Powered Flight Ob- servances during 1959." The an- nouncement of the award was made in the spring of 1960 by General, the Honourable George R. Pearkes, V.C., then Minister of National Defence.

John Alexander Douglas McCurdy was born at Baddeck, Cape Breton Island, Nova Scotia, on August 2, 1886. He was the second son of Arthur W. McCurdy, a former editor of the *Cape Breton Island Reporter,* who, in 1885, had become secretary, and then assistant to Dr. Alexander Graham Bell, inventor of the telephone. Thus began John McCurdy's relationship with Dr. Bell, which was to last until Dr. Bell's death on August 2, 1922. John McCurdy was also the grandson of the Honourable David McCurdy, once a legislator in the Province of Nova Scotia.

John McCurdy received his early education at Baddeck Academy and, in 1902, at the age of sixteen, he entered the University of Toronto's School of Practical Science. He graduated as a mechanical engineer in 1907. In this same year, Dr. Bell invited John Mc- Curdy to help him carry out his tetrahedral kite experiments during the summer months. Dr. Bell firmly believed in the tetrahedral principle of con- struction due to its remarkable stability in

the air. As a young lad, John McCurdy spent many happy and pleasant hours in Dr. Bell's laboratory under the influence of this great man.

Frederick Walker "Casey" Baldwin first met Dr. Bell in the summer of 1906 at Dr. Bell's estate, Beinn Bhreagh (Gaelic for "Beautiful Mountain"), near Baddeck, Nova Scotia. He was twenty-four years of age and had just graduated in mechanical engineering from the University of Toronto, and John Mc- Curdy, then in his junior year in Science at Toronto University, had invited him to spend a couple of weeks with him at Baddeck. So, Casey Baldwin was taken to Beinn Bhreagh by his friend, John McCurdy. Dr. Bell, nearly sixty years of age at the time, took an instant liking to Casey Baldwin and asked him to come back in the fall (1906), after he had finished his summer course at Cornell University, to build a tower for him on top of Beinn Bhreagh to show that the tetrahedral principle could be applied to engineering structures and withstand the force of the winds that swept across the Bras d'Or Lakes on Cape Breton Island. Incidentally, Casey Baldwin was the grandson of the Honourable Robert Baldwin, former Premier of Upper Canada and one of the Fathers of Confederation.

Dr. Bell invited these two engineers to help him because he needed them in his work, and he did not have the amount of technical knowledge required to put a man into the air in one of his man- carrying structures. Therefore, he sought competent engineering advice to do this.

In the spring of 1907, Dr. Bell visited Glenn Curtiss at his motorcycle and engine shop at Hammondsport, New

York, hoping to obtain the delivery of an engine he had ordered earlier. Later, Dr. Bell offered Glenn Curtiss a bonus if he would deliver another engine to him at Baddeck in person. This he agreed to do. Since Dr. Bell, John McCurdy and Casey Baldwin had no experience with engines, Dr. Bell invited Glenn Curtiss to come to Baddeck to help them.

At this time, Glenn Curtiss was doing very well for himself in the engine-manufacturing business, and was a most knowledgeable man on engines. In fact, he was building one of the best motorcycle engines in North America at Hammondsport.

When Glenn Curtiss returned to Baddeck in the late summer of 1907, Dr. Bell engaged him to help solve their engine problems. Glen Curtiss' interest had been aroused during his earlier visit that summer to deliver the engine to Dr. Bell at Baddeck.

At this time, Lieutenant Thomas Selfridge was making a study of flying machines for the United States Army, and was particularly interested in the *Cygnet* experiment. Lieutenant Selfridge was an Officer in the United States Army Balloon Corps and had met Dr. Bell on one of his visits to Washington. He had also visited Baddeck during the summer of 1907 at Dr. Bell's invitation to observe their experiments. So Selfridge was posted to Baddeck by President Theodore Roosevelt at the personal request of Dr. Bell.

These men worked throughout the summer months of 1907 on Dr. Bell's tetrahedral kite, the *Cygnet*. They experimented by towing kite models with a motor boat when the breeze was right, measuring wind velocities and altitude, testing engines and propellers. Dr. Bell was usually with them. As a matter of fact, they lived in Dr. Bell's house at Beinn Bhreagh.

One evening in September, 1907, Mrs. Bell, while talking with the men, suggested that they should form an

association to carry out their projects. She, herself, was quite willing to provide funds for the work of any association that might be formed.

So it was that the Aerial Experiment Association of Halifax, Nova Scotia, was formed on October 1, 1907, at the suggestion, and under the sponsorship of Mrs. Bell, who donated the total sum of $35,000 towards the work of this newly formed association. Mrs. Bell donated $25,000 for the first year, and was later to donate a further $10,000 for the association's extended period of six months. She had just sold some property that she had inherited, which had increased in value, and was prepared to use the money. Besides John McCurdy, the other members of the association were Dr. Alexander Graham Bell (1847-1922), Casey Baldwin (1882-1948), Glenn Curtiss (1878-1930) and Thomas Selfridge (1882-1908).

The creation of the Aerial Experiment Association was "for the purpose of carrying on experiments relating to aerial locomotion with the special object of constructing a successful aerodrome," as stated in the article of agreement. The association was created only for the period of one year. In Dr. Bell's words, "it was a co-operative scientific association, not for gain but for the love of the art and doing what we can to help one another."

During the remaining months of 1907, they were still working in Baddeck on Dr. Bell's tetrahedral kite, the *Cygnet*, which was 42 1/2 feet from tip to tip. It was a large man-carrying kite with over 3,000 small tetrahedral cells which were covered with bright red silk. Although strong enough to carry a man, it required an engine to get it off the water.

The *Cygnet* was the association's first project. It was ready for trial on December 6, 1907, and flown over the Bras d'Or Lakes for a test. Selfridge lay face down in the man-carrying kite, and he was covered with rugs to keep him

warm. The kite was then put on a raft called the "Ugly Duckling," which was towed behind the steamboat *Blue Hill*. The kite took off successfully and rose to a height of 168 feet above the water. After remaining in the air for seven minutes it started to descend. As it neared the water, smoke from the funnel of the steamer blew between the ship and the kite. This obscured the view of the men who were to cut the tow-line when the kite reached the surface, and the kite was dragged along the water. Selfridge had a cold ducking, but fortunately he was not hurt. Alas, the *Cygnet* was demolished, and with it the opportunity of putting an engine in it. However, valuable information had been obtained from the experiment.

After this, they decided to go to Hammondsport, where Glenn Curtiss lived, as his engine shop would be nearby. Also, there were hills in the vicinity, and a large lake where their experiments could be continued.

The early months of 1908 found them at work building a glider at Hammondsport. This was called the *Hammondsport Glider*. With it, they made some fifty glides, ranging in distance from ten feet to 100 yards. They received many a hard bump from being unable to always control the glider. Then, in the late spring, the glider crashed one day and it was destroyed.

With this experience, their own ideas, and the information they had on other flying machines, they set out to build their first powered machine, known as Drome No. 1. This was called Selfridge's *Red Wing*. The name *Red Wing* came from the red silk covering.

While all members of the association worked together, each one was to have a machine named after him and, in theory, he was to be mainly responsible for his own design. And this was Selfridge's machine. When it was finished, it was fitted with iron sleigh runners to facilitate its take-off for its first trial flight.

Dr. Bell's tetrahedral kite, Drome No. 5, Cygnet II, under construction at Baddeck, N.S., on September 12, 1908. Note the silk used in the kite.

Photo courtesy of Gilbert H. Grosvenor Collection, Library of Congress.

However, Tom Selfridge was away on business at the time, so Casey Baldwin was chosen as the one to make the flight for him. Conditions were right for a test flight on March 12, 1908, so its first trial flight was made from the frozen surface of Lake Keuka, near Hammondsport. Casey Baldwin climbed into the first aeroplane with a cockpit. Several men took hold of the wings to hold the craft back as the engine was being started. After going about 200 feet, the machine left the ice. Casey Baldwin and his *Red Wing* were airborne. He flew the *Red Wing* for a measured distance of 318 feet, 11 inches, at a height of ten feet before he brought the machine down for a a smooth landing. The machine had an air-cooled engine on which each cylinder had its own carburetor. While preparing for this flight, Glenn Curtiss, John McCurdy and several of the factory workers were on skates, which was just as well as it turned out, for, on first starting the engine, the machine had moved off, fortunately away from the shore, with no one inside to control it. Eventually, those on skates caught up with it and hauled it back to the starting point for its actual test flight.

It is claimed that this was the first *public* aeroplane flight in North America. Casey Baldwin became the first Canadian to fly a powered aircraft, and the first British subject to fly. Also, Casey Baldwin was the fourth man to fly a powered aircraft on the North American continent.

On March 17, 1908, the *Red Wing* made another flight. Unfortunately, it was its last flight. Casey Baldwin was at the controls again. This time he was caught in a stiff breeze and the machine came down heavily, flipped, and the wing struck the ice, wrecking the machine. But Casey Baldwin was not hurt. The *Red Wing* had lasted exactly five days. The crash proved to Casey Baldwin that shifting the pilot's weight was not enough to keep the machine stable!

Next, designs were under way for the construction of another machine, known as Baldwin's *White Wing*. It was covered with white silk, as there was no more red silk left! Since the accident to the *Red Wing* had shown that lateral control was essential, the design for the *White Wing* included movable wing tips. John Mc-Curdy called them hinged tips or "little wings." These wing tips were to give lateral control while flying the machine. They were connected to the pilot's seat so that he could correct the machine when it tilted.

Also, in addition to movable wing tips, which later were called ailerons, Baldwin's *White Wing* had a tricycle un-dercarriage, supported by bicycle wheels with pneumatic tires. It was one of the first aircraft with a wheeled undercarriage of any sort to be designed in North America. Otherwise, the *White Wing* resembled the *Red Wing* in appearance.

The *White Wing* was built in two months' time. Casey Baldwin test flew the machine on May 18, 1908. He flew a distance of 279 feet at an altitude of ten feet at Hammondsport. Also, the other three members of the association made their first flights on the *White Wing*. Dr. Bell, himself, never flew. Tom Selfridge made his first powered-flight the next day, May 19, 1908; Glenn Curtiss made his first powered-flight on May 22, 1908, for a distance of 1,017 feet in 19 seconds; and John McCurdy made his first powered-flight on May 23, 1908. John McCurdy made the last flight on the *White Wing*. Apparently, he was unable to control the machine and it plunged to the ground and was wrecked. Five flights had been made on the *White Wing* covering distances from 20 feet to 300 yards.

Now it was time for Glenn Curtiss to design Drome No. 3. He named it the *June Bug*, perhaps because it was first flown during the month of June. Glenn Curtiss' design followed those of the first two machines, but the drome was more

solidly built. He first flew the *June Bug* on June 20, 1908, and had a successful flight. He flew a distance of 456 feet. The *June Bug* made over 100 flights, ranging from short distances to two and a half miles. John McCurdy also flew the *June Bug* for a distance of two miles.

With Glenn Curtiss piloting the *June Bug* on July 4, 1908, he won the Scientific American Trophy for a heavier-than-air machine flying the first measured kilometre under test conditions.

By now, John McCurdy was ready to start on the design for Drome No. 4, which was to be his machine. It was called the *Silver Dart*.

At this time a decision was reached to stay in Hammondsport for the summer of 1908, rather than return to Baddeck where Dr. Bell was carrying out ex-periments with another tetrahedral kite. Besides, they wanted to stay close to Glenn Curtiss' engine shop, since he was the expert on engines. However, Casey Baldwin did return to Baddeck to be with Dr. Bell.

Many flights were made in Ham-mondsport during the summer of 1908 on the *June Bug* by John McCurdy, Glenn Curtiss and Tom Selfridge. Their experience was growing each day. Unfortunately, at this time, Tom Selfridge was recalled to Washington by the United States Army. Meanwhile, John McCurdy was hurrying to complete his drome; and Glenn Curtiss was trying to put the *June Bug* on floats so it would fly from the water. In this, he was un-successful.

Work on their projects was stopped for a time due to the sudden death of Tom Selfridge at Fort Myer, Virginia, on September 17, 1908. His death was the result of an accident to a machine flown by Orville Wright, in which Tom Selfridge was an observer for the War Depart-ment. He was the first person to lose his life in the crash of a powered aeroplane. Orville Wright was badly injured.

The association held a meeting in

The Silver Dart *on the ice of Baddeck Bay, N.S., on February 23, 1909, with John McCurdy at the controls, just about to make its first flight in Canada.*
Photo courtesy of Gilbert H. Grosvenor Collection. Library of Congress.

Washington shortly after Tom Selfridge's accident, and decided to continue its work for another six months, until March 31, 1909. Tom Selfridge's father voted on his behalf. Otherwise, the life of the association would have automatically expired on September 30, 1908.

The *Silver Dart* was now completed. It was powered by a 35 h.p. water-cooled engine, designed and built by Glenn Curtiss. It had a 42-foot wing span. It was test flown by John McCurdy on December 6, 1908. It flew well and made a good landing. John McCurdy made ten more flights before January, 1909, when the *Silver Dart* was shipped by rail to Baddeck. It was said that Dr. Bell, with his sure instinct for history, wanted one of the association's machines flown in Canada. Its longest flight at Hammondsport was for a mile and a half, but it made many shorter flights. Also, many experiments were made, and further experiences gained.

Glenn Curtiss was continuing his work on the *June Bug* at this time. It was re-named the *Loon*, as he was attempting to make it fly off the water. Dr. Bell had made suggestions how this might be done. But Glenn Curtiss did not succeed in his attempts. So the *Loon* was stored away for the winter in January, 1909. John McCurdy and Glenn Curtiss returned to Baddeck to be with Dr. Bell and Casey Baldwin.

At Baddeck, Dr. Bell was awaiting the arrival of an engine for his tetrahedral kite, known as Drome No. 5; while Casey Baldwin was continuing his experiments with hydrodromes.

The new Curtiss engine for Dr. Bell's tetrahedral kite arrived at Baddeck on February 11, 1909, and it was installed in the kite. The first tests of the kite were made on February 22, 1909. A propeller was broken during the tests, which were unsuccessful. However, it was decided to make another propeller for the kite. In the meantime, on February 23, 1909, the new Curtiss engine was taken from the

kite and put in the *Silver Dart*.

Then John McCurdy took the *Silver Dart* for a test flight on the afternoon of February 23, 1909. John MacDermid's one-horse sleigh was pressed into service to tow the craft on to the ice. Eight of Dr. Bell's staff pushed the craft along the ice. Someone cranked the propeller, and John McCurdy took off in the *Silver Dart*, headed into the slight breeze, and flew for about three-quarters of a mile above the frozen Bras d'Or Lakes at a height of approximately 60 feet at a speed of about 40 m.p.h. Then the *Silver Dart* made a perfect landing!

On this memorable date, February 23, 1909, John McCurdy made the first flight in Canada, and the British Empire.

One hundred and forty-six people had gathered on the ice at Baddeck to watch this flight of a heavier-than-air machine. Few of the spectators at that flight could have dreamed of the day when the Dominion of Canada would be spanned by commercial aircraft operating on schedules.

By the standards of the day, John McCurdy wrote, "the *Silver Dart* was quite a heavy craft to perform so well, and so flawlessly. Together, including my weight and that of the engine, the total weight of the aircraft was 960 pounds."[1]

"And just to prove that the *Silver Dart's* first flight in Canada was no mere stroke of luck, I took it up for another flight the next day, February 24, 1909, and flew for four and one-half miles. The day after that, on February 25, 1909, I took the aeroplane on a flight of some 20 miles over the Baddeck countryside."[2] Then in March, 1909, John McCurdy flew the *Silver Dart* several times for distances up to 20 miles over the Baddeck area. Its performance was outstanding.

The *Silver Dart* proved to be the best

machine that the association developed. Actually, John McCurdy was the only person ever to fly the *Silver Dart*.

Wide publicity was given to John McCurdy's flight in the *Silver Dart* on February 23, 1909, and the Board of Commissioners of Baddeck Centre, when they met the next day, February 24, 1909, passed the following resolution:

"Whereas the first flight of an airship within Canada was made successfully at Baddeck yesterday, the twenty-third day of February, in the year one thousand nine hundred and nine, an event of historic importance, coupling as it will with the fact, the name of our worthy and honoured citizen, Dr. Graham Bell, under whose auspices the flight was made, the name of the bold aeronaut, Douglas McCurdy, a Baddeck boy, born and bred, and the name of our home Baddeck, where this notable event took place.

RESOLVED that these facts are well worthy of being recorded on our public records, and further resolved that copies of this resolution be sent to Dr. Graham Bell, and Mr. Douglas Mc-Curdy with the congratulations of the village of Baddeck Centre on their well merited success."[3]

In his reply, Dr. Bell wrote these prophetic words:

"This may seem to be a small matter at the present moment; but when flying-machines have become common, and Aerial Locomotion a well recognized and established mode of transit, the origin of the art in Canada will become a matter of great historical interest, and people will look back to the flight made on February 23, 1909, as the first flight of a flying machine in the Dominion of Canada."[4]

Even though the *Silver Dart* had now flown in both Canada and the United

The Silver Dart *taking off the ice of Baddeck Bay, N.S., on February 23, 1909, with John McCurdy at the controls, making its first flight in Canada.*
Photo courtesy of Gilbert H. Grosvenor Collection, Library of Congress.

States, other flight tests continued to be made, as well as experiments with the kite *Cygnet II* at Beinn Bhreagh. The *Cygnet II* was a huge 'plane, or kite, which followed the tetrahedral cell kite principle favoured by Dr. Bell. It did not make any flights.

These were the projects that the Aerial Experiment Association had carried out during its short life span before it came to an end on March 31, 1909, by time limitation. The objective of the association had been achieved with great success. This was, indeed, an interesting chapter in the early history of flying.

Dr. Bell, excited over the flights of the *Silver Dart*, and, in an attempt to help John McCurdy and Casey Baldwin in their effort to promote flying machines, set out for Ottawa and spoke to the Canadian Club on March 27, 1909. Many distinguished guests attended the luncheon, amongst whom were His Excellency Earl Grey, the Governor General; the Prime Minister, Sir Wilfrid Laurier; and other gentlemen, including the Honourable, Sir Frederick Borden, the Minister of Militia and Defence.

With the expiration of the Aerial Experiment Association, John McCurdy and Casey Baldwin formed Canada's first aircraft manufacturing organization, the Canadian Aerodrome Company of Baddeck, Nova Scotia, on March 31, 1909, to take over the association's work. The company was backed financially by Dr. Bell.

Meanwhile, John McCurdy and Casey Baldwin continued to make demonstration flights in the east in the hope of inspiring an interest in the possibilities of their machines, and persuading the Canadian Government to finance further "aerodrome" work by demonstrating the *Silver Dart*. However, they were successful in being invited to come to Ot-

tawa to give demonstration flights before officials of the Department of Militia and Defence. Therefore, the *Silver Dart* was crated and shipped to Ottawa and Petawawa Military Camp, Ontario, for this purpose.

On August 2, 1909, John McCurdy took the *Silver Dart* for a flight before military officials at Petawawa Military Camp. The *Silver Dart* made four successful demonstration flights, but crashed on its fifth flight. John McCurdy was unhurt, except for a broken nose.

John McCurdy described it this way in 1959:

"As a matter of fact, the *Silver Dart* behaved like a perfect lady until I took her to Petawawa in a vain attempt to convince army officials that there might be a future for aeroplanes in Canada's defence set-up. Here, I had not taken into consideration the way that soft sand could drag on a plane's wheels and, after taking the *Silver Dart* up for four good flights, I nosed her over and made her into kindling wood on the fifth try."[5]

So the historic *Silver Dart* came to a tragic end at Petawawa. Today, a monument and a bronze plaque mark the place where the *Silver Dart* came to rest. The remains of this historic 'plane were later shipped to Baddeck.

Meanwhile, the Canadian Aerodrome Company of Baddeck, Nova Scotia, was continuing to build "aerodromes." During its life span, the company built three of them: *Baddeck I*, a biplane, completed in July, 1909; *Baddeck II*, a biplane, completed on September 11, 1909; and a *Hubbard* monoplane, completed on March 16, 1910.

Baddeck I and *Baddeck II* each had 40-foot wing spans, while the *Hubbard* had a 33-foot, 11-inch wing span. Each of these aircraft had a Kirkham engine,

which was considered to be an improvement over the Curtiss engine used in the *Silver Dart*. Kirkham had worked with Glen Curtiss in Hammondsport. *Baddeck I* had a 42 h.p. engine; while *Baddeck II* and the *Hubbard* each had a 40 h.p. engine. Each engine had six cylinders.

In spite of the unfortunate mishap to the *Silver Dart*, John McCurdy and Casey Baldwin were still keen on demonstrating their aircraft to officials of the Department of Militia and Defence.

So, *Baddeck I* was shipped to Petawawa Military Camp upon its completion, where it was assembled to make further demonstration flights before the Militia Council. *Baddeck I* had new structural features, including the first enclosed fuel tanks, and the first wing radiators. The first demonstration flight was made on August 11, 1909; and the second one on August 12, 1909, for a distance of 300 feet. These flights were successful and were made by John McCurdy, with Casey Baldwin watching. However, while John McCurdy was making another demonstration flight on August 13, 1909, the *Baddeck I* stalled and crashed, and was damaged. John McCurdy had flown a distance of 210 feet. He was unhurt. This was a great disappointment for John McCurdy and Casey Baldwin who had worked so hard to get this far.

After being repaired, *Baddeck I* was successfully flown for short distances by John McCurdy at the Montreal Aviation Meet on June 27 and June 28, 1910. Then on June 30, 1910, *Baddeck I*, while being flown by John McCurdy, crashed for some reason or other, probably because of high winds, and was destroyed. Its remains were later shipped to Baddeck.

Baddeck II, completed in September, 1909, was first flown on September 25, 1909, from the Aerodrome Park at Baddeck and made four successful flights that day. On September 28, 1909, John

A closeup of John McCurdy at the controls of the Silver Dart.
Photo courtesy of Gilbert H. Grosvenor Collection. Library of Congress.

McCurdy made three successful flights over 300 feet long. Then on September 29, 1909, Casey Baldwin made two short flights. On September 30, 1909, John McCurdy and Casey Baldwin made three more flights each. On one of these flights, Casey Baldwin flew a distance of 2,640 feet. Then during the first week of October, 1909, John McCurdy made six flights covering the length of the field, and Casey Baldwin made one for the same distance. On October 13, 1909, John McCurdy flew some 2,376 feet. The flights continued through until December, 1909. John McCurdy made a two-mile flight on October 21, 1909; a seven-mile flight on October 23, 1909; a sixteen-mile flight on November 1, 1909; and a five-mile flight on December 13, 1909.

John McCurdy made a special demonstration flight of three-quarters of a mile before Governor General Earl Grey on December 8, 1909. His Excellency had travelled all the way by train to Cape Breton to see these flights. It was raining at the time of one of the flights, but he insisted on standing in the rain to see the demonstration flight at Baddeck. The Governor General remained there for a week.

During February and March, 1910, John McCurdy flew Baddeck II off the ice at Baddeck Bay. On one flight on March 3, 1910, he flew for eleven miles and another for nine miles the same day. In all, John McCurdy made twenty-three flights from the ice at Baddeck Bay that winter. Casey Baldwin flew as a passenger with John McCurdy on three of these flights. Major G. S. Maunsell, Director of Engineering Services from Militia Headquarters, Ottawa, visited the Canadian Aerodrome Company at Baddeck in March, 1910. He watched John McCurdy make several flights. Then Major Maunsell flew with him as a passenger for a distance of two miles on March 9, 1910. Again, that same day, Major Maunsell flew with John McCurdy

as a passenger for the same distance. These were successful flights.

However, these successful flights did nothing to change the government's attitude.

It was at this time that John McCurdy and Casey Baldwin offered to sell their two "aerodromes" (Baddeck I and Baddeck II) to the government for $10,000, and, also, they would instruct the men who would fly them for the government. But their offer was declined.

The Militia was impressed with the demonstration flights and did attempt to obtain funds to assist the pioneer Canadian Aerodrome Company in their "aerodrome" experiments. However, the government refused to grant any funds for this work at that time. So the work of the Canadian Aerodrome Company ceased at Baddeck about a year after the company was formed.

The Hubbard monoplane, completed on March 16, 1910, first flew on April 9, 1910, piloted by Hubbard himself. It was the first Canadian-built aeroplane to be exported!

Casey Baldwin did no more flying after 1911. Later, he became internationally known for the development of devices used in naval and aerial warfare.

John McCurdy then turned to barn-storming and during this period became one of North America's best-known pilots. His skill as a pilot brought him fame on the exhibition flying circuit in the United States. In October, 1910, he set a world speed record in a Curtiss biplane at the Belmont Park International Aviation Meet.

In the years leading up to World War I, he campaigned tirelessly for the establishment of a Canadian military flying corps, though without much success initially. Sir Sam Hughes, then Minister of National Defence, dashed his hopes with the statement that aeroplanes would never play a part in modern warfare! World War I proved John McCurdy's theories right, of course, and

after the war the Canadian Air Force was formed.[6]

John McCurdy held Pilot's Licence No. 18, dated October 5, 1910, issued by the Aero Club of America, under the authority of the Fédération Aeronautique Internationale. He was the first of two Canadians so licensed. The other one was William Stark of Vancouver, who held Licence No. 110.

In August, 1911, "flying meets" were held in the east at Toronto and Hamilton. A number of flights were made successfully. Charles F. Willard, a pilot from the United States, and John McCurdy were at the air meet, amongst others, and engaged in an aerial race from Hamilton to Toronto by 'plane on August 2, 1911. John McCurdy was the first to arrive at Toronto, covering the distance of 35 miles in 36 minutes.

Another of these pilots was James V. Martin from the United States who had made some successful flights in his "flying machine" of the day. He flew to Hamilton, Ontario, in July, 1911, only to have his machine come to an unfortunate resting place on the marshlands of Hamilton Bay. While Pilot James Martin luckily escaped being hurt, the flying machine had to be removed from the bay by manpower — and it was young Robert Dodds, later Director of Civil Aviation for Canada, who was engaged to provide the manpower, and to dismantle and remove the machine from Hamilton Bay! For this work he received One Dollar — the first money he received for working on an aeroplane — and the desire to pilot one of these flying machines. And he later became a pilot!

In February, 1915, the British War Office requested the Canadian Government to enlist candidates for the Royal Flying Corps and the Royal Naval Air Service. Therefore, in the spring of 1915, Curtiss Aeroplane and Motors Limited was organized, with John McCurdy as President, to manufacture Curtiss JN-4's. With the help of the British Government,

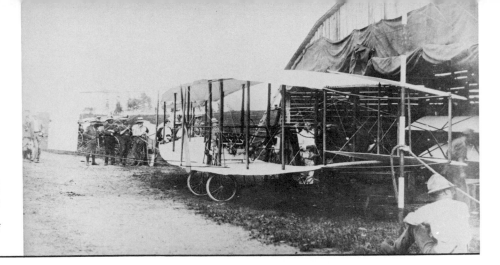

Baddeck I *at Petawawa, Ontario, in August, 1909, ready to make demonstration flights before officials from the Department of Militia and Defence and others.*

Photo courtesy of Gilbert H. Grosvenor Collection. Library of Congress.

he also opened and ran the Curtiss Flying School, established in the spring of 1915 by Curtiss Aeroplane and Motors Limited of Toronto to teach flying to assist in the war effort. A flying field was established at Long Branch for flying training, and a seaplane base at Hanlan's Point, without doubt the first official bases set up in Canada. Through this school, young Canadians were trained for the Royal Flying Corps and the Royal Naval Air Service. These young men learned to fly at their own expense and paid their own way to England to serve with the Royal Flying Corps and the Royal Naval Air Service.

John McCurdy gave up flying in 1916 when his eyesight began to fail, but never did he lose his interest in aviation.

John McCurdy renewed his association with the aircraft field in 1928 when he joined Reid Aircraft Company of Cartierville, Quebec, which had been formed

The Committee of Award for the year 1959 consisted of the following members:

Chairman: Air Commodore M. Lipton, Chief of Operations, Air Force Headquarters, Department of National Defence, Ottawa.

Members: Mr. M. M. Fleming, Controller, Civil Air Operations and Regulations, Department of Transport, Ottawa.

Mr. G. C. Hurren, Vice-President, Royal Canadian Flying Clubs Association, Ottawa.

Mr. R. N. Redmayne, General Manager, Air Industries and Transport Association, Ottawa.

Captain G. C. Edwards, Deputy to Assistant Chief of Naval Staff, (Air and Warfare), Naval Headquarters, Ottawa.

Secretary: Flight Lieutenant R. A. Roane, Chief of the Air Staff Secretariat, Air Force Headquarters, Department of National Defence, Ottawa.

earlier in the year (incorporated in February, 1928) by aircraft designer Walter T. Reid, to manufacture the Reid Rambler. As a result of a merger in January, 1929, Reid Aircraft became Curtiss-Reid Aircraft Co. Ltd., with John McCurdy as President.[7] By 1935, the Curtiss-Reid Aircraft Co. Ltd. was absorbed by the Noorduyn Aircraft Co. Ltd., headed by Bob Noorduyn, who manufactured the well-known *Norseman* aircraft.

At the outbreak of World War II in 1939, John McCurdy went to Ottawa to become Assistant Director General of Aircraft Production with the Department of Munitions and Supply, and later Director of Purchasing as well. Still later, he became Special Assistant to the Financial Adviser in the department.

John McCurdy was appointed Lieutenant Governor of the Province of Nova Scotia on August 12, 1947. Throughout his career, he served his country with distinction. He retired to private life on October 1, 1952.

On February 23, 1959, the R.C.A.F. made him an Honorary Air Commodore. It was during this same year that he was awarded the Trans-Canada Trophy in recognition of his meritorious service in the cause of Canadian aviation during the previous fifty years, and for his outstanding contribution to the success of the 50th Anniversary of Powered Flight Observances during 1959. Canada commemorated the 50th Anniversary of powered flight with the issue of a stamp bearing the image of the *Silver Dart*.

The Honourable Leon Balcer, Minister of Transport, presented the Trans-Canada Trophy to the Honourable J. A. D. McCurdy on November 2, 1960, at the annual meeting of the Air Industries and Transport Association held in the Chateau Frontenac in Quebec City, Quebec.

Two years later, on June 25, 1961, the Honourable John Alexander Douglas McCurdy, D.Cn.L., M.B.E., M.E., D.Eng., LL.D., Honorary F.C.A.I., died in Montreal of bronchial pneumonia, with complications. He was 74 years of age. He had a memorable career, first as an engineer, then inventor, pilot, industrialist, flying instructor, public servant and as a representative of the Crown. It had now come to an end. At the time of his death, he was the sole surviving member of the famous Aerial Experiment Association, established in 1907.

He received an honorary degree of Doctor of Laws from Boston University in 1949; and also received an honorary degree of Doctor of Canon Law from King's College, Halifax. He was made a Knight of Grace, Order of St. John of Jerusalem (K.G.St.J.). He was made an Honorary Fellow of the Canadian Aeronautical Institute (now the Canadian Aeronautics and Space Institute), the highest honour the institute can bestow, and his name is perpetuated by the institute's annual McCurdy Award, the premier Canadian award in the aviation technical fields. He was named a member of Canada's Aviation Hall of Fame in 1973. Also, he was made a Companion of the Order of Flight (City of Edmonton).

NOTES

[1] Hon. J. A. D. McCurdy as told to H. Gordon Green, "I Flew the Silver Dart," *Weekend Magazine*, February 7, 1959.

[2] *Ibid.*

[3] Article on the Aerial Experiment Association, *Canadian Aviation,* August, 1934.

[4] Ibid.

[5] Hon. J. A. D. McCurdy as told to H. Gordon Green, "I Flew the Silver Dart," *Weekend Magazine*, February 7, 1959.

[6] *Aircraft,* August, 1961.

[7] *Ibid.*

Major-General W. G. Leach.
Photo courtesy of the Department of National Defence.

1960

W. G. Leach

Citation: in recognition of his contribution to the cause of Canadian aviation through his research in the field of high altitude physiology, and for the courage and devotion to duty he displayed in conducting this research

Major-General W. G. Leach, C.D., B.A., M.D., (then a Wing Commander), while a Medical Officer with the R.C.A.F. Institute of Aviation Medicine in Toronto, Ontario, was awarded the Trans-Canada Trophy for meritorious service in the advancement of aviation in Canada during 1960, "in recognition of his contribution to the cause of Canadian aviation through his research in the field of high altitude physiology, and for the courage and devotion to duty he displayed in conducting this research." The announcement of this award was made on April 21, 1961, by the Honourable Douglas S. Harkness, Minister of National Defence.

In making the announcement, the minister said that during his research work, Major-General Leach continually exposed himself to explosive decompression and periods of anoxia at high atmospheric altitudes despite the fact that no observations had ever been made which recorded the effects of this exposure. The personal courage he displayed in the pursuit of his research was beyond the call of duty, and has resulted in greater safety for people the world over who fly in high-altitude aircraft.

For a number of years, Major-General Leach conducted specialized research into the effects of anoxia and explosive decompression in high-altitude aircraft, with emphasis on these problems as applicable to the new generation of turboprop and jet passenger aircraft which have now been introduced into air line and military service throughout the world. The results of this research have received national and international acclaim, and have provided a base for

further research in many countries. Major-General Leach's work has also resulted in improved air line and military crew-training techniques and the design of new oxygen equipment.

Wilson George Leach was born on September 28, 1923, at Chalk River, Ontario, where he received his early education. He attended high school at Pembroke, Ontario.

When a teen-ager, he joined the R.C.A.F. on June 1, 1942, as an E.C.2, and was given flying instruction. He received his pilot's badge and was commissioned as a Pilot Officer on July 9, 1943. After further instruction, he became a flying instructor serving in various positions in Training Command at a number of Canadian bases until the end of World War II.

At the end of World War II, he left the service to further his education, as he had decided to become a medical doctor.

He attended the University of Western Ontario in London, Ontario, from 1946 to 1952, where he received his medical training. He used his service gratuities to help him with the costs of his education, as far as possible.

Leach rejoined the R.C.A.F. Reserve in 1949 as a Flying Officer. He was then posted to the R.C.A.F. Station at London, Ontario. While there, he had become an R.C.A.F. regular on March 17, 1952, and was promoted to Flight Lieutenant on June 1, 1952. Also, this same year, 1952, he received his medical degree.

Leach interned at the Victoria Hospital at London, Ontario, and took post-graduate training for a year at the University of Western Ontario at London, Ontario, where he specialized in

The Honourable Douglas Hardness, Minister of National Defence (left) presenting the Trans-Canada Trophy to Major-General W. G. Leach on November 2, 1961.

Photo courtesy of Air Transport Association of Canada.

biophysics. He was transferred to the R.C.A.F.'s Institute of Aviation Medicine in Toronto, Ontario, in 1954, where he was a Research and Development Medical Officer.

An announcement was made in April, 1961, by the Honourable Douglas S. Harkness, Minister of National Defence, that Wing Commander Leach, while a Medical Officer with the R.C.A.F. In-

---

The Committee of Award for the year 1960 consisted of the following members:

Air Commodore L. J. Birchall, Chief of Operations, Royal Canadian Air Force, Department of National Defence, Ottawa.

M. M. Fleming, Controller, Civil Air Operations and Regulations, Department of Transport, Ottawa.

G. C. Hurren, Past President, Royal Canadian Flying Clubs Association, Ottawa.

A. C. Morrison, General Manager, Air Industries & Transport Association, Ottawa.

Captain V. J. Wilgress, Deputy to Assistant Chief of Naval Staff, Naval Headquarters, Department of National Defence, Ottawa.

stitute of Aviation Medicine in Toronto, had been awarded the Trans-Canada Trophy in recognition of his contribution to the cause of Canadian aviation, through his research in the field of high-altitude physiology, and for the courage and devotion to duty he displayed in conducting this research. Also, in 1961, he was promoted to Wing Commander.

The Honourable Douglas Harkness, Minister of National Defence, presented the Trans-Canada Trophy to Major-General Leach on November 2, 1961, at the annual meeting of the Air Industries and Transport Association held in Quebec City.

During the years that Leach was a Research and Development Medical Officer with the R.C.A.F. Institute of Aviation Medicine in Toronto, he rose in rank to become a Group Captain on August 30, 1965. Also, he successively held appointments as project officer in the High-Altitude Chamber Unit; was Officer Commanding of the High-Altitude Physiology Section; and was Officer Commanding the Operational Medical Establishment.

Then in 1966 he was transferred to the Department of National Defence Headquarters at Ottawa, Ontario, where

he became Director of Medical Staffing and Training in the Surgeon General's Office.

Three years later, in 1969, he attended the National Defence College in Kingston, Ontario, for a one-year period.

He was promoted to Brigadier-General on July 1, 1970. Also, he became Deputy Surgeon General of Operations on the staff of the Surgeon General. Then, in 1971, he became Deputy Surgeon General. In April, 1971, Major-General Leach was named Queen's Honorary Surgeon, an appointment he will hold for the duration of his present Canadian Armed Forces' appointment.

On March 5, 1976, he was promoted to the rank of Major-General, and also appointed Surgeon General, which position he holds today.

In recognition of his military service, Major-General Leach was awarded the Canada Decoration, and later a Clasp. He was named a member of Canada's Aviation Hall of Fame in 1973. He was made a Companion of the Order of Flight (City of Edmonton).

1961

Weldy Phipps showing the normal Super Cub wheel compared with the enlarged ones he designed for the two-place 'plane. The 35-inch tire using low pressure permits landings on terrain that would wreck other aircraft.
Photo courtesy of Norman Avery.

Welland W. "Weldy" Phipps

Citation: in recognition of his contribution to the cause of Canadian aviation through his development of landing gear which permits the exploitation of the short field characteristics of light aircraft operating from unprepared surfaces in the Arctic

Welland W. "Weldy" Phipps, C.M., while Vice-President and Operations Manager of Bradley Air Services of Carp, Ontario, was awarded the Trans-Canada Trophy for meritorious service in the advancement of aviation in Canada during 1961, "in recognition of his contribution to the cause of Canadian aviation through his development of landing gear which permits the exploitation of the short field characteristics of light aircraft operating from unprepared surfaces in the Arctic." The announcement of the award was made on March 23, 1962, by the Honourable Douglas S. Harkness, Minister of National Defence.

In making the announcement, the minister said that the balloon-tire landing gear, which Mr. Phipps had developed, had proved itself more versatile each year since it was first tried out in 1958.

It was while Mr. Phipps was flying in the Arctic in 1953 that he conceived the idea of using small aircraft (light planes) for light transport duties, because of the relatively high costs of using helicopters in the Arctic. His five years of effort reached fruition in 1958 when he flew two government geologists from the Department of Mines and Technical Surveys north in a light aircraft, a PA-18 Piper Super Cub, equipped with special large balloon tires of his own design. He covered 30,000 square miles of territory in 300 flying hours at a cost of some $12,000. Two helicopters did a similar job in 1955, but further helicopter operations were cancelled because of the high costs, the announcement continued.

Welland Wilfred "Weldy" Phipps was born in Ottawa, Ontario, on July 23, 1922, where he received his education.

He joined the Royal Canadian Air Force as a teen-ager in July, 1940, and became a Flight Engineer. He trained at Brandon, Manitoba, St. Thomas, Ontario, and Macleod, Alberta. He went overseas in 1941 and was posted to No. 409 Squadron, R.C.A.F., in England. Later, Weldy Phipps, then a Sergeant, was assigned to night bomber operations with No. 405 Squadron, R.C.A.F. During bombing operations over Essen, Germany, his Halifax bomber was shot down on the night of April 3, 1943. He had completed twenty-eight bombing raids and was within a few trips of a complete tour when this happened. He parachuted safely to the ground, but was taken prisoner. He spent two years as a prisoner of war in Germany before he and another POW, Flying Officer Hugh Clee of Vancouver, escaped during a 450-mile forced march to escape the Russians. During this time Weldy Phipps lost between twenty-five and thirty pounds. They were shot at, but they survived and escaped unharmed and made their way to the Allied lines in less than a week in April, 1945. During his internment he had been promoted to Warrant Officer.

He returned to Canada in 1945 after the war was over, and attended Nepean High School to continue his education. Like many other Canadian airmen, Weldy Phipps got his start in aviation while with the R.C.A.F. as a Flight Engineer. He did not learn to fly until after the war,

His first job was with Atlas Aviation Limited of Ottawa, a charter company, in 1946. Weldy Phipps was then encouraged to take flying instruction and obtain his pilot's licence and his air engineer's licence. This he did.

First, he received Private Pilot's Licence No. 4868, dated May 16, 1946; and Air Engineer's Certificate No. A-2218, dated June 25, 1946. As the years went by, his certificate was endorsed to include the following aircraft types: Piper J.3, Globe Swift, Piper PA, Republic RC 3, Aeronca 7AC and 11AC, Anson V, DHC-2 Beaver and Lockheed P-38.

Then Weldy Phipps received his Commercial Licence in 1947; his first Public Transport Pilot's Licence in 1948; followed by his Airline Transport Licence No. AT-577, dated May 15, 1953. When this licence was lost, it was replaced by AT-644, dated January 28, 1957. Also, he held Restricted Radio/Telephone Operator's Certificate No. 45331, dated November 16, 1964. (His original radio licence was issued around 1947.) His Aircraft Maintenance Engineer's Licence, Category A and B, was re-issued on March 23, 1971 (originally Licence No. YZM 567, issued about 1950.) He also holds a licence as a Master of Small Craft (Marine), dated August 5, 1975.

In 1948, Weldy Phipps left Atlas Aviation to fly as a staff pilot for Rimouski Airlines (later to become Quebecair), where he remained for one year.

He joined Spartan Air Services Limited of Ottawa, in 1949, first as a chief pilot, and rose to become Operations Manager and then Assistant Manager. He had previously headed up the company's Research and Engineering Division, and was Operations Manager from 1954 to 1956. He was Chief Pilot and Maintenance Superintendent from 1952 to 1954.

While employed with Spartan Air Services, Weldy Phipps completely modified the nose section of a high-altitude Lockheed Lightning P-38 aircraft used on high-altitude (35,000 feet) aerial photographic work to take a larger camera. The nose housed the photographer and his equipment. This modification was made to Spartan's fleet

of P-38's and proved most satisfactory and even increased the cruising speed of the aircraft by 30 m.p.h. The introduction of this system meant a 16-fold increase in mapping operations of the Arctic in preparation for the building of the Distant Early Warning Line.

To facilitate the use of these aircraft on Arctic surveys, Weldy Phipps took work crews into two points in the north and supervised the construction of two airports; one at Gary Lake, 200 miles northwest of Baker Lake, and one at Esker Lake in the Ungava District.

In 1953, Weldy Phipps conceived the idea of using light aircraft for light transport work because of the relatively high costs of using helicopters in the Arctic. Prior to this, the geologists used dog teams and canoes mainly in the coastal areas. They could only cover from 400 to 600 square miles in a season.

He flew north in 1954 with a self-designed tractor-type landing gear over tandem wheels. His experience with this gear brought about trials with standard tandem gear produced by aircraft manufacturers for two-place aircraft.

He also captained four-engined Yorks while making supply runs during the building of the Distant Early Warning Line from 1955 to 1957. While flying in supplies, he made landings on hastily prepared strips on ice surfaces, when something better was not available.

In 1958, Weldy Phipps joined Bradley Air Services of Carp, Ontario, with Russell Bradley as a partner. He was Vice-President and Operations Manager. While with this company he began his work to perfect the balloon tire-type wheels for aircraft operating in the Arctic. The Phipps' undercarriage design consisted of greatly oversized balloon tires, 25 inches on a four-inch hub, using seven pounds of air pressure. The tires were made by Goodyear to fit a Piper PA-18 Super Cub, and were known as "Phipps Special." They permitted landings and

take-offs in the most forbidding terrain. The Super Cub's average speed was only 90 m.p.h. Weldy Phipps felt that the whole secret of light aircraft success in the Arctic was the balloon tires, even though they slowed down the Super Cub's speed by about 20 m.p.h.

One of Phipps' first ventures during the summer of 1958 in a Super Cub sparked the Arctic oil rush for which drilling was allowed to progress.

While Vice-President of Bradley Air Services, Weldy Phipps was issued a one-year permit to explore for oil and natural gas in the Arctic Islands. His permit covered 67,000 acres on South Melville Island, some 800 miles from the North Pole. He called it a small holding as large oil companies have permits for areas as large as 15 million acres. If he found there were excellent prospects for finding gas or oil, he would form a company, he explained.

Then, in 1959, Weldy Phipps returned to the Arctic with five Super Cubs from Bradley Air Services using his improved landing gear. The tire size was increased from 25 to 35 inches, with a width of 24 inches, and pressure reduced from seven to four pounds. These big tires take up the shock of landing and permit a take-off from rough ground. During this season, in a three-month period, two Super Cub aircraft on geological survey work covered 100,000 square miles on Banks and Victoria Islands. Two more Super Cub aircraft carried geologists on oil work around Bathurst and Prince of Wales Islands. Another served both expeditions. The five Super Cubs logged 3,000 landings on balloon tires without a single mishap. The geologists were all left within a short walk of their objectives, instead of having the usual long treacherous hike to reach the areas where they wanted to be.

Weldy Phipps carried out a mercy mission for the U.S.A.F. in 1959 when he airlifted an ailing man from Ward Hunt Island on the roof of the world to

ᐊᖅᓕᕋᔪᓪᐊ
VOTE FOR
W.W.(Weldy) Phipps
ᓂᔾᐊᓂᐊᐳᕐ ᐊᖅᓕᕋᔪᓚᐊᓂᒡ
N.W.T. COUNCIL MEMBER
HIGH ARCTIC

Alert, on the northern tip of Ellesmere Island, after a 700-mile dash. American aircraft could not land at the point and their helicopters could not be staged to the area in time, so Weldy Phipps and his Super Cub were called upon to carry out the errand of mercy in this austere world.

Eight PA-18 Super Cubs were flown north in 1960 under Weldy Phipps' direction. A Beaver was also fitted with balloon tires (45 inches on 10-inch hubs with seven pounds of pressure). In addition to the four oil companies the fleet served, the Jacobsen-McGill Expedition was moved around Axel Heiberg Island collecting vital scientific information. They could not have financed their explorations by any other means of transportation.

The Beaver alone logged 600 hours in three and one-half months in 1960 and achieved the same performance the following year.

Perhaps the most exciting challenge for Weldy Phipps' Cub came on November 12, 1960 at 1:00 A.M. in the form of an S.O.S. from the Department of Health and Welfare in Ottawa. A whooping cough outbreak had swept through the Eskimo settlement at Grise Fiord on Ellesmere Island, 260 miles from Resolute, Northwest Territories, and all attempts by the R.C.A.F. and American forces to land a doctor had proven futile. So Weldy Phipps and Dr. A. H. Stevens of Ottawa were rushed north to Resolute from Ottawa in an R.C.A.F. aircraft, a distance of some 2,400 miles. The Dakota was captained by Flight Lieutenant Al Richards. However, the Dakota encountered a violent Arctic blizzard en route and developed mechanical trouble, and had to make an emergency landing at Great Whale River on the east side of Hudson Bay. After the engine trouble had been rectified, Al Richards took off the next day for Resolute, where Weldy Phipps and Erwin Keller, another Arctic pilot, assembled a

Super Cub in weather 30° below zero F. in four hours. Two of Bradley's Super Cubs had been stored at Resolute for the winter.

Weldy Phipps flew Dr. A. H. Stevens the 260 miles from Resolute in his Super Cub, with the R.C.A.F. Dakota flying along with him providing navigation for him to Grise Fiord. They nearly froze because the Cub's heater failed to compete with the Arctic temperatures! Time did not permit the installation of instruments in the Cub; but, in any case, the gyro-activated instruments were not winterized and so were useless. A crude flare path had been set out at the Eskimo settlement to guide them to a landing on the sea ice. Cans of gasoline had been set afire by the R.C.M.P. to provide a light. The Cub bounced to a short halt on the sea ice. The tires had absorbed the shock. The doctor took off on a six-mile dog team ride to treat the Eskimos, while Weldy Phipps took care of the Cub for the next three days.

When the doctor returned, he and Weldy Phipps left Grise Fiord's rugged coast of high, sheer cliffs, in the Super Cub, and contacted the Dakota to provide the navigation for them on the return flight to Resolute through extreme cold and ice-crystal fog. Then they boarded the Dakota and left for Ottawa. Another mission accomplished!

The Department of Northern Affairs, Wildlife Service, was able to carry out its first comprehensive survey of migratory birds using Cubs in 1961. Their previous surveys had been on a lesser scale and costs had not permitted the use of aircraft.

Since his early landing gear tests had taken place, Weldy Phipps' gear had been modified for Beaver and Otter aircraft, and twin Otters. The two de Havilland Otters flew on the Polar Shelf Expedition with great effectiveness. They were operated by McMurray Air Service of Uranium City.

The development of the landing gear for the PA-18's was that of Weldy Phipps from the very first idea, through the planning and engineering stages, to the actual construction of the components. He personally conducted the flying tests on location just to prove his theories. It was the idea, the physical and mental achievement of one man. Work from the start was pushed by Weldy Phipps — and more than once he was told he was crazy! But this did not stop him from carrying through with his idea.

The balloon tires were accepted for use on several types of light aircraft in time for the 1961 summer operations in the Arctic. The tundra tire, as it was sometimes called, was very fat, a low-pressure over-size type that proved most effective for operations from very soft surfaces.

Weldy Phipps' idea allowed government geologists to increase the number of Arctic surveys which, in turn, resulted in northern drilling operations. He also flew mercy missions in a Super Cub out of areas where military aircraft could not operate.

Briefly, Weldy Phipps replaced the standard gear on a PA-18 Super Cub with large balloon tires and landed on any reasonably level surface in the Arctic. It was his landing field. It sounded simple, but there were various consequences, if care was not taken to land properly.

And, for his resolve to succeed in his effort to develop a 35-inch tire using low pressure to permit landings in the Arctic, he was awarded the Trans-Canada Trophy for 1961. On March 23, 1962, an announcement was made by the Honourable Douglas S. Harkness, Minister of National Defence, that Mr. Welland Phipps had been awarded the Trans-Canada Trophy in recognition of his contribution to the cause of Canadian aviation through his development of landing gear which permitted the ex-

A Piper Cub aircraft with 35-inch tires belonging to Bradley Air Services of Carp, Ontario.
Photo courtesy of Norman Avery.

ploitation of the short field characteristics of light aircraft operating from the unprepared surfaces in the Arctic. He had been rewarded for his resolve to succeed!

The presentation of the award of the Trans-Canada Trophy to Mr. Weldy Phipps was made by John Baldwin, on behalf of the Minister of Transport, on November 7, 1962, at the Air Transport Association of Canada's annual meeting held in the Seigniory Club at Montebello, Quebec.

Weldy Phipps formed Atlas Aviation in 1962, and moved its main base of operations to Resolute, Northwest Territories, on Cornwallis Island, about 80 miles from the North Magnetic Pole on Prince of Wales Island. The airport had a 6,000 ft. landing strip. Weldy Phipps was President, of course. As operator and owner of Atlas Aviation, he ran the most northerly charter business in

---

The Committee of Award for the year 1961 consisted of the following members:

Chairman: Air Commodore L. J. Birchall, Chief of Operations, Air Force Headquarters, Department of National Defence, Ottawa.

Members: Mr. M. M. Fleming, Controller, Civil Air Operations and Regulations, Department of Transport, Ottawa.

Mr. G.C. Hurren, representing the Royal Canadian Flying Clubs Association, Ottawa.

Mr. F.R. Kearns, President, Air Industries and Transport Association, Ottawa.

Captain V. J. Wilgress, Director of Naval Aircraft Requirements, Naval Headquarters, Department of National Defence, Ottawa.

Secretary: Group Captain G. F. Jacobsen, Assistant to the Chief of the Air Staff, Air Force Headquarters, Department of National Defence, Ottawa.

Canada. Thus began a phase of his career that was to bring him personal fame and fortune. Flying in the Arctic became a year-round operation for Weldy Phipps soon after he formed Atlas Aviation, instead of just a seasonal occupation. Later, he closed his Ottawa office, sold his home, and moved his wife and family to Resolute — or, rather, he had his wife, Fran, do this for him!

Being within close proximity to the North Magnetic Pole meant that directional or magnetic compasses were useless. He had to use astro navigation, which meant taking fixes on the sun, moon and stars. He had an astro compass fitted to the windshield of his 'plane and took bearings on the sun as he flew along — when the sun happened to shine. On dull days, he had to fly by visual contact. Of course, there were no weather reporting stations or radio facilities to assist him along the way. Radio instruments developed by Bradley engineers gave him a range of 1,500 miles or more when conditions were favourable.

Weldy Phipps bought his first twin-engined Otter in 1967. He succeeded in getting registration markings CF-WWP for his Otter. These are his initials, of course, and his call letters were Whisky Whisky Papa!

Then there was the time in the spring of 1967 when Weldy Phipps' chief pilot, Dick de Blicquy, landed CF-WWP on skis on Air Force Glacier, near Tanquary Fiord, Northwest Territories, on northern Ellesmere Island, to pick up a British and Canadian mountain-surveying party. Unfortunately, he couldn't start the engine to take off, so he radioed to Weldy Phipps for advice. Weldy Phipps' advice was to get a hammer and tap the fuel pump. But Dick de Blicquy was unable to reach the aircraft to do this. So Weldy Phipps flew in himself and landed near the stranded machine on the glacier. With him he carried a hammer and a new fuel pump, just in case. He went to

the Otter and climbed up to the starboard engine, warmed up the pump with a stove, then tapped it with the hammer a few times or so. The Otter's engine started up, and everything was fine — much to the amazement of the R.A.F. men who had been amused by Weldy Phipps' advice in the first place!

It was reported in the fall of 1968 that a small Canadian 'plane was waiting on the edge of the Great Polar Ice Pack for the weather to clear to make a daring attempt to pluck an injured British explorer from an Arctic ice floe before winter darkness made the operation impossible. It was Weldy Phipps, who ran a charter service from Resolute on Cornwallis Island, who planned to fly to the camp of the Wally Herbert Expedition. Allan Gill was one of a four-man British team of explorers attempting to cross the Great Polar Ice Pack from Point Barrow, Alaska, to Spitzbergen, Norway, via the North Pole. They had hoped to make the trip in sixteen months. The expedition's headquarters had decided to evacuate geophysicist Allan Gill, 37, who had suffered a slipped disc in a fall a month earlier. Their headquarters said the injury forced the group to camp and delayed plans for the first surface crossing of the Arctic Ocean via the North Pole. At this time, Weldy Phipps was weatherbound at Isaachsen on Ellef Island, one of the Queen Elizabeth Islands, 2,000 miles north of Winnipeg. Also, it was reported at the time that the Royal Canadian Air Force had dropped many tons of relief supplies to the expedition.

When this trans-Arctic expedition from England ran into difficulties because of Allan Gill's injury, they were camped on the ice about 50 miles from the United States Ice Island, and Navy research station, designated T-3. T-3 was 600 miles northwest of Isaachsen, at that time. Weldy Phipps had received a message from England asking if he could make a flight to the expedition's position

A Piper Cub with big wheels, flown by Weldy Phipps, shown in an Arctic "landing field."
Photo courtesy of Norman Avery.

and evacuate Allan Gill. Weldy Phipps said that he could. His negotiations were with the B.B.C. who immediately despatched a three-man crew to Resolute to accompany him on the flight. On their arrival at Resolute, Weldy Phipps flew them to Isaachsen. The weather at Isaachsen was not good but the delay of three days or more was because of difficulties in communicating with Point Barrow, Alaska. Point Barrow was the headquarters of the United States research group on T-3. Ice Island, T-3 was the limit of Weldy Phipps' fuel range and it was imperative that their radio beacon be switched on, and that a flare path be lit for his arrival. At that latitude, and late in the season, the sun was already well below the horizon.

Weldy Phipps finally received a message from Point Barrow that the beacon would be switched on at the time he requested and a flare path would be lit. So they left Isaachsen as scheduled although they could not pick up their beacon, which they considered was due to the extreme range. At his point of no return, he was still unable to receive the beacon but decided to continue on the gamble that, if the beacon did not come on, he would pick up the lights. About thirty minutes from his estimated time of arrival at T-3, the beacon came on the air which was a godsend as the lights were not visible until they were practically overhead! On landing at T-3, the B.B.C. got in touch with the powers that be in England and 33-year old Wally Herbert on the ice. Instructions were received

from England to evacuate the entire expedition!

Wally Herbert, who was determined to complete his polar sea crossing, advised Weldy Phipps not to attempt a landing at his camp as there was no room to land and the ice was very thin. Prior to leaving Resolute, Weldy Phipps was told that the landing conditions at Herbert's camp were excellent. Herbert also rejected suggestions that he use dogs to find a place to set a flare path. After three or four days with his Twin Otter poised on the roof of the world on T-3, Weldy Phipps, in his wisdom, concluded that, under no circumstances, would Wally Herbert jeopardize his chances of completing his expedition by assisting him to land at the expedition's location, so Weldy Phipps and his party returned to Resolute. Allan Gill recovered through the winter and the expedition members continued their journey.

Weldy Phipps was elected as a member of the Northwest Territories Council in Yellowknife in December, 1970. Of course, he covered his constituency by aircraft, and could take time to view the austere beauty of the Arctic world. Most of his 2,500 constituents of the High Arctic were Eskimos.

By early 1971, Arctic-wise Weldy Phipps had 17,000 flying hours to his credit, much of it in the pure cold air of the Arctic when -10° F. was considered to be a reasonably mild day!

Weldy Phipps landed at the North Pole on April 4, 1971, with his wife Fran, the first woman to step on the North Pole, to

set up a radio beacon to help guide pilots. It was -25°F. at the time. Weldy Phipps had ideas about flying tourists in his ski-equipped Twin Otter, CF-WWP, from Resolute Bay to Lake Hazen on Ellesmere Island, and then on to the North Pole. The cost would be $2,500 for a four or five-day round trip from Montreal or Toronto to the North Pole; but his plans to inaugurate the first tourist flight to the North Pole were abandoned. The weather was too capricious. He did, however, fly a business man from St. Petersburg, Florida, to the North Pole in 1970, just because he wanted to see the North Pole!

There were no hangars for their aircraft at Resolute, which meant that Weldy Phipps had to work on engines outside at -30° F., or whatever the temperature was, often freezing and blistering his fingers. To assist him, large heavy canvas engine covers, or hoods, were made for him by his sister in Ottawa, Mrs. Geraldine Trudel, so he would have some protection from the penetrating Arctic cold when he was working on the engines. The covers were shipped north to Resolute, by air or by boat. Her assistance was invaluable to him in so many ways.

During the winter there was darkness for twenty-four hours, which meant that outside repairs or maintenance work had to be done with a light, often taking many hours. And the cold of the High Arctic penetrates through every layer of clothing. Winter is a dangerous and difficult time to fly in the hostile world of the Arctic. Weldy Phipps was the only northern pilot who flew in Arctic daylight and darkness. And he was tops at both.

The Trans-Canada Trophy being presented to Weldy Phipps (centre) by John Baldwin (right), on behalf of the Minister of Transport, on November 7, 1962. At the left is D. N. Kendall, then Vice-President of the Air Transport Association.

Photo courtesy of the Air Transport Association of Canada.

Flying was second nature to him; even so, landing in the darkness was pretty risky. There is no sun from early November to the end of January.

During his ten years as President, Chief Pilot and Chief Maintenance Engineer of Atlas Aviation at bleak Resolute Bay, he rescued reckless adventurers, provided aircraft parts to others for damaged aircraft, and took food and supplies to stranded parties in the Arctic regions on the roof of the world, while carrying out his operations throughout the Queen Elizabeth Islands, the Parry Islands, the Sverdrup Islands, Prince of Wales Island, Ellesmere Island, Axel Heiberg Island, Devon Island, and others, even as far as Greenland. Also, he made a number of flights to the North Pole for scientific purposes — and one to see about inaugurating tourist flights to the North Pole! In addition, during his Arctic flying career, he made many emergency flights. Some of these, and perhaps most, resulted in the actual saving of lives.

Through the years his curiosity about the north had been satisfied; he had seen the austere beauty of the Arctic in the winter, and its fragile charm during its short summer period.

It has been said that you can't realistically call Weldy Phipps a "bush pilot," since the Arctic area over which he flew hasn't seen a tree since before

the last Ice Age! But he was an Arctic pilot flying in his Arctic world, which has a quiet beauty of its own, at times. He was wise in the ways of the Arctic. And he flew the first commercial flight to the North Pole in 1972 with the famous Twin Otter, CF-WWP, known in the Arctic as Whisky Whisky Papa.

During these years as President of Atlas Aviation, his fleet of ten aircraft increased in value to around $2,000,000. He had three twin-engined Otters (worth approximately $500,000. each), a single-engined Otter, a Beaver, a Super-Cub, a Piper Apache, a Piper Aztec (on lease), a Beechcraft and a DC-3. He had nine pilots or so working for him, including one Eskimo pilot, and seven others on his staff. They lived in interconnected trailers at Resolute, which he had built for them by a carpenter that he engaged to do the work. Here he remained until the fall of 1972 when he sold Atlas Aviation Limited to Kenting Limited of Calgary for a reported figure of $1,000,000 or so.

He was named a member of Canada's Aviation Hall of Fame in 1973. He was made a Companion of the Order of Flight (City of Edmonton). He was appointed a Member of the Order of Canada in January, 1976.

Also, it has been said that Weldy Phipps is a legend in Canadian bush

flying although he never really wanted it that way. He is stocky, good natured and warm hearted, and flew for a living, not for romance. Nevertheless, he was not able to avoid becoming a legend. He helped introduce to northern exploration the fat-wheeled Piper Cub — a little two-man aircraft with souped-up engines mounted on wheels three feet in diameter. With only four pounds of pressure in their tires, the planes could — and did — land in incredibly short space of snow, ice, slush, mud, sand or moss, because the fat tires acted almost as snowshoes.

Weldy Phipps of Almonte, Ontario, often called an old Arctic hand, ex-air line president and owner, pilot, engineer, northern politician (as he was elected a member of the Council of the Northwest Territories in December, 1970), retired at the age of 50, in 1972, to lead a more leisurely life with his family on Prince Edward Island, where he acquired property somewhere on the northeast coast. After going to Prince Edward Island, he took a two-year sabbatical to travel by boat to the Islands of the Caribbean, to Bermuda, to Florida, and the Bahamas. Today, he and his wife, Fran, are busier than ever in planning and building their home for themselves and their eight children, amongst other things.

1963

Frank A. MacDougall

Citation: in recognition of his contributions to Canadian aviation over the preceding 40 years

Frank A. MacDougall, B. of Sc.F., while Deputy Minister of the Ontario Department of Lands and Forests, Toronto, Ontario, was awarded the Trans-Canada Trophy for meritorious service in the advancement of aviation in Canada during 1963, "in recognition of his contributions to Canadian aviation over the preceding 40 years." The announcement of the award was made on March 18, 1964, by the Honourable Paul Hellyer, Minister of National Defence.

In making the announcement, the minister said that Mr. MacDougall developed the use of the department's aircraft for the administration of Game and Fisheries' Regulations, for wildlife surveys, for the movement of inspectors and other officers on forest management duties, and for restocking lakes and streams with game fish fingerlings dropped from the department's aircraft.

For his continued interest and example in the use and development of aircraft as a pilot and air engineer, he contributed, in a large measure, to the development and progress of Canadian aviation in its practical application and to the production of original Canadian aircraft, which has brought many benefits to the Canadian people.

Frank Archibald MacDougall was born in Toronto, Ontario, on June 16, 1896. He received his early education in Carleton Place, Ontario. Then he entered Queen's University in Kingston, Ontario, in 1915, but did not complete his course, as he decided to enlist in the Royal Canadian Artillery to serve overseas. He was one of those gassed at Vimy Ridge in France.

When the war was over, he returned to Canada, and decided to continue his education. So, he entered the University of Toronto to study for his degree in forestry. This he received in 1923. Also,

while attending Toronto University, he was employed by the Province of Ontario during the summer months to assist in work of the Forestry Branch.

Upon his graduation in 1923 with a degree in forestry (B. Sc.F.), Frank MacDougall joined the permanent staff of the Department of Lands and Forests on May 15 and became assistant forester of the Pembroke and Sault Ste. Marie districts. Then in 1924 he became district forester of the Sault St. Marie district. It was in the spring of 1924 that the Ontario Provincial Air Service was formed by Roy Maxwell.

While District Forester, Frank MacDougall used to yearn to be able to fly an aircraft. So, one day he definitely made up his mind to get a pilot's licence and set out to take flying instruction from George H. R. Phillips, who was with the Ontario Provincial Air Service, and was the winner of the Trans-Canada Trophy for 1931. He completed his lessons and received his Commercial Pilot's Licence No. 678, dated May 1, 1930, and later his Air Engineer's Certificate. He could now officially fly the department's aircraft on forestry protection work and in apprehending poachers.

In 1931 he was appointed Superintendent of Algonquin Provincial Park, which is the largest and oldest provincial park in Ontario, and also district forester of the Algonquin District. He was known as the first flying Superintendent of Algonquin Park, and in earlier days used to fly Fairchild KR-34, CF-AOH, for a time.

Frank MacDougall's experience in using aircraft in forestry work was broadening as time went by, and he received his Transport Pilot's Licence No. 165 on May 18, 1939.

While holding these various positions in the department, and as a pilot, he

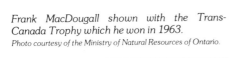

Frank MacDougall shown with the Trans-Canada Trophy which he won in 1963.
Photo courtesy of the Ministry of Natural Resources of Ontario.

became convinced of the usefulness of aircraft in the protection of forests and in the administration of the provincial parks.

The experience which Frank Mac-Dougall had acquired through the years in forestry work, including his experience as a pilot, eventually led to his appointment as Deputy Minister of Lands and Forests in 1941. He then became known as the flying Deputy Minister. In April, 1946, he became responsible for the administration of fish and wildlife when the Department of Game and Fisheries was amalgamated with the Department of Lands and Forests.

Having a particular interest in the usefulness of aircraft in forestry work, Frank MacDougall took action to expand and develop the department's air services for the purpose of detecting forest fires from the air, and in suppressing them by means of water-bombing from the air. His department was directly responsible for developing the water-bombing tanks to equip its aircraft fleet. This method of combatting forest fires from the air has since been adopted by many other protective air services.

Frank MacDougall's experience as a pilot for thirty-two years, while flying through the northern areas, led him to take active steps to suggest how the Canadian-designed and built Beaver and Otter aircraft should be developed to meet northern bush requirements. He gave both stimulus and initiative to the development of these world-famous aircraft by placing orders for them with The de Havilland Aircraft Company, even before the aircraft had flown. Through Mr. MacDougall's foresight and decision, the Ontario Department of Lands and Forests operated the largest fleet in the world of government-owned aircraft on forestry protection services. The successful results have, undoubtedly, brought great economic advantage to Ontario, and to Canada as a whole.

The first customer for the now ubiquitous de Havilland Beaver was the

Ontario Department of Lands and Forests. As forty aircraft were involved, it was not surprising that de Havilland Aircraft paid close attention to the requirements of the department. These new aircraft were to replace the veteran Norseman aircraft which had served admirably through the years, but were not as suitable for this type of flying as the Beaver. Frank MacDougall was in the foreground advocating a suitable replacement.

Frank MacDougall spent ten years as the first flying Superintendent of Algonquin Park, establishing a pattern for successive superintendents after he became Deputy Minister in 1941. It is said that he once remarked that the introduction of the aircraft to the job of overseeing the 2,700 square-mile Algonquin preserve reduced the task to "something like that of running a nice big farm." Columnist Bruce West of the Toronto *Globe and Mail,* an old friend of his, wrote: "Usually, amid the smoke and grime of a big forest fire, MacDougall could be found sitting on a stump somewhere discussing operations with some veteran ranger. Not as a white collar big shot from Queen's Park but as bushman to bushman."

Then one day in the spring of 1964 came the announcement by the Honourable Paul Hellyer, Minister of National Defence, that Frank MacDougall had been awarded the Trans-Canada Trophy for the year 1963 in recognition

of his contributions to Canadian aviation over the preceding forty years.

The presentation of the award of the Trans-Canada Trophy to Frank Mac-Dougall was made by the Honourable Arthur Laing, Minister of Northern Affairs and National Resources, on November 2, 1964, at the Air Transport Association

---

The Committee of Award for the year 1963 consisted of the following members:

Chairman: Air Commodore C. G. Ruttan, Chief of Operations, Royal Canadian Air Force, Department of National Defence, Ottawa.

Members: Air Commodore D.S. Blaine (Ret.), Assistant to the Chairman of the Air Industries Association of Canada, Ottawa.

Mr. M. M. Fleming, Controller, Civil Air Operations and Regulations, Department of Transport, Ottawa.

Mr. G. C. Hurren, Honorary Vice-President, Royal Canadian Flying Clubs Association, Ottawa.

Mr. A. C. Morrison, Executive Director, Air Transport Association of Canada, Ottawa.

Captain V. J. Wilgress, Deputy to Assistant Chief of Naval Staff, Ottawa.

Secretary: Flight Lieutenant W. H. Nichols, Chief of Air Staff Secretariat, Royal Canadian Air Force, Department of National Defence, Ottawa.

Frank MacDougall standing on the pontoon of CF-OBY, a Beaver DHC-2 seaplane belonging to the Department of Lands and Forests, Ontario, which he flew on forestry operations.
Photo courtesy of the Ministry of Natural Resources of Ontario.

of Canada's annual convention held in the Empress Hotel in Victoria, British Columbia.

As a forester, Frank MacDougall was internationally known. He was consulted by Ethiopia for advice on tree planting; Belgium on game management; and Chile on forest resources.

So successful was he in using the aircraft against poaching, which during the thirties had been a major problem, that the illegal practice was practically wiped out. He averaged some 20,000 air miles a year flying over the 2,700 square miles of Algonquin Provincial Park, and during his whole career logged over 5,500 flying hours. Even after he became Deputy Minister, right up to the time of his retirement, he continued to fly his

Beaver, CF-ODO, which was based at Toronto Island Airport.

After forty-three years of service with the Department of Lands and Forests, the last twenty-five of them as Deputy Minister, this veteran bush pilot retired on June 16, 1966, on his 70th birthday. On June 13, three days before his retirement, he had passed his regular pilot's medical with an A-1 rating.

He was named a member of Canada's Aviation Hall of Fame in July, 1974. He was made a Companion of the Order of Flight (City of Edmonton).

Frank MacDougall died at the age of 79 on June 27, 1975, at the Toronto General Hospital. He was married and had three children.

This administrator and pilot was a

rather quiet person, and was known as a man of few words. He had a kind and generous nature, characterized by warmth. He was just as much at home in an aircraft as he was in his spacious office at Queen's Park in Toronto.

Though first a forester, he had long been an influential and respected figure in Canadian aviation. He early recognized the value of the aircraft in forest protection work and was instrumental in building up the Air Services Division (earlier known as the Ontario Provincial Air Service) of the Department of Lands and Forests, into what is believed to be the largest organization of its kind in the world.

1966

Philip C. Garratt

Citation: Nil

Philip C. Garratt, A.F.C., retired Vice-President and Managing Director of The de Havilland Aircraft of Canada, Limited, Toronto, Ontario, was selected by the Honourable Paul Hellyer, Minister of National Defence, as honorary winner of the Trans-Canada Trophy for the year 1966, at a testimonial dinner held in his honour at the Chateau Laurier in Ottawa on March 30, 1966. The dinner honouring Mr. Garratt was sponsored by the Air Industries Association of Canada, and was in recognition of his fifty years' contribution to aviation in Canada.

With this honorary award to Mr. Garratt, the Trans-Canada Trophy was brought out of retirement and reinstated, following a number of representations made to the Minister of National Defence. It was last awarded for the year 1963.

As the trophy had been retired, there was no Committee of Award set up to choose a winner of the Trans-Canada Trophy for 1966 through regular channels. However, with Mr. Paul Hellyer making this honorary award to Phil Garratt on this occasion, an irregular pattern was followed which brought the trophy out of retirement.

1967

Robert A. "Bud" White

Citation: in recognition of his outstanding achievement in setting the Canadian absolute altitude record of 100,110 feet on December 14, 1967

Colonel Robert A. "Bud" White, C.D., B.A.Sc., M.B.A. (then Lieutenant Colonel), while Senior Test Pilot of the Aerospace Engineering Test Establishment, located at the Canadian Forces Base, Uplands, Ontario, was awarded the Trans-Canada Trophy for meritorious service in the advancement of aviation in Canada during 1967, "in recognition of his outstanding achievement in setting the Canadian absolute altitude record of 100,110 feet on December 14, 1967." The announcement of the award was made on October 1, 1968, by the Honourable Leo Cadieux, Minister of National Defence.

Colonel White flew a specially modified CF-104 Starfighter on twelve successful runs above 95,000 feet before reaching 100,110 feet on December 14, 1967. He headed a government and industry team effort which exercised much of Canada's national aerospace research and development capability in achieving this Canadian record.

Robert Allan "Bud" White was born in Sudbury, Ontario, on December 11, 1928. He received his early education at Kirkland Lake, Ontario, where he grew up. He then moved to Toronto where he attended Upper Canada College.

During the summers of his two years at Upper Canada College, he worked with Imperial Oil Limited on their oil tankers in Venezuela. He graduated from Upper Canada College in 1948.

Bud White won an Air Cadet scholarship in 1948, and entered the first post-war class of those attending the Royal Military College at Kingston, Ontario. After his graduation, he joined the R.C.A.F. and took flying instruction at Centralia, Ontario. Previous to this, he had received flying lessons as a teen-ager at Tripp Flying School and Leavens

Brothers Northern at Larder Lake, Ontario, during 1945-1946, and later at Barker Field, Toronto. He was issued Private Pilot's Licence No. 5466, dated August 8, 1949, endorsed for Aeronca 7AC aircraft, at Toronto. He received his R.C.A.F. pilot's wings in the summer of 1951, and was promoted to Flying Officer on June 1, 1952. This same year, 1952, he received his diploma in Mechanical Engineering from the Royal Military College.

Following this, he attended the University of Toronto and received his Bachelor of Science degree in Mechanical Engineering in June, 1953.

Upon receiving operational training on F-86 Sabres at Chatham, New Brunswick, he was posted to No. 427 Fighter Squadron at 3 Fighter Wing, Zweibrucken, Germany, on a three-year tour of duty. Upon his return to Canada in 1957, he became a Resident Staff Officer at the University of New Brunswick in Fredericton. He was promoted to Flight Lieutenant on June 1, 1958, while at Fredericton. Then he spent a summer on the staff of the Central Flying School in Trenton.

Bud White spent 1959 at Farnborough, England, attending the Empire Test Pilots' School. After his graduation, now an engineering test pilot, he returned to Canada and was sent to the Climatic Detachment of the Central Experimental and Proving Establishment of the R.C.A.F. at Namao in 1960. While in Namao (Edmonton), he became the Establishment's Detachment Commander at Northwest Industries Ltd. at Edmonton Municipal Airport. Here he conducted flight tests on T-33 and C-119 aircraft for the R.C.A.F. During this period, he received a commendation for saving his crew and a C-119 Boxcar aircraft during an engineering flight test.

He went to Los Angeles, California, in 1962, where he was one of four Canadians 'loaned' to the United States Air Force to support the American Space Programme. Because of his engineering test pilot's background, he was assigned to the Mercury programme and the Gemini Launch Vehicle programme. He also participated in the first two Mercury and the first four Gemini Launches from Cape Kennedy, Florida, as one of the seventeen-man special programme office team which managed and controlled the U.S.A.F. support to the National Space Programme. While on this work, he was promoted to Squadron Leader on August 13, 1963.

Upon his return to Canada in 1965, he was sent to Toronto to attend the last course at the R.C.A.F. Staff College there. After this he returned to the Aerospace Engineering Test Establishment at Uplands, Ontario, as Officer Commanding Flying Operations.

Bud White was promoted to Wing Commander (Lieutenant-Colonel under the Canadian Armed Forces) on August 1, 1967, and became senior test pilot with the Aerospace Engineering Test Establishment.

While Colonel White was senior test pilot with the Aerospace Engineering Test Establishment, he set the Canadian absolute altitude record of 100,110 feet on December 14, 1967, in a highly modified CF-104 Starfighter. Colonel White tells about his flight in the March, 1968, edition of *Sentinel*:

"In December of 1966 my U.S.A.F. Exchange Test Pilot, Capt. Jim Reed, came to me with an exciting idea. It was this: beat the Russians and capture the World's Absolute Altitude Record for Canada in Centennial Year.

"Of the hundreds of records in the realm of aeronautical competition, only six are termed "World's Absolute" by the International Aviation Federation,

(the FAI), the governing body for aerospace records. Not only is "Altitude" one of these six, but it is well known by the general public and greatly coveted by the technical community. Over the years, the World's Altitude Record has been hotly contested by the major powers; in one year alone, 1959, it was held in turn by the Russians, the U.S. Navy, and by the United States Air Force. In 1961 Colonel Georgi Mossolov captured the record for Russia in a rocket-boosted MIG-21, called E-66A, when he attained 113,892 ft. His record still stood in 1967, beating it by the requisite three percent became our goal!

"Our attempt would be based on three keystones. First we would use our high speed "pacer" aircraft CF-104 Number 700. It was lighter than a standard Starfighter and it could be easily modified and instrumented. Secondly, we would take advantage of the high energy jet winds along the axis of the St. Lawrence valley to increase our total kinetic energy. By starting our pull-up from within the core of a jet wind, we estimated that we could increase our maximum height by some 5,000 feet for every 50 knots of jet wind. Finally, we felt that we could improve our zoom profile over that achieved by the Americans in their 1959 record flights. We postulated that by initiating our pull-up from 35,000 to 40,000 feet and then pulling only low levels of "G" we would carry more energy into the vertical, and thus reach greater heights.

"Our proposal drew enthusiastic support from Canadian Forces Headquarters, and General Allard personally approved the Centennial Project on 14 August 67. We were off and running!

"Our first task was to get an uprated engine, and it was here that Materiel Command and Orenda joined the Centennial team. Simultaneously, we

began to modify "700". We had to extend the inlet cones to better position the shock wave across the engine intakes for the higher supersonic speeds. Lockheed Aircraft Corporation helped by lending us the cone extensions and helping us mount them. The electrical system was completely revised as we added two new batteries and a "zoom" inverter. And the pressurization system had to be changed out of all recognition. Captured by the spirit of it all, most of us worked well into the night and almost every week-end for five months!

"In 1959 when Capt. Joe Jordan of the U.S.A.F. captured the world's altitude record, the existence of the F-104 "flat-spin" was unknown. Since then, however, a number of Canadian and American pilots had to jump out of 104's. Lockheed studies revealed a stable and deadly spin mode, and it was apparent that if we were not extremely cautious our Centennial zooms could easily get us into a flat spin. So we had to approach our task with unique instrumentation. Principally this meant an extremely sensitive vane to measure angle of attack, an instrument panel that would allow the entire zoom manoeuvre to be flown on instruments, and a power system that would not arc out in the low density conditions of inner space.

"The Flight Research Section of the National Aeronautical Establishment (NAE) came up with the design of an "Alpha" vane to measure angle of attack. They fabricated the vanes, tested them in their wind tunnels and installed them on our Centennial "Bird". NAE gave us a great deal of help!

"We needed full pressure suits! The Institute of Aviation Medicine secured these for us through the Surgeon General of the U.S.A.F., and in September Major Ron Hayman and I flew down to Tyndall Air Force Base in

Florida to pick them up.

"Later on we obtained valuable assistance and special check-out gear from the Physiological Test Squadron at Edwards Air Force Base.

"We finally got airborne in the first week in October, and our first task was to work the speed up to Mach 2.4 and determine engine performance. We progressed cautiously, but even then we ran into serious control and damper problems before we could start into perfecting the zoom manoeuvre.

"Starting from Mach 2.0 and 25 degrees climb angle, we gradually began to increase our Mach number and climb angle. During these days it seemed as if problem followed problem. Always the team overcame them, sometimes with almost superhuman effort, but time began to run out on us. Too soon Ron Hayman had to leave for the R.A.F. Staff College in Bracknall! Then on our 29th flight, 1 got to 96,000 feet from Mach 2.2 with a light following wind. I felt we had it made!

"But then we began to have engine inlet guide vane problems. We tried everything, but it wasn't until we had changed engines and re-scheduled inlet guide vanes that we got our thrust back. And lo and behold, a light jet stream was still overhead!

"By the third flight on the 14th of December, the engine was producing the required thrust, and N.A.E.'s T-bird located the jet wind core to the south of Ottawa. Profile "David" (after my eldest son!) was filed with Air Traffic Control and the countdown for our 41st flight began. Scores of Air Traffic controllers in Toronto and Montreal began vectoring aircraft around our profile airspace, and Ottawa Terminal Control began to clear our route. Profile "David" traversed the most densely travelled air-space in Canada, between Toronto and Montreal, at high speeds, and required a most unique

arrangement with the Department of Transport. (But, by then, we had worked together for two and one-half months and everything went like clockwork!)

"I took off and began my climb out to the west of Ottawa, while Jim Reed in the chase (a standard CF-104) carefully checked me over. At 35,000 feet, I dumped cabin pressure and checked out my suit during the climb to 47,000 feet. At 100 miles west of Ottawa, I started a slow turn around to the east, and DRTE (Defence Research Telecommunications Establishment) Satellite Tracking System at Shirley's Bay began to track by beacon. Their tracking data was the vital bit of "proof" we needed to establish any record of our height. Once DRTE had me on "autotrack", I went full power and dove to 35,000 feet. I was supersonic almost at once, and by 35,000 feet was up to Mach 1.4. I continued to accelerate! Bypass on! Through T-2 Reset! Mach 2.0! Shirley's Bay told me to switch antennae. Mach 2.35! A gentle ramp up to 39,000! Mach 2.4! Pulling 2.4G! At 57 degrees pitch angle I seemed to be going straight up! My angle of attack. "Alpha" gauge was centered, so I was right on zoom schedule. At 75,000, the afterburner blew out, and at 84,000 I shut the engine down to prevent it overheating.

"From the time I had established my climb angle, at about 70,000 feet, I was just like a fly riding on an artillery shell! I could control the altitude, but I could make almost no change in the trajectory. Altitude control was critical, and, with the gyroscopic effect of the still-rotating engine, any loss of control could get me into a flat spin! Following my "Alpha" gauge, I gradually began to push my nose down as "700" arced over the top. Almost Zero "G", and over the top at 65 knots; but I'm still supersonic! Dive brakes out as I start to accelerate downward, and a gentle

turn towards home. The Mach number continues to rise as I re-enter, even with maximum braking angle of attack, it rises to Mach 1.8 when I reach 60,000 feet and relight the engine. "Relight!!" This is the one word from me that relieves the people on the ground, who are sweating it out with me. Then events come in quick succession as DOT radar vectores me home, my chase catches me, checks me over and we come straight in because of my low fuel.

"When DRTE told me I had peaked at 100,110 feet, I was discouraged. It was apparent to me that we were not going to be able to beat the Russians. The following day, I confirmed this on our 42nd flight, and terminated the program.

"Now that time is eroding some of the pangs of failure, I can see that we did something significant. First of all, we got to 100,110 feet and proved it, to the satisfaction of the Royal Canadian Flying Clubs Association, who monitored all of our flights for the F.A.I. We established a Canadian national altitude record that has only been beaten by one other pure jet in the world. And, of the 25 zoom flights, we managed to make 12 flights safely above 95,000 feet. No one else has ever spent that much time in a jet at those levels!

"But I think the main benefit was that we exercised all of our national aerospace research and development organizations. In the same way that an operational squadron exercises to enhance its combat readiness, we exercised our capabilities, and all of us, individually and collectively, gained valuable experience that could not have been acquired in any other way. Moreover, we obtained data about the CF-104 that can be directly related to the operational CF-104 squadrons in Europe.

"But the thing about the Centennial

Project that I will always remember best was the way people worked

---

The Committee of Award for 1967 consisted of the following members:

Major-General W. K. Carr, Commander, Training Command, D.N.D., Ottawa

D. A. Golden, Air Industries Association of Canada, Ottawa

R. W. Goodwin, Department of Transport, Ottawa

W. M. McLeish, Canadian Aeronautics and Space Institute, Ottawa

W. P. Paris, Royal Canadian Flying Clubs, Ottawa

A. C. Morrison, Air Transport Association of Canada, Ottawa

Commodore P. F. Russell, Director General Operations, Maritime, D.N.D., Ottawa

Brigadier-General E. A. Amy, Director General Operations, Land, D.N.D., Ottawa

Brigadier-General E. P. Bridgland, Director General Aerospace Systems, D.N.D., Ottawa

Brigadier-General D. R. Adamson, Director General Aerospace Systems, D.N.D., Ottawa

Colonel M. F. Doyle, representing Director General, Postings and Careers, D.N.D., Ottawa

together, especially our ground crew. Every man on the team worked his heart out to capture the record for Canada. And you can't ask for more than that!"

Then came the announcement by the Minister of National Defence, the Honourable Leo Cadieux, in October, 1968, that Lieutenant-Colonel R. A. White had been awarded the Trans-Canada Trophy in recognition of his outstanding achievement in setting the Canadian absolute altitude record of 100,110 feet on December 14, 1967.

The Honourable Leo Cadieux, Minister of National Defence, presented the Trans-Canada Trophy to Colonel White on October 24, 1968, at a dinner hosted by the minister and attended by surviving former winners of the Trans-Canada Trophy held at the Canadian Forces Base, Rockcliffe Officers Mess, to mark the occasion.

In 1969, Colonel White became Director of Cadets at the Royal Military College at Kingston, Ontario.

He received his Master's degree in Business Administration from Auburn University in 1972, while attending the U.S.A.F. Air War College at Maxwell Air Force Base, Montgomery, Alabama.

Upon his return to Ottawa, he joined the Directorate of Policy Co-ordination and Review with the Department of National Defence in the office of the Vice-Chief of the Defence Staff.

He was promoted to Colonel on February 15, 1975; and was posted to North Bay, Ontario, on August 6, 1976, as Commander of the Canadian Forces Base there.

He was awarded the Canada Decoration, with Clasp, in recognition of his military services; and he was made an Officer of the Order of Military Merit for his flying and leadership of the joint industrial-government-military Centennial Team. He was awarded the Trans-Canada Trophy for 1967. Also, he was named a member of Canada's Aviation Hall of Fame in 1973, and made a Companion of the Order of Flight (City of Edmonton).

Colonel White is married; and he and Mrs. White have two boys and two girls. The family resides in North Bay. They enjoy skiing, fishing and camping.

1973

M. W. "Max" Ward

Citation: in recognition of achievements in the field of air operations, in pioneering new areas and in advancing the cause of aviation

M. W. "Max" Ward, President of Wardair Canada (1975) Ltd., Edmonton, Alberta, was awarded the Trans-Canada Trophy for 1973, "in recognition of achievements in the field of air operations, in pioneering new areas and in advancing the cause of aviation."

The announcement of the award was made at the annual meeting of the Canadian Aeronautics and Space Institute held in Edmonton, Alberta, on May 15, 1973.

Maxwell William "Max" Ward was born in Edmonton, Alberta, on November 22, 1921, where he received his education.

He joined the Royal Canadian Air Force in 1940 at nineteen years of age, and was given a course in flight instruction. He received his commission as a Flying Officer. He was then assigned duties as a Flight Instructor, serving at a number of R.C.A.F. stations in Canada during World War II.

Max Ward began his career as a commercial pilot flying for Northern Flights Limited from a base at Peace River, Alberta, to Yellowknife, Northwest Territories, in 1945. He had received his Limited Commercial Licence No. C-2332, dated June 18, 1945. Northern Flights was founded by Jack Moar, and was an ambitious effort to establish air transportation in the Yellowknife district with war surplus Cessna T-50's and Tiger Moths. During the years that he flew for Northern Flights, Max Ward flew the Peace River-Yellowknife-Hay River route, which now forms a segment of the Pacific Western Airlines' system.

It was in 1946 that Max Ward decided to establish his own charter service at Yellowknife. He formed a company known as Polaris Charter Company Limited of Yellowknife. His total capital consisted of his war gratuity, which he applied as a down payment on the purchase of a $10,500 Fox Moth, CF-DJC. This same year, young Ward,

Max Ward in Fox Moth, CF-DJC, belonging to his company Polaris Charter Company Limited of Yellowknife, N.W.T., established in 1946. He ran his company single-handed hauling supplies into the mining exploration camps in the area.

Max Ward standing beside a replica of his original Fox Moth at Seattle, Washington, on May 2, 1973, the day that the company took delivery of its first Boeing 747, which is shown in the background.

Photo courtesy of Wardair Canada.

operating single-handed from dawn until dusk, hauled prospectors and supplies into the mining exploration camps that were springing up in the area. In addition to flying the Fox Moth, he maintained it, cleaned it, loaded it and ran the business all by himself. His activities helped in establishing the Consolidated Discovery Mine by speeding up the movement of men and supplies during the early development stages.

Then, in 1947, the Air Transport Board made it mandatory for every air carrier in Canada to obtain an Air Transport Board charter. Since Max Ward did not have a charter licence, he was encouraged by Romeo Vachon, a Member of the Air Transport Board, to form a partnership with George Pigeon, a veteran bush pilot, who was in possession of a charter licence. They organized a company in 1948 called Yellowknife Airways on a 50-50 basis. Max Ward contributed his Fox Moth from the Polaris Charter Company to the assets of the new company, while George Pigeon contributed a Stinson 104. However, George Pigeon quite suddenly sold his interest in the company in 1949, and Max Ward decided to liquidate his share as well, since, he said, he had lost everything he had in the partnership, as he was pretty green behind the ears at the time. This unfortunate lesson taught him much about business dealings.

For a period of time after this, Max Ward gained valuable experience as a bush pilot flying for Associated Airways of Edmonton, whose operations extended over the Yellowknife area and as far afield as Aklavik and Coppermine and the Arctic Islands. The money he earned from this work helped to pay off the debts resulting from his partnership venture with George Pigeon.

Max Ward went to Lethbridge around 1950 where he built houses to earn enough money to help him start a company of his own again. For years he had visualized a type of air service that

would play a valuable role in the development of the Northwest Territories; and his cherished ambition was to be achieved within two years.

After much persistence, patience and impatience, and many trials, he sought and finally received a Class 4 Domestic Charter Commercial Air Service licence from the Air Transport Board to operate from a base at Yellowknife. Thus, Max Ward returned to Yellowknife, Northwest Territories, his former base of operations, where he formed his new company, which he called Wardair Limited. He organized Wardair Limited of Yellowknife, Northwest Territories, in 1952, entirely on his own, without the aid of any outside capital.

On June 2, 1952, Max Ward took delivery of Otter No. 5 from The de Havilland Aircraft, and Wardair Limited started operations immediately the Otter arrived at Yellowknife Bay.

There was a surging movement of men and supplies through Yellowknife — prospectors, drill crews, Indians hired for claim staking — all in urgent need of transportation. Max Ward introduced a new concept of regular and reliable service and the new air line was strained to the limit of its capacity from the start.

Max Ward bought a new Beaver in 1954. And in 1955 he bought an Otter to add to his rapidly expanding organization. Then, in February, 1956, he took delivery of a third Otter. In 1957, he added a Bristol Freighter to his fleet, which was fast contributing to the swift development of Canada's farthest frontier. This Bristol Freighter was a new concept in charter flying from Yellowknife into the remote regions and permitted the transport by air of heavy equipment to locations on the fringe of the Barren Lands.

During this period, Max Ward took time off to get his Airline Transport Licence No. XDA-796, dated October 3, 1958, which is still in good standing today.

Max Ward's flying activities were many and varied. The movement of prospecting parties out into the field and the freighting of supplies and equipment into mining camps in the area formed a substantial percentage of the total. His 'planes were called upon to haul an endless variety of mixed cargo, ranging from Caterpillar tractors and diesel power plants, weighing a ton, to baby cribs, floor lamps and packages of pins, as well as carrying doctors, nurses, missionaries, geologists, cows, horses and hay!

It was under the most extreme subzero operating conditions that Max Ward was able to provide uninterrupted air service to a pioneer segment of Canada's population scattered over a vast territorial area. He contributed a great deal of technological know-how to problems of cold weather operation and the development of flying techniques suited to a land where few, or no navigational aids then existed. His flying activities played no small part in the development of our rich mineral resources in the Northwest Territories, notably Hottah Lake, Marion Lake, Pine Point, Coppermine and Yellowknife.

The company's name was changed from Wardair Limited of Yellowknife, Northwest Territories, to Wardair Canada Ltd., with its head office in Edmonton, Alberta, in 1961. Max Ward then added a DC-6 to his aircraft fleet.

Wardair Canada Ltd. continued to serve the north but expanded into the international charter field in that year, 1961, and has never looked back. Max Ward now held a Class 9-4 International Non-Scheduled Charter licence for his company. Since that time, Wardair Sales Offices have been established in most of the major centres across Canada, as well as in London, England.

Then in 1966 Wardair Canada entered jet operations with a Boeing 727 and the company's fleet now include Boeing 707 and Boeing 747 aircraft on the international runs; and Twin Otters and a

Max Ward (right) with the man who was Wardair's chief pilot of northern operations for many years. This was at Yellowknife, N.W.T., in the early 1950s; with CF-IFP, a single-engine de Havilland Otter in the background.

Photo courtesy of The de Havilland Aircraft of Canada Ltd. via Wardair Canada.

Bristol Freighter on the northern runs.

In September, 1967, the company went public, with the majority of the shares being held by members of the family.

During the past fourteen years or so, Wardair Canada has established a reputation second to none anywhere in the world for efficient operations and service to the travelling public. From an aircraft utilization standpoint, the company has achieved utilization rates which are among the highest recorded for the various aircraft in operation. Servicing and maintenance of Wardair Canada's fleet has been maintained at the highest levels, and the company's safety record has been outstanding.

The personal dedication and leadership demonstrated by Max Ward in making these notable achievements possible have, without doubt, been largely responsible for the success of his enterprise. Through his ability to lead and to inspire others, he has created an efficient team of enthusiasts dedicated to the pursuit of excellence in every facet of the company's operations, and the results of this are evident for all to see.

Max Ward's achievements in the field of operations, in pioneering new areas and in advancing the cause of aviation,

The Committee of Award for the year 1973 consisted of the following members:

Major-General D. W. Goss, Department of National Defence, Ottawa.

Mr. I. S. Macdonald, Director of Fleet Planning, Air Canada, Montreal

Mr. E. J. Bobyn, National Research Council, Ottawa

Mr. J. P. Uffen, Director of Research and Technical Design, The de Havilland Aircraft of Canada, Downsview, Ontario.

Wing Commander, J. G. Wright, President, JGW Systems, Ltd., Ottawa.

have been outstanding indeed; and for this he was awarded the Trans-Canada Trophy for 1973.

The presentation of the award of the Trans-Canada Trophy to Max Ward was made by Mr. W. T. Heaslip, then President of the Canadian Aeronautics and Space Institute, on May 15, 1973, at the institute's annual dinner held in Edmonton, Alberta.

Max Ward was presented with the Billy Mitchell Award in September, 1971; was made a Companion of the Order of Icarus in 1973; was awarded the Trans-Canada Trophy for 1973; was named a member of Canada's Aviation Hall of Fame; was made an Officer of the Order of Canada on July 1, 1975; and was made a Companion of the Order of Flight (City of Edmonton).

Today, Wardair Canada Ltd. is the largest Canadian international air charter carrier. Wardair Canada flies to Europe, England, the Caribbean, the United States, the Orient, the South Pacific, Hawaii, and so on.

Mr. and Mrs. Max Ward reside in Edmonton. They have two sons and two daughters.

It was reported in the *Ottawa Journal* of March 7, 1977, from Edmonton, that Wardair Canada (1975) Ltd., plans on buying more jets! The report said that Wardair Canada was buying four long-range, wide-bodied passenger jet aircraft to serve its rapidly expanding holiday charter market. It reads as follows:

"The four aircraft, including spare power plants, spare parts, equipment and new power plant overhaul facilities at Edmonton International Airport, will cost $213.1 million, said Maxwell W. Ward, founder and President of the international charter airline.

"The Edmonton-based company will take delivery of the aircraft: two Boeing 747's and two McDonnell Douglas DC-10's over the next 26 months.

"The 747's each carry 456

passengers and are advanced models of the two 747's which Wardair now has in service. They will cost about $50 million each.

"The DC-10 Trijets, the first McDonnell Douglas Jumbo jets sold to a Canadian airline, will cost about $40 million each. Ward said these aircraft have long-range, intercontinental capability and will carry 301 passengers.

"Mr. Ward also announced that Wardair has made arrangements to sell its two 183-seat Boeing 707's.

"They will be sold for a total of $14.5 million and will be taken from the Wardair fleet in May, 1978, after the two DC-10's arrive, he said.

"The first of the 747's is scheduled for delivery next March and the second will be delivered in April, 1979.

"Financing arrangements are being completed through commercial banks.

"By the time the fourth aircraft is delivered in the spring of 1979 our available aircraft seats will have been increased by nearly 100 per cent," he said.

"Larry Dickenson, Director of Commercial Sales for Canada and Alaska with McDonnell Douglas, said there are 230 DC-10's in service throughout the world.

"The seating in the aircraft ordered by Wardair will prove a high level of passenger comfort," he said.

So these are Max Ward's grand plans for Wardair Canada's future! Is it any wonder that Max Ward has been referred to as "Canada's giant of the air charter business?"

In addition, Max Ward ordered two DASH 7 airliners from The de Havilland Aircraft of Canada in the summer of 1977 at a cost of around $9,500,000. These airliners are to be based at Yellowknife, and are to be used for passenger and freight operations. It is planned to add them to the Wardair Canada fleet in March and June, 1978.

1974

Robert H. "Bob" Fowler, O.C., F.C.A.S.I.
Photo courtesy of The de Havilland Aircraft of Canada Ltd.

Robert H. "Bob" Fowler

Citation: in recognition of having contributed to the progress of aviation in Canada

Robert H. "Bob" Fowler, O.C., F.C.A.S.I., while Chief Engineering Test Pilot with The de Havilland Aircraft of Canada, Downsview, Ontario, was awarded the Trans-Canada Trophy for 1974, "in recognition of having contributed to the progress of aviation in Canada." The announcement of the award was made at the annual meeting of the Canadian Aeronautics and Space Institute held in Ottawa on May 14, 1974.

Mention was made in the citation of Robert Fowler's efforts in assisting in the development of STOL operating criteria and flight programmes, as well as his research in the human factors involved; the development of flight controls and propulsion systems for low-speed, steep-gradient (high-angle) approaches; and his work with the augmentor wing Buffalo jet research aircraft in association with the National Aeronautics and Space Administration.

"When participating in engineering flight test programmes, Mr. Fowler's ability to perceive problems and communicate with his engineering associates have made his contributions invaluable in the design and development of Canadian aircraft," the citation read.

Robert Howden "Bob" Fowler was born in Toronto, Ontario, on September 19, 1922. He attended Vaughan Road Collegiate in Toronto, Ontario, prior to joining the R.C.A.F. in 1941.

He first learned to fly as a youth at the age of eighteen at the old Barker Field, Toronto, in a J-3 Cub, in 1940 and 1941. He soloed after only six hours of flight instruction over a period of fourteen months!

It was reported in *Canadian Aviation* (June, 1974) that it involved a lot of fibbing every time Robert Fowler went back to Barker Field to try to book

another half-hour, so as to try to give them the impression that it was only last week and not four months ago that he had been there for the last half-hour. He recalled riding up Dufferin Street on a bicycle, parking the bike behind a hangar, taking the bicycle clip from his pants and putting it in his pocket, and then shaking out the pant leg to look very operational as he walked inside the hangar!

Then, when he joined the R.C.A.F. in 1941 he was given further flying instruction. He went overseas in December, 1943.

While Robert Fowler was with the R.A.F.'s 2nd Tactical Air Force, he flew forty-eight missions in B-25's on day and night low and medium-level raids over Europe in 1944.

Following discharge from the R.C.A.F. at the end of World War II, he studied law at the University of Toronto for one year in 1945-46. Then it was back to flying again, as he received his Limited Commercial Certificate No. C-3137, dated May 25, 1946.

With a keen interest in flying, he became Chief Pilot for the Dominion Gulf Company (Gulf Oil Company) in 1947, flying a Grumman Goose. This company was the original developer of the airborne magnetometer for anti-submarine use during World War II, and introduced it into use in an extensive geophysical exploration programme.

In 1949, Robert Fowler joined Spartan Air Services of Ottawa, and spent three years in the Arctic and other parts of Canada engaged in high-altitude photo survey and airborne magnetometer operations. He flew modified Lockheed P-38's, flying as high as 35,000 feet on photo operations.

Then Robert Fowler joined The de Havilland Aircraft of Canada as a test pilot in March, 1952. And he's still

The first flight of the seaplane version of the Twin Otter on October 1, 1966. It is aircraft No. 1. The first flight of the Twin Otter landplane was on May 20, 1965. Bob Fowler is at the controls.

Photo courtesy of The de Havilland Aircraft of Canada Ltd. by Tony Honeywood.

learning what it's like to be a test pilot. He has remained with this company for twenty-five years. He became Chief Production Test Pilot in 1957; and has been Chief Engineering Test Pilot since 1959. Robert Fowler received his Senior Commercial Certificate No. SC-301, dated March 14, 1953, the year after he joined de Havilland.

While employed with The de Havilland Aircraft of Canada, he completed a four-year Industrial Management Extension Course at the University of Toronto during the evenings from 1970 to 1974.

Robert Fowler's experimental engineering flight test career began with the final flight testing and certification flying of the Caribou aircraft, the last piston-engined aircraft to be designed and produced at de Havilland Aircraft.

This was followed by an extended period of research flight testing at de Havilland Aircraft during which the aerodynamic and human factors' aspects of fixed-wing, steep-gradient approaches and landings were explored in a research aircraft utilizing modulated jet thrust. This work marked the means by which The de Havilland Aircraft of Canada embarked on the development of its line of turbine-powered aircraft.

Robert Fowler performed the first flight of the prototype PT-6A turboprop engine, which was later used in the Turbo Beaver, Twin Otter and DASH 7 aircraft; and the first flight and initial development flight testing of the prototype General Electric YT-64 turbo-prop engine, which was later used in the de Havilland Buffalo aircraft. He also performed the first flights and much of the subsequent development testing and certification of the Turbo Beaver, Buffalo and Twin Otter aircraft, all of which have found wide acceptance in world markets. Most recently, from 1975 to 1977, he performed the first flight and much of the development flying of de Havilland's DASH 7, the world's first STOL airliner.

The flight testing of these aircraft saw the development of high-lift devices, flight controls, and propulsion systems which permitted precise control of aircraft and thrust at very low approach and landing speeds.

Robert Fowler has participated in the initial development flight test work associated with the modification of a Buffalo aircraft to incorporate the air cushion landing system, designed by Bell Aerospace Corporation.

In the recent stages of development of augmentor-wing technology at de Havilland Aircraft, he took part in all augmentor-wing 3 degree and 6 degree of freedom simulations at the NASA/AMES (National Aeronautics and Space Administration/Ames Flight Research Center, Mountainview, California), and participated as a NASA-appointed test pilot in the flight testing of the augmentor-wing jet research aircraft at the AMES Flight Research Center in Mountainview, California.

Robert Fowler has gained wide experience in the operation of STOL (Short Take-Off and Landing) aircraft as the concept of the STOL aircraft has developed. As a result, he has participated in programmes concerned with the development of STOL operating criteria and in flight programmes with the FAA (Federal Aeronautics Administration), NASA and the Department of Transport.

His principal projects with de Havilland Aircraft have been the certification of the Caribou aircraft; single and twin-engine, steep-gradient/modulated jet-thrust research aircraft; Beaver crosswind-gear flight development programme; Caribou crosswind-gear flight research programme; first flights of prototype U.A.C. PT6A turboprop engine; first flight and initial development GE YT-64 turboprop engine; first flight and development of the Turbo Beaver; first flight and development of the Buffalo aircraft; first flight and development of the Twin Otter, land, ski and seaplane; and first flight and development of the de

Havilland DASH 7 STOL airliner.

Robert Fowler has flown over 12,000 hours on over sixty-five types of aircraft.

In recognition of having contributed so much to the progress of aviation in Canada, Robert Fowler was awarded the Trans-Canada Trophy for 1974.

The presentation of the award of the Trans-Canada Trophy to Mr. Robert Fowler was made by Mr. Frank Thurston, then President of the Canadian Aeronautics and Space Institute on May 14, 1974, at the institute's annual banquet held in the Chateau Laurier in Ottawa, Ontario.

Robert Fowler is a member of the Society of Experimental Test Pilots and a Fellow of the Canadian Aeronautics and Space Institute, the highest honour the institute can bestow; and in 1975 he was made an Officer of the Order of Canada. He is a design approval representative test pilot for the Canadian Department of Transport.

A test pilot is involved with a new aircraft from the moment it has begun as an idea, right on through its early design stages until the moment it is certified to be flown by its purchasers. This involves the making of decisions as to the quality of the flight controls it will have, their characteristics as to feel and response, and effort required to fly the new aircraft.

The Committee of Award for the year 1974 consisted of the following members:

Chairman: Mr. J.P. Uffen, Director of Research and Technical Design, The de Havilland Aircraft of Canada, Downsview, Ontario.

Members: Mr. E. J. Bobyn, National Research Council, Ottawa.

Mr. Harry Halton, Canadair Limited, Montreal.

Mr. D. L. Mordell, North Troy, Vermont, U.S.A.

Brig. Gen. M. Doyle, Department of National Defence, Ottawa.

The DASH 7 taken shortly after it's first flight on March 27, 1975. At the left is A. W. "Mick" Saunders, who flew with Bob Fowler on the first flights of the Buffalo, Twin Otter and DASH 7. Bob Fowler is shown in the centre; while Mr. B. B. Bundeman, then President of The de Havilland Aircraft of Canada Ltd., is shown on the right. The DASH 7 is the world's first STOL airliner.

Photo courtesy of The de Havilland Aircraft of Canada Ltd. by Ron Nunney.

The test pilot has a great deal to do with the systems management aspects of the new aircraft, which involves the actual panels on which the fuel, hydraulics, electrical, de-icing, avionics, pressurization, heating and air-conditioning, and several other systems are controlled. Time passes so quickly in each one's lifetime that Robert Fowler finds that sometimes it is difficult to believe that one's ideas in all of these sort of things are actually taken seriously, when it seems like only yesterday that he was riding a bike up to Barker Field to spend a hard-saved five dollars on

another half-hour of dual instruction on a Cub.

The role of a test pilot carries much responsibility. In developing the handling qualities of a new aircraft, a test pilot has a great deal to do with the safety with which it will perform its role. This gives him a sense of direct responsibility to those who fly the aircraft and to the many people who will be flying in it in the future. Men such as Robert Fowler face many risks and unknown dangers and problems each time they test fly an aircraft to ensure that the aircraft will be safe for those who later fly them.

Without doubt, these test pilots are a special kind of person who make sure that nothing has been overlooked in the development of the aircraft before it is certified safe to fly. Robert Fowler is one of these very special persons. Yet he remains a retiring person, warm-hearted and patient, and is extremely modest about his accomplishments. His sense of humour serves him well in his day-to-day tasks.

Robert Fowler and Mrs. Fowler reside in Weston, Ontario. They have five children, four girls and one boy.

The DASH 7 on its way back to Downsview Airport on March 27, 1975. Bob Fowler is at the controls.

Photo courtesy of The de Havilland Aircraft of Canada Ltd. by Ron Nunney.

1975

John A. M. "Jack" Austin

Citation: in recognition of his long and active service to the air transport industry

John A. M. "Jack" Austin, B.A.Sc., retired President of Austin Airways Limited of Toronto, Ontario, was awarded the Trans-Canada Trophy for 1975, "in recognition of his long and active service to the air transport industry."

The announcement of the award was made at the annual meeting of the Canadian Aeronautics and Space Institute held in Montreal in May, 1975.

John Alexander MacDonald "Jack" Austin was born in Renfrew, Ontario, on September 30, 1912, where he received his early education. He attended the University of Toronto's Faculty of Applied Science and Engineering, graduating in 1934 with a B.A.Sc.

In 1933, while still in university, Jack Austin started to take flying lessons from The de Havilland Aircraft of Canada at the company's airfield. He received Private Pilot's Licence No. 1511, dated October 2, 1934. His flying instructor was Leigh Capreol.

It was on March 1, 1934, that Jack Austin and his brother Charles entered into a partnership and formed Austin Airways Limited. Leigh Capreol was employed with the company under a managerial contract, for a time. He was also a pilot.

The company started its flying operations with two Waco cabin aircraft and a Tiger Moth. One of the Waco aircraft was equipped for the use of a stretcher, and it was believed to be the first commercial air ambulance in Canada. The Tiger Moth aircraft was the original of its type in Canada. Later that year, the company bought a Fox Moth.

Also, this new company reopened the Toronto air harbour, which was then located at the foot of Yonge Street, for its summer operations. Winter operations were carried out from the Toronto Flying Club field, then at Wilson and Dufferin Streets. The company's first flights were made into the Little Long Lac mining area, to permit prospectors to stake the area.

Austin Airways was incorporated on May 22, 1935, under letters patent from the Dominion of Canada.

Austin Airways also purchased the assets of Eclipse Airways of Chapleau, Ontario, in 1935, which included one Waco aircraft. This aircraft was transferred to the company's new base at Sudbury, Ontario. This was the beginning of the company's first expansion to the north. Also, this same year, the company traded its Tiger Moth for a Fleet Model 7, which was believed to be the forerunner of the Fleet Finch.

Jack Austin obtained his Air Engineer's Certificate in 1936, and became a licensed air engineer. That was the year of the Moose River Mine catastrophe. Austin Airways' aircraft participated in this rescue mission. Also, Chapleau was opened as a sub-base in 1936 to serve the Halcrow-Swayze mining area.

During the period in 1936 when major forest fires were raging out of control in northern Ontario, Austin Airways' pilots, including Jack Austin, began flying forest fire patrols for the Government of Ontario to suppress these forest fires. A noteworthy flight this same year was when Pilot Frank Fisher of Austin Airways flew one of the company's Wacos from Corner Brook, Newfoundland, to Toronto, refuelling at Sydney, Nova Scotia, Saint John, New Brunswick, and Longueuil, Quebec, en route. Jack Austin was the co-pilot and air engineer on this flight, which was for mining purposes. Jack Austin did much flying for his company through the years.

Jack Austin's company opened a sub-base at Temagami, Ontario, in 1937, to service mining interests and tourists flying into the area. Austin Airways started a flying school at Sudbury this same year to give flying instruction. A great number of the students from this school saw service with the R.C.A.F. One of them was Rusty Blakey, who was still an active pilot with the company in 1974. In fact, he had never flown for any other company. The company did aerial photography flying for mapping and forest inventory under contract with the Ontario Government during 1937.

Another sub-base was opened at Gogama, Ontario, and one at Biscotasing, Ontario, to provide air service to the mining development areas. Aerial photographic work continued during 1938; and a Fairchild 51/71 was purchased for this purpose.

During the World War II years, civil flying was restricted to essential services only, such as fire suppression, aerial photography, timber sketching and supplying the mining industry. During this period, the company traded the Fleet aircraft for two Aeroncas, and a Bellanca was purchased to serve the mining interests.

In 1943, Jack Austin opened another base at Nakina, Ontario. This was opened initially for the purpose of handling commercial sturgeon fishing. But the purpose was twofold; one to benefit the native fishermen and the other to create Canadian export funds, as the product was sold chiefly to the United States.

In the early winter of 1944, Jack Austin and Gordon Mitchell, one of the company's pilots, flew to Moosonee in Fairchild 71, CF-BVI, to do charter work for the Departments of Indian Affairs and National Health and Welfare. This covered the settlements on the east and west coasts of James Bay. Upon the completion of this charter trip, another one was made for Mr. Cowan, District Manager of the Hudson's Bay Company,

which covered the west coast of James Bay.

It was at this time that Mr. Cowan asked Jack Austin if he would be interested in establishing an air service to the area and, if so, he said that he would use his efforts to have the mail transferred to Austin Airways for delivery. Up to this time the mail had been handled by vessel in summer and by dog team in winter. This marked the beginning of the company's service to the James Bay and Hudson Bay settlements. In later years, this service was operated as a Regular Class 2 service and extended from Timmins, Ontario, and Sudbury, Ontario, to the south; to Hudson Strait on the east; and Port Severn on the west coast.

The Austin brothers continued to expand their operations and opened a base at South Porcupine in 1945 to serve the Timmins-Porcupine area, as well as the Moosonee operations. The company also continued to expand its fleet of aircraft, and in 1945 purchased a Fleet Freighter, a twin-engined aircraft, for its various operations. The following year, the company purchased its first two Norseman aircraft, which were built by Bob Noorduyn's company, Noorduyn Aircraft Company. These were a start on replacements for the Bellanca and Fairchild aircraft, as the company had decided that the Norseman would be more suited to northern bush operations.

Disastrous fires broke out in the Chapleau and Mississauga regions in 1948. Eventually these two fires merged and raged throughout the area, virtually wiping out the mature growth of white pine. Jack Austin arranged to have Austin Airways brought in to help the Ontario Government bring the forest fires under control. All of the company's pilots participated in this effort, including Jack Austin.

Then Jack Austin received his Commercial Pilot's Certificate No. 5087, dated March 7, 1950; and he was also the holder of an Air Engineer's Certificate.

Austin Airways continued its programme of expansion and Jack Austin purchased two Anson Mark V aircraft in 1950. They were both equipped for electro-magnetometer survey work. These aircraft were under contract to the Canadian Nickel Company Limited to assist in locating mineral deposits. In the following years, many discoveries were made. Also, Austin Airways assisted in the discovery of the mine at Thompson, Manitoba, that now belongs to the International Nickel Company of Canada. The company's Anson aircraft were still on survey work for the same company when Austin Airways was sold.

By 1952 Jack Austin had purchased a Canso aircraft, and contracted it to the Canadian Nickel Company Limited, which operated mostly from Churchill north to the Ferguson Lake-Baker Lake area. Jack Austin says he owes a great deal to Mr. R. D. Parker, former President of the Canadian Nickel Company Limited (also former Vice-President of the International Nickel Company of Canada), for his encouragement and assistance in having his company use larger aircraft in its operations. The operations were carried out on an I.F.R. (Instrument Flight Rules) basis, generally, using facilities on the northern end, as mutually provided for between the Canadian Nickel Company and Austin Airways.

The company further expanded by purchasing assets and contracts from Nickel Belt Airways of Sudbury in 1952, under the guidance of Jack Austin. In addition, Austin Airways opened a base at Geraldton, Ontario, for the development of Manitouwadge mining development.

When the Mid-Canada Line was under construction during 1955-56, Jack Austin was appointed Chairman of Group A Operating Committee, which acted on behalf of all the participating carriers. As Chairman, he was responsible for the actions and efforts of the committee. The committee consisted of those carriers using Canso or DC-3 aircraft.

The participating carriers were, in addition to Austin Airways, Mont-Laurier Aviation, World-Wide Airways, Northern Wings, Quebecair, Maritime Central Airways, Wheeler Airlines, Dorval Air Transport, Arctic Wings, Central Northern Airways, Boreal Airways and Eastern Provincial Airways.

Jack Austin's aim was to prove that these companies could operate together to provide efficient service in time of an emergency. As such, Austin Airways liaisoned with the Bell Telephone Company, the prime contractor for the Trans-Canada Telephone System, the Department of Defence Production and the Department of Transport. While working with the Department of Transport, Jack Austin produced a common operations manual, mutual despatchers and a common pool of spares. The operation was a complete success and proved that competitors could work together towards a common cause.

It was at the end of 1957 that Charles Austin sold his interest in Austin Airways to his brother Jack Austin; then Charles retired from participation in the affairs of the company at that time, leaving the business in the hands of Jack Austin, as President.

Austin Airways developed its own winter air strip at Moosonee to permit the operation of heavy aircraft on skis and on wheels. The company accomplished this by clearing the muskeg and providing drainage ditches, then impacting the surface snow and keeping it dragged and rolled. This air strip served the company's operations until 1970 when the government finally put in a permanent air strip.

During the initial stages of the Mid-Canada Line, Jack Austin's company provided the beacons and radio facilities in the company's own area of James Bay and Hudson Bay. Eventually, the R.C.A.F. put in beacon facilities, and

some radio guidance at Winisk and Great Whale River; while the Department of Transport established a beacon at Moosonee. These were after-the-fact installations.

Austin Airways operated a Class I Service between Timmins and Kapuskasing in 1958-59 when Air Canada abandoned the service since it was not making a profit on the run.

When Austin Airways' licence for operation into the James Bay and Hudson Bay areas was upgraded from Class 3 to Class 2, Jack Austin made a concentrated effort to develop a regular service using a combination of Canso and DC-3 aircraft. This combined use of a Canso and DC-3 aircraft was necessary due to the lack of air strips. Most of the settlements were without permanent air strips and this required the use of amphibious aircraft in summer, and DC-3 wheel-ski-equipped aircraft during the winter months. Unfortunately, in spite of the company's best efforts, this condition still exists and the outposts still experience, to some degree, the problems of break-up and freeze-up. To accomplish this service, the company installed its own radio system, including beacons where necessary, and during the following year had most of the route approved for the company's I.F.R. operations.

Jack Austin's company carried out flying operations for the Gravity Survey Division of the Dominion Observatory through the years from 1950 to 1970. This took the company's aircraft with their pilots over many of the provinces, including the Northwest Territories.

In conjunction with the Aircraft Industries of Canada Limited, Jack Austin developed the first water-bombing kit for Canso aircraft. He says, very modestly, that the real credit should go to Joe Lucas of the Aircraft Industries of Canada and to Jim Bell of Austin Airways.

Austin Airways, under its President,

Jack Austin, carried out ice reconnaissance flights for the Meteorological Division of the Department of Transport in the Hudson Strait and Davis Strait areas from 1961 to 1963.

Jack Austin was active in the development of the Povungnituk Tourist Accommodation. Povungnituk is one of the main centres of the Eskimaux (now Inuit) culture. It is also noted for its sport fishing. To assist the native population in developing these resources, Austin Airways not only purchased the materials and supplies required for them to construct their tourist accommodation, but flew them in. This accommodation consisted of houses built from local stone, but equipped with windows, floors, partitions and furniture, which had to be flown in. This was quite a large undertaking for Austin Airways.

During 1966, Jack Austin's company established major maintenance facilities at Mount Hope, Ontario (Hamilton Civic Airport). This same year, the company's operations extended as far as Baffin Island when Austin Airways commenced flights to the Penny and other Ice Caps for scientific surveys for the Department of Energy, Mines and Resources. These flights continued through to 1971.

Then during the Air Canada strikes in 1966 and 1969, Austin Airways operated essential scheduled services linking Timmins, Sudbury and Toronto.

Jack Austin, along with Tom Wheeler, President of Wheeler Airlines Ltd. of St. Jovite, Quebec, received the first award of honorary life membership in the Air Transport Association of Canada in 1967.

Austin Airways built a large maintenance facility building at the Moosonee air strip in 1972 at its own expense. This was an important facility since the company needed it for the handling of passengers, mail and goods. The company also built a terminal building in 1972-73 at Timmins Airport for its use.

Then, immediately following the

Jack Austin (left) receiving the commemorative plaque from Mr. Ian Macdonald, then President of the Canadian Aeronautics and Space Institute, on the occasion of the presentation of the Trans-Canada Trophy on the evening of May 14, 1975.

Photo courtesy of Jack Austin.

withdrawal of Air Canada passenger service between Timmins and Sudbury, Jack Austin's company commenced a unit toll service between these points, operating twice daily on week days, and once daily on Saturdays and Sundays. This was a substantial increase in service over Air Canada's.

While Austin Airways ceased flying operations from Toronto in 1938 to concentrate on northern development, the head office remained there. Charter operations were carried out from all bases, in addition to the Class 2 and Class 3 services linking northern settlements. The charter operations covered many purposes. Some of these included the handling of sportsmen for fishing and the annual goose hunts. Native students were flown from their homes to their schools and returned at the end of the school term. Austin Airways employed a number of Indians as agents at the various points they served.

However, in the fall of 1974, Austin Airways Limited, with its headquarters at Toronto Island Airport, Toronto, Ontario, was taken over by White River Air Services Ltd., of White River, Ontario. Austin Airways was Canada's oldest air line. Jack Austin sold his controlling interest to White River Air Service Ltd. The transaction involved the transfer of all issued shares of Austin Airways.

Jack Austin's company, Austin Airways, was essentially a bush air line through the years. It employed 25 pilots, and operated a fleet of 21 aircraft, such as Cessnas, Beavers, Norseman, Otters, DC-3's, Cansos and three of the four Avro Ansons remaining on the Canadian Civil Aircraft Register, so it was reported. In all, Austin Airways employed over 100 people. The company had bases at Sudbury, South Porcupine, Timmins, Nakina, Geraldton, Moosonee, Moose Factory and at Kapuskasing, Ontario. It provided charter and non-scheduled air service to northern communities and outlying areas.

In addition to being President of Austin Airways Limited, Jack Austin had a twenty-year record of participating in the development of the Canadian air transport industry through his many memberships in the old Air Industries and Transport Association and, since 1962, in the new Air Transport Association of Canada. He became a director of the Air Industries and Transport Association in 1955, and held this position for three years, and was honorary treasurer from 1956 to 1958. From 1959 to 1962 he was the association's Vice-President, Transport. When the A.I.T.A. became "Industry" and "transport" in 1962, Jack Austin became the first President of the newly formed Air Transport Association of Canada. Then he was a director of the

---

The Committee of Award for the year 1975 consisted of the following members:

Chairman: Mr. H. Halton, Vice-President, Engineering, Canadair, Montreal.

Members: Mr. D. L. Mordell, North Troy, Vermont, U.S.A.

Mr. H. W. Seagrim, Executive Vice-President of Air Canada, Montreal.

Brigadier-General K. R. Greenaway, Sr. Science Adviser, Department of Indian Affairs and Northern Development, Ottawa.

Colonel J. A. G. Diack, Director of Aerospace Maintenance, Department of National Defence, Rockcliffe, Ontario.

Air Transport Association of Canada from 1963 to 1966; and Vice-Chairman from 1968 to 1970.

Jack Austin has been known as one who has worked steadily since 1934, through good times and bad times, quietly and efficiently without government assistance, and in those forty years he built up an air service to the outlying regions that has brought great benefit to all Canadians. He managed his business for forty years, and many of his employees were with the company for over twenty-five years.

Then, in 1975, the authorities took notice of Jack Austin's forty years of service which he had given towards the development of the Canadian air transport industry. He was awarded the Trans-Canada Trophy in recognition of his long and active service to the industry.

The presentation of the award to Mr. Jack Austin was made by Mr. Ian Macdonald, then President of the Canadian Aeronautics and Space Institute, on the evening of May 14, 1975, at the institute's annual banquet held in the Chateau Champlain in Montreal.

Jack Austin was named a member of Canada's Aviation Hall of Fame in 1975. He was made a Companion of the Order of Icarus (Hall of Fame); a Companion of the Order of Flight (City of Edmonton); and a member of the Order of Polaris (Government of the Yukon Territory).

He is married. Mr. and Mrs. Austin live in Toronto. They have two daughters.

1976

David C. Fairbanks, D.F.C.
Photo courtesy of Mr. Fred W. Hotson.

David C. Fairbanks

Citation: in recognition of the valuable service that he contributed to the development of Canada's STOL aircraft in his capacity as a test pilot for over 20 years

Squadron Leader David C. Fairbanks, D.F.C., former Manager of Flight Operations, with The de Havilland Aircraft of Canada Limited, Downsview, Ontario, was awarded the Trans-Canada Trophy posthumously during 1976, "in recognition of the valuable service that he contributed to the development of Canada's STOL aircraft in his capacity as a test pilot for over 20 years."

The announcement of the award was made at the annual meeting of the Canadian Aeronautics and Space Institute held in Toronto in May, 1976.

David Charles Fairbanks was born in Ithaca, New York, U.S.A., on August 12, 1922, where he received his early education, and attended high school.

When only eighteen years of age, this young American hitch-hiked from Ithaca, New York, to Canada in the bitter cold of January, 1941, so that he could join the R.C.A.F. However, he was turned back at the Buffalo Peace Bridge with only twenty cents in his pocket. Not one to give up easily, he tried again in February, 1941, but this time he used a more formal approach, and succeeded in entering Canada. He found his way to Toronto and enlisted in the R.C.A.F. there.

David Fairbanks began his training as a pilot in the R.C.A.F. at No. 21 Elementary Flying Training School at Chatham, New Brunswick, on Fleet Finch II trainers. He received his wings as a pilot on November 21, 1941.

He was sent to No. 9 Service Flying Training School, Summerside, Prince Edward Island, to continue his training. After a posting to Trenton, Ontario, he was moved to No. 13 Service Flying Training School at St. Hubert, Quebec,

where he served as a flying instructor for a two-year period.

David Fairbanks was promoted to Flying Officer and posted overseas in February, 1943, where he flew Spitfires and Tempests with 501 and 274 Squadrons. He then became Commanding Officer of No. 274 Squadron. He served entirely with R.A.F. Squadrons, and had an outstanding operational career.

His record showed the destruction of fifteen enemy aircraft with four damaged ones and, in a three-week period alone, he destroyed seventy-two enemy locomotives and vehicles. He was awarded the Distinguished Flying Cross on December 9, 1944, with a first Bar on January 26, 1945, and a second Bar at the end of the war. He was reported missing shortly after shooting down his fifteenth enemy aircraft. But, he had been shot down and taken prisoner on February 28, 1945, and David Fairbanks spent the rest of the war in a German prison camp. He was liberated in April that year.

On his release from the R.C.A.F. in October, 1945, he held the rank of Squadron Leader.

After a brilliant career as a fighter pilot in the Royal Canadian Air Force during World War II, he returned to the United States to attend Cornell University in Ithaca, New York. He received his Bachelor's Degree in Mechanical Engineering in 1950.

Following his graduation, David Fairbanks emigrated to Canada and went to Montreal, where he joined the Dominion Bridge Company Limited, at Lachine, as a design engineer in 1950. He remained with the company for a

David Fairbanks, D.F.C., World War II pilot, who flew Spitfires and Tempests with 501 and 274 R.A.F. Squadrons, and then became Commanding Officer of No. 274 Squadron.
Photo courtesy of Fred Hotson of The de Havilland Aircraft Ltd.

David Fairbanks, D.F.C., while with the 401 City of Westmount Squadron in the early 1950s, as a reserve pilot.
Photo courtesy of Fred Hotson of The de Havilland Aircraft Ltd.

year. During this period, he joined the R.C.A.F. 401 City of Westmount Squadron (Reserve), where he flew Harvards and Vampires. He served as a Squadron Leader in the "Auxiliary."

He was associated with Sperry Gyroscope of Canada Limited, Montreal, as a Sales Engineer and Assistant Aeronautical Sales Manager from 1951 to 1955. He spent two years in Canada and two in England, where he flew with the R.A.F. No. 504 Auxiliary Squadron, flying the Meteor 8 and Sabre E.

David Fairbanks joined The de Havilland Aircraft of Canada as a test pilot in 1955, flying Beavers, Chipmunks and Otters. He received his Commercial Pilots Licence No. ULC-7110, dated January 11, 1955.

He was the co-pilot on the first flight of the DHC Caribou on July 30, 1958.

David Fairbanks was Captain of a round-the-world demonstration tour of the Caribou in 1964. He covered 38,000 miles and flew through twenty-eight countries. In the fall of 1967 he delivered a number of Twin Otter floatplanes to the Amazon Delta of Peru.

From 1970 through to 1972, he took part in a series of NAFEC STOL (National Aviation Facilities Experimental Centre) (Short Take-Off and Landing) evaluation flights near Atlantic City, New Jersey, in conjunction with the United States Federal Aeronautics Administration and the Canadian Department of Transport to determine standards for future Short Take-Off and Landing criteria.

Also, David Fairbanks organized ferry deliveries within de Havilland Aircraft and participated in many such flights, including one in a Twin Otter, from Toronto to New Zealand via the Pacific.

He was a demonstration pilot for all de Havilland aircraft types at major world air shows, including Farnborough and Paris, and on numerous world tours.

As Manager of Flight Operations for The de Havilland Aircraft, David Fairbanks had complete responsibility for all test flying and all matters pertaining to the company's flight operations around the world.

His expertise in the development of STOL aircraft was widely recognized by his flying colleagues and his advice and guidance was constantly sought by the regulatory authorities in both Canada and the United States regarding the establishment of STOL operating procedures.

It was during this twenty-year period with flight operations for the company that he demonstrated the Beaver, Twin Otter, Caribou and Buffalo aircraft in some eighty countries around the world with great skill and credit to his own company and to the Canadian aircraft industry.

David Fairbanks was actively engaged in pilot engineering liaison studies in connection with the de Havilland DASH 7 at the time of his sudden death on February 20, 1975.

___

The Committee of Award for the year 1976 consisted of the following members:

Mr. H. C. Eatock, Assistant Chief, Aerodynamics Engineering, Pratt and Whitney Aircraft of Canada Limited, Montreal.

Professor W. J. Rainbird, Chairman, Division of Aerothermodynamics, Faculty of Engineering, Carleton University, Ottawa.

Colonel W. E. Castellano, Director of Aeronautical Engineering, Canadian Armed Forces, Department of National Defence, Ottawa.

Mr. H. S. Fowler, Sr. Research Officer, National Research Council, Ottawa.

Mr. B. G. Jones, Vice-President, Engineering and Maintenance, Eastern Provincial Airways Limited, Gander, Newfoundland.

Major-General G. A. MacKenzie, Chief of Air Doctrine and Operations, Department of National Defence, Ottawa.

Then, in May, 1976, the Canadian Aeronautics and Space Institute announced that David Fairbanks had been awarded the Trans-Canada Trophy for 1976 posthumously for having contributed so much to the development of Canada's STOL aircraft in his capacity as a test pilot for over twenty years.

When David Fairbanks returned to Canada following his graduation from Cornell University, he maintained his association with military flying through the R.C.A.F. Auxiliary Squadrons Nos. 401 and 411. In the course of his flying career, he logged over 8,000 hours on some eighty aircraft types.

David C. Fairbanks died on February 20, 1975, at the age of 53, two weeks after suffering a heart attack at the official unveiling ceremonies for The de Havilland DASH 7 airliner at Downsview, Ontario. He and Mrs. Fairbanks made their home in Toronto.

Photography, music and mathematics were his hobbies, when he wasn't flying or away on tours. He also enjoyed sailing, swimming, skiing and reading.

He was a member of the Canadian Aeronautics and Space Institute, and the American Society of Mechanical Engineers.

As a young man, David Fairbanks, D.F.C., had a distinguished World War II record as a fighter pilot while serving with the R.C.A.F. in Canada and overseas; and an equally distinguished record with The de Havilland Aircraft of Canada as a test pilot for over 20 years. As a test pilot, he also knew what it was like to face unknown dangers and problems each time he test flew an aircraft. But David Fairbanks was a unique person — a test pilot — who faced these unknown dangers and risks to ensure that the aircraft he was testing would be safe to fly. He shouldered his responsibilities well.

Yes, his contribution in the field of aeronautics in Canada was significant.

1977

A/V/M. A. E. Godfrey, M.C., A.F.C., V.D.
Photo courtesy of the R.C.A.F.

A. Earl Godfrey

Citation: in recognition of his outstanding achievements in the field of air operations

Air Vice-Marshal A. Earl Godfrey, M.C., A.F.C., V.D., p.s.a., i.d.c., of Gananoque, Ontario, was awarded the Trans-Canada Trophy for 1977, "in recognition of his outstanding achievements in the field of air operations."

The announcement of the award was made at the annual meeting of the Canadian Aeronautics and Space Institute held in Quebec City on May 18, 1977.

Albert Earl Godfrey was born on July 27, 1890, in Killarney, Manitoba. When he was four months old, his parents moved to Vancouver, and settled there. So Vancouver was to become his home town.

He attended Dawson School in Vancouver — and it was there that he got his start for a career in the service. In 1902, when Earl Godfrey was twelve years old, Sergeant-Major Bundy went to the school one day to select some boys to form a bugle band for the 6th Duke of Connaught's Own Rifles (D.C.O.R.'s) — and Earl was one of the boys chosen for the band. He advanced quickly from a bugler to a sergeant. In his studies, he specialized in mechanical engineering.

Earl Godfrey began his colourful career in the aviation world in 1912, on the day he first built an aeroplane in his own basement in Vancouver. From 1911 to 1913, he worked around with Billy Stark and Bill Templeton, also aviation pioneers, on the first two aeroplanes that ever flew in British Columbia.

When the war of 1914-1918 broke out, Earl Godfrey joined the 11th Canadian Mounted Rifles (C.M.R.'s) in Vancouver, in January, 1915, as a trooper. Subsequently he transferred to the 1st Canadian Pioneer Battalion to speed his departure for England and France, and he went overseas with this unit in

November, 1915. His ambition was to become a member of the Royal Flying Corps.

However, his Commanding Officer, Colonel Hodgson, would not hear of this and said that he must first serve in France before transferring to the Flying Corps. Nevertheless, the turning point was soon to come. Earl Godfrey had been with his battalion in the front line at Yprés when the Germans broke through the Canadian lines capturing Sanctuary Wood, taking many of the battalion as prisoners. From that experience, he concluded that the only way to resist the Germans was by equipping every man with a machine gun. This he set out to do in his own way and, while he was in France, he utilized his engineering knowledge and invented an automatic rifle. This was an invention of an adjustment in the recoil mechanism of a Ross rifle which converted it into an automatic rifle. Colonel Hodgson was so impressed with his invention that he showed it to General Arthur Currie, the Corps Commander. At his request, a few days later, Earl Godfrey demonstrated the rifle to General Currie and Brigadier-General Odlum. Earl Godfrey was highly commended for his invention of the automatic rifle, which was sent to the Inventions Board in London.

When General Currie was shaking Godfrey's hand bidding him good-bye, he mentioned that, if there was ever anything he could do for him, he should not hesitate to get in touch with him. Earl Godfrey, with his thoughts foremost on flying, quickly said that he wanted to join the Flying Corps — and General Currie listened eagerly.

Within a week his wish was fulfilled, and his application was approved. One day early in August, 1916, he received his commission as Second Lieutenant and

The Fairchild seaplane which S/Ldr. Godfrey (standing beside propeller) and S/Major Graham (centre) used to fly the first air mail between Ottawa and Vancouver for the Civil Government Air Operations in September, 1928. This picture was taken just before the flight started on September 5, at 7:00 a.m.
Photo courtesy of the Department of the Interior.

was transferred from the Canadian Overseas Forces in France directly to the British Royal Flying Corps in France, and served as an observer with No. 10 Army Co-operation Squadron, which was equipped with B.E. 2-C's. Earl Godfrey was now a member of the Royal Flying Corps and his long and interesting career in flying was beginning.

His first Commanding Officer in the Royal Flying Corps was Major Mitchell who became Air Chief-Marshal, Sir William Gore Sutherland Mitchell, K.C.B., C.B.E., D.S.O., M.C., A.F.C.; and finally Usher of the Black Rod in the British House of Commons. It was under Major Mitchell's guidance that Godfrey received his early Air Force training.

Godfrey later joined No. 25 (Two-seater Fighter) Squadron equipped with F.E. 2-B's. It was in this Squadron that he was first credited with shooting down two enemy aircraft. One of his pilots in No. 25 Squadron was a Captain Shirtcliffe, a New Zealander, and it was a coincidence that, nearly twenty-five years later, Air Vice-Marshal Godfrey greeted his son who came to the Dominion in the 1st Contingent of Australians and New Zealanders to train under the British Commonwealth Air Training Plan.

Another fellow officer of No. 25 Squadron who went on many a bombing raid with Godfrey across the German lines in 1916 had risen to the rank of Air Chief-Marshal, Lord Tedder, K.C.B., C.B., etc.

In January, 1917, Godfrey returned to England to train as a pilot and obtained his wings at Netheravon where Colonel William Barker, V.C., D.S.O., M.C., with Bar, was also in training.

Godfrey returned to France in March and joined No. 40 Squadron equipped with French Nieuports, single-seater fighters. It was in this squadron that young Godfrey first excelled as a fighter pilot. He was officially credited with shooting down seventeen enemy aircraft and two kite balloons, and was awarded the Military Cross.

Godfrey was a great believer in fire-power and, while he was in No. 40 Squadron, the Germans brought out single-seater fighters with two front guns. He was not to be outclassed, so he made a gun mounting for his Nieuport for two Lewis guns. So, he had the first British single-seater fighter in France equipped with two guns, which was the forerunner of the multi-gun.

It was under Earl Godfrey's guidance that Major E. "Mick" Mannock started off on his notable career as he was in Godfrey's patrol over the lines the day he shot down his first enemy aircraft. Major Mannock was officially credited with fifty enemy aircraft and was awarded the V.C., D.S.O. and two Bars, M.C. and Bar, and was killed on July 26, 1918, a short time before armistice was signed.

Late in September of 1917, Godfrey was transferred to Home Defence, and took part in the first night defence battles over London, flying in No. 44 Squadron with the 1st Sopwith Camel Night Flying Squadron against Zeppelins and Gothas. He received his promotion to Flight Lieutenant in this squadron.

In May, 1918, the Royal Air Force transferred him to Canada, and he was appointed Commanding Officer of the School of Aerial Fighting at Beamsville, Ontario. He was promoted to Squadron Leader at this time. This was the largest training station the Royal Air Force had in Canada. Here pilots received their final course in aerial gunnery and aerial fighting before going overseas. At this command Godfrey received the Air Force Cross for his meritorious work. After the armistice he returned to England for a short period to carry out duties with the Royal Air Force until December, 1919.

Upon his return to Canada he entered the Civil Government Air Operations Branch and took part in fisheries patrol along the Pacific coast.

Godfrey did not remain away from the service for very long, for in 1922 he was

called back to the Canadian Air Force to take over the post of Commanding Officer at Camp Borden early that year. He returned to the Canadian Air Force as a Flight Lieutenant. In the summer of 1922, on July 12, he became Commanding Officer (Air Station Superintendent) of the Ottawa Air Station. When Squadron Leader C. MacLaurin, D.S.C., was killed in a flying boat accident on the west coast, Godfrey replaced him as Commanding Officer of the Vancouver Air Station in October, 1922. The Vancouver Air Station was one of the first to be established in Canada, and that was in the summer of 1920 at Jericho Beach on English Bay.

The Canadian Air Force became the Royal Canadian Air Force on April 1, 1924, and Godfrey was promoted to Squadron Leader at this time, while still stationed at the Vancouver Air Station.

Godfrey was posted to Andover, England, in 1925, to take a Staff Course at the Royal Air Force Staff College. After graduating, he returned to Ottawa about the middle of 1926, to the position of Superintendent, Civil Government Air Operations.

It was the summer of 1926 that he met Dalzell McKee, an American civil pilot from Pittsburgh, Pennsylvania, who was in Canada planning to make a flight to Hudson Bay in his Douglas seaplane. As Dalzell McKee's seaplane's take-off performance was too restricted, the Douglas Aircraft Company of Santa Monica, California, suggested that he return the aeroplane there for certain modifications. Dal McKee thought he would like to fly the seaplane there, going by way of Vancouver. In the meantime, he would forget about his flight to Hudson Bay. With the idea of flying across Canada to Santa Monica, he asked the Royal Canadian Air Force if one of its officers might accompany him on this trip as a pilot. As Godfrey had already been detailed to visit the R.C.A.F. units at Vancouver, High River,

Winnipeg and sub-units, he was the one chosen to accompany Dal McKee on the flight, as first pilot and navigator.

So, in September, 1926, Captain James Dalzell McKee, accompanied by Squadron Leader Earl Godfrey, left on their historic flight across Canada from Montreal to Vancouver and then on to San Francisco. This was the first flight made across Canada in a seaplane. The trip across Canada was made in thirty-four hours and forty-one minutes over an elapsed period of nine days.

This transcontinental flight was a never-to-be-forgotten experience for Godfrey — thrilling, yet arduous and daring. Flying in the early days was a great venture in itself, as the pilots did not have radio or navigation aids — nor did they even have airports or landing fields as we know them today. The R.C.A.F. had a few seaplane bases that were suitable for seaplane landings, but a lot of planning was required for these flights. For instance, the amount of gas and oil required at each stopping place had to be foreseen, and shipped in by train in advance. A formidable task was seeing that their water-cooled engine did not freeze during the cold weather. Upon arrival at each place, much improvisation had to be done, and the job of a pilot was no easy one, as the care of the 'plane was his responsibility. So a venture of this nature entailed much labour, forethought and initiative to go with the challenge it presented. Earl Godfrey possessed all of these attributes — and was the right man in the right place for such a trip.

He returned from this most colourful trip with a wealth of experience, especially about flying conditions in Canada.

In the spring of 1927, Dal McKee returned to Canada and was making preparations for another flight across Canada, which would take him down the Mackenzie River to Aklavik and Herschel Island and from there through the colourful gold dust "Trail of '98" to the Yukon and Alaska, and down the Pacific coast to Vancouver, returning to Montreal by a new route. On this flight, Godfrey was to fly Dal McKee again, and use the same Douglas seaplane that they used the year before. The Douglas Aircraft Company had modified the seaplane since their trip across Canada in 1926, which greatly improved the seaplane's performance. They were to be accompanied by Lieutenant Earl S. Hoag of the American Army Air Corps, Washington, a friend of Dal McKee and well-known among Pittsburgh aviation circles also, and Squadron Leader (later Air Vice-Marshal) A. Tom Cowley, who was then with the office of the Controller of Civil Aviation. They were to fly Vedette flying boats.

Earl Godfrey flew the Douglas seaplane from Ottawa to Vickers in Montreal to have it equipped with a new type of Short floats for their 1927 flight. Also, a Pratt and Whitney engine was installed in the Douglas — the first engine of this type ever to be installed in any aircraft in Canada. Earl Godfrey test flew the "experimental" seaplane and also test flew the two Vedette flying boats. One of these Vedettes was flown to Dal McKee's camp at Lac la Pèche, Quebec, so he could get in some practice flying before leaving for their trip across Canada. Earl Hoag also flew from Montreal to Lac la Pèche in the Vedette with Earl Godfrey. All three returned to Vickers Aircraft Company in Montreal in this Vedette.

But it seemed that this transcontinental and northern trip was never intended to take place. Dal McKee and Earl Hoag discussed which one of them would fly the Vedette to Lac la Pèche, and Earl Hoag thought it best for Dal McKee to pilot the flying boat, while he would be the co-pilot. About an hour after they left for Lac la Pèche on June 9, 1927, Godfrey left in another Vedette for Ottawa.

When Godfrey arrived home in Ottawa that night and entered his house, the telephone rang. Squadron Leader Basil Hobbs was at the other end of the line. Hobbs informed him that Dal McKee had just been killed in an accident, while attempting to land his Vedette on Lac la Pèche — on the evening of June 9, 1927. Earl Godfrey was stunned.

Aviation and the country had lost a wonderful friend in Dal McKee's death.

Nevertheless, Dal McKee's and Earl Godfrey's trip the year before had gone down in history, to be commemorated by the "Trans-Canada Trophy".

In September, 1928, Godfrey obtained a civil aircraft from Mr. Sherman Fairchild of the Fairchild Aircraft Corporation, Long Island, New York, to make a flight across Canada carrying the first air mail for the Civil Government Air Operations. The first leg of the seaplane flight from Ottawa to Vancouver, carrying the first trans-Canada air mail, was made in three days. Sergeant-Major Graham went along as air engineer. At ten after six on the evening of September 8, Godfrey brought his Fairchild seaplane down on the water at Jericho Beach, British Columbia. He left Ottawa on the morning of September 5. They covered a distance of 3,300 miles in about thirty-two hours. Just before reaching his goal, Godfrey was met by Flight Lieutenant Hull of the R.C.A.F. at Vancouver, who flew out over the Fraser River to meet him and escort him in. Godfrey said the trip was practically uneventful and was carried out almost on schedule.

As soon as Godfrey arrived, he was met by his parents. He said that they had averaged a little over 100 miles an hour for the entire distance and could have made the whole flight in two days' flying time from daylight to darkness, if the weather had been good. As it was, they ran into several spells of bad weather. The worst part of the whole flight was down the Thompson and Fraser canyons from Ashcroft, British Columbia, until they sighted New Westminster. At

A/V/M. A. E. Godfrey congratulates S/Ldr. Green on the success of the attacks, and on his promotion from F/Lt. to S/Ldr., which was announced while they were on patrol. From left to right: A/V/M. Godfrey, G/Capt. Clare Annis, O.B.E., Commander of the Station and S/Ldr. Green, September, 1943.
Photo courtesy of the R.C.A.F.

Kamloops they ran into heavy forest fire smoke which continued all the way through. The visibility was nil. They were flying at 4,000 feet above the river when they ran into the smoke. They continued for a short distance but were flying blind and had to turn back and fly under the smoke pall. They came down the Fraser River only 1,000 feet above the river and had to bank sharply around the walls of the canyon. It was mighty bumpy down in the canyon, and several times Sergeant-Major Graham lost his seat as particularly bad bumps struck him. Godfrey had great praise for the weather reports and forecasts supplied to them by Sir Frederick Stupart, Director of the Meteorological Service, Toronto.

At Vancouver, for their return journey, via a more northerly route, they picked up two senior Air Force officers, Group Captain J. Lindsay Gordon, Director of Civil Government Air Operations, and Wing Commander L. S. Breadner, and started the return trip via Prince Rupert, Prince George and the Peace River. They ran into thick smoke beyond Peace River Crossing and crashed while attempting to land. They were not found for twelve days.

It was a coincidence that, on the day Godfrey crashed on the Peace River, the only boat that was operating on the river also ran on the rocks and sank. She was a Hudson's Bay Company's boat loaded with a cargo of freight, cattle and a large number of passengers. The boat sank before the 'plane crashed as Godfrey and his passengers saw the wreck in the river looking like an old derelict and had no idea it had only just gone down. He crashed about 100 miles farther down the river near a place called Carcajou.

Later that evening, when the wind changed and the smoke cleared, a trapper found the crew on the bank of the river with a fire, trying to dry their clothes. For the next twelve days Godfrey and his three companions bunked in with the trapper in his 12 by 12 log cabin.

The first few days a pall of smoke covered the surrounding country making it impossible for the party to be found by an aircraft.

About two days after the crash it finally dawned on the trapper that a small boat pushing a small scow had gone down river and it was possible it might return before the freeze-up, so a constant watch was kept. Finally one evening, just before dark, the sound of a motor was heard off in the distance. When darkness came, they had a large bonfire going to attract attention. The boat came in close enough for them to call to each other. When the men aboard heard who it was, the boat pulled in to shore. In the boat were General A. D. McRae, M.P. for Vancouver, a friend of Godfrey, and the operator of the boat. The general had been down to Fort Vermilion on an exploratory cruise.

They told them the story of their plight. General McRae then made arrangements for Group Captain Gordon and Wing Commander Breadner to be taken on board the boat for Peace River Crossing. They had no accommodation for any more. The boat was to return later for Godfrey and Graham.

After a series of misfortunes — such as engine trouble, running on the rocks — General McRae and his party finally arrived at Peace River Crossing four days later and word was flashed across the country that the missing fliers had been found and all were well.

Godfrey and Graham arrived back at Peace River Crossing by boat just one month after they had left there by 'plane. That was the unfortunate end of the return flight of the first Ottawa to Vancouver air mail flight.

In April, 1930, Godfrey was promoted to the rank of Wing Commander. He remained as Superintendent of Flying Operations with the Civil Government Air Operations. In 1931 he took over Command of the Ottawa Air Station at Rockcliffe, Ontario, for his second tour of

duty. He commanded Trenton Air Station from 1936 to 1938. He was promoted to Group Captain in April, 1938. Then, in the fall of 1938, he organized No. 1 Training Command with its headquarters in Toronto, Ontario. He attended the Imperial Defence College in London, England, in 1938-39. In October, 1939, he was promoted to Air Commodore.

Before returning to Canada after the war broke out in 1939, Godfrey made an inspection tour of the Maginot Line and all Royal Air Force bases in France and some French bases, obtaining first-hand information. He returned to Canada in October, 1939, and was posted to the Western Air Command Headquarters at Jericho Beach, Vancouver, as Air Officer Commanding on October 19, 1939.

In September, 1940, Godfrey was appointed Aide-de-Camp to Earl Athlone, Governor General of Canada.

During the latter part of March, 1941, Godfrey was posted to the Eastern Air Command as Air Officer Commanding. He remained there until the end of July, when he returned to the Western Air Command where he remained until the end of 1941. He was transferred to Royal Canadian Air Force Headquarters, Ottawa, as Deputy Inspector General for Western Canada.

In June, 1942, he was promoted to Air Vice-Marshal and in January, 1943, he took over the duties of Deputy Inspector-General for Eastern Canada in which position he remained until his retirement from the Service on June 8, 1944.

During his two years of inspection work, the Air Vice-Marshal visited every R.C.A.F. establishment in Canada, Newfoundland, Labrador and Alaska, holding parades, inspecting and speaking to the personnel, giving some praise and words of encouragement. Being keen on flying, he travelled by air to visit all the coast defence stations, often taking over the controls himself. He was the type of person who appreciated efforts put forth in the line of duty — and did not hesitate to voice his appreciation, whether for himself, or on behalf of the Royal Canadian Air Force; and he was always on the alert to notice a job that was well done. This Air Vice-Marshal was, after all, an ambassador to the men and women in the service, more especially since he was appointed Deputy Inspector-General. In the course of his duties, he covered thousands of miles each year. And how did he travel? By air, of course, unless it was inopportune — as his love for flying never waned. While Deputy Inspector-General, it was his responsibility to implement constructive recommendations in the interests of the R.C.A.F., so that the efficiency of its operations would be increased, thus maintaining the enviable reputation of the R.C.A.F.

While Deputy Inspector-General in 1943, Air Vice-Marshal Earl Godfrey visited one of the larger R.C.A.F. bases at Gander, Newfoundland, to make one of his routine inspections. It was from this station that giant Liberator bombers of the North Atlantic Squadron normally operated on convoy and anti-submarine duties. On the day that he was addressing his men reports were being received at the station that enemy submarines were in the waters nearby. In the talk he had given that day he had said, "When the history of this war is written there will not be one of you here today who will not be proud to say, "I served in Newfoundland." It is a pleasure to visit this station to see and talk to the boys who, nearly every day, are hundreds of miles out over the ocean, liable to attack a German submarine or even be attacked by a submarine." Within a few hours after his address, one of the four-motored Liberator bombers of the North Atlantic Squadron became engaged in a gun battle with a U-boat, and had one of its motors put out of action by gunfire. Two other aircraft were also engaged in other U-boat attacks. As the Air Vice-

Marshal wanted to have a first-hand picture of one of these battles of the Atlantic, he went to get some rest so that very early the next morning he could take his place to man one of the guns of the turret in a Liberator bomber that would be on patrol the next morning. Before he went to the hangar, he had spoken to the crews of the Liberators who made the attacks the night before, and had arrived back around midnight. They were then having a snack.

"I wouldn't miss this for anything," he said just before taking off on what was to be a fifteen-hour and fifteen-minute convoy patrol.

Earl Godfrey was one of eight members of the Liberator's crew to take part in two attacks. He manned one of the turret guns. The Squadron Commander was Squadron Leader Fred "Bunt" Green of St. Thomas, Ontario. Godfrey is one of the few, if not the only Air Vice-Marshal in Canada, to handle the guns of a Liberator during an attack by an enemy submarine.

Whenever Earl Godfrey flew anywhere, he always liked to discuss whatever might be new in aeronautics with his pilot, when he was being piloted, rather than doing the piloting. His boundless energy and enthusiasm kept him always forging ahead to ascertain what were the latest and newest developments in flying.

He received the King's Jubilee Medal in 1935 and the Coronation Medal in 1937.

Godfrey retired from the R.C.A.F. on June 8, 1944, climaxing his long and meritorious career in the military aviation world.

Air Vice-Marshal Earl Godfrey was advised by Mr. J. P. Beauregard, President of the Canadian Aeronautics and Space Institute on February 18, 1977, that he had been awarded the Trans-Canada Trophy in recognition of his outstanding achievements in the field of air operations for 1977. It was said that his dedication to the advancement of flying in Canada was not confined to a

single spectacular feat; but his service to aviation in Canada was invariably performed behind the scenes and always as a participant out of the public eye.

The presentation of the award to Air Vice-Marshal Godfrey was made by Mr. J. P. Beauregard, President of the Canadian Aeronautics and Space Institute, on May 18, 1977, at the institute's annual meeting held in Quebec City.

Ever since the early days of his youth, Godfrey has been a keen sportsman and a well-known athlete. He was thrice British Columbia motorcycle champion — in 1911, 1912 and 1913 — when he won the five-mile championship race on a half-mile dirt track at Hastings Park, Vancouver. He also won the twenty-five-mile Northwest Championship in Seattle, Washington, in 1913. He was considered one of the best dirt track motorcycle racers on the Pacific coast in the early days. His favourite sports today are trapshooting, boating, fishing and hunting, and he is particularly en-

The Committee of Award for the year 1977 consisted of the following members:

B.G. Jones, Vice-President of Operations, Eastern Provincial Airways, Gander.

A. W. Fia, Vice-President of Bristol Aerospace, Winnipeg.

J. A. Tully, Engineer, Standard Aero Engines, Winnipeg.

Major General G.A. MacKenzie, Chief, Air Operations, Department of National Defence, Ottawa.

H. S. Fowler, Sr. Research Officer, National Research Council, Ottawa.

R. H. Fowler, Chief Engineering Test Pilot, The de Havilland Aircraft of Canada, Limited, Toronto.

Dr. H. I. H. Saravanamuttoo, Faculty of Engineering, Carleton University, Ottawa.

thusiastic about boating.

Air Vice-Marshal and Mrs. Godfrey live in Gananoque, Ontario. They have two daughters, both married; one lives in Ottawa, the other in Montreal.

He is a quiet-spoken person, with a serene manner. He has a keen sense of humour, and cherishes friendship.

The wise guidance which Air Vice-Marshal Earl Godfrey gave to the Royal Canadian Air Force in the field of aviation was of inestimable value. He was credited with a number of firsts in pioneering aviation, including the historic trans-Canada seaplane flight in 1926, and the equally historic flight which he made across Canada in 1928 carrying the first air mail from Ottawa to Vancouver. Also, he was the inventor of an automatic rifle.

So, on the eve of the Fiftieth Anniversary of the award of the Trans-Canada Trophy, a most fitting tribute was paid to Air Vice-Marshal Earl Godfrey, who piloted Captain James Dalzell McKee's Douglas seaplane on its historic flight across Canada, from Montreal to San Francisco via Vancouver, in September, 1926. It was because of this historic flight that the Trans-Canada Trophy, also known as the McKee Trophy, came into existence in 1927.

Photo courtesy of the National Museum of Science and Technology.

A/V/M. A. Earl Godfrey, M.C., A.F.C., V.C., after being presented with Trans-Canada Trophy on May 18, 1977, in Quebec City.

APPENDIX "A"
List of 22 Light Aeroplane Clubs, or Flying Clubs at the outbreak of World War II

Halifax Aero Club,
P.O. Box 392,
HALIFAX, Nova Scotia

Cape Breton Flying Club,
P.O. Box 209,
SYDNEY, Nova Scotia

Saint John Flying Club,
Municipal Airport,
MILLIDGEVILLE, New Brunswick

Montreal Light Aeroplane Club,
CARTIERVILLE, P.Q.

Ottawa Flying Club, Inc.,
P.O. Box 380,
OTTAWA, ONTARIO

The Flying Club of Kingston,
P.O. Box 52,
KINGSTON, ONTARIO

Toronto Flying Club,
R.R. #1,
DOWNSVIEW, ONTARIO

Hamilton Aero Club,
Civic Airport,
HAMILTON, ONTARIO

St. Catharines, Flying Club,
ST. CATHARINES, ONTARIO

Brant-Norfolk Aero Club,
BRANTFORD, ONTARIO

Kitchener & Waterloo Flying Club,
R.R. #1,
WATERLOO, ONTARIO

London Flying Club,
P.O. Box 611,
LONDON, ONTARIO

Border Cities Aero Club,
Walker Airport,
R.R. #1,
ROSELAND, ONTARIO

Lakehead Flying Club,
P.O. Box 52,
FORT WILLIAM, ONTARIO

Winnipeg Flying Club,
P.O. Box 2265,
WINNIPEG, MANITOBA

Brandon Flying Club,
BRANDON, MANITOBA

Regina Flying Club,
Municipal Airport,
REGINA, SASKATCHEWAN

Moose Jaw Flying Club,
Airport,
MOOSE JAW, SASKATCHEWAN

Saskatoon Flying Club,
P.O. Box 613,
SASKATOON, SASKATCHEWAN

Calgary Aero Club,
Municipal Airport,
CALGARY, ALBERTA

Edmonton and Northern Alberta Aero Club,
Municipal Airport,
EDMONTON, ALBERTA

Aero Club of B.C.,
Vancouver Municipal Airport,
Sea Island,
EBURNE, BRITISH COLUMBIA

Reproduced from Encyclopedia Canadiana published by Grolier Limited, by kind permission.

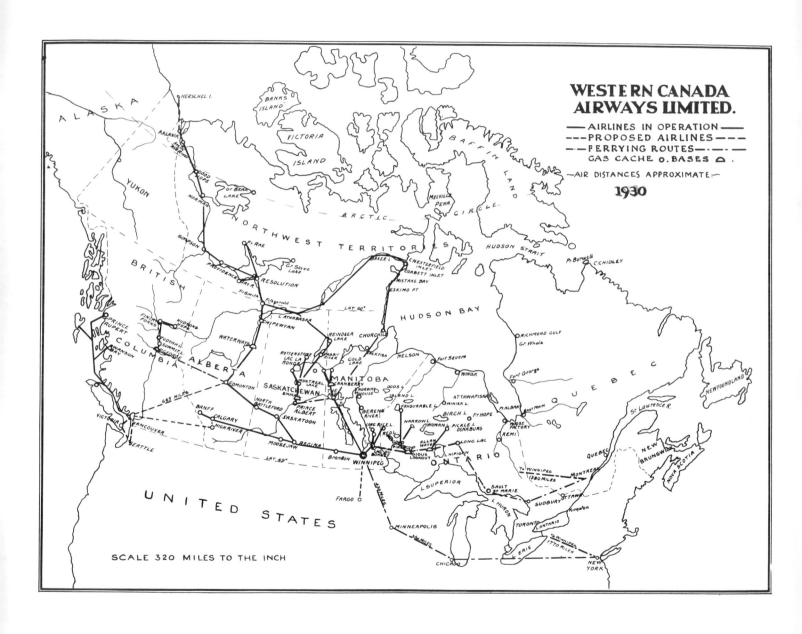

WESTERN CANADA
AIRWAYS LIMITED.
——— AIRLINES IN OPERATION ———
------PROPOSED AIRLINES------
—·—·— FERRYING ROUTES —·—·—
GAS CACHE o. BASES △ .

—AIR DISTANCES APPROXIMATE—
1930

SCALE 320 MILES TO THE INCH

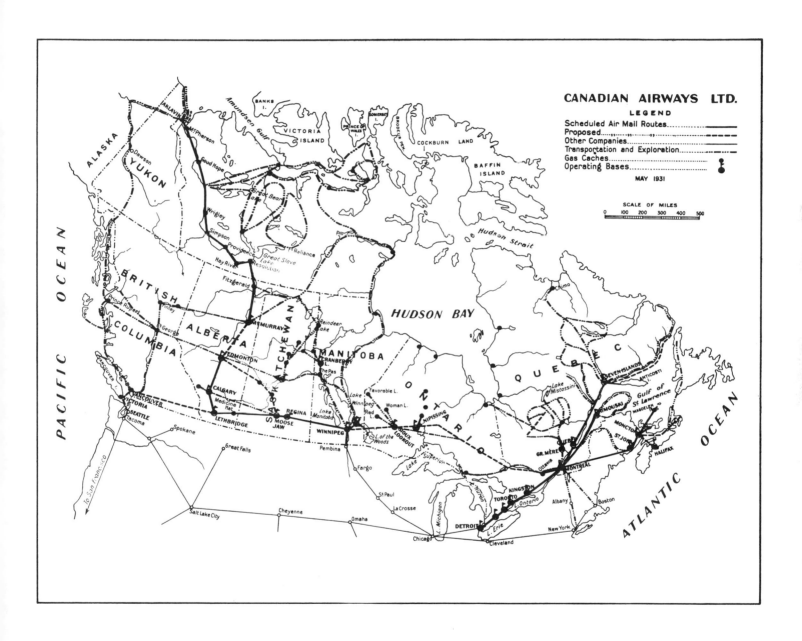

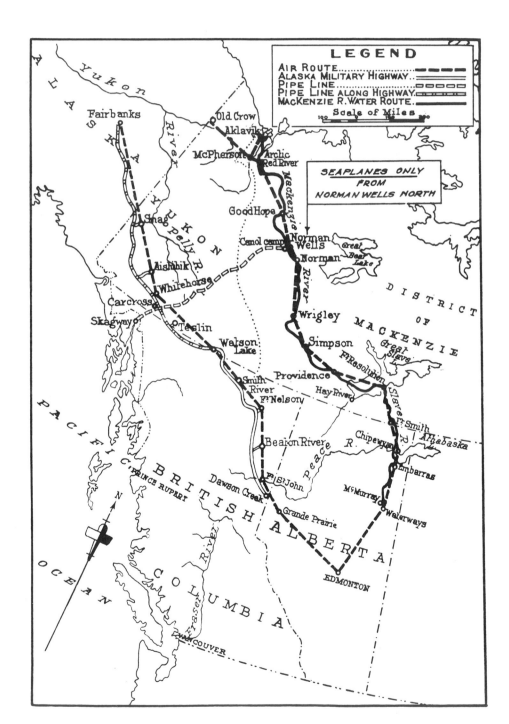

LEGEND

AIR ROUTE	_ _ _ _ _
ALASKA MILITARY HIGHWAY	- - - - -
PIPE LINE	▭▭▭▭
PIPE LINE ALONG HIGHWAY	▭▭▭
MACKENZIE R. WATER ROUTE	•••••••

Scale of Miles

*SEAPLANES ONLY
FROM
NORMAN WELLS NORTH*

ALASKA

Yukon River

Fairbanks

Old Crow

Aklavik

McPherson · Arctic Red River

Pelly R.

Snag

Good Hope

Mackenzie

YUKON

Canol camp · Norman Wells · Norman

Great Bear Lake

Aishihik

Whitehorse

DISTRICT

Carcross

Skagway · Teslin

River

Wrigley

OF

Great Slave

MACKENZIE

Walson Lake

Simpson

Ft Resolution

PACIFIC

Providence

Hay River

Smith River

Ft Nelson

Slave R.

Ft Smith · Athabaska

Chipewyan

R.

Beaton River

Peace R.

Embarras

BRITISH

PRINCE RUPERT

Dawson Creek

Ft St John

McMurray · Waterways

ALBERTA

Grande Prairie

OCEAN

COLUMBIA

River

EDMONTON

VANCOUVER

Fraser River

N

This map shows the air route from Edmonton to Whitehorse and Fairbanks, which was known as the Northwest Staging Route during World War II; the Alaska Highway from Dawson Creek to Whitehorse and Fairbanks, known as the Alaska Military Highway during World War II; the Canol Pipe Line; the pipe line along the highway; and the Mackenzie River Route from Edmonton to Aklavik.

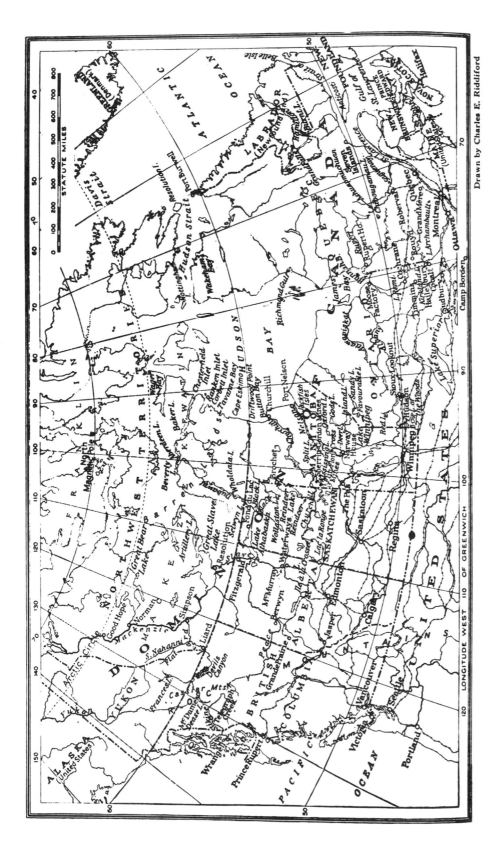

This map shows many of the places reached by Canada's aviation pioneers.

Drawn by Charles E. Riddiford

Index